MacWEEK Upgrading and Repairing Your Mac

Lisa Lee

The Don Crabb Macintosh Library

Hayden
Books

MacWEEK Upgrading and Repairing Your Mac

Library of Congress Catalog Number: 95-081203
ISBN: 1-56830-249-5

97 96 95   4 3 2 1

Interpretation of the printing code: the rightmost double-digit number is the year of the book's printing; the rightmost single-digit number is the number of the book's printing. For example, a printing code of 95-1 shows that the first printing of the book occurred in 1995.

Publisher
Don Fowley

Acquisitions Editor
Karen Whitehouse

Development Editor
Brian Gill

Copy Editor
Pete Kuhns

Technical Editor
Terry Rawlings

Publishing Coordinator
Rosemary Lewis

Marketing Manager
Ray Robinson

Marketing Coordinator
Meshell Dinn

Interior Designer
Anne Jones

Production Manager
Kelly Dobbs

Manufacturing Coordinator
Paul Gilchrist

Production Team Supervisor
Laurie Casey

Graphic Image Specialists
Clint Lahnen, Laura Robbins,
Craig Small, Todd Wente

Production Team
Angela Calvert, Jennifer Eberhardt, Tricia Flodder,
Erika Millen, Gina Rexrode, Beth Rago, Erich Richter,
Christine Tyner, Holly Wittenberg

Indexer
Brad Herriman

Contents at a Glance

Contents

Dedication

This book is dedicated to my mom and dad. This book is also dedicated to the memory of my cousin Warren Eng.

Acknowledgments

Many people helped bring this book to you, some of whom I have never met and others who have spent generous amounts of time providing me with information, support, and wisdom.

This book would not be in your hands if not for the people at Hayden Books, especially Brian Gill, Karen Whitehouse, and Pat Gibbons. Their experience, work, and avidness for Macintosh have been the driving force behind bringing this book to you.

Thanks also go to the technical reviewers of the manuscript, especially Mike Neil, Terry Rawlings, and John Yen.

Special thanks for technical and all other kinds of support go to Don Crabb, Jordan Mattson, Brian Gilmer, Larry Abrams, Bill Cockayne, Karen Tanner, Suzanne Lamar, Jennifer Cavaliere, Lupe Silva, Leo Judge, JP Garcia, Steve Orens, Phil Hayes, Tom Lopez, Tim Holmes, Tim Stahlke, Chad Williams, Donna LaBarge, Suzanne Andrews, Jim Murphy, Laura, Jackie, Julie, Jason, and BMUG staff, volunteers, and presenters who taught me tons of things about Macintosh computers.

I would also like to thank Steve Birchall, Kelley Boylan, Shelley Brisbin, Peter Durso, Ken Grey, Michael Kent, Darien Kruss, Jack McShea, Tom Negrino, John Rizzo, Jeff Roback, and Peter Stoller for their excellent work on the first edition of this book—much of which you will find in this book.

No Macintosh computers or Macintosh products were exploited, hurt, or killed to bring you this book.

—Lisa Lee, November 1995

About the Author

Lisa Lee is an engineer at Apple Computer and has special interests with animation, writing, and music. She has spent the past years consulting for several Macintosh hardware and software companies and has a propensity for using great software products.

Her early Macintosh years were spent volunteering with BMUG, where she helped start up the first multimedia special interest group, contributed to editing and writing for the BMUG newsletter, and helped Derrick Schneider, Hans Hansen, and Tim Holmes bring you the book *Zen and the Art of Resource Editing: BMUG's Guide to ResEdit.*

INTRODUCTION

Welcome to Macintosh

When you have a Macintosh, it's natural to wonder what your options are for expanding, maintaining, and using your computer. If you are looking to buy your first computer, or a second, there are many Macintosh models to choose from. Products designed to work with the Macintosh also span a massively greater range of products compared to the computer models with which they work. Combining these two create hundreds and thousands of hardware and software possibilities and opportunities. These opportunities include making your Macintosh faster and bigger so that it can do neat and cool things. It also includes the inevitable problems and possibly repairs.

This book discusses upgrades and repairs for Macintosh hardware, System software, and general software products. Taking these topics, the book can be divided into four basic sections: Core Macintosh products, Upgrades, Troubleshooting/Repair, and Reference material. Core Macintosh products include Macintosh basic hardware and software for the Mac. This section makes up the first 5 chapters of the book, where you'll learn about the Mac and how its hardware and software work. This is designed to help you understand the Mac a little better so that you can make better decisions when upgrading or repairing your Mac.

The upgrades section of the book is divided into three chapters. Topics such as installing an internal hard drive, internal CD-ROM drive, and memory are covered in the hardware chapter. The software chapter covers popular applications and the latest System software.

The section on troubleshooting consists of three core chapters, plus a chapter on when it's time to replace your hardware or software. Chapters 8 through 10 cover hardware, software, printer, and network products. Chapter 11 discusses when you should finally break down and get some new equipment/software. An in-depth discussion of tax and business benefits is included.

Appendices at the back of the book contain all the materials referenced in the book, including a complete list of Macintosh models with major features, a virus listing, Macintosh error codes, and a glossary. Top ten lists for troubleshooting hardware, software, and networks are included, too. System software tables include a history of Macintosh System software, and a complete listing of control panels and extensions for System 7.5 and a brief description of each piece of software.

Things to Do with This Book

All the information in this book can be consumed in small or large amounts. You can use this book as a reference, as general reading for understanding Macintosh products and extended features for your computer, or for sharing with others who may have questions about Macintosh computers. If you have a Mac and are curious about how something works on your Mac, what a particular expansion port does, or which System Enabler file your Mac needs to start up, you can find this information in the first few chapters of this book. If your Mac is having a problem running software, accessing installed hardware, or printing, you can find pertinent information in the troubleshooting sections of this book.

Things Not Covered in This Book

This book does not cover network administration for large or sophisticated networks. It also does not cover corporate, client/server business upgrade paths or options. These 'higher end' solutions for computing are reserved for other network and computer references.

In each product section only the most common or popular manufacturers are discussed. This does not mean other products are not comparable, or possibly better than those discussed in this book. There are also many Macintosh hardware and software products, I chose to cover selected products in selected categories. References to additional Macintosh product resources are provided, and locations for shareware and freeware software are also included.

Happy Upgrading and Repair Thoughts

This book can help you make upgrades and repairs to your Macintosh by providing you with product-specific information and unraveling how the technologies work. One of the best things about owning a Macintosh is that there are more than 20 million other people out there who have a Mac, too. This book contains standard and accumulated knowledge that will hopefully bring you pleasant and enjoyable upgrade and repair experiences with your Macintosh computer. Here's to happy upgrading and repair thoughts for everyone!

When You Must Spend Money

Whenever you decide to spend money on your Macintosh, keep in mind that technology is continually improving. Products and technology available today will almost certainly be shadowed by less-expensive and more-powerful technology tomorrow. In addition, new technologies are being introduced and made available to the public in shorter and shorter amounts of time.

This chapter introduces you to upgrade and repair options, and shows you general troubleshooting and repair procedures to help you understand your Macintosh better. You will read about ways to spend less money on the upgrades and repairs your Mac does need, and also what upgrades and repairs cost nothing. You will find more specific answers elsewhere in this book.

How do you decide what to buy today to continue to have usable technology tomorrow? Try to keep in mind all the things you would like to accomplish using your Macintosh. Also, decide how quickly or slowly you want to adopt new technologies. Think of more cost-effective ways to use the technologies you want, such as using a local service bureau or hiring a consultant. When you know which technologies you can afford, the knowledge will help you find out how much money to spend now, how much you can spend later, and also what you do not need.

Note

Keep in mind you always have an option to sell your current system in lieu of upgrading or repairing it. Whether your system has no expansion options, or the most expansion available, you still may want to make a strategic change in how you want to use your Macintosh.

Issues to Consider Before Spending Money

Before you decide to spend money on an upgrade, repair, or new system, consider your short-term computing goals. Try to answer the following questions:

- What kinds of work do you plan to do on your Macintosh?

- How much hard drive space or multiple hard drive space do you need for daily and backup use? Should you purchase another hard drive or removable media mechanism, to store your data *prior* to selling your current model and purchasing another Macintosh?

- What type of monitor is adequate for your work? Can your existing Mac handle the type of work you plan to do in the future? Features and limitations of specific Mac models limit their variability with hardware (14" vs. 21" monitors on LC models) and software (FPU-dependent, memory-intensive applications).

- How many colors do you need to work with, and can your existing monitor handle this requirement? If you plan to be doing publishing, photography, and art work, this can be very important.

- How much memory will you use for running System software and application software?

- Is a color printer more appropriate than a black-and-white printer?

- Are there any other peripherals you may need to use in addition to the keyboard and mouse?

- Will you also need to use other types of peripherals, such as a camera, scanner, speakers, or digitizer?

- How much new or existing technology do you plan to adopt in the future? This can include new hardware, System software, or applications.

Example configurations

The following three sample computer configurations illustrate the type of equipment required for publishing, small business, and home use. This information is provided as a baseline to help show you some possibilities of the hardware and software involved with configuring your Macintosh.

Desktop publishing

Macintosh computers are used more in desktop publishing than in any other industry. They are commonly used by publishers, advertising agencies, fanzine magazines, and newsletter lay-out personnel at major corporations. Desktop publishing, which involves photography, page layout, writing, editing, and printing, is used by single-owner newsletter publishers and large-volume magazine, book, and newspaper publishers.

A desktop publishing system generally needs:

- At least 40 MB of memory for four-color separation and other high-end color publishing. (More memory is always better.)

- At least 500 MB of hard drive space; 2G is preferred.

- Internal or external CD-ROM drive for access to media.

- A removable media drive such as a Zip, SyQuest, optical, Bernoulli, or external hard drive. Several additional devices may be necessary depending on the media formats used by other publishing clients, collaborative workgroups, or service bureaus. Other alternatives include using a recordable CD drive to master backups and transfer publishing content, finished material, or large sized media.

- For backups, a DAT drive or removable media drive is highly recommended.

- A large screen monitor (maybe two or three monitors). The second and third monitor can be helpful when viewing large images and page layouts simultaneously.

- Extended keyboard.

- Mouse or graphic pen tablet (or both).

- A powerful CPU (and even multiple CPUs for acceleration or multitasking). A common upgrade is to add a graphics accelerator for accelerating image redrawing and manipulation.

- Adequate network connectivity (such as a modem, network cabling between Macintosh computers, and Ethernet or LocalTalk transceivers) to send the finished work to the printer.

- LaserWriter (at least 600dpi) that can be used to sample or test the published output before sending it out for high-end or high-volume publishing.

- Software applications such as Adobe Photoshop, Kai's Power Tools, Adobe PageMaker or QuarkXPress, a word processor, World Wide Web HTML editor, and server software.

Small business

The small business owner also has been able to take advantage of the Macintosh computer's capabilities. A business manager can now perform many automated tasks simply and easily. The tools that make this possible are software for spreadsheets, databases, presentations, appointment tracking, reference material, and project planning. With this software, a small number of employees can now track daily, weekly, monthly, and quarterly sales with the click of button; review service requests, inventory, and budgets; and create reports for customers and other business associates. These capabilities and advantages can help a small office with one Macintosh or a large multinational corporation with hundreds and thousands of Macintosh computers across the globe.

A small business system generally needs:

- At least 8 MB, preferably 24 MB, of memory (spreadsheets can be very large in memory as well as on the hard drive).

- A 500 MB (preferably 1 GB) hard drive.

- An internal or external CD-ROM or DAT drive for backups and access to data and information.

- Network capabilities for either modem or live Internet connection.

- At least one medium-sized monitor (if not two: one for calendaring, the other for work).

- Extended keyboard.

- Mouse.

- External projection device for vivid presentations.

- Portable or desktop printer for correspondence, reports, presentations, and labels.

- Software applications for creating, tracking, managing, billing, paying, communicating and planning projects and products.

- Additional hard drives for mobile information, backups, and media storage.

- Color media output for creating, reproducing, and tracking business content originating from VCR, film, slides, and overhead media.

- A powerful, fast CPU (if not many multitasked or multiple CPUs) to maintain productivity.

Home computing

For home computing, the Macintosh has no equal. The Mac has introduced home users to the most innovative and entertaining software and revolutionary educational tools available. Macintosh online services enable users to chat or send mail to other users nearby or around the world, and provide a wealth of published information.

Home users recently have had more multimedia software technologies and applications become available. QuickTime, for example, is multimedia technology used in many CD-ROM educational, recreational, and entertainment software titles. Hollywood has also adopted multimedia to bring you interactive entertainment accompanying many of today's popular movie and television shows. Home users can use multimedia—specifically a video camera connected to a Macintosh video-in and video-out ports (or add-on card supporting video input and output)—to create video archives of adventures, the family tree, and a picture book of friends and relatives.

A Macintosh for home use should have:

- At least 8 MB of memory (preferably 24 MB).

- At least 120 MB (preferably 500 MB to 1 GB) of hard drive space.

- Extended keyboard.

- Mouse.

- Printer (optional).

- A 14" or larger color monitor. The screen size should be 640×480 or higher.

Getting in over your head

With technology changing so rapidly, many feel that it is harder and harder to make a cost-effective computer purchase. Some Mac owners feel that whatever model you buy today, it will be slower and outdated tomorrow by a new model or software that is only created for another model. Similarly, if you don't buy something because you want to wait for a better 'deal', you may end up waiting for a very long time, if ever, to buy a computer.

The rewards of buying an expensive computing system are that you can fuel a business and quickly make back the money you initially invested in the computer system. Although you don't need every whistle and bell for a computer to run a small business or publish a newsletter or book, investing in an effective computer system can add up to a significant cost.

How much Macintosh do you need?

When investing in computer systems, try not to spend all of your budget on every available technology. Instead, try to define what features and options you need now, versus the things you can put on 'hold'. Generally hardware prices, especially for hard drives and other peripherals, change more frequently than software prices. By holding off on hardware purchases you will almost always have more time to find the best value for your dollar.

This doesn't mean you don't need the most expensive system. Apple's high-end Macintosh models usually offer the fastest performance, most expandability, and the latest in hardware and software technology. The most expensive system can also mean a more productive system, permitting you to get more work accomplished in less time.

Is 8 MB of memory enough?

Almost all current Macintosh models have at least 8 MB of memory as a minimal memory configuration. Earlier models shipped with 4 MB of memory, and many low-cost models had only one memory expansion slot. If you plan on using the traditional System Folder, plus software applications that are not memory hungry, an 8 MB Mac easily can meet your computing needs.

More memory gives you the added luxury of having multiple applications open at the same time, saving time and the hassle of launching and quitting each application. Additional Apple System software technologies such as QuickDraw GX, PowerTalk, QuickDraw 3D and OpenDoc require at least 16 MB of memory and also adequate amounts of hard drive space.

When not to spend money

To save headaches and cash, you need to decide what you do need and the things you don't need. If you're sure you have the perfect system in mind, and Apple suddenly introduces some new technology that "you can't live without," it's always best to wait. In general, first introductions of new technologies for hardware, software, or system software generally require some fine tuning and bug fixing. A good general practice is to wait for new technologies to be tried by others who can afford to spend time troubleshooting. Many products are exceptional, such as Apple's Power Macintosh, IOmega's Zip drives, System 7.0, 7.1, and 7.5, and most revisions to widely used applications. Nevertheless, wait until the bugs are eliminated, and follow the technology's progress through discussion groups on the Internet or online forum.

Upgrading and Repairing the Mac, a Quick Tour

Many hardware and software repairs are mandatory when the hardware or software ceases to function, or a peripheral prevents you from using the Macintosh. If a repair is more expensive than replacing a product, the best choice is obvious. Forget the repair and upgrade the hardware/software. Because hardware and software products are constantly being improved, you can often get more performance and features at a lower cost than the original product you purchased.

Hardware and software problems

Inherent with any computer are hardware and software problems. Hardware problems can vary from defective memory modules to a bad motherboard. Software problems can consist of an even wider variety of symptoms—from system software not starting up to software that freezes your computer when you try to print or save a file. If these problems occur, what does this mean to you and your computer system? More importantly, is the problem a clue you should upgrade your Macintosh, repair the problem yourself, or ask for help?

Note

For more details on troubleshooting, see the sections on troubleshooting in Chapters 9, 10, and 11.

Diagnosing a problem can be unexpectedly time consuming if you don't have a set method for localizing the cause or source of a problem. Try to keep a log of regular hardware and software maintenance. Also, when a problem occurs, note the steps you take during trouble-shooting. If you are able to find a workaround to a problem, make a note in your log; this may help you prevent a hardware or software problem in the future.

Generally, there is nothing software can do to correct nonfunctional hardware. You must replace defective hardware with new, properly working hardware. If you have a software failure, however, you can try a few quick and easy steps to correct the problem, such as reinstall a backup of the original software, look for an update for the software, or go back to a previous version of software that works on your Macintosh. This section discusses recommended steps to take when a hardware or software problem first occurs.

1) When was the first time the problem happened on this Mac?

If your Macintosh initially ran fine for days, weeks, months, or years, you may want to note the latest software changes or tasks you performed on your Macintosh prior to seeing the problem occur. It is possible you may have added incompatible software or hardware to your system.

2) Does this problem occur on another Macintosh?

If you have access to another Macintosh (the same model can be more helpful for trouble-shooting), and it has the same System software version as your system, try reproducing the problem on the second Macintosh. (Try not to copy any files from the troubled System Folder to the second system.)

Warning

Reproducing the problem on the second machine probably isn't a good idea, if it's something as serious as a general system failure.

If you suspect your Macintosh is too slow, you may want to perform a similar task on another Macintosh model sharing the same configuration as yours to compare task times and, if possible, identify any System software differences between the two systems. Slow performance can indicate the need for a faster processor, more memory, a faster modem, or a larger or second hard drive.

3) Is there any software that can diagnose this problem and fix it?

Apple includes Disk First Aid 7.2 with its System software which can repair most types of damaged file systems. This program is located on Apple's Disk Tools floppy disk; for Performa models, this program is on the Performa Utilities floppy disk; on Power Mac models with a CD-ROM, it is included on the Power Macintosh CD.

Symantec sells commercial software that has more features than Apple's Disk First Aid 7.2 (or Drive Setup 1.0.2 for Power Macintosh), and also includes full customer support and regular upgrades. Norton Utilities is the most popular hard drive maintenance software for Macintosh. It performs tasks similar to Apple's Disk First Aid, but has several additional features for maintaining your Macintosh.

If your Mac file system is in great condition, but has unexplained crashes or odd system behavior—a computer virus may be at fault. Disinfectant 3.6 is a free software application that can scan and repair almost all known Macintosh viruses. It is available through most Macintosh ftp sites on the Internet and through online services and user groups (such as the Berkeley Macintosh User Group).

Note

Software viruses are computer code that attach to other software code and cause either System software or application software to behave oddly or crash inexplicably. Viruses can also corrupt hard drives and slow down hard drive performance. Some viruses can even erase hard drives.

If you use your computer regularly, it is good practice to run virus protection software to keep your Macintosh in good working condition. If you have a backup of your software available on a tape, hard drive, or floppy disk, and you suspect a virus, you can restore your work-in-progress instead of trying to recover a damaged file or contents of a folder on the damaged volume.

A *backup* is a second copy (some consultants recommend keeping three backups) of some or all of your software. This can include System software as well as any valuable work-in-progress or archived files stored on internal or external hard drives. Back-ups can be performed by backup software such as Dantz' Retrospect Remote, or by manually copying or duplicating files to floppies, hard drive, DAT tape drive, or pressed to a CD-ROM. Remember to back up your software regularly.

Repairs versus upgrades

Hardware repairs fall into two categories: hardware items worth fixing and those not worth fixing. Affordable items that are easy to replace and cost from $1 to $300 are memory, cables, floppy drives, keyboard, mouse, hard drives, CD-ROM players, floppy disks, removable media drives and media, power supplies, and miscellaneous buttons or knobs on your main computer or peripherals. One or a few of these items will eventually need partial or full replacement during the life of your computer; these repairs are worth fixing.

The hardware that is not worth fixing includes the pricier ticket items. When a repair is equal to the cost of a new system, buy a new system. Repairing old hardware does not guarantee another problem will occur sometime in the near future. Hardware not worth fixing includes monitors, motherboard failure, or multiple parts not working on the motherboard, graphics, accelerator, and complete system damage (such as a large-scale fire, water, or electrical damage).

1

Repairing software usually has much less overhead involved and can be a simple reinstallation of software, or an upgrade for a bug fix. An error message, slow performance or warning messages help you become aware of impending problems. If you have been using your software regularly, and then discover a message such as 'the application was unable to launch,' the software may have previously crashed or a virus might be present. Try to keep a duplicate set of backup disks available and check the hard drive and make sure it is virus free before reinstalling any software. If all applications are behaving oddly, you may want to run some diagnostic software such as Apple's Disk First Aid or Norton Utilities to see if there may be possible file system damage in addition to a possible virus infection.

What is worth upgrading and what is not?

If you are adding or replacing hardware, look for at least a 50% increase in hardware performance. For software, performance and new features should be compared to the price of the upgrade, as well as the amount of memory and additional (if any) hard drive space required.

Although most Macintosh models can benefit from a processor accelerator or replacement upgrade, some models may not take advantage of the add-on hardware due to limitations of the motherboard's data bus input and output speeds or SCSI access times. Access times to SCSI and other devices depend largely on the hardware used in the product, and also on the version and configuration of system software of the Macintosh. Some extension software, for example, can slow down overall software performance as much, if not more than a defragmented hard drive or slow data bus.

For both hardware and software upgrades, do not rely on published specifications when upgrading subsystems in your Mac. Rather, run diagnostic software on your Mac to see if the upgrade is performing to your requirements. Keep in mind that your Mac System software configuration and hard drive access times can have a noticeable impact on add-on hardware as well as application software performance. For more information on upgrade products and the most common repairs refer to Chapters 6, 7, and 8.

Don't bother upgrading...

Some Macintosh models only support a certain amount of memory. The first LC Macintosh computers only supported 10 MB of memory. In addition, most low-cost Macintosh computers only have one expansion slot for adding or upgrading new features. Desktop models can require expensive upgrades for improving graphics, SCSI, or network performance. If you cannot justify the cost of a particular upgrade, it may be more economical to rent a hardware product or preconfigured Macintosh to do specific high-end tasks.

The main criteria when considering an upgrade is to compare the cost of an upgrade against the cost of a new CPU upgrade. If a newer Macintosh model is less expensive than the upgrade required for your existing Mac, keep your current model and spend the upgrade on a second CPU. Because LocalTalk networking is built into every Macintosh, you can connect a serial cable to two Macintosh computers (or LocalTalk drop boxes) to share files and folders between the two computers without having to install any internal hardware products.

A final alternative

An alternative to purchasing an upgrade is to become a seed site for a particular vendor or vendor's hardware or software product. A *seed site* is a company or person who is legally approved by a vendor to review and provide feedback on a product prior to its commercial release. Seed sites usually are able to obtain a free copy of the finished product in return for the information they return to the company. Generally, if you are not a specialist with the product you are working with, you won't be as valuable to the software or hardware company.

Seed sites are also referred to as *beta test sites* in the industry. Individuals and companies who are given the privilege to use a pre-released product must provide bug reports as well as feedback on the features of the product. Problems that are found must be reproducible, and communicated quickly and clearly to those who are responsible for fixing bugs found in the product. As a seed site, it is valuable to provide constructive feedback within a fast (one week or less) turnaround time to make an impact on the product. Most hardware and software companies rely on seed sites to determine real-world compatibility and usability of a product before the product is given to the masses. If you want to be considered as a seed site for a product, try to contact the product manager; be prepared to explain why you are qualified to be a seed site.

This is simply one of a large number of alternatives to upgrading and repairing your Macintosh. If you are looking for specific information, you should use the Index or Table of Contents of this book to find the specific information you need. This book makes upgrade/repair recommendations wherever possible.

Understanding Your Mac

In this chapter, you can read about general information on the Macintosh CPU, as well as specifics on internal and external hardware configurations on the oldest through to the latest Macintosh models. If you need specific information on one model only, still try to skim through the other parts of the chapter so that you can gain a better understanding of the Macintosh.

PowerPC and 68K Machines

Macintosh is best known for its ease of use, exceptional integration of hardware, System software, and superior applications. Aside from the all the clever features available, the processor chip is also a well thought-out device.

Apple has traditionally used Motorola processors in all its Macintosh models and, until recently, used only 68000-based processors. For example, the 68LC040 processor is found in almost all the latest non-Power Macintosh computer models. With the introduction of the PowerPC chip in 1994, Apple brought its exceptional Mac design to a new level of hardware performance. Today, Apple's Macintosh computers are available with either a 68LC040 or PowerPC-based CPU. Apple also has cross-platform DOS systems that use a 66MHz 486DX processor as a daughter board (in addition to a 68LC040 or PowerPC processor) to run DOS or Windows software from the same hard drive.

Apple's current product line consists of desktop, portable, and low-cost Macintosh models. Desktop Macintosh computers, such as the 9500, 8500, and 7500 Power Macintosh computers, are the larger high-end systems. Portable Macintosh computers are called PowerBooks and can use the same software as any other Macintosh. Low-cost Macintosh computers include the popular LC product line and most Macintosh Performa computers. Most low-cost models, such as the LC 580 and Power Macintosh 5200/75, are all-in-one hardware solutions that include the monitor, speakers, and microphone built into the hardware case.

The following Macintosh computers use a 33MHz 68LC040 processor and run System 7.5 software:

Performa 630 series
Performa 580
PowerBook 190/66 and 190c/66 models (see Figure 2.1)

Figure 2.1   Macintosh PowerBook 190/66 with Apple's latest 68LC040 processor.

PowerPC-based Macintosh computers include:

9500
8500
7500
7200
8100/100(AV)
7100/80(AV)
6100/66
PowerBook 5300, 2300 and 5200, 5300, 6200, and 6300
Performa models are mentioned later in this chapter.

If some of this seems a little fuzzy to you right now, read on; it will all be explained briefly.

Note

In addition to introducing more Power Macintosh computers in 1995, Apple licensed its operating system and hardware technology to several companies, including Power Computing, Radius, and DayStar. These companies have introduced the first "clone" Power Macintosh computers as well as new System configurations and upgrade options for Macintosh owners.

Why PowerPC?

The power of any computer model is the processor. Apple's joint venture with IBM and Motorola produced the PowerPC processors, which are the first RISC processors used for Macintosh. Prior to the PowerPC, Macintosh computers used Motorola's 68000, 68020, 68030, and 68040 processors—CISC processors.

Note

Two types of processors are used in computers today: RISC and CISC. RISC stands for *Reduced Instruction Set Computing*. A simplified set of instructions is recognized by the chip in comparison to a larger instruction set supported by traditional CISC architecture. The characteristics of the RISC chip are a product of many physical design changes to the processor, which allow RISC chips to manage data more efficiently than CISC chips. CISC stands for *Complex Instruction Set Computing*. The primary difference between CISC and RISC is that CISC processes its instructions by executing a predefined sequence of micro-instructions (also known as microcode) that can take more than one System clock pulse to process. RISC processors can perform similar complex tasks faster than CISC because RISC processors can execute multiple instructions simultaneously; RISC chips break down complex tasks into several simple instructions.

Differences among PowerPC processors

Aside from the difference in form factor between the PowerPC 601–604 versus PowerPC 603 Macintosh computers, a common question asked is, why buy a 603 if I can buy a 604? Power Macintosh computers differ slightly from their 680x0 predecessors. The 601 processor was the first implementation of RISC architecture, which was improved upon with the 603 and 604 processors. The 603 processor offers the same compatibility as the 601, but is clocked much faster. It is a low-power, smaller cache version of the 601 chip, designed for Macs and other computers with a smaller power supply.

The 604 processor is the newest PowerPC processor, offering faster processor speeds and a smaller dye size. Macintosh computers with this processor require DIMMs instead of SIMMs because of the different processor architecture and performance. The 604 (found in PCI Power Macs) and 603e-based (found in Power Macintosh PowerBooks) Macintosh computers also use a newer emulator that improves software emulation performance. Connectix's SpeedDoubler offers similar software emulation for the 6100, 7100, 8100, and LC500 and 6200 models. The Apple/IBM/Motorola alliance has also announced a 620 processor. The 620 chip is a full 64-bit implementation of the PowerPC architecture, and will most likely be used in servers and workstations.

601 Processor

The PowerPC 601 was the first PowerPC chip produced by the Apple/IBM/Motorola alliance. Its design was heavily lifted from the IBM POWER architecture used in IBM's RS/6000 workstations. The PowerPC 601 brought the power of these high-end workstations to the desktop Macintosh.

The 601 has three *execution units*, which are the parts of the processor that handle instructions. An instruction is the basic unit that defines software. Instructions tell the execution units to perform various functions such as add two integers together, multiply two floating point values, or control program flow. All PowerPC instructions are 4-bytes long, and these instructions are stored in main memory or on disk as part of the application.

The 601 has one Integer Unit, one Floating Point Unit, and one Branch Processing Unit. The Integer Unit performs functions on integer values, such as basic math, logical operations, and comparisons. The Floating Point Unit performs the same type of functions on floating point numbers. The Branch Processing Unit is used to control the flow of the program, and it tells the processor where it should fetch the next instructions from main memory. (The PowerPC 601 also has a 32K cache that contains both instructions and data.)

The 601 is capable of dispatching three instructions to each of these functional units each clock cycle. This basically means it can do three things at once. The capability to process more than one instruction at once is called *Superscalar processing*. Because Superscalar processors can perform more than one operation each clock cycle, it is not accurate to compare the processor speed of processors with different designs.

The PowerPC 601 chip is made up of 2.8 million transistors and is available in 50 to 110 MHz versions. The original PowerPC 601 measures 11 × 11 mm and consumes 9.2 watts. Later versions of the 601 consume much less power and are significantly smaller in size.

603 Processor

The PowerPC 603 processor was the next iteration of the PowerPC architecture, and was designed to be about as fast as a 601, but much smaller and less power-hungry. The 603 has the same number of functional units as the 601, but adds a special unit to load and store data from main memory. The 603 also has two smaller caches instead of one large cache as found in the 601. The 603 has an 8K cache for instructions and another 8K cache for data. This split cache design is more efficient for handling data and instructions.

The PowerPC 603 in made up of 1.6 million transistors and is available in 50 to 80 MHz versions. The PowerPC 603 measures 7.4 × 11.5 mm and consumes 2.5 watts at 80 MHz. Because of the smaller caches, the 603 doesn't perform as well as the 601 when running emulated 68K code. To alleviate this problem, the PowerPC alliance designed the PowerPC 603e, which is similar to the 603, but has one 16K cache for instructions and one 16K cache for data. The 603e also has an additional integer unit.

The PowerPC 603e is made up of 2.6 million transistors and is available in 50 to 100 MHz versions. The PowerPC 603e measures 8.4 × 11.67 mm and consumes 3.0 watts at 80 MHz. Because the 603 was designed to be a low-power chip, it is perfect for portable computers and low-cost desktop systems. The 603 also has a number of dynamic power-saving features. When a functional unit is not processing an instruction, for example, it automatically powers itself down, then turns itself back on when needed. The 603 can also "power-down" to save power. The capability to "doze" and "sleep" the processor makes it more efficient, and allows for longer battery life in portable designs.

604 Processor

The PowerPC 604 processor is the current iteration of the PowerPC architecture. This chip is designed to be much faster than the 601 and has the capability to work in multi-processor systems.

The PowerPC 604 has two Integer Units, one Floating Point Unit, one Branch Unit, one Special Register Unit, and one Load Store Unit. The 604 also contains 16K of Instruction Cache and 16K of Data Cache. Special systems are designed into the chip that allow a result from one unit to be available to other units for the next processor cycle. All these capabilities were designed for high-end Mac desktop platforms; as such, the 604 was not designed with power consumption in mind—10 watts is consumed at 100MHz.

The PowerPC 604 comprises 3.6 million transistors and is available in 90 to 150 MHz versions. The 604 measures 12.4 × 15.8 mm in size.

Hardware versus software performance

A faster processor does not necessarily mean faster system software or application performance. Overall system performance on Macs, in general, can be affected greatly by the simple addition of extensions and control panels in the System Folder. Virtual Memory, personal File Sharing, background printing, and background software calculations (such as finding items or counting folder contents) can slow your Macintosh down to a crawl.

This, of course, is the dilemma most users face. Customize the Mac to death and take a huge performance hit, or turn everything off and enjoy a fast, Zen-like Macintosh. You can have both by using an Extension Manager like Now Startup Manager, Conflict Catcher, or the Extension Manager in System 7.5, along with custom extension sets. If you're planning on doing a lot of processor-dependent work, you can use the minimal extension setup to avoid software incompatibilities or conflicts. If entertainment and adventure are your objectives, you can turn all the extensions "on," and spend time customizing and exploring software.

For those who want to use DOS or Windows on their Macs, hardware solutions almost always perform faster than software solutions. The speed of an additional processor added to a Macintosh is most limited by the slot and data bus speed of the Macintosh motherboard. Cross-platform hardware solutions have potentially higher performance, but also higher maintenance variables than a software solution.

Apple provides 486DX processors that can run with either the 630 or 6100 Macs. On the 630, the Intel processor includes 4 MB of onboard memory (expandable to 32 MB). The 6100 shares its motherboard memory with the added Intel processor. With the introduction of the PCI Macintosh, Apple will probably introduce newer dual-processor products, replacing the 486 processors with Pentiums. Keep in mind that with additional hardware, high data-bus speeds, and the limitations of adding two processors to one motherboard, unique hardware problems may occur.

Software solutions for running applications from other platforms generally cost less than their hardware counterparts, provide lower maintenance, and higher compatibility, although they generally will be slower. Insignia's SoftWindows 2.0 emulates the 486 processor and supports DOS and Windows and PC applications. Because SoftWindows is software, it uses a standard set of drivers to interface with Macintosh hardware, such as the hard drive, CD-ROM, and floppy drives. This can be a real timesaver if you do not have the configuration expertise of DOS or Windows, but want to run software applications using sound or CD. If performance is not critical for your cross-platform needs, purchase a faster Macintosh and choose software emulation so that you can use your non-Macintosh software now, then add a hardware solution later.

PCI-based Power Macs

The 9500, 8500, 7500, and 7200 Power Macintosh computers are the first models to support PCI (Peripheral Component Interconnect) expansion slots. PCI is an expansion slot standard that is commonly used in Intel-based PC computers for graphics, networking, and other speed-dependent hardware. Most Macs use the NuBus type of expansion slot for these peripheral add-ons. Many Macintosh products available for PCI Macintosh computers are also available for NuBus or PDS expansion slots. However, you should always check with the hardware vendor to make sure product specifications, models, and formats have not changed or been discontinued. These current Mac models with PCI slots are pictured in Figures 2.2 through 2.6. (For more information on these Macintosh computers, see Appendix G.)

Courtesy of Apple Computer, Inc.

Figure 2.2 Power Macintosh 8500/120: AV and telephony technology built-in.

Courtesy of Apple Computer, Inc.

Figure 2.3   Power Macintosh 7500/100: a smaller desktop footprint and upgradable processor.

Courtesy of Apple Computer, Inc.

Figure 2.4   Power Macintosh 7200: a 75 or 90MHz 601 processor that can be upgraded to a 7500 motherboard.

Figure 2.5 Power Macintosh PowerBook 5300/117: Apple's first PowerPC portable.

Figure 2.6 Power Macintosh PowerBook 2300: Apple's first PowerPC Duo Mac.

PCI-based and PowerBook Power Macintosh computers have additional System software native to these Macintosh models. This special System software was first released as version 7.5.2. System 7.5.3 will support all Macintoshes, including PCI-based computers.

Apple's introduction of PCI Macintosh computers is likely to attract clone manufactures that want to produce this type of Mac. Current Macintosh clone makers, such as Power Computing, Radius, and Daystar are expected to introduce PCI Macintosh clones soon. Power Computing is planning to offer Power Macintosh clones that support both PCI and NuBus slots!

Available PCI products

PCI products available for the 9500, 8500, 7500, and 7200 models include graphics acceleration, network, SCSI, storage, DOS compatibility, data acquisition, and PCI to NuBus conversion cards. PCI-based networking products include support for Ethernet, Token-Ring, ATM, and FDDI protocols. SCSI and storage products provide disk array, SCSI-2, caching, and RAID controller acceleration. Orange Micro has a DOS and OS/2 compatible PCI card, and National Instruments has instrument control and data acquisition cards for PCI slots—PCI-MIO-16XE-50, PCI-1200, and PCI-DIO-96 DAQ. In addition, the following selected PCI products are available for Power Macintosh computers.

Adaptive Solutions PowerShop

Adaptive Solutions, Inc., offers PowerShop, a PCI card that provides high-resolution graphics acceleration for Photoshop and Kodak high-end digital cameras. This card includes 4 MB of memory onboard and runs through four chips with 16 DSPs (digital signal processors) each—a total of 64 DSPs that accelerate a variety of Photoshop functions. This software installs and runs transparently within Photoshop. A NuBus version of this product is also available.

> $2,000 Estimated Street Price
> Adaptive Solutions, Inc.
> Beaverton, Oregon
> (503) 690-1236, (800) 482-6277

National Instruments LabView

National Instruments is a leading supplier of data acquisition and instrument control products for the Macintosh. LabView, an all-graphic programming language designed to work with instrumentation applications, works with National Instruments' plug-in boards. National Instruments introduced four PCI boards for the PCI Power Macintosh computers, and an accelerated version of LabView for Power Macintosh.

> National Instruments PCI-MIO-16XE-50, PCI-1200, and PCI-DIO-96 DAQ 6504
> Bridgepoint Parkway
> Austin, TX 78730
> (800) 433-3488, (512) 794-0100

AsantéFAST 10/100 adapters

Asanté Technologies is the leading worldwide manufacturer of high-performance Ethernet networking products for Macintosh. Asanté offers the new AsantéFAST 10/100 adapters as a Macintosh and PC solution for ethernet networks. This PCI card provides plug-and-play convenience and supports NWay10Mbps and 100Mbps operations automatically.

Asanté FAST 10/100 PCI Adapter
821 Fox Lane
San Jose, CA 95131
(800) 662-9686

Farallon Fast EtherTX 10/100 PCI

Farallon plans to introduce a complete line of Fast Ethernet networking products based on the IEEE 100BASE-TX standard. The first product Farallon intends to ship is a PCI 10/100 Fast Ethernet interface card. The Fast EtherTX 10/100 PCI card is based on 3Com's 10/100 Fast Ethernet chipset and will support both 10BASE-T Ethernet and 100BASE-TX Fast Ethernet. A single RJ-45 connector autosenses between 10BASE-T and 100BASE-T, making migration to Fast Ethernet practical and affordable. The Fast EtherTX card fully supports Apple's Open Transport and Open Firmware specifications and also works on PCI-based PCs.

Farallon Computing, Inc. Fast EtherTX-10/100
2470 Mariner Square Loop
Alameda, CA 94501
(510) 814-5000, (510) 814-5030

Raven Pro PCI

MicroNet is a leader in the development of data storage solutions for Macintosh computers. Raven Pro PCI is designed for performance and versatility. Single and dual channel options are high-performance, enabling the Raven Pro to keep up with the high bandwidth available with PCI. The software manager provides RAID 0 (disk striping) as well as RAID 1 (mirroring) for ultimate high-speed performance and fault-tolerant data storage.

MicroNet Raven Professional PCI Disk Arrays
80 Technology Drive
Irvine, CA 92718
(714) 453-6000

DPT PACI SmartCacheSCSI, Smart RAID controller
140 Candace Drive
Maitland, FL 32751
(407) 830-5522

FWB PCI SCSI JackHammer

FWB is the leading developer of high-performance, high-fault tolerant RAID solutions for Macintosh. The FWB PCI SCSI JackHammer FAT and WIDE SCSI-3 accelerator card and the FAST and WIDE SCSI-3 SledgeHammer for PCI disk arrays are the first two PCI products. All FWB storage products, including RAID, hard disk, tape, SyQuest, optical, CD-ROM, and CD-Writer are fully compatible with PCI-based Power Macintosh computers.

FWB, Inc. PCI SCSI JackHammer and SledgeHammer
1555 Adams Drive
Menlo Park, CA 94025
(415) 833-4615

Orange Micro PCI and NuBus platforms

Orange Micro provides PCI and NuBus cross-platform solutions for Macintosh. Orange Micro provides 486 processors as a high-performance hardware solution for running DOS and Windows on Macintosh computers.

Orange Micro, Inc. PC400
1400 N. Lakeview Avenue
Anaheim, CA 92807
(714) 779-9332

Power Macintosh product lines

Power Macintosh models include the following:

- 603-chip based, low-cost, all-in one LC5200 and 6200 Macs with a PDS expansion slot, built-in stereo speakers, and optional TV tuner.

- High-end desktop 601 and 604-based 9500, 8500, 7500, and 7200 Power Macs with PCI expansion slots, AV capabilities, larger level 2 caches built-in, and internal four-speed CD-ROM players.

- 603e-based 2300 and 5300 PowerBook Macs with support for PC cards, docking, external monitors, and larger internal hard drives than previous PowerBook models.

The PowerPC Processor is a joint effort between Apple, Motorola, and IBM, producers of the 601, 603, and 604 processors used in Power Macs. The high-end 620 PowerPC processor is the newest processor. As of press time, Apple has not announced a Macintosh that will use the 620 PowerPC chip.

PCI, Peripheral Component Interconnect, is an industry standard expansion card format for graphics acceleration, video, network, SCSI, and other hardware expansion device support traditionally found in the PC/DOS industry. PCI devices for Macintosh have Macintosh-compatible software drivers and offer lower-cost expansion solutions than previous NuBus expansion slot products available for previous Macintosh computers. PCMCIA, recently renamed PC, is a removable card format Apple originally used with its Newton product line, and has adopted as removable media for modems and networking cards for PowerPC-based PowerBooks.

Power Macs also support new and existing Apple technologies such as Geoport, AV input and output, telephony, speech-to-text and text-to-speech, QuickTime, QuickDraw GX, PowerTalk, QuickDraw3D, Open Transport, QuickTime Video Conferencing, AppleShare, Apple Remote Access, QuickTime VR, Personal Filesharing, AppleTalk, Virtual Memory, and stereo sound input and output. Power Macs can also run DOS and Windows software with the addition of Apple's PC daughterboard or with software applications such as Insignia's Soft Windows 2.0, which can emulate Intel 486 processor calls.

What is native software?

Native software is software created specifically to run on the PowerPC processor. This processor, used in all Power Macintosh computers and their clones, replaced the 680x0 Macintosh processor. The Power Macs can also run traditional 68K Macintosh application software through a software emulator. The 68K emulator is software that intercepts 68K code and acts as the 680x0 processor chip, although it really is a PowerPC processor chip.

Software applications that contain Power Macintosh and traditional 680x0 (also known as 68K) code are known as *fat* applications. A fat application will run Power Macintosh native software if launched on a Power Mac, and 68K software if launched on a traditional 68K Macintosh. Fat applications generally take up more hard drive space than 68K-only or PowerPC-only code.

> ### Note
>
> A fat application can be returned to a 68K application by deleting the 'cfrg' resource from the application using Apple's ResEdit 2.1.3.

68K product lines

Although Apple recently discontinued most of its 68040-based Macintosh computers, these machines can meet most user's price/performance goals and are a great short-term solution for those who don't plan to invest in native software. The most popular desktop 68040 models were the Quadra 800, 840AV, and 650, which offered the fastest 68040 speeds available with the FPU-supported 68040 processor. The 840AV is the fastest 68K Macintosh—40MHz.

The LC630, Quadra 630, and related Performa models are still the most popular Macintosh models sold today. The optional TV tuner lets you frame-grab live video, and one PDS slot is included for expansion. A PowerPC card can be added to the 630 Macs, too; however, it blocks the PDS slot and prevents the addition of a PDS card. The PowerBook 190/66, 190cs/66, and 150 all use 33MHz 680LC040 processors and are still on Apple's price list as of this printing. The PowerBook 150 is the low-cost portable Macintosh, with a 9.5 inch backlit passive-matrix display. The 190 model supports PC card expansion and is an all-in-one PowerBook similar to the 150, but with an optional color screen.

Why would I want a 68K machine?

For many, using a 680x0 Macintosh offers excellent compatibility, minimal software and hardware upgrades, lower exposure to new problems, and quicker learning curves for new technologies. Probably one of the greatest benefits is that the 68040-based Macintosh can run 68K applications faster than the software emulator on Power Macintosh.

When shopping for a Macintosh, keep in mind what software you plan to use—68K or Power Macintosh—what versions have the features you want, any related upgrades for longer term use, and whether 68040 Macs offer a better price/performance solution than a Power Macintosh.

Performa

Macintosh Performas are identical to their traditional Macintosh model counterparts. The Performa 631, for example, uses the same motherboard as the Macintosh 630; System software, however, is configured differently. For example, Performa System software has a Performa Utilities floppy disk, but no Disk Tools disk found with traditional Macintosh System 7 software. Also, only one installation option is available for Performa System software.

To install Performa System software for the hard drive, you start the Macintosh from the Performa Utilities floppy disk and launch the Apple Backup/Restore application. This will request additional backup floppies. If you start from a Performa CD, Performa automatically loads the backup files. The backup will restore a System Folder to the hard drive.

All Performas also include software bundles. Software bundles range in content from applications, to dictionaries and, if the Performa has an internal CD, multimedia CD titles. If you purchase a Performa with an internal CD, you receive a CD with a full backup and restore of System software and all bundled software applications. Keep in mind that you can only perform a complete restore of either the System software, the software bundle, or both. You cannot install only one application from the CD or bundle. In addition, each Performa CD will start only on the Performa it shipped with.

68K Performa models

Macintosh Performa are available with 68LC040 and PowerPC processors. Software bundles are similar on both 68K and PowerPC models. Each model has a unique hard drive and memory configuration and comes bundled with additional hardware such as VRAM, an internal modem, or a TV tuner card.

Performa 630 series–68K Performas

The Performa 631CD is based on the Quadra and LC 630 Macintosh models. It has 8 MB of memory, 500 MB hard drive, and carries Apple part number M4148LL/A. The Performa 631 comes bundled with a 14" Performa Plus Display (.28 Dot Pitch), Apple Design keyboard,

14.4 bps Fax/Modem by Global Village Communications, Inc. (with Send Fax S/W), and double-speed CD-ROM. System 7.5 comes pre-installed on all Macintosh computers, including Performa models.

Macintosh Performa 638CD is also based on the Quadra and LC 630 Macintosh, but has a slightly different hardware configuration. The 638CD includes 8 MB of memory, 350 MB hard drive, Apple TV Tuner card, 1 MB VRAM, and carries Apple part number M3599LL/A. Additional hardware bundled with the 638CD include the 14" Performa Plus Display (.28 Dot Pitch), Apple Design keyboard, 14.4 bps Fax/Modem by Global Village Communications, Inc. (with Send Fax S/W), and double-speed CD-ROM. Performa System software 7.5 comes pre-installed on the hard drive.

The Macintosh Performa 640CD DOS Compatible is also based on Apple's 630 Macintosh product line, but this Mac carries an Intel processor attached to the motherboard as a separate processor for DOS or Windows. It includes 12 MB of memory, 500 MB Hard Disk, and carries Apple part number M3939LL/A. The processors used by this dual-platform product are the Motorola 68LC040-66/33MHz processor and Intel's 486DX2-66MHz processor. The Performa 640CD also includes an Apple Multiple Scan 15" Display (.28 Dot Pitch), AppleDesign keyboard, 14.4 bps Fax/Modem by Global Village Communications, Inc. (with Send Fax S/W), and double-speed CD-ROM.

PowerPC Performas

Power Macintosh Performas feature the same System software and hardware as Power Macintosh computers. These computers, however, are much faster and more adaptable, should you ever decide to add peripherals internally.

Performa 5215CD

Macintosh Performa 5215CD is based on the Power Macintosh 5200/75 LC computer. The 5215CD includes 8 MB of memory, 1GB hard drive, and carries Apple part number M4107LL/A. Additional hardware bundled with the 5215CD includes the Apple Multiple Scan 15" Display (.28 Dot Pitch), AppleDesign keyboard, 14.4 bps Fax/Modem by Global Village Communications, Inc. (with Send Fax S/W), and quad-speed CD-ROM. This Performa uses System software 7.5.1 and enabler 406, which is pre-installed on the hard drive.

Performa 6116CD

Macintosh Performa 6116CD is based on the Power Macintosh 6100 computer. The 6116CD has 8 MB of memory and 700 MB internal hard drive. Additional hardware bundled with the 6116CD includes the Apple 14" Performa Plus Display (.28 Dot Pitch), AppleDesign keyboard, 14.4 bps Fax/Modem by Global Village Communications, Inc. (with Send Fax S/W), and Apple internal double-speed CD-ROM drive. This Performa has System 7.5 pre-installed on the internal hard drive.

Performa 6220CD

Macintosh Performa 6220CD is based on the Power Macintosh 6200CD computer. The Performa 6220CD has a built-in TV tuner card, 16 MB of memory, 1GB internal hard drive, and carries Apple part number M4104LL/A. A monitor is not included with this bundle. Additional hardware for the 6220CD includes the AppleDesign keyboard, internal quad-speed CD-ROM, and a 14.4 bps Fax/Modem by Global Village Communications, Inc. (with Send Fax S/W). System 7.5.1 and enabler 406 are pre-installed on the internal hard drive.

Performa 6200CD

Macintosh Performa 6200CD is based on the Power Macintosh 6200/75 LC computer. The Performa 6200CD has 8 MB of memory, 1GB internal hard drive, and carries Apple part number M4100LL/A. Additional hardware includes Apple Multiple Scan 15" Display (.28 Dot Pitch), AppleDesign keyboard, 14.4 bps Fax/Modem by Global Village Communications, Inc. (with Send Fax S/W), and Apple internal quad-speed CD-ROM. System software 7.5.1 and enabler 406 are pre-installed on the internal hard drive.

Mac Clones

The first Macintosh clones are based on the Power Macintosh 8100/100 and 8100/110, both of which run System 7.5.

Power Computing

Power Computing introduced two Macintosh clones in mid-1995: the Power 100 and Power 110. Both computers are similar to Apple's 8100/100 and 8100/110. Power Computing's sales approach is to let you build your own system; pricing information for your custom Mac clone can be obtained on the World Wide Web site at www.powercc.com. All models have a 30-day money-back guarantee, lifetime technical support, available on-site service, and a variety of hardware configuration options, such as an internal removable-media drive. These models also include software bundles pre-installed on the internal hard drive.

Power Computing's fastest model is the Power 120, which has a 120MHz 601 PowerPC processor and 256K level 2 cache (with optional 512K and 1 MB caches also available), 8 MB of memory expandable to 200 MB, built-in video support for 17" VGA displays, internal 3.5" hard drive ranging in size from 356 MB to 4GB, internal floppy drive, built-in Ethernet, two high-speed serial ports, internal quad-speed CD-ROM player, 16-bit audio input and output capabilities, 3 NuBus expansion slots, and high-speed SCSI port. Keyboard, mouse, and System software are included with all models.

Power Computing will probably introduce Power Macintosh clones with 604 and 601-based PCI clone models in the near-future that will give customers the option of combining NuBus or PCI slots via daughter cards that extend from the main motherboard. Some of the 604 and 601-based models will also support processor upgrades.

Power Computing Corporation
12337 Technology Blvd.
Austin, TX 78727
(800) 999-7279, (800) 708-6227 Technical Support

Radius

Radius introduced its first Macintosh clones in the fall of 1995: Radius System 100 and 81/110. These clones, based on Apple's 8100/100 and 8100/110 models, offer custom graphics configurations or completely customizable systems. Radius Systems come standard with 16 MB of memory, built-in Ethernet, 16-bit audio support, and internal quad-speed CD.

The 81/110 features open-ended configurability, and can be configured with a 730 MB or 2GB hard drive in addition to Radius NuBus video acceleration products. The Radius System 100 model includes a 2GB hard drive, software bundle with Adobe Photoshop, accelerated 24-bit super resolution color, Adobe Photoshop acceleration, and accelerated SCSI disk for optimized graphics performance. The Radius System 100 also offers 1600×1200 resolution, QuickDraw acceleration, PhotoEngine acceleration, and real-time CMYK acceleration for Photoshop using the Radius Thunder IV GX 1600 graphics accelerator card.

Another Radius offering is the PowerUser 110MHz clone (similar to the 8100/100). This tower-shaped case, with three NuBus slots for expansion, quad-speed internal CD, built-in video support, also includes a 256K level-2 cache and a 2GB internal hard drive. The Power-User model does not include a monitor and keyboard in the base price, but is bundled with System 7.5. The PowerUser 110MHz is only available from MacWarehouse.

Radius, Inc.
215 Moffett Park Drive
Sunnyvale, CA 94089
(408) 541-6100, (800) 227-2795

PowerUser clones
MacWarehouse
PO Box 3013
1720 Oak Street
Lakewood, NJ 0871-3013
(800) 710-9926

DayStar

DayStar is best known for its accelerator products, but recently became an Apple clone licensee. DayStar has not announced a clone model to date, but it announced products that take advantage of multiple processors in a Power Macintosh. Multiple processing involves adding PCI or NuBus accelerator hardware and software to a Macintosh. At press time no additional information on DayStar clone products was available. More information on DayStar's accelerator products can be found in Chapter 6.

Apple WorkGroup Servers

Apple's WorkGroup Servers are Macintosh computers configured to be dedicated servers. Workgroup servers are designed to work as dedicated servers on an AppleTalk network. If other computers on the network use AppleTalk, they can also access the Macintosh server. A server is not intended to be used by a regular computer user, however; it is configured by an administrator so that other users with a variety of access privileges can store and share information by moving files and folders to the server. Any Macintosh can be a server if Personal Filesharing is turned on in the System software, or by installing AppleShare software. You would then create users and groups and select the items you want to share on the network.

Workgroup servers are based on Macintosh desktop models but come with additional hardware, such as an internal DAT drive for backups, larger internal hard drive, and an internal CD-ROM drive. The server includes bundled server software that is not installed on the hard drive. The bundled software can be used for backups, server administration, network troubleshooting, and configuration. Higher-end server models offer faster processors (faster than are available on desktop models) and more internal storage space. Newer WorkGroup Servers also have slightly altered front cases: the floppy drive is located in the lower middle half of the case, the DAT drive at the top of the front case, and the internal CD or removable media drive in the upper middle section of the case.

WorkGroup Servers run the latest version of AppleShare software—Apple's server software. AppleShare allows a server administrator to create individual users and groups of users with a variety of access levels for access to files and folders on the server's internal or external hard drives. AppleShare includes networking tools to facilitate analysis of network performance and troubleshooting and also facilitates server backups of critical information from client users.

For more information on Apple's WorkGroup Servers, call a local Apple dealer or Apple (408) 996-1010. Valuable alternative resources include Apple's Web page site at www.info.apple.com; their ftp site—ftp.info.apple.com—and Apple's Product Central area on eWorld or AppleLink.

A Brief History of Macintosh Computers

The first Macs—the XL, 128K, 512K, 512Ke, Plus, and SE—were first introduced in 1984 and used the 16 MHz 68000 processor. The Mac Portable and PowerBook 100 (a miniaturized version of the Portable and Classic Macintosh) also used this chip. The first systems came with a keyboard, mouse, and floppy drive, one serial port, a 9" black-and-white 1-bit screen, and a port for an additional floppy drive.

Courtesy of Apple Computer, Inc.

Figure 2.7   The 128K Macintosh.

Courtesy of Apple Computer, Inc.

Figure 2.8   The 512Ke Macintosh.

Courtesy of Apple Computer, Inc.

Figure 2.9 The Macintosh Plus.

Courtesy of Apple Computer, Inc.

Figure 2.10 The Portable Mac.

In 1987, Apple introduced its largest , most expandable Macintosh: Macintosh II. Code-named Paris, this was the first 68020-based Macintosh, the first Mac with color, and the first Mac with six slots for adding video, network, sound, and accelerator cards. In 1990, Apple introduced its second and last 68020-based Macintosh with a new product line—LC, for low-cost Macintosh. The Macintosh II featured six NuBus expansion slots and two internal floppy drives, as well as internal hard drive. The Macintosh II grew into the IIx and IIfx models, then was discontinued and replaced by the Quadra 900 and 950 with a tower case.

In 1993, Apple introduced the first AV (audio video) Macintosh computers and consolidated the now discontinued Quadra line of 68K Macintosh computers. The 840AV and 660AV models support speech recognition, video input and capture, video output, and two-speed internal CD drives that no longer require a caddy. The 840AV was the fastest 68040 Macintosh Apple released, using a 40MHz 68040 processor compared to 33MHz 68040 and 68LC040 processors in alternate models. The delineation between the Centris and Quadra product lines, all of which use 68LC040 or 68040 processors, is that the Quadra line consists of faster 68040 processors matching the same form factor as the Centris line.

The LC was the first low-cost Macintosh, with the most popular form factor ever. Form factor is the size of the case that holds the motherboard, power supply, hard drive, floppy drive, and external ports. It was one of the first models to feature sound input and included a microphone. Following the LC were the LCII, LCIII, LC475, Quadra 605, and Performa 400, 405, 410, 450, 460, 475, 476, and 477. The LC line expanded to include all-in-one Macintosh computers (models that have built-in monitors) such as the LC550, 575, and Power Macintosh 5200/75 LC and 5300/100 LC models.

These low-cost Macintosh computers are designed for customers who are limited in desk space and who do not plan to expand their Macintosh beyond the addition of one card. The LC expansion slot uses the PDS (processor-direct slot) format. Desktop models and Power Duos also incorporate the PDS format, although the Power Duo uses its PDS slot to dock with additional devices.

The Macintosh Portable was the first 68000 portable Macintosh, and was reborn in the PowerBook 100. Since the first portable, PowerBook models have existed in two form factors: the all-in-one and Duo. All-in-one PowerBooks include the 140, 145B, 150, 160, 165, 165c, 170, 180, 180c, 520, 520c, 540, 540c, 190c/cs, and 5300 series models. PowerBook Duos can be expanded through the use of a portable mini-dock or a desktop-based dock. Duo models include the 210, 230, 250, 270, 270c, 280, 280c, and 2300. PowerBooks have since evolved into the Power Macintosh PowerBook 190/66 and 5300/100 and 5300/117. PowerBook Duos took portability a step further, with a model that had no floppy drive, one processor-direct slot (PDS), one serial port, and room for an internal modem. These models could be docked into a variety of expansion ports, including the DuoDocks consisting of additional VRAM, two NuBus slots, additional internal hard drive and floppy drive.

The first Power Macintosh computers were introduced in 1994 and included the 6100/60, 7100/66, and 8100/80 models, which also sported an AV graphics card option. They share the hardware case first used on the Quadra 610, 650, and 800. Since their introduction new models contain faster processors and require System 7.5. Faster Power Macintosh models are the 6100/66, 7100/80, 8100/100, and 8100/110. Over one million Power Macintosh computers were sold in their first year of release, and have sustained immense popularity due to exceptional software and hardware performance.

What Makes a Mac a Mac

Like all computer platforms, Macintosh computers rely on a number of common pieces of hardware to function. Some of the most important pieces are obvious: a CPU, RAM, floppy disk drive or hard disk drive, monitor, and keyboard. Macintosh computers also include a number of features exclusive to the Macintosh line. You may have used Mac hardware so often you forgot what makes a Mac a Mac. This section focuses on the Macintosh elements designed into Macs over the past 10 years.

ADB

The Apple Desktop Bus (ADB) is most commonly used for connecting a keyboard and mouse to your Macintosh. It can also be used to connect additional input devices, such as a second keyboard, pointing device, graphics tablet, or hardware key. Up to 27 ADB devices can coexist on an ADB port. The more devices connected to a single port, however, the slower the performance. Pen-based drawing and writing tablets and joysticks can also use the ADB port instead of the serial port. Most Macs, except for PowerBook Duos, have at least one ADB port; higher-end models have two. For more information on keyboards, mice, and other Macintosh input devices see Chapter 4.

Cache

A disk cache uses a predetermined amount of DRAM memory to process file system instructions. The disk cache can improve file system performance by reducing the need for the CPU to read and write files and folders to the hard drive. The cache size is set in the Memory Control Panel, which is a part of System 7.

Macintosh computers support a disk cache and a processor cache. Some Power Macintosh computers can have an additional processor cache added to the motherboard. These are called Level 2 caches and range in size from 256K to 1 MB. The Level 2 cache is a special type of RAM that is added to a processor direct (PDS) slot. (Level 1 cache is a part of the PowerPC processor and is faster than RAM.) Another advanced Mac processor, the 68040, has an internal cache built into it. You can turn on or off the built-in cache using the Cache Switch control panel.

Cache cards can also be added to a Macintosh computer's NuBus, PDS, or PCI expansion slot to improve performance. Keep in mind that caches are only effective at certain sizes. For example, if you select a 2 MB cache, it may not provide any more performance than a 1 MB cache because of motherboard data bus speed limitations or the slow speed of another hardware component on the motherboard.

CD-ROM

Internal CD-ROM players are a standard feature on all desktop and low-cost Macs. The speed of the internal unit varies from 2x (double-speed) to 4x (quad-speed). CDs used in these players can be formatted for any CD player speed, but must be formatted for the faster speed drive to take advantage of its faster performance. CDs supported include traditional audio CDs, Kodak PhotoCDs, Macintosh formatted CD-ROMs, and some DOS data CDs formatted for Macintosh.

CD-ROMs were available externally for Macintosh when the IIci was introduced in 1989. The Apple SC CD-ROM drive was Apple's first external CD mode. Compared to Apple's current 600e internal or external CD ROM drive, the SC has an extremely slow, almost unusable access time. The original SC drive also has problems with dust interfering when reading CD media.

Apple's first internal CD-ROM player, the 150, shipped with the Quadra 650, 610, and 800 models, and the Performa 600. The SC, SC+, and 150 CD Players require CD caddies, or jackets, for their player mechanism. The Power Macs introduced the first caddyless, 2x internal and external CD-ROM players—the 300i and 300e. The 600i and 600e look almost identical to the 300 series models, except they have a faster access speed (4x).

CPU

The Central Processing Unit (CPU), also referred to as "processor," is the engine of a computer. The type of processor and its clock speed determine how a Mac can be upgraded. Macintosh computers use Motorola CPUs, which began with the 68000, and then evolved into the 68020, 68030, 68040 (and 68LC040). The new PowerPC chips—the PowerPC 601, 603, 603e, and 604—were developed by Apple, Motorola, and IBM, and are based on RISC technology. Previous 68K Motorola CPUs were CISC processors, which require complex research and development to increase the speed and shrink the size of the processor chip. Macintosh software created for PowerPC chips is two to four times faster than the same software created for 68K Macintosh computers.

Apple also provides cross-platform solutions: Mac users can put an Intel processor daughtercard on the Macintosh motherboard. Intel processors available for the Mac are 66MHz 486 SX and DX chips. These hardware solutions are certified to be compatible with Windows 95 in addition to Windows 3.1 and DOS. See Appendix G for more specific information on Apple's cross-platform Macintosh computers.

Ethernet

Ethernet is a fast, productive networking protocol that enables computers to transfer information across a network. It is a common network protocol in most businesses and schools because it supports local and wide area networks and allows access to the Internet. Apple has supported Ethernet network cards since the Mac II was introduced; Ethernet is available as a built-in or add-in option in all current Macintosh computers available today.

Two types of Ethernet networks exist—10BASE-T and Coaxial (Thin Net). Each format requires a different type of Ethernet transceiver on the Macintosh; if both formats exist on a network, a converter is required to convert the two formats. Ethernet, as well as LocalTalk networks, require a beginning and end Macintosh on the network. If Macs are "looped" into the network several times, or improperly terminated on the physical network, network performance will decrease and some Macs may not function properly.

Floppy Drive

A floppy drive reads floppy disks. All Macs, except for PowerBook Duos and models before the IIci, contain internal 1.4 MB floppy drives. 1.4 MB floppy drives can read 1.4 MB, 800K, and 400K formatted floppies. With additional software, such as PC Exchange 2.0, these floppy drives can also read Intel/DOS/Windows PC floppies, Apple II/IIgs/Prodos floppies, and UNIX file formats.

Floppy disks can be used for short-term data storage, including backups. These are also the least expensive and most readily available removable media for computers today. Since every model has a floppy drive, it is the easiest way to move files from one Macintosh to another. Keep in mind that access times for floppy disks are the slowest access rates existent compared to other removable media.

Hard Drive

Hard drives store files and folders, such as System software and applications. A hard drive consists of several pieces: a power supply, hard disk, SCSI in and out ports, and a SCSI ID counter. An internal hard drive uses the power supply connected to the motherboard of the CPU; external hard drives use a dedicated power supply. The hard disk is the physical disk that a mechanical "arm" or "head" writes information on and reads information from. Most hard drives have two SCSI 50-pin connectors: one for connecting the drive to the Macintosh, and a second for continuing the SCSI daisy chain to another SCSI device. The SCSI ID counter must be set to an ID number unique to the hard drive (SCSI ID 0 and 7 are reserved for the Macintosh internal hard drive and motherboard).

The "soft" side of a hard drive is a File System that consists of a catalog and directory representing all the contents on the hard drive. Faster hard drives provide faster data throughput to the processor and SCSI chips on the motherboard. A good general rule for purchasing a hard drive is to buy one with the most storage capacity for the most money you can afford to spend. Next to memory, you can never have enough hard drive space, either. Over the past years, the price and size of hard drives have become more cost effective than, comparatively, memory.

Hard drives were first added to Macintosh SE models. These early Macs contained about 20 MB of hard drive space. 40 MB and 80 MB drives were standard sizes for hard drives until the IIfx was introduced. Its high-end configuration had a 160 MB hard drive. Current desktop and PowerBook Power Macintosh models contain hard drives ranging in size from 230 MB to 2GB. Hard drives up to 9GB are also available for Macintosh computers from third-party mail order vendors.

IR

Infra-Red is relatively new hardware technology available on Macintosh low-cost, desktop, and portable models. IR can be used as a traditional remote control interface and is commonly found on home stereo and televisions. To use infra-red as a close range network solution, you must have two units with compatible infra-red hardware and software within three feet of each other.

Note

One popular, but frowned upon use for infra-red was during mid-terms or finals. Students used this harmless technology to share information.

Infra-Red was first used in the Newton to "beam" business cards from one Newton to another. The 630, 5200, and 6200 desktop Macs and 190, 5300, and 2300 series PowerBooks have internal IR to communicate between Macs or to control the built-in TV tuner. Third-party products include IR-based technology that can simulate network functionality. This is the first wireless solution for Macintosh networking, and works efficiently in closely knit workgroup offices.

LocalTalk

LocalTalk is a smaller bandwidth (slower) network protocol than Ethernet that is built into every Macintosh via the Printer serial port and AppleTalk System software. It is a low-cost, built-in solution for any Macintosh, and enables Macintosh computers to talk to each other and to printers. If more than two Macintosh computers exist on your LocalTalk network, additional LocalTalk "drop boxes" can be purchased to create a LocalTalk network of Macs. LocalTalk supports a maximum of 32 nodes, or Macintosh devices per "zone" before network performance is affected. When networking Macs together, be sure to minimize the network cable length to maximize network performance (the shorter the network distance, the faster the network performance).

Microphones

Microphones can be used to input sound to a Macintosh; the Mac can then output the sound to a variety of media, including floppy disks and CD-ROM. Early Macintosh computers could not record sound. MacRecorder was first introduced in the late 1980s as an external device that plugged into the serial port and allowed the Mac to record sound through a microphone, or directly from another audio source. Stereo sound could be simulated by using two Mac Recorders—one used the Printer port, the other the modem port. The IIsi, LC, and Quadra 900, and Quadra 700 were the first Macs to have sound input hardware and System software. PowerBooks, Color Classics, and other all-in-one Macs have microphones built into the Macintosh case. Live and pre-recorded audio can be controlled by the Sound control panel.

Apple introduced speech technology with the Quadra 840AV and Centris/Quadra 660AV, permitting text-to-speech and speech-to-text (PlainTalk technology) capabilities on Macintosh. Speech technology required a DSP chip on the first AV models; the PowerPC chip processes speech on the Power Macintosh computers. The microphone for this technology is much more sensitive and a tad larger than the original microphone sold and included with IIsi and LC Macintosh computers. All current Macintosh models use the PlainTalk microphone for any type of sound input to Macintosh.

MIDI

MIDI—Musical Instrument Digital Interface—is a standard in the music industry for controlling musical instruments. Macintosh computers can also use the MIDI standard through the use of additional hardware, which is most commonly attached to the Macintosh serial and/or microphone port. MIDI enables a Macintosh to become a MIDI keyboard controller and musical workstation for digital audio. MIDI can also be used to control non-musical MIDI compatible hardware devices, such as home electronics and appliances. For a more in depth explanation of sound, MIDI, and music on the Macintosh, see Chapter 11.

Modems

Modems connect your Mac to other computers and online services through phone lines. Modems come pre-installed in your Macintosh modem serial port or can be purchased separately. Internal and external modems usually cost between $100 and $300. This is a small fee considering the amount of information and people you can access by adding one to your Mac.

Modems enable your Macintosh to connect to Bulletin Board Services; online services such as America Online, Prodigy, or eWorld; and to the Internet. With additional software, modems can also function as telephone answering machines and telephone systems.

NuBus/PCI Slots

NuBus slots are part of almost every desktop Macintosh model. NuBus slots enable you to upgrade your Macintosh with network, graphics, SCSI, data controlling, and accelerator cards. NuBus slots and other Macintosh expansion slots are limited by power and physical dimension specifications. For this reason, upgrades cannot exceed the data bus speed of the motherboard, or the size of the Macintosh case. Apple introduced the NuBus expansion slot beginning with the Macintosh II, and included this slot standard with all Macs up through the first Power Macintosh (LC, all-in-one, and PowerBooks excluded).

NuBus slots accept many types of NuBus expansion cards and can be used to extend the number of monitors or network connections on your Macintosh. Most accelerator cards are also available for NuBus slots, which increase a Mac's processing, graphics, and SCSI performance. Smaller form-factor Macs such as the Centris/Quadra series or the Power Macintosh 6100 (these Macs share the same external case/form factor) have a PDS (Processor Direct Slot) that accepts a special "L-shaped" card to accommodate NuBus cards.

The Mac II, IIx, and IIfx have six NuBus slots, which is more than any current Mac. However, these models lacked other features such as built-in Ethernet, video, and sound—standard on all modern Power Macs. The last Macs to have NuBus slots included from one to five slots.

Desktop Macs introduced in 1995 have PCI (Peripheral Computer Interconnect) expansion slots. These slots are incompatible with NuBus, and are physically smaller in size. PCI cards currently include video, networking, graphics accelerators, PowerPC accelerators (cards with one or more PowerPC processors), and SCSI accelerators. PCI cards are a standard format in the PC/DOS industry. Compatibility of a PC PCI card is only possible if the PCI card includes a Macintosh software driver.

Power Macintosh computers with PCI slots can use NuBus cards with the addition of a PCI to NuBus conversion card. The Power Computing company is expected to offer Power Macintosh clones that will support PCI and NuBus slots. This is a good upgrade solution if you currently use NuBus cards that you want to continue to use with a faster PowerPC platform. Keep in mind that you may want to consider the power consumption and performance of PCI and NuBus card combinations installed together in a particular Macintosh computer.

LC Macs have one PDS (Processor Direct Slot) for video, acceleration, or networking cards. The PDS varies across the LC line; not all PDS cards work with all LC models. The LC II, for example, has a slightly different PDS slot than the LCIII, LC475, and LC5200. The LC, LCII, and LCIII also had the option of using an Apple IIe PDS card. These were discontinued with the LCIII in 1994.

PowerBooks introduced in 1995 have PCMCIA (also known as PC) expansion slots that accept Type I or II PC cards, such as networking, modem, or hard drive cards. Previous PowerBook models allowed an additional monitor to be connected, but these lacked expansion slots. PowerBook Duos include a variety of DuoDocks, the largest of which can hold two NuBus cards, an internal hard drive, FPU, and VRAM.

Other networks

With the 840AV and 660AV Macs, Apple introduced Geoport. Geoport works with Geoport-compatible serial ports, and requires a hardware "pod" that provides modem, telephony, and other telecommunications features. More information on Geoport is available in Chapter 11.

PowerBooks and PowerBook Duos lack Ethernet connections because of power consumption problems and expansion port limitations. Some third-party vendors such as Farallon have created EtherWave transceivers that allow a PowerBook's LocalTalk port to connect to an Ethernet network, enabling the PowerBooks to access a faster network bandwidth.

RAM

RAM (Random Access Memory) is used for applications (DRAM—dynamic random access memory) and video/monitor displays (VRAM—video random access memory). DRAM, commonly referred to as RAM, or the generic term "memory," is used by software to store memory management, data manipulation, and other types of information sent to it by applications and System software. Memory is perhaps the most frequent Macintosh upgrade.

A good general rule is to double or triple the amount of memory you think you need to allow for software growth. Many Macintosh models have a limited number of memory expansion slots. The Power Mac 6100, for example, only has two memory slots. Memory must be added in twos to be recognized by other hardware and System software. If you initially purchase two 4 MB memory modules, then realize you need more memory, you will need to either move the 4 MB modules to another Macintosh, or sell them and buy two 8 MB or 16 MB memory modules to complete the upgrade. High-end desktop models have four to sixteen memory expansion slots.

Note

When software is launched, a predetermined amount of memory is allocated for the application to run, permitting the application to interact with other files, System software, and hardware. The proper amount of installed memory is critical for running software. Software additions, such as virtual memory, are not comparable in performance to the addition of hardware memory, especially if you want to use your Macintosh for multimedia or for publishing large text or image documents.

The size of the memory SIMM (single-inline memory module) or DIMM (dual-inline memory module) in Macintosh computers differs. A SIMM is the small board on which the memory chips are soldered. Macintosh SIMMs vary in size for desktop and low-cost models from 30-pin to 72-pin SIMMs. The IIfx and first LaserWriter printers used the same size memory SIMMs (64-pin SIMMs). PowerBooks and Duos have unique SIMMs designed for their single memory expansion slot. The PowerBook 170 and 140 series used one type of memory module; the PowerBook 520 and 540 series use another; and the Duos (all models) use another memory module format.

The 9500, 8500, 7500, and 7200 PCI-based Macintosh computers introduced in 1995 all use 168-pin, 64-bit DRAM DIMMs. Early Macintosh computers (introduced in 1986) used 30-pin SIMMs, ranging in speed from 60 to 120 nanoseconds. The LCIII, Quadra 800, 650, and 610 series introduced in 1992 up through the first Power Macintosh computers used 72-pin SIMMs, a common SIMM size in DOS PC computers.

ROM

ROM stands for Read-Only Memory. Every Mac has a ROM chip set. The Macintosh ROM, commonly referred to as the Macintosh Toolbox, is the heart of every Macintosh.

It holds the System software and hardware drivers in a chip, which cannot be altered. ROM has fast access, and is responsible for speedy performance of software interacting with hardware. The ROM chip itself resides on the motherboard and is labeled with Apple's copyright stamp.

ROMs vary in size: the first Macs had 128K of ROM; today's Power Macs have 4 MB of ROM. Macintosh ROMs allow the Macintosh to start up, perform calls to the Toolbox, and talk to various hardware components. This information can also exist (and does) in Macintosh System software; however, the ROM allows increased performance and access to hardware information. This may change as Apple updates Macintosh system software to be completely native for Power Macintosh hardware.

SCSI

SCSI, also known as Small Computer System Interface, is most commonly used on the Mac to connect internal hard drives and CD-ROM players to the rest of the Macintosh system through the motherboard. Internally, the SCSI cable is a flat, multi-pin cable extending from the motherboard to the hard drive. Externally, SCSI cables are used to connect hard drives, scanners, CD-ROM players, display devices, printers, and a variety of removable media hardware devices. These connect to each other using 25-pin or 50-pin SCSI cables. PowerBooks use a smaller 30-pin SCSI connector for the PowerBook-end of the cable, extending to a 50-pin connector for external SCSI devices.

SCSI can support up to seven SCSI devices through a *daisy-chain*, which is a string of SCSI peripherals connected to the back of a Macintosh. Macintosh desktop models have 25-pin SCSI connectors. Most hard drives, scanners, and SCSI peripherals have two 50-pin connectors. Daisy-chaining two hard drives requires one 25 to 50 pin cable (Mac to hard drive) and a 50 to 50 pin cable (hard drive to hard drive). The total length of the SCSI cable should not exceed seven feet to ensure communication integrity across the daisy chain.

Each SCSI device must have a unique identification number (ID) usually located at the rear of the SCSI device (sometimes only accessible inside the case of the SCSI device). Keep in mind that the internal hard drive is always SCSI ID 0; the Macintosh is SCSI ID 7. Macs with internal CD players usually set this device to SCSI ID 3.

Only the physical last SCSI device in the daisy chain must be terminated for all the SCSI devices to be accessible by the Macintosh. SCSI Probe 3.5 is free software that can show you which SCSI devices are visible and accessible to your Macintosh. SCSI cables vary in content and quality; not all SCSI cables are alike. In troubleshooting a SCSI problem, try swapping SCSI cables with different SCSI devices to see if the problem disappears.

Serial I/O

Serial I/O, also known as serial input and output, is a standard Macintosh feature that supports printers, networks, and peripheral devices added to a Macintosh. Macintosh serial ports can be used for communicating directly with many peripherals. A serial cable can be attached from one Macintosh serial port to another to link the two computers through Personal File sharing and other networking features.

When you connect a serial cable from a Macintosh serial port to a Printer's serial port you can print. To allow multiple Macs access to a printer, you can purchase network transceivers that connect to the Macintosh serial port. Cables connect to other transceivers, which in turn connect to a printer. Transceivers are small boxes that support LocalTalk or Ethernet networking protocols. Some transceivers have green, orange, and red lights to indicate successful or unsuccessful network connections between the Macintosh and another network device.

Speakers

Speakers are popular internal and external multimedia equipment for Macintosh. A set of external speakers can greatly enhance playback of multimedia software and audio CDs when played on the Mac's CD-ROM drive. Macintosh computers come with an internal speaker that plays 8-bit monophonic sound (newer models play 16-bit stereo). External speakers or headphones can also be attached to the Macintosh sound output port. Apple has two external speaker models that connect to the sound output port via mini-plug; third-party speaker manufacturers, including Sony, Yamaha, and Bose, also manufacture external speakers.

Virtual Memory

Virtual Memory is a part of Apple's system software; when turned "on" Virtual Memory increases the amount of physical memory by creating a special "swap space" on the hard drive. The swap space used by Virtual Memory is reserved in an invisible file on the hard drive. Virtual Memory settings are controlled through the Memory control panel. Full features of the Memory control panel are covered in Chapter 5.

Virtual Memory increases performance on a Power Macintosh and reduces application memory requirements. To get the same benefits, you must set virtual to 1 MB more than the amount of physical memory installed on your Mac. For example, if your Mac has 24 MB of installed physical memory, turn Virtual Memory on and set it to 25 MB. When you restart your Macintosh, open "About This Macintosh" from the Apple Menu in Finder. It should show you how much physical memory is available, plus how much additional Virtual Memory (logical memory) is recognized and available to your Mac.

Virtual Memory can also be used to increase the amount of memory available to applications by two or three times, depending on how much free space is available on the hard drive. Unfortunately, increasing Virtual Memory by such factors will slow down any Macintosh because Virtual Memory uses the hard drive to swap out the contents of physical DRAM. The use of Virtual Memory on 68K Macintosh computers is not recommended when using multimedia software (QuickTime, QuickDraw 3D, CD-ROM titles, and so on) or other hard drive-intensive applications.

Macintosh Family Price and Performance Considerations

The best way to determine whether you are getting a good deal on a computer is to measure its price versus performance value. Price/performance can be measured with used and new Macintosh models and, depending on the software applications you will be running, will be an excellent indication of the best model to purchase. Price-to-performance measurements are moving more in favor of the customer and less in favor of manufacturers as technology continues to advance. You can buy faster and less expensive computing power now than ever before.

The measurement of price to performance involves comparing the processor, clock speed, and price of the Macintosh you want to buy to a similar new model in the same price range. Chances are that the newer model may offer considerably more performance than the model you are considering. For example, compare the Power Macintosh 5200/75 against the Power Macintosh 7500/100 and the 6100/66. The 5200 uses the PowerPC 603 processor, which many critics feel offers almost the same performance as the 6100/66. However, if you compare the 5200 and 6100 to the Power Macintosh 7500, which has a 100 MHz 601 processor, you pay a few hundred dollars more and have access to more technology, more room for memory and hard drive expansion, and can upgrade to a 604 processor in the future. If you compare the 7200/75 or 90 Power Macintosh computers to the 6100/66 and 5200/75, you still get a better price-to-performance ratio. In addition, the 7200 has the option to upgrade to a 7500 in the future. This upgrade path is not available with the 5200 and 6100 models.

Similar price-to-performance comparisons can be applied to low-cost models, such as 68030 Macintosh computers and 68040 and 68LC040 models. For desktop, portable, and low-cost systems, consider how many applications you plan to use that require a 68040, versus how much you want to spend to upgrade to PowerPC software. In general, you want the fastest processor you can find that meets your price range.

Another price to performance element to keep in mind is that higher-end Macintosh models include larger hardware configurations. This means you get more memory, hard drive space, and external ports in addition to a faster processor and larger case. The Power Macintosh 8500 and 9500, for example, are available in 32 MB memory configurations with 2GB hard drives. In comparison, the Power Macintosh 5200 is only available in 8 MB and 16 MB configurations with 1GB hard drives.

Your System Software

System software enables the CPU and associated hardware to run other software applications. Apple's System software runs when you first start up the computer and continues as control panels, extensions, and other System software load into memory. System software enables the user to customize settings such as mouse movement, clicking speed, and to select desktop patterns.

In order for the Macintosh to boot and run properly, it must have two essential pieces of System software in the System Folder: the System File and the Finder file. Only one active System Folder can exist on each hard drive volume. If more than one System Folder exists, your Mac may have startup problems or problems running application software because it won't know which Finder or System File from which it should launch.

This chapter will discuss the many versions of System software that have been available for the Mac—through System 7.5.2 and future software updates.

A History and Feature Guide

This section covers the System software used on Macintosh models since the Macintosh II, which included version 6 of the System software. Information for each version includes a general description of the features in the System software and the Mac models that can support the software.

System 6.x

Contents—Four 800K floppies or two 1.4 MB floppies, uncompressed.
Requirement—at least 2 MB of memory, bootable from hard drive or floppy.
Main features—MultiFinder, and Finder modes, single Control Panel window.
Macintosh models supported—Plus, SE, SE/30, II, IIx, IIcx, IIci, IIfx, LC, IIsi, Classic, PowerBook 100.

The first color Macintosh—Macintosh II—shipped with System software version 6.0.1. Prior to System 6, Apple had released a number of System software versions, primarily for the Plus and SE models. The most stable version for the Mac was version 4.1. System 6.0.1 added color to the Macintosh, although initially you could see color only on a color monitor attached to a color-support video card installed in a Macintosh II. 8-bit QuickDraw was first built into the II, SE/30, IIx, and IIcx ROMs, and supported more than the black-and-white mode of the Plus and SE models. 32-bit QuickDraw was added to ROMs when the IIci was introduced.

System 6 did not contain any compression of its System software files; if a user needed to replace a System software file, he or she could click-drag the file without having to run the installer.

System 7

Contents—six 1.4 MB floppies, uncompressed.
Requirements—at least 4 MB of memory; 68000 or higher processor; and an internal hard drive (at least 4 MB of hard drive space).
Main features—32-bit operating system, MultiFinder-only, separate control panel files and icons, color icons, aliases, interapplication communication, Balloon help, process/application manager, color desktop patterns.
Macintosh models supported—Plus, SE, SE/30, II, IIx, IIcx, IIci, IIfx, LC, IIsi, Classic, Quadra 900, 700, PowerBook 100, 140, 170 (with System 7 .0.1).

System 7.0 was introduced in the first quarter of 1991. Engineers worked on its various components for three years or more, creating Apple's most updated System software version in its history. Millions of Macintosh owners upgraded their systems with System 7, and developers have created thousands of System 7-savvy applications since its introduction. One new feature enabled users to drag and drop an extension, control panel, or system file, such as a sound, over the System Folder. The System asked you if you wanted these items placed in the appropriate folder located inside the System Folder.

With System 7.0, Apple introduced a new, redesigned operating system for its developers, an updated user interface with more color support, and a number of new features. QuickTime 1.0 followed the release of System 7.0 and pioneered software synchronization technology for creating multimedia applications on the Macintosh.

System 7.1

Contents—seven 1.4 MB floppies, uncompressed (compressed for 840AV/660AV).
Requirements—4 MB of memory; 68000 or higher processor; and an internal hard drive (approximately 5–7 MB of space).
Main features—Font folder, Worldscript I and II, System Enablers, separate control panels for specific CPUs (control strip for PowerBooks, energy saver for LCs, speech software for the AV Mac), and the Apple CD-ROM player.

System 7.1 was introduced in 1992 and was the first commercial, retail version of Apple's System software. International support was simplified in 7.1, and the Font folder was added. Also, the System Enabler file was introduced, permitting Apple to release a new Macintosh computer by creating a unique System Enabler file rather than an entire operating system to support the new hardware. System 7.1 introduced only a few, but relatively critical features compared to System 7.0. System Enablers are either names (for Duos and Power Mac models) or numbers (for LCs and Performas). For a complete list of System 7.1 and 7.1-based System Enabler files, see Appendix D.

Another new feature of System 7.1 is the Font folder that can manage up to 128 font suitcases. Keep in mind that suitcases can be merged and can hold multiple font families. The Font folder can recognize a font suitcase dragged or dropped over System software and asks you if you want the font suitcase to be placed in the Font folder.

The first PowerMacs—such as the 6100, 7100 and 8100, plus the Quadra and Performa 630 and PowerBook 150—shipped with System 7.1.2. System 7.1.2 contained native System software for the Power Mac. The Quadra 630 and PowerBook 150 computers included support for their internal IDE hard drive and new System Enabler files.

System 7.1 Pro

Contents—twelve 1.4 MB floppies, uncompressed and compressed.
Requirements—Apple Macintosh or PowerBook computer with at least 4 MB of RAM (5 MB recommended); hard disk; and Apple SuperDrive floppy disk drive.
Main features—PowerTalk 1.0, which includes mail send/receive, and server mounting capabilities. Additional features include digital signatures, business cards, and mail gateways to other mail services such as the Internet.

System 7 Pro, or System 7.1.1, introduced PowerTalk 1.0, Apple's mail and server access technology. PowerTalk introduced the Key Chain metaphor for storing server passwords, and included drag-and-drop technology for creating and sending mail to other PowerTalk users. PowerTalk also works with software gateways to manage mail sent via Internet between PowerTalk sites.

System 7 Pro doesn't run on the Macintosh 128, Macintosh 512, Macintosh Plus, or Macintosh XL.

System 7.5

Contents—eight 1.4 MB floppies compressed, or CD-ROM. Note that floppy disks for QuickDraw GX (two 1.4 MB floppies) and PowerTalk (one 1.4 MB floppy disk) are not included in the seven floppy disks.

Requirements—4 MB of memory; Mac Plus or larger Macintosh; and at least 5 MB of hard drive space.

Main features—Apple Guide 1.0, MacTCP 2.0.4, Thread Manager, Drag and Drop, Apple Menu Options, Extension Manager, larger desktop patterns, WindowShade, QuickTime 1.6.2, and Sound Manager 3.0.

System 7.5 was introduced in 1994 and supports Macintosh computers, including all 680x0 models from the Mac Plus through the first Power Macintosh computers. System 7.5 includes PowerTalk 1.1, QuickDraw GX, QuickTime 1.6.2, and Sound Manager 3.0. In 1995, QuickTime 2.0 and 2.1, QuickDraw 3D 1.0, and OpenTransport 1.0 were introduced with the first PCI-bus Power Macintosh computers. OpenDoc 1.0 is another technology Apple introduced in late 1995. Each of these technologies is discussed later in this chapter in the section "Additional System Software." Also see Chapter 7, "Buying Software Upgrades."

System 7.5 has a special feature that enables you to perform a "clean" install of System software. This can be accomplished by launching the System 7.5 installer, then typing ⌘-Shift-K. This will bring up a dialog window with two options: Update Existing System Folder and Install New System Folder. Choose the latter and a new System software folder will be created, without using any previous System files or resources.

System 7.5.1

Contents—Four 1.4 MB floppies compressed (System update that comprises a partial System disk set with no de-install options); or CD-ROM.

Requirements—Any Macintosh with System 7.5.

System Updates began with System 7.0.1, when Apple created a way to bring its customers bug fixes and System software modifications between the larger System software releases. System Update 3.0 was created for System 7.1.

System Update 7.5 version 1.0 changed the version number of System software to 7.5.1. The LC5200, 6200, 5300, and 6300 LC Mac models use System 7.5.1 with a System Enabler file (406) as its System software. System Updates are bug fix and performance enhancement releases of System software. System Update 7.5 version 1.0 is free and fits on four 1.4 MB floppy disks. This update is available on most online services, as well as Apple's ftp, Web, and support sites.

System 7.5.2

Contents—13–15 1.4 MB floppies, or CD-ROM.

This version update applies only to the newest Macintosh computers—9500, 8500, 7500, 7200, PowerBook 5300, 190, and 2300. Each computer model listed above has a CPU-specific floppy disk set and CD-ROM. System 7.5.2 is the System software version for all of these Macintosh models. For more information on these Mac models, see Chapter 2.

Additional System Software

Apple has introduced over the past seven years a number of extensions to its System software that enable the Macintosh to do things that only computers costing 10 to 100 times more could do just 10 years ago. For example, Apple's release of QuickTime 1.0 in 1991 shook the professional graphics world by enabling Mac users to create, edit, and output complete films on the Mac.

QuickTime 2.1

QuickTime enables sound and images to be synchronized with System software and hardware components. This software is also available in playback mode for Windows PCs. QuickTime 2.0 is most commonly used in multimedia software such as educational, game, and 3D software.

Since version 1.0, QuickTime has grown from one extension to three: QuickTime, QuickTime Musical Instruments, and QuickTime PowerPlug (for Power Macintosh).

QuickTime 1.6.1 was the first version of QuickTime to use a minimum amount of memory if the technology is not being used by other software. QuickTime 1.6.1 only occupies about 20K of memory when not in use. The amount of memory QuickTime uses directly depends on how much another application relies on QuickTime—usually about 800K of memory.

QuickTime runs on color-capable Macintosh computers equipped with a 68020 processor or better, 4 MB of memory, and versions 6.0.7 or later of the Macintosh operating system.

QuickTime 2.0 recommended using the Multimedia Tuner 2.0.1 with QuickTime 2.0. The Multimedia Tuner is an extension file that fixes some bugs with QuickTime 2.0 and improves QuickTime playback performance. The Multimedia Tuner extension is not needed with QuickTime 2.1, which incorporates these fixes.

QuickDraw 3D 1.0 or 1.0.3

QuickDraw 3D is Apple's newest multimedia technology that enhances application features, the interface, and interactivity. QuickDraw 3D software can also work with 3D-extendable hardware, also available from Apple. With this software and 3D-extendable hardware, Macs can now play high-end 3D software, such as interactive virtual reality packages, that was previously unavailable because of hardware speed limitations.

QuickDraw 3D also influences the World Wide Web by providing interactive 3D interfaces for Web page content. 3D technology enables a user to move a software object into or out of a window of an application. An object can also be rotated, edited, added onto, lit with one or more light sources, and rendered. *Rendering* involves projecting a pattern or image onto the surface of the 3D object.

This technology is currently available only for the Power Macintosh. QuickDraw 3D includes a QuickDraw 3D extension and several QuickDraw 3D libraries. A Macintosh with 16 MB of RAM and an internal hard drive is required to run QuickDraw 3D.

Open Transport 1.0

Open Transport is a superset addition to AppleTalk network technology. AppleTalk is available on every Macintosh and in every version of System software. Open Transport includes MacTCP and additional networking services such as Ethernet.

Open Transport 1.0 requires a minimum 100K–300K of memory (depending on your Macintosh model) with networking software "off." With AppleTalk "on" an additional 600K of memory is required; MacTCP requires an additional 100K.

Newer Mac models also include Open Transport 1.0.8 for network System software, except for the PowerBook 5300, 190, and 2300 computers. If your Mac has software compatibility problems with Open Transport 1.0 and you have a copy of System 7.5, the workaround is to remove the four or five Open Transport-named library files located in the Extensions Folder in the System Folder, as well as the AppleTalk and TCP/IP control panels from the Control Panels folder. Copy the MacTCP Control Panel (version 2.0.4) from System 7.5 to the System Folder and Restart. Network performance may not be as fast as it was with Open Transport 1.0.7 installed. Nevertheless, application compatibility and functionality should be restored.

QuickDraw GX 1.1.2

QuickDraw GX is an extended set of graphics features for desktop publishing, printing, and imaging. QuickDraw GX's most accessible advantage is with desktop printing. QuickDraw GX supports all LaserWriters, the StyleWriter, and a few other Macintosh printer models. Third-party printer drivers are also available for QuickDraw GX. An icon of each printer is created on the desktop by QuickDraw GX, enabling you to drag a file to the printer icon to print a file, instead of having to open the application and the file and then select File, Print.

QuickDraw GX provides a number of other amazing publishing features, including the following:

- Greatly enhanced graphics capabilities. Because QuickDraw GX is an object-based model (shapes are the basic building blocks for everything), all graphic primitives can be distorted, or transformed in many ways.

- Simplified printing and print management via a new, customizable print architecture and user interface.

- The capability to create "portable" documents from any application, enabling other users to print and view documents without having the original application or fonts.

- Powerful type and text capabilities. When used in conjunction with updated or new applications, these features enable you to display and print any typeface in any of the world's myriad script systems. Other typographical capabilities of QuickDraw GX include the following:

    —Creation of layouts from descriptions of text, styles, and other information
    —Automatic creation of contextual forms and ligatures
    —Manual and automatic kerning, tracking, and letter spacing

—Sophisticated justification with support for Arabic kashidas
—Determination of the caret(s) for some locations within the text
—Support of applications' line-breaking decisions with fast measurement routines
—Automatic reordering and rearrangement of text for languages such as Arabic, Hebrew, and Hindi

QuickDraw GX consists of the QuickDraw GX extension, printer drivers, Power Mac libraries, and additional printer description and font files. QuickDraw GX runs on 68020, 68030, or 68040 Macintosh systems, and requires System 7.5 and approximately 5 MB of hard drive space. QuickDraw GX is also optimized for the PowerPC chip, so that applications can access the speed and performance of PowerPC technology. If running QuickDraw GX and PowerTalk with System 7.5, 16 MB of memory is required.

PowerTalk 1.2.3

PowerTalk enables you to send and receive mail on your Macintosh. This program also lets you set a server password, manage send/receive files, manage mail recipients and catalogs, and create mail applications. The PowerTalk technology provided in System 7.5 is the "client" side of PowerTalk. Apple also has a PowerTalk server solution that manages all PowerTalk users on a network and stores files sent to other PowerTalk users.

PowerTalk consists of two PowerTalk extensions: a PowerTalk folder in the System Folder, which stores your confidential server password information, and the PowerTalk folder in the Apple Extras folder. PowerTalk requires at least 16 MB of memory if running with QuickDraw GX and System 7.5, a Macintosh 68020 or faster running system, and an internal hard drive.

PlainTalk 1.4.1

Speech-to-text technology is currently available on the Power Macintosh and 840/660AV Macintosh only. PlainTalk includes several "voices" that "talk" to you. Each voice occupies a specific amount of memory, depending on the sound quality of the voice and the number of PlainTalk syllables it supports.

PlainTalk consists of the SpeechManager extension, plus additional files for voices. Speech-to-text requires at least 12 MB of memory, System 7, and an internal hard drive.

OpenDoc 1.0

OpenDoc introduces a new structure for Macintosh applications. Instead of one application with innumerable features, OpenDoc has parts. Each part can be one or several features, and depending on which part you use, the Menubar changes to show the Menu for that part. There is no Quit menu item; instead OpenDoc automatically quits when you close your last document.

OpenDoc consists of a number of extensions and library files for both 68K and Power Macintosh. It requires at least 2 MB of memory for the container piece, and any number of parts that individually can range in size from 10K to one or more megabytes. 16 MB of memory is required for optimal performance; also required are System 7.5 and an internal hard drive.

Performa System Software

Performa System software is nearly identical to traditional System software for Macintosh. The first Performa System software version was 7.0.1P, followed by 7.1P through 7.1P6. Performa System software is no longer distinguished differently from traditional System software. Original Performa software, such as Launcher Control Panel and the Performa Control Panel, are now a part of System 7.5. Performas also share the same System Enabler as their Macintosh counterpart. The current version of Performa System software is 7.5.1.

All Performa models include an uninstalled version of At Ease, which is Apple's security software that can be configured to simplify access to a Macintosh. Performa System software does not include an installer; instead, the Apple Backup Utility on the Utility Disk in the Performa System software disk set restores the Performa System software and all bundled software.

Performas also do not ship with a copy of System software; users are requested to create a backup of the system when they start up their Performa the first time. If your Performa has a CD-ROM player, the CD-ROM included with the computer contains both the System software and software bundle and will only start up the Performa it was created for.

Performa Software Bundles

The software included in each Performa varies from model to model. Educational titles from Broderbund (Grandma & Me) and other well-known Macintosh educational software developers are usually included. ClarisWorks, Quicken (check management software), *American Heritage Dictionary*, At Ease, typing, and calendaring usually are also included in a Performa software bundle. These titles all come pre-installed on the internal hard drive of the Performa, and in some cases the user must contact the publisher to obtain manuals.

Macintosh System software, such as System 7.5, is essential software you must use on your Macintosh. In addition to System software Apple has new extensions, such as QuickTime, QuickDraw GX, QuickDraw 3D, Open Transport, PowerTalk, and OpenDoc. These technologies may require an upgrade (which is what this book is all about!) unless you have a new Power Macintosh with at least 16 MB of memory. More information on System software can be found on online services, and via Apple's ftp and World Wide Web pages.

Understanding Your Mac Extras

Although many Macintosh models are complete computer systems right out-of-the-box (such as PowerBooks, LC5200, 580, 575, and 550 models), many more models consist only of the CPU case and mouse. Your Macintosh Extras consist of a first (or second) monitor, keyboard, mouse (or other pointing device), and additional hardware for file storage, networking, television, multimedia input and output, and printing. Macintosh Extras are any Macintosh hardware or software that is not included in the box with your Macintosh computer. This chapter reviews Apple's Macintosh Extra products as well as commonly recognized third-party vendors who provide comparable Macintosh Extra products. Additional vendors who sell Macintosh Extras can be found in Chapter 9. This includes the Macintosh Product Registry, a quarterly publication that lists Macintosh hardware and software products. It is accessible through America Online, eWorld, and Apple's Web page and can also be found online in the Redbook product registry, or in bookstores and magazine stands.

ADB Peripherals

ADB stands for Apple Desktop Bus. This port is usually located at the back of a Macintosh, or on the sides of an Apple keyboard. The ADB cable has four pins and allows you to connect a variety of input devices such as a mouse, keyboard, and graphics tablet to your Macintosh. The following section discusses several kinds of ADB devices, and includes addresses and phone numbers for selected ADB device manufacturers.

Keyboards

Not to be confused with musical keyboards, computer keyboards resemble the typewriters from which they originated. Many other input methods are available, but the keyboard remains the most common and familiar device for inputting text and numbers into a computer. Preference for a particular keyboard design, size, ergonomics and color are mostly subjective to personal tastes as well as your height, plus the size and shape of your hands.

Some people are concerned with compactness because they don't want to give up desk space. Others want big keyboards bristling with lots of keys and LEDs. Touch typists have particular preferences about the mechanical resistance of the keys and the overall layout and dimensions. The little bumps on the D and K keys are there for touch typists. These bumps on the *home keys* are what keep your fingers in the right place. In other situations (retail and industrial), you may need waterproof and dustproof keyboards. You should try typing on the keyboard you want to buy before making a purchasing decision.

Note

Take care to place your keyboard at a comfortable height. Long hours of typing can lead to carpal tunnel syndrome if your hands and wrists are at uncomfortable angles. Ideally, your hands and wrists should be flat, not bent. Most keyboards have a height adjustment, but you shouldn't use them; the back of the keyboard should be kept down, not up. Wrist rests can help level your wrists, and are an essential accessory. Look for one that is soft and that raises the wrist up to as flat an angle as possible. The section "Keyboard Accessories" discusses wrist rests in more detail.

Alternative keyboard layouts

Apple provides System files that add recognition of special symbols unique to various languages to its operating System. Each country is responsible for creating a unique version of System software to meet the specific hardware and software configuration needs. Japan, for example, has a version of System software which supports full Kanji language characters. The System software is also designed to work with the Kanji keyboard hardware to support English character input on a Kanji keyboard.

Note

Kanji characters are also known as 2-byte characters to denote the additional size of each typed character. Roman-based languages, such as English use 1-byte characters.

In the U.S., Apple provides foreign language support with language kits, which contain custom pieces of System software and keyboard drivers and layouts to support both English and another language. Apple's Language Kits for Japanese and Chinese dialects are examples of software products containing 2-byte System software extensions and keyboard files which are accessible with English System software.

Keyboard layouts enable Macintosh System software to recognize custom symbols used by specific countries on any Macintosh keyboard. There are also dozens of Roman keyboard layouts. Roman keyboard layouts include the English, French, and Spanish languages. Custom Roman keyboard layouts exist for the U.S., Britain, Canada, France, Switzerland, Germany, Spain, Sweden, Norway, and Italy. If you have custom keyboard layouts installed in your System Folder, they will appear in the Keyboard Control Panel. You can only use one keyboard layout at any given time on your Macintosh, although you can change your keyboard layout without restarting your computer. Additional keyboard layouts for other languages are also available from Apple and all are designed to be used with System 7. If you do business internationally, you may want to buy these foreign language keyboard layouts.

Another option on Mac keyboards is the ability to change the standard QWERTY keyboard layout. In the early days of the mechanical typewriter, engineers had to find a way to make people type more slowly to keep the long metal keys from jamming. The QWERTY layout was the solution, and we're more or less stuck with it because that's what everyone knows and has learned. Several more efficient systems have been developed since then; the Dvorak layout is the best known. Although not quite as popular as QWERTY, the Dvorak layout puts the alphanumeric keys in an order that promotes faster typing.

An alternative to the traditional keyboard that allows alphanumeric input is the *chording keyboard*. These strange-looking devices usually are curved to fit the hand and have a button for each finger. Use the buttons in various combinations (like playing chords on the piano) to enter all the letters of the alphabet. You have to spend some time learning to use one of these alternative keyboards, but you can enter data extremely quickly with them. Court stenographers use similar devices because of their allowance for speed. Moreover, chording keyboards can be useful for people with disabilities.

If your work involves extensive numeric entry, you should have a numeric keypad. The typewriter-style row of numbers across the top of keyboards frustrates most people. Many keyboards, such as Apple's extended keyboards, have a numeric keypad built in, but you can buy one as a separate Apple Desktop Bus (ADB) accessory. Some keyboards also offer the option of an adjustable numeric keypad to accommodate left-handed numeric entry.

Selected keyboards

The following keyboards from Apple and third-party vendors represent a cross-section of those available. Ergonomic considerations should motivate your choice far more than the number of keys on the panel.

Apple keyboards

Apple Design Keyboard. Apple's current full-size keyboard has function keys and a right-hand numeric keypad; this keyboard works with all Macintosh computers with an ADB port. It is lighter in weight than previous extended keyboard models, and has height adjustments on the top-most corners of the bottom of the keyboard.

$90 average street price

Apple Extended Keyboard II. The Extended Keyboard II has all standard keys plus function keys, arrow keys, a numeric keypad, and other special keys (often useful when you're connected to a DOS machine or a mainframe and need special characters). The II model has a flatter profile, along with height adjustment, to reduce strain on the wrist.

$170 average street price (The Apple Extended Keyboard II is currently discontinued.)

Apple Adjustable Keyboard. You can split this keyboard in two and adjust the angle and placement of each segment. The main section splits in the middle, and the two halves pivot apart. You can change this keyboard's arrangement whenever you feel the need. Built-in wrist pads help to relieve strain. The numeric keypad detaches completely, and all the function keys are on this segment. The Adjustable Keyboard has all the keys of the Extended Keyboard, plus audio input controls for the built-in microphone on recent Macs.

$100 original average street price (The Apple Adjustable Keyboard is currently discontinued.)

Apple Keyboard II. Apple's basic keyboard occupies a small amount of desktop space. It includes the numeric keypad and cursor control keys, but lacks the function keys and other goodies on the extended keyboard.

$90 original average street price (The Apple Keyboard II is currently discontinued.)
Apple Computer, Inc.
One Infinite Loop
Cupertino, CA 95014
(408) 996-1010, (800) 776-2333

ADB Industrial Keyboard

Ruggedly made to survive in factory environments, this keyboard is a good choice for those who are developing Mac-based industrial, laboratory, or assembly line systems.

$480 SRP
Business Technology Manufacturing
42-20 235th St.
Douglaston, NY 11363
(718) 229-8080 Voice

MacPro and TrakPro

This is an ergonomic and configurable extended keyboard for all Macintosh computers with ADB ports. Key Tronic offers a complete line of Macintosh input devices, and has been producing Macintosh keyboards since the Macintosh II. In addition to its custom trackball and configurable components, its standard features are similar to those found on Apple's extended keyboard, such as a separate numeric keypad, top-row function keys and directional arrow keys.

$179 SRP MacPro Plus
$249 SRP Trak Pro
Key Tronic Corp.
P.O. Box 14687
Spokane, WA 99214
(509) 928-8000, (800) 262-6006

TrackBoard Keyboard

This keyboard gives users a full-function, extended keyboard and an easy-to-use trackball in a single, space-saving package. The TrackBoard product includes a trackball located on the keyboard plus three built-in buttons which work in conjunction with the trackball. It works with any Macintosh with an ADB port.

$179.95 SRP
Datadesk International
7869 W. Day Road NE
Bainbridge Island, WA 98110
(206) 842-5480, (800) 248-4001

Kensington Notebook KeyPad

PowerBook users who frequently enter numeric data might want to buy Kensington's Notebook KeyPad to make up for PowerBook's lack of a keypad. The Notebook KeyPad requires an ADB port; you must have a dock if you want to use it with a Duo.

$119.95 SRP, $149.95 SRP with adding machine software
Kensington Microware
2855 Campus Blvd.
San Mateo, CA 94403
(415) 572-2700 Voice
(415) 572-9675 Fax

Keyboard accessories

Keyboard accessories can prolong the life of your keyboard and can make the use of it more comfortable and pleasant. Accessories can even protect equipment from dust, damage, and other naturally occurring but unwanted environmental fallout. Two popular accessories that business owners should consider when using their Macs are keyboard covers and wrist pads:

- Keyboard Covers. Many companies make nylon dust covers, which are useful in environments with pets and small children (such as home offices) to prevent damage from falling objects and spilled liquids. For retail (especially point of sale with food handling) and industrial use, tough plastic skins keep dust and liquids out. Touch typing can be slightly more difficult when these covers are placed over the keyboard.

- Wrist Pads. There are a variety of wrist pads available for both keyboard and mouse. Wrist pads sit in front of a keyboard or mouse and raise your wrist closer to the level of the keyboard keys. The pads usually consist of a combination of firm and soft materials to provide both comfort and support to your hand. Many wrist pads use variations of neoprene as cushioning material in the wrist pad. If you use your keyboard or mouse extensively, wrist pads can help reduce wrist strain and hand fatigue.

Overview of the mouse

The mouse, or pointing device, has been one of the Macintosh's more innovative and distinctive features throughout its history. Researchers at Xerox PARC originally developed the concept of a pointing device, and Apple was the first company to introduce this device commercially on the Lisa computer. Since then, the mouse has become a standard in the personal computer industry because it is the best way to move the cursor and selected items around onscreen. Apple has always offered a single-button mouse, though others boast several buttons.

In the beginning, Apple used a dedicated, unique port for the mouse. Because it accommodated only one mouse and no other devices, Apple changed over to a more flexible port for input devices, beginning with the SE, called the *Apple Desktop Bus*. ADB accommodates several input devices at the same time, such as a mouse, keyboard, graphics tablet, and trackball. ADB does not provide much electrical power, so you have to limit the number and type of ADB devices you connect to your Mac and avoid those with relatively large power requirements.

Generally, you can connect five or six ADB devices with no loss of power. Apple recommends less than three ADB devices be connected to your Mac at any given time. All Macintosh input devices now use the ADB port; if you have a pre-SE Mac, finding input devices for the old serial mouse port is becoming increasingly difficult. Some input devices, such as graphics tablets, require their own serial port connection. Newer graphics tablets are designed solely for ADB ports and offer reasonable performance, in addition to cordless pens for input.

Tip

For your own comfort, you might want to raise the mouse an inch or so off the desktop. Many people simply put a book under the mouse pad. This helps keep your wrist more in line with your arm. Also, consider using a wrist rest for your mouse as well as for your keyboard. Too much bending of the wrist can create conditions for the development of carpal tunnel syndrome.

Care and feeding

Over a period of daily use, the mouse ball picks up dirt particles and gets sticky and unreliable. To avoid this, use a mouse pad. They're inexpensive (often given away as advertising items), and keep contamination out of the mouse's rolling mechanisms. Mouse pads also provide a more efficient and consistent rolling surface. Choose one with a nice photo or graphic image, and it will brighten up your working environment.

Even a mouse pad can't keep all dirt out of the roller. Periodically, you need to open the mouse and clean it (see your Apple manual for instructions). You can buy mouse cleaning kits with swabs and fluid at most computer shops. Cleaning usually requires using a Q-tip™ or similar dust-free cloth to remove dirt and dust from the mouse's internal rolling parts, which are the main contacts to the main rolling ball of the mouse.

Selected mice

What are the differences among mice? You can find hundreds of third-party mice on the market, some larger or smaller footprints, extra buttons, or well-conceived ergonomics. Cordless mice were introduced a few years ago, and usually work with a device connected to your Mac's ADB port. Alternatives such as Nintendo-like game controllers, joysticks, touchpads, and Felix (pseudo-joystick) offer interesting input methods for the control of your cursor. A variety of mice and mice alternatives are discussed in this section.

Apple Desktop Bus Mouse II

Apple has gone through several generations of mouse design. The original serial mouse was square and tall. At the time of Mac SE introduction (with its ADB port), Apple brought out the Desktop Bus Mouse, a low-profile version shaped to fit the hand more easily. The newest design, Desktop Bus Mouse II, has softer, more rounded contours than previous models, and a larger button.

> $80 average street price
> Apple Computer, Inc.
> One Infinite Loop
> Cupertino, CA 95014
> (408) 996-1010, (800) 776-2333

MouseMan

MouseMan is curved to fit the contours of the human hand. Choose either the right- or left-handed version for the best comfort.

> $129 SRP
> Logitech
> 6505 Kaiser Dr.
> Fremont, CA 94555
> (510) 795-8500 Voice
> (510) 792-8901 Fax

Mouse alternatives

Traditionally, an Apple mouse is included in the box along with the computer. Yet, many feel uncomfortable dragging the mouse around a mouse pad. Others do not like coming to the edge of a mouse pad or mouse cable when trying to complete a critical task. Mouse alternatives include trackballs, touch pads, graphics tablets, and touch screens. The following includes a brief description of selected trackball and touch pad products.

QuePoint

A touch surface similar to those found on newer PowerBooks. The QuePoint enables you to point and click, by moving your finger along the smooth surface.

$98 SRP
MicroQue
5211 Greenpine Drive
Murray, UT 84123
(801) 263-1883

GlidePoint

Another touchpad alternative to the mouse, ALPS also develops the touchpads used in 520 and 540 series PowerBooks. It features a limited lifetime warranty, and with software allows you to adjust the finger-to-cursor tracking ratio. The GlidePoint is a strong competitor to the mouse and trackball.

$70 average street price
Alps Electric, Inc.
3553 North First Street
San Jose, CA 95134
(800) 720-ALPS (2577)

Mouse accessories

Mouse accessories are great impulse items at computer shows. You can buy a mouse suit, with whiskers and ears, or a racing car shell to dress up your mouse. Super-fast ball bearing suspensions and Teflon sliders can soup up performance. All these whimsical items, though of dubious value in improving performance, certainly make using your Mac more fun.

Trackballs

Trackballs offer some advantages over the mouse, and were among the first alternatives. Essentially, a trackball is nothing more than an upside-down mouse. Trackballs do not require additional software to access the point-and-click functionality of a regular mouse. Software is needed to use additional features, such as programming the second button, or dual button programmability. They're a great asset for playing many computer games because of their speed. Trackballs also make many common operations in paint and drawing programs easier, and can be less stressful on your wrist compared to a mouse.

One important benefit when using a trackball rather than a mouse is that your hand stays in one position. This can be both good and bad. If you experience shoulder pains from moving the mouse around, a trackball can provide welcome relief. On the other hand, that little bit of mouse movement exercises the arm and shoulder. Leaving the hand in one position on the trackball for extended periods of time (such as when you scroll through a series of database records during pruning and updating operations) can create ideal conditions for carpal tunnel syndrome. The best approach is to switch between mouse and trackball to provide physical relief and variety of movement.

Trackballs are convenient in many situations, particularly when you're working with graphics applications. In contrast to using a mouse, you do not run the risk of running out of mouse pad room when trying to draw lines, shapes, or edit pixels in a graphics image. Trackballs can also be programmed to select special key combinations. In graphics applications, this can help automate magnifying an image or selecting a certain graphics tool before using the trackball.

Kensington TrackBall Turbo Mouse 4.0

One of the more popular trackballs, Turbo Mouse has two buttons; Click and Click-Lock. Click-Lock makes moving graphic objects easy. You can program it via the Control Panel so that holding the two buttons simultaneously carries out one of seven commands (Close, Save, Print, and so on). Kensington also sells various trackballs in several colors and styles (including an 8-ball).

> $169.95 SRP
> Kensington Microware
> 2855 Campus Blvd.
> San Mateo, CA 94403
> (415) 572-2700 Voice
> (415) 572-9675 Fax

MacTrac

MacTrac 2.0 is similar to other trackball products. Its included control panel software makes it easy to customize the use of the trackball with the three buttons surrounding the trackball. You can program command-key functions to any of the three buttons or swap buttons for easier left-handed use. Tracking speed can be adjusted from super-precise to super-fast. It is 100 percent compatible with System 7.5 and Power Macintosh.

> Microspeed, Inc.
> 5005 Brandin Ct.
> Fremont, CA 94538
> (510) 490-1403, (800) 438-7733

Stingray

With a unique, smooth ergonomic look that is designed to fit in the natural arch of the hand, this trackball is raised in the center of the base unit and has two buttons on each side. It's comfortable to use, though the trackball does not spin as freely as others.

> $99.95 SRP
> CoStar
> 100 Field Point Rd.
> Greenwich, CT 06830
> (203) 661-9700, (800) 426-7827

Joysticks

Joysticks enhance the fun of playing action games or sitting in the cockpit of a flight simulator. Similar to the mouse or a trackball, they move the cursor and let you select options by pressing buttons. Most joysticks are ADB devices.

Many companies make joysticks, and the more common game pad. However, finding a good joystick is difficult. Ruggedness is a key factor for uninhibited game play, so stay away from cheaper models. Number of buttons, ergonomics, and programmability are all important. Prime factors are ease of control and rapidity of firing. Highlights of some of the better, well-known joystick models can be found in the following pages.

MouseStick II

The MouseStick II uses optical sensing to provide smooth control with up to 1200 lines of resolution. This joystick comes with customized control settings for many popular games; you can even create your own custom settings. MouseStick II has five independent user-definable buttons, plus a full-size padded handle with adjustable tension. It is a popular joystick for use with flight simulation games (see Figure 4.1).

Figure 4.1 Gravis' MouseStick II uses optical sensing for increased sensitivity.

Advanced Gravis Computer Technology
3750 N. Fraser Way
Burnaby, BC, Canada V5J 5E9
(604) 431-5020 Voice
(604) 431-1184 Fax

Thunderstick–Mac

Thunderstick offers dual thumb buttons on the comfortable handle, and x and y axis centering adjustments. This joystick makes aerial simulations and arcade games exciting.

$69.95 SRP
Microspeed, Inc.
5005 Brandin Ct.
Fremont, CA 94538
(510) 490-1403, (800) 438-7733

QueStick II

QueStick uses a custom Motorola chip onboard to accommodate game-specific control sets. It has a special ADB address assigned by Apple to avoid conflicts with the mouse (which you can leave connected). With the QuePrefs Control Panel you can assign specific functions to the controls (two buttons and a switch) for each game and player. Or you can select a QueSet from the library of game sets for many popular games. QueStick also provides keystroke emulation for games that work better with keystrokes than with firing buttons. The joystick handle is contoured to fit your hand comfortably, and trim pads allow you to center it precisely. The Power On LED changes color when you press any button. Cushioned feet prevent slipping and help to avoid marring tabletops.

$49.95 SRP
MicroQue
5211 Greenpine Dr.
Murray, UT 84123
(801) 263-1883 Voice
(801) 263-2886 Fax

Graphics tablets

If you do serious graphics work or enjoy drawing with a pen-based object as opposed to a mouse or trackball, you might need a graphics tablet. True enough, you can draw and paint with the mouse, but not with the degree of control that a pen and tablet provide. For those who have highly developed skills with pen and ink or brushes and paint, a pressure-sensitive pen and tablet provide the familiar feedback of working with these real-world tools.

Tablets are an alternative to the mouse and can be used in almost any application. For example, editing a spreadsheet or a database is easier if you can tap directly on the cell or field you want to change and not have to slide the cursor all over the screen. Complex applications, from DTP to CAD, often have special palettes and function keys; tapping on them saves time. Tablets also can be helpful for people entering music into a notation application via its note palette.

The biggest differences are the following:

- Working area. This factor refers to the actual size of the tablet's pressure-sensitive input area. Bigger tablets are more expensive; smaller tablets can be more comfortable if you like to hold them in your lap as you would a sketch pad.

- Resolution. The resolution of a tablet is measured in the number of divisions per square inch. If you create finely detailed illustrations or complex CAD documents, you need more expensive models that support higher resolutions. The down side of high resolution tablets is that the amount of data throughput increases and processor performance seems slower due to the large amounts of data being processed.

Pressure-sensitive pens emulate real-world tools, and with compatible software, enable you to work onscreen just as you would on canvas. Press down on a brush, and the stroke widens. Press lightly on a watercolor brush for a tiny drop of color. Nearly all major graphics applications such as Painter and Photoshop support pressure-sensitive pens. Also, most pens are now cordless, freeing the user from the inconvenience of an attached and length-limited cord. Many pens do not require batteries, which usually means that all the position and pressure sensing takes place on the tablet.

Tablets historically have been serial devices because the ADB port is not fast enough to handle the amount of data they can generate. Some manufacturers, however, have introduced products that work with the ADB port. The most noticeable difference between serial and ADB-based tablets is speed—ADB is slower than printer and modem serial ports. Tablets also tend to draw more power than most ADB devices can sustain; you must be careful about the number of ADB devices on the chain.

You need a fast Mac (at least a IIci if you work in 24-bit color) to use tablets—68040 or Power Macintosh are preferred. Even though the ADB driver in System 7.5 is not native, native applications will process the pen data throughput much more efficiently and faster. Slower Macs take longer to display what you draw, and can destroy the creative impulse. However, smaller tablets seem to have better performance. Remember that these performance issues rarely apply to serial-based graphics tablets.

Graphics tablets allow artists to use a more natural and familiar method for inputting designs. Drawing with a pen makes a traditionally trained artist feel at home, and can save paper and real-world tool costs in the long run. The pen can also function like a mouse for cordless point-and-click access, as well as for dragging desktop items.

ArtZ

Small and inexpensive, Wacom's ArtZ is a popular ADB cordless pen and tablet package that enables you to create Mac graphics in traditional ways. This lap-size entry-level tablet gives you the feel of working with a sketch pad and pencil, on a 6 × 8-inch working area. The batteryless, cordless pen resembles a traditional pen. ArtZ senses 120 levels of pressure to simulate real-world tools such as pens, pencils, crayons, paintbrushes, pastels, and markers. ArtZ overcomes the speed limitation of ADB, with a tracking speed of 140 dpi. Wacom also sells a separate weighted pen which may feel more comfortable to some artists.

$449 SRP
Wacom Technology
501 SE Columbia Shores Blvd., Suite 300
Vancouver, WA 98661
(206) 750-8882
(800) 922-6613

DrawingSlate II

CalComp tablets were developed for CAD applications at Lockheed. Engineers liked them so much the company formed a consumer division to market them as computer peripherals. These tablets range from entry-level to mid-performance, and are available in sizes of 6×9 inches, 12×12 inches (A size), and 12×18 inches (B size). Drawing Slate II supports increased resolution of 2540 lines per inch and accuracy of +/- 0.01 inches.

$395 to $595 SRP
CalComp Digitizer Division
14555 N. 82nd St.
Scottsdale, AZ 85260
(602) 948-6540
(800) 458-5888

Microgrid Ultra ADB

Definitely for high-end users, Microgrid tablets offer working area, resolution, and other features that professional illustrators, desktop publishers, and users of CAD applications need. The backlit models can facilitate tracing or animation artwork.

$3299 to $5499 SRP; 17×24 inches to 44×60 inches (opaque)
$7499 to $8699 SRP; 36×48 inches to 44×60 inches (backlit)
Summagraphics
8500 Cameron Road
Austin, TX 78754
(512) 873-1239 (phone or fax)
(800) 444-3425

Touch screens

Touch screens function the same as graphics tablets, except your finger is the pen. Touch screen surfaces are transparent, so that you can see the screen beneath them (see Figure 4.2). They're useful for self-running demos (especially HyperCard-based demos), and public information kiosks that permit people to operate the computer simply by tapping buttons onscreen. Touch screens replace the keyboard and mouse completely in these situations or can complement them in office and home use. Almost all are ADB devices, and are completely compatible with the Macintosh and its applications.

Figure 4.2   Touch screens permit the user to interact directly with an image.

The attraction to touch screens is their directness and immediacy. In this respect, they surpass the mouse as a pointing device. The downside is that they require the user to be within arm's reach of the CRT screen so that he or she can place a finger on the surface. The problems of radiation and electromagnetic fields become much greater the closer you are to the monitor or electromagnetic source. For casual, occasional use at a kiosk, this probably is not significant. For continual daily use at home or in the office, a touch screen might not be a good idea. On an LCD screen, however, the use of a touch screen avoids this problem.

Touch screens enable you to create interactive information kiosks and store demonstration software. The direct user response of a touch screen ("To select an item, please tap the button on the screen") makes them ideal for situations involving the general public.

Edmark TouchWindow

The Edmark Touch Window is an ADB device that is a low-cost way to implement touch screen technology.

$335 SRP
Edmark
6727 185th Ave. NE
PO Box 97021
Redmond, WA 98073
(206) 556-8400
(800) 426-0856

Elo ADB Touchscreen Controller

The Elographics Touchscreen uses a clear glass panel with their IntelliTouch surface acoustic wave sensing device. Fast response and high resolution (greater than 900 touch points per square inch) make this ADB device ideal for kiosk applications.

> $290 SRP
> Elo TouchSystems, Inc.
> 105 Randolph Rd.
> Oak Ridge, TN 37830
> (800) 356-8682

Mac 'n' Touch

Install Mac 'n' Touch over your monitor's screen as if it were a glare filter. Each system includes an ADB controller, a polished or etched ClearTek 1000 touch sensor, driver software and installation and set-up instructions. This input device is perfect for self-running in-store demos or kiosks because it eliminates the need for a mouse.

> Call for pricing, it varies depending on the monitor.
> MicroTouch Systems, Inc.
> 300 Griffin Park
> Methuen, MA 01844
> (508) 659-9000 Voice
> (508) 659-9100 Fax

TouchMonitors

TouchMonitors have factory installed touch screens. They are available in 14-, 17-, and 19-inch monitor sizes. All Elo TouchMonitors are UL listed, CSA certified, FXX Class A verified and are available with Elo surface wave (IntelliTouch) or resistive (AccuTouch) Technologies. Both can be used with a finger or gloved hand.

> $970 to $2800 plus controller SRP
> Elo TouchSystems, Inc.
> 105 Randolph Rd.
> Oak Ridge, TN 37830
> (800) 356-8682

Pen/handwriting devices

Pen input has become a popular solution for vertical markets, but still has many mainstream analysts and users confused about its future. Some people enjoy the convenience; others can't imagine why anyone would want pen input. These devices will never replace the keyboard, but they have an application, along with voice input and bar code readers. If you don't think so, check out what the UPS and Federal Express drivers carry with them (or at least watch the ads on TV). These pen input notebooks capture and transmit information for the package tracking system so that the company can tell you precisely where your package is at any given moment. Some systems even digitize your signature with time and date stamping.

In conditions such as these, pen input is far better than paper and pencil, and impractical for keyboard-based devices. So far, the Windows market has more pen input hardware and software than the Mac market. All Windows systems use single-character recognition software rather than word recognition software. Single character recognition is slower to input and recognize, but is ideal for numerical entry.

What can you do with pen input for the Mac? Consider a nurse checking on patients. He or she can write down the vital signs by filling out a series of electronic forms on a tablet. When finished, the nurse plugs the tablet into a docking station, which downloads all the data. Doctors can access each patient's information at their convenience from a computer connected to the system, or via modem. In the business world, a salesman making field calls can fill out an electronic order form and send it back to the office via modem. The form does all the calculations, and with no errors resulting from data re-entry. Shipping can take place within minutes if necessary.

Pen input systems

Pen input systems use a graphics tablet or touch screen to enable you to enter data by writing it or drawing it. Generally, they go one step further with software that converts your graphical input into word processor text and neater drawings (real circles, boxes, and straight lines instead of approximations).

MacHandwriter

MacHandwriter is a package that includes a cordless pen, an ADB tablet, and recognition software. This device uses a block printing system to recognize individual characters on a grid (see Figure 4.3). MacHandwriter does not recognize cursive handwriting or entire words, as does the Apple Newton MessagePad, but understands individual letters. For tasks such as filling out forms, taking sales orders, entering data into medical records, or taking inventory, MacHandwriter often is a better choice than a keyboard. You can also use it as a standard graphics tablet. One of the more successful products in the Windows market, MacHandwriter is now available in a Mac version.

$399 SRP
Communications Intelligence Corp
275 Shoreline Dr., 6th floor
Redwood Shores, CA 94065
(415) 802-7888 Voice
(415) 802-7777 Fax

Figure 4.3 The MacHandwriter can recognize individual handwritten block letters.

Apple Newton MessagePad 120

Most people haven't thought about the Newton MessagePad as an alternative input device for the Mac. But with the Connection Kit, you have a direct route into your desktop Mac or PowerBook. Use the Newton MessagePad to take handwritten notes while you're on the phone, to jot down random flashes of thought, or to make quick sketches of great ideas. Later, download the data files to your Mac and use your regular applications to flesh out your ideas. At least you won't be starting from scratch, and you won't have a wall full of unrelated little yellow sticky notes. Think of the Newton MessagePad as a portable Mac input device with handwriting recognition and temporary data storage. The 120 model is available in 1 MB and 2 MB memory configurations and has a large library of software available as well.

$400–$600 average street price
Apple Computer

Bar code and magnetic stripe readers

Bar codes solve many problems, but usually don't come to mind when discussing personal computers. Supermarket checkouts leave the impression that bar codes require big, expensive hardware; Figure 4.4 proves otherwise. This simple, yet obscure technology can increase productivity and efficiency as much for you as for Fortune 500 companies. To view bar codes on your Macintosh, you need to install the bar code font in your font folder of your System Folder. To print bar codes, you generally need the resolution of a laser printer, but dedicated mailing label printers from CoStar and Seiko can print postal bar codes successfully with thermal printing technology.

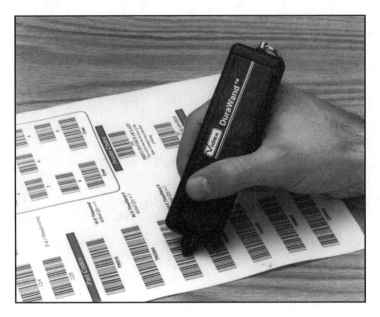

Figure 4.4 The Durawand portable bar code reader.

A bar code represents an identification number for an item using patterns of lines and spaces. After the bar code reader decodes the number, the computer looks up the corresponding item in its database. At that point, you have access to all the information about that item. In the supermarket, the decoded product identification number triggers the computer to enter the price into the cash register. At the same time, it deducts the item from the store's inventory. This kind of system works well for small businesses that deal with many individual items, such as video rental shops. In addition, bar codes can help businesses track files in a large office, track patient records in a hospital, or manage merchandise in a mail order operation.

The key to bar codes' usefulness is that they trigger the release of information. Bar code readers simply automate entry of the ID number. You can do the same thing by typing numbers on a keyboard, or even by using a voice recognition system. Many bar code formats are in use, each adapted for the needs of that particular industry. The best known is the Universal

Product Code (UPC) found on virtually all retail items. The Postal Service and legal industry use their own bar codes. Various formats, including three of nine and two of five, are suitable for vertical applications developers.

Bar codes can do interesting things. For example, a bar code can trigger the computer to turn off the lights through an X-10 control system, program a VCR, or change the channel on the TV through an infrared transmitter. Just point a bar code reader at the appropriate code on a laser printed list, and the Mac executes the command for you. You can activate macros this way—log onto an online service, check your mail, and log off—just by moving a light pen across a bar code with a descriptive name printed next to it.

Closely related to bar codes are the magnetic stripes on the backs of credit cards and ATM cards. The advantage of magnetic stripes is that you can change and update the information stored on the cards. Bar code and magnetic stripe readers typically are serial port or ADB devices.

Selected Bar Code and Magnetic Stripe readers

Bar code and magnetic stripe readers are powerful technologies for automating data entry. We regularly see bar code applications in supermarkets, for looking up prices and decrementing the inventory. Many video rental shops use them to look up customer data and track rentals and returns. Any business that deals with large numbers of individual objects can benefit from bar code tracking.

Magnetic stripes can store a fair amount of data—and you can change that data whenever necessary. They are especially useful for pseudo-money systems (amusement park rides, mass transit, and so on). In these applications, the end-user "buys" a certain amount of money and "spends" it by sliding the card through a reader, which updates the data on the card.

Bar Code Reader

The Synex Uniscan 300 Bar Code Reader translates bar codes (UPC, Code 39, EAN, Codabar, and 2 of 5) directly into Mac data with its onboard firmware. Because this device uses the ADB port, it requires no external power supply or driver software, and is made rugged for industrial applications. Synex also sells software for printing postal bar codes.

> $279 SRP
> Synex
> 692 10th St.
> Brooklyn, NY 11215
> (718) 499-6293 Voice
> (800) 447-9639

DataDesigns

DataDesigns offers many products, including combination magnetic stripe and bar code readers. Models include DD MagScan, DD MaxiBar, DD MaxiScan, DD MiniBar, DD ScanImage, and DD ScanPlus.

$395–$3950 SRP
DataDesigns
PO Box 781741
San Antonio, TX 78278
(800) 706-0780
(210) 697-0780

DuraWand

DuraWand is a portable, pen-like bar code reader for the Mac.

$495 SRP; DuraWand
$100 SRP; software
$859 SRP; complete system
Videx
1105 NE Circle Blvd.
Corvallis, OR 97330
(503) 758-0521 Voice
(503) 752-5285 Fax

OmniWand

OmniWand enables you to take the bar code reader away from the Mac, collect data, store it, and download it into the Mac later. It has a lightweight but durable cast metal case, a choice of input modules, and a serial interface.

$1235 SRP
Videx
1105 NE Circle Blvd.
Corvallis, OR 97330
(503) 758-0521

Percon Series 10, Series 20

A standard bar code reader with light pen and cable that also reads magnetic stripe cards.

$540–$605 SRP
Percon
1720 Willow Creek Circle, Suite 530
Eugene, OR 97402
(503) 344-1189 Voice
(800) 873-7266

TPS Bar code and magnetic stripe readers

TPS makes a variety of bar code readers. The TPS magnetic stripe readers also can record and verify data stored on the cards.

$369–$2795 SRP
TPS Electronics
2495 Old Middlefield Way
Mountain View, CA 94043
(415) 988-0141 Voice
(800) 526-5920

Alternative input devices

Input devices in this section represent some of the more imaginative methods for inputting data and operating computers. These are useful devices, however, that may be the most realistic in a given situation. The chording keyboard, for example, solves problems for people who use the phone constantly, or suffer from carpal tunnel syndrome. Voice input and control has become a rapidly growing field of interest since the introduction of the AV Macs and the Power Macs. For those working with virtual reality applications, 3-D imaging, musical performance, dance, or architectural walkthroughs, a glove, headgear, or a sock fitted with motion sensors allows you to manipulate objects in space. As strange and esoteric as these input devices may seem, they all deserve serious consideration. Many of them are even more useful in vertical applications for the physically challenged.

Though these alternative input devices may seem strange at first, they all have practical uses. In many cases, if you need them, you can't get along without them.

The Bat

The Bat uses a totally unorthodox process for entering alphanumeric characters. Often called *chording keyboards,* The Bat requires you to press combinations of keys, as if you are playing chords on the piano. The Bat has only seven keys that you punch in various combinations to produce every available character on extended-type keyboards, including ⌘, option, and control keys. Your hand fits comfortably on the curved device with its built-in wrist rest. Your four fingers rest over the four home keys, and your thumb accesses the three thumb buttons. Most people can learn the alphabet in about an hour or two, and soon work up to speeds of 25 to 30 words per minute. Macros can increase entry convenience, just as word processors offer automatic typing of commonly used words and phrases. One unit is sufficient (either the right- or left-handed model), though some users prefer to have both available for added convenience. The Bat works well whenever you have only one hand free and the other is operating another keyboard, the mouse, or a graphics tablet. Musicians entering MIDI data, telephone sales staff, desktop publishers, PowerBook users on a crowded plane, and others could benefit from this unique device. The Bat also serves the needs of many disabled people.

$495 dual, $295 single (choose right- or left-handed model) SRP
Infogrip
1141 E. Main Street
Ventura, CA 93013
(800) 397-0921 Voice
(805) 566-0880 Fax

PowerSecretary

PowerSecretary translates spoken words into word processor text using Apple's PlainTalk software technology. It first recognizes the spoken sounds (phonemes) and converts them to the most likely letters and combinations. Then, using a 120,000 word dictionary, it finds the correct words and displays them in your document at rates up to 45 words per minute. PowerSecretary takes dictation within most applications that include text and numbers, such as spreadsheets and databases and vertical applications in the medical and legal fields. PowerSecretary adapts itself to each user, and improves efficiency whenever users need hands-free entry. It also serves as a voice control system, similar to its other product, Voice Navigator.

Note

PowerSecretary runs on 68040-based and Power Macs, and requires a 16-bit sound card (except on AV models, which already have one). The sound card can be one of the better quality cards used for digital audio recording and editing, though a less expensive one (under $300) works just as well for this purpose.

$2495 SRP plus 16-bit sound card
Articulate Systems
600 W. Cummings Park, Suite 4500
Woburn, MA 01801
(617) 935-5656 Voice
(800) 443-7077
(617) 935-0490 Fax

Voice Navigator II

Voice Navigator II enables you to operate your Mac with voice commands. After it learns your particular vocal inflections, it executes any menu item, Finder function, application command, or keyboard shortcut. It's all done with software, but the package includes a good super-directional microphone.

$699 SRP
Articulate Systems
600 W. Cummings Park, Suite 4500
Woburn, MA 01801
(617) 935-5656 Voice
(617) 935-0490 Fax

Options for the physically and cognitively challenged

If you've ever suffered a temporary disability such as a sprained wrist or carpal tunnel syndrome, you probably took advantage of Apple's Easy Access control panel. Fortunately, the Mac offers many possibilities for adapting to users with short-term and permanent special needs.

Many standard input devices have already opened doors for the physically challenged. Just use your imagination and a mouse, for example, and you may be able to adapt one for a particular person. Several companies also make specially designed input devices, but you have to hunt them down; unfortunately, these companies rarely advertise in computer magazines, nor do they exhibit at computer shows. Larger user groups (Boston Computer Society, Berkeley Mac Users Group) often have special interest groups devoted to special needs. If you don't live within traveling distance to one of these large groups, use an online service to join one of their forums. This way you can keep up-to-date on what's currently available.

Alternative keyboards and mice, touch pads, and voice input and control make computers more accessible to the physically and cognitively challenged. With hardware and software extension, computers provide a means for many disabled people to communicate with the world. Speech synthesis enables them to hold conversations and to talk on the phone. To speed up and simplify the conversational exchange, word predictive software guesses and suggests frequently used sequences of words.

Bar code readers can make the Mac speak by allowing easy access to a database of commonly used words and phrases. You can point the bar code reader at a printed sheet with the code next to each phrase and the Mac either types it automatically, or speaks it. Panasonic uses a similar system for programming VCRs. Another way to use bar codes would be to turn lights on and off, or to operate appliances through the X-10 control system. America Online, one of the most popular online service providers, features the capability of using your Macintosh to read the mail, or other online content using Apple's PlainTalk software (Speech Manager extension).

Many of these devices are highlighted in earlier sections, but are also listed here because of their application for special needs individuals. Many developers have even created new software that extends the Mac interface with hardware and software especially for this market.

The Bat

The Bat requires only one hand to operate, which can help people with permanent and temporary disabilities. It's small and lightweight, which makes it ideal for tight spots, such as on a wheelchair. See the section "Alternative Input Devices" for a more thorough description of this product.

> $495 dual, $295 single (choose right or left hand model) SRP
> Infogrip
> 1145 Eugenia Pl., Suite 201
> Carpinteria, CA 93013
> (800) 397-0921 Voice
> (805) 566-1079 Fax

Headmaster Plus

Headmaster Plus substitutes for the mouse. This head-mounted pointer (see Figure 4.5) helps those who cannot use their hands to control the Mac. A breath-activated puff switch clicks the mouse button. Headmaster Plus works with software that displays a keyboard onscreen so that users can point at letters and type them.

Figure 4.5   The Headmaster Plus provides mouse control for the physically challenged.

$1195 SRP, Remote adapter $495
Prentke Romich
1022 Heyl Rd.
Wooster, OH 44691
(800) 262-1984 Voice
(216) 263-4829 Fax

Ke:nx

Ke:nx (pronounced *connects*) provides many methods of alternative computer access with a package of hardware and software functions for the disabled. You plug the input device into the Ke:nx controller box, and the software opens menus, launches applications, and so on. The company offers over 100 hardware and software products.

$780 SRP
Don Johnston, Inc.
1000 N. Rand Rd., Bldg. 115
PO Box 639
Wauconda, IL 60084
(708) 526-2682 Voice
(800) 999-4660
(708) 562-4177 Fax

PowerSecretary

PowerSecretary transcribes spoken words into computer data, which is a perfect substitute for those who are unable to operate a keyboard.

Note

PowerSecretary runs only on 68040-based Macs and requires a 16-bit sound card (about $300).

$2495 SRP plus 16-bit sound card
Articulate Systems
600 W. Cummings Park, Suite 4500
Woburn, MA 01801
(617) 935-5656 Voice
(617) 935-0490 Fax

IntelliKeys

IntelliTools makes a variety of input devices for the disabled, such as alternative keyboards.

$250–$315 SRP
IntelliTools
5221 Central Ave., Suite 205
Richmond, CA 94804
(510) 528-0670 Voice
(510) 528-2225 Fax

Monitors

Good monitors illustrate in vivid detail the Macintosh environment. When purchasing a monitor, consider what type of applications you will use, what type of work you will perform, the amount of time your average session on the computer will be, and what kind of lighting or environmental characteristics your Mac will be in. In general, less expensive monitors will have curvier picture tubes, lower picture quality or less support for peripheral monitor connections. Even high-resolution monitors like Sony's 14" RGB display, available from Apple and Sony are not perfect. The tube has a very fine line about two-thirds of the way down the screen which some interpret to be a hardware flaw in the picture tube, but is actually a design limitation of the hardware.

Understanding monitors

From the simple Mac Plus monochrome 9-inch monitor to a 37-inch 24-bit multisync monster, the monitor market is chock-full of singular and multifunction displays that match your job, budget, and eyes. Although monitors are not usually built to fulfill only one function, some are more capable than others in meeting the needs and demands of certain professional niches.

Color publishing is one niche market for which monitor manufacturers have built special displays. Access to display configuration is crucial for exacting color work—choosing a lower-end monitor that might only have a brightness knob and on/off switch may impede professional results. Many high-end color publishing monitoring systems, such as products offered by Radius and Kodak, come with hardware calibrators that measure and adjust the screen color and many display configurations automatically. These calibrators compensate for room light, screen angle, and even paper texture. Manufacturers strive for nearly perfect WYSIWYG (What You See Is What You Get) results, so that the image on the color display is as close as possible to the printed output.

The engineering field is another professional niche that requires special purpose monitors. Sharp and bright contrast, low flicker, and large screen sizes are necessary to display thin lines accurately on blueprints and spec charts. For engineering, high-resolution monochrome and gray-scale displays fit the bill without the added cost and machine power needed to reproduce color. The Sigma MultiMode 150, described later in this chapter, is an example of this kind of monitor.

Multisync or multiscan monitors

Multisync, autosync, and multiscan refer to monitors that have the capability to draw the screen at different aspect ratios based on internal Mac hardware capabilities. For instance, a multisync monitor can give you the correct WYSIWYG on your 16-inch or 17-inch monitor at 832 × 684 pixels; or switch to a 640 × 480 pixel aspect ratio. Because 640 × 480 is the standard 13-inch screen aspect ratio, it actually blows everything up larger, spread over the full 17 inches of picture tube. Remember this if your eyesight is suffering or if you are planning a presentation.

Some monitors can sync to several different aspect ratios, enlarging or reducing the picture considerably. If the hardware and software are available, a multisync monitor can usually switch modes on-the-fly (in System 7.5, by closing the Monitors control panel without restarting the Macintosh). On-the-fly video switching enables you to select instantly a lower 640 × 480 desktop size or change to a higher density 832 × 684 desktop size. This type of monitor can even draw screens with aspect ratios found on larger monitors. One trade-off is that the picture size shrinks as the aspect ratios exceed the WYSIWYG aspect ratio of that particular multisync monitor. These features are available with all Apple multisync monitors and can come in handy for switching from publishing to interactive multimedia software.

Multisyncs for years have been available outside the Mac-exclusive sales community; Mac owners looking to buy a multisync monitor can find good prices in the larger and more competitive PC/Windows market. This makes them roughly the same price as single-sync monitors made specifically for Macs. A number of multisync models are available for a PC machine; inline or "pass-through" plug adapters reconfigure the monitor's pinouts to fit Macs. Check with your vendor for plug adapters that fit your particular brand of monitor. Most computer stores that carry Macs have these inexpensive adapters.

Adapters are also available that enable you to select aspect ratios by setting dip-switches on the plug itself—this is handy if you have a multisync monitor, but no "switch-on-the-fly" software.

Non-Macintosh monitors

Just as multisync/multiscan monitors have migrated from PC machines to Mac displays, so have VGA and Super VGA monitors—once made exclusively for PC and workstation computers. If the VGA or SVGA monitor outputs the same aspect ratio that your Mac's onboard display circuitry or NuBus board is capable of generating, a simple cable adapter is all you need to use VGA and SVGA monitors on the Macintosh. The main advantage to using these monitors is that you can get excellent quality for less money.

One of the best places to find inexpensive VGA and SVGA monitors is in *Computer Shopper Magazine,* which you can buy at most large newsstands. As big as a tabloid-sized phone book, *Computer Shopper Magazine* is filled with hundreds of dealers hawking PC peripherals. These dealers can tell you which cable-end adapter your Macintosh needs for their particular VGA/SVGA display.

NTSC monitors

NTSC monitors are not recommended as a main computer display because they are interlaced: the horizontal lines are drawn sequentially. The even horizontal lines (2, 4, 6, and so on) are drawn in the first field, and the odd lines (1, 3, 5, and so on) are drawn in the next field, all within the span of 1/30 second. Both fields display so quickly (1/60 per second) that they appear to be one image. The refresh rates are half that of non-interlaced monitors, making the picture appear to flicker. This visible flicker quickly becomes hard on the eyes and is not recommended for detailed work.

NTSC monitor technology is old by video standards, dating back to the 1940s. Throughput bandwidth was so constricted that the video signal had to be split between separate fields of odd and even lines to get it to the viewer. Each bandwidth signal was sent down the line one after another, separately. Both lines would write to the screen so quickly that the eye perceived both fields as a single image. Nevertheless, this technology still produces a visible flickering that resembles a strobe light; definitely harsh if watched over time. Computer (or noninterlaced) displays write an entire frame rather than individual fields of information, making the image displayed sharper and reducing flicker.

Animators and desktop video creators are two types of professionals who need to work with NTSC and computer displays. These professionals eventually "print to tape" Macintosh-based art, animation, and video, and need to switch frequently between the computer monitor and an NTSC monitor. This switch frequency ensures that no size, movement, or color discrepancies occur between the two output modes. Currently, most NTSC output color boards for the Macintosh output RCA, composite, and S-Video signals.

NTSC monitors with the hardware capability to switch from overscan to underscan are perfect for desktop video professionals and animators. *Overscan* refers to the tendency of NTSC screen displays to fall off the perceived edge of the picture tube; *underscan* moves the entire display to the center of a smaller aspect ratio screen so that the entire image is visible.

Radius' VideoVision Telecast and RasterOps Mediatime boards have the capability to use NTSC-interlaced displays right next to your primary noninterlaced monitor, and can perform overscan, underscan, and many other color configurations.

Apple monitors

Apple monitors have earned world reknown for image crispness and system software compatibility. Since the first black-and-white Apple monitors, Apple has introduced more color monitor models into its line of imaging products. Virtually any Apple monitor will plug into the built-in video port of any 68040 or Power Macintosh model and work on startup if the Macintosh model supports external monitor video connections or video cards.

Almost all Apple monitors share a 15-pin connector that plugs into the video port or video card port located at the rear of the case. This is also referred to as a DB15 connector. Apple Portrait and 2-page displays initially shipped with larger connecting cables, which Apple replaced with 15-pin ended cables for better plug-in compatibility. For Power Macs, a 15-pin to multi-pin connector is required to connect to the built-in video port at the back of the Power Macs. PDS or NuBus video cards which have DB15 (15-pin) video connectors can also be added to Power Macs and do not require a multi-pin adapter connector to be utilized.

Most people buy monitors at the time of the CPU purchase, and Apple Mac dealers usually sell Apple monitors with CPUs. Many Apple monitors feature high-quality Sony Trinitron picture tubes, and have set the standard for picture quality. Although they are not usually feature-laden displays, the Apple monitor line is beginning to feature basically configured multisync monitors. Apple monitors are well-built, not overpriced, and cover the spectrum of sizes from 12-inch to 21-inch. See Table 4.1 for information about Macintosh displays.

AppleVision 1710AV

Image quality is the first concern of anyone buying a monitor, and the AppleVision 1710AV is outstanding in this area. It features internal self-calibration technology, eliminating the need to spend time and money to maintain accurate color calibration. The AppleVision 1710AV provides automatic screen-to-print matching using Apple's unparalleled ColorSync 2.0 technology. The 1710AV can also be adjusted to compensate for many of the effects of ambient lighting and CRT aging using its intuitive Macintosh software. This software also provides control over all screen functions, including geometry, brightness, contrast, and variable color temperature.

Features: Tilt/swivel base; automatic degaussing, offers a range of resolution modes—up to 1,280 × 1,024 pixels. Includes built-in high-quality stereo sound and directional microphone capable of voice recognition; built-in intelligence also is provided to ensure that your monitor remains calibrated.

Description: The AppleVision 1710AV is an exceptional audiovisual display combining multiple-scan capabilities with the next-generation Trinitron tube. It offers a host of advanced Apple DigitalColor technology features, and boasts built-in speakers and a microphone. It features plug-and-play compatibility with DOS and Windows software-based computers as well as Macintosh and Power Macintosh systems.

Compatibility/Requirements: Power Macintosh, Quadra, Centris, Macintosh II (with video card), and PowerBooks, System software version 7.1 or later; or any Mac running a Display card from Apple; plug-and-play compatible with DOS/Windows/IBM PC machines using supplied adapter. See Table 4.1.

Apple Multiple Scan 14 Display

The Apple Multiple Scan 14 Display uses multiple-scan technology, allowing you to choose between different resolutions without restarting your computer. This capability gives you the flexibility to adjust your display to suit the particular application in which you are working on-the-fly. The display's integrated front-panel stereo speakers and easy-access headphone jack are also a perfect addition for multimedia applications.

Features: Tilt/swivel base; Degausses automatically, offers a range of resolution modes–up to 800 × 600 pixels. Also features built-in high-quality stereo sound and easy-access headphone jack.

Description: The Apple Multiple Scan 14 Display (14-inch picture tube; 12.4-inch diagonal viewable image size) is a high-quality color monitor designed to be the optimal solution for working with today's multimedia applications. Surprisingly affordable, this display combines the flexibility of multiple-scan technology with the multimedia advantage of built-in stereo speakers to give you an outstanding price/performance value.

Compatibility/Requirements: Power Macintosh, Macintosh LC, Macintosh Quadra, Macintosh Centris, Macintosh Performa, Macintosh II, and PowerBook computers. System software version 7.1 or later. Compatible display card required for use with Macintosh II. Cable adapter required for use with some Macintosh LC, Macintosh Performa models, and PowerBook computers.

An affordable cable adapter kit is available from Enhance Cable Technology. Call 1-800-343-2425 and ask for the Multiple Scan 17 Display adapter kit.

Apple display history

Table 4.1	Macintosh Display Configurations		
	Macintosh Portrait Display (15")	*Apple ColorPlus 14" Display*	*Macintosh Color Display (14")*
Part number	M0404	M2346LL/A	M1198LL/B
Pixels	640 by 870	640 by 480	640 by 480
Resolution	80 dpi	68 dpi	68 dpi
Screen refresh rate	75 Hz	66.7 Hz	66.7 Hz
Dot pitch	80 dpi	0.28 mm	0.26 mm
Macintosh LC & LCII w/256K VRAM SIMM	16 colors	16 colors	16 colors
w/512K VRAM SIMM (768K total)	256 colors	256 colors	256 colors
Macintosh LCIII w/512K soldered on	16 grays	256 colors	256 colors
w/256K VRAM SIMM (768K total)	256 grays	32,768 colors	32,768 colors
Macintosh LC 475 & Quadra 605 w/ two 256K VRAM SIMMs (512K total)	16 grays	256 colors	256 colors
w/two 512K VRAM SIMMs (1,024K total) replaces two 256K SIMMs	256 grays	32,768 colors	32,768 colors
Macintosh IIcx, II, IIx, & IIfx w/Macintosh Display Card 8•24	256 grays	16.7 million colors	16.7 million colors
Macintosh IIsi & IIci	16 grays	256 colors	256 colors
w/Macintosh Display Card 8•24	256 grays	16.7 million colors	16.7 million colors
Macintosh IIvx w/two Macintosh 256K VRAM SIMMs (512K total)	256 colors	256 colors	256 colors
w/two 512K VRAM SIMMs (1,024K total) replaces two 256K SIMMs	32,768 colors	32,768 colors	32,768 colors
w/Macintosh Display Card 8•24	256 grays	16.7 million colors	16.7 million colors
Macintosh Centris 610, 650, Quadra 650 w/512K soldered on w/Macintosh VRAM Expansion Kit (1,024K total)	16 grays	256 colors	256 colors
	256 grays	32,768 colors	32,768 colors

Apple Audio-Vision 14 Display (14")	Macintosh 16" Color Display (17")	Macintosh 21" Color Display	Apple Performa Display	Apple Performa Plus Display
M5814LL/A	M1044Z/A	M5812LL/A		
640 by 480	832 by 624	1,152 by 870	640 by 480	640 by 480
68 dpi	70 dpi	79 dpi	68 dpi	68 dpi
66.7 Hz	75 Hz	75 Hz	66.7 Hz	66.7 Hz
0.26 mm	0.26 mm	0.26 mm H × 0.29 mm V	0.39 mm	0.29 mm
16 colors	16 colors			
256 colors	256 colors			
256 colors	256 colors	256 colors	256 colors	
32,768 colors	256 colors	32,768 colors	32,768 colors	
256 colors	256 colors	16 colors	256 colors	256 colors
32,768 colors	32,768 colors	256 colors	32,768 colors	32,768 colors
16.7 million colors	256 colors	256 colors	16.7 million colors	16.7 million colors
256 colors	256 colors	256 colors		
16.7 million colors	256 colors	256 colors	16.7 million colors	16.7 million colors
256 colors	256 colors			
32,768 colors	32,768 colors			
16.7 million colors	256 colors	256 colors	16.7 million colors	16.7 million colors
256 colors	256 colors	16 colors	256 colors	256 colors
32,768 colors	32,768 colors	256 colors	32,768 colors	32,768 colors

continues

Table 4.1 Macintosh Display Configurations, CONTINUED

	Macintosh Portrait Diplay (15")	Apple ColorPlus 14" Display	Macintosh Color Display (14")
Macintosh Quadra 660AV w/1,024K soldered on	256 grays	32,768 colors	32,768 colors
Macintosh Quadra 700 w/512K soldered on	16 grays	256 colors	256 colors
w/Macintosh VRAM Expansion Kit (1,024K total)	256 grays	256 colors	256 colors
w/three Macintosh VRAM Expansion Kits (2,048K total)	256 grays	16.7 million colors	16.7 million colors
Macintosh Quadra 800 w/512K soldered on	16 grays	256 colors	256 colors
w/Macintosh VRAM Expansion Kit (1,024K total)	256 grays	32,768 colors	32,768 colors
Macintosh Quadra 840AV, 900, & 950 w/1,024K soldered on	256 grays	32,768 colors	32,768 colors
w/two Macintosh VRAM Expansion Kits (2,048K total)	256 grays	16.7 million colors	16.7 million colors
Macintosh Performa 400, 410, & 430 w/512K VRAM SIMM	256 colors	256 colors	256 colors
Macintosh Performa 405 w/256K VRAM SIMM	16 colors	16 colors	16 colors
w/512K VRAM SIMM (512K total) replaces 256K SIMM	256 colors	256 colors	256 colors
Macintosh Performa 450, 460, 466, & 467 w/512K soldered on	16 grays	256 colors	256 colors
w/256K VRAM SIMM (768K total)	256 grays	32,768 colors	32,768 colors
Macintosh Performa 475 & 476 w/two 256K VRAM SIMMs (512K total)	256 grays	16 grays	256 colors
w/two 512K VRAM SIMMs (1,024K total) replaces two 256K SIMMs	256 grays	256 colors	32,768 colors
Macintosh Performa 600 w/two 256K VRAM SIMMs (512K total)	256 colors	256 colors	256 colors
w/two 512K VRAM SIMMs (1,024K total) replaces two 256K SIMMs	32,768 colors	32,768 colors	32,768 colors
w/Macintosh Display Card 8•24	256 grays	16.7 million colors	16.7 million colors

Apple Audio-Vision 14 Display (14")	Macintosh 16" Color Display (17")	Macintosh 21" Color Display	Apple Performa Display	Apple Performa Plus Display
32,768 colors	32,768 colors	256 colors	32,768 colors	32,768 colors
256 colors	256 colors	16 colors	256 colors	256 colors
256 colors	256 colors	256 colors	256 colors	256 colors
16.7 million colors	16.7 million colors	256 colors	16.7 million colors	16.7 million colors
256 colors	256 colors	16 colors	256 colors	256 colors
32,768 colors	32,768 colors	256 colors	32,768 colors	32,768 colors
32,768 colors	32,768 colors	256 colors	32,768 colors	32,768 colors
16.7 million colors	16.7 million colors	32,768 colors	16.7 million colors	16.7 million colors
16 colors	256 colors	256 colors		
16 colors	16 colors			
256 colors	256 colors	256 colors		
256 colors	16 colors	256 colors	256 colors	
32,768 colors	256 colors	32,768 colors	32,768 colors	
256 colors	16 colors	256 colors	256 colors	
32,768 colors	256 colors	32,768 colors	32,768 colors	
16 colors	256 colors	256 colors		
32,768 colors	32,768 colors	32,768 colors		
16.7 million colors	256 colors	256 colors	16.7 million colors	16.7 million colors

continues

Table 4.1   Apple Display Configurations, CONTINUED

	Macintosh Portrait Diplay (15")	Apple ColorPlus 14" Display	Macintosh Color Display (14")
Macintosh Performa 600CD w/two 512K VRAM SIMMs (1,024K total)	32,768 colors	32,768 colors	32,768 colors
w/Macintosh Display Card 8•24	256 grays	16.7 million colors	16.7 million colors
PowerBook 180c, 165c, 165, 160, & 180	16 grays	256 colors	256 colors
PowerBook Duo 210, 230, 250 & 270c w/Duo Dock or MiniDock 512K soldered on	16 grays	256 colors	256 colors
w/Duo Dock & 512K VRAM SIMM	256 grays	32,768 colors	32,768 colors

Apple AudioVision 14-Inch Display

This rather small 14-inch display uses a crisp Sony Trinitron picture tube and a flat, high-contrast screen. A built-in microphone is sculpted into the center of the chassis around the screen, helping make this "Star Trek"-looking monitor the current bells-and-whistles leader of all Apple displays.

One drawback to the pioneering AudioVision monitor is that it may be uncomfortably small for multimedia work, which may require another monitor just to hold floating menus, palettes, and drag-around tool boxes; a 16-inch display like the Macintosh 16-inch Color Display is a better size for multimedia work.

Features: Built-in stereo speakers and microphone; tilt/swivel base; inputs for ADB; audio inputs.

Description: The first in a class of displays, the Apple AudioVision monitor features onboard stereo sound that is unexpectedly good. Ergonomically designed with ADB and sound input plugs in the side panel, the AudioVision is an excellent step toward the future of Macintosh displays combining sound and vision (see Figure 4.6).

Compatibility/Requirements: All color-capable Macintosh models and color/gray-scale generating PowerBooks with a variety of color depths depending on hardware card or VRAM installed.

Size/Resolution: 14-inch screen; 640 × 480 pixels/70 dpi

Screen Refresh Rate: 66.7 Hz

Dot Pitch: 26 mm

Regulatory Approval: EnergyStar rated

Apple Audio-Vision 14 Display (14")	Macintosh 16" Color Display (17")	Macintosh 21" Color Display	Apple Performa Display	Apple Performa Plus Display
32,768 colors	32,768 colors	32,768 colors		
16.7 million colors	256 colors	256 colors	16.7 million colors	16.7 million colors
256 colors	256 colors	256 colors	256 colors	
256 colors	256 colors	256 colors	256 colors	
32,768 colors	32,768 colors	32,768 colors	32,768 colors	

Figure 4.6 Apple AudioVision monitor.

Macintosh 16-Inch Color Display

Features: Tilt/swivel ADB output, microphone; headphone/external speaker outputs

Description: The Macintosh 16-inch monitor displays high-quality color utilizing a Sony Trinitron picture tube with a flat, high-contrast screen. Like the AudioVision 14-inch monitor, the 16-inch monitor features ADB and sound input/output plugs onboard (but no speakers or microphone). An effective antiglare/antistatic monitor coating keeps reflection down and dust off.

Compatibility/Requirements: All color-capable Macintosh models and color/gray-scale generating PowerBooks with a variety of color depths depending on hardware card or VRAM installed.

Image Size/Resolution: 832 × 624 pixels/70 dpi

Screen Refresh Rate: 75 Hz

Dot Pitch: 0.26 mm

Regulatory Approval: Swedac and MPR II rated for low-frequency magnetic emissions

Macintosh 14-Inch Color Display

Features: Tilt/swivel base; automatic degaussing

Description: The Macintosh 14-inch color display monitor utilizes the same Trinitron picture tube as its workhorse predecessor, the Applecolor 13-inch monitor, but is 40 percent more energy efficient and 50 percent brighter. High-contrast glass helps keep its picture among the consistently best-rated small monitors available for the Macintosh.

Compatibility/Requirements: All color-capable/NuBus equipped Macintosh models and color/gray-scale generating PowerBooks with appropriate VRAM or Color display board.

Image Size/Resolution: 640 × 480 pixels/70 dpi

Screen Refresh Rate: 66.7 Hz

Dot Pitch: 0.26 mm

Regulatory Approval: Swedac and MPR II rated for low-frequency magnetic and electrical emissions; ISO 9241 compliant ergonomic design

Macintosh 14-Inch Color Plus Display

Features: Tilt/swivel base; automatic degaussing

Description: This monitor utilizes a shadow mask display technology rather than the brighter Trinitron picture tube. While lacking the crispness of the more expensive 14-inch display, the Color Plus is the budget choice for Mac users who need inexpensive, adequate color. This display is compatible with all color-capable Macs and most 8- and 24-bit video cards for the Mac.

Compatibility/Requirements: All color-capable Macintosh models and color/gray-scale generating PowerBooks with a variety of color depths depending on hardware card or VRAM installed.

Image Size/Resolution: 640 × 480 pixels/70 dpi

Screen Refresh Rate: 67 Hz

Dot Pitch: 0.28 mm

Regulatory Approval: Swedac and MPR II rated for low-frequency magnetic and electrical emissions. ISO 9241 compliant design.

Apple Multiple Scan 17 and 20 Displays

Introduced in 1994, Apple's 17" and 20" color monitors offer similar features found in PC multisync displays. The Multiple Scan displays can change the size of your desktop on the fly—if you have System 7.5 software installed—and provide front-panel access to size and screen alignment. Apple's multisyncs also offer 15-pin video cable output that plugs into the Macintosh video/monitor port without the need for a cable adapter. For the Power Macintosh a 15-pin to multi-pin connecter is still required to connect to built-in video, but is not required to connect to Power Macintosh PDS or NuBus video cards with Apple's standard DB15 (15-pin) connector.

Features: Tilt/swivel base; automatic degaussing

Description: The Apple Multiple Scan 20 Display uses a 20-inch Trinitron picture tube for crisp contrasty color—and lots of it. The only multisync monitor from Apple, the Apple Multiple Scan 20 features a high-quality, antistatic, antiglare bonded panel, with digital controls for brightness, contrast, horizontal and vertical size and centering, convergence, rotation, pincushion, white point, and power. The AMS 20 can switch resolutions on-the-fly using Apple's System 7.5 control panel, and is also IBM PC compatible (with the addition of a plug adapter).

Compatibility/Requirements: Quadra; Centris Macintoshes; or any Mac running 24AC Display card from Apple; plug-and-play compatible with DOS/Windows/IBM PC machines using supplied adapter.

Image Size/Resolution: 640 × 480 pixels; 832 × 624 pixels; 1024 × 768 pixels; 1152 × 870 pixels; 1280 × 1024 pixels

Screen Refresh Rate: 67 Hz at 640 × 480 pixels; all other resolutions at 75 Hz

Dot Pitch: 0.31 mm

Regulatory Approval: MPR II rated for low-frequency magnetic and electrical emissions; EPA EnergyStar compliant (while in Energy Saver mode).

Macintosh 21-Inch Display

Description: The Macintosh 21-inch display incorporates a flat face plate, gray filter glass, relatively small 0.26 mm dot pitch, and easy-to-reach ADB and sound ports onboard. Although this is not a Trinitron monitor, it can sharply display two entire 8 1/2 × 11-inch pages of color text and graphics side by side in sharp focus.

Features: Tilt/swivel base; automatic degaussing; antiglare screen; ADB; microphone; onboard sound outputs

Compatibility/Requirements: All color capable Macs except LC/LCII/LCIII, IIsi, IIVX (unless 8/24 card is installed).

Image Size/Resolution: 1152 × 870 79 dpi

Screen Refresh Rate: 75 Hz

Dot Pitch: 0.26 mm

Regulatory Approval: MPR II rated for low-frequency magnetic and electrical emissions; EPA EnergyStar compliant (while in Energy Saver mode).

Macintosh Portrait Display

Description: Though beginning to show its age, the Portrait Display can display one full 8 1/2 × 11-inch page in monochrome. This may be all you need if you produce flyers or must design full pages separately with no two-page spreads. Portrait displays are workhorses in the journalism world. You probably can find a used one at a very low price.

Features: Antiglare screen; ADB plug onboard

Compatibility: Color Macs except for LC/LCII; IIvx onboard video; Performa 400/410/430/405/600 onboard video.

Image Size/Resolution: 640 × 870 pixels/80 dpi

Screen Refresh Rate: 75 Hz

Dot Pitch: 0.29 mm

Regulatory Approval: MPR II rated for low-frequency magnetic and electrical emissions

Macintosh 12-Inch RGB Display

Description: The Macintosh 12-inch RGB display utilizes a shadow mask display technology rather than a brighter Trinitron picture tube. The 12-inch monitor is the lowest priced color monitor available from Apple, and provides Mac users an affordable color monitor.

Features: Tilt/swivel brightness and contrast controls

Compatibility/Requirements: All color-capable Macintosh models and color/gray-scale generating PowerBooks with a variety of color depths depending on hardware card or VRAM installed.

Image Size/Resolution: 512 × 384 pixels/64 dpi

Screen Refresh Rate: 60 Hz

Dot Pitch: 0.28 mm

Regulatory Approval: Swedac and MPR II rated for low-frequency magnetic and electrical emissions

Macintosh 12-Inch Monochrome Display

Description: The Macintosh 12-inch monochrome display is the lowest priced monitor available from Apple. Though it isn't good for graphics, publishing, or multimedia, it is useful as a second "tools screen" monitor in many Mac setups. The 12-inch monitor is the least expensive of the line, and is a quality monochrome display, offering sharp contrast with its Page White phosphor screen and dark glass.

Features: Antiglare brightness and contrast controls

Compatibility/Requirements: All NuBus-equipped Macintosh model PowerBooks using either onboard video or one-bit display card

Image Size/Resolution: 640 × 480 pixels/76 dpi

Screen Refresh Rate: 35 Hz

Dot Pitch: 0.28 mm

Regulatory Approval: Swedac and MPR II rated for low-frequency magnetic and electrical emissions

Performa monitors

Performas are bundled with lower-image quality 14" monitors with a larger dot-pitch size and a 640×480 display. These monitors can be hard on your eyes; if you are considering a Performa, you may want to consider a Performa bundle that includes a monitor with better image resolution, or a traditional Macintosh model.

Compatibility: SVGA, multisync, and compatibility with other Apple monitors

Third-party monitors

More than a dozen companies offer Macintosh displays in several sizes. If you are buying or recommending a monitor, you have your work cut out for you. The best advice is to call the companies, ask about competing models, ask them to send literature, and cross reference their comments.

The following monitors are a cross-section of the best displays chosen from several third-party vendors. All have tilt-swivel bases for adjusting the viewing angle of the monitor. These monitors are great alternatives to the Apple monitors in the same class, or have exceptional features for specialty applications. They can also be used with PC computers with the addition of a PC-compatible cable adapter.

Sony 15", 17" through 20" multisyncs

Sony has several monitor models with a range of features that work with Macintosh and PCs. Sony monitors do not include any additional software or cable adapters. Cable adapters that convert the monitor cable to the Apple standard DB15, 15-pin built-in video connector, are necessary to connect Sony multisync monitors to Macintosh 680x0 and Power Macintosh video cards. Separate cables are also necessary for the multi-pin Power Macintosh built-in video connector.

Sony Multiscan 15sf

This monitor features great image quality in a compact, affordable monitor size. Although the diagonal viewable area of the monitor is 14", the tube size of the Trinitron display is 15". It supports resolutions up to 832 × 624. Sony's Digital Multiscan™ technology optimizes image geometry and focus. Color temperature control also facilitates consistent color accuracy across monitors. The Trinitron tube is vertically flat and is coated with anti-glare silica, minimizing glare. It meets EPA Energy Star and VESA guidelines for power management.

Sony Multiscan 17sf

This monitor offers the same, sharp Trinitron display quality as the 15sf model. It has 16.1" of maximum viewable image size, with the diagonal tube size being 17". It supports resolutions up to 1024 × 768 and incorporates the same Digital Multiscan technology found in the 15sf monitor. It also meets EPA Energy Star and VESA guidelines for power management.

Sony Multiscan 20se

This 20" Trinitron display offers 19.1" of viewable image size and supports resolutions up to 1152 × 870. In addition to the Digital Multiscan technology found in the 15sf and 17sf models, the 20se also offers three color temperature presets and adjustable hue and saturation intensity (HSI) control. A 17se model is also available and supports the same resolutions as the 20se, but with a 17" Trinitron tube and 16" of viewable image size.

NEC 15", 17 through 21" multisyncs

NEC uses a different tube technology than Sony's Trinitron technology. In addition to the monitor, you receive monitor resolution changing software created by Alysis and cable adapters for Macintosh 15-pin built-in video. NEC monitors, like Sony monitors, can be connected to both Macintosh or PC video cards or built-in video connectors, and both vendors have established popular reputations in the computer and consumer industries as producers of high-quality products.

NEC MultiSync 4FGe 15-Inch Color Display

Description: The 4FGe (see Figure 4.7) is a recommended alternative to the Apple 14-inch monitor line, and carries some of the latest cutting-edge technology available for an accurate and high-quality color display. Stacking up favorably against traditional Trinitron-based monitors, the NEC 4FGe's Invar alloy shadow mask allows more light to be processed with less heat, giving a higher contrast and brighter image than other monitors in its class. NEC uses Radius' switch-on-the-fly software for its multisync monitors, as well as the innovative NEC AccuColor system, which allows individual adjustment of the degree of color from each of the three RGB color guns. Another innovation is NEC's Intelligent Power Manager software, which automatically places the monitor into a low-energy sleep mode during low-usage periods. The sleek, attractive outer shell design of the NEC monitors comes from frogdesign™, the same company that designs Macintosh, NeXT computers, and many other innovative, award-winning industrial design products. NEC monitors are also fully compatible with Power Macs with a free cable supplied from NEC.

Features: AccuColor control system; 12 user-controllable digital configurations available from front panel; tilt/swivel base

Figure 4.7   NEC MultiSync 4FGe 15-inch color display.

Compatibility/Requirements: All color-capable Macs and color/gray scale PowerBooks with appropriate VRAM or display board

Image Size/Resolution: Optimum resolution occurring at 1024 x 768 pixels; capable of 640 × 480 pixels, 832 × 624 pixels, 1024 × 768 pixels

Screen Refresh Rate: 75 Hz

Dot Pitch: 0.28 mm

Regulatory Approval: Swedac and MPR II rated for low-frequency magnetic and electrical emissions. Reduced Magnetic Field technology; ISO 9241 compliant ergonomic design.

Portrait Pivot 1700

Description: Based on the Radius Pivot line of displays, the Portrtait Pivot 1700 can be used in both portrait and landscape orientations simply by tilting the monitor 90; the picture automatically switches modes. The Radius Pivot line has been discontinued. The Portrait Pivot has .26mm dot pitch, and is a multisync monitor featuring switch-on-the-fly Dynamic Desktop monitor control software. Its anti-reflective Silica Glass coating helps provide better focus, clarity, and brightness. Aside from its unique swivel capability, the Portrait Pivot's picture ranks among the best of the small monitors available for the Macintosh. With Portrait Display Lab's three-year warranty, the Portrait Pivot is one of the best buys and—literally—the most flexible monitor for the Mac (see Figure 4.8).

Figure 4.8   The Portrait Pivot 1700 is based on Radius' PrecisionColor Pivot.

Features: Multisync; turn display physically on its side and have picture remain oriented; tilt/swivel base; separate horizontal and vertical centering.

Compatibility/Requirements: Color capable Macs and PowerBooks with appropriate VRAM or color display card installed

Image Size/Resolution: 640 × 480 pixels, 864 × 640 pixels, 1024 × 768 pixels/81 dpi

Screen Refresh Rate: 72 Hz at 864 × 640 pixels (decreases as the screen sizes increases)

Dot Pitch: 0.26 mm

Regulatory Approval: Swedac and MPR II rated for low frequency magnetic and electrical emissions. ISO 9241 compliant ergonomic design. UL, CSA, TUV; FCC Class B; Canadian DOC B.

Philips Brilliance 1720 17-Inch Color Display

Description: The Philips Brilliance line of displays (see Figure 4.9) feature workstation-level performance for a variety of professional color applications. The Brilliance 1720's wide array of onboard electronics autosyncs to nine separate display resolutions, including VGA, SuperVGA, and all Mac resolutions. Unusually high refresh rates (for example 76 Hz in 1280 × 1024 pixel aspect ratio) make it exceptionally flicker-free. AGRAS (antiglare, antireflection, and antistatic) tube coating, EBU tube phosphors, and 0.27 mm dot pitch provide a sharp and unusually bright display. Unique to the Brilliance monitor series is an onboard LCD display panel for clear identification of selected modes and adjustment configuration, which features an auto shut-off to minimize distraction.

Figure 4.9   Philips Brilliance 1720 17-inch color display.

Features: Microprocessor controlled fixed-mode frequencies and onboard memory of user settings; onboard LCD display window; tilt/swivel base; separate horizontal and vertical sync.

Compatibility/Requirements: Color-capable Macs and PowerBooks with appropriate VRAM and hardware; DOS/Windows/IBM PC, Workstations, and X-Terminals

Image Size/Resolution: Maximum resolution of 1600 × 1280 pixels, with optimum resolution at 1280 × 1024 pixels; capable of VGA 640 × 480 pixels, 640 × 400 pixels; SVGA 800 × 600 pixels; Quadra 832 × 624 pixels; XGA 1024 × 768 pixels; 1280 × 1024 pixels.

Screen Refresh Rate: 60 Hz, 67 Hz, 70 Hz, 72 Hz, 73 Hz, 75 Hz, 76 Hz, 87 Hz depending on resolution

Dot Pitch: 0.27 mm

Regulatory Approval: Swedac and MPR II rated for low-frequency magnetic and electrical emissions. ISO 9241 compliant ergonomic design.

Sigma MultiMode 150 19-Inch Gray-scale Monitor

Description: Many industrial designers do not need color. Gray-scale and monochrome monitors require less power, which means that they throw less dangerous emissions, last longer, and are cheaper to run. Highly recommended is the Sigma Designs Multimode 150 19-inch high-resolution gray-scale display (see Figure 4.10). With the highest refresh rates and maximum resolution of any gray-scale monitor for the Macintosh, the Multimode 150 meets the needs of engineers working with highly detailed and premium-quality graphics. The Sigma also features on-the-fly resolution switching, hardware pan and zoom, and block-transfer mode. Block-transfer mode enables the monitor to utilize QuickDraw acceleration. This wide array of features makes the Sigma 150 an excellent choice for exacting gray-scale work.

Figure 4.10   Sigma MultiMode 150 19-inch gray-scale monitor.

Features: Tilt/swivel base; block-mode transfer; Swedac and MPR II rated for low-frequency magnetic and electrical emissions

Compatibility/Requirements: Any Mac with onboard video or NuBus-capable Mac with appropriate display card (such as Apple 4/8 or 8/24 card).

Image Size/Resolution: Optimum resolution at 2048 × 1536 pixels; capable of syncing to 2048 × 1536 pixels/150 dpi, 1664 × 1200 pixels/120 dpi, 1280 × 960 pixels/92 dpi, 832 × 600 pixels/60 dpi, 640 × 480 pixels/46 dpi, 512 × 384 dpi

Screen Refresh Rate: 76 Hz to 116 Hz over range of resolutions

Dot Pitch: 0.28 mm

Virtual Vision NTSC Monitor

The Virtual Vision monitor is designed for Mac video professionals who need an NTSC television monitor to produce Desktop Video or animation. To use this monitor, you also need a video card with an NTSC converter and output to switch in and out of noninterlaced to interlaced mode.

Available from Virtual Vision (1-800-758-7060), this interesting device (coined "personal entertainment eyeware") is basically a pair of stylish wraparound, dark but transparent eyeglasses outfitted with a small heads-up display NTSC monitor inside the glasses—with virtual screen size in excess of 60 inches. Stereo sound using strategically placed speakers on the arms of the eyeglasses also is provided. The onboard TV tuner with antenna has outstanding reception and is smaller and lighter than a camcorder battery (see Figure 4.11).

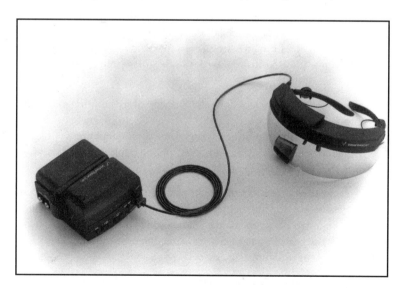

Figure 4.11   Virtual Vision NTSC monitor.

Deluxe models have RCA inputs for stereo audio and video inputs right on the portable power supply. These inputs make the monitor flexible for desktop video as well as heads-up camcorder shooting, eliminating the need to look through the camera eyepiece to record. It definitely takes some getting used to and can cause a mild form of motion platform imbalance after you take them off, but only if you move around with them on. These glasses attract a lot of attention, which can be an added factor if you're out shooting video for your next multi-media project. (Tip: Carry business cards.)

Compatibility/Requirements: Any NuBus Macintosh equipped with an NTSC converter that has an RCA video output.

External Storage Drives

Hard drives are the most common Macintosh peripheral. The standard connection format for internal and external hard drives is SCSI. Hard drive vendors, such as Apple, APS, LaCie, MicroNet, and FWB add additional firmware and software drivers that interface SCSI and IDE with Macintosh hardware components and System software.

Whether this popularity is due to the hard drive's relatively long storage reliability, decent speed, or low cost per megabyte, the hard drive's popularity is so widespread that it is often thought of as an integral part of the computer. It is not: the computer does not need a hard drive to operate. Other media can act as bootable storage for the Mac, making hard drives a peripheral. Among Mac users, however, the hard disk is the storage medium of choice.

Hard disks rely on machined aluminum, glass, or ceramic that is about 1/8 inch thick and is contained in a sealed drive mechanism. Called platters, these disks are covered with a coating that is magnetized by the drive's actuator head. Older disks are coated with an oxidized iron particulate. Many new high-performance drives use a much thinner metal plating, or thin-film media that allows bits to be packed tighter for more storage and faster access time per disk.

The hard drive is often compared to a phonograph because of its spinning platter and "stylus" that retrieves information. The stylus on a hard drive is an electromagnet at the end of a read/write armature that can create or find information on the spinning platters. A hard disk stays magnetized even when it is not plugged in and, like a phonograph, it records a lasting (but erasable) impression that can be read again when you need to access it.

Generally, the larger the drive, the more platters it will contain, although higher density platters and data compression are slowing that trend. All platters rotate on the same spindle, and each platter has its own armature stylus. As the platters spin, they create a thin air cushion upon which the read/write head floats as it moves across the drive surface. This gap is so thin it is measured in microns, or millionths of a meter.

Each platter is broken up into tracks. These tracks form concentric circles that emanate from the hub of the platter to the perimeter. As information is sent by the drive controller, it passes through the armature, magnetizing the particles on the platter tracks, forming binary patterns, or bits.

Understanding hard drives

Apple and a healthy number of hard drive vendors make up the Macintosh hard drive market. Like any thriving third-party market, fierce competition among vendors keeps the technology advancing, while prices steadily drop.

Drives are not just plain "storage" anymore; they are an integral part of various computer solutions. The wrong disk drive can limit the specific goal of a computer professional. A server, for example, requires large reliable hard drives, or arrays of hard drives set up with fault-tolerant disk mirroring. If a video-editing workstation is being put together, sustained throughput level is more important than access speed. PowerBook owners looking for an internal drive need a hard drive with low heat and power requirements. Many veteran users simply want to maintain access to a large number of applications and files if they have grown beyond the single internal drive. They need accessible, rewritable storage rather than specialized drive features.

Consequently, the market for SCSI hard drives is large; hard drives from 20 MB to 9GB (9000 MB) are available, each with its own set of features, speed, reliability, and quirks. But each one will run just fine from your Macintosh (unless you own a Mac 512 or 128, which do not have SCSI ports). Keep in mind that with present System software, the Macintosh cannot address storage partitions larger than 2GB contiguously—drives larger than 9GB are partitioned and appear as individual drives (or volumes) on your Mac's desktop. This limit will be doubled in the next incarnation of System software, and most likely raised to much higher limits as digital video and large volume transfers become more and more prevalent.

The need for faster, less expensive, and higher-quality hard drives is quickly being addressed by new generations of super-fast Apple models such as the 840AV and Power Macs. These new Macs have the speed to work with large server configurations, multimedia applications, color-image processing, video, and other storage-intensive, speed-thirsty applications.

Speed

Like the CPUs they plug into, hard drives are constantly increasing in speed and steadily decreasing in cost. The difference between a popular hard drive line and a dead-end one is determined by three very basic factors: speed, reliability, and price—in that order. Speed, for hard drives and other peripherals, equals efficiency and means the latest technology was probably built into the drive.

To put the relative speed of hard drives in perspective, a decent hard drive will access information 10 times faster than a floppy disk, but nearly 100 times slower than RAM. Hard drive access time—the time it takes your computer to show you what you asked for—is always being decreased as the technology becomes more refined and competition increases. Overall drive speed is measured using a combination of spindle speed and latency time. The slowest part of the hard drive mechanism causes the overall speed of the drive to increase.

Generally, newer drives are faster than older drives because even the lower-end model lines have benefited from the trickle down of newer technology.

Internal and external hard drives

The SCSI hard drive is a contained mechanism that requires a power cord and a SCSI port either internally—in one of the Mac's allotted drive bays—or externally in a box containing a power supply and internal SCSI connector (see Figure 4.12 for a cutaway view of an internal drive mechanism). To install an external hard drive, you simply plug it into the SCSI port of the Mac, or daisy-chain it from another SCSI device (see Chapter 9 for more information about connecting SCSI peripheral devices together).

Figure 4.12   Cutaway of a hard drive.

External devices always cost more money than their internal counterparts—enclosures, power supply, shielding, and cooling add up to roughly an extra hundred dollars for an external device as opposed to an internal one that piggybacks the Mac components.

Most external drive vendors do not actually manufacture the drive mechanisms they sell; instead they simply buy the mechanisms from a small handful of hard drive manufacturers—Seagate, Quantum, Micropolis, or DEC—and place them in external enclosures with their company name on them. This is important to note when you read the fine print on hard drive warranties to see who is responsible for fulfilling the warranty on the drive.

This is not to say that all external drive enclosures are the same; the quality varies widely. For the same reason that a Ferrari engine is not dropped into a Pinto chassis, an expensive, high-tech drive mechanism that holds all your data should be installed in a high-quality external enclosure, with the best shielding and internal components, and connected to your Mac with the best cables available (see Chapter 9 for more information on cables and terminators).

You should look for the following features in an external enclosure:

- Full-Metal RF/EMI (radio frequency & electromagnetic) shielding. Many poor-quality drives use metal paint on the enclosures. This is a poor, cheap substitute for shielding. Look for enclosures with a full metal jacket instead.

- Quality power supply. Does the hard drive have an onboard fuse and surge suppresser? Also, the more watts the power supply puts out the better.

- Switchable active termination. Only a few companies offer this feature on their external enclosures, but it is very desirable. Switchable active termination supplies terminate power on their own rather than rely on the Mac's power supply to push power down the line into the drive through SCSI. Termination problems can be minimized here—terminating your guesswork about previously invisible problems.

- Decent fan cooling. Look for a drive with a removable dust screen that you can clean and replace.

The best enclosures with all these features and more are available from APS Technologies, one of the larger third-party drive resellers.

External enclosures come in many different shapes and sizes. Portable external drives in enclosures from Liberty Systems (408-983-1127) are the smallest in the industry, not much bigger than the mechanism itself. Though their smallest drives don't have fans to cool them, their portability is renowned.

Zero-Footprint drive enclosures (or enclosures that fit underneath an integrated Mac Plus/Classic/SE without any extra footprint) are the same color as Macs. When purchasing an external drive enclosure, most companies will offer just about any shape you require, at no extra charge.

Note

All of Apple's current Macintosh computers have 1.4 MB floppy drives that can read and format 1.4 MB and 800K floppy disks as well as read 400K floppies. External floppy drives are available through Apple or Apple retailers for PowerBook Duos only. These external floppy drives plug into a mini-dock that in turn connects to the Duo's processor direct slot.

Physical versus storage size

The physical size (as opposed to the storage capacity) of hard drives is based on the diameter of the platter inside the drive mechanism itself. Hard drive mechanisms fall into three general drive measurements:

- 2.5 inch (also known as 1/3 Height or Low-Profile drives). Flatter than a pack of cigarettes, these drives go into PowerBooks and other tight places where power requirements are low, and heat must be kept to a minimum.

- 3.5 inch (also known as half-height or internal-sized drives). The size most often found inside Macs and external hard drives. Half-height drives have the best power-to-weight ratio of all sizes and are the most widely available. These drives have enhanced spindle speeds and better platter coatings, which make them faster and with more storage capabilities than the full-height drives they replace.

- 5.25 inch (also known as Full-Height or Winchester drives). Seldom found in Macs anymore, the full-height drives pull too much power, generate too much heat, and take up too much space to be a forward-looking choice for new desktop computers, although the Mac II, IIX, IIfx, and Quadra 900/950 can all utilize full-height drives.

Users who are upgrading need only be concerned about the physical size of the drive if it's going to be mounted inside the Macintosh; externally, the drives are hidden away in their own enclosures. Regardless of the size of the hard drive, they plug into the Mac the same way, and are recognized the same by the Macintosh.

RAID disk arrays

Redundant Array of Inexpensive Disks (RAID) technology was developed to increase performance by using normal existing drive technology rather than making the Single Large Expensive Drives (SLEDs) faster. RAID systems coordinate several linked drives to read/write in parallel—effectively doubling the access and latency speed of either drive. To accomplish this, the CPU must distribute data to two individual drives through two separate SCSI busses. This allows it to write twice the normal amount of data in the same time as one drive—making read time twice as fast. RAID arrays can be set up to perform disk mirroring, which is also called a fault tolerant setup that basically writes the same data to two different drives; should either drive crash, the data is safe and a new drive can replace the old drive.

At least two drives are required for an array setup, although more can be added. Two SCSI inputs are required on the Mac itself. Currently the only Macs that have two internal SCSI bus controllers are the Quadra 900/950, and the Power Macintosh 8100AV. If a second SCSI input is required for your system, an additional NuBus SCSI driver card can be added so that the two drives can be run off individual busses.

RAID has five possible implementation levels. Each performs a specific kind of task:

- RAID Level Zero (also known as formatting with Data Striping) reads and writes data in parallel to matched drives on the line in user-specified chunks called segments. Level Zero RAID drive setups are usually expensive, but they represent the highest possible performance for SCSI of any Mac configuration. Mac users who require the fastest SCSI throughput available should check out a RAID Level Zero Disk Array.

- RAID Level 1–5. Levels 1–5 perform disk mirroring as well as combinations of striping and mirroring in different configurations. Levels 1–5 do not provide the performance of RAID Level 0; however, they are more than adequate for fast data backup and information management.

For your purposes, Level Zero is probably more important. RAID Levels 1–5 may be of little use because this system relies on matched sets of hard drives as backup systems rather than more cost-effective backup, such as DAT.

Disk problems

There are two general kinds of hard drive problems: software and hardware crashes.

- Software crashes do not compromise the disk's physical integrity or firmware (the drive's onboard circuitry and mechanics). Any lost data can usually be recovered using a disk utility program. Many times software crashes can be attributed to viruses or SCSI address or termination problems, which can be solved by changing cables, SCSI ID numbers, or with recovery and anti-virus programs.

- Hardware crashes are among the most feared situations of computer users. Usually through no fault of your own, a drive will crash irrecoverably. This phenomenon is also known as die, go down, check out, eat it, suck your life away—all phrases meant to be spat out bitterly over mixed drinks. They say there are two kinds of drives: those that crash, and those that have crashed. Be prepared—back up!

A drive failure will happen eventually. That's why drive manufacturers have a MTBF rating for each drive, which stands for an estimated *Mean Time Before Failure* for that particular drive. Though drives do not automatically stop working after a certain amount of hours in operation, the MTBF rating is more of a general "guesstimate" of a drive's life span based on the reliability of its parts.

Although no single factor prevails, hard drive crashes can usually be traced to a few weaknesses:

- Damaged drive controller. A part of the controller assembly fails to perform. Your data may be intact, but there is no way to read the disks—you cannot simply open the case and replace it. (Well, you could if you were in a "clean" room with microparticulate clothing and breathers, but not everyone has access to these kinds of facilities.) Environmental factors, voltage spikes, and static electricity can blow out the delicate capacitors and onboard electronics found on the controller.

- Spindle failure. This main moving part is central to the drive's existence. When its lubricant is gone, the spindle will grind as the drive spins, telling you to back up your data and to get rid of the drive while you can. Sometimes the problem can be too much lubricant, which will cause stiction—a condition where the drive platters refuse to spin without some kind of push—usually a good shake will get the drive started, but will eventually kill it, too (and it looks rather silly to clients, similar to kicking your TV when guests are over).

- Erratic platter movement (head crash). This kind of crash is caused by the platters wobbling as they spin, like a poorly loaded washing machine. The actuator head will begin contacting the platter, finally damaging it by physically scratching the platter and destroying both the read/write head, the platter, and all the information contained on it. This condition creates the same sound as fingers on a chalkboard—unmistakable and shrill. You will not forget this sound, especially if this drive was your main source of storage.

Data on drives with these problems is going nowhere but in the garbage, unless you decide that your data is worth spending a lot of money to recover. If so, you can have the platters removed and placed in a new drive mechanism where they can be re-read.

Other less destructive hardware crashes can be attributed to media errors—bad sectors of the platters that cannot be successfully charted by the Mac and the drive controller. Software utilities, such as Hard Disk Toolkit from FWB Technologies or Anubis from Charismac can format the drive around the bad sectors. All new drives should be tested for bad sectors, and if more than a few bad sectors are found, the drive(s) should be returned.

There is no real way to foresee or prevent a major hardware crash. The best you can do is back up your drive regularly, and keep your warranty information at hand for your drive. Many drives feature excellent warranties of three and even five years for hardware failure.

Hard drives and formatting software

When you purchase a hard drive, it will already be formatted as one volume to work with your Macintosh. The software used to format the hard drive, also known as hard drive formatting software, is included on the hard drive. If you wish to add additional volumes to your hard drive (this will reduce the initial size of the hard drive into two, three, or more smaller sized volumes) you can launch the software and configure your hard drive prior to copying additional files to it. You can also use hard drive formatting software to reformat the hard drive should the Macintosh file system become damaged or corrupted. Always backup all data on the hard drive before reformatting it.

Note

When new System software is introduced, you should upgrade your drivers on your hard drive as well as your hard drive formatting software.

Apple hard drives/HD SC Setup

Apple's internal and external hard drives can be formatted or updated with Apple's software HD SC Setup and for Power Macs, 630, and PowerBook 150 Drive Setup. The current version of this software is HD SC Setup is 7.3.2. Power Macs, and any Macs with IDE hard drives require Apple's Drive Setup 1.0.2 application. Apple's external hard drives currently ship with a copy of LaCie's Silverlining formatting and partitioning software.

APS

Alliance Peripheral Systems Technologies is well-known for its technical support as well as great prices on hard drives, DAT drives, and removable media. When you purchase an internal or external hard drive from APS, you also receive their hard drive formatting software, and an archive of Macintosh shareware software. APS also has a popular external hard drive casing, the SR2000, which is part of all of its available external hard drives.

APS hard drives
APS Technologies
5131 Deramus
Kansas, City, MO 64120
(800) 677-3294, (816) 920-4109 (Int'l Sales)

LaCie

LaCie has been providing Macintosh hard drives, and its formatting software Silverlining for many years. LaCie has a variety of models and specialize in high-performance hard drive solutions. Like APS they advertise regularly in magazines such as MacUser and Macworld.

LaCie hard drives
La Cie Ltd.
8700 SW Creekside Pl
Beaverton, OR 97005
(503) 520-9000, (800) 999-0143

MicroNet

A popular and longtime Macintosh hard drive provider, MicroNet offers great service and prices for their internal and external drives. MicroNet's formatting software shares common features, such as Silverlining and FWB Hard Drive Toolkit, allowing multiple volume partitions and diagnostic checking features.

MicroNet hard drives
MicroNet Technology
80 Technology
Irvine, CA 92718
(714) 453-6000, (800) 800-3475

FWB Hard Disk Toolkit

FWB, located in Silicon Valley, provides Hard Disk Toolkit software with its drives. The software formats Mac drives and partitions hard drive volumes with an easy-to-use interface. FWB supports Apple SCSI Manager 4.3.1 and SCSI 2 formats; the software also has a RAID Toolkit for formatting hard drives to work as RAIDs. RAID consists of software that splits data and sends it to two equal size hard drives. Macs recognize the RAID drives as one volume. This arrangement allows the fastest SCSI access possible for Macintosh applications and System software.

Hard Disk ToolKit 1.8, RAID ToolKit
FWB, Inc.
1555 Adams Drive
Menlo Park, CA 94025
(415) 325-4329

Drive7

Drive7 is a hard drive formatting software application that supports any Macintosh hard drive, IDE hard drives, and traditional SCSI-type Macintosh hard drives.

Drive7
Casa Blanca Works, Inc.
148 Bon Air Center
Greenbrae, CA 94904
(415) 461-2227

Other software for hard drives

Hard drive size-doubling software arrived on the Macintosh scene about two years ago and, in general, provides a realistic alternative to purchasing a physical hard drive. This software, however, has many inherent problems that have not made this type of product popular. Doubling software doubles the size of a hard drive by reformatting the sector sizes of the hard drive platter. Software companies include eDisk, SuperDisk (Alysis), Stacker, and Times Two.

eDisk, More Disk Space, SuperDisk
Alysis Software
1331 Columbus Avenue, 3rd Floor
San Francisco, CA 94133
(415) 928-2895, (800) 825-9747

Stacker for Macintosh
Stac Electronics
5993 Avenida Encinas
Carlsbad, CA 92008
(619) 431-7474, (800) 522-7822

Disk Doubler

Symantec's file compression software can free up hard drive space. If you have a number of folders and files as backup or data you don't use very often, Disk Doubler immediately decompresses the information when you double-click on data's folder or file. This slows launch time of applications, but enables you to get a few more megabytes out of your existing hard drive.

Symantec Corp.
10201 Torre Ave
Cupertino, CA 95014
(800) 441-7234, (800) 626-8847 (in CA)

StuffIt 1.5.1/StuffIt Deluxe

The original file compression software for Macintosh, Aladdin's StuffIt products support a wide variety of file compression options. Some of the supported options include StuffIt 1.5.1 (which is freely distributed on the Internet and online services), BinHex, and zip (commonly used on PCs). StuffIt 1.5.1 and StuffIt Deluxe can compress, expand, split and join files similar to DiskDoubler (by Symantec) which uses its own file compression technology. StuffIt also provides password encryption and self-expanding archives.

Aladdin Systems, Inc.
165 Westridge Drive
Watsonville, CA 95076
(408) 761-6200

Other removable media

Removable media is a popular alternative to purchasing a hard drive for extending hard disk storage, archiving, and backing up files. Most removable media involve a player device and removable cartridges. The biggest cost of using and maintaining removable media is the cost of the removable cartridges, and tracking the data you put on them. To keep up with all the changes you make to several removable media, it is a good idea to keep a short log of what you keep on your removable media cartridges and *when* you put the content on the cartridges. Zip and SyQuest media, the two most popular removable media, appear on your desktop via an icon, similar to internal or external hard drives. DAT and other tape mechanisms do not have icons representing the drive on the desktop, and need software to access the data stored on the tape.

Zip drives are the latest and most popular removable media today. The initial model, introduced by IOmega in 1995, is a SCSI device that uses floppy-sized cartridges that can store up to 100 MB per disk. A newer model, capable of storing 1GB of data will also be available soon. The reason these drives are popular is their relatively low cost for the removable media player device, as well as the cartridges.

SyQuest introduced the first popular removable media format: SyQuest removable 44 MB cartridges and players. These SCSI devices have reasonable access times and provide a low-cost (compared to purchasing one or many hard drives), efficient, reliable solution to data storage and quick access to backup files. SyQuest's current models can use 88 MB or 200 MB cartridges in addition to the original 44 MB. SyQuest also provides a newer, smaller, SCSI-based removable cartridge format, utilizing 3.5" removable disks that can hold up to 135 MB. The cost of this new technology is similar to IOmega's Zip drive.

Recordable CD-ROM players

CD-ROM has grown to be an affordable and entertaining media format. Recently, recordable SCSI CD players have also become popular because they can write up to 600 MB of stored information on a write-once, read-many CD. After the recorder creates a CD, it can be used in any Macintosh CD-ROM player as a back up, audio, or multimedia CD. Popular models have mechanisms that are manufactured by Olympus, Sony, Kodak, Yamaha, and Phillips.

Eastman Kodak Co.
Writable CD (software)
901 Elmgrove Rd.
Rochester, NY 14653
(716) 724-4000, (800) 235-6325

DAT drives (tape backup media)

DAT drives are tape backup media that can store anywhere from 1GB to 140GB of information on 4mm or 8mm tape cartridges. Apple includes these drives in their WorkGroup Server line of Macintosh computers as internal drives. Other popular DAT drive vendors are APS, MicroNet, and RUMI. These drives are generally less expensive than an external hard drive mechanism, but cannot provide immediate access to data.

APS has a full product line of DAT drives. APS's Hyper QIC model is its most affordable DAT solution, and provides up to 2GB of backup storage. It can compress 3–4GB of data with additional software compression. APS includes a copy of Retrospect Remote with its DAT drives in addition to a 2-year warranty and 30-day money-back guarantee.

APS Technologies (Alliance Peripheral Systems)
6131 Deramus
Kansas City, MO 64120
(800) 235-3707

http://www.apstech.com

FWB, like APS is well-known for its hard drive and CD products. FWB also has a HammerDAT product line which is compatible with Macintosh II or larger, 4 MB of memory, System 6.0.5 or later. The HammerDAT product line consists of the 2000, 4000, and 8000 DDS drives which offer 2GB to 4GB of native storage capacity, or 8G or more compressed. Cabling, media and Restrospect Remote software are included with its DAT products.

$1389–$4099 SRP
FWB, Inc.
1555 Adams Drive
Menlo Park, CA 94025
(415) 325-4329

MicroNet offers two lines of DAT drives. Its Premier and Advantage drives range in price from $1075 to $4295 SRP.

MicroNet Technology, Inc.
80 Technology
Irvine, CA 92718
(714) 453-6000, (800) 800-3475

Magneto optical drives

Magneto optical drives offer the largest amount of data storage; however, they have considerably slower access times compared to hard drives and most other removable media drives. Magneto optical drives allow you to write and rewrite data to a CD-type media cartridge. These drives use 3.5" and 5.25" removable media, usually a CD-size disk in a permanent casing. The external casing is very similar to that of a floppy disk. They can store 120 MB to more than 1GB of data on one disk. One pitfall to using magneto optical drives is that the software drivers vary from drive maker to drive maker. If you plan to share magneto optical information across different brand magneto optical devices, make sure that differing drives can read each other's formatted CDs. Also keep in mind that the magneto optical cartridges range in price from $20–$40 each.

Note

Magneto optical CD media cannot be used with CD-ROM drives. Many magneto optical CD media are not recognized across differing brands and product lines, either.

Alliance Peripheral Systems offers a full range of magneto optical products supporting 230 MB to 1.3GB of storage. The APS 230 MB MO and APS 1.3GB MO have one- and two-year warranties, respectively. The 1.3GB model includes a 4 MB cache and uses Sony MO 1.3GB media cartridges. The 230 MB model uses Olympus MO 230 MB media.

$499.95–$1699.95 SRP
APS Technologies (Alliance Peripheral Systems)
6131 Deramus
Kansas City, MO 64120
(800) 235-3707

http://www.apstech.com

Pinnacle Micro offers a complete line of single and multiple magneto optical product lines. They originally introduced the 3.5" magneto optical drive which can store up to 120 MB of data. Its current 3.5" model, Tahoe-230, holds up to 230 MB of data and can work with a Mac Plus or larger. Pinnacle Micro offers 5.25" magneto optical drives as well as removable media supporting Macintosh II or larger computers. Storage capacities of their magneto optical products range from 120 MB to 120GB.

$795–$39,995 SRP
Pinnacle Micro
19 Technology
Irvine, CA 92718
(714) 727-3300, (800) 553-7070

FWB, a leader in hard drive and removable media technology has a complete product line of HammerDisk Optical Drives. The HammerDisk E230 and 230 3.5-inch magneto-optical drives offer 128 MB to 230 MB of data storage . The HammerDisk 1300HH and HammerDisk 1300FMF 5.25-inch multifunction drives offer 650 MB to 1.3GB capacities. Cabling, media and software are included.

$929–$3289 SRP
FWB, Inc.
1555 Adams Drive
Menlo Park, CA 94025
(415) 325-4329

Printers

Choosing a printer for your Macintosh can be daunting because of the number of different printer categories and the large range of models in each category. For example, inkjet printers alone vary from a portable monochrome printer for $300 all the way up to a large format color inkjet that prints billboards for $30,000 or more.

Printing technology has evolved into a number of commercially available low-cost options. Mac users benefit from this vast selection of technologies; one of these methods will undoubtedly be perfect for your needs:

- Dot Matrix

- Inkjets

- Lasers

- Portable inkjet or thermal wax

- Color Printers: Dye Sublimation, Inkjet, Laser, and Thermal Wax

Assessing your needs now and in the future is your best approach to finding the right printer. If you want to print letters with your color logo on the letterhead, you might have the letterhead printed traditionally and then purchase a less expensive monochrome printer to print text on the letterhead. This method is much more cost effective because a monochrome printer has a lower maintenance curve and consumables cost.

Printers are more capable of paying for themselves than other Mac components; they last a lot longer than your other peripherals because their moving parts are often replaced as part of the duty cycle. For example, an old dot matrix impact printer is still useful for producing triplicate receipts because that is all that's required of it.

The printer you choose will be determined by the job you need to do; there is no single do-it-all printer. For instance, you can print your letters on a dye sublimation printer—if you don't mind paying $3 a page for special paper. A laser printer at a fifth the cost of that dye sublimation printer will do a much better and faster job on your letters.

For many users, choosing a printer is really a question of money; this is where your research can be a valuable resource. Used printers are a wise and frugal choice. With the addition of new ink or toner, a used printer is as good as new.

Shopping for a printer

When shopping for a new printer, always check to see what the competition offers. For instance, if you like an Apple model printer, chances are that Hewlett-Packard is playing leap frog with Apple by moving to a less-expensive higher resolution. Another company is probably right on HP's trail, working hard to put out higher performance at lower cost. If you can afford to impulse buy, stick to the big players: Apple, Hewlett-Packard, QMS, or Canon. If your little printer company (with the flashy ads and speed/resolution/price claims) goes out of business, you could be left with a dead-end peripheral.

If you are bargain hunting and warranty is not a huge issue, check out America Online's Classifieds for some of the heaviest trafficking of used Mac printers. The usual common sense warnings apply here, however: know exactly what you are getting and who you are buying from. Get their home phone number and any online references, and ask for shipping confirmation numbers before sending money. America Online is a great resource for all penny-pinchers. Sometimes you can even tell if a new printer you are interested in is actually a dud by emailing folks with the printer for sale and impartially asking them about the unit. People can be surprisingly frank online, and will often flare about how poor or incredible a given printer is, which is infinitely more valuable than the sales materials you get at a trade show or from a dealer.

Dot matrix overview

Dot matrix printers were the first printers available for Macintosh computers and are the missing link between typewriters and Macs. Dot matrix printers take bitmaps from the Mac and use an impact head and ink ribbon to shuffle back and forth across the page, line by line, dot by dot, impacting the ink ribbon and the paper. These printers are slow, noisy, and of low quality, but are the most inexpensive of all printers. They are also the least expensive to maintain because of their inexpensive print ribbons, which are available from most office supply stores.

If you handle payrolls using triplicate checks, create carbon paper forms, or need sheet feeding, the dot matrix printer is the only way to go.

Apple ImageWriter II

The first type of printer sold by Apple for the Macintosh was the dot matrix ImageWriter, and even today the same printer is compatible with every Macintosh sold. Slower than even the slowest inkjet, with poor resolution, the only advantage the venerable ImageWriter II has over other printers is that it can print on carbon forms and continuous tractor-fed forms. This common use in business is the only thing keeping these printers on the market. An optional LocalTalk interface allows networking, and its three separate resolutions allow somewhat faster operation in basic draft mode.

Method: Impact Dot Matrix
Media: Fabric ink ribbon
Speed: 2 ppm, draft; 1/2 ppm, Near Letter Quality
Maximum dpi: 160
Paper Format: Cut sheet or fanfold continuous (tractor feed)
Interface: Serial Din cable

Inkjet overview

Compared to lasers with the same resolution, inkjets are a bargain. The problem with this technology is that ink will absorb into the paper slightly, spreading out unevenly from its impact point. For this reason, inkjet printers are finicky; they print crisper images on coated or even synthetics rather than more absorbent cotton and light weave paper stocks, which absorb more ink and decrease the resolution. Large black areas or overlapping color areas will soak a page with wet ink, which can dry unevenly, resulting in blacks that aren't that black, and ruined texture. Savvy inkjet owners now know that photocopying the inkjet-printed page using a slight reduction delivers the appearance of laser prints with truer blacks and uniform paper texture.

Inkjet printers are fairly slow (2–6 pages per minute for black-and-white printouts) and mostly PostScript-incompatible. However, inkjets are easy to maintain, lightweight, quiet, inexpensive, and most are LocalTalk networkable right out of the box. You can refill the ink cartridges yourself in most cases with either a refill kit, a syringe and water-based black ink, or even with more ecological soy inks. Note that if your cartridge has run dry, the small sponge inside the cartridge or the print head may have dried out and become unusable. Most ink cartridges will go for months without needing a change and cost between $15 and $40. Some InkJet models also use ink more efficiently than others, making the ink in the cartridges last longer. Table 4.2 lists specifications of several inkjet printers.

Table 4.2 Inkjet Printer Specifications

	Apple Computer	*GCC Technologies*	*Hewlett-Packard*
PRODUCT	**STYLEWRITER 1200**	**WIDEWRITER 360**	**DESKWRITER**
Phone	(408) 996-1010	(617) 275-5800	n/a
Toll-free phone	(800) 776-2333	(800) 422-7777	(800) 851-1170
List price	$270 street price	$1699	$365
Maximum speed (in pages per minute)	3	4	3
Resolution (in dots per inch)	360	360	300

	Apple Computer	GCC Technologies	Hewlett-Packard
Paper capacity (in sheets)	100	75	100
Paper capacity (in envelopes)	15	n/a	n/a
Number of fonts included	64	21	4
Levels of Gray	over 100	33	33
Warranty period (in years)	1	1	3

Apple StyleWriter 1200

Apple's StyleWriter 1200 is small and quiet, and the print is good enough for most personal printer needs. With its "GrayShare" software, the StyleWriter is not only a true gray-scale output device, but a networkable one as well—albeit with a host Mac as the center of the hub. The StyleWriter 1200, with no onboard page processing unit, takes its page description from the host Mac—the faster your Mac, the faster your printing. The StyleWriter's service cycle is approximately five hundred pages before a $20 ink refill cartridge is required. If you are printing lots of graphics, however, you will need to refill sooner.

Method: Thermal Inkjet
Media: Water-based ink
Speed: 3 ppm
Maximum dpi: 360
Paper Format: 8 1/2 × 11-inch standard paper
Interface: LocalTalk/Serial Din cable

Hewlett-Packard DeskWriter

The StyleWriter 1200's main competitor, Hewlett-Packard's remarkable DeskWriter, has become the best-selling inkjet printer in the world (see Figure 4.13). This printer's use is completely transparent on the Mac, plus its low price, compatibility, excellent support, and nearly maintenance-free operation make it the printer to beat.

Interestingly enough, the DeskWriter is not a grayscale device. Its 300 dpi dithered simulation of grayscale actually looks better than the StyleWriter's output using its GrayShare printer driver at 360 dpi. The DeskWriter can be LocalTalk networked, or just connected to the serial port. Duty cycle for the DeskWriter is just as forgiving as the StyleWriter's, with perhaps more options for refilling and recycling the cartridges. Although not as small as the StyleWriter 1200, the DeskWriter feels more sturdy because it has fewer plastic parts tenuously attached than Apple's printer.

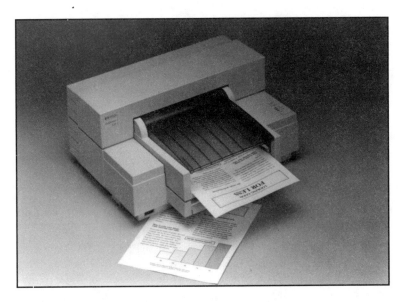

Figure 4.13   Hewlett-Packard DeskWriter.

Method: Thermal Inkjet
Media: Water-based ink
Speed: 2 ppm
Maximum dpi: 360
Paper Format: 8 1/2 × 11-inch standard paper
Interface: LocalTalk/Serial Din cable

Laser printer overview

Dozens of manufacturers turn out laser printers for personal and business use and every niche
in between. The huge number of models is most evident when examining the difference in
models at the low and high end—from the basic non-PostScript models at $600 to 17 pages
per minute, PostScript-ready, 600 dpi monsters that sort, staple, and clear paper jams by
themselves.

Laser-print technology actually uses a laser that reads the data stream from the print description source—the PostScript or QuickDraw bytes streaming from the print controller. The
laser "etches" an electrostatic image on a spinning metal drum that attracts and applies the
positively charged dry black toner, transferring it to your paper as it rolls under the rotating
drum. From there, the paper makes its way under a hot fuser that dries and permanently solidifies the toner on the page.

Two classes of laser printers are available: the personal laser printer and the business, or
workgroup, printer. Personal printers are priced just above inkjets—$600–$2000, depending

on features such as horizontal/vertical resolution, networking capability, onboard RAM, PostScript, DOS/Windows support, and, of course, speed. Personal lasers are aimed at the light print requirements of an individual or even a small business.

Business laser printers are meant for larger groups and a greater workload, and usually have onboard PostScript, built-in Ethernet, simultaneous connection to many different platforms, as well as large paper feeders, and higher-tolerance print engines that last longer and require less attention. Business printers range in price anywhere from $1,500–$12,000. Duty cycles vary from printer to printer, but will be much greater for workgroup lasers because of their higher load tolerance and larger toner needs. See Table 4.3 for specifications of several laser printers.

Table 4.3   Personal and Workgroup Laser Printer Specifications

	Phone	List Price	Imaging language	Processor clock rate
Apple Computer Personal LaserWriter NTR	408/996-1010	discontinued $1179 original	Adobe PS Level 2	AMD 29000 RISC/16MHz
Apple Computer LaserWriter 4/600, Personal LaserWriter 300	408/996-1010	$900 $689	Adobe PS Level 2 QuickDraw QuickDraw	NA NA NA
Apple Computer LaserWriter Select 300	408/996-1010	discontinued $839 original		
Apple Computer Computer Laser-Writer Select 310	408/996-1010	discontinued $1079 original	Adobe PS Level 1	AMD 29205 RISC/16MHz
Digital Equipment Corporation DEClaser 1152GB	508/467- 8078 508/493-5111	$699	Adobe PS Level 2	68000/ 16MHz
CC Technologies PLP II	617/275-5800 800/422-7777	$659	QuickDraw	NA
GCC Technologies BLP Elite[1]	617/275-5800 800/422-7777	$879 to $1398	Adobe PS Level 1	68000/ 16.67MHz
GCC Technologies BLP Eclipse[2]	$1099 - 4 $1799 - 8	n/a	n/a	
Lexmark LaserPrinter 4039-10R	606/232-2000 800/358-5835	$1599	Clone PS Level 1	AMD 29200/16MHz
Lexmark LaserPrinter 4039-12R	606/232-2000 800/358-5835	discontinued $1999 original	Clone PS Level 1	AMD 29200/16MHz

continues

Table 4.3 Personal and Workgroup Laser Printer Specifications, CONTINUED

	Phone	List Price	Imaging language	Processor clock rate
NEC SilentWriter Model 640	508/264-8000 800/632-4636	call	Adobe PS Level 2	
NewGen Systems Corporation TurboPS/300p^2	714/641-8600 800/756-0556	$1995	Clone PS Level 1	Weitek
NewGen Systems Corporation TurboPS/400p^3	714/641-8600 800/756-0556	$2595	Clone PS Level 1	Weitek
Okidata OL850	609/235-2600 800/654-3282	$1999	Adobe PS Level 1	68000/ 12.5MHz
QMS PS-410	205/633-4300 800/631-2692	$1595	Adobe PS Level 1	68020/ 16MHz
QMS 420 Print System	205/633-4300 800/631-2692	$1995	Clone PS Level 2	68020/ 20MHz
Samsung Electronics America Final 8000	201/229-4000 800/466-0262	$1995	Adobe PS Level 1	Intel i960/16MHz
Texas Instruments MicroLaser Plus PS17	800/527-3500	$1199	Adobe PS Level 1	16MHz
Texas Instruments MicroWriter PS23	800/527-3500	$949	Adobe PS Level 1	
Texas Instruments MicroLaser Turbo	800/527-3500	$1799	Adobe PS Level 2	Weitek

	Number of fonts provided	TrueType rasterizer built-in	RAM model/ maximum	Standard SIMMS for RAM upgrade
Personal Laser-Writer NTR	64	Yes	3MB/4 MB	Yes
Personal LaserWriter 300	39	NA	512K/512K 2M virtual	NA
LaserWriter Select 300	39	NA	512K/5 MB 2.5M-7.5M virtual	Yes
LaserWriter Select 310	13	No	1.5 MB/5.5 MB	Yes
DEClaser 1152	17	No	2 MB/4 MB	Yes
PLP II	21	No	1 MB/1 MB	Yes

	Number of fonts provided	TrueType rasterizer built-in	RAM model/ maximum	Standard SIMMS for RAM upgrade
BLP Elite	17	No	2 MB/4 MB	No
BLP Eclipse	17	Yes	2 MB/6 MB	No
LaserPrinter 4039-10R	39	No	2 MB/16 MB	Yes
LaserPrinter 4039-12R	39	No	4 MB/16 MB	Yes
SilentWriter Model 95F	35	No	2 MB/5 MB	No
TurboPS/300p	35	Yes	3 MB/16 MB	No
TurboPS/400p	35	Yes	4 MB/16 MB	No
OL850	65	No	2 MB/6 MB	No
PS-410	45	No	2 MB/6 MB	No
420 Print System	39	No	6 MB/10 MB	Yes
Finale 8000	35	No	2 MB/18 MB	No
MicroLaser	17	No	.5 MB/4.5 MB	No
Plus PS17MicroWriter	23	No	2 MB/4.5 MB	No
PS23MicroLaser	35	No	2.5 MB/ 10.5 MB	No

	SCSI port for font hard disk	Other controller upgrades	Turbo Addt. software included	Print engine/ maximum speed (in pages/min.)
Personal LaserWriter NTR	No	No	No	Canon LX/4
Personal LaserWriter 300	No	No	No	Canon/4
LaserWriter Select 300	No	PostScript ($399)	No	Fuji-Xerox/5
LaserWriter Select 310	No	No	No	Fuji-Xerox/5
DEClaser 1152	No	No	No	Canon LX/4
PLP II	No	PostScript	No	Oki OL-400/4
BLP Elite	No	No	No	Oki OL-400/4
BLP Eclipse	No	No	No	Oki OL-400/4
LaserPrinter 4039-10R	No	No	No	Lexmark/10

continues

Table 4.3 Personal and Workgroup Laser Printer Specifications, CONTINUED

	SCSI port for font hard disk	Other controller upgrades	Turbo Addt. software included	Print engine/ maximum speed (in pages/min.)
LaserPrinter 4039-12R	No	No	No	Lexmark/12
SilentWriter Model 95F	No	No	No	Minolta/6
TurboPS/300p	optional	No	No	Canon LX/4
TurboPS/400p	optional	No	No	Canon LX/4
OL850	No	No	Adobe Type Manager	Oki OL-800/8
PL-410	No	No	No	Canon LX/4
420 Print System	No	No	No	Canon LX/4
Finale 8000	No	1200 dpi $995	No	Samsung/8
MicroLaser Plus PS17	No		No	Sharp/9
MicroWriter PS23	No		No	Samsung/5
MicroLaser Turbo	No		No	Sharp/9

	Resolution (dots/inch) /Resolution enhancement	Paper capacity (first tray/ second tray) in sheets	Paper sizes supported
Personal LaserWriter NTR	300x300/No	70/250 opt.	letter, legal, A4 executive envelopes
Personal LaserWriter 300	300x300/Yes	100/No	letter, legal, A4, executive envelopes
LaserWriter Select 300	300x300/Yes	250/500, 30 envelopes opt.	letter, legal, A4 executive envelopes
LaserWriter Select 310	300x300/No	250/500, 30 envelopes opt.	letter, legal, A4 executive envelopes
DEClaser 1152	300x300/Yes	70/250	letter, legal, A4 executive envelopes
PLP II	300x300/No	250/200	letter, legal, A4,B5
BLP Elite	300x300/No	250/5	letter, legal, A4, B5
BLP Eclipse	300x300/No	250/5	letter, legal, A4, B5
LaserPrinter 4039-10R	600x600/Yes	200/600 opt.	letter, legal, A4, B5, envelopes

	Resolution (dots/inch)/ Resolution enhancement	Paper capacity (first tray/ second tray) in sheets	Paper sizes supported
LaserPrinter	600x600/Yes	200/600 opt.	letter, legal,
Silent Writer	300x300/Yes	250/250 opt.	A4, B5, envelopes letter, legal, A4, A3
TurboPS/300p	300x300/opt.	70/250 opt.	letter, legal, A4
TurboPS/400p	400x400/Yes	70/250 opt.	letter, legal, A4
OL850	300x300/Yes	200/200 opt.	letter, legal, A4, executive
PL-410	300x300/No	70/250 opt.	letter, legal, A4, B5 executive
420 Print System	600x600/No	70/250 opt.	letter, legal, A4, B5 executive
Finale 8000	300x300/No	250/250	letter, legal, A4 executive
microLaser	300x300/No	250/500 opt.	letter, legal A4, B5, envelopes invoice
microWriter PS23	300x300/No	250/500 opt.	letter, legal, A4, B5, envelopes
microLaser Turbo	300x300/No	250/500 opt.	letter, legal, A4, B5, executive

1 An 8-ppm version is available for $1349.
2 The 8-ppm version, $1799, also includes resolution enhancement.
3 The TurboPS/660p, with a faster controller and 600 x 600-dpi resolution, also sells for $1995.
4 No list price; check with dealer.
5 Company did not supply information.

Workgroup/Business Laser Chart

	Phone	List	Maximum Engine Speed (in ppm)
LaserWriter 16/600 PS	408/996-1010 800/776-2333	$2298 average street	16
LaserWriter Pro 810	408/996-1010 800/776-2333	$4899	20
PageMarq 20	713/378-8820 800/345-1518	$3599[A]	20

continues

Workgroup/Business Laser Chart, CONTINUED

	Phone	List	Maximum Engine Speed (in ppm)
LZR2080	818/887-8000 800/334-3174	$4995-$5495	20
Eclipse 8	617/275-5800 800/422-7777	$1799	8
SelectPress 600	617/275-5800 800/422-7777	$4499	8
LaserJet 4M	800/752-0900	$2399	8
LaserJet 4si MX	800/752-0900	$5499	17
Unity 1200XL-O 800/950-6868	612/944-9330	$8995	8
IBM 4039 16L	800/426-2468	$3399	16
Turbo PS/6608	714/641-8600 800/756-0556	$4995	8
Okidata OL850	609/235-2600 800/654-3282	$1999	8
860 Print System	205/639-4400 800/523-2696	$4595	8
1725 Print System	205/639-4400 800/523-2696	$4999	17
MicroLaser Pro 600	800/527-3500	$2198	8
MicroLaser XI Turbo	800/527-3500	$3649	16

	Engine Manufacturer	Best Resolution (in dpi)	PostScript Level
LaserWriter 16/600 PS	Canon	600x600	2
LaserWriter Pro 810	Fuji/Xerox	800x800	2
PageMarq 20	Fuji/Xerox	800x400	2
LZR2080	Fuji/Xerox	800x800	2
Eclipse 8	Okidata	300x300	2
SelectPress 600	Toshiba	600x600	2
LaserJet 4M	Canon	600x600	2
LaserJet 4si MX	Canon	600x600	2
Unity 1200XL-O	Toshiba	1200x1200[B]	1
IBM 4039 16L	Lexmark	600x600	1
Turbo PS/6608	Canon	600x600[C]	1

	Engine Manufacturer	Best Resolution (in dpi)	PostScript Level
Okidata OL850	Oki Electric	300x300	1
860 Print System	Canon	600x600	2
1725 Print System	Canon	600x600	2
MicroLaser Pro 600	Sharp	600x600	2
MicroLaser Xl Turbo	Sharp	300x300	2
	Manufacturer of Postscript Interpreter	TrueType Rasterizer	RAM (base model/ maximum)
LaserWriter Pro 16/600 PS	Adobe	Yes	8 MB/32 MB
LaserWriter Pro 810	Adobe	Yes	8 MB/16 MB
PageMarq 20	Adobe	Yes	4 MB/20 MB
LZR2080	Adobe	No	8 MB/32 MB
Eclipse 8	Phoenix Technology	Yes	2 MB/6 MB
SelectPress 600	Phoenix Technology	Yes	8 MB/16 MB
LaserJet 4M	Adobe	No	6 MB/32 MB
LaserJet 4si MX	Adobe	No	10 MB/26 MB
Unity 1200XL-O	Microsoft	Yes	32 MB/48 MB
IBM 4039 16L	Phoenix Technology	No	4 MB/16 MB
Turbo PS/6608	Weitek	No	12 MB/96 MB
Okidata OL850	Adobe	No	2 MB/4 MB
860 Print System	QMS	No	12 MB/32 MB
1725 Print System	QMS	No	8 MB/32 MB
MicroLaser APro 600	Adobe	Yes	6 MB/22 MB
MicroLaser Xl Turbo	Adobe	No	2.5 MB/10.5 MB
	All Ports Active/ Emulation Switching	SCSI Port for Font Hard Drive	Ethernet
LaserWriter Pro 16/600 PS	Yes/Yes	Yes	built in
LaserWriter Pro 810	Yes/Yes	Yes	built in
PageMarq 20	Yes/Yes	Yes (built in)	built in
LZR2080	Yes/Yes	Yes	optional
Eclipse 8	Yes/No	No	built in
SelectPress 600	Yes/No	Yes (built in)	built in
LaserJet 4M	Yes/Yes	No	optional

continues

Workgroup/Business Laser Chart, CONTINUED

	All Ports Active/ Emulation Switching	SCSI Port for Font Hard Drive	EtherNet
LaserJet 4si MX	Yes/Yes	No	built in
Unity 1200XL-O	Yes/Yes	Yes	built in
IBM 4039 16L	Yes/Yes	No	optional
Turbo PS/6608	Yes/Yes	Yes	optional
Okidata OL850	Yes/Yes[D]	No	No
860 Print System	Yes/Yes	Yes	optional
1725 Print System	Yes/Yes	Yes	optional
MicroLaser Pro 600	Yes/Yes	No	optional
MicroLaser Xl Turbo	Yes/Yes	No	optional

	Standard Paper Tray Capacity (in sheets)	Maximum Paper Size (in inches)
LaserWriter Pro 16/600 PS 250	8.5x14	
LaserWriter Pro 810	3 trays (250 each)	11x17
PageMarq 20	3 trays (500 each)	11x17
LZR2080	3 trays (250 each)	11x17
Eclipse 8	250	8.5x14
SelectPress 600	250	11x17
LaserJet 4M	2 trays (100/250)	8.5x14
LaserJet 4si MX	2 trays (500 each)	8.5x14
Unity 1200XL-O	250	12x19.5
IBM 4039 16L	500	8.5x14
Turbo PS/6608	250	11x17
Okidata OL850	200	8.5x14
860 Print System	2 trays (250/100)	11x17
1725 Print System	2 trays (500 each)	8.5x14
MicroLaser Pro 600	500	8.5x14
MicroLaser Xl Turbo	200	8.5x14

[A]*Estimated street price, base configuration.*

[B]*Manufacturer's claim.*

[C]*Upgradable to 1200 by 600 dpi for accuracy of the company's support technicians. Macworld uses a point system, including bonuses and demerits, to derive the final rating. Ratings are for companies, not individual products.*

[D]*Accomplished by software.*

Apple's Laserwriter Plus introduced the beginning of desktop publishing for Macintosh. It has been followed by a wide range of PostScript-based printers and is a standard in the computer industry for desktop publishing. In 1995, Apple introduced its first Color LaserWriter printer, which accompanies its ink-jet and longstanding favorite dot-matrix printer, the ImageWriter II. Other popular makers of Macintosh printers include Hewlett-Packard (HP), Canon, and Epson. All Macintosh printers ship with Windows printing software, and are perfect as network printers because of their Macintosh and PC compatibility.

When purchasing a printer, cost is usually proportional to the quality, or resolution (dots per inch, or dpi) of the printed text or image, and the pages per minute the printer is capable of producing. Current PostScript laser printers support 600 dpi; PostScript-based inkjet printers also can handle this resolution. LaserWriters usually have better type quality than ink jet printers due to the nature of the print ink media (toner cartridge versus ink cartridge). However, most laserwriters do not offer a low-cost color solution like the inkjets.

LaserWriter 4/600 PS

The Apple LaserWriter 4/600 PS is an affordable black-and-white PostScript laser printer that is ideal for home, education, and small-business users who require outstanding print quality, PostScript capability, and RAM expansion options.

As easy to own as it is to buy, the LaserWriter 4/600 PS connects via the Macintosh computer's built-in LocalTalk port, and features an attractive, compact design. It also provides state-of-the-art energy efficiency. Yet for all its simplicity and operation, the LaserWriter 4/600 PS offers a host of advanced capabilities. It features outstanding print quality using Adobe PostScript Level 2. The LaserWriter 4/600 PS also comes with 64 PostScript and TrueType fonts. As your printing needs become more sophisticated, the LaserWriter 4/600 PS supports a 4 MB RAM Upgrade, which expands both the printer's memory cache and its ability to print documents that contain large numbers of downloadable fonts.

Apple LaserWriter Select 320

The Apple LaserWriter 320, currently discontinued, is a personal laser printer that can stand up to the rigors of small workgroups—and it's fast enough to do it over a standard LocalTalk network. With full support of PostScript Level 2 and Apple's FinePrint resolution enhancement as a standard feature, the 320 outputs excellent quality, including detailed text and graphics. At 15.4 pounds, it is actually lighter than an ImageWriter, and has roughly the same size "footprint." Street and used prices well under $1000 make this printer a steal.

Type: Personal Laser Printer
Method: Laser
Media: Dry toner
Speed: 4 ppm
Languages: PostScript Level 2
Maximum dpi: 300
Paper Format: Letter, legal, executive, A4, envelopes

Interface: LocalTalk serial cable
RAM (Base/Max.): 2 MB/4 MB
Number of fonts: 35 PostScript, 35 Intellifont, 10 TrueType

Hewlett-Packard 4MP

The HP LaserJet 4MP is a direct descendent of the hugely popular HP LaserJet in the DOS world (see Figure 4.14). Like the 4M, the 4MP does everything well. Closer in performance to a workgroup printer, and at a street price of around $1400, the 4MP is priced closer to a personal printer with twice the performance. Its 600 dpi print engine, combined with HP's Microfine toner and RET (HP's resolution enhancement technology), make output look sharp and clean—and nearly typeset.

Figure 4.14   Hewlett-Packard LaserJet 4MP Printer.

A host of inputs, including LocalTalk, serial, and parallel (PC), make the MP universally networkable. If you have a Mac and PC, the "hot switching" feature allows seamless switching for multiplatform usage. The 20 MHz RISC processor and onboard cache enable you to print 4 pages per minute at the highest resolution. HP seems nearly fanatical about recycling and energy savings; most of its Mac line is EnergyStar compliant (consuming less than 15 watts in Powersaver mode), and toner refilling and cartridge recycling is encouraged.

Type: Personal/Entry Level Business Laser Printer
Method: Laser
Media: Microfine toner
Speed: 4 ppm

Languages: PostScript Level 2, PCL 5
Maximum dpi: 600
Paper Format: Letter, legal, executive, A4, envelopes, mailing labels, postcards, 3-by-5-inch index cards
Interface: LocalTalk, Serial, BiTronics parallel
RAM (Base/Max.): 6 MB/22 MB
Number of fonts: 80 Scalable

Apple LaserWriter Pro 810

The Apple LaserWriter Pro 810 is Apple's largest postscript printer, with capabilities beyond anything Apple has offered previously. A true workgroup laser, the 810 can withstand the onslaught of multiple users on different platforms printing all day. By printing at 400 dpi (standard mode), with full support of PostScript Level 2 and Apple's FinePrint resolution enhancement, the Pro 810 outputs detailed text and graphics. This printer also supports 300, 600, and 800 dpi for letter-size paper and requires additional memory for larger paper sizes. The 810 has onboard send-and-receive fax capabilities with the addition of a special plug-in cartridge available from Apple. A 600,000-page duty cycle is respectable turnaround for a drum change and check up, and the large toner cartridges will print 11,000 pages before replacement. Three 250-page paper cartridges ensure a lower attention level as well.

Type: Workgroup Laser Printer
Method: Laser
Media: Dry toner
Speed: 20 ppm
Languages: PostScript Level 2, PCL 4+
Maximum dpi: 400 default; capable of 800
Paper Format: Tabloid, letter, legal, executive, A4, envelopes, transparencies
Interface: LocalTalk, TCP/IP, NetWare IPX, Digital LAT
RAM (Base/Max.): 8 MB/32 MB
Number of fonts: 64 Scalable

QMS 860 Plus

The QMS 860 Plus is a graphics powerhouse that can support multiplatform workgroups that need imagesetter-like quality (see Figure 4.15). The 860 Plus supports multiple users on different platforms simultaneously—including DECs, PCs, UNIX, IBM mainframes, and Macs. At 1200 × 600 dpi (standard mode) the 860 Plus Print System 810 outputs excellent quality text and graphics. A 600,000-page duty cycle, toner cartridges print cycles of 6,000 pages, and a 250-page paper cartridge/100-sheet multipurpose tray are not quite up to snuff with other workgroup printers, but are excellent for a printer that really should be used only for final proofs.

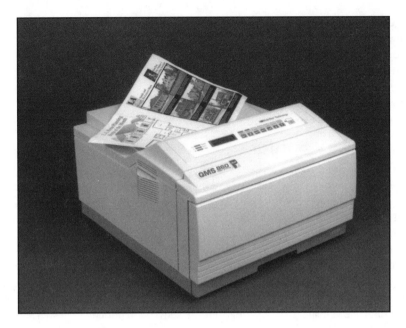

Figure 4.15   QMS 860 Plus Printer.

Type: Workgroup Laser Printer
Method: Laser
Media: Dry toner
Speed: 20 ppm
Languages: PostScript Level 2, PCL 4+, ESP (auto emulation sensing/switching)
Maximum dpi: 1200 × 600 default
Paper Format: Tabloid, letter, legal, executive, A4, envelopes, transparencies
Interface: LocalTalk, TCP/IP, NetWare IPX, Digital LAT, Centronics Parallel, EtherTalk
RAM (base/max.): 24 MB/32 MB
Number of fonts: 39 Scalable

Additional PostScript and non-PostScript printers

LaserWriter 16/600, LaserWriter 12/600, and LaserWriter Select 360 are all Apple 600 dpi printers that support PostScript Level 2 and PCL 5 print languages. The 16/600 has built-in support for Ethernet or LocalTalk networks, 8 MB memory built-in (expandable to 16 MB), 16 pages per minute print speed, and a SCSI port for attaching external hard drives to store fonts. LaserWriter 12/600 has similar features, but only prints 12 pages per minute. The LaserWriter Select 360 has a smaller form factor than the previously mentioned models, includes 7 MB of built-in memory (expandable to 16 MB), prints 10 pages per minute, and also has an expansion option for a built-in fax modem.

Portable printer overview

Fueled by the success of Apple's PowerBook line of laptop computers, the new portable printer market provides a number of excellent printing choices for Mac travelers.

Portable models available for Macs use either thermal wax transfer printing or inkjet technology. Thermal wax doesn't smear when wet, or mottle when printing large black areas; cartridges are somewhat more expensive, however, and don't last as long as inkjet cartridges—usually 20-150 pages per cartridge. All of these printers are fairly easy to deal with for replacing print media, such as paper, and print fewer pages per cartridge. See Table 4.4 for information about several portable models.

Table 4.4   Specifications of Portable Models

	Apple Computer	Eastman Kodak	GCC Technologies	Mannesmann Tally
Product	Portable StyleWriter	Kodak Diconix 701	WriteMoveII	MobileWriter PS
Phone	(408) 996-1010	(716) 724-4000	(617) 275-5800	(206) 251-5500
Toll-free phone	(800) 776-2333	(800) 344-0006	(800) 422-7777	(800) 843-1347
List price	$449	$479	$599	$999
Maximum speed (in pages per minute)	1/.5 best mode	3	NA	6
Resolution (in dots per inch)	360	300	360	300
Paper capacity (in sheets)	1 (100-sheet tray) optional)	30	1	80
Number of fonts included	39	4	0	35
Warranty period (in years)	1	3	1	1

Apple Portable StyleWriter

Apple's Portable StyleWriter is small and quiet, and the print quality is good enough for most personal printer needs (see Figure 4.16). At 4.5 pounds and less than two inches high, it fits inside a briefcase. Like the StyleWriter 1200, the portable lacks an onboard page-processing unit—the faster your Mac, the faster your printing. The Portable StyleWriter uses rechargeable Ni-Cad batteries; an automatic sheet feeder is optional; PostScript compatibility is not an option. The Portable StyleWriter's service cycle is 500 pages before a $19 ink refill cartridge is required.

Figure 4.16 The Apple portable stylewriter.

Method: Inkjet
Media: Water-based ink
Speed: 1.5 ppm (in fast mode)
Maximum dpi: 360
Paper Format: Single 8 1/2 × 11-inch standard paper
Interface: RS-422 Serial port

Mannesmann Tally MobileWriterPS

The MobileWriterPS from Mannesmann Tally is the only portable that is not only a fully featured PostScript printer, but its 6-page-per-minute processing speed is better than most personal printers (see Figure 4.17). LocalTalk is built-in—unlike any other portable. At 8.3 pounds and with a $999 list price, it is twice as heavy and twice as expensive as the Portable StyleWriter, but offers traveling computer users professional-quality options not found on other portable models.

Method: Thermal wax transfer
Speed: 6 ppm
Maximum dpi: 300 × 300
Paper Format: 8 1/2 × 11-inch, legal, A4
Interface: LocalTalk and Centronics Parallel

Figure 4.17 Mannesmann MobileWriterPS is a full-featured, mobile PostScript printer.

Color printers

From the portable to the industrial, color Macintosh printers are available for simple individual needs and for large printing company requirements. Color models output the same or similar quality using color laser, color inkjets, thermal wax, and dye sublimation media. Unlike monochrome black-only printers, a color Mac printer's speed is measured in minutes per page rather than pages per minute. Generally, it takes four times as long to print a color page than a black-and-white page; the Mac needs to process the page description, which is roughly four times larger. In addition, the printer must make separate color passes over the page to lay down the "dither" pattern that combines primary color dots, fooling the eye into seeing other shades.

Color printing on plain paper is problematic on most devices, and impossible on dye sublimation printers—they require special coated paper. Plain paper used in liquid inkjet models looks splotchy because of uneven ink absorption and saturation that makes the page buckle. Solid ink printers are a good solution, but are not as affordable as inkjet.

Like most Mac peripherals, getting the best takes the most money and maintenance. Dye sublimation printers, with photographic quality output, cost around five dollars a page. Obviously, this is not the kind of machine to which you send fifty proofs before you get one right.

Business graphics users who need to create more eye-catching pie charts and basic graphics may be impressed with the new generation of inkjet color printers. Although photographic quality is forsaken on these printers, lower maintenance, better speed, and plain paper capability are benefits.

Table 4.5 provides more information about a number of color printers that use laser, inkjet, thermal, or dye sublimation.

Apple Color StyleWriter 2400

The Apple Color StyleWriter 2400 is an affordable ink-jet printer that provides high performance for both color and black-and-white printing. Whether you use the Color StyleWriter 2400 to print your household budget, your child's latest art project, a class handout, or a customer presentation, you'll appreciate the quality and convenience of this printer's fast-drying, water-resistant ink. It's extremely simple to set up and features a compact, attractive design that fits easily into any work space. In addition, the Apple Color StyleWriter 2400 uses an automatic power on/off control that complies with the EPA's Energy Star conservation guidelines.

The Apple Color StyleWriter 2400 produces output with impressive quality, offering 720×360 dpi resolution for edge smoothing on black-and-white pages and 360×360 dpi resolution for pages with color or gray-scale images. Its speed is also impressive; it prints up to 5 pages per minute in black-and-white and up to 0.33 pages per minute in color. Through Apple's ColorShare technology, the Apple Color StyleWriter 2400 can be shared by users on a LocalTalk, EtherTalk, or TokenTalk network. You can also choose to add the optional LocalTalk module for a direct connection to a LocalTalk network.

Method: Thermal Inkjet
Media: Water-based ink
Speed: 5ppm – b&w, .33 ppm color
Maximum dpi: 360
Paper Format: 8 1/2 × 11-inch standard paper
Interface: LocalTalk/Serial Din cable

Apple Color SW 2200

Even if your travels are simply from one desktop MacOS System to another, the portable Color StyleWriter 2200 is the perfect way to add color printing capability to all your work sites. Weighing only 3 pounds and featuring a compact design that lets it fit into a standard briefcase, the Color StyleWriter 2200 is anything but small when it comes to features. It offers impressive 360×360 dpi resolution for color printing—and even higher resolution for printing in black and white. The speed of the Apple Color StyleWriter 2200 is also impressive: It prints up to 5 pages per minute in black-and-white and up to 0.33 page per minute in color.

Method: Thermal Inkjet
Media: Water-based ink
Speed: 5ppm – b&w, .33 ppm color
Maximum dpi: 360
Paper Format: 8 1/2 × 11-inch standard paper
Interface: LocalTalk/Serial Din cable

Color LaserWriter 12/600 PS

The Color LaserWriter 12/600 PS is comparatively much larger in size to the LaserWriter 600 and 630. It is a high-quality PostScript laser printer that provides high-resolution text and images in color and black-and-white. It's ideal for anyone who is looking for convenient, high-quality color printing at an affordable price. Until now, high-quality color printing involved expensive specialized equipment that wasn't even an option for most computer users.

With 12 MB of RAM built-in, 600 dpi, and output of 12 pages per minute for monochrome and 3 pages per minute for color, the Color LaserWriter 12/600 is comparable to Apple's best high-end LaserWriters as well as higher-end color printers. Another similarity to Apple's printer line is the ease of setup. This printer ships with everything you need to get started printing impressive color documents right away. In fact, it requires only six supplies, four toner cartridges, one fuser, and one oil bottle. This contributes not only to its convenience, but also to its affordability. The Apple Color LaserWriter carries a suggested retail price of approximately $7000.

Method: Laser
Media: Toner
Speed: 12 ppm
Maximum dpi: 600
Paper Format: 8 1/2 × 11-inch standard paper
Interface: EtherTalk, LocalTalk/Serial Din cable, parallel
RAM (Base/Max.): 12 MB/40 MB
Number of fonts: 64 Scalable TrueType, 30 scalable PostScript

Table 4.5   Color Printer Specifications

Product	Company	Phone	Price
Apple Color Printer	Apple Computer	408/996-1010 800/776-2333	$699
HS-1PS	Brother International	908/356-8880 800/284-4357	$6995
Canon BJC-820	Canon Computer Systems	714/438-3000 800/848-4123	$800
CJ-10 Color Bubble-Jet Copier with IPU	Canon Computer Systems	714/438-3000 800/848-4123	$6695

continues

Table 4.5   Color Printer Specifications

Product	Company	Phone	Price
Jolt PSe	Dataproducts Corporation	818/887-8000 800/980-0374	$4995
HP DeskWriter C	Hewlett-Packard	800/752-0900	$649
HP DeskWriter 550C	Hewlett-Packard	800/752-0900	$719
HP PaintJet XL300	Hewlett-Packard	800/752-0900	$2795
HP PaintJet XL300-PS	Hewlett-Packard	800/752-0900	$3995
IBM 4079 Color Jetprinter PS	Lexmark International	606/232-2000 800/853-6100	$3495
Phaser III PXi Color Printer	Tektronix	503/682-7377 800/835-6100	$6995

Product	Page-Description Language	Standard Ports/Optional Ports/All Active
Apple Color Printer	QuickDraw	SCSI/none/NA
HS-1PS	BR-Script Level1	L, P, S/none/yes
Canon BJC-820	QuickDraw	P, SCSI/none/yes
CJ-10 Color Bubble-Jet Copier with IPU	QuickDraw	SCSI/none/none
Jolt PS	Adobe Level 2	L, P, S/none/yes
HP DeskWriter C	QuickDraw	L, S/none/yes
HP DeskWriter 550C	QuickDraw	L, S/none/yes
HP PaintJet XL300	QuickDraw	L, P, S/1/yes
HP PaintJet XL300-PS	Adobe Level 2	L, P, S/1/yes
IBM 4079 Color Jetprinter PS	PhoenixPage Level 2	L, P, S/none/yes
Phaser III PXi Color Printer	Adobe Level2	L, P, S/Ethernet, Token Ring/yes

Product	Emulations/ Autosensing	RAM (base model/ maximum)	Resolution (in dots per inch)
Apple Color Printer	NA/NA	NA/NA	360
HS-1PS	HPGL, PCI.4/yes	10 MB/26 MB	300
Canon BJC-820	Epson LQ-2550/no	NA/NA	360
CJ-10 Color Bubble-Jet Copier with IPU	NA/NA	NA/NA	400
Jolt PS	HPGL, PCL4/no	6 MB/10 MB	300
HP DeskWriter C	NA/NA	NA/NA	300

Product	Emulations/ Autosensing	RAM (base model/ maximum)	Resolution (in dots per inch)
HP DeskWriter 550C	NA/NA	NA/NA	300
HP PaintJet XL300	NA/NA	2 MB/18 MB	300
HP PaintJet XL300-PS	HPGL/2, PCL5/yes	6 MB/18 MB	300
IBM 4079 Color Jetprinter PS	HPGL/yes	4 MB/16 MB	360
Phaser III PXi Color Printer	HPGL/no	10 MB/22 MB	300

Product	Number of Fonts	Paper Sizes	Tray Capacity (in sheets)
Apple Color Printer	64	A, A3, A4, Igl, B	100
HS-1PS	35	A, Igl	100
Canon BJC-820	3	A, A3, A4, Igl, B	100
CJ-10 Color Bubble-Jet Copier with IPU	0	A	90
Jolt PS	39	A, A4, Igl, B	200
HP DeskWriter C	13	A, A4, Igl, B	100
HP DeskWriter 550C	35	A, A4, Igl, B	100
HP PaintJet XL300	35	A, A4, AB, Igl, B, B4	200
HP PaintJet XL300-PS	35	A, A4, AB, Igl, B, B4	200
IBM 4079 Color Jetprinter PS	35	A, A3, A4, Igl, B	100
Phaser III PXi Color Printer	39	2	200

Scanners

Scanners enable you to scan text, film, and printed media into your Macintosh quickly and effortlessly. Scanner hardware is available in flatbed and handheld formats, and offers a wide range of image resolution. Handheld scanners are small and portable, but difficult to use. Flatbed scanners offer convenience and good performance. Drum scanners usually belong in service bureaus because of their cost and lengthy learning curve, but they provide the highest quality possible for high-end, four-color printing. (A few models are migrating down to the desktop level.) Still-video cameras enable you to capture still and moving images on location, just like ordinary cameras, and to download electronic data files directly into your Mac.

Acquiring and editing images requires a faster Mac with much more RAM and disk storage space than needed in office work. This rest of this chapter offers guidelines for how much up-grading is appropriate. You will read about the various types of scanners that are available, the Photo CD option, and standard software for scanners. This includes a brief discussion of

Photoshop filters, which can be used to communicate with your scanner software drivers to send data directly from the scanner into Photoshop. Photoshop filters support an open-ended software module format, commonly referred to as filters. Other image editors have similar features which can extend the functionality and ease-of-use between hardware and software products. This section also looks at still-video cameras and capture boards.

Note

Handheld scanners pose significant ethical and legal questions because they are so easy to use casually. Flatbed scanners with document feeders and OCR software are even more dangerous. For example, you can capture a cartoon out of the paper and send it by email to a friend. You can scan a magazine article, run it through OCR software, and pass it on to a colleague. Both of these situations fall under the *fair use doctrine,* as long as you give the creator credit. Fair use allows you to scan the cartoon and the article to keep in your personal reference library in much the same way you make photocopies. You also can pass on a copy or two to friends and quote brief passages in a review.

However, the temptation to steal copyrighted material leads many people into legal trouble. If you use that cartoon in the company newsletter, or copy and paste the magazine article into a document as if it were your own writing, you are violating copyright law. Large-scale distribution, whether free or for-profit, is another situation you want to avoid because that amounts to publishing copyrighted material. Obtaining permission to use copyrighted materials usually involves a simple phone call, but you must make that call. In every case, you should give proper credit to the author or artist and the copyright owner. After all, you would expect the same fair treatment for your own efforts.

Handheld scanners

In the past, when flatbed scanners were relatively scarce and expensive, handheld models were popular. In fact, the progenitor was Thunderware's ThunderScan, which used the old Apple ImageWriter dot matrix printer. This clever design put an optical sensor into a surrogate ribbon cartridge for the ImageWriter and took advantage of the printer's mechanism to move the scanning device across the paper and to advance the paper. The next step in development was to put the sensor into a handheld package, and add a light source, a motor, and little rubber wheels to push it down the page. These little scanners work fairly well, except for keeping them at a perfect right angle to the edge of the original. In addition, almost all hand-held scanners only scan an area four inches wide. Some come with a plastic guide, and devices such as The Tray are beginning to appear in the stores.

Most handheld scanners scan an area about half the width of a page, and provide 8-bit gray scale and 400 dpi resolution. Some color models have appeared, but seem to have disappeared (in favor of flatbed models). Differences in optical quality and in the motor and drive mechanism affect the clarity of the image. Most handheld scanners use the serial port. The operating software can stitch the two halves of an 8 1/2 × 11-inch page together. Most come with entry-level OCR and/or image editing applications.

Flatbed scanners

Flatbed scanners are currently the ideal desktop device for inputting text and graphics. They are superior to handheld scanners because they provide controlled conditions for the scanner to move the sensing device down the page at a precise rate without losing alignment. This becomes even more important for three-pass color scanning, because all three scans must be identical except for the color data when the images go to the printing press.

Think of a flatbed scanner as a copy machine without a printer. Your laser printer becomes the output device. The advantage is that you can use your Mac to edit the image before you print it. For a simple page copying operation, you can adjust the contrast, brightness, gamma curve, and other parameters to print a satisfactory copy from difficult originals, especially photos. With the Mac and appropriate software, you can crop and resize the image, and then place it in a document along with text and other graphics.

Differences among flatbed scanners are diminishing. All flatbed scanners use CCD sensors, so their basic performance is similar. Because of the amount of data they generate, flatbed scanners typically are SCSI devices. Nearly all offer 24-bit color, 300 dpi resolution, come bundled with operating and editing software, and sell for about $300. Almost no scanners lack 24-bit color capability. A few are reaching into greater color depths, and this trend will be an area of increasing competition. Some use a single-pass method for sensing the levels of the three primary colors (either RGB or CMY), while others scan the image once for each color. Single-pass scanners are not necessarily faster than triple-pass models.

Some of the first questions to ask when comparing scanners are: Is the light source a full spectrum source, or just an ordinary bulb with the right wattage? Does the scanner use the same light source for each pass, with color filters, or does the system use three different light sources? As the sources age, their intensities relative to each other change, causing inconsistencies in the scanned values. If so, can you adjust their output periodically? How sharp are the scanned images?

The overall clarity of the optical system affects the quality of the scanned image, just as it does with a camera. Another factor is the steadiness of the mechanism. The quality of the motors that move the scanning mechanism down the page, the smoothness of the bearings, and the accuracy of the guide tracks affect the clarity. Tiny amounts of jittering can blur the image.

Drum scanners

Generally speaking, drum scanners belong at a printing company or a specialized color separation shop. Unless you or a person on your staff knows how to operate a drum scanner, you will get better results by going to a professional color separator. Moreover, you need to be doing a high volume of in-house work to make a drum scanner a feasible investment. The advantage is that you have close control over the entire process.

In most cases involving high-quality four-color printing, you will make a scan on a flatbed to use for placement on your layout, then go to a separation shop for the final high-quality drum scan. Drum scans are required if you plan to publish coffee table books, fashion magazines, posters, or product packaging.

Drum scanners use photomultiplier tubes to amplify the light before it reaches the sensing device, which is of higher quality than in desktop models. This enables them to measure a wider dynamic range of intensity levels; drum scanners also generate 12 bits rather than 8 bits for each of the three colors. As a result, drum scanners capture more subtleties of detail in highlights and shadows.

You must be able to wrap the original around the drum (not always possible), which spins at a high rate while the scanning head moves down the length of the drum. Better optical systems on these machines provide sharper, clearer images, and you can enlarge small originals without encountering fuzziness. Another advantage of the drum configuration is that the scanning head can be within millimeters of the surface (not separated by a sheet of glass, as in flatbeds). The high speed of the rotating drum also permits use of a stronger, more focused light beam without damaging the original.

Shopping for scanners

When shopping for a scanner, think not only about what you will do with the scanner, but also about your plans for the media you scan. Will you use scanned images only for onscreen reference, laser printer output, or in typesetter output? Do you plan to use scanned data in printed publications, or in multimedia presentations? What about Optical Character Recognition (OCR)? The best scanner for you depends more on what you want to do with the images than on the kinds of images you want to capture.

You can choose from handheld, flatbed, and drum scanners for desktop use with the Mac. Nothing beats the handheld models for convenience, especially for scanning text and numerical data in columns and small images. For larger documents, and for work requiring resolutions greater than 400 dpi with 24-bit color depth, the flatbed models work well. Desktop drum scanners bridge the gap between in-house production departments and service bureaus, but their cost and learning curve make them viable only for companies with a high volume of scanning and color separation work.

To help you decide further, you should consider the options available for high-end scanning at service bureaus. If you work only with photographs, you can use the Kodak Photo CD system and completely avoid the scanner. In other situations, you may want to have your color separation service provide you with a high-resolution scan (usually via SyQuest cartridge) so that you can do your own color correction, resizing, cropping, and retouching.

Scanner resolution is more important than any other scanner feature. Scanners usually have two different resolutions: optical resolution and interpolated resolution. *Optical resolution* refers to the resolution the scanner actually scans at and captures—this figure is more meaningful. Software algorithms can boost that resolution through interpolation; hence, the interpolated resolution advertised with scanners.

The reason why optical resolution is more important is that the clarity and accuracy of a 300 dpi optical scan interpolated to approximate 600 dpi resolution is not the same as a true 600 dpi optical scan. (A scanner with 600 dpi optical resolution can interpolate to 1200 dpi.)

Be sure you know which figures you are evaluating because many salespeople are uncertain on this point. The clarity of the scanned image also depends on the quality of the optical system, and on the transport mechanism for the scanning head. The most effective way to compare scanners is to scan the same image on several different brands and see what the results look like.

Another factor that distinguishes one scanner from another is the software that is bundled with it. For example, nearly all scanners include Photoshop image editing software; sometimes it's the full version, but often the Photoshop Light Edition (LE) is included, which isn't nearly as useful. Look for plug-in module software for your scanner to create a simple interface between the scanner and Photoshop.

Setting up for scanning: RAM and disk space

Before you scan, prepare by putting as much RAM into your Mac as possible. Scanner files are large—a letter-size page can take up to one megabyte as a TIFF file. For 24-bit color at 300 dpi, it will be one megabyte for each of the three passes. If you need to have more than one document open at the same time, the RAM requirements escalate dramatically. Virtual memory relieves some of the problem, but is much slower. Aside from the scanned image, your image editing application will be large, and you probably will want to have your page layout application open. The following table shows some typical examples of scanned photographs. All are intended for output on an imagesetter at 1270, scanned at 266 dpi actual size with a 133 lpi screen (see Table 4.6).

Table 4.6   Typical compressed photo sizes.

Size of Original	TIFF	LZW (Compressed)
3 x 5	3.44 MB	2.1 MB
4 x 6	4.6 MB	3.1 MB
5 x 7	7.1 MB	4.6 MB

Obviously, you need comparable amounts of hard drive storage space to handle the files you create with your scanner. SyQuest cartridges are the accepted medium for moving files between you and service bureaus. For your active library of images, you need one or more high capacity hard drives, or possibly an optical drive. For long-term storage, tape backup is relatively inexpensive.

For efficiency in editing, you must have the fastest Mac you can afford, preferably outfitted with plenty of video RAM and video display accelerators. Dedicated image processing cards (such as SuperMac's ThunderStorm or DayStar's Charger accelerator) are also useful. You can work on a slower Mac, but anything as slow or slower than a IIcx becomes frustrating.

Photo CD

Kodak's Photo CD format enables you to skip the scanning process entirely. You simply take 35mm photos and send them to a Photo CD processing lab. They come back to you not as prints but as scanned data files on a CD-ROM disc. You can access them on the Mac by using a CD-ROM drive. You can also view these images on a TV set with audio CD players that are Photo CD compatible. The images are stored in five different resolutions on the Photo CD disc, so that you can use a low-resolution image (smaller data file) for placement, color correction, and retouching, and send the highest resolution version for color separation and printing.

Photo CD is more beneficial for video-based work than for printing. It was conceived as a consumer medium for viewing on a TV set rather than as a means for acquiring images for four-color printing. Photo CD images work well in desktop video and multimedia applications, but require careful color correction to use for printing. Photo CD scanners at the processing labs use a YCC format that stores data about hue, saturation, and brightness; you first must convert Photo CD files to CMYK format for four-color separations suitable before printing. Moreover, you may find yourself spending a lot of time correcting problems such as low contrast, washed out highlights, and a yellow emphasis. If you work with Photo CD images extensively, you should invest in software that addresses these problems directly, such as PhotoImpress from Purup and ColorExtreme from Human Software. Both are available from the PrePress Direct Catalog, (800) 443-6600.

Ofoto

If you have a flatbed scanner, you really need Ofoto. It's the best scanning software available for the Mac because it automates most of the tedious setup work that you must do before scanning an image. With this program, you can throw an image into your flatbed scanner, click a button, and Ofoto returns a perfect scan most of the time. If not, you can make a few adjustments with its onscreen controls and fix it. Ofoto does what a human operator normally does, but faster and more accurately. First, it makes a low-resolution prescan to check the overall range of values for brightness, contrast, and so on. After finding out what it needs to know, Ofoto makes the actual scan, with optimized settings and high resolution. You don't even need to align the original with the edge of the scanning area; Ofoto automatically rotates the image!

Photoshop, Kai's Power Tools, and accelerators

Photoshop is the editing application of choice. Nearly every scanner includes it and a plug-in module for that model. With Photoshop, you can retouch photos and other images with the software equivalent of all the darkroom tricks. You can punch up a purple, play down a gray, or adjust the contrast and brightness of an image. You can fix many kinds of problems by copying a color and texture into a paint tool and brushing it over a similar area. For example, if a strand of hair is sticking out, you can brush it out with a sample of background color, or a sample of skin color if it's over the face. You can paste another person into a photo and it will look as if they were both present when the photo was taken. You can make two-faced, five-legged cows if you want to. Photoshop also has an extensive library of filters for improving photos and for creating special effects. After you've made all the changes, you can create four-color CMYK separations, complete with control over parameters that previously were the province of prepress shops, such as undercolor removal, gray component replacement, undercolor addition, and ink density.

Kai's Power Tools adds numerous special effects and filters to Photoshop. Fractals, spherizing, intensity sharpening, color sharpening, and gradient patterns are among its capabilities. The CD-ROM version has additional expert modes and filters, power tips, and how-to tutorials.

If you find yourself editing images frequently, you probably will develop a need for special-purpose accelerators. The calculations involved in applying Photoshop filters can tie up your Mac for long periods of time. The faster your Mac, the better; anything less than a IIci can be annoying. Accelerator cards that replace the CPU with a faster chip are only a partial answer, as are video display accelerators—both are important if you want faster performance. Dedicated graphics accelerators are also useful. For example, SuperMac's ThunderStorm accelerator off-loads the number-crunching tasks to two dedicated Digital Signal Processing (DSP) chips. DayStar's Charger performs a similar function.

Cataloging your graphics

Mac users with scanners quickly acquire enormous libraries of images. Organizing them is a problem because you end up with file names such as *Bird, Bird2,* and *Bird On Tree.* A better way to keep track of all types of graphic images is with a *pictorial database.* It catalogs the images by file name plus any keywords you assign to them. To find all the bird images with the characteristics you need (birds in flight, flocks, or only the blue birds), just search for the proper criteria. The software displays all the images from the Find command as miniaturized (thumbnail) sketches—the onscreen equivalent of a light table. This cataloging method simplifies the process of finding the ugly vulture you need to illustrate a story on financial misfortune.

One of the more versatile databases, Aldus Fetch, catalogs scanned images, Photo CDs, clip art, drawings, and QuickTime movies. You can catalog an image with a drag-and-drop operation; Fetch stores the index of the image and its thumbnail in a common pictorial database. The program searches for images on your hard disks, floppies, Photo CDs, and CD-ROMs and is compatible with many DTP and editing applications. A newer product, Kudo Image Browser, by Imspace, adds AppleScript capability so that you can automate image placement into catalogs and perform other repetitive operations.

OCR software

Optical Character Recognition software turns scans of printed text or numbers or both into computer characters. Early OCR software merely generated basic ASCII characters and made many spelling errors that took time to correct, even with a spelling checker. In 1988, Caere introduced OmniPage, the first usable OCR software for the Mac, for just under $1000.

It understood formatting, which is important to Mac users (who are largely page layout experts). Italics, boldface, point sizes, special characters, and even typefaces were recognizable with this program. OmniPage also was able to separate graphics from text, follow text wrapped around graphics, and understand multiple columns. It pushed the error rate to 5 percent, which was a remarkable achievement in its time. More recent versions improved this error rate, and are less expensive. In 1990, Caere put the software into ROM and mounted it on a handheld scanner that can output formatted text directly into a word processor, spreadsheet, or database. That package retailed for under $695.

In 1994, Xerox introduced TextBridge—for now, the most error-free OCR software available. It typically sells for less than $100. At that price, it should be in the software library of everyone who has a scanner. It's useful for inputting lists of names and addresses, columnar financial data, and other tedious tasks around the office. Another potential use is for research projects. You can mimic the convenience of an online database search—using your own library of printed materials. Scan and OCR all those articles and papers you need to read, and use the Find command in a word processor or database manager to search for references to keywords. If you do business with the government, you can scan and OCR portions of the Federal Register every day to check for changes in the laws and regulations affecting your company. OCR is now at a price and performance level to make it a tool everyone can use to increase productivity.

Accessories and software

Many manufacturers offer automatic document feeders as optional accessories, which are especially useful for OCR work involving long documents. Transparency adapters, another option, hold small objects such as 35mm slides firmly in position.

Photoshop dominates the Mac market as the preferred editing software. Therefore, most scanner manufacturers bundle it with their hardware. Bundling actually helps to keep prices down because the scanner companies don't have to develop their own software. Because of the modular nature of Photoshop, the scanner company simply needs to supply a Photoshop plug-in that interfaces the hardware and the software. This also makes using the scanner much simpler to use.

Scanner models by type

Scanners are among the more popular Mac peripherals. As the field has expanded, prices have come down, and fancy features have become standard. At first, handheld scanners were the big sellers, but flatbeds are replacing them. Though convenient, the handheld models are difficult to use and lack the refinements of the flatbed models. Drum scanners typically belong in pre-press shops, though some companies are introducing smaller scanners with impressive resolution for the desktop Mac market.

Selected handheld scanners

The following describes some of the most well-known and reliable handheld scanners. Shades of gray, relative price, and resolution are important considerations that should influence your purchase.

ScanMan Model 32

ScanMan senses 32 shades of gray, making it suitable for scanning photos and line art (see Figure 4.18). Its hardware resolution is adjustable from 100 to 400 dpi, and its scanning width is 4.2 inches. A plug-in module for Digital Darkroom simplifies operation. ScanMan comes bundled with CatchWord Pro OCR software.

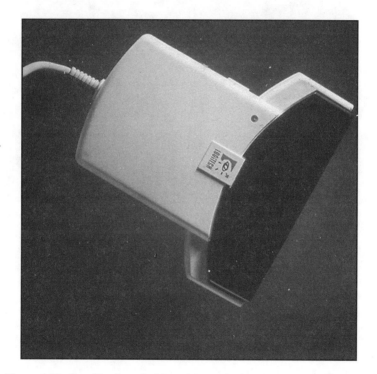

Figure 4.18 ScanMan is perfect for quick scans of text.

$599 with Digital Darkroom SRP
Logitech
6505 Kaiser Dr.
Fremont, CA 94555
(510) 795-8500 Voice
(510) 792-8901 Fax

OmniScan

A hand-held scanner with OCR software built-in, OmniScan (see Figure 4.19) inputs format-ted text from printed pages directly into your applications. OmniScan software also sends and receives faxes. It supports 400 dpi resolution and runs with a Mac Classic or larger, 4 MB of memory, and a hard drive. It supports 8-bit grayscale, and can capture a variety of formats, fonts, and styles.

Figure 4.19   OmniScan is designed for text.

$595 SRP
Caere
100 Cooper Ct.
Los Gatos, CA 95030
(408) 395-7000 Voice
(408) 354-2743 Fax

LightningScan 400

LightningScan 400 provides 400 dpi optical resolution and includes ThunderWorks scanning and editing software, Olduvai's Read-It! OCR software, and SnapGuide, a snap-on plastic scanning guide.

$399 SRP
Thunderware
21 Ontario Way
Orinda, CA 94563
(800) 628-0693 Voice
(510) 254-3047 Fax

LightningScan Portable

A battery-powered handheld scanner for PowerBook and Duo users is now available. This scanner weighs only one pound and connects to the serial port. It has 400 dpi resolution, and includes charger, ThunderWorks, SnapGuide, and Read-It!.

> $449 SRP
> Thunderware
> 21 Ontario Way
> Orinda, CA 94563
> (800) 628-0693

The Tray

This simple plastic device turns your hand-held scanner into something more like a flatbed scanner. It has a tray frame to hold the document, with guides for the sliding holder. Place your scanner on the holder, and it glides smoothly down the document.

> $39.95 SRP
> Tiger Software
> (800) 666-2562

Selected flatbed scanners

The following scanners are well-known and reliable. Shades of gray or levels of color, relative price, scanning surface area, and resolution are important factors you should consider.

Apple Color OneScanner

Introduced in 1993, the Apple Color One Scanner offers a wide range of features when combined with the included Ofoto 2.0 software. Ofoto 2.0 supports PICT, TIFF, EPS, and MacPaint file formats. The Color OneScanner supports 75 to 1200 dpi through software interpolation, or 300 dpi. It requires System 7.0 or later System software.

> $899 average street price
> Apple Computer
> One Infinite Loop
> Cupertino, CA 95014
> (408) 996-1010, (800) 776-2333

Apple OneScanner

The OneScanner, with 8-bit (256 shades) gray scale and 300 dpi resolution offers entry-level performance. This scanner includes Ofoto.

> $299 average street price
> Apple Computer

HP ScanJet IIcx

The ScanJet IIc offers 24-bit color, 400 dpi optical resolution, and single-pass scanning. Printer calibration matches scanned image colors to a wide variety of color printers. A 300 dpi, 8-bit version—the ScanJet IIp—is available for $599 SRP.

> $1199 SRP, Document Feeder $559 SRP
> Hewlett-Packard
> PO Box 58059, MS #511L-SJ
> Santa Clara, CA 95051
> (800) 752-0900 Voice

Epson ES-800C

The Epson ES-800C scans 24-bit color with a single pass at up to 800 dpi resolution, interpolated to 1600 dpi. A package with the ES-600C (600 dpi resolution), and Photoshop 2.5 LE is available for $999 SRP.

> $1499 SRP with Photoshop 2.5, Kai's Power Tools, SCSI cable
> Epson America
> 20770 Madrona Dr.
> Torrance, CA 90503
> (310) 782-0770 Voice, (800) 289-3776
> (310) 782-4235 Fax

Microtek ScanMaker IIHR

With optical resolutions of 300 to 600 dpi, the IIHR can produce interpolated resolution up to 1200×1200 dpi with a maximum of 2400 dpi. It operates with 24-bit color depth, switchable to 8-bit gray scale, 4-bit OCR, and 1-bit line art depths for greater convenience. Includes a color calibration application, and Photoshop LE.

> $799 to $849 SRP
> Microtek Lab
> 3715 Doolitle St.
> Redondo, CA 90278
> (310) 297-5000 Voice, (800) 654-4160
> (310) 297-5050 Fax

Microtek ScanMaker III

This new flatbed scanner pushes performance levels into 36-bit color depth (billions of colors), with optical resolution of 600×1200 dpi (interpolated to 2400×2400 dpi). The advantages of its expanded dynamic range include smoother color gradations, denser color values, and increased detail in shadow and highlight areas. The III comes with the full version of Photoshop and a plug-in module.

> Approx. $3500 SRP

Microtek
Silverscanner

Silverscanner scans in 24-bit color at 300 dpi, interpolated to 600 dpi.

> Approx. $1499–$2099 SRP with Photoshop
> LaCie
> 8700 SW Creekside Pl.
> Beaverton, OR 97005
> (503) 520-9000 Voice, (800) 999-0143
> (503) 520-9100 Fax

UMAX UC1260

The UC1260 has an optical resolution of 600 × 1200 dpi, and interpolated resolution of up to 2400 × 2400 dpi, at a 24-bit color depth. UMAX scanners are three-pass machines, but still fast. A single light source with three filters maintains consistent intensity on all three passes. This program comes with the full version of Photoshop and a plug-in module. Transparency adapters ($895 SRP) and document feeders ($495 SRP) are optional.

> Approx. $2495 SRP with Photoshop and plug-in module
> UMAX Technologies
> 3353 Gateway Blvd
> Fremont, CA 94538
> (510) 651-8883 Voice (800) 562-0311
> (510) 651-8834 Fax

UMAX UC 630 LE

The UC 630 LE is one of the more popular scanners for its quality and low price. It has an optical resolution of 600 × 300 dpi, at 24-bit color depth, and comes with Photoshop LE and a plug-in module. The 630 LE uses the same optional transparency adapter and document feeder as the UC1200.

> Approx. $999 SRP with Photoshop LE
> UMAX Technologies
> 3353 Gateway Blvd
> Fremont, CA 94538
> (510) 651-8883 Voice
> (510) 651-8834 Fax

Slide scanners

These special-purpose scanners are designed for professionals who need to scan slides. Many flatbed scanners have optional transparency adapters, but dedicated slide scanners are more efficient for high volumes, and provide higher resolutions.

Nikon Coolscan

Coolscan uses three LED light sources (RGB) to minimize heat buildup. An internal version for the Mac fits into a vacant disk drive bay. It accepts mounted 35mm slides and filmstrips, and captures 24-bit RGB color with resolution up to 2700 dpi.

$1595 internal version, $1795 external version SRP
Nikon Electronic Imaging
1300 Walt Whitman Rd.
Melville, NY 11747
(516) 547-4355 Voice
(516) 547-0305 Fax

Microtek ScanMaker 35T

The ScanMaker 35-T offers 24-bit color with maximum resolution of 1828 dpi. It accepts 35 mm slides in portrait or landscape orientation, and filmstrips. Photoshop LE and a plug-in module are included with this device.

$999 SRP
Microtek Lab, Inc.
3715 Doolittle Drive
Redondo Beach, CA 90278
(310) 297-5000, (800) 654-4160

Selected drum scanners

Drum scanners use higher quality sensors and optical systems than typical flatbeds, and can capture a wider range of colors (12 bits instead of 8 bits) with a better signal-to-noise ratio. These devices require a skilled operator and are practical only for high-volume production departments.

ColorGetter II

The ColorGetter II handles both transmissive and reflective originals ranging in size from 35mm slides to 14-inch photos. It scans in a single pass with 2000 scan lines per inch (another model works at 4000 lpi), with 12 bits per color (instead of 8-bit flatbeds). ColorGetter II can scan 5400 dpi in more than 2000 steps, without interpolation. The extra 4 bits capture a wider range of intensity values. The ColorGetter II fits on a desktop, and requires at least a Mac II or faster, with large amounts of RAM and disk storage.

$35,750 SRP; ColorGetter Ii Prina
$41,450 SRP; ColorGetterII I
$47,450 SRP; ColorGetter II Pro
Optronics, An Intergraph Division
7 Stuart Rd.
Chelmsford, MA 01824
(508) 256-4511 Voice
(508) 256-1872 Fax

Crosfield Magnascan Plus

The Magnascan Plus has interchangeable drums to accommodate originals of various sizes. This scanner can produce the highest quality scans available, but requires knowledge and experience in printing technology. It connects to a Mac IIfx or Quadra with large amounts of RAM and disk space.

$99,000 SRP
Du Pont Printing and Publishing
Barley Mill Plaza 18-1130
P.O. Box 80018
Wilmington, DE 19800
(800) 538-7668 Voice

ScanMate Magic

This entry-level desktop drum scanner delivers the extended dynamic range of drum scanners (12 bits per color), and connects to your Mac via SCSI. Unlike most drum scanners, its sensing device is a photodiode, a less expensive, solid state version of the photomultiplier tube. Magic offers 2000 dpi resolution with a scanning area of 10 × 12 1/2-inches, plus a Photoshop plug-in.

$19,000 SRP
$1,650 SRP; Color Quartet (closed loop color calibration/separation software)
Desktop Training Professions
6 Bedford Farms
Bedford, NH 03110
(603) 626-5551
(603) 669-7456 (fax)

OCR software

OCR software can facilitate text input into your Macintosh computer and must be used with a scanner. OCR products, such as Caere's OmniPage product line, Expervision's TypeReader, and CTA's TextPert support optical character recognition with most scanners. LightSource's Ofoto 2.0 and Photoshop 2.0 (or later version, when used with scanner plug-in software) support easy-to-use image scanning features that also work with a wide range of scanners and file formats. If you are looking to scan more than text, Ofoto, and Photoshop enable you convert paper graphics into your computer.

LightSource Ofoto

Ofoto is a complete solution for taking the original scanned image to the final printed page. It automatically makes all adjustments and color corrections to compensate for errors in the chain so that the final output looks like the original. Simply print out its calibration page on the particular printer, copy machine, or fax machine you will use. For four-color printing, make your electronic separations of the calibration page, send them to your typesetting service bureau, and ask your printer to run the calibration page on the unused portion of a large sheet on the next job you take to them. When you scan the actual printed page, Ofoto closes the loop and creates a preferences file for that device or chain of devices. The next time you scan a photo you plan to print on your laser printer, for example, select the preference file and you will notice improved quality on photos. Select the preferences for "Joe's Fax Machine" and you can send him a laser printout corrected for the anomalies of Joe's fax machine. Best of all, select the preferences for the Heidelberg press at Friendly Printing, and your four-color work will look amazing.

$295 SRP
Ofoto 2.0
LightSource, Inc.
17 E. Sir Francis Drake Blvd.
Larkspur, CA 94939
(415) 925-4200, (800) 994-2656

Caere's OmniPage Professional

OmniPage Professional, version 5.0 is Caere's high-end text recognition software. It requires a 68030, 68040, or PowerPC processor, 5 MB of memory, and 15 MB of free hard drive space. It features Caere's newest OCR technologies, and is the most accurate and easy-to-use character recognition software available for Macs. It features 6- to 72-point font recognition, an interactive spell checker, recognition of up to 13 foreign languages, 24-bit color image editing, and 3D character recognition. Omnipage Direct, OmniPage Lite, and WordScan are smaller versions of OmniPage Professional, offering fewer features and are often included as a software bundle with many scanner products. These can usually be upgraded to OmniPage Professional for approximately $100.

$695 SRP
OmniPage
Caere Corp.
100 Cooper Ct.
Los Gatos, CA 95030
(408) 395-7000, (800) 535-7226

ExperVision TypeReader Professional 1.0

ExperVision offers TypeReader Professional 1.0 for Macintosh 68020 or larger computers with 6 MB of memory (8 MB recommended), 9.5 MB of free hard drive space and System 6.0.5 or later. It uses a more sophisticated technology to implement its character recognition and can read any page of type and any type of page. It recognizes more than 2,000 fonts in size from 5 to 64 points, stylized or nonstylized can work with degraded documents such as faxes and photocopies.

$395 SRP; TypeReader
$495 SRP; TypeReader Professional 1.0
$99 SRP; ExperFax 2.0

ExperVision, Inc.
48890 Milmont Drive, #108D
Fremont, CA 94538
(408) 428-9988, (800) 732-3897

CTA TextPert 4.0

TextPert offers optical character recognition for Macintosh Plus or larger with at least 1 MB of memory. It requires a hard drive and scanner, similar to OmniPage and TypeReader. TextPert also has a Developer's ToolKit which allows other software developers to include OCR technology in their software.

$695 SRP; TextPert 4.0
$1,200 SRP; TextPert Developer's ToolKit
TextPert 4.0
CTA, Inc.
25 Science Park
New Haven, CT 06511
(203) 786-5828, (800) 252-1442

Digital Cameras: A Visual Alternative

An alternative to scanning images into your Macintosh is to "grab" them. Frame-grabbing video, or the process of taking still images of objects from digital cameras, is similar to scanning three-dimensional objects. Digital cameras are used with computers for a wide range of applications: collecting family photos, pictures for insurance claims, and as images in web pages, CD-ROM titles, and QuickTime movies. Apple's first digital camera, the QuickTake 100, was introduced in 1993, and followed-up by the QuickTake 150 in 1995.

Like printers, digital camera prices vary depending on the image resolution. For handheld devices, the amount of memory available to store captured images varies from model to model. The cameras are primarily designed to capture still images rather than moving objects. Desktop-based cameras offer still frame and multi-frame grabbing capabilities for color and black and white images. High-end digital cameras are not as cost-efficient as their analog camera counterparts; low-cost solutions, however, such as Apple's QuickTake models enable you to download files immediately. You don't need to wait at a photo shop for an hour, pay additional development costs, or pay for pictures that aren't worth printing.

Digital camera products

Selected digital cameras are discussed in the following pages. The digital camera market is still relatively new, so expect the technology to continue to improve and drop in price over the next two years. In general the lower cost digital cameras offer more limited features, or lower image quality than their high-end counterparts. It's a good idea to view actual digital camera output before making a purchasing decision. Many worldwide web site pages use digital cameras to display static or updated images. Viewing theses pages can give you a general idea of the image quality provided by digital cameras.

Apple QuickTake 150

Apple's QuickTake 150 is similar to its predecessor, the QuickTake 100, except for newer ROM and more memory for image storage; additional lenses (for close-ups) are also included with Apple's 150 model. If you have a QuickTake 100, you can upgrade for a fraction of the price of the original camera. Both cameras have high- and standard-resolution modes, and come with software to communicate with either a Macintosh or PC/Windows computer. Image resolution is 640×480, 24-bit color (millions of colors); at this resolution, the 150 can store up to 16 high-quality images. 32 standard-quality images can be stored at a lower resolution, or a combination of the two types of images can be used. QuickTake software for downloading digital images requires a 68020 Macintosh or later, 5 MB of memory (8 MB for the Power Macintosh), 10 MB of hard drive space, system 7.1 or later.

$699 SRP
Apple Computer, Inc.
One Infinite Loop
Cupertino, CA 95014
(408) 996-1010, (800) 776-2333

AV Macintoshes can have a video camera connected directly to the Macintosh. With additional software, these cameras can provide video frame capture, editing, and playback features for business, personal, or entertainment use. Combined with sound software and multimedia hardware, you can turn your Macintosh into a video production system.

QuickCam

Connectix's QuickCam can capture both still-frame and multi-frame grayscale images to your Macintosh. This is an economical solution for low-cost multimedia. Video conferencing software enables you to see and speak with another QuickCam user on a network or across modems.

$149 SRP
Connectix Corp
2600 Campus Drive
San Mateo, CA 94403
(415) 571-5100, (800) 950-5880

FlexCam

This uniquely designed flexible orb incorporates a video camera and microphone that sits on your desktop. The camera is connected to a flexible 'neck' that simplifies pointing and shooting. FlexCam can also be used to capture audio and video input from a VCR, video conferencing systems, and other standard NTSC video devices. Software requires a Macintosh II or faster and an NTSC or PAL video capture card.

$595 SRP
$795 SRP; FlexCam Pro

VideoLabs
10925 Bren Road E.
Minneapolis, MN 55343
(612) 988-0055

Kodak Digital Camera 40

The Kodak 40 is ideal for business applications. Features include fully automatic picture tak-ing, built-in automatic flash, 756 × 504 resolution, storage for 48 images, and 24-bit color support. Exposure control helps you take better pictures; optional lenses increase the Kodak's versatility. Software requirements include System 7.1 or later and a Macintosh II (or faster) system that supports 32-bit QuickDraw.

$995 SRP
Eastman Kodak Company
Digital & Applied Imaging
901 Elmgrove Road
Rochester, NY 14653
(800) 235-6325

External Speakers and Microphones

All Macs have an internal speaker for audio CD or software sound playback. External mono-phonic or stereo speakers can also be connected to the Macintosh's sound output port, and can greatly enhance multimedia and game software interactivity. Apple has two external speaker models available; a number of systems are available from third-party manufacturers such as Sony, Yamaha, and Bose. If you have an external CD-ROM player, the addition of external speakers can make your Macintosh much more enjoyable. In addition, by merging Macintosh sound output with the CD audio output, you can take advantage of dual source sound output.

Apple began shipping models with sound input capabilities with the IIsi, LC, Quadra, and PowerBook. Performas do not include a microphone in the CPU box, and can be purchased separately from Apple for a small price. The current Apple microphone was first introduced with the Macintosh 840AV and 660AV models, which support speech recognition technol-ogy. Power Macs also support speech recognition; all other Macintosh models only support text-to-speech playback and traditional sound recording.

PlainTalk

In the span of 20 years, computers have come from simple calculators to actually talking with us and working with our voice commands, as in the case of the Macintosh AV computers. Apple's PlainTalk technology uses two components: TTS, or Text-To-Speech, which reads computer documents, and SR, (Speech Recognition), which enables you to control the Mac with voice-activated scripts.

TTS, or Text-To-Speech, is relatively straightforward technology that reads to you; TTS is used in less polished forms such as the Talking Moose and other utilities. The AV series DSP architecture isn't necessary to run TTS. Practical applications of TTS—spelling, spacing, and meter—are amusing but are outweighed by RAM requirements. Voice samples alone take up 5 MB; the extension itself is another megabyte. Because TTS only works with the latest versions of TeachText, Mac users with a short supply of RAM simply cannot load it. Some high-tech users may find TTS helpful in proofreading; low-tech writers will stick to the standard and cheaper red-pen method.

PlainTalk's SR module is much more interesting and more advanced. Imagine talking to your Mac, and having your Mac talk back to you. Unlike TTS, Speech Recognition can only be used on an AV-equipped Mac. SR is written so that users can speak in conversational tones rather than unnatural patterns where the user has to pause to allow the computer to catch up.

As good as this software is, consistent and accurate recognition is rare when you use the uni-directional PlainTalk Microphone included with AV Macs. The Jabra EarPHONE (619-622-0764), however, provides virtually perfect recognition. EarPHONE (see Figure 4.20) actually senses the resonance of the speaker's head instead of listening for projected sound waves, which can be fouled with crosstalk and other noises in the room. As the speaker talks, the skull around the mouth resonates and the Jabra device senses these vibrations—this is probably the most space-age input device yet devised for the Mac. The Jabra EarPHONE is the only product Apple endorsed as an upgrade for its own microphone.

Figure 4.20   The Jabra EarPHONE senses the resonance of your mouth and head.

The EarPHONE supports other AV-capable functions, such as telephony. The Jabra EarPHONE can be used as a phone receiver and voice input system, as well as a voice-activated speed dialer that allows 20 previously stored phone numbers to be activated when you say the number's password.

When the PlainTalk SR module hears the command Quit, Find, Cut, and so on, it sends a message to begin a macro, or *script,* that executes the command. Both the native AppleScript/ AppleEvents and the latest incarnations of QuicKeys™ can handle the macro's execution and scripting duties.

4

If It Ain't Broke, Do You Fix It?

The biggest fear when upgrading software is that somehow it won't work the same way as the previous version, or will introduce new software problems that may require other software or hardware upgrades. Before you settle on an upgrade, consider and answer these questions:

1. Is there a new feature you would like to use on your computer?

2. Is the technology able to work with your System's present memory, hard drive, and peripheral configuration while improving or preserving overall System performance?

3. If you need to make changes, over what period of time will it take you to update your System to use this new feature, and will another new feature or technology be available that will be more compelling for you to use at that time?

4. Are the changes in the upgrade necessary to continue using the features in the current version of the software?

Most Macintosh products, especially packages with popular features, are tested before the product is released to customers. Testing can vary from product to product and version to version; most Macintosh software that is System 7.5-compatible has regular upgrades to remedy performance, feature, or bug fix requirements. The initial software release usually is fine-tuned after several weeks of commercial availability. Of course, if a new Macintosh model arrives, new problems that were previously unknown in the software may crop up on a newer model Mac, or specific configuration of a new model. These problems are usually fixed and made available free to customers via online services, as well as directly through hardware vendors, software distributors or the software publisher.

Whether you are certain about upgrading, or have doubts, this chapter discusses the benefits of preventative maintenance and offers simple suggestions for overcoming common pitfalls with your Macintosh hardware and software. We will also walk through backup strategies, including a brief summary of using Retrospect Remote software to backup your hard drive. Understanding some basic troubleshooting concepts can help you set up your Macintosh to run at its ultimate efficiency and productivity. Applying the optimal setup of your computer environment, such as placement of your computer, dealing with static, power surges, connectors, and safety issues can improve your productivity and prevent costly repairs, such as minimizing hardware and software loss in the event of a disaster. In some cases this information can help you spend less on an upgrade, delay purchasing an upgrade, or overcome an upgrade altogether. Other concepts and processes also discussed in this chapter include System software and application compatibility with your Mac.

In this chapter, you will learn how to deal with the problems you may encounter with System 7—frozen screens, system crashes, incompatibility between hardware and software, and incorrect memory settings. Common error messages, such as Error Type 11 and 39, what they mean and suggestions for making these messages go away are discussed covering all Macs. You will become familiar with System 7.5 as well as 7.1 features, such as using a RAM disk, your memory control panel, troubleshooting tools, and processor incompatibilities.

Customizing Your Macintosh Software

Macintosh consists of Apple's hardware, System software, and software applications. Macintosh hardware provides the processor engine, memory, storage space, expansion slots, and connectivity. Macintosh software consists of applications, extensions, control panels, desk accessories, shared libraries, and code resources. The software side of Macintosh can have absolutely no impact on software's performance running on the hardware, or can cause all kinds of software conflicts, slow performance, and sporadic freezes or crashes. All of these experiences enrich the Macintosh culture. When you try shareware, freeware, or commercial software that has been integrated with System software or runs as a standalone application, it won't take long for you to decide whether to sacrifice software and hardware compatibility for a new feature.

Customizing and experimenting with your Macintosh is something all Macintosh users eventually do. If you decide to experiment, you are strongly recommended to have a full backup of your System software, preferably on another hard drive, or on a removable or tape storage device. After you have a backup, adding in one or several extensions or applications is a great adventure. If a software conflict occurs, or if you don't like a feature, move the System software file out of your extensions or control panels folder to prevent it from loading at startup.

Minimal System software configuration optimizes hardware performance

A minimal System Folder can take on many different types of configurations. The core of System software consists of two files (System and Finder); as a result, these are the contents of an absolute minimal system. Many features in applications may not be available, installable, or usable if you only have these two files in your hardware. The System Folder on the Disk Tools floppy disk is the most easily accessible minimal System Folder configuration available; you don't need to run the installer or hand install any pieces to use this configuration. Unfortunately, the System Folder on Disk Tools does not support many features in applications or perform many regular features of System software, which are automatically available when you choose the Easy Install option included with the System software CD or floppy disk set.

If you have a Performa, your minimal System Folder is located on your Performa Utilities floppy disk. Keep in mind that Performa System software is only available in one configuration, the restored backup of the System Folder. Performa System software does not have a software installer that must be used to install System 7.5 and later versions. For more information on Macintosh Performa see Chapters 2 and 3.

> ### Note
>
> These minimal System scenarios assume you are not running any application installers that place Extensions or Control Panels in the System Folder.

When you purchase your Macintosh, it will have the equivalent of a System 7.5 Easy Installation; the default setting for installing System software. You can create a minimal System Folder with this installation by turning off all Extensions and Control Panels (except for the software you want to use). For multimedia, this would be QuickTime 2.1 and Apple's CD-ROM 5.1 (or newer) software, plus any CD-ROM data format conversion files, such as the ISO-9000, and audio CD extensions. A minimal System Folder configuration for word processing would include only the printer driver and any application-specific fonts or other System software. Deactivating extensions, control panels, fonts, and printer drivers by using an Extension Manager (such as Conflict Catcher) or moving these files out of the System Folder, then restarting will also free up memory, and increase your System software performance.

Preventative Maintenance: Upgrades You Should Do First

If you aren't upgrading your Mac's hardware or software, you should still perform a few preventative maintenance steps regularly. Preventative maintenance not only helps you become more familiar with your Macintosh, but also helps you identify small problems before they snowball. Hardware maintenance also reduces the time it takes to isolate problems. You don't need to be a rocket scientist to perform preventative maintenance on your Macintosh. For example, two of the smartest things you can do require only pen and paper: write down when and where you purchased your Macintosh and peripherals, and make a list of the critical files and applications on the hard drive.

Overview of hardware maintenance suggestions

Tasks you can perform regularly on hardware range from dusting and vacuuming the area around your computer regularly, to checking power and connection cables to make sure all cables are firmly seated in each hardware device. Make sure each piece of hardware is placed in an area with appropriate ventilation, and is away from magnetic sources such as stereo speakers, magnets, televisions, or other computers. Your Macintosh monitor image can become wavy or distorted if another magnetic source is nearby. Older monitors tend to have less magnetic shielding than newer monitors. If peripherals are connected to your Macintosh, try to keep them on a clean, flat surface to avoid falls and loose cable connections.

If you have pets or pests, check for pet hair or pests entering your Macintosh through open slots or ventilation areas on the external case. Dust and its ilk can also make a mouse slower and less responsive over time. This can be due to dust accumulating around the contacts located underneath the mouse.

Backing up your software may be an investment you overlook when you initially purchase your computer system, however, it is the most critical preventative maintenance you can perform on your Macintosh. You can perform a backup many different ways. You can use an application with or without the addition of floppy disks, an external hard drive, removable media, or DAT drive. The easiest way to back up files is to copy the file or folder to a floppy disk or external hard drive while you are working on a file.

Retrospect Remote is an easy to use backup application that works with either hard drives or DAT drives. You can schedule full or incremental backups for times when your computer is not in use, and have the backup software complete the computer's shutdown when the backup is finished. Retrospect Remote is also accelerated for Power Macintosh.

Performa users have an Apple Backup Utility included with their System software. The application is located on the Performa Utility floppy or Performa CD-ROM, and can back up a small number of files, or your entire hard drive. Keep in mind that if you use floppies for backups, you may get a bad disk (from bad or defective sectors) over time. If you miss one disk in a floppy backup, you can't restore anything from the floppies.

Ventilation and heat

Computers route electricity through many components. A single CPU chip can contain well over 1 million transistors. Electric current running through all those switches in such a small physical area generates a lot of heat.

Many computers, printers, and peripherals rely on airflow to cool these components before they reach temperatures that may cause internal damage. Ventilation holes are a staple of almost every computer-related device. Many others also include a small fan to increase the amount of air that circulates inside the compartment.

Think of your computer equipment as an entity that needs to breathe. Here are some guidelines for providing plenty of oxygen and maintaining airflow:

- If you are uncomfortable, so is your computer equipment. These electronic components were designed to run reliably in room-temperature environments. If your particular climate is excessively hot, and you can't "turn down" the heat, find ways to improve the airflow inside your equipment.

- Do not cover the vents. This includes placing books, papers, or anything else on top of, or against any computer equipment that would obstruct airflow.

- Keep your computer equipment out of direct sunlight and away from incandescent or halogen lightbulbs. These sources of light generate a fair amount of heat.

- Do not place computer equipment near building heat vents or radiators. Ideally cool air should enter the devices.

- If you use a dust cover for your computer equipment, wait several minutes after shutting off the device before covering it. The cover will trap heat inside rather than let it dissipate out the vents.

If you need to improve the airflow inside your Macintosh, you may want to install additional internal and external fans.

Dirty air

With all this air flowing inside your computer equipment, it's no surprise that dust and other contaminants begin to collect on your components. Your body has several lines of defense against these airborne invaders; your computer does not.

Dust obviously makes its way into your computer by being pulled through cooling vents (thanks to your fan). When dust lands on computer chips, it acts as an insulator and the chips actually get hotter. When dust lands on your floppy disk drive heads, they damage the floppy disk surface, resulting in data loss.

Some airborne contaminants contain chemicals that accelerate the erosion of metallic parts inside your computer. Tobacco smoke is particularly harmful because it becomes sticky and gummy as it builds up, allowing dust to become glued to even more surfaces inside your equipment. Another effect of tobacco smoke is that your equipment chassis becomes discolored.

Hair spray, air freshener, furniture polish, and other airborne fluids also make their way into your computer equipment, land on your keyboard, and stick to the front of your monitor. Keep these things away from your computer if at all possible.

Electric power concerns

Just as air flowing through your computer equipment can be contaminated with pollutants, so can the electricity that feeds your equipment be contaminated. Usually this "dirty" electricity is caused by fluctuations in power. Although dirty electricity doesn't discolor your computer or make it sticky, it can cause component failure and increase the likelihood of data loss.

When you plug an appliance into an electrical outlet, you are supposed to receive a steady alternating current (AC) of electricity at 60 Hz (cycles per second). Here are some possible anomalies that destroy this steady, clean power:

- *Spike (impulse).* When the voltage increases dramatically for a brief moment, circuits that are not prepared to handle that amount of power can overload. Spikes account for 7.4 percent of power disturbances.

- *Surge.* A longer, larger, and more dangerous spike usually caused by lightning strikes or the dissipation of power from the switching off of large nearby appliances. Computer components receiving surges are prone to premature failure. Surges account for 0.7 percent of power disturbances.

- *Sag (brownout).* The most common type of power problem is a reduction in AC voltage for a period of time from a few seconds to a few days. Sags are typically caused by starting up other electrical devices that have high power requirements (such as air conditioners). Computer equipment is "starved" of electricity and cannot function properly; resulting in system crashes or loss of data. Sags account for 87 percent of power disturbances. A blackout, in comparison, is a complete loss of AC voltage which can be caused by wind, storm, or local disaster.

- *Chronic low line voltage.* This condition is similar to a sag, but is the result of faulty wiring or insufficient power distribution to an area. The damaging effects are identical to sags.

- *Noise.* Electromagnetic Interference (EMI) and Radio Frequency Interference (RFI) are two kinds of noise that disrupt the smooth flow of power. Many kinds of natural and artificial phenomena, including lightning and radio transmitters, can be responsible. Computers behave erratically when fed with noisy power.

Notice that most power fluctuations are the result of under-voltage conditions, such as sags, brownouts, and blackouts. Even when the occasional surge or spike attacks, computer manufacturers have designed their systems to be reliable in all but the worst cases. Nevertheless, many people still feel more comfortable with a front line defense against power dangers.

The preferred method of protecting your computer equipment is to plug it into a special device, which is in turn plugged into the electrical outlet. Several categories of these protectors exist, and they can be bought at many hardware or office supply stores.

Surge suppressors

This passive device contains circuitry that is designed to dissipate incoming voltage exceeding tolerable levels. Surge suppressors provide reasonable protection against spikes and surges headed toward your computer equipment; sags and other low-voltage anomalies are not eliminated. A surge suppressor is a required accessory for anyone with a computer. Which would you rather have destroyed due to a power surge: a $15 device or your $5,000 computer system?

Here are some features found on good surge suppressors:

- On/off switch to control all devices attached to the suppressor

- Extension cord

- Status lights to tell you if the surge circuitry is functioning (without these you have no way of knowing)

- Multiple, individually monitored outlets to provide different levels of protection for various components

- Noise filter to reduce EMI and RFI occurrences

- Circuit breaker that disengages when surge suppression stops functioning to prevent additional spikes from reaching your computer equipment

- Power off/power on alarm that sounds a buzzer when power is lost or when it comes back on

- Warranty and/or monetary reimbursement if the suppresser fails to protect your computer equipment

- Telephone line and/or cable TV protection to prevent surges from harming this equipment

Also make sure that the suppressor you are buying has been approved by Underwriters Laboratories (UL) for product safety.

Don't be fooled, however, by look-alike power strip extension cords that have no surge protection. These devices, while useful for other types of electric appliances, do not keep your computer equipment from being harmed.

Power conditioners

Power conditioners include all the features of the better surge protectors and also actively monitor incoming electrical current to detect and eliminate incoming electrical spikes. During brownouts, some power conditioners can draw additional current from the AC line to provide the computer equipment with the correct amount of voltage for reliable functioning.

Uninterruptible power supplies

Uninterruptible power supplies (UPS) provide power conditioning features, as well as redundant (backup) power sources in the event that main power is lost. A UPS charges its battery cells whenever power is available. When the incoming voltage drops below normal operating parameters, the battery switches on to deliver electricity to dependent devices.

The time it takes to switch to battery backup when AC power fails is a critical factor in choosing a UPS. If the computer equipment is not supplied with power for more than a few cycles (each lasting 1/60th of a second) it experiences electrical "starvation" and could shut down, resulting in data loss.

Some UPS models are not designed for computer use and allow several cycles to pass before backup power is initiated. UPSs intended for use with computer equipment begin functioning in battery mode if only one cycle is dropped. This type of UPS is said to operate in *standby* mode and is the most commonly sold form of battery backup.

A UPS that operates in *online* mode is always feeding the attached equipment from the battery and, therefore, does not need to switch to battery power in the event of AC failure. The size of the battery charger used in this type of UPS must be large enough to handle both the continual draw of power from attached equipment and the recharging of the battery cells. Another design limitation to online UPSs is that they generate significantly more heat than a standby UPS. This loss of efficiency significantly increases the cost of running an online UPS over the lifetime of the unit.

You need to choose the proper size UPS for the equipment you will use with it. The amount of electricity the batteries can deliver is measured in watts. The amount your UPS can deliver during a power failure must exceed the total wattage required by the devices plugged into it.

Listed are some wattage requirements for a few Macintosh computers and peripherals. For your specific configuration, look on the back or bottom of each component you intend to protect with a UPS.

Macintosh IIcx	78 W
Macintosh 13-inch color monitor	52 W
Macintosh IIsi with color monitor	130 W
CD-ROM Drive	32 W
LaserWriter	585 W
19-inch color monitor	104 W
Quadra 900 with 21-inch color monitor	312 W

If your particular piece of equipment does not state its wattage, you can calculate watts by multiplying volts times amps.

Power cycling (On/Off)

One consideration when setting up a good computing environment is to maintain a constant operating temperature for your Macintosh that is within acceptable values. There are two ways to do this: leave your computer continuously powered off, or leave your computer continuously powered on. The latter is one of the best ways to improve your workstation's life and reliability.

The reasons behind this are simple: when a computer is first powered on, every component inside is scrambling for power at the same moment. This puts an incredible strain on the power supply to meet the demands of the rest of the System. The stress only increases with each additional SIMM, expansion board, or internally powered device that you add to your Macintosh.

Consider the example of a hard drive motor. It takes much more power for the motor to spin up from 0 RPMs to 3600 RPMs than it does to maintain a constant velocity. One common malady of hard drives is their failure to start up. If they are left on continuously, the chance of this type of failure is practically eliminated.

It is perfectly safe to leave your Macintosh and peripherals on for 24 hours a day, year-round. Some would argue that the additional electricity required exceeds the cost of a single repair— but this is easily dismissed. More and more of today's computers and peripherals are designed to meet the Environmental Protection Agency's Energy Star rating, which requires that computers and peripherals have a "sleep mode." This energy saving feature is described later in this chapter under the section "Energy Star Issues."

Even small monitors can generate enough heat to warm a room by a few degrees if left on continuously. If you don't yet have an Energy Star rated monitor, you can turn yours off if you plan on being away for more than an hour. If you choose to keep your monitor on, buy a screen saver program that will blank the display to prevent phosphor burn-in that occurs when the same image is left on over a long time. Newer low-phosphor monitors that are immune to burn-in, and Energy Star monitors that will shut themselves off after a period of non-use may eventually eliminate this requirement.

Static electricity

Like a miniature spike, the sudden discharge caused by static electricity can, although rarely, harm computer equipment. Controlling static is a concern when working inside the computer's case and in climates where the relative humidity remains fairly low for extended periods of time.

To thwart the possibility of static affecting equipment, implement one or more of these preventive measures:

- Place an electrically grounded mat near or underneath your computer equipment and always touch it prior to using your computer. Most grounding kits available for purchase also include a wrist strap to ground you, too.

- Use an anti-static spray near your computer equipment on a regular basis.

- Install special static-reducing carpet around your computer area.

- Never plug anything into or unplug anything from your computer equipment while it is turned on. This includes mice, keyboards, monitors, SCSI devices, and network cables.

If a computer receives a static discharge, it will sometimes lock up or freeze and require restarting. Other times certain components, like the Apple Desktop Bus (ADB), will cease functioning completely.

Warning

Always turn off power BEFORE connecting or disconnecting hardware from your Macintosh computer.

Vibration

Like temperature changes, vibration can cause parts that should not move to move, resulting in loose connections. More harmful, however, is the probability of data loss due to hard drive malfunction.

Place your workstation and peripherals on solid, level desks. Don't stack devices on top of one another unless you are sure of their stability (see Figure 5.1). Avoid excessive vibration from slamming desk drawers or dropping books on your desk surface. Even slamming your office door can cause vibrations that may be harmful to your equipment.

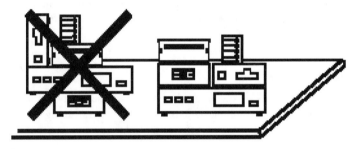

Figure 5.1   Stacked peripherals should be stable.

An often-overlooked source of vibration comes from playing loud music in the immediate vicinity of your workstation. Finally, always turn off any computer or peripheral before you move it.

Dust and pollutants

Although dust inside your Mac can be annoying, it is fairly easy to clean out. Dust and dirt inside your mouse or keyboard, however, can be an ongoing headache. With all the nooks and crannies on a standard keyboard, it's surprising that small insects don't make a home in them more often. Heaven knows there's enough food inside the typical keyboard to keep a family of beetles happy for a month! The mouse (computer variety) is also known for collecting bits of dirt and grime; after all, it is constantly being rolled around on a desk or pad. The ball picks up whatever it touches and deposits it inside the case.

To keep your keyboard free of excess material (not to mention beetles), follow these guidelines:

- Don't eat near your computer. This rule sounds obvious, but many workers sit at their desks during lunch. Inevitably crumbs accumulate inside the keyboard.

- Don't drink near your computer. When soft drink cans are opened, a fine mist of carbonated water, sugar, and flavoring is likely to be released into the air. Where this concoction falls is your guess; just make sure it doesn't settle in your keyboard or mouse.

- Don't use any kind of spray near your computer. Glass cleaner, furniture polish, hair spray, and air fresheners all contain some liquid that could fall into your keyboard. This sticky liquid will lodge other crumbs and dust between, under, and around the keys, decreasing their sensitivity when you touch them.

- Don't smoke near your computer. Besides discoloring computer cases, the chemicals in cigarette smoke are also sticky and can cause a film to form on your monitor, inside your mouse, and on your keyboard.

- If you want to prevent "stuff" from falling into your keyboard, buy a clear molded cover that fits over the keys and the case like a second skin. To keep your mouse dust free, just wipe the surface you use it on a couple of times a day with a dry, lint-free cloth.

If it's too late to prevent your keyboard and mouse from becoming filled with dirt, read about cleaning input devices in Chapter 4.

Radio Frequency Interference (RFI)

When your workstation experiences problems that you cannot diagnose, don't rule out the possibility of invisible radio frequency interference. You can trace it to any device that emits radio waves, including:

- Portable telephones

- Microwave ovens

- Some motion sensors

- Wireless intercoms (and baby monitors)

Sometimes the only treatment necessary is to move the offending device farther away from your computer, or reorient it so it faces another direction. In extreme cases, special shielding around the computer, its cables, or the offending device is necessary.

If some other device near your computer displays symptoms of RFI, keep in mind that your workstation itself could be causing the interference. Turn off your computer and see if the troubled device shows signs of improvement.

Preparing for breakdowns

As with most other electrical appliances, parts that are not solid-state—parts that rely on some sort of motion during their function—usually break down. These include power switches, floppy drives, CD-ROM drives, keyboard keys, mouse buttons, all forms of removable storage devices, and printers. Purely electrical systems rarely fail on their own, although they may fail due to something as simple as a static discharge. To minimize the possibility of a moving part breaking, move as many of these parts as little as possible. When it's not possible to constrain movement, have a spare.

One such example is a Mac SE/30 that was used as a file server. After a single static discharge on a dry winter day, the Apple Desktop Bus (ADB) ports failed; it could no longer use a keyboard or mouse. It cost over $250 in parts alone to replace the main logic board, just to recover the use of these input devices.

The replacement part took nearly two weeks to arrive, but that didn't hinder the use of the Mac as a file server. Any function that was necessary to perform could be done using Farallon's Timbuktu, a utility that allows one Mac to take control over another across a network—just like operating your television by remote control.

If a major component such as a main logic board needs repair, you can pretty much count on losing the functionality of that piece of equipment for the time it takes to get a replacement part installed. To minimize these downtime headaches and prevent component failure, follow these guidelines:

- If you use your computer for several hours day to day, leave your workstation on all the time. By reducing the number of times your system warms up and cools down, you decrease the amount of thermal stress on each component. PowerBook and PCI Power Macs have energy saver modes which put the Mac to sleep if you are not using it while the computer remains on.

  If you use your computer every once in while, with several days or more than twelve hours passing without touching the computer, it is okay to leave your computer powered off. This saves electrical power, and powering on will not add extensive stress to your hardware.

- Always ground yourself before you touch your workstation. You can use a wrist strap provided in most static kits, too. Small amounts of static electricity have been known to wipe out a perfectly functioning component or two. Touch something else before you touch your Mac.

- Plug your computer equipment into a surge protector to keep it safe from harmful spikes and surges.

- Use a waterproof dust cover on all equipment after hours. If a small fire starts somewhere in your building, the sprinkler system will start a downpour of water. Even the thinnest dust cover will keep your workstation from getting totally soaked. This measure will also keep your equipment dry if a rainstorm rips a hole in your roof.

- Keep spare parts on hand. Depending on the number of workstations you are responsible for, you may want to keep an entire workstation around just for its parts. It's much easier to troubleshoot and repair a faulty video card, mouse, or CD-ROM drive after you first replace it with a new one.

- Know your service provider. Contact your computer dealer or repair center and find out about their policies, prices, and availability before you need them.

- Know your nearest rental company. In a crunch, you may need to rent an entire workstation or just one component. Find out what various peripherals are available and their costs.

Now that you are aware of some environmental conditions that can cause minor problems with your computer equipment, examine some more aggressive forms of danger: theft and natural disaster.

Physical security: theft prevention

The first defense against computer theft is not to advertise that you have computers. Nevertheless, if you can't keep thieves from eyeing computer equipment, at least you can keep them from walking away with it. Several things you can do to secure your Macintosh and its peripherals include:

- Register all hardware with the manufacturer. By notifying the manufacturer who you are, you have a greater chance of recovering any stolen property should it ever be found.

- Keep workstations out of view of passing street or foot traffic. Put workstations in offices, or use partitions in an open-space environment. After working hours, close windows and use dust covers on all equipment. The less thieves know about what you have, the less likely they will attempt to steal it.

- Lock and bolt the computers to a desk or other immovable object. Several options are available. Metal tabs can be placed into special slots on the back of most Macs. Cables can be run through the slots and attached to a secure object. Special plates can be attached to desks; Macs can then be held securely with clamps. Also, metal cages or frames can be mounted around the Mac and locked down, preventing their removal.

- For portable Macs, a cable is attached, or the Mac is placed inside a lockable case. For employees who spend time in airport or bus terminals, there is even a motion-detector for PowerBook Macs that sounds a high-decibel alarm if the PowerBook is moved without entering the proper access code.

- It's a bit more tricky to lock down peripheral devices such as removable storage drives, monitors, and printers because they come in a variety of shapes and sizes. Consider having these components permanently tattooed in a highly visible place to discourage would-be thieves. Don't just slap on some metallic label with your company name, though. These labels can be pulled off rather easily with pliers and some adhesive remover. Instead, engrave your company information into the case where it cannot be removed or easily covered.

- Don't forget to lock your doors and have a professional alarm system installed at your workplace. It may also be beneficial to hire a security consultant for a day to examine your office for potential break-in locations. A graphic design firm that was robbed had dozens of Macs in a supposedly secure environment. The firm had a sophisticated alarm system wired to all the doors and windows. Yet they didn't prepare for thieves crawling up over the doors into the ceiling and down into the office. Now this firm has motion detectors installed inside the office, and all the Macs are securely locked to desks.

Natural disasters: loss prevention

Fire, flood, hurricane, tornado, earthquake, lightning. These natural phenomena should make you think seriously about the possibility of a disaster striking your department. Preparing for a breakdown and preparing for a disaster is like the difference between night and day. A breakdown may require an extra spare part in the file cabinet; a disaster may require a spare roof over your head. In other words, it's going to be a lot more difficult to do it right.

Here's an example of preventing disaster downtime: an insurance company was devastated by a fire—everything was lost. But within two days' time the entire Macintosh department was back to work. How was this possible? Because the company had prepared a written disaster recovery plan. This plan helped the Mac department assemble every necessary electrical system, network management, and communication device in a remote trailer. The company had a source for temporary replacement computers, and kept accurate daily backups off-site. Several employees were able to work at home on their personal systems and retrieve data by modem. Because the company planned and thought of every contingency, what could have been a downfall became no more than an annoying obstacle.

To prepare for a disaster, either natural or accidental, consider these recommendations:

- Have proper insurance to cover all your computing needs. Full disaster coverage will mean the difference between getting up and running in days, weeks, months, or years. The companies that survive disasters are those that believe in insurance.

- Maintain current and complete off-site backups of your data. It's not enough to create backups and leave them in your office if your entire building is destroyed. For more information on backups, see Appendix B.

- Create an accurate and reproducible network topology map. Think of your network as a jigsaw puzzle. If all the pieces were suddenly dismantled and strewn about, could you put it back together again? The topology should also include a list of hardware and software models and serial numbers. Many software companies will send replacement disks if you experience a disaster—but only if you can provide the proper serial numbers.

- Locate a suitable source of power and phone lines for temporary placement. Will there be enough electricity to re-create your department elsewhere, or will you have to bring your own generators? Can the phone company run the number and type of lines you will need?

- Create a list of employees with their own workstations at home. These employees will become an invaluable resource during the time you are rebuilding the department because they can continue to work.

While some of these steps may seem obvious and others exhausting, all are a necessary part of a disaster plan. But they are probably the smallest part. The really exhausting work is preparing a written plan, descriptive to the smallest detail, that can be brought into action on a moment's notice. All information needs to be accessible and current, and a team needs to be ready to execute the plan and manage it throughout the recovery process. Remember the five Ps:

Prior Planning Prevents Poor Performance

Employee off-site use policies and protections

Accidents happen. Even the most careful people can have a bad day and misplace or drop something. Before you allow employees to take computer equipment out of their offices, make sure you have policies in place to cover all possible accidents.

Whether equipment is going off-site to a client's office or to an employee's home, the same guidelines must apply. The employee must be responsible for the proper care and use of the equipment at all times. Have employees check out each computer or peripheral device that leaves the office, and sign their names to accept responsibility for its care. Check with your insurance company to see if it will cover equipment that has been removed from the office. Employees who want to use company-owned equipment in their homes may have to purchase their own insurance.

Besides taking responsibility for the equipment, employees should be aware that everything taken out must be in the same condition when it is returned. If an employee takes out a PowerBook, it should return with a charged battery. Virus detection software should be a requirement for all hard drives.

Another consideration with storage devices in particular is software. There should be a strict policy regulating the addition of software on portable Macs or hard drives that leave the office. If an employee takes out a hard disk, it should return without any additional extensions or control panels that change the operation of the computer. Any data that was added to the drive is also the employee's responsibility to remove.

Energy Star issues

Computing devices that meet certain requirements by the Environmental Protection Agency (EPA) can be advertised as Energy Star compliant (see Figure 5.2). An Energy Star device uses as little electricity as possible while operating. If left unattended for a specified time, Energy Star devices will automatically enter a low-power "sleep" mode. Macintosh PowerBook computers, PCI Power Macintosh, low cost Macintosh computers, and most printers are Energy Star compliant.

EPA POLLUTION PREVENTER

Figure 5.2 Energy Star compliant devices can carry this logo.

Manufacturers that build computers, monitors, and printers to meet these specifications are encouraged to display the Energy Star logo on their products.

Warranty considerations

Apple Computer provides a one-year warranty on all products it manufactures. Apple will repair defects in the product at no charge. If unable to restore your product to good working order after a reasonable number of attempts, Apple will, at its option, replace or refund the product's purchase price.

If you would like to contact Apple to find your nearest Apple-authorized service provider within the United States, call 1-800-538-9696, extension 525. You will need to provide the service center with a bill of sale to verify the original date of purchase.

Some Apple products may qualify for on-site or express freight repair within the United States. Call 1-800-SOS-APPL (1-800-707-2775) between 6 a.m. and 6 p.m. Pacific time, Monday through Friday, excluding holidays. You can also call a participating authorized service provider during normal business hours. You will be asked for the model and serial number of your product and the date of purchase. See a copy of Apple's one-year limited warranty that came with your equipment for more information.

Other companies may provide similar warranties for their own products. Nearly all warranties do not apply to damage caused by accident, abuse, misuse, misapplication, or service provided by non-authorized service providers (including upgrades and expansions).

Safety considerations

Sometimes it's difficult to be prepared for adequate safety of your Macintosh. Here are some safety practices that should always be followed when working near any electrical appliance, including computers and their peripherals.

- Always turn off a computer or peripheral if:

    Frayed power cords are visible.
    Liquid has spilled into the case.
    Excessive moisture forms on the case.
    The device has been dropped.
    You want to clean the case.

- Never operate your computer or peripherals if:

  The cover is off.
  Any internal parts have been removed.
  It is not electrically grounded properly.

Failure to follow these recommendations may result in personal injury to yourself or others. In addition to possible bodily harm, data loss may occur if the hard drive becomes subjected to stray electric charges or vibration.

Although studies have not been entirely conclusive, there is a growing concern regarding the health of those who work on or near computer equipment for many hours a day. The emissions of static discharge, magnetic fields, radiation, and even noise from your computer could have long-term effects that we are not yet aware of. Products are available, however, that reduce or eliminate all of these emissions from your workstation, usually in the form of a shield placed around an offending peripheral.

Regular maintenance

To prevent unnecessary service or loss of data, here are some general guidelines for maintenance that should be applied on a regular basis. Of course, your needs may vary from these. Some of these concepts are covered in later chapters.

Daily

Every day, you should take a moment to examine your computer equipment for the following:

- Check for proper ventilation.

- Wipe off any accumulated dust from the monitor.

- Check the status lights (if available) on the surge suppressor to make sure it is functioning.

Weekly

These tasks should be performed about once a week, or more often as needed.

- Inspect input devices (keyboard, mouse, trackball) and clean if necessary.

- Perform a virus detection sweep on the hard drive.

- Check all input and output connections on your computer equipment to ensure that they are securely fastened.

- Back up recently changed files on the hard drive.

- Wipe away fingerprints or dirt from the monitor screen.

Monthly

- Remove excess dust from the ventilation holes in and around your computer equipment.

- Defragment and optimize the hard drive to improve its performance.

- Rebuild the desktop file by holding the ⌘ and Option keys down through the entire startup process until you are prompted to rebuild the desktop.

- Perform a backup of the entire hard drive.

Hard Drive Backup

If you have ever lost a file you were working on, you know how important it is to have a recent backup of part or all of your hard drive. A backup is the process of copying the file(s) or folder from your hard drive to another hard drive or floppy disk. Backups are preventative maintenance, allowing you to recover your work should your initial file, folder, or hard drive stop working for some reason. This section covers backup strategies, discusses backup media, and using backup software.

Because not everyone works the same way with computers, there cannot be just one way to back up data. The "Schedules" and "Types of Backups" sections give you examples of backup schedules and selecting files for backups. Some forms of media are better suited for holding backup data, and these are discussed under "Backup Media." Three popular software utilities for creating and maintaining backups are discussed in "Backup Software."

It will never happen to me

In many states, it is mandatory for licensed drivers to have auto insurance. Even those who have never been involved in an accident appreciate the fact that if they ever are, they will not have to bear the financial burden alone. The same philosophy holds true for backing up your hard drive. You may consider it a burden to your time and budget. But it beats having to re-install your System software, re-load each of your applications and re-create each of your documents. And don't forget that Murphy's Law states that if your hard drive ever does die, it will be right before your deadline to complete a project, or right before you finish re-editing a large document.

Backup strategies

Successful implementation of any plan relies on having a solid strategy; backups are no exception. The first two questions we need to answer to develop our strategy are: Which files do we need to back up, and how often do we back them up?

The following sections examine some of the different kinds of files that exist on your hard drive and what their roles are.

Applications

These are the actual programs you run to make things happen on your computer. There are two general categories of applications: those that create files, and those that perform a task. Many people separate the latter group into a folder called "utilities" somewhere on their hard drive.

Look around and see if you can locate the master disks that were used to originally install your applications. If you have them (although you should always have a copy as well), you can re-load the applications if you ever have to. If you have applications that were not loaded from master disks (like shareware utilities downloaded form an online service), you should consider making one backup of them on a floppy disk, second hard drive, or removable cartridge for safekeeping.

These files don't contain data that changes; therefore, they don't need to be backed up regularly. If you will be backing up to a large media device (fixed hard drive, DAT, removable hard drives), you may want to create one working backup of each of your installed applications to facilitate its recovery. It's easier to restore the 15 MB of files that make up your word processor from a backup than it is to go through the loading process with each of the 13 floppy disks that those files are compressed on.

Application helpers

Many applications come with extra files that provide additional features or learning experiences. These helper files may be dictionaries for your word processor, a set of clip art for your presentation software, a set of predesigned macros for your spreadsheet, or a set of Apple Guides for specific applications. In many cases they are not critical to launching or using the main features of the application. If you need to, they also can be reloaded from the master disks or their copies.

These files usually don't contain data that changes and don't need to be backed up regularly. However, any helper files that you create or modify such as macros, dictionaries, style sheets, and Apple guides should be backed up with your normal documents.

Documents

Inside these files are the results of your work—many hours or months may have gone into their creation. Documents include word processed text, photos, illustrations, databases, spreadsheets, page layouts, sounds, movies, presentations, and modem connections settings. Another type of less-obvious document is the settings files and preferences that many applications create when they are installed or launched on your Mac. While they are commonly deposited in the Preferences folder inside the System Folder, they are occasionally found in other locations on your hard drive or System Folder. Many people overlook these files because they did not explicitly create them, but they should be treated as documents, nonetheless.

One problem many people have regarding their documents is that they can't remember what's inside the file named "My Letter" or the file named "My Letter 2." The Macintosh operating system allows you to create file names consisting of up to 31 characters. When naming new files, take advantage of this feature to create a descriptive name and date for your file. This can save time when trying to find and recover backups with lots of files, or lost data on an isolated hard drive.

Note

System 7 has a Find File feature built into Finder, allowing you to search for files by many criteria, including date, name, and version.

System files

Your System Folder typically contains hundreds of files, each of which can be classified into one of several types: control panels, extensions, fonts, Apple menu items, preferences, startup items, and the System and Finder files, just to name a few. Luckily, the Macintosh System creates custom folders to contain most of these special types of System software files. Because they are all placed in their proper folder, it's easier to locate, update, deactivate, and install them.

You should have at least one backup of your entire System Folder (or at least the System, Finder, and all the folders mentioned previously) in case you experience a System software problem. This is a little different than a hard drive crash, but the results can be just as frustrating if you do not have a speedy way to restore your hard drive and software to previous 'working' conditions. For additional hard drive troubleshooting, see Chapters 9 and 10.

Schedules

There are no magic formulas or calculations you can use to determine how often you should perform backups. It's really up to you to decide what data on your hard drive is at risk at any given time. I know some people who back up their systems every day, and others who only backup whenever they work on a critical project, or feel it has been too long since the last backup. Both of these solutions are acceptable, although it is best to backup your hard drive at regular intervals if you use your Mac regularly. However, customizing when you backup allows you to provide yourself with the proper amount of security for your data, as well as timely access to it should a problem occur.

In any situation, always rotate your backup media. For example, if all your files fit on a single disk, you want to use at least three disks for backing up. The first reason is that you never want to overwrite your last backup. The second reason is that if you experience a progressive disk failure or virus attack, you will have more than one earlier backup from which to recover files.

Usually several driving factors are noticeable in a backup strategy. One factor is the number of computers that need to be backed up and the need for higher capacity devices to store the data. Another factor is that the more valuable the data, the more frequently backups need to be performed. Finally, the larger the amount of data that needs to be backed up and the more frequently backups are performed, the higher the chance that one or more of the functions should be automated.

In developing your backup schedule, be sure that the time span between backups encompasses the greatest amount of work you are willing to re-create. If you only backup on a weekly basis, you could find yourself having to re-create a week's worth of files. If you back up nightly, the most data you could lose is one day's worth. Unfortunately, you cannot equate the amount of data lost with the amount of time it will take to recover that data. In the worst case scenario, even the proper backups of your files, it could take several hours to re-format a hard drive, install System software and applications, and restore the lost data.

Keep in mind that to formulate a backup strategy for more than one Macintosh, you need to study, and sometimes regulate, how the computer operators around you work.

Types of backups

Once you figure out how often your backups need to occur, you need to determine how the backups will actually take place. No matter which method you decide to use, there is one factor that you have to contend with: time.

Perhaps the most common excuse for not having a current backup of valuable data is "I didn't have time." Face it—depending on the number and size of the files you are dealing with, it could take a number of hours to manually copy each of them to another storage device. Time is a luxury that very few people have. The last thing you want to worry about is making additional copies of your work just in case something goes wrong.

If the issue of time is of concern to you, use a combination of hardware and software solutions that don't require the manual insertion of disks or the selection of individual files. However, if the prospect of spending extra money for an automated backup system is not feasible, perhaps a less-automated solution is for you.

Following are several methods to automate or speed up the backup process. Some require the use of additional hardware or software which may not be a part of your current Mac environment. To implement a good backup strategy, the purchase of additional equipment may be necessary at this time. Some of the software packages we discuss at the end of this section can also automate backups, with the added ability to perform backups on selected files.

Keep documents separate

One way to simplify the backup process is to have all your document files in one location, rather than scattered all over your hard drive. Optimally, you should store your System and applications on one hard drive and your documents on another to reduce disk fragmentation. If you don't have multiple hard drives or System 7.5, create a folder named "Documents" or "Active Projects" and store all your current work in it (see Figure 5.2). Within this folder, your files can be further categorized if necessary. At some point, a document is finished, and can be moved out of the working folder and into a "completed" folder. When you prepare to execute a backup, identify the working folder, and back up the files in it.

Sorting files by date

The Macintosh Operating System allows you to view files in a window via a number of attributes which are set in the Views Control Panel. The modification date shows a window with files sorted by modification date. By doing this, you can easily bring the most recently changed documents to the top of any window (or folder) for easier selection.

Perform backups during off-hours

In most cases, once you begin a backup, you do not have to stay around to watch it execute. Dragging files to a networked file server or onto a removable cartridge are both procedures that, once started, complete by themselves. Keep in mind that if you wait until Friday at 5 p.m. to begin your backup, you won't actually have the backup files in your hand until Monday morning. This makes your backup media vulnerable to environmental hazards (fire, water sprinklers, electrical failure or theft) and defeats its purpose. For this reason, you should consider making your backup day another day of the week.

Backup across a network

When several Macs are networked together, gathering files to be backed up can be simplified with the use of System 7's File Sharing capabilities. Assign one Macintosh with a large hard drive to be the collection site. Enable File Sharing, and if necessary 'Guest' access, on this Mac, and specify a sharable collection folder. All the other users can use the AppleShare icon in Chooser (located in the Apple menu) to log on to the collection Mac and to download the files they want backed up onto the hard drive. This way all files are on one Mac and can be organized more efficiently for backup onto a removable drive or tape drive.

Backup media

Every desktop Mac comes with a floppy disk drive. This is probably the first exposure that Mac users have to storage capabilities besides their internal hard drive. As the number of files you work on increases, however, the relatively small capacity of floppy disks becomes apparent. What other choices do you have for storing your backups? Read on.

Several forms of storage media are available for Macintosh computers:

- Floppy disk

- Fixed hard disk drive

- Removable cartridge

- Magneto-optical disk

- CD-ROM (Compact Disc-Read Only Memory)

- DAT (digital audio tape)

Choosing where to store your backup data is almost as much a task as choosing what to back up. The most important thing to remember is never to store your backups on the same device as your originals. If that device fails, you've lost both copies of your files. Another consideration is the physical location of your backup media, which is covered at the end of this section "Physical Security of Backups."

Each of these media types requires a different drive in order to be usable, so if you're considering a purchase, keep in mind the cost of the drive in addition to several disks or tapes. Some of these media types are magnetic in nature and others depend on optical technology. All except the CD-ROM are capable of both reading and writing data (CD-ROMs can only be written to once), and they all may be displayed on your Macintosh desktop as icons. The main difference between these various devices is their capacity.

Tape is designed for backup; it's fast, reliable, and inexpensive. If you're just backing up your own drive, use floppies or a removable cartridge. They can serve double-purpose as both backup media and expandable storage devices. Tape backup systems have been around for years, but until recently, they have all relied on analog technology. The new crop of digital tape formats, with DAT leading the pack, promises to store your data faster, cheaper, and with more options than before.

DAT

Digital audio tape (DAT) is a magnetic media format that looks like a miniature version of a VHS tape. It is a sequential access device, which means that the physical type must be rewound or forwarded to position it at the read/write head. Other types of disks, called random access, allow the head to move to the data.

For its price, DAT provides the greatest amount of storage capacity per dollar. A typical 1.3GB (1300 MB) tape only costs around $8. Compare this to a $20 or $50 removable cartridge that stores 80 to 100 MB. DAT is also fast when compared with most other removable media. Also, a DAT is small enough to fit in your shirt pocket.

Depending on the specific brand of drive you purchase and the length of tape you use, different configurations are available for current DAT technology. In fact, breakthroughs in compression and SCSI transfer have helped DAT to improve dramatically.

Everything else

The other media types are useful for specific backup needs. For instance, optical media is not subject to harm when placed near a magnetic field. Magnetic media is useful when the data needs to be retrieved instantly, or even updated several times a day. CD-ROM recorders can be purchased for about $2,000 that let you create "read-only" discs. Although somewhat slower than other media, CD-ROM can store approximately 600 MB of non-changing data on a single disc. Even floppy disks have their use when storing smaller files that need to retain their transportability and accessibility from one Macintosh to another. For more information on external storage devices, see the "External Storage Drives" section in Chapter 4.

Backup software

Not everyone needs to use specialized backup software to create and maintain a backup. If you are only responsible for the files on one Macintosh, you may be able to drag-and-drop the files onto a floppy or other removable disk.

If you are responsible for an office full of Macs, however, you may want to consider using software that was designed to handle the arduous task of manipulating thousands upon thousands of files. Some programs even use an existing network to facilitate the collection of files to be backed up.

CD-ROM and DAT drives require that you use some software to write to them, because they cannot be mounted to the desktop when empty.

The following consists of a summary of three popular backup software applications available for Macintosh.

Retrospect

Company: Dantz Development Corporation (510-253-3000)

No matter what you are backing up to, Retrospect can handle it. The program can write to floppy disks, removable cartridge drives, and nearly every tape backup device that can be plugged into a Macintosh. In fact, Retrospect is bundled with most tape drives you can buy. Besides having some very sophisticated, yet easy-to-use backup features, this application can also archive your data. In this case, the files are copied to another device and then erased from the original hard drive.

Besides being fully featured for the backup needs of a single workstation, Retrospect has an add-on component called Retrospect Remote that allows backup of one or several networked Macs to a central Macintosh computer location. It is not necessary for these Macs to use File Sharing in System 7, you just need to install the Retrospect Remote Control Panel on the Mac you want to backup.

Retrospect is a perfect solution for any backup needs, and is especially well-suited to handle complex search criteria for multiple Macintosh computers.

DiskFit Pro

Also from Dantz, this smaller sibling to Retrospect is designed with the same ease-of-use in mind. Nearly all settings needed to complete a backup can be made from a single window. DiskFit Pro is best suited for backing up an individual Macintosh to floppy disks, hard disks, removable cartridge media, optical disks, or a combination of these. It can however, be used over a network with System 7 File Sharing to gather data from several Macs.

The collection of your backup disks (DiskFit Pro cannot backup to tape drives) is called a SmartSet. Each disk in the set contains a small catalog file that is part of a master catalog of all the files. By saving catalog information on each disk, files can be restored even if the master catalog in the set is lost. After you have created a full backup of your files, only incremental backups are needed to write the changes to the SmartSet.

All backup data is written as normal files to the target media. Although this process of writing data is slower than creating one large file per disk, it simplifies retrieval of individual files that can be easily dragged back onto your hard drive. For files that are too large to fit entirely on your target disk, DiskFit Pro splits them into smaller segments that will automatically be joined during a restore. DiskFit Pro does not implement any file compression features during a backup.

As part of the running sequence, files and folders may be excluded from the backup and unattended backups can be initiated. DiskFit Pro even has an option to shut off your Macintosh after it completes a backup.

To help you remember when it's time to make your next backup, a control panel is included with the package. DiskFit Pro Reminder can be scheduled to notify you at a specified time on certain days of the week that a backup needs to occur.

Redux Deluxe

Company: Inline Software (203-435-4995 or 800-453-7671)

If you like programs that mostly run by themselves, then consider Redux Deluxe. Launch the application and choose Backup. After identifying your source disk and target disk, Redux Deluxe automatically names your backup disks and erases them if desired. That's it. Now for the options.

Your files will be written in one of two formats: normal or proprietary. It depends on how much data you have selected to backup. If the data exceeds the space on your target disk, the files will be written in a compressed format to multiple disks. Otherwise the backup is written normally, as executable files.

Redux Deluxe can create backups on floppy disks, hard disks, removable cartridges, tape, or network volumes. The normal operation of the program replaces files that have changed since the previous backup, adds new files, and removes old ones. To prevent this usually undesirable feature, you must choose Anchor Deleted Files from the application's File List. If a backup is stopped for any reason, Redux Deluxe can resume from the point at which it left off.

One option called Filters provides the ability to restrict which files are backed up by specifying them by name, date, type, and creator. For more customized file selection, a script can be created that enables the use of phrases such as "Check all items newer than one week." These scripts can be saved to disk and opened in other copies of Redux Deluxe, eliminating the need to type them more than once. Unattended backups can be initiated, and the activity reviewed in a log.

Other backup solutions

Other software packages can perform routine backups and file synchronization. Most have similar features to the programs reviewed here and differ only by their user interface. Before buying a program make sure it can handle your backup needs for today, and grow with you to meet your backup needs for tomorrow as well. Magazines like Macworld, MacUser, and MacWEEK can help keep you updated on the latest changes, features, and flaws with Macintosh backup utilities.

Physical security of backups

You now have the knowledge to create and implement a backup strategy. But this doesn't mean you have reached the end of understanding backups. There are a few pointers you should follow to keep your backups (the actual disks, cartridges, or tapes) safe and secure in case they ever need to fulfill their intended purpose.

- Keep magnetic media away from magnetic fields. These include the unlikely "bell" telephones, electric motors, and fluorescent lamp ballasts.

- Enable the write-protect tab or mechanism on your backup media. This prevents someone from accidentally erasing your data.

- Follow the same storage procedures as you would for "live" data. Don't let the backups get too hot, too cold, wet, bent, or dusty.

- Consider locking the backups in a safe or vault, especially if your data is confidential in nature.

- If you put your backups into a safe, be sure to note what temperature the safe is rated for. Most "document" safes only keep the internal temperature from reaching 451 degrees Fahrenheit (the charring point of paper). Computer media needs to be kept much cooler than that or it will melt.

- Create alternating sets of backups. For example, if your entire backup fits on one tape, use two or more tapes to store your backups. This way when one is being used to execute a backup the others are safely put away and nearly as current.

- Keep your backups physically far away from your original data.

Off-site storage of backups

Continuing with the idea of keeping your backups safe, it is worthy to note the most important way you can keep your backup media in good physical shape: store backups far, far away from the source of their files.

Besides hard drive failure and accidental software erasure of your valuable files, it is also possible that you will experience data loss from one of more of the following: natural or accidental disaster (flood, earthquake, fire, electrical malfunction), theft, and computer virus (see

Appendix E for a Virus List). By keeping your physical backups in a different office, building, city, or state, you can avoid losing both your original data and your backups to the same tragedy.

Operating System and Software Maintenance

System software and software applications are the most critical products on the hard drive. Once you purchase an application, or System software, you should make a copy of the original floppies as a backup, and use the backup to install onto the hard drive. If for any reason the software becomes corrupted or you experience problems, you can always re-install from your backups.

Startup problems and odd freezes

Common startup indications include the sad Macintosh icon, chime sounds, a question mark flashing inside a floppy icon, and failure to arrive at your Desktop. These errors can occur more or less frequently on your Macintosh depending on how many others have access to your Macintosh hardware and System software folder, and how frequently hardware is upgraded, changed, and/or swapped from other Macintoshes. Generally, if you are the only user of your Macintosh, you will rarely have hardware or startup problems, except if you use a large number of extensions in your System software and upgrade applications frequently.

Flashing question mark inside floppy icon

This usually indicates the hardware was unable to locate a System Folder on a bootable CD, floppy disk, or hard drive from which to start. To work around this problem, start up from your Disk Tools floppy disk, or if you have a Performa your Utilities Disk or Performa CD. If you have a System Folder, it can become de-blessed, or deactivated by moving the System file or your model's System Enabler out of the System Folder. Starting up from the floppy will allow you to move or copy the System Enabler to the System Folder on the hard drive, after which your Macintosh should successfully start. If you have hardware devices attached to your Macintosh, this situation may be caused by a SCSI ID conflict, or non-terminated SCSI daisy chain. The worst case for this situation is your hard drive may be "dead". Either the hard disk itself may be damaged or the mechanism which reads and writes to the disk.

Chime sounds

If you hear chime sounds after turning your Macintosh on, or after restarting, it is possible you may have a hardware problem. If memory was recently added to your motherboard, it could be a defective DRAM SIMM. If DRAM or VRAM was not recently added, it could mean failure of one or more hardware components on your motherboard. This can include a bad connection to a serial port, or ADB connection, to a bad chip on the motherboard.

Sad Macintosh

The sad Macintosh icon will appear before the 'Welcome to Macintosh' message. Basically, the sad Macintosh icon indicates you have a hardware problem with your Macintosh. Occasionally the sad Mac error can occur if the programming switch on some Mac models is pressed while starting up. It can also occur if you have a defective or nonfunctional memory SIMM installed on your motherboard. Sometimes a workaround for the sad Macintosh can be to restart your Mac.

Startup problems can also occur while extensions load. Extensions are software that modify System software tables at startup. These files are located in the extensions folder in your System Folder. If a conflict between extensions occurs, you need to move one, both, or all extensions out of the System Folder and restart. You can also hold down the 'Shift' key during startup (this prevents extensions from loading at startup).

Basic overview & troubleshooting tips

Identifying and resolving a problem on your Macintosh is similar to solving a mystery or puzzle. A simple problem is a problem that can be reproduced. More complex and often difficult problems to troubleshoot are ones that occur at one point in time without providing the user with any clues, and result in infrequent or odd problems at some point in the future.

If you have a trouble-free, customized System software folder, it's a good idea to make a backup of its contents to have it handy in case an unexpected software emergency occurs. For any given problem on your Macintosh, try some of these suggestions to see if the problem can be eliminated.

1. Try to recall exactly what you did before the problem occurred. Also, try to remember any error messages or hardware sounds that occurred and are symptomatic to the problem.

2. Check the version of your System software, application software, and any shareware you may have installed.

3. Make sure all hardware connections are well-connected and cables are tangle-free.

4. See if the problem goes away by turning off your System software extensions (hold down the 'Shift' key at startup).

5. Try starting from your Disk Tools or Performa Utilities floppy to see if the problem still occurs.

6. Remove any software preferences associated with the problem and restart.

7. Set software back to factory defaults (if this option is available for the product) and restart your Macintosh.

Recurring Type XX Errors and their cures

System Errors or Bus Errors of type 1, 3, 11, 25, 39, and 43 occur often on Macintosh computers. These errors indicate software problems that can cause a Macintosh to crash, freeze, or basically cease to work. These errors can be caused by old software that is incompatible with System 7.x, corrupt software, file system problems, or viruses. A number of software applications can help you fix most of the corruption and diagnose System software problems. In addition, most publishers provide software upgrades that often correct System software incompatibilities.

These problems can occur often on your Macintosh depending on how many files you moved from an earlier model Mac, how many other users are allowed to install or copy software to your Mac, and which software you like to use on your Macintosh. (Your favorite software may have known conflicts with other extensions or applications.) All of the Macintosh error types and their meanings are listed in Appendix A.

Error Type 11

If you have a Power Macintosh, Error Type 11 often occurs with improper loading into memory of Apple's emulator on startup. Try restarting your Macintosh to see if this corrects the problem.

Error Type –25

Error Type –25 occurs when you are out of memory. This error can occur if you have too many applications already open on your Macintosh. Select the application menu located on the far right corner of the Finder menubar. If you see several applications listed in this menu, quit one or all applications to free-up memory so that you can launch another application. Be sure to save any files you may need before quitting the application.

This error can also mean your application may simply need more memory at launch time to overcome this error message. To increase your application's memory partition, select the file, then select Get Info from the File menu, and enter a few hundred additional K of memory into the editable text field at the lower right corner of the Get Info window. If the application launches, you will not be able to change the application's memory partition number.

If the error message still occurs, try turning off all Extensions at startup (by holding down the 'Shift' key at startup), then launch the application. If the application launches successfully, you may want to consider purchasing additional memory for your Macintosh, as the extensions loading were occupying memory your application needed to launch successfully.

Error Types 1 and 3

Type 1 and 3 errors usually occur when an application is launched. The application may not be 32-bit clean, it may have an incompatibility with System software, or an incomplete or corrupted software application or file may be initiated during the application's launch procedure.

To resolve type 1 or 3 errors:

1. Try reinstalling your software from original floppies (or CD-ROM) to see if the error message disappears.

2. If it does not, try putting your System software in 24-bit mode if your Macintosh model supports it. Power Macs and other current Macintosh models no longer have this option.

3. Try to launch the application with an earlier version of System software or on another Macintosh with the same or earlier version of System software.

4. If you are using a Power Macintosh, try turning Modern Memory Manager off in the Memory control panel and restarting your Mac.

You are trying to determine if the application is having a problem launching specifically on your Macintosh, or if the problem may be with the application and System software compatibility. These errors can occur with newer Macs running older software and/or newer versions of software and System software extensions on any Mac.

Error Type –43

Error Type –43 is a File not Found error message. This can occur if your software package is incomplete, or if your file system or Finder is corrupted. Try running Apple's Disk First Aid 7.2 (located on your Disk Tools or Performa Utilities floppy) to check the hard drive's file system.

In addition, make sure you run version 3.6 of Disinfectant regularly to ensure no viruses are corrupting or erasing files on the hard drive. If no problems are found, try reinstalling your software package to see if the error message goes away.

Error Type 39

Error Type 39 is an end-of-file error message. This can occur on Performa with the Launcher file. To correct the problem, try re-installing an original backup of the software file or application that's creating the error message.

If the error message occurs with all or several applications, check the application's version number and creation date by selecting the application's icons and Get Info information from the File menu. If the creation date is prior to 1990 (prior to System 7.0), the file may not be 32-bit clean (which is preferable because System software runs in 32-bit mode). Try checking your online services library (on AOL, keyword 'software'), or Macintosh ftp site for a newer version of the software. Most commonly used Macintosh shareware has been updated over the years. If a newer application does not exist, you may have to kiss this software good-bye to eliminate more crashes in the future.

Disinfectant 3.6 (or a newer version), Apple's Disk First Aid 7.2 (or newer), and Apple's HD SC Setup or Drive Setup are all free software applications that can help identify, and repair or prevent problems with Macintosh hardware or software. These Apple software packages are located on the Disk Tools floppy disk, which is a part of the System software disk set. Apple's Disk First Aid checks the hard drive's file system for errors in the catalog and directory.

Disinfectant 3.6 is freeware available on most online services, Macintosh ftp sites, and user groups. Norton Utilities 3.1.3 (or newer version), Conflict Catcher 3.0.1, Apple Diagnostics, and Symantec Anti-Virus for Macintosh are commercial software products that can diagnose, identify, and help prevent hardware and software problems.

More problems, causes, and solutions

System 7 is several years old now, and has proven to be no more problematic than System 6. Overall, it's more extensible, more versatile, and just plain more useful than System 6. Each new System software release has brought System 7 more functionality (and therefore more software), adding features to applications that just don't work in System 6. However stable this new base of code, more features means more places to look for a problem when things go wrong—more settings, extension files, and more control panels.

To make problem solving a bit more complex, not all versions of System 7 are alike. System 7.1 changed the way fonts were handled, and System 7.5 added major new software such as PowerTalk and QuickDraw GX. (See Chapter 3 for details of the various versions of System software.)

Regaining control of a frozen Mac

A *frozen screen*, also referred to as a hung computer, is a common method the Mac uses to deal with an upset stomach (temporary or systemic software conflicts in RAM). Babies burp, but the Mac hangs. The Finder or your application just stops dead in its tracks in the middle of whatever it was doing, suspended in time. Sometimes you can move your cursor around freely, not realizing your screen has frozen. In this case, you will notice that the buttons and menus don't work, and are mere pictures. Other times, your cursor freezes on the spot along with the rest of the screen, or disappears altogether. In any of these cases, you have lost control of your Mac.

You can do several things to regain control of a frozen Mac. Preferably, you will want to regain control without having to shut off the power because cutting the Mac's power with open applications can damage them.

1. Wait a minute or two. Make sure your Mac really has hung up, and is not just working out a complex problem or waiting for a network procedure. If a watch indicator or time thermometer is displayed, make sure it is frozen as well—if it is moving, your Mac is working. In normal operation, indicators and thermometers can stop for a short while if the Mac is too busy doing something else, so be sure to study them for any motion.

2. If your screen really is frozen, press ⌘+period. This step can stop a process that has gone haywire and is running in loops. If you get control of your application, save your data immediately.

3. If ⌘+period doesn't work, force your application to quit by using ⌘+Option+Escape. This works in the Finder as well as in any other application. A warning that unsaved changes will be lost will appear, and then give you the option to force a quit or to cancel (see Figure 5.3). These aren't the greatest of options; forcing your application to quit will result in the loss of any work you did since the last time you saved, and pressing Cancel returns you to a frozen screen. Unfortunately, you don't have much of a choice at this point.

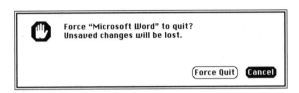

Figure 5.3   *Forcing an application to quit is one way to release a frozen screen.*

4. If you have successfully returned to your application (step 2) or to the Finder (step 3), save your work if you need to, then quit out of any applications that may be open and shut down your Mac by using the Finder's Shutdown command in the Special menu. Start up as normal. You can also select Restart, but Shutdown will reset RAM more effectively.

5. Sometimes hitting the Force Quit button and evoking the message shown in Figure 5.3 will do nothing—the Force Quit dialog box also freezes. If your screen is still frozen, hit the restart switch, located on the front or side of most Macs, and on the back of PowerBooks.

6. Occasionally, the restart button will be ineffective as well. Shut off your Mac using the power off button located on the back or in the front of your Macintosh.

7. If all else fails, remove the power cord from the AC outlet. Use this step as a last resort if your power button isn't responding. In this case, you may have a cabling misconfiguration or malfunction that is playing games with the voltages in your power system.

System crashes

You know your Mac has crashed when you receive a message with a bomb icon in it saying something very informative such as, "Sorry, a system error has occurred." A system crash is more serious than a frozen screen; you cannot gain control of your Mac without restarting.

The crash message sometimes contains two buttons, Restart and Resume. Always try the Restart button first because pressing Resume usually results in a frozen System crash window. Quite often the Restart button won't work either, forcing you to hit your Mac's restart switch or shut off the power.

Tools for frozen screens and crashes

If you aren't happy with a choice of staying frozen or forcing a quit without having the chance to save your data, software tools are available that will help when your Mac hangs and crashes.

NowSave from Now Software will save your file every time a certain number of keystrokes is hit, or after a certain number of mouse clicks or minutes. You can set a different save frequency for each application, and you can set NowSave to create a buffer of your most recent keystrokes, which you can recover in case you need to restart.

Fixing the problem

Occasionally, your Mac will freeze or crash only once; the sole time it occurs may not be indicative of any problem. In these cases, restarting the Mac will get you up and running without any further problems. Other times, the problem will come back again to haunt you. Continuing crashes and frozen screens are usually caused by software—document files, applications, or System software that have been corrupted or are conflicting with each other. Occasionally, the problem will be with your hard disk; a good hard disk utility may help locate and fix the problem (see Chapter 12).

Whether the cause is software, a problem is easier to track down if it occurs repeatedly: it predictably occurs when a certain set of conditions are met. It may be a particular application that needs to be reinstalled, or a conflict between two or more extension files or control panels. Random crashes are more difficult to pinpoint, and you may resolve the problem only after reinstalling most of your application and System software, without ever discovering exactly what was broken. Here are some configurations prone to freezes and crashes:

- **Multiple System Files**. An easy thing to check for are multiple copies of the System file (use the Find command in the Finder). You should have no more than one System file on each disk or partition. Two system files can cause random crashes and frozen screens because both fight for control of the Mac.

  You can break this rule if you use a program designed to manage more than one System file and System Folder. System Picker and Blesser are shareware or freeware utilities that can be found on many computer bulletin boards and disk collections of shareware. With any of these programs, you select the System Folder that you want to use, and the program prevents any others from loading into memory. This is useful if you are trying out different versions of System software, and want to switch back and forth between them. It is a safer practice, however, to decide on one System and delete any others.

- **Conflicts.** A common cause of crashes and frozen screens is extension file conflicts. Applications can also be incompatible with each other, although this rare.

A utility that can help is Help! from Teknosys. Help! looks at all your System software and applications, and notes whether you have any files that are known to be incompatible. It can also tell if there are damaged files, or if duplicate copies of software exist, including fonts or device drivers.

- **Other Possible Problems.** If the problem only happens in an application, try reinstalling the application from the original set of floppy or CD-ROM disks. You can also try reinstalling the System software from your Apple disks.

Repeatable or random crashes can also be caused by software that is incompatible with your Mac's processor, or an incorrect setting in the Memory control panel. These are discussed next.

Processor incompatibilities

Incompatibilities between older software and newer CPU chips are common in the PC world, but are rare in Macintosh computing. Apple has done a better job than any other operating system manufacturer in successfully making compatibility with future hardware a reality. Decade-old applications written for the 68000 CPU can run flawlessly on Macs using 68040 and PowerPC chips.

However, incompatibilities do occur when software developers don't follow Apple programming guidelines; software that runs fine today unexpectedly crashes with a new model of Mac. The bad news is that even major software houses are guilty of occasionally producing software that doesn't work on new Mac product lines. The good news is that major incompatibilities have only occurred three times during the Mac's history.

The first time was in 1987 with the introduction of the Mac II, which used the 68020, a processor that was not used for very long in Macs. All applications have long since been rewritten to compensate for any incompatibility. There were no incompatibility problems with the 030 chip, but when the first Quadras were introduced, the 68040 chip caused some problems. The third time was at the introduction of the Power Macs in 1994.

68040 incompatibility

Besides the PowerPC chips, the 68040 has been the main chip used in Macs built for the past few years. These include all Quadra models, the LC III, LC475, LC575, LC580, most Performas, and the last 68K PowerBook 500 series and Duo models. Almost all software written today is completely compatible with 68040 CPUs, but you may have some older versions of applications which are not 32-bit clean, or not 68040 processor-savvy that will crash on these machines.

Fortunately, most of the incompatible applications will run if you disable the cache in the 68040 processor. You can do this in the Cache Switch control panel. This control panel gives you a choice of two settings: Faster (cache is enabled) and More Compatible (cache is disabled). More compatible mode is noticeably slower than Faster mode. Caches are discussed in Chapter 2, "Understanding Your Mac."

PowerPC compatibility

Application software incompatibility rarely occurs with the PowerPC chips in Power Macs. In fact, more compatibility problems occurred when the first 040 Macs were launched than with Power Macs. The incompatibilities that do occur with Power Macs are usually older extension files or control panels. One workaround for addressing error messages accompanying 68K software on a Power Mac is to turn of Modern Memory mode in the Memory control panel. Then restart your Macintosh for the change to take effect. Native applications run faster with Modern Memory Manager selected.

Programs that don't work on the Power Mac include older versions of MacDraw from Claris, After Dark screen saver 1.0 and 2.0 from Berkeley Systems, and Symantec's Think C before version 6.0.1. Some older versions of Apple's networking software won't work on Power Macs, namely AppleTalk Remote Access version 1.0, AppleSearch 1.0, and AppleShare 4.0 AU/X, Apple's version of UNIX for the Mac, also won't run on Power Macs, but Power Macs can run Apple's PowerOpen, based on IBM's UNIX. The first versions of Connectix Virtual and RAM Doubler didn't work because they make calls directly to the memory management unit in 68030 and 68040 chips. Version 1.5 and later versions of RAM Doubler have fixed incompatibilities with Power Macs (except for the PCI Macs; at press time, Connectix released a fix for RAM Doubler and PCI Mac incompatibilities). Keep in mind that many software applications and extensions have their own software incompatibilities with other software in addition to Apple's software products.

Still, almost all Mac applications ever written will run on Power Macs. The phrase "Power Mac compatible" used by some software companies doesn't really mean much because EVERYTHING is compatible. The logo/phrase that is significant is "PowerPC software," which can take advantage of the PowerPC chip and will run many times faster than non-native software. However, native software is completely incompatible with non-Power Macs—it won't work on 68000, 68020, 68030, or 68040 processor Macs.

Some vendors combine two sets of code on their installation disks—one for 680x0 and one for PowerPC—along with an installer program that can recognize which type of Mac you have; these are called "fat" applications. Others sell two different versions in separate boxes. If you plan to purchase software accelerated for Power Macs, look for the red "Accelerated for Power Macintosh" label on the software or hardware packaging.

To get the best speed from your hard disk, Power Mac users should also format their disk with formatting software. Disk Toolkit from FWB, can take advantage of at least version 4.3 of SCSI Manager, part of the System software shipped with Power Macs. Hard disks formatted with software that is not SCSI Manager 4.3-savvy will run significantly slower. Unfortunately, the drives Apple shipped on the first Power Macs were not formatted with this software, and are not as speedy as they could be. If you were one of the early Power Mac pioneers, you should consider reformatting your Power Mac's hard disk with some of the new formatting software.

5

Memory control panel settings

System 7's Memory control panel (see Figure 5.4) controls what the Mac does with available RAM. This control panel can set aside portions of your Mac's RAM to be used for functions other than the normal RAM function. Normally, RAM holds portions of software and data the CPU uses when it runs applications. The four settings—Disk Cache, Virtual Memory, 32-bit addressing, and RAM Disk—dramatically affect the performance of your Mac, and also prevent or cause crashes, depending on the software you're running. Any changes you make to any of these settings take effect only when you restart your Mac. Newer Macintosh models, beginning with the Quadra 840AV, and extending into the Power Macs, PowerBook 150 and Quadra 630 only support 32-bit mode. Power Macs have two settings for memory management, modern and traditional.

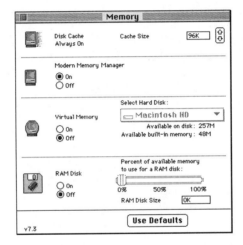

Figure 5.4   *The Memory control panel.*

Disk cache

The Disk Cache (incorrectly called "RAM cache" in System 6) is a section of RAM used to hold portions of applications and data files frequently used by the CPU. Applications are too big to fit entirely into RAM, so the disk cache acts as a kind of RAM overflow container to hold application information. Because accessing RAM is many times faster than accessing a hard disk, using the RAM cache will speed up your Mac.

Unlike System 6, the disk cache in System 7 is always on, at a minimum setting of 32K. Increasing this amount will increase your Mac's performance, but the rate of increase becomes negligible at some point. In addition, the disk cache takes away the amount of RAM available to applications, so you don't want to set it too high; likewise, too little available RAM will prevent some applications from launching. A good rule of thumb is to set 32K for each megabyte of total RAM in your Mac, or 256K for an 8 MB machine. Disk Cache is the least critical of the Memory settings as far as System 7 problems go, because it won't cause your Mac to crash.

Virtual Memory

Virtual Memory is a feature of System 7 that uses an invisible file on your hard disk as if it were real RAM to extend the RAM available for applications. Virtual Memory is slower than real memory for many reasons, one of which is that a hard disk is slower than RAM.

Not all Macs can use Virtual Memory. Macs with a 68000 processor cannot use it. Macs with both a 68020 and the optional 68851 PMMU chip (such as a MacII) can use Virtual Memory, but the original LC can't because there is no slot for the 68851. All 68030, 68040, and PowerPC Macs can use Virtual Memory. Don't worry too much if you don't know what your Mac model can do—if your Mac can't use Virtual Memory, it won't be available in the Memory control panel.

Older driver software for hard disk drives may be incompatible with System 7's Virtual Memory. In these cases, you can simply upgrade with a later driver. The Apple HD SC Setup or for Power Macs, Quadra or Performa 630 and PowerBook 150, the Drive Setup 1.0.2 utility that comes with Mac Disk Tools floppy and System installer disks will update the driver for Apple hard drives. For other hard drives, you can use driver update software such as FWB Software's Hard Disk Toolkit (see Chapters 9 and 10 for more information on this product).

Even if you can run Virtual Memory, you may decide to keep it turned off if you have a 680x0–based Mac. The biggest problem with Virtual Memory in non-Power Mac models is speed, or lack of it. Virtual Memory can reduce your speedy Quadra to a crawling whimper. Not only is a hard disk slower than real RAM, but Apple's implementation of the Virtual Memory technology is not the best in the computer industry, as its disk access is not very efficient. You should definitely avoid using Virtual Memory in PowerBook Macs on battery power. Virtual Memory keeps the hard disk constantly spinning, and will quickly drain your battery.

The story is different for Power Macs, where Virtual Memory works better than it does in 68020, 030, and 040 Macs. Your Power Mac will require less memory to run software, and will run faster if Virtual Memory is set to 1 MB more than the amount of physical memory installed in your Power Mac. If you double the amount of virtual to physical memory, your Power Mac will still be slower than if Virtual Memory were turned off, but it won't bring the machine down to a crawl.

Follow one rule if you decide to use Virtual Memory on any Mac—use it sparingly. Virtual Memory should be a temporary method of getting you through a RAM jam, either until your requirement for more memory ends, or until you can buy more real RAM.

When you first turn on Virtual Memory on a 68K Mac, the default setting adds on enough Virtual Memory to double the amount of RAM in your Mac. On a Power Mac, Virtual Memory's default is set to 1 MB more than the amount of physical memory. (As Figure 5.4

shows, the display shows the total amount of memory, real RAM plus virtual.) It is best not to increase this amount, but rather to decrease it to the minimum amount you think you will need.

Tip

Another way to improve the performance of Virtual Memory is to set it up on a disk or partition that does not contain System software and applications. This way, the disk calls that are busy servicing Virtual Memory do not compete with the disk needs of application and System software.

32-bit addressing

The 32-bit addressing option in the Memory control panel refers to the number of address bits available for addressing memory. When set to 32-bit, your Mac can recognize 2 to the 32nd power of memory. This is equivalent to 4GB of memory, half of which is set aside to manage motherboard hardware component input and output, the other half is available for recognizing physical memory installed on the motherboard. With 32-bit addressing turned off, the data path is reduced to 24 bits.

In 24-bit mode, your Mac can see a maximum of 16 MB of memory. Of the 16 MB, 8 MB is used for memory mapped to support NuBus and other hardware on the motherboard. The remaining 8 MB is available to support physical memory. In 24-bit mode, Virtual Memory is also limited to 14 MB total (virtual plus real RAM) with 32-bit addressing turned off. Generally, you should keep 32-bit addressing turned on, not only for the memory benefits, but to prevent some modern applications from crashing. However, you may need to turn 32-bit addressing off when running an older application that is not "32-bit clean." Macintosh LC and LCII computers only support a maximum of 12 MB of Virtual Memory.

If you have an old Mac, you may find yourself unable to turn on 32-bit addressing—Macs with a 68000 CPU do not support 32-bit addressing—the original Mac, the 512K, 512Ke, Mac Plus, Mac SE, the first Mac Classic, the original Macintosh Portable, and the PowerBook 100. The Classic II and Color Classic have 68030 CPUs, and do support 32-bit addressing.

Some older Macs (the Mac SE/30, II, IIx, and the IIcx) have the right CPU, but lack the code in their ROM chips to support 32-bit addressing. This latter group can be 32-bit-enabled with the addition of an extension file called MODE32, available from Apple, Connectix (the original developer), and from many electronic bulletin boards and online services.

RAM disk

A RAM disk is the opposite of Virtual Memory: it diminishes the amount of RAM available to applications to create a virtual storage disk (see Figure 5.5). This disk mounts on the desktop like any other disk, and allows you to copy software to it by dragging and dropping icons.

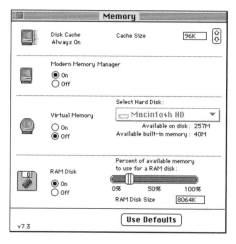

Figure 5.5   *Configure the size of a RAM disk from the Memory control panel.*

However, there are two big differences between a virtual disk and a real disk:

1. A virtual disk is much faster than a real disk because RAM is faster than a hard disk. Applications copied to a RAM disk will run faster than from the hard disk. You can even make a RAM disk your startup disk, if you create a pared-down System Folder that can fit on a RAM disk. In addition, PowerBook users can gain extra battery life by using a RAM disk because RAM uses far less power than a real hard disk.

2. A virtual disk is only a temporary container for files. Like the rest of RAM, a RAM disk is erased when the power is turned off. This means you will lose your data and applications whenever you shut down, during a power failure, when your PowerBook battery dies, and when your Mac crashes. (You can, however, restart your Mac and retain files kept on a virtual disk.) For this reason, data on a RAM disk should be frequently saved to a floppy or hard disk.

System 7.x problems

You may run into a few other problems with System 7 that warrant some attention.

Vanishing files

Users of versions 7.0 and 7.0.1 of the System software may experience problems with files and folders disappearing. This was a bug in the System software that Apple fixed with a program called System 7 TuneUp and in System 7.1. This bug causes the Finder to lose track of a file in the list of files that is kept on the hard disk.

System 7 TuneUp is a small program that installs some lines of code in your System file. When System 7 TuneUp has been installed, you'll see a bullet (•) next to the version number in the About This Macintosh dialog box, as in 7.0.1•.

If you have System 7 TuneUp installed, or have System 7.1 or later and are still missing files, you may have a problem with the directory on your hard disk. A disk repair program such as Norton Utilities can often fix these types of problems (see Chapter 7). Another thing you can try for disappearing files and folders is to rebuild the Desktop, as described in the next section.

Rebuild the desktop

Rebuilding the Desktop is a procedure that can solve Finder problems as well as speed up a drive that has become sluggish. Every Macintosh disk has at least one invisible desktop file which is a database of every file on the disk. It keeps track of file names, their locations, and all the information in the Get Info box, including anything you may have typed in the Comments field. Floppies have a single desktop file. Hard disks, CD ROMs, and other storage devices bigger than 2 MB have two invisible files called Desktop DB and Desktop DF. (System 6 uses a single desktop file.)

The desktop files continue to collect new information every time you add or move a file or folder, and need to be rebuilt from time to time to get rid of older information about files that have been deleted. To rebuild the desktop files, hold down ⌘+Option while starting up the Mac. For each volume or partition on a hard drive you have attached to your Mac, a dialog box will come up asking you if you want to rebuild the desktop files for that disk (see Figure 5.6). The drawback to rebuilding the desktop files is that you lose the text you may have typed in the Comments field in the Get Info dialog boxes for each file.

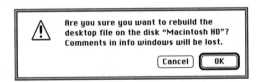

Figure 5.6 *Periodically rebuilding the Desktop can improve performance.*

This dialog box also appears when you restart after switching from System 6 to System 7. You should choose OK in this case to prevent any problems with your files. If your Mac wants to rebuild your desktop file, and you didn't press ⌘+Option or switch system versions, you may have a problem with your disk. Go ahead and choose OK to rebuild the files, but run a disk repair utility afterward to check it out.

Broken aliases

An alias is broken when it no longer brings up its parent file when you double-click on it. (Broken aliases are sometimes referred to as "orphaned.") This can happen when you change the path to the original file by moving it to another hard drive. Trading up to a new hard disk by copying your files will break all your aliases, even if you give the new hard disk the same name as the old one. You can also confuse an alias if the original file is on a network and your network link isn't established, such as when AppleTalk is turned off in the Chooser, your network cable is unplugged, or some other problem occurs.

An easy fix is to drag the old alias to the trash, empty the trash, and create a new one. However, this could be difficult if you have a lot of aliases in several folders. The shareware programs called Alias Assassin and Auto Assassin, available on ZiffNET/Mac on CompuServe and on eWorld, will find and delete dead aliases for you. Now Software's Now Utilities contains a program called Now Profile that will find dead aliases and duplicated files for you. Another commercial product called Server Tools from Santorini Consulting and Designs of San Francisco includes a utility called Disk Cleaner, which creates a list of dead aliases, duplicate files, and empty folders.

Preventing and Curing a Virus

As our society becomes more dependent on computers, software virus stories have been popping up in national news, newspapers, books, movies, and online services. Viruses can be written for any computer platform, and can result in unexpected crashes, loss of hard drive space, corruption of some or most of your system and applications or files, and at worst, can erase the contents of your hard drive.

Macintosh has a number of virus protection software that should be run regularly on the hard drive. The intervals at which you should run virus protection software are determined by:

- The number of people, besides you, who use the Macintosh

- Whenever files are downloaded from the Internet

- The Mac's connection to other floppy disks or hard drives

- Whether the Macintosh contains critical applications, files, and so on

The more of these criteria that apply to your Macintosh, the more frequently you will want to back up and run virus protection software on the system. An alternative is to use Symantec's S.A.M. (Symantec Anti-Virus for Macintosh) which will check for viruses at pre-determined times, including floppies or hard drives/removable media as they are inserted or mounted onto the Desktop. For a listing of most known viruses see the Virus List in Appendix E located at the back of this book.

Hardware Upgrades

Purchasing an upgrade for your Macintosh can be a no-brainer, or a virtual mind-boggler. This chapter focuses on the best way to research the upgrades you should consider, and the best ways to buy these upgrades. Some of the tools you can use during your research include benchmarks, vendor and product information, and price, feature, and performance comparisons.

Two software applications are well-known benchmark applications for Macintosh: Speedometer and MacBench. These benchmarks are one form of data that can help in your decision to purchase an accelerator upgrade or a new Macintosh.

Benchmarks Versus Practical Experience

Benchmark software runs on the computer and produces a series of performance numbers. Benchmarks can help you determine how your current System performs compared to slower or faster Macintosh models, and can also measure the performance of hardware upgrades, such as accelerator cards.

Benchmarks test a variety of number crunching and chip-dependent processes on a computer System and are used to determine price performance ratios, and software and hardware performance on new and existing computer systems. Unfortunately, software benchmarks generally do not run real-world processes. Sometimes applications software runs well with benchmark software, but has slower performance when you use the software for a real world task.

Another consideration is whether the benchmark application is written for 68K or PowerPC processors (or both). If you run a 68K benchmark application on a PowerPC Macintosh, you will receive benchmarks on the 68K emulator running on the PowerPC chip. The more appropriate benchmark to run on a PowerPC Macintosh is benchmark software written for (accelerated for) Power Macintosh. This will provide native performance results on the Macintosh, which should be two to four times faster than the 68K emulator.

Benchmark software for Macintosh include Speedometer 4.0 and MacBench 2.0. If you run specific software applications regularly, or perform specific tasks with System software, such as the Scrapbook, Notepad, or Calculator, use this software to determine whether certain tasks are taking less or more time than usual on your Macintosh.

Speedometer

Speedometer 4.01, published by Scott Berfield, is available on most online services and Macintosh ftp sites. The suite of benchmark tests include benchmarking Whetstones, Dhrystones, Sieve of Erathosthenes, plus additional tests including Towers, Quick Sort, Bubble Sort, Queens, Puzzle, Permutations, Fast Fourier, F.P. Matrix, Int. Matrix, and Sieve measured in seconds (these will be explained in a moment). Color Benchmark tests run in monochrome, two bit, four bit, and eight bit.

Speedometer also enables you to view general hardware information, such as the type of processor you have and the ROM version and size. The System software version on your Mac, such as the version of 32-bit QuickDraw and Finder, can also be checked. You can also use Speedometer and its common benchmarks to compare your Macintosh to previous Macintosh models:

- **Whetstones.** The Whetstones test is designed to test the Mac's calculation capabilities. It is a floating point test with a special emphasis on the use of transcendental functions.

- **Dhrystones.** The Dhrystones test is designed to exercise almost every other part of the System that the Whetstone test does not address. This test principally manipulates strings of data to test the speed at which the computer can access and move memory. Like the Whetstones test, the actual results of this test are presented as the number of iterations per second. The author of Speedometer points out that according to some in the computer science community, "the Dhrystones test does nothing, but it does it very well."

- **The Towers of Hanoi.** Solves the famous Towers of Hanoi puzzle for a stack of 14 disks. Its main purpose is to serve as a simple index of raw CPU power.

- **Quicksort.** Employs a standard QSort algorithm applied to a random array of 5,000 elements. Its main purpose is to serve as a simple index of raw CPU power.

- **Bubble Sort.** Sorts a random array of 5,000 elements using the standard bubble sort technique. This measure of raw CPU power is also a painfully slow way to sort anything.

- **The Queens Problem.** Exercises the classic Eight Queens Problem 250 times. Its main purpose is to serve as a simple index of raw CPU muscle.

- **Puzzle.** The Puzzle test is derived from the Stanford Mix (a suite of benchmark tests from Stanford University) and has been rewritten for the Mac. This test uses dynamically allocated memory to perform complex calculations utilizing matrix manipulations and integer multiplication. The performance of this test is a good index of the CPU's raw speed.

- **Permutations.** Recursive test is adopted from the Stanford Mix. It calculates a 10×10 matrix in all possible permutations. The performance of this test is a good index of the CPU's raw speed.

- **Fast Fourier Analysis.** This is a real-world test. Fast Fourier Analysis is a recursive calculation that uses a lot of floating point math in the calculation. It is heavy in addition, subtraction, multiplication, and the use of some transcendental functions, but not as much as the Whetstones test.

- **Floating Point Matrix Multiply.** This test multiplies two 40×40 floating point matrixes. This is usually used as a test of floating point math, but is also an index of general CPU performance.

- **Integer Matrix Multiply.** This test performs matrix multiplication of two 40×40 integer matrices. It is a test of integer math and general CPU performance.

- **The Sieve of Eratosthenes.** This classical test benchmark uses a simple repetitive algorithm to find all prime numbers up to 8,190. It is an index of the CPU power and its integer math capability.

- **Color QuickDraw Tests.** The Color QuickDraw Tests are available for machines that possess Color QuickDraw in ROM. The same test can be run in each of four basic graphics modes—1-bit (monochrome), 2-bit (four colors), 4-bit (16 colors), and 8-bit (256 colors).

  When selected to run, the Color test module presents a dialog box from which test(s) to run are selected. Only those modes supported by an available video card are available, and the current mode will be preselected. This may cause strange effects on the desktop and any other active programs. If altered for the test, the screen will be set back to normal when the test is completed.

  Each test draws a series of empty and filled geometric shapes. Copies of those shapes are moved around the window and then scrolled out of the way.

When the tests are complete, the results will be displayed in two columns. The first column—ABS.—is the amount of time (in seconds) to complete the test. The second column—RAT.—is a ratio of the time taken to complete the test versus the time a Mac II took with an Apple 8-bit card to do the same. The higher the RAT. number, the better.

Performance Rating Tests

The Performance Rating Tests are designed to test the performance of a machine in a real-world situation. The four tests are run in sequence with individual results displayed. The value determined for each tested subsystem is a ratio of the subsystem's performance to that of a Macintosh Classic. A Classic should score approximately 1.0 on all four tests. When all the tests are complete, a weighted result is generated as the PR (Performance Rating) for the System under test. The higher the PR, the better.

- **The CPU Test.** This benchmark tests the basic operations of the processor. The test is written in assembly language so that behavior at the processor level is known. The first part of the test is a Bubble Sort of a 1,024 element array. The array is then copied and manipulated in several ways using various additions, subtractions, ANDs, and ORs.

- **The Graphics Test.** The Graphics test is to the monochrome test of the Color QuickDraw tests module. The difference here is that scrolling is done in larger steps. The test draws a series of empty and filled shapes and copies those shapes around the window. It then scrolls the whole image out of the window. If a color machine is used, the screen will be temporarily set to monochrome during this test and will be reset afterwards.

- **The Disk Test.** The Disk test is designed to spot potential performance problems with hard disks. The test creates a one megabyte file on disk and proceeds to read and write to it in various-sized blocks. All disk access is done through the File Manager, which is similar to the disk writes performed by normal applications.

  The disk test is good at pointing out fragmentation problems (due to the large size of the test file). If the file has to be created across several discontinuous parts of the disk, the performance will be slow. If surprisingly bad results are obtained from this test, a disk optimizer program such as MacTools or Public Utilities is recommended.

- **The Math Test.** The Math test exercises floating point and integer math calculations. The breakdown of the test is roughly 75 percent integer and 25 percent floating point operations. The floating point operations do not include any transcendental functions in this test.

The old performance rating

The values from each of the four tests are combined using the following formula:

PR = (0.4xCPU) + (0.3xGraphics) + (0.2xDisk) + (0.1xMath)

This formula gives you the Performance Rating (PR) for the Macintosh under evaluation. The PR represents a ratio of the performance between the Mac being tested and a plain vanilla Macintosh Classic.

CPU performance is 40 percent of the overall performance (PR), graphics is 30 percent, disk speed is 20 percent, and math performance is 10 percent. If the tester disagrees with this formula, or if it does not represent the type of work the Mac performs (or will perform), the values for each test are displayed and saved with the average so that the user can rework these figures. One strong feature of this program is that all test results can be exported to a text file for importing into a spreadsheet or database.

The new performance rating

As of Version 3.22, a new PR is calculated (the previous PR is called the Old PR) using a new formula designed to correct for a mathematical calculation problem in the formula. The formula used for the Old PR tends to bias the results toward whichever value is highest. This may present an inaccurate assessment of machine performance (PR).

If an accelerated Classic has a math processor a million times faster than a standard Classic, the PR should not be 10000.9! If only 10 percent of the machine's capability is accelerated, the formula for the Old PR gives incorrect results. As a result, the New PR is calculated as follows:

PR = 1/ (0.4/CPU + 0.3/GRAF + 0.2/DISK + 0.1/MATH)

Both values are calculated and displayed in the PR window. The Preferences dialog enables you to choose the value you want to use for the Analysis Graphs (see Figure 6.1).

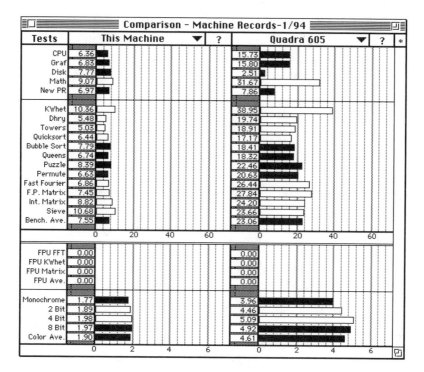

Figure 6.1 Results of Speedometer test of all systems are displayed in bar-graph format.

System information

In addition to being an excellent source of performance information, Speedometer can also display the System information about a Macintosh. The System Information Window displays information on hardware, graphics, versions, and other miscellaneous data on any Mac running System 6.05 or later.

Four sections make up the System Information display; click on the appropriate icon to see that section's information (see Figure 6.2). One piece of information is the same on each screen: the User Name.

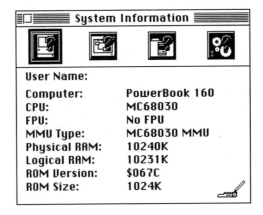

Figure 6.2 The System Information Window.

The Hardware icon displays the User Name and the following information:

- **Computer.** The model of the computer on which the test is being run.

- **Native CPU.** The processor in use.

- **Nominal CPU.** The processor emulated.

- **FPU.** The Floating Point Unit type, if one is present.

- **MMU Type.** The Memory Management Unit type, if one is present.

- **Physical RAM.** The amount of RAM installed.

- **Logical RAM.** The amount of accessible RAM (may include Virtual Memory).

- **ROM Version.** The version number of the ROMs.

- **ROM Size.** The size of the ROMs in kilobytes.

The Audiovisual icon displays the following information:

- **QuickDraw Version.** The version of QuickDraw in use.

- **Display Manager.** Present or not present.

- **Current Depth.** The bit depth of the active display.

- **Maximum Depth.** The maximum bit depth of the active display.

- **Screen Size.** The size in pixels of the active display.

- **Resolution.** The Dots Per Inch of the screen horizontally and vertically.

- **Outline Fonts.** Present or not Present.

- **Stereo Output.** Present or not Present.

- **Stereo Input.** Present or not Present.

- **16 Bit Audio I/O.** Present or not Present.

- **Speech Manager.** Present or not present.

The Version icon displays the following information:

- **System Version.** The version of the System software in use.

- **Finder Version.** The version of the Finder in use.

- **A/UX Version.** Present or not present

- **QuickTime Version.** The version of QuickTime in use.

- **AppleTalk Version.** The version of AppleTalk installed.

- **Time Manager.** The version of Time Manager in use.

- **Text Edit.** The version of Text Edit in use.

- **Communications Toolbox.** The version of the Communications Toolbox installed.

- **Script Manager.** The version of the Script Manager installed.

All version information comes from the System Folder, except for AppleTalk. The presence of the version in this window does not necessarily indicate that the file in question is installed or in use.

The Miscellaneous icon presents information about System Managers, including:

- **Addressing Mode.** 24- or 32-bit mode.

- **Alias Manager.** Present or not present in your System software.

- **Apple Events.** Present or not present in your System software.

- **Scripting Support.** Present or not present in your System software.

- **Scriptable Finder.** Scriptable or non-scriptable.

- **Help Manager.** Present or not present in your System software.

- **Easy Access.** Present or not present in your System software.

- **CloseView.** Present or not present in your System software.

- **Power Manager.** Present or not present in your System software.

Speedometer analysis reference

The System comparison capabilities of Speedometer are the most useful and powerful parts of the program. The Analysis Window enables you to compare graphically the performance of a System to other systems. In addition, the user can compare the performances of other Macs to each other. This can be especially useful if the user is thinking about buying a new Macintosh or accelerator and wants to know how well it will perform. Registered users of Speedometer receive a Machine Record File that contains performance ratings for most of Apple's Macintosh models.

Speedometer 4.02 is an excellent shareware program. A registered copy should be in every power users' and MIS worker's toolkit. The registration fee is $40, and includes documentation, upgrades, general support (unavailable for nonregistered users), and the satisfaction that you are contributing to one of the most helpful software programs made. (Site licenses are available from the author.)

Speedometer can be obtained from major bulletin board systems such as CompuServe, Genie, America Online, and AppleLink, and through local user groups. Send registration and mail orders with $40 to:

Scott Berfield
26043 Gushue Street
Hayward, CA 94544

Version 4.02 is now available and accommodates the new Power Macintosh line. The new benchmark-reference Macintosh is the Quadra 605 (replacing the Mac Classic).

MacBench

MacBench 2.0, published by Ziff-Davis Labs, benchmarks the same Mac subsystems as Speedometer. MacBench uses four tests to disk, processor, video, and floating point calculations on the Mac. The processor and floating point exercises test how fast the computer processes calculations. The processor benchmark tests how well (quickly) the RAM and central processor work together. The floating point test provides an index of how well the Macintosh handles floating point calculations.

Like Speedometer, MacBench can be used to evaluate System changes and upgrades. One common use for MacBench is to compare results before and after modifying a Mac.

MacBench attempts to provide real-world results from its tests by mimicking the way users normally work with their Macs. Although MacBench does not run the actual applications common in most offices, it does exercise Macs identically to the actual operations performed by these applications. The authors of MacBench use several popular Macintosh applications—Microsoft Excel, Microsoft Word, and Claris' FileMaker Pro—to test the most common routines used in these programs. However, MacBench will function fine even if you don't have these applications.

MacBench tests the disk, processor, and video subsystems separately. The core tests performed in these subsystems are a disk mix (see Figure 6.3), processor test, FPU test, and video mix test. Each score is then compared to the results from an LC III. The user can customize tests or record special test suites for examination. The rest of this section discusses each subsystem test in detail.

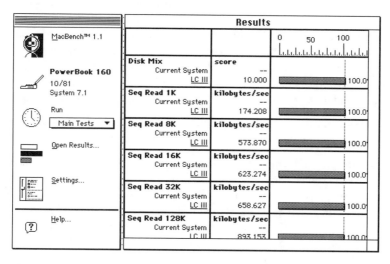

Figure 6.3 The main screen of MacBench 1.1, showing the Disk Mix test.

The processor subsystem

The processor subsystem test exercises the CPU, RAM, RAM cache (if present), and any accelerators in the System. This test measures the Mac's fundamental processing power in conjunction with its use of RAM. The test is designed to mimic several common tasks used in common applications and normal day-to-day operations. The main function during the test is a search and sort of data read to memory and some integer math calculations. Floating point calculations are also performed using the built-in floating point routines.

One important application of this test is to verify how effectively a particular model Macintosh uses its CPU in conjunction with its RAM. In cases like the Mac IIsi and Mac IIci, which use System RAM instead of VRAM, lower scores are expected. Fast processors that accommodate RAM and cache memory will score highest on this test.

The floating point subsystem

Floating point calculations—multiplication, division, addition, subtraction, and square roots—are performed in this test. A hardware FPU is not necessary to perform these tests because MacBench can use Apple's built-in FPU emulation software or the actual hardware FPU running in the main processor System to step through the test. If no hardware FPU is found by MacBench, a software version is used. The user can select the software version of the test in Settings if desired.

The video subsystem

The video controller (built-in or card) is tested in conjunction with any accelerators and a monitor. The video test executes common QuickDraw commands and operations found in everyday applications. The video mix yields an overall score for the Mac's video subsystem and is composed of nine separate tests. As expected, these tests transfer screen data to and from the monitor, move it around, scroll, and draw common geometric shapes. The way objects are drawn are based on common redraw methods of popular Mac applications. The results of the tests are calculated as a weighted harmonic mean of the individual results. If the test is run separately, MacBench displays the results as "operations per second" and no weighting is applied to the results.

MacBench provides the user with the option of running all the tests in one session, a set of selected tests, a single subsystem test (like the video test), or an individual test.

The authors of the program remind the user that MacBench tests basic subsystems in the Macintosh, not actual applications or application code. Changing or upgrading a Macintosh System with a faster processor or accelerator almost never results in the exact performance increase (due to the upgrade) being transferred to a software application performance gain. That is, accelerating video performance by 50 percent does not result in a 50 percent gain in performance in applications currently in use on the System. Keep in mind that most applications do more than display graphics. Thus, the performance enhancement of an upgrade is related directly to the amount of time the application displays graphics. The effect on sorting a large number of records will be largely unchanged if video performance is enhanced. If the performance of a sorting operation is inadequate, another kind of upgrade is required.

The disk subsystem

The hard disk System in a Macintosh is more than a disk drive. For this reason, MacBench tests the disk controller (on the motherboard or SCSI card), the disk cache, and any associated hardware. Overall, this test is a measure of how well a Macintosh handles disk transactions. The individual disk tests read and write blocks of data from a test file in a sequential process. The sizes of data blocks used in the tests are 1, 8, 16, 32, and 128K.

The disk mix provides an index of the overall performance of the hard drive System. The disk mix measures the typical disk usage of the profiled applications. Essentially, the disk mix acts as a disk-intensive application that exercises disk activities. The test employs the Macintosh System File Manager to simulate a real-world application. One use for this test (recommended by the developers) is to assess the proper setting for the disk cache in a System.

System information button

MacBench also provides basic System data. The System Information button displays information on the Macintosh model, processor type, FPU, ROM version, addressing mode selected, RAM, Virtual Memory, MMU, System software, and loaded extensions. In addition, the user can obtain information on video cards, SCSI volumes, and selected test settings. If the user decides to publish benchmark data obtained by MacBench, the licensing agreement stipulates that it is mandatory that the system information mentioned above be included the test file.

MacBench requires:

- Macintosh Plus or greater

- System software 7.0 or later

- 4 MB RAM minimum

- A minimum 8 MB free hard drive space; 32 MB is optimal

MacBench uses a hardware FPU if one is available; if not, MacBench uses a software emulator to complete the tests.

Test settings and results

Test settings can be changed by clicking on the Settings button or the Settings menu item in the Tests menu (settings cannot be altered for preset test suites, however):

- The user can specify which hard drive is used for the hard disk test.

- The user can specify whether the hardware FPU or software version is to be used in the FPU tests.

- Specific video cards can be selected for the video tests if more than one is present.

The MacBench results window displays:

- The name of the tests that are run.

- The score the Macintosh received on the test. If more than one results file is open, MacBench displays each result file.

By default MacBench will compare all the results to an LC III. The user can change this comparison to any Macintosh that has available data. Test results are displayed as a bar-graph and are compared to the System whose values represent 100 percent (in Figure 6.4, the Mac LCIII).

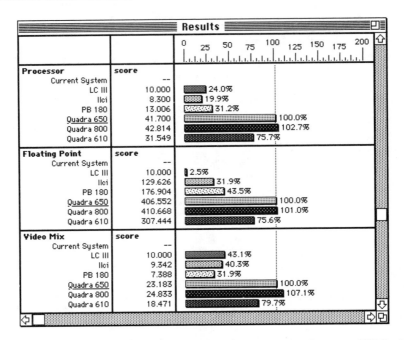

Figure 6.4 Macintosh benchmark results from MacBench 1.1. Courtesy of Ziff-Davis Benchmark Operations.

In the second column, note that units for individual tests are different from those for "mix" tests. Individual disk tests are reported in kilobytes per second, arcs tests are reported as arcs-per-second, and so on. The higher the numbers, the better.

Comparing results to another Macintosh

To compare a specific Macintosh model, open a published or saved record file from within MacBench and display the results. Ziff-Davis publications, such as MacUser, publish reviews of Macintosh systems with their MacBench results. According to the MacBench license agreement, users who want to publish benchmark records of systems must disclose certain information on the System(s) in the data file. As a general rule the user is expected to provide the following:

- Identify the exact System unit name; amount of secondary RAM cache, if any; CPU accelerator processor speed and type, if any; amount of RAM; hard disk size and size of hardware hard disk cache, if any, of the computer used for the test. For example: Apple Macintosh IIci with 32K external RAM cache, WXY Corp. 33 MHz 68040 XYZ CPU accelerator, 8 MB of RAM, and 80 MB hard disk or Apple Power Mac—6100 with 60 MHz PowerPC—601 CPU, 8 MB of RAM, and 250 MB hard disk.

- Identify the exact display name, video card name (or onboard video, if applicable), amount and type of video RAM, display resolution, and color depth, as in this example: Apple Macintosh 21-inch Color Display using onboard video with 1 MB of VRAM and running at 1152×870 pixels with 256 colors.

- Identify the operating System version (such as System 7.1), size and type of software disk cache, if any (such as 32K System 7.1 disk cache), and any other special conditions used to achieve the result, such as disk compression utility ABC version 1.1 enabled.

Please consult the license agreement included with a copy of MacBench for details concerning the specific data required for published benchmarks.

Getting copies of other Ziff-Davis benchmarks

MacBench is provided free of charge on 3 1/2-inch disks. To obtain a copy, send your name, address, phone number, and the names of the benchmarks required to Ziff-Davis at the following address. Normally benchmarks will arrive via U.S. mail in four to six weeks.

Ziff-Davis Benchmark Operation
Attn.: MacBench Technical Support
One Copley Parkway, Suite 510
Morrisville, NC 27560
`http://www.zdnet.com`

MacBench is available on ZiffNet/Mac in both the MacUser Forum and the MacWEEK Forum as a self-extracting archive called MACBEN.SEA. To get a free copy of MacBench, just download the file MACBEN.SEA from one of these forums:

- If you are using the MacUser Forum, type GO MACUSER and download MACBEN.SEA from Library section 3—MacUser Utilities.

- If you are using the MacWEEK Forum, type GO MACWEEK and download MACBEN.SEA from Library section 6—Benchmarking.

CPU Upgrades

Upgrading your processor is the fastest and easiest way to accelerate your Macintosh. Apple's latest Macs provide upgrade slots on the motherboard that accept special processor daughterboards. Other Macintosh models support the addition of a cross-platform Intel processor, enabling you to run PC/Windows applications on the Macintosh. Keep in mind that only some Macintosh computers can have the processor chip upgraded (PowerPC as well as 68040 models), and these may be limited to a specific type of accelerator.

Processor Upgrades to the main motherboard

Early Macintosh models had processors soldered directly to the motherboard, eliminating the possibility of a processor upgrade. PowerBooks currently have their processors soldered onto the motherboard. Many of the 68040/68LC040-based Macintosh models have removable processor chips that support processor upgrades. The most common processor upgrades are the addition of an FPU to a 68LC040-based LC Macintosh or Performa model, and the replacement of a 68040 chip with a 68LC040 processor (increases processor speed and adds a floating-point unit to the motherboard).

One thing you CANNOT do is add a PowerPC processor to a 68040 processor slot. The PowerPC chip won't fit into the 680x0 chip footprint (also known as *dye size*), and the PowerPC processor was not created to be interchangeable with 680x0 chips. This is due to speed limitations of the other chips on the motherboard and changes to the ROM, hard drive, and other hardware components.

Apple also has Intel processor upgrades for 68K and PowerPC Macintosh computers. Intel processors on daughterboards are added to the Macintosh motherboard and share memory, ports, and other components. To switch the monitor from one platform to the other you must press command-space bar. Apple uses Intel 486DX processors on the daughterboard that are Windows 3.1 and Windows 95 certified compatible. Software emulation—another way to run PC/Windows applications—enables you to run Mac and PC applications simultaneously on the Mac desktop.

Installing accelerators

Most accelerators require software and hardware components before they can be recognized by System software. Most 68K accelerators require the addition of DRAM SIMMs on the accelerator card before they are attached to the motherboard. PowerPC accelerators are designed to use the DRAM on the 68LC040 or 68040 motherboard; accelerator designs vary from vendor to vendor.

Install the hardware card into the appropriate Macintosh slot it was designed for, then install the accelerator software on the Macintosh. Restart, and you should be able to turn the accelerator 'on' and define any preferences you may want to use on startup. Restart your Macintosh again to activate the accelerator software settings, then try running your software applications with the benchmark software described earlier to see if there is a performance increase.

Apple is actively pursuing owners of traditional Macintosh systems that accept PowerPC (PPC) upgrades and encouraging them to make the transition to the new architecture. A number of upgrade kits and upgrade cards are available that enable Mac owners to upgrade their systems to PowerPCs. In addition to Apple upgrades, third-party options are available that can be inexpensive routes to PowerPC computing.

Understanding accelerator cards

PowerPC and 680x0 accelerators have been a popular choice for increasing raw hardware speed on existing Macintosh models. Accelerator card upgrades, which have been available for many years, can increase Mac performance without the need to buy a new computer.

Accelerator cards are the best choice for increasing performance if a lot of money has been invested in an existing Macintosh or exchanges aren't possible. Users of older Macintosh models that have considerable money invested in (older) RAM, hard drives, or software that cannot be used with the PowerPC should purchase third-party accelerator boards. Fortunately, there is an accelerator for just about every Mac and every Mac operation. The real question is when do you begin to experience diminishing returns. As you continue to buy accelerators for an aging Mac, there comes a point when the amount of money invested in accelerators equal the cost of a new, more efficient Mac with all the accelerator functions built in. Only you can decide the breaking point, but it might help to know that sentimentality has no place in the resale market.

Accelerator boards (as opposed to CPU upgrades) only speed up certain information paths, such as the SCSI bus or QuickDraw graphic routines. Some cards are application-specific, such as the Radius' PhotoEngine board (covered later in this section) which speeds up Adobe Photoshop. If you work with Photoshop or another professional application, and it is the only program you need to speed up, look for the application-specific accelerators covered later in this section.

One criticism against accelerators is that speeding up the clock and processor is only partially effective because the data bus through which data flows to the processor still runs at its original (slow) speed. This creates a bottleneck in the System that the processor cannot alleviate. To get around the data bus bottleneck, designers usually add high-speed Static-RAM (SRAM) to the accelerator. SRAM acts as a cache between the main memory and the accelerator. In older compact Macs and some 020-based designs, the main memory was added directly to the accelerator card to bypass the data bus. Some new PowerPC accelerators use a high-speed cache and RAM onboard the accelerator to optimize performance.

This configuration, though better from a performance standpoint, sometimes justifies the purchase of faster RAM memory. On the whole, the use of slow SIMMs causes the accelerator to use more wait-states, slowing the System. Furthermore, the addition of SIMM sockets and memory management chips increases the cost of the board; vendors will not apply this design to low-cost or a wide range of products given the cost-sensitive nature of the current market. Macs have never been more inexpensive. Their low cost seriously affects the accelerator market because the cost of an accelerator card is closer to the cost of an entire Mac System.

Factors that affect the performance of accelerated Macs include:

- The amount of native (motherboard) RAM

- The RAM's speed

- The native SCSI transfer rate

- Data bus speed and width (how many bits wide is the bus and the clock speed at which it is running)

- Hard drive performance

- The presence of an FPU or coprocessor if it is needed for a specific application

Not all accelerator cards are designed the same; some cards are better engineered than others. For example, apparently equal 33 MHz 040 cards do not perform identically even though the core CPU is the same. What the buyer gets in a more expensive card is better performance and reliability because of better engineering.

Compact Macs such as the Mac Plus, SE, and Classic all have slow SCSI ports and slow processors (relative to 68040 and PowerPC). Large file access will necessarily be slow in these systems if the SCSI port is not enhanced. 68030- and 68040-based Macs offer more efficient System architectures and CPU design (caching), and include the Paged Memory Management Unit (PMMU) for Virtual Memory.

Accelerator boards made for the compact Macs connect or solder onto the host machine's 68000 chip or, if one is available, use the PDS slot on the motherboard. The Mac Plus has no expansion slot; upgrades require a clip for the accelerator to mount above the main logic board over the 68000, or require direct soldering of the accelerator or connector socket to the 68000. Because of this last condition, Plus owners who are faint of heart may want to have the upgrade done at a dealer or Apple-authorized service shop. Heat dissipation in early compact Macs like the Plus has always been a problem. For this reason, these units required fans for hefty upgrades like full accelerator boards. In contrast, most modular Macs have pop-in PDS card accelerators. On the whole, any qualified service center can install and test any board with little risk of damage.

Upgraded Macs that have old or original parts and subsystems may turn out to be unreliable. It may be wise to upgrade power supplies, floppy drives, and internal cables if you are considering spending a lot on an accelerator. As far as problems with the upgrade are concerned, watch for AppleTalk, printer, and general extension and application software compatibility problems with accelerators.

Selected accelerators

Like any market, Mac accelerator makers come and go. Some accelerator manufacturers come from the comparatively huge PC market and dip their adapted PC product into the Mac market. In addition, existing third-party Mac accelerator manufacturers will adapt an existing accelerator for one type of Mac and re-release it as something else. Although these scenarios sound like unreliable approaches to Mac accelerator engineering, a number of companies have successfully adapted accelerators from PC designs and designs for older Macs.

The companies covered in this section are particularly interested in the Macintosh computer's future development. Each manufacturer has several years of Mac platform development, or has a product so good that not listing it would be a disservice. As new accelerators become available, read the reviews, call the manufacturer, and find out from computer groups or online chatter how the accelerator performs.

As a general rule, the closer the product is to an actual Apple Macintosh CPU product, the more compatible the product will be. Apple endorses and licenses its own CPU hardware and System level software to third-party developers who can then make boards or peripherals that are equally as compatible as the Apple equivalent. Apple-approved Macintosh clones, such as DayStar, Power Computing, and Radius offer 100 percent compatibility with Macintosh software, and have Apple's full support. Be wary of processor products which cannot promise 100 percent compatibility with Macintosh software.

The following sections describe in detail recommended Mac accelerator boards from a number of manufacturers. Performance, compatibility, and any installation requirements for each board are discussed.

BrainStorm Plus/SE Accelerator

The BrainStorm Accelerator more than doubles the speed of a Macintosh SE/Plus, making it faster than a Macintosh II. Graphics operations are doubled on the Plus and tripled on the SE, and hard drive transfer rates are claimed to be five times faster. The BrainStorm Accelerator can make your computer dramatically more responsive when launching programs, scrolling documents, manipulating graphics, printing, calculating spreadsheets, and using a database.

The BrainStorm Accelerator uses Bus Acceleration to achieve this lightning performance. Unlike other accelerators, which must wait for the slow chips on the original 8 MHz Macintosh motherboard, the BrainStorm Accelerator incorporates a specially designed chip that reconfigures the Macintosh bus to operate at 16 MHz. In conjunction with a 16 MHz CPU, this bus speed allows the existing memory and input/output chips to operate at two to three times their original speed.

The BrainStorm Bus Accelerator (BBA) chip also more than doubles the speed of the SCSI interface on the Macintosh motherboard. This chip operates a SCSI hard drive with a one-to-one interleave at its top speed, further boosting overall performance. The BrainStorm Accelerator's fast SCSI reduces the time you wait for the hard drive by more than half, reducing one of the most serious Macintosh performance bottlenecks found on older models like the Plus and SE.

The BrainStorm Plus/SE Accelerator works with an extensive list of programs, including Microsoft Excel and Word, PageMaker, all Claris software, and nearly every other application, INIT, and CDEV available for the Plus/SE. BrainStorm guarantees compatibility with any Macintosh software that adheres to Apple's programming guidelines, and supports standard Apple System software, including System 7.

System requirements for this accelerator include the following:

- RAM must be 100 nanoseconds or faster

- System Software 6.0.4 or later

- Some SCSI hard disks may need updated drivers

BrainStorm requires that an authorized repair shop perform the upgrade on the Plus; an authorized upgrade is optional for the SE. End-user installation on an SE requires a separate tool set available from BrainStorm.

$189 SRP
$199 SRP; SE model
BrainStorm Products
1145 Terra Bella Avenue
Mountain View, CA 94043
(415) 964-2131

DayStar Value 040 Card

DayStar produces a family of lower cost 68040 and 68LC040 upgrades for the Mac LC, LC II, Performa 400, 405, and 430. The Value 040 is available in speeds ranging from 33 MHz to 40 MHz, has an optional Ethernet Module, and a 128K SRAM cache. The Value 040 boosts a Mac LC up to a Centris 610 or even a Quadra 840AV (see Figure 6.5).

Figure 6.5   DayStar Value 040 Card.

The Value 040 uses the same technology as DayStar's Turbo 040, which received *MacWEEK* magazine's "five star," excellent overall rating. The Value 040 consumes less power than the Turbo 040 because it was designed to run on the Mac LC. The Value 040 is available in 33 MHz and 40 MHz speeds and does not require an adapter. An optional 128K Static RAM cache increases performance by an additional 70 percent. The Value 040 also works with the memory you already have, so there are no hidden costs.

The Value 040 supports an optional Ethernet Module that allows users to add a standard Quadra-style, AUI Ethernet transceiver to their Mac LC. Now Mac LC users do not have to sacrifice high-speed networking when adding an accelerator board. The Ethernet Module supports Direct Memory Access (DMA) to motherboard memory for the fastest performance possible. The Ethernet Module works with any Apple compatible Ethernet transceiver that supports thick, thin, or 10BASE-T cabling.

The Value 040 is 100 percent compatible with all Centris and Quadra compatible software, including Apple System 6, System 7, QuickTime, Virtual Memory, and AppleTalk Remote Access (ARA).

The included AutoCache software allows most applications that are not 68040 compatible to switch to 68030 cache mode automatically. Once a 68040 incompatible application is added to the AutoCache list, the Value 040 transparently switches cache modes while the application is open and reverts to the standard mode when the application is closed.

The board can plug directly into the motherboard PDS, or with a DayStar SlotSaver adapter, can plug into the CPU socket to leave the PDS and inline NuBus slot open.

> Processor: Motorola 68040 microprocessor and 128K SRAM cache (optional on 33/40 MHz board models)
> CPU speed: 33 and 40 MHz
> $849 SRP; 33 MHz with Math Chip
> $999 SRP; 40 MHz with Math Chip
> $649 SRP; 33 MHz
> DayStar Digital, Inc.
> 5556 Atlanta Hwy.
> Flowery Branch, GA 30542
> (404) 967-2077, (800) 532-6567

DayStar Quad 040 Centris/Quadra 68040 Accelerator

The Quad 040 combines a 40 MHz 68040 processor with a 128K SRAM secondary cache to increase the performance of the Centris 610, 650, and 660AV, and Quadra 700, 800, 900, and 950. The Quad 040 can make the Centris and Quadra faster than the Quadra 840AV at a fraction of the cost of buying a new machine.

The Quad 040 provides several other features and enhancements:

- A QUIC (Quadra Universal Interface Connector) slot

- PDS design

- Plugs directly into the motherboard PDS or—with a SlotSaver adapter—plugs into the CPU socket to leave the PDS and inline NuBus slot open

- Transparent operation of non-68040 compatible applications

- Works with existing motherboard memory

The Quad 040 uses the same technology as DayStar's Turbo 040—a 40 MHz 68040 CPU with a secondary 128K Static RAM cache. The Quad 040 also provides a QUIC (Quadra Universal Interface Connector) slot, which is a high-speed expansion connector for DayStar and other third-party products. The QUIC allows daughter cards to communicate at the Mac's Processor Direct Slot (PDS) speed and bypass the relatively slow NuBus interface. DayStar offers the Charger QUIC daughtercard to upgrade the Quad 040 to the same functionality as the Image 040, which is used for high-performance Adobe Photoshop processing.

The PDS design of the Quad 040, unlike NuBus-based accelerators, synchronizes with the motherboard. This allows the board to take advantage of the Centris and Quadra machines' faster motherboard memory, video, and SCSI subsystems. The PDS architecture with the 128K cache enables the Quad 040 to achieve the absolute fastest performance possible while ensuring 100 percent compatibility with existing hardware.

The Quad 040 also has a "universal" design that supports seven Macintosh models. This card installs in seconds into the PDS of the Centris 650, Quadra 700, 800, 900, and 950. The Quad 040 supports the Centris 610 and 660AV with the addition of a low-cost adapter.

Because the Quadra's PDS connector is inline with a NuBus slot, the addition of a PDS card blocks a NuBus slot. To overcome this obstacle, users can purchase a low-cost SlotSaver adapter that provides a slot for the Quad 040. This adapter connects to the CPU socket, leaving the motherboard's NuBus and PDS connectors open for other boards. (This approach is very successful with the DayStar Mac II family of PowerCache accelerators.)

The Quad 040 is 100 percent compatible with all Centris and Quadra software. It supports System 7, including QuickTime, Virtual Memory, and AppleTalk Remote Access (ARA); and supports all Centris and Quadra compatible hardware, including busmasters and accelerated video cards.

> Processor: Motorola 68040 CPU with 128K SRAM cache
> Speed: 40 MHz
> Onboard Features: Apple-licensed ROMs and bundled imaging utilities
> $999 SRP
> DayStar Digital, Inc.
> 5556 Atlanta Hwy.
> Flowery Branch, GA 30542
> (404) 967-2077, (800) 532-6567

DayStar Image 040 CPU Accelerator for Quadra/Centris Macs

The Image 040 is faster than Apple's fastest non-RISC Mac, the Quadra 840AV. The Image 040 uses the same Motorola 40 MHz 68040 CPU found in the Quadra 840AV. It also provides a 128K Static RAM cache and a twin 64 MHz DSP graphics engine to further enhance performance. This combination allows any Quadra or Centris machine to run applications up to 30 percent faster than the Quadra 840AV (see Figure 6.6).

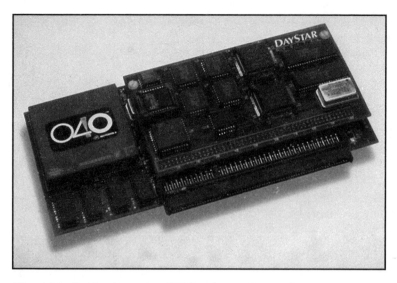

Figure 6.6   DayStar Image 040 CPU Accelerator Upgrade Card.

The Image 040 provides "Adobe Charged" performance for speed gains of up to 500 percent in Adobe Photoshop and other imaging applications that use the Photoshop plug-in standard. The Image 040 also features twin AT&T DSPs for imaging application acceleration. The Quadra 840AV provides a built-in AT&T DSP 3210 that excels in floating point environments, such as speech recognition and audio applications. The Image 040's twin DSP architecture is better suited for the acceleration of integer-based operations, such as those found in imaging applications.

The Image 040 is bundled with DayStar's "Adobe Charged" software, including Charger Suites Vol. 1 with PowerPreview as well as Kudo Image Browser, Storm PicturePress 2.5, XAOS Tools' Paint Alchemy, and Kodak's Photo CD Access & Sampler. Additional software modules are available to accelerate Kodak Precision Color Management and Kodak Photo CD Access & Sampler.

The Image 040 is 100 percent compatible with all 610, 650, 660AV, and Quadra 700, 800, 900, and 950 hardware. The board plugs directly into the motherboard PDS. With a DayStar SlotSaver adapter, it can plug into the CPU socket so that the PDS and inline NuBus slot remain open.

Processor: Motorola 68040 microprocessor
Speed: The CPU has 40 MHz and the twin DSP chips have 64 MHz
Onboard Features: Apple-licensed ROMs and bundled imaging utilities

   $1599 SRP;
   $109 SRP; adapters

DayStar Digital, Inc.
5556 Atlanta Hwy.
Flowery Branch, GA 30542
(404) 967-2077, (800) 532-6567

DiiMOCache 040/50 Accelerator

The DiiMOCache 040 Accelerator is a 68040 PDS card running at 50 MHz with a 128K cache. This card comes in several models; the only difference is the plug adapter for each particular Mac. The plug adapter leaves the NuBus and PDS slots free for other cards (in most cases). This card is as fast as a 68040 upgrade gets, and is capable of accelerating a Macintosh up to 350 percent. The card accelerates all CPU intensive functions, and offers twice the performance of most 68040 Macs.

The DiiMOCache is available for the Macintosh Quadra 605, 610, 630, 650, 660AV, 700, 800, 900, and 950, and Centris 610 and 650. The card is compatible with System 7 and later.

Processor: Motorola MC68040
Processor Clock Speed: 50 MHz
$899 SRP
DiiMO Technologies, Inc.
12201 Technology Blvd., Ste. 130
Austin, TX 78727
(512) 335-0421, (800) 503-4466

Vandal

The Vandal 030 SE Accelerator line uses a 68030 PDS card with a 256K data cache and built-in video output support for single and dual page monochrome monitors. Three different models running at 33 or 50 MHz can accelerate the SE beyond the IIfx. Aided by an onboard FPU coprocessor running at the same speed as the CPU, the Extreme cards also have slots onboard for the addition of SIMMs to further enhance performance.

This card is compatible with the Mac SE and requires 4 MB of RAM. All standard Macintosh software, including System 6.0.7, System 7, and later, is 100 percent compatible with this card.

Processor: Motorola MC68030
Processor Clock Speed: 33 or 50 MHz
$399.99 SRP; 50MHz
$304.99 SRP; 33MHz
Extreme Systems
1050 Industry Drive
Tukwila, WA 98188
(206) 575-2334, (800) 995-2334

Radius Rocket, Rocket 25i, Rocket 33, and StageTwo Rocket

Radius introduced the first Macintosh accelerators for Macintosh Plus and SE models. This company now has a Rocket line of 33 and 40 MHz NuBus card accelerators for 68030 and 68040 Macintosh models with a NuBus expansion slot. Multiple rockets can also be installed and used in the Macintosh with the addition of RocketShare software, bundled with Rocket accelerator hardware.

Radius Rockets are NuBus-based processors that run on models ranging from Mac IIsi up to the Quadras. Rockets are powered by various Motorola 68040 chips, from 25 MHz to 40 MHz. A basic Rocket increases the processing speed of the original Mac II up to six times, even exceeding Quadra performance in some cases; higher-end StageTwo Rockets run as fast or faster than a stock 840AV Quadra. All Rocket 68040 processors (except for 25i) include an integrated math coprocessor that is ideal for CAD, 3-D rendering, and scientific analysis applications—programs that use floating-point instructions. The low-cost Rocket 25i, without the integrated math coprocessor, is best suited for integer-based publishing and productivity applications, such as page layout, drawing, word processing, and presentations.

Radius Rockets include a flexible memory architecture with eight SIMM slots that support 4 to 128 MB of standard 30-pin DRAM. The Rocket also includes a processor direct slot for additional add-on cards made by Radius for such functions as graphics and video acceleration.

Rockets include several software enhancements to further improve System performance. When used with Radius display interfaces, Rockets provide QuickDraw acceleration for faster screen response. The built-in QuickDraw acceleration and Radius display interface provides faster screen response for routine operations such as scrolling, window resizing, and area fills. Some CAD applications are designed to take advantage of Rocket's QuickCAD display list processing techniques to accelerate zooms and redraws.

RocketWare allows the user to specify cache settings by application for maximum speed and compatibility. MODE32x from Connectix is also included, which enables Rockets in Macintosh II, IIx, and IIcx computers to address more than 8 MB of memory with System 7. Rockets are compatible with Radius RocketShare multiprocessing software, which utilizes multiprocessing on supported tasks such as 3-D rendering.

Application cache and compatibility settings can be adjusted so that you can specify the cache mode used by the 040 for each application for maximum speed and compatibility. A built-in Processor Direct Slot provides a high-speed, 100 MB per second interface for future expansion options. StageTwo Rockets have advanced onboard DSPs derived from the DSP booster used as add-ons to other Rockets. These StageTwo DSPs work directly with Adobe Photoshop, accelerating many of the onboard image processing filters.

The accelerator card fits into a NuBus slot. Software must be installed, and the card software requires System 7 or later and at least 4 MB of RAM on the motherboard and card. The 40 MHz card is more compatible with System 7 or newer than previous hardware cards. Earlier cards can have intermittent incompatibilities with some Mac II models and software using sound, or non-Apple software drivers; the 40 MHz card does not have these problems.

Processor: Motorola MC68040
Processor Clock Speed: 25, 33, or 40 MHz
$700–900 avg. street price; 25–40 MHz Rocket
$299 avg. street price; RocketShare
Radius Inc.
215 Moffett Park Drive
Sunnyvale, CA 94089
(415) 541-6100, (800) 227-2795

DayStar FastCache Quadra

DayStar FastCache Quadra works in any Quadra or Centris with a PDS slot (see Figure 6.7). The FastCache works transparently inside the Quadra, with no software or hardware incompatibility. The FastCache contains 128K of high-speed Static RAM (or SRAM), which holds data and instructions just outside the CPU for "zero-wait" state processing. AutoCache software included from DayStar allows switching between 030 and 040 cache modes automatically.

Figure 6.7 The FastCache Quadra provides static RAM cache for Quadras and the Centris 610.

This cache card is 100 percent compatible with all Macintosh hardware and software that runs on the Quadra/Centris line (the Centris 610 requires an adapter supplied by DayStar). The FastCache installs in the PDS (Processor Direct Slot) of the Centris/Quadra line. The FastCache is CDEV controlled.

$299 SRP; FastCache Quadra Universal 128K for Quadra 610, 650, 700, 800, 900, 950, and Centris 610
$139 SRP; FastCache Quadra 128K for Quadra 700, 900
DayStar Digital, Inc.
5556 Atlanta Hwy.
Flowery Branch, GA 30542
(404) 967-2077, (800) 532-6567

DiiMOCache 128K Cache Card

DiiMOCache 128K Cache Card is available in two versions: one for the LCIII and Performa 450, and one for the Mac IIci and IIsi (adapter board included). For the LCIII, Performa 450, and IIci, the card plugs directly into the PDS; for the IIsi, the DiiMOCache card ships with a dual slot adapter for other cards such as Ethernet and video. Both versions offer an optional FPU chip as well. The DiiMOCache Card works transparently, with no software or hardware incompatibility. Like the DayStar FastCache, the DiiMOCache Card contains 128K of high-speed Static RAM (or SRAM), which holds data and instructions just outside the CPU for "zero-wait" state processing. DiiMO's five-year warranty and free technical support are attractive features for a cache card (see Figure 6.8).

Figure 6.8 DiiMOCache 128K Cache Card.

This card is one hundred percent compatible with all Macintosh hardware and software (System 6.0.5 or System 7) when run on the Macintosh for which it was designed. The DiiMOCache card installs in the PDS (Processor Direct Slot).

$129 SRP; IIci
$179 SRP; IIsi
$230 SRP; IIsi (with 20 MHz math coprocessor)
$129 SRP; LCIII, Performa 450
$209 SRP; LCIII, Performa 450 (with 35 MHz math coprocessor)
DiiMO Technologies, Inc.
12201 Technology Blvd., Ste. 130
Austin, TX 78727
(512) 335-0421, (800) 503-4466

Sonnet upgrades

For Macs without math coprocessing chips onboard, Sonnet Technologies provides a full line of processor and FPU chips that provide a noticeable improvement when working with math intensive applications such as spreadsheets, CAD, and graphics applications. Some programs, particularly high-end modeling and rendering programs, will not even open on a Mac without an FPU. Others run comparatively slower on 68030 processors.

The addition of an FPU to a 68LC040 involves changing the processor chip on the motherboard. Sonnet offers 25 and 33 MHz 68040 processors that replace the 68LC040 on the motherboard. This FPU upgrade option is available for Centris, Performa, Quadra 475, 605, 610, 650, 630, and LC 475, 575, 580 Macintosh models. Sonnet FPU upgrades for IIsi, LCII, LCIII, 550, and Performa models with an FPU socket on the motherboard use Motorola 68882 math coprocessors in their 68020/68030 upgrade cards. No software is required (see Figure 6.9).

Figure 6.9   Sonnet FPU/PMMU upgrades.

These FPU upgrades work with all Mac models that do not have math coprocessors. The processor or math coprocessor plugs in like a board, or snaps in like a chip. All Macs automatically recognize a math coprocessor after it is installed. Properly installed, Sonnet FPU accelerators do not void the Apple warranty, but must be installed by an Apple authorized service provider.

> $200–300 avg. street price; 25–33 MHz 68040 processor
> $400–700 avg. street price; 40MHz 68040 SpeedsterPDS accelerator for IIci, IIsi, IIx, IIcx (with and without FPU and 128K cache)
> $250–600 avg. street price; 40–50MHz 68040 QuadDoubler accelerator card for Centris and Quadras
> $100–$190 avg. street price; 25 MHz 68020 to 33 MHz 68030 LC, LCII, and Mac II accelerators
> Sonnet Technologies, Inc.
> 18004 Sky Park Circle
> Irvine, CA 92714
> (714) 261-2800

Digital Eclipse PowerBook FPU upgrades

FPU upgrades are also available for selected PowerBook models from Digital Eclipse:

> $329 SRP; PowerBook 140 F25
> $349 SRP; PowerBook 160 F/33
> $339 SRP; PowerBook 145 and 160 FPU
> Digital Eclipse Software, Inc.
> 5515 Doyle Street, Ste. 1
> Emeryville, CA 94608
> (510) 547-6101, (800) 289-3374

Thunder/24 GT and PrecisionColor Pro 24X 24-Bit Display Accelerator Cards

Radius' Thunder/24 GT currently stands at the top of the Mac display accelerator hill: it provides the best onscreen performance of any Mac graphics card available—delivering up to 20 times faster performance than Power Macintosh built-in video. The Thunder/24 supports resolutions of up to 1,600 × 1,200 pixels at 8-bit color, displaying 92 percent more information than the highest resolutions provided by built-in video; this accelerator can also provide up to 1,152 × 870 at full 24-bit color. Thunder/24 GT provides these amazing resolution depths using highly optimized ASICs (Application Specific Integrated Circuits) that are designed to deliver fast 32-bit QuickDraw acceleration.

Radius' PrecisionColor Pro 24X supports full 24-bit color at resolutions up to 1,152 × 870 with onboard high-speed QuickDraw acceleration and NuBus block transfer support. This card comes with Dynamic Desktop software, enabling hot-key resolution and bit depth switching on-the-fly, and is built on a 6.5-inch NuBus 90 design.

The Thunder/24 GT and Precision Color Pro 24X are compatible with any regular color NuBus-capable Mac supporting regular specified NuBus card length (and not the seven-inch-only card length supported by the Quadra 605 and others).

$1749 SRP; Thunder/24 GT
$1399 SRP; PrecisionColor Pro 24X
Radius, Inc.
215 Moffett Park Drive
Sunnyvale, CA 94089
(415) 541-6100, (800) 227-2795

Radius PhotoEngine

PhotoEngine's four 32-bit digital signal processors deliver Adobe-charged Photoshop acceleration for resamples, filters, mode conversions, and onscreen graphics acceleration for fast viewing of CMYK files. The 7-inch NuBus 90 design fits in all NuBus Macintosh slots, including the Centris/Quadra 610 and Power Macintosh 6100.

Because this is an application-specific product, compatibility is limited to Photoshop. Any Macintosh with a NuBus slot, including the Power Macintosh, is compatible. This card is compatible with System 7.1 and later versions.

$1099 SRP
Radius, Inc.
215 Moffett Park Drive
Sunnyvale, CA 94089
(415) 541-6100, (800) 227-2795

FWB SCSI JackHammer SCSI Accelerator Card

The SCSI JackHammer is a RISC-based, Fast/Wide SCSI-2 accelerator board for the Mac that transfers data directly to NuBus or PCI at rates of up to 20 MB per second (see Figure 6.10). This is a 700 percent improvement over most native NuBus SCSI ports. The JackHammer increases the performance of hard drives, disk arrays, magneto optical, DAT, and other storage devices. Prepress, graphics art, and digital video users will be pleased with the leap in disk access performance; QuickTime users will also see an enormous jump in disk access time.

The JackHammer delivers data to and from the Mac at the speed of any hard drive currently on the market. Built-in SCSI Manager 4.3 software allows the computer to off-load drive management tasks to the JackHammer, freeing up the CPU to perform other tasks. Advanced features such as disconnect/reconnect, tagged command queuing, and asynchronous I/O maximize the performance of today's sophisticated Fast SCSI-2 drives. Because the JackHammer installs in a NuBus slot, it does not actually replace the onboard SCSI port, which can still be used.

Figure 6.10 FWB SCSI JackHammer Card.

The PCI SCSI JackHammer and SledgeHammer provides a Fast and Wide SCSI-2 RISC coprocessor for Power Macintosh computers with PCI. The PCI SledgeHammer family of disk arrays delivers the latest in RAID 0 performance and RAID 1 fault tolerance. Available in capacities from 2GB to 24GB, these arrays can attain sustained data transfer rates of up to 32 MB per second and are ideal for color publishing, multimedia, digital video, and networks.

All FWB products are fully compatible with the relevant NuBus, PDS, or PCI Macs and SCSI I, II, and Fast/Wide SCSI-2 drives. The JackHammer card installs in a NuBus slot; PCI models install in Power Macintosh PCI slots.

40 MHz RISC-based SCSI processor
33 MHz/sec DMA transfer rate
NuBus (or PCI) block mode transfer
16-bit wide SCSI-2 connector
Active SCSI termination
Two-year warranty
$499 SRP; PCI SCSI JackHammer
$699 SRP; PCI Fast 20/40 JackHammer
FWB, Inc.
1555 Adams Drive
Menlo Park, CA 94025
(415) 325-4329

PowerPC Upgrade Options

PowerPC upgrades use two different designs: a full logic board upgrade that completely transforms the older Macintosh to a new PowerPC (PPC) model, or a user-installed PPC upgrade card that plugs into the Mac's logic board and offers accelerated performance at a fraction of the price of a full upgrade or new Macintosh.

At the top of the heap are the full logic board upgrades for owners of the Macintosh IIvx, IIvi, Performa 600, Quadra (or Centris) 610, Quadra (or Centris) 650, Quadra (or Centris), and Quadras 800 and 840AV. Table 6.1 lists of common upgrades and the Macs for which they are designed.

Table 6.1 Power Macintosh Upgrade Specifications	
Microprocessor	PowerPC 601 Integrated floating-point processor Integrated 32K cache Runs at twice the clock speed of host Macintosh
Cache	1 MB onboard level-2 cache
Installation	User installed in the Motorola 68040 processor-direct slot
ROM	Includes 4 MB Power Macintosh ROM
Operating environment	Temperatures: 50 to 131 degrees F (10 to 55 degrees C) Relative humidity: 5 to 95 percent noncondensing Maximum altitude: 10,000 feet (3,048 meters)

Tables 6.2 and 6.3 include general operating specifications on the PPC 601 chip, Apple-supplied upgrade (logic board kits and upgrade cards), and general clock speed information on the Apple Upgrade Card compared to the present 040-based systems. Keep in mind that DayStar's PowerPC upgrades discussed in the beginning of this section have almost identical hardware and software compatibility compared to Apple's PowerPC upgrade card. Also note that the Quadra 840AV, 800, Power Mac 8100/80, 8100/100 and 8100/110 can also be upgraded to the Power Macintosh 8500 motherboard.

Table 6.2 Macintosh Upgrade Compatibility				
Macintosh *Model*	*6100/60* *6100/60AV*	*7100/66* *7100/66AV*	*8100/80* *8100/80AV*	*Upgrade* *Card*
Quadra 900, 950			•	•
Quadra 840AV			•	
Quadra 800			•	•
Quadra 700				•
Quadra/Centris		•		
Quadra/Centris 650		•		•
Quadra/Centris 610	•			•
Mac IIvx, vi, P600		•		

Table 6.3 Power Macintosh Upgrade Card Specifications		
Macintosh	*Motorola 68040 Speed (MHz)*	*Upgrade Card Speed (MHz)*
Quadra 630	33	66
Quadra 605	25	50
LC580	33	66
LC 575	33	66
LC475	25	50
Performa 631, 635, 636, 637	33	66
Performa 575, 577, 578	33	66
Performa 475, 476, 477	25	50
Quadra 950	33	66
Quadra 900	25	50
Quadra 800	33	66
Quadra 700	25	50
Quadra 650	33	66
Quadra 610	25	50
Centris 610	20	40

Logic board upgrades

Any Mac that is upgraded with a logic board is identical to its corresponding Power Macintosh. As shown in Table 6.2, a Quadra 610 converts to a 6100/60; a Quadra 650 converts to a 7100/66; and a Quadra 800 converts to a Power Macintosh 8100/80. AV options are also available.

Keep in mind that RAM purchases are necessary for some owners of converted (upgraded) Macintosh systems. The Macintosh IIvx, for instance, requires additional RAM, which adds to the cost of the upgrade.

Power Macs, Centris, and Quadras use the 72-pin SIMMs. The Power Macintosh uses 80 ns, 32-bit, 72-pin SIMMs in pairs, although the 5200, 5300, 6200, and 6300 models can have 72-pin SIMMs added one at a time. See the following section on upgrading RAM for additional information on Power Macintosh memory upgrades. Owners of Macintosh computers that use the older 30-pin SIMMs need to buy additional RAM for their Power Mac upgrades. PCI Power Macs use 70 ns, 64-bit, 168-pin DIMMs, which again are different from previous memory SIMM sizes.

Peripherals and NuBus cards should be compatible with the new System, although some ROMs on video cards require updates from the manufacturer. Users of the 6100/60 require an adapter for 7-inch NuBus cards. The 9500/132 Power Macintosh computer has PCI expansion slots for graphics cards, and do not have VRAM on the motherboard. The 9500/120 is bundled with a graphics card. 8500, 7500, 7200, 6300, 6200, and 5200 Power Macintosh computers have onboard VRAM supporting between 1 MB to 4 MB of total VRAM, support built-in video, and do not require a video card to connect a monitor to these models.

Apple continues to offer logic board upgrades to 6100, 7100, and 8100 models. Upgrades for the AV versions cost an additional $100 to $400, depending on the model. PowerPC upgrade cards are still available from Apple for the Quadra/LC 605, 475, 575, 580, and 630 Macintosh and Macintosh Performa models. These range in price from approximately $300 to $700 SRP.

The PPC upgrade card

A PPC upgrade card is available for every 68040 Macintosh made. Owners of older Macs, such as the Quadra 700 and 900, should consider this upgrade path. The PPC Upgrade Card is a PDS-based plug-in, and works in every Quadra and Centris computer with a standard PDS slot. The PPC upgrade card has no SIMM socket for its own RAM.

Apple's Upgrade Card

The Power Macintosh Upgrade Card adds a PowerPC 601 chip that runs at twice the clock speed of the host System (see Figure 6.11). Actual performance gained from the upgrade depends largely on the software and tasks run on the System, but estimates are in the 200 to 300 percent range for actual systems. The retail price of the upgrade card is about $700.

Figure 6.11 Power Mac Upgrade Card.

Benchmark data for standard and converted Quadras and Power Macs is provided in Table 6.4. The data is derived from MacBench 1.1 results from Ziff-Davis Benchmark Operations. According to the MacBench scoring conventions, the LC III receives a score of 10 on all tests and is the default reference Macintosh for comparisons. Note that the speed increase gained by running native applications depends largely on the model tested. Table 6.5 presents data for the PowerPC Upgrade Card only.

Table 6.4   Performance Ratings for Common Macs and Their Power Macintosh Counterparts

Macintosh	Disk Perf.	Processor	Floating Pt.	Video	Overall PR
Classic	2.51	0.75	0.58	1.06	0.94
Macintosh IIvx, vi	10.24	7.37	151.01	9.08	9.30
Performa 600	10.69	6.34	7.05	7.91	7.47
Quadra 610 Centris 610	18.42	31.55	307.44	18.47	24.94
Quadra 650 Centris 650	18.25	41.7	406.55	23.18	29.64
Quadra 660AV Centris 660AV	16.05	31.79	307.61	22.14	25.69
Quadra 700	11.04	30.04	305.28	23.17	22.37
Quadra 800	19.07	42.81	410.67	24.83	31.10
Quadra 840AV	19.16	49.06	476.45	30.21	34.80
Quadra 900 Quadra 9500	6.62	40.73	399	27.23	30.19
Power Mac 6100/60	19.44	112.62	3219.34	25.44	38.97
Power Mac 6100AV/60	19.74	180.15	3395.93	30.02	44.69
Power Mac 7100/66	20.71	166.05	4184.89	34.11	47.88
Power Mac 7100AV/66	20.73	166.43	4156.23	19.78	36.71
Power Mac 8100/80	23.11	234.08	4470.74	36.54	53.78

Table 6.5   Performance Rating of PowerPC Upgrade Cards

Macintosh	Processor	Floating Pt.	Video Perf.	Disk Perf.	Overall PR
Power Mac 8100/80	240	4525	36	22	52.32
Power Mac 7100/66 L2	200	4330	35	20	48.56
Power Mac 7100/66	165	4180	33	19	45.32

continues

Table 6.5   Performance Rating of PowerPC Upgrade Cards, CONTINUED

Macintosh	Processor	Floating Pt.	Video Perf.	Disk Perf.	Overall PR
Power Mac 6100/60 L2	175	3435	30	17	41.53
Power Mac 6100/60	120	3220	25	16	35.89
Quadra 950+ Upgrade Card	165	2000	17	21	33.73
Quadra 700+ Upgrade Card	125	400	22	15	32.87
Quadra 950	40	310	24	22	31.33
Quadra 700	30	140	23	15	24.74

Upgrade card limitations

What advantages does a new Mac or a logic board upgrade have over the Upgrade Card? First, remember that the Upgrade Card from Apple cannot be installed in every Macintosh. The logic board upgrade is practically equivalent to a Power Macintosh; the only question is whether the internal hard drive, CD-ROM, and other hardware can handle this performance improvement. If not, consider a new Mac. A full logic board upgrade adds extra features other than just speed—additional bit-depth and resolution support and 16-bit sound might be important in your work.

Finally, the performance of the Upgrade Card is limited because it relies on the old logic board and bus of the host Macintosh. Apple has tried to minimize this limitation by including 1 MB of secondary RAM cache on the Upgrade Card. Regardless, the design of the logic board on a full-fledged Power Macintosh is better optimized for performance and yields better results than an accelerated Macintosh with a 601 chip.

Apple's PowerPC Upgrade Card does not have an expansion slot of its own onboard. After it is installed, it may block the NuBus slot in the host Mac. Centris and Quadra 610 owners have to completely forfeit the slot after installation.

Because the general effectiveness and simplicity of the upgrade card appeals to owners of older Macs, accelerator-maker DayStar Digital has licensed technology from Apple for its own PPC upgrade cards. Two PDS cards are available from DayStar: one that runs at 66 MHz and another that runs at 80 MHz. Suggested retail prices are $1,400 to $2,300 for the upgrades.

DayStar PowerPro 601 PowerPC Upgrade Card for Centris and Quadra

DayStar is well aware of the shortcomings of the Apple designs and has engineered a higher performance System in their PowerPro cards. For instance, the DayStar cards run at a fixed clock speed regardless of which Mac is hosting them (in contrast to the clock-doubled cards).

This gives Quadra 610 owners the option of running an 80 MHz System, in contrast to the Upgrade Card that only doubles the clock to 50 MHz.

The DayStar cards include SIMM sockets so that the 601 can access RAM quickly without having to go back to the main logic board. Currently, four 72-pin sockets are included with the PowerPro 601 cards, yielding a maximum of 128 MB of RAM with the DayStar System. The PowerPro 601 also has a slot for extra RAM cache.

The ideal user for the DayStar card needs to run 040-emulated software and native code software side by side in his or her workstation. The 040 code is expected to run without a performance degradation typical in the currently emulated systems.

The PowerPro 601 was the first third-party PowerPC coprocessor available for the Mac. This card plugs directly into the PDS connector of the Macintosh Quadra 650, 700, 800, 900, and 950, and Centris 650 computers. This PowerPC processor-based upgrade card is currently available in 66 and 80 MHz speeds. PowerPro 601, with its high-performance memory and cache options, upgrades the Quadra or Centris to Power Macintosh 7100 and 8100 levels of performance (see Figure 6.12).

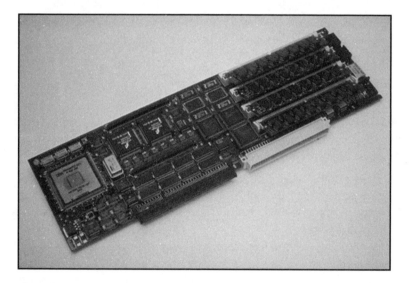

Figure 6.12   DayStar PowerPro 601 PowerPC upgrade card.

The PowerPro 601 uses genuine Apple PowerPC ROMs. This ensures that users who purchase DayStar upgrade cards have the same level of compatibility with current Macintosh hardware and software products. This includes Macintosh software emulation capabilities found on Apple's Power Macintosh. In addition, users who want to avoid running in emulation can reboot Macs that have been upgraded with a PowerPro 601 and operate at full Quadra/68040 processor speeds. This option is important to many users who plan to switch to PowerPC over the course of the next years. The ability to use a 68040 processor for software applications is not available for those who purchase a new Power Macintosh System or logic board upgrade.

The PowerPro's plug-and-play design is more convenient than Apple's Power Macintosh logic board upgrades—no board switchouts. DayStar's 100 MHz and 80 MHz PowerPro 601 boards can support any of six different Quadra and Centris platforms.

The PowerPro 601 works with memory already installed on the Macintosh computer; in addition, DayStar designed the card to support up to 128 MB of additional RAM using the same 80 ns 72-pin SIMMs required by Power Macintosh computers. Memory added to PowerPro 601 is also contiguous with Macintosh existing memory: it is contiguous to the motherboard memory. This feature works transparently and does not require changes to the current Mac configuration. When the Mac is run in 040 mode, it still has access to the memory on the PowerPro 601. These capabilities, and the option of adding DRAM (Dynamic Random Access Memory) to a PowerPC-based, processor-based upgrade card is unique to DayStar's PowerPro 601.

The PowerPro 601 has an "asynchronous" design, which means it can run at the maximum speed of the processor, independent of the motherboard's speed. Other manufacturers' boards, such as Apple's PowerPC Upgrade Card, use "synchronous" designs. Synchronous designs cannot take advantage of 80 MHz speeds because they can only double the speed of the motherboard on which they are installed. This asynchronous design and the advantages inherent in it should appeal to high-end users who need maximum levels of performance all the time.

The PowerPro 601 plugs directly into the PDS connector of the Macintosh Quadra 650, 700, 800, 900, 950, and Centris 650. It is compatible with all applications that are compatible with the Apple Power Macs of the same speed and RAM configuration.

> Processor: PowerPC 601 microprocessor
> Speed: 100, 80, and 66 MHz versions
> Onboard Features: Apple-licensed PowerPC ROMs, support for up to 128 MB of additional memory, high throughput 64-bit memory access, optional 1 MB secondary cache, asynchronous design, and bundled imaging utilities
>
> $2,149 SRP; 80MHz
> $1,399 SRP; 66MHz
> $1,699 SRP; 66MHz with cache bundles
> $2,299 SRP; 80MHz with cache bundles
> DayStar Digital, Inc.
> 5556 Atlanta Hwy.
> Flowery Branch, GA 30542
> (404) 967-2077, (800) 532-6567

Other PowerPC upgrade issues

Unfortunately, the upgrade to PowerPC may not be complete with just RAM and upgrade cards. Some other important details must be addressed before proceeding with an upgrade to a PowerPC.

Upgrading a Macintosh to a new PowerPC model requires a major overhaul of the System, including upgrading the hardware, software, and video card firmware. You'll need to examine the modifications and updates to device drivers, System software changes, and general upgrade problems and costs associated with switching over to native application software. Without maximizing the System all the way around, the Macintosh will not perform reliably at its top speed.

This section highlights areas you will need to consider for PowerPC compatibility

Hard drive issues

One of the most notable changes to a new PowerPC System concerns the SCSI System and drivers. The new ROMs from Apple include a revised SCSI Manager (version 4.3) that requires a new driver for top performance. Without this driver upgrade in a converted System, expect slowdowns in disk performance. Most of the major drive manufacturers have already upgraded their drivers. The current version of the SCSI driver is version 4.3.1, which is available in Apple's System Update release for System 7.5. If one of the upgraded commercial hard disk drivers is not available, use Apple HD SC Setup version 7.3 or Drive Setup 1.0.2 or later to update the drivers on Apple-supplied hard drives. For other drives, a commercial formatter is required.

Video card issues

High-end users of accelerated video cards are experiencing problems after switching over the old cards to the new Power Macs. Many cards require a ROM upgrade to be compatible with the Power Macintosh System. In most cases, this upgrade is free (or at least inexpensive) and comes directly from the card's manufacturer.

If the card's ROM is out of date with the Power Mac, performance slows appreciably (perhaps 20 percent of the original speed). Use one of the benchmark programs discussed earlier in this chapter to measure the video performance of the card in both the old and the new Mac. This should tell you whether a ROM upgrade is required. Keep in mind that all video/ monitor INITs and CDEVs are also candidates for native code upgrades.

Logic board upgrade recommendations

The following recommendations apply to Power Macintosh upgrades only. Use these as guidelines during your research.

- **Macintosh IIvx/vi, Performa 600.** The Apple logic board upgrade kit is the only real choice for IIvx owners considering converting to the Quadra 650 or a fast accelerator card. The conversion kit results in a completely new, modern Power Macintosh.

- **Centris and Quadra 610.** Centris and Quadra 610 owners should probably opt for the logic board upgrade from Apple. The complete conversion to the Power Macintosh 6100/60 is only about $300 more than the Upgrade Card price. The expanded features and better performance of the 6100 are worth the extra cost.

- **Centris/Quadra 650, Quadra 800.** These owners have the broadest choice of logic board upgrades or the upgrade cards. Apple's upgrade card is certainly the least expensive solution, especially for 650 owners. The decision must be whether the lack of performance and features of the least expensive card matter. Most owners of these Macs are probably best suited to go the logic board upgrade route. Unless you heavily depend on 68K software applications, the 650 and 800 are not entry-level Macs and it is safe to assume that owners of these models will prefer to maintain the same positions in the product line as they had before PowerPC.

- **Quadra 700, 900, and 950.** Owners of these Macs can select from either the Apple Upgrade card or the DayStar PowerPro 601 card. If price is no object and performance is key, the DayStar card is currently the best choice. The Apple card still provides acceptable performance at an attractive price, however.

- **Quadra, Quadra 840AV.** Assuming that buyers of these Macs are interested in advanced multimedia features, the only real choice here is to opt for the Apple logic board upgrade and try to keep pace with the changing standards in AV technology. If performance and compatibility with 680x0 software is the primary consideration, the upgrade cards with accelerators are certainly good choices. Be aware of software and video card ROM compatibility issues, however.

Apple's logic board upgrades are available for IIvx, Centris, and Quadra computer owners. You should equally consider DayStar accelerator cards as well as Macintosh clones. Many of the logic board upgrades available for 68K-based models offer Power Macintosh performance with the 601 processor, but not with the 604 processor. If an upgrade looks attractive, consider selling your old Mac and buying a new one. The cost of the new model may be greatly decreased by rolling the proceeds of the sale into a purchase. Depending on the model, the upgrade to a new Mac from the sale of an old one may cost less than simply upgrading.

Table 6.6 shows the Apple part numbers and descriptions of the currently available Power Macintosh upgrade options. Also included are part numbers for the CD-ROM upgrades and mounting kits. Please consult an Authorized Apple Reseller in your area for details on conversions and Mac upgrades. Remember that in most cases these upgrades are not do-it-yourself kits; they require Apple-certified technicians to install, test, and submit the new warranty.

Table 6.6   Power Macintosh Upgrade Information: Apple Upgrades and Part Numbers

Upgrade Option	Order No.	Notes
Power Macintosh Upgrade Card	M2843LL/A	Includes System 7, complete setup, learning, and reference documentation. All necessary hardware and installation instructions are included.
Power Macintosh 6100 series NuBus Adapter Card	M2337LL/A	This is specifically for the 6100 motherboard, which cannot use the NuBus Adapter from previous models.
DOS Compatibility Card	M3581LL/A	Intel Processor, which is added onto the 6100 logic board.
Power Macintosh	M2343LL/A	Includes System 7, 6100/60 Logic complete setup, learning Board Upgrade and reference documentation. All necessary hardware and installation instructions are included. 8 MB RAM and video adapter are included.
Power Macintosh 6100AV/60 Logic Board Upgrade		M2901LL/A Includes System 7, complete setup, learning and reference documentation. All necessary hardware and installation instructions are included. 8 MB RAM and S-video to composite video adapter are included.
Power Macintosh 7100/66 Logic Board Upgrade	M2474LL/A	Includes System 7, complete setup, learning and reference documentation. All instructions are included. 8 MB RAM and 1 MB VRAM are included.
Power Macintosh 7100AV/66 Logic Board Upgrade	M2840LL/A	Includes System 7, complete setup, learning and reference documentation. All necessary hardware and installation instructions are included. 8 MB RAM, 2MB VRAM, and S-video to composite video adapter are included.
Power Macintosh 8100/80 Logic Board Upgrade	M2344LL/A	Includes System 7, complete setup, learning and reference documentation. All necessary hardware and installation instructions are included. 8 MB RAM and 2 MB VRAM are included.
Power Macintosh 8100AV/80 Logic Board Upgrade	M2902LL/A	Includes System 7, complete setup, learning and reference documentation. All necessary hardware and installation instructions are included. 8 MB RAM, 2 MB VRAM, and S-video to composite video adapter are included.

continues

Table 6.6   Power Macintosh Upgrade Information: Apple Upgrades and Part Numbers, CONTINUED

Internal CD-ROM Upgrades	Order No.
AppleCD 300i Plus internal	M3152LL/A
Adapter kit for 6100/60 or AV	M2846LL/A
Adapter kit for 7100/66 or AV	M3126LL/A
Adapter kit for 8100/80 or AV	M2847LL/A

RAM

Most likely the first upgrade any Macintosh owner will pursue is to increase the RAM, or memory, in the System. Random Access Memory (or RAM, or DRAM—dynamic random access memory) is temporary (volatile) memory the computer uses to store information and process data that is loaded from the hard drive when a program is launched or when data is manipulated.

Computers store most information on magnetic disks, also commonly referred to as hard drives. When the computer needs a piece of information, it reads the information from the disk drive and places its contents in RAM. Only when the data is in RAM can the computer work on it. The more RAM the computer has, the more programs and data that can be loaded at one time. Similarly, very large documents such as 24-bit scanned color images or large databases can be accessed and manipulated quickly if there is enough RAM to accommodate the entire file. Macintosh is a cooperative multitasking operating System. This permits a user to have several programs open and running concurrently as long as enough RAM is available to support the programs and their files.

The Macintosh uses dynamic-RAM, or DRAM, chips to store and process data. DRAM (being dynamic) requires that a refresh signal be sent to the memory on a regular (periodic) basis to refresh the memory and retain its contents. Another form of RAM, referred to as static-RAM, is used elsewhere in newer Macs and does not require this refresh signal.

The designs of older Macs required that DRAM be refreshed 60 times per second. This rate equaled the refresh rate of the monitor because the DRAM was shared with the video circuitry in the Mac. The block of memory the video display refreshed every 1/60 of a second is referred to as the *screen buffer*, which holds screen data necessary to paint the next display picture.

The video circuitry depends on the DRAM during its screen updates; because of this dependency, Macintosh systems need to update the screen buffer and DRAM contents concurrently. The design reduced the complexity of the Macintosh but took a toll on performance. Because the microprocessor had to wait for the video system to finish its screen drawing and painting routines before it could access RAM, resulting memory access was slow. The effects of this DRAM-based display in the Macintosh IIsi and IIci can be seen clearly by using a program like MacBench 2.0 or Speedometer 4.0 to benchmark test the performance of the video system.

Later 680x0 Macintosh models revised this design. The screen data formerly placed in RAM is now allocated to a special kind of memory called *video random access memory,* or VRAM. A video management chip is in charge of updating the VRAM every few milliseconds and except for interruptions from other processes, the CPU is free to access RAM whenever it needs it. Power Macintosh computers use a configuration similar to the IIci and IIsi; they use DRAM for video display instead of VRAM. However, performance is not affected due to improved memory subsystems in the hardware architecture.

The amount of information stored in a RAM chip is measured in kilobits (kbit) or megabits (Mbit). Presently the most common sizes for RAM purchased as upgrades for Macs are 1-Mbit, 4-Mbit, 8-Mbit, and 16-Mbit chips. These bits must be combined into larger 8-bit bytes for the Macintosh to use. Thus eight 1-Mbit DRAM chips must be wired together to form a block of memory commonly found and used in Macintosh systems. These eight chips are soldered together on a circuit board to form a 1 MB Single In-line Memory Module (SIMM). The SIMM module is the basic Macintosh memory upgrade part ordered from memory producers. SIMMs have a 32-bit data path; DIMMs have a 64-bit data path.

Note

IBM PC-type computers use a 9-chip version of the 72-pin SIMM, which can be used in Macintosh computers. The ninth chip is disregarded by the Macintosh System and causes no complications.

RAM considerations

Before purchasing SIMMs or DIMMs, several physical factors need to be checked. First, identify the physical size required by the Mac for a SIMM or DIMM. Several Macs require low-profile 30-pin SIMMs, which stand shorter than regular SIMMs. Most newer Macs require low profile SIMMs; if in doubt, these SIMMs are a safe bet. Low profile SIMMs work in all Macs as long as the speed and pin-outs are correct. Composite SIMMs are large inexpensive SIMM modules built-up of many smaller SIMMs. They are less expensive, but occupy more space and are problematic. Avoid purchasing composite SIMMs or DIMMs whenever possible. Before purchasing memory, you may want to verify whether you will be purchasing a noncomposite or composite SIMM or DIMM from the vendor.

Memory speed

Another important specification that should be checked when upgrading is the RAM access time (in nanoseconds, ns) or RAM speed. The speed of RAM chips given for each Macintosh states in Table 6.7 is the maximum time required for the Macintosh to successfully read to and write from the SIMM.

Table 6.7 Macintosh Desktop System RAM Configuration

System	RAM Soldered Onboard	Number of SIMM Sockets	Possible SIMM Sizes	Physical RAM Configs (MB)	Speed (ns)
128	128K	0	n/a	128K	n/a
512/ 512Ke	512K	0	n/a	512K	n/a
Plus	0	4	256K, 1 MB	1, 2.5, 4	150
SE	0	4	256K, 1 MB	1, 2, 2.5, 4	150
SE/30	0	8	256K, 1 MB, 4 MB	1, 2, 4, 5, 8, 16, 17, 20, 32	120
Classic	1	2	256K, 1 MB	1, 2, 2.5, 4	150
Classic II	2	2	1 MB, 2 MB, 4 MB	2, 4, 6, 10	100
Color Classic	4	2	1 MB, 2 MB, 4 MB	4, 6, 8, 10	100
LC	2	2	1 MB, 2 MB, 4 MB	2, 4, 6, 10	100
LC II	4	2	1 MB, 2 MB, 4 MB	2, 4, 6, 10	100
LC III	4	1	1 MB, 2 MB, 4 MB, 8 MB, 16 MB, 32 MB	4, 5, 6, 8, 12, 20, 32	80
LC 475	4	1	1 MB, 2 MB, 4 MB, 8 MB, 16 MB, 32 MB	4, 5, 6, 8, 12, 20, 32	80
LC 520	4	1	1 MB, 2 MB, 4 MB, 8 MB, 16 MB, 32 MB	4, 5, 6, 8, 12, 20, 32	80
LC 550	4	1	1 MB, 2 MB, 4 MB, 8 MB, 16 MB, 32 MB	4, 5, 6, 8, 12, 20, 32	80
LC 575	4	1	1 MB, 2 MB, 4 MB, 8 MB, 16 MB, 32 MB	4, 5, 6, 8, 12, 20, 32	80
Performa 200	2	2	1 MB, 2 MB, 4 MB	2, 4, 6, 10	100
Performa 400, 405, 410, 430	4	2	1 MB, 2 MB, 4 MB	2, 4, 6, 10	100
Performa 450	4	1	1 MB, 2 MB, 4 MB, 8 MB, 16 MB, 32 MB	4, 5, 6, 8, 12, 20, 36	80
Performa 460, 466, 467	4	1	1 MB, 2 MB, 4 MB, 8 MB, 16 MB, 32 MB	4, 5, 6, 8, 12, 20, 36	80
Performa 475, 476	4	1	1 MB, 2 MB, 4 MB, 8 MB, 16 MB, 32 MB	4, 5, 6, 8, 12, 20, 36	80
Performa 550	4	1	1 MB, 2 MB, 4 MB, 8 MB, 16 MB, 32 MB	4, 5, 6, 8, 12, 20, 36	80
Performa 600	4	4	256K, 1 MB, 2 MB, 4 MB, 16 MB	4, 5, 8, 12, 20, 68	80
Mac TV	4	1	1 MB, 4 MB	5, 8	80

System	RAM Soldered Onboard	Number of SIMM Sockets	Possible SIMM Sizes	Physical RAM Configs (MB)	Speed (ns)
II	0	8	256K, 1 MB, 4 MB	1, 2, 4, 5, 8, 17, 20	120
IIx	0	8	256K, 1 MB, 4 MB	1, 2, 4, 5, 8, 16, 17, 20, 32	120
IIcx	0	8	256K, 1 MB, 4 MB	1, 2, 4, 5, 8, 16, 17, 20, 32	120
IIci	0	8	256K, 512K, 1 MB, 2 MB, 4 MB	1, 2, 4, 5, 8, 16, 17, 18, 20, 24, 32	80
IIfx	0	8	1 MB, 4 MB	4, 8, 16, 20, 32	80
IIsi		1	4 256K, 512K, 1 MB, 2 MB, 4 MB	1, 2, 3, 5, 9, 17	100
IIvi	4	4	256K, 512K, 1 MB, 2 MB, 4 MB, 16 MB	4, 5, 8, 12, 20, 68	80
IIvx	4	4	256K, 512K, 1 MB, 2 MB, 4 MB, 16 MB	4, 5, 8, 12, 20, 68	80
Centris 610	4	2	4 MB, 8 MB, 16 MB, 32 MB	4, 8, 12, 20, 36, 40, 44, 52, 68	80
Centris 650	4 or 8	4	4 MB, 8 MB, 16 MB, 32 MB	4, 8, 12, 16, 20, 24, 28, 32, 36, 40, 44, 48, 52, 56, 60, 64, 68, 72, 76, 80	80
Centris	4	2	4 MB, 8 MB, 16 MB, 32 MB	4, 8, 12, 20, 36, 40, 44, 52, 68	70
Quadra 605	4	1	1 MB, 2 MB, 4 MB, 8 MB, 16 MB, 32 MB	4, 5, 6, 8, 12, 20, 36	80
Quadra 610	4	2	4 MB, 8 MB, 16 MB, 32 MB	4, 8, 12, 20, 36, 40, 44, 52, 68	80
Quadra 650	8	4	4 MB, 8 MB, 16 MB, 32 MB	8, 12, 16, 20, 24, 28, 32, 36, 40, 44, 48, 52, 56, 60, 64, 68, 72, 76, 80, 84, 88, 92, 96, 104, 108, 112, 120, 136	80
Quadra	4	2	4 MB, 8 MB, 16 MB, 32 MB	4, 8, 12, 20, 36, 68	80
Quadra 700	4	4	1 MB, 4 MB	4, 8, 20 24, 28, 32, 36, 40, 52, 64	80

continues

Table 6.7   Macintosh Desktop System RAM Configuration, CONTINUED

System	RAM Soldered Onboard	Number of SIMM Sockets	Possible SIMM Sizes	Physical RAM Configs (MB)	Speed (ns)
Quadra 950	0	16	1 MB, 4 MB	4, 8, 12, 16, 20, 24, 28, 32, 36, 40, 52, 64	80
Quadra 800	8	4	4 MB, 8 MB, 16 MB, 32 MB	8, 12, 16, 20, 24, 28, 32, 36, 40, 44, 48, 52, 56, 60, 64, 68, 72, 76, 80, 84, 88, 92, 96, 104, 108, 112, 120, 136	60
Quadra 840AV	0	4	4 MB, 8 MB, 16 MB, 32 MB	8, 16, 32, 64, 128	60
Power Macintosh 6100/60 or 66	8	2	4 MB, 8 MB, 16 MB, 32 MB	8, 16, 24, 40, 72	80
Power Macintosh 7100/66 or 80	8	4	4 MB, 8 MB, 16 MB, 32 MB	8, 16, 24, 32, 40, 48, 72, 80, 136	80
Power Macintosh 8100/80, 100 & 110	8	8	4 MB, 8 MB, 16 MB, 32 MB	8, 16, 24, 32, 40, 48, 56, 64, 72, 80, 96, 104, 112, 120, 136, 144, 152, 160, 168, 176, 184, 200, 208, 216, 224, 232, 264	80
Power Macintosh 9500/120 or 132	0	12 168 pin DIMM	4 MB, 8 MB, 16 MB, 32 MB, 64 MB, 128 MB	16 MB–768 MB	70
Power Macintosh 8500/120	0	8 168 pin DIMM	4 MB, 8 MB, 16MB, 32 MB, 64 MB, 128 MB	16 MB–512 MB	70
Power Macintosh 7500/100	0	8 168 pin DIMM	4 MB, 8 MB, 16 MB, 32 MB, 64 MB, 128 MB	8 MB–512 MB	70
Power Macintosh 7200/75 & 90	0	4 168 pin DIMM	4 MB, 8 MB, 16 MB, 32 MB, 64 MB, 128 MB	8 MB–256 MB	70
Power Macintosh 6200/75	0	2 72-pin SIMM	4 MB, 8 MB, 16 MB, 32 MB	8 MB–64 MB	70
Power Macintosh 5200/75	0	2 72-pin SIMM	4 MB, 8 MB, 16 MB, 32 MB	8 MB–64 MB	70
Power Macintosh 6100/66 DOS Compatible	8	2 72-pin SIMM	4 MB, 8 MB, 16 MB, 32 MB	8 MB–72 MB	80

System	RAM Soldered Onboard	Number of SIMM Sockets	Possible SIMM Sizes	Physical RAM Configs (MB)	Speed (ns)
Apple Workgroup 68 Server 60	4	2	4 MB, 8 MB, 16 MB, 32 MB	4, 8, 12, 20, 36, 40, 52,	80
Apple Workgroup Server 80	8	4	4 MB, 8 MB, 16 MB, 32 MB	8, 12, 16, 20, 24, 28, 32, 36, 40, 44, 48, 52, 56, 60, 64, 68, 72, 76, 80, 84, 88, 92, 96, 104, 108, 112, 120, 136	60
Apple Workgroup Server 95	0	16	1 MB, 4 MB	4, 8, 12, 16, 20, 24, 28, 32, 36, 40, 48, 52, 64	80

Generally speaking, the faster the Macintosh, the faster the memory required. Keep in mind that a SIMM rated faster than the maximum access time required for a particular Mac will work fine, so buy the fastest RAM you can afford so that it can be transferred to a newer (faster) machine in the future without the need for new memory.

In most cases you can install RAM yourself, unless opening the Mac involves strange tools or complex procedures. You should be warned, however, that parts in both in the Mac and the SIMM are delicate, sensitive to static, and intolerant of oil and dirt. Consult installation instructions from Macintosh user groups, online services, or qualified technicians if there is any doubt about the installation. Damaged SIMMs and SIMM sockets are expensive to repair and replace. Most companies that sell SIMM upgrades can provide static guard kits as well as detailed installation instructions to guide you.

SIMM Pin-out

Most older Macs use a 30-pin SIMM. PCI Power Macs use a 64-bit SIMM packed on a 168-pin DIMMs. 6100, 7100, 8100, 5200, 5300, 6200, 6300 Power Macs, and most 68K Macs, including the Quadras, use a 32-bit SIMM packaged on a 72-pin SIMM. The Macintosh IIfx and many LaserWriter printers use a different variety altogether: a 64-pin SIMM. Make sure you know which SIMM is used in your Mac before venturing to the phone or store.

Another consideration: don't assume that any combination of SIMM upgrades is possible. The Macintosh IIci, for example, does not accept 2 MB SIMMs. The upgrade from 8 MB goes directly to 16 MB, a steep jump and an expensive upgrade. In contrast, the Macintosh IIsi upgrades from 5 MB to 9 MB using two 2 MB SIMMs.

All desktop Macintosh models introduced since February 1993 use 72-pin SIMM slots for their RAM. These models include LCIII, LC 475/605 series, LC 500 series, LC 630 series, Quadras, Centris, the first Power Macintosh and Performa equivalents. This type of SIMM is considered by many as an industry standard and is widely available for other types of computers (IBM PCs and PC clones).

When PC designed SIMMs are used with Macintosh computers the ninth parity bit is omitted, which is part of the so-called "industry standard." The same applies to 30-pin SIMMs that are manufactured for use with PCs. The ninth parity bit in 72-pin SIMMs installed in Macintosh slots is ignored and should not present any problems. However, you should test the SIMM in all banks of the Macintosh model you intend to use.

Not all "industry standard" SIMMs are guaranteed to work in all Macintosh systems. In other words, these Macintosh models might require the "higher" quality SIMMs that meet industry standards. Apple recommends that you buy 72-pin fast-paged mode SIMMs with access times of 60 ns or faster (80 ns for the Macintosh LCIII).

Composite SIMMs

Apple does not support composite SIMMs for the 72-pin SIMM form factor. Composite SIMMs are manufactured using a smaller or older memory technology, such as a 16 MB SIMM made of rows of 4 MB chips. These SIMMs are not recommended for use in Apple computers. If you have not installed memory before, you may want to consider purchasing memory from a Macintosh vendor who can provide installation instructions and support, versus a PC-only memory vendor. A PC-only vendor may be less expensive, but may not be able to provide you with the correct SIMM or SIMM installation information should any questions or problems arise.

Note

Designations for 32-bit SIMMs from manufacturers and vendors are confusing. Macintosh 72-pin SIMMs are specified as follows:

1×32-80/60	=	4 MB SIMM, 80 ns or 60 ns
2×32-80/60	=	8 MB SIMM, 80 ns or 60 ns
4×32-80/60	=	16 MB SIMM, 80 ns or 60 ns
8×32-70/60	=	32 MB SIMM, 70 ns or 60 ns

RAM requirements by task

The size of your workspace or RAM determines how many programs and how much information you can work with at one time. Whether you are working on a memo, spreadsheet, or graphics, it all takes up space in memory. The larger the item or the number of items, the more RAM you need.

Often when working on a project, you may have more than one program running, or more than one source of information at hand. Depending on the task, you may be using a word processor, database, spreadsheet, and email application. If information for a report is in the spreadsheet and enough RAM is not available, you have to save the report, open the spreadsheet, copy the information from the spreadsheet to the Clipboard, quit the spreadsheet, launch the report, and paste the information into the report. This entire process can be accomplished faster and easier if the computer has more RAM and can run all the programs at once under MultiFinder in System 6.0.7 or Apple's System 7 operating systems.

One common reason to upgrade memory is to take advantage of operating System features found in System 7. To take advantage of System 7, a Macintosh requires at least 4 MB of RAM for most practical uses. System 7.5, Apple's latest revision of System 7, also runs in 4 MB of memory; however, QuickDraw GX, PowerTalk, and other new System software technologies require 16 MB to run. Additional System software technologies such as Open Transport, OpenDoc, and QuickDraw 3D can require up to 24 MB to run all the additional features for these System software products.

Differences exist in the way System 7.x and 6.0.x use memory. 6.0.x and earlier System software only support a 24-bit operating System. While running 6.0.x, the Macintosh is in 24-bit mode and the address space starting at $00 0000 through $7F FFFF (8 MB) is reserved for System RAM. The SIMM sockets use the entire range of $00 0000 through $7F FFFF, which equals 8 MB of RAM. The first Macintosh computers, such as the Mac Plus and SE, only supported a maximum of 4 MB of memory, so this was not a real problem until newer hardware architectures and larger memory SIMM sizes became available.

Consequently, with 24-bit addressing enabled, installing four 4 MB SIMMs would give you 8 MB of usable RAM. The memory configuration under "About This Macintosh" (About the Finder with System 6) only shows 8 MB is available. The remaining memory is assigned to the System partition or heap. This extra memory assigned to the System is unusable. To access more than 8 MB of memory for program use, 32-bit addressing must be enabled in your Memory Control Panel in System 7.

With System 7, you have the option of turning on 32-bit addressing in 32-bit clean ROM computers (all models after the II, IIx, SE/30, and IIcx, with the exception of the AV, 630, PowerBook 150, and Power Macintosh models, which operate in 32-bit mode all the time). The Memory control panel turns on and off 32-bit addressing and requires a System extension if an older Mac is used. MODE32 is required on computers running System 7 versions prior to 7.1, or the 32-Bit System Enabler installed on computers running 7.1 will enable 32-bit operation for the Mac II, IIx, SE/30, and IIcx models. This permits the operating System to address memory above 8 MB in systems that physically support more than 8 MB of RAM.

In 32-bit mode, the Macintosh II family of computers (which includes the Macintosh SE/30) has the address space starting at $0000 0000 through $3FFF FFFF (1 GB) reserved for System RAM (see Figure 6.13). NuBus RAM cards may use address $0000 0000 through $3FFF FFFF to add System RAM. The SIMM sockets use addresses $0000 0000 through $07FF FFFF, which equals 128 MB of RAM. By noting these settings and using the Memory Control Panel and MODE32, the user can access all the RAM specified for his or her particular Macintosh.

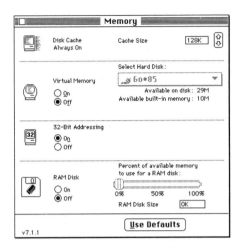

Figure 6.13 The Memory control panel is used to activate 32-bit addressing under System 7.

In general, the benefits of additional RAM are as follows: the user can have multiple applications open at the same time under System 7 (or MultiFinder in System 6), the user can allocate more RAM to a particular application to squeeze higher performance from the application and open more (or larger) documents, newer versions of favorite applications that require more RAM can be loaded, and a RAM disk can be created for top speed and (in the case of PowerBooks) battery power savings.

No matter how much physical memory is installed in a Macintosh, there are software tools available to optimize the use of this precious resource. The software described in the following sections can help you extract every last free byte of RAM.

MODE32 and the 32-Bit System Enabler

System 7 allows the Macintosh to address more than 8 MB of RAM. Whether a user can access this RAM depends on the model Macintosh. The ROMs in the older Macs—Macintosh II, IIx, IIcx, and SE/30—are not 32-bit clean. That is, they don't allow the Mac to address the full 32-bit address and thereby limit the amount of RAM that can be accessed. The problem was critical enough for Macintosh customers that a fix was developed by Connectix Corporation, later licensed by Apple, and is now available free via online services, users' groups, and with many Connectix products. Apple engineers later developed a patch of their own called the 32-bit Enabler, which was created specifically for System 7.1. It is recommended for use on the machines mentioned in this paragraph. You must use one of these products if you have one of these Macs with "dirty ROMs" to access more than 8 MB of RAM installed on the motherboard.

RAM Doubler

Two products have emerged that enable users with low-memory Macs to avoid the trouble and expense of a full-blown RAM upgrade: RAM Doubler from Connectix and OptiMem from Jump Development Group. RAM Doubler is an inexpensive solution to out-of-memory errors and doesn't rely on the installation of SIMMs. This program uses several RAM tricks to double the amount of RAM available in any Macintosh with a PMMU installed.

Foremost among its methods for squeezing more RAM out of a Macintosh is dynamic re-mapping of RAM contents. RAM Doubler takes charge of unused memory allotted to applications and reallocates it for use by other applications. In addition, RAM Doubler compresses RAM contents that are unlikely to be called (or used) again. In low-memory situations, RAM Doubler uses hard drive space as a Virtual Memory swap area, but only places low priority routines and data there, reserving the actual RAM for frequently accessed code. The program runs as an extension to the operating System and requires no setup or intervention from the user.

Double-clicking on the installer places the RAM Doubler extension components in the System Folder. After you restart, select "About This Macintosh" and you should see the total amount of memory double the amount of built-in memory on your Mac. This indicates RAM Doubler has successfully loaded and is running on your Mac.

Don't expect to dedicate all the "new RAM" to a single memory hungry application like Photoshop, however. A single application can only have as much RAM as is physically present in the System. RAM Doubler does not work with more than 128 MB of physical RAM either. RAM Doubler requires System 7, 32-bit clean applications, and does not run with System 7's Virtual Memory.

RAM Doubler version 1.5.2 has many bug fixes, is compatible with Power Macintosh, and is a recommended choice for expanding any amount of RAM in any Macintosh (see Figure 6.14). If you have an earlier version of RAM Doubler, upgrades are free and are recommended to increase software compatibility and performance. Unfortunately, RAM Doubler does not work with older non-PMMU Macs like the SE and PowerBook 100. In addition, compatibility problems exist with Virtual Memory schemes used in such programs as multimedia applications. There is also a small degradation in performance depending on application and user work habits, but most reports are that it is almost unnoticeable.

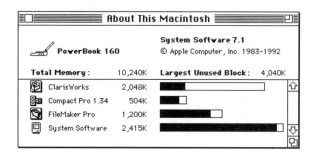

Figure 6.14 Connectix RAM Doubler effectively doubles the amount of RAM in PMMU-based Macs.

$99 SRP
Connectix Corp.
2600 Campus Drive
San Mateo, CA 94403
(415) 571-5100, (800) 950-5880
America Online: keyword **Connectix**

OptiMem

Jump Development Group's OptiMem works as a control panel in the System Folder to increase the amount of available RAM in Macintosh computers. The main feature of OptiMem's System is that unlike RAM Doubler, which requires a PMMU, OptiMem works on 68000-based Macs and allows the user to select which applications are affected in memory optimization and which are left alone. In this way programs such as ACI US 4D and Now Startup, which are not compatible with RAM Doubler, can still be used.

OptiMem utilizes a method of reclaiming unused RAM allocated to applications by dynamically resizing the walls of the memory partitions set in the Get Info window for every application. OptiMem automatically resizes the memory allocated to an application to reduce the amount required until more is called for by the program. It cuts down on the consequences of low-memory usage, such as when the Finder closes windows spontaneously and applications quit due to out-of-memory errors.

Because OptiMem actively adjusts the memory partitions of applications, it is helpful in resolving problems of RAM fragmentation common in high-memory Macintosh systems (see Figure 6.15). OptiMem is a smart program that tries to learn how programs are used so that it can optimize RAM automatically. OptiMem even warns you when a low-memory condition occurs so that corrective actions can be taken before problems result.

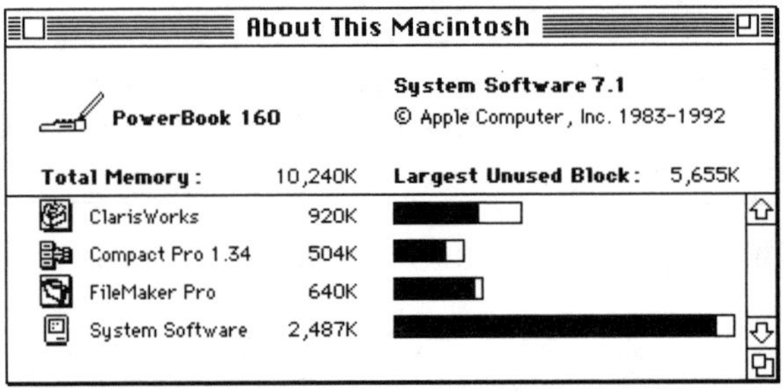

Figure 6.15 OptiMem in use.

One fact often missed when evaluating these products is that OptiMem and RAM Doubler can be used together. Although they are in the same class of programs, they use different approaches to allocating memory. The two programs should not be thought of as identical by any means.

$129 SRP
Jump Development Group
1228 Malvern Avenue
Pittsburgh, PA 15217
(412) 681-2692

Opening Your Mac to Install Upgrades

Opening the case of the Macintosh is required in almost every upgrade. A few of the newer models, such as the all-in-one LC series, provide a logic board accessible through a hatch located in the rear of the case. Through this hatch the logic board slides out and is easily serviced. Most models require opening the Macintosh case, however; and if access to the SIMM slots is blocked, you must also remove the hard drive, power supply, CD ROM, or floppy drive.

Before you upgrade a Mac, read this section for a few tips on opening the case and accessing inner parts of the computer. Keep in mind that recent design changes have resulted in a range of variations in case designs and logic board layouts. Familiarize yourself with the layout and case features of your Macintosh before proceeding.

Safety issues

Opening any piece of electronic equipment endangers the electronics and the repair person. Don't take any risks; follow basic safety guidelines. Garnishing an upgrade with unnecessary repairs is the last thing any Macintosh owner wants to do. The following steps will help you remove the case safely:

1. Shut down the computer gracefully (preferably by selecting Shutdown in the Special menu).

2. Turn off the computer and all devices connected to it.

3. Unplug the Macintosh from its main power connection (wall or surge suppresser) to eliminate any chance of connecting with the AC power. In some Macs, the AC plug is exposed in the back of the unit and can be grabbed or touched accidentally.

   While working on the Mac, it is important that you are at the same potential as the component on which you are working (see step 6). If a voltage potential exists between you and the Mac (or a circuit board), charge will flow from where it is concentrated to where it is depleted. This flow may create a spark, which can damage electronics.

4. Disconnect all devices connected to the Macintosh.

5. Place the computer on a clean anti-static work surface. Avoid wearing metal jewelry and clothing that collects static electricity. Carpeted floors should also be avoided.

6. Wear a wrist strap connected to the ground shield or plane of the chassis or circuit board to discharge static buildup. Touch the power supply case with one hand to dissipate excess charge if needed. Don't become disconnected from the Mac or circuit board while working on the unit or touch anything that might be charged, electrified, or at a different potential. If electric tools are to be used, select only those with grounded tips and contacts.

7. Handle the SIMMs and any other circuit boards by the edge. Avoid touching the metal contacts. Avoid the high voltage areas of the Mac or monitors. Areas and objects around the CRT, video section, and power supply should not be touched or probed.

Compact Macs (all-in-one designs)

Compact Macs include the Mac Plus, SE, SE/30, and Classic. To safely access the inside of these computers, follow the steps in this section.

1. Place the Mac face down on a work table. Open it by using a T-15 Torx driver with a long handle that can reach inside the hand hole at the top of the Mac. Remove the two screws inside the hand hole and any on the rear panel. (On the Mac Plus another screw is inside the battery hatch on the rear panel.)

2. Remove the programmers' switch from the side of the Macintosh.

3. Use a case cracker (or spreader) to loosen the case from around the front bezel. Work the spreader carefully and gently around the whole seam along the case to prevent cracking or marring the edge. If no case cracker is available, a wide, flat putty knife can often be substituted.

4. Remove the RF foil shielding from the base of the unit.

5. Wear an anti-static wrist strap and attach it to the metal chassis inside the case. If the Macintosh is a Mac Plus it may be necessary to discharge the CRT flyback transformer before attaching the wrist strap.

5a. For the Mac Plus: The CRT is discharged by attaching a 10 MB-ohm resistor to the tip of a screwdriver and attaching the other end to a ground connection. Ground one end of the resistor by attaching a long wire and clipping it to one end of the resistor and attach it to a ground point like the chassis. Poke the other end that is fixed to the end of the screwdriver under the suction cup where the flyback attaches to the monitor. Make sure you are not touching any metal and hold the screwdriver by the plastic handle. Make contact for about 60 seconds and the circuit should be discharged. Newer Macs from the SE on usually have a modified flyback transformer with an integrated dump resistor that discharges the CRT voltage after shutdown. Wait 30 seconds or so for this to work. Check the voltage with a meter if in doubt.

If you are not sure of this procedure, contact a service center for help. This part can be dangerous.

6. Remove all cables that connect the logic board to the analog board. The floppy drive and SCSI ribbon cables also need to be removed. It is often a good idea to remove the circular connector and wires at the rear of the picture tube too, in case the unit is bumped while working on it. A broken tube is an expensive repair.

Modular Macs

Most modular Macs are simple to open. There are at most several screws at the rear of the unit that have to be removed or loosened to free the lid. In most cases, one screw is all it takes; usually the lids lift right off. For the IIsi, retaining tabs secure the top onto the case; these have to be lifted slightly. In the IIvx and related models, one screw secures the top and the lid. Remove this screw then slide the lid forward a few inches and then up. In other cases like the Quadra 700, 800, and 900, a bit more disassembly is required to access the SIMM sockets. The removal of the hard drive bay and the logic board may be required to access the SIMM sockets in some modular Macintosh computers, such as the Quadra 800, 840AV, and Power Mac 7100, 8100, and 8500.

Mac Portable

The case of the Macintosh Portable is opened by pushing two release tabs at the rear of the unit and then lifting up. The Macintosh Portable does not use any screws to seal the case or to connect the motherboard to any other hardware component.

PowerBooks

Disassembly of a PowerBook depends on the model. For the **PowerBook 100**, follow these steps:

1. Remove the battery first.

2. Close the PowerBook (screen down) and lay it top down on a table.

3. Remove the screws and rubber tabs from the bottom of the case. Some screws can be removed with a Phillips screwdriver.

4. Flip the unit over and release the monitor fasteners before opening the case. The monitor should now be free and the keyboard should be accessible.

To open a **PowerBook 140, 145, 160, 165, 165c, 180, 180c, 520, 520c, 540, or 540c and Power Mac series PowerBooks,** follow these steps:

1. Remove the battery and close the unit.

2. Lay it top down.

3. Using T-8 and T-10 Torx drivers, remove the screws on the bottom and the lone screw under the rear flap near the internal modem port.

4. Separate the two pieces of the case carefully. Very delicate cables inside the case have to be disconnected gently. The case comes apart as a clam-shell fitting.

5. Flip the unit over so that the screen is up and open the case. Expert RAM installers do not have to completely remove the top of the PowerBook's case or disconnect the ribbon cables to install the RAM cards. If you separate the case about two inches, you should have enough room to install the RAM card.

Disassembly of the Duos is the same as PowerBooks except that after the screws are removed from the bottom of the case, flip the unit over and open the screen. The keyboard should be loose. Lift the keyboard up and fold over gently. The RAM card installs in the upper right corner inside the case.

Installing RAM

On the whole, the installation of extra RAM is a simple matter, once you know how to do it. Beginners may have some problems finding the correct SIMM or DIMM sockets and may confuse them with VRAM sockets common in the newer Macintosh. Additionally, seating the SIMM or DIMM correctly in the socket often presents a challenge.

Several models of SIMM sockets are available and in use at Apple for different models of Mac. The Mac Plus, for example, used an angled all-plastic socket in which the SIMMs are inserted straight up and then pushed back into the seated locked position. In contrast, the Mac II family has more head-room for SIMMs inside the case and uses a straight-up socket in which SIMMs are inserted at an angle to the socket and then folded up to lock into position at right angles to the logic board. Many Mac II models use the all-plastic sockets as well.

A common problem that occurs after installing SIMMs or DIMMs is they do not make adequate contact with the small fingers or pins that line the interior of the socket. A common practice among installers is to gently rock the SIMM or DIMM back and forth in the socket two or three times before locking it in place to help seat the SIMM or DIMM properly along its edge. Do not push or rock the SIMM or DIMM with great force, however; the metallic surface on the edge connector contacts can give way and ruin the SIMM or DIMM. One source of failure in less expensive SIMMs or DIMMs, even those installed properly, is from the metallic coating: one or more "fingers" will either oxidize or be "punched" through by the sharp contact in the SIMM socket. Additionally, the socket contacts can be bent and moved out of proper alignment, thereby ruining the socket.

When locking the SIMM or DIMM in place, guard against the SIMM or DIMM not seating all the way back in its socket. Make sure the SIMM or DIMM locks properly in place with the retaining clip or bails. Early SIMM sockets were entirely plastic and prone to loose or broken retaining clips. This was a major source of problems. If an old Mac is encountered with all-plastic SIMM sockets, move the bails very slowly and carefully away from the edge of the card when installing or removing SIMMs. Modern sockets have metal bails that definitely improve reliability.

A complete list of the memory specifications for Macintosh desktop computers is given in Table 6.7. Please consult this table for specific configurations and requirements. Other resources for installing memory, which are also free on most online services, are SIMM Stack 4.6 (or newer) and BMUG's SIMM Stack 1.0 (or newer). These are both Hypercard stacks that have detailed graphics of most Macintosh motherboard layouts with instructions on how and where to install the memory SIMM(s).

Compact Macs

Some simple rules should be followed when adding RAM in a compact Macintosh. Please consult Table 6.7 for information on where SIMM sockets are located and what possible upgrades are available:

- When filling a row of SIMM sockets, the row must be either completely full or empty. No partially filled rows are permitted.

- Rows must have the same SIMMs in each socket. No mismatching of values or speeds is permitted. All SIMMs in a row must be the same size (MB) and speed (ns).

- When in doubt as to where to place new SIMMs in a multi-socketed logic board, put the largest SIMMs in the first row or bank. You will usually be right.

Mac Plus

A stock Macintosh Plus comes with 1 MB of RAM—four 256K SIMMs. The maximum RAM for a Plus is 4 MB. When installing a memory upgrade in a Plus, the SIMM bank A must be filled first with the highest value SIMMs (see Figure 6.16). When installing 1 MB SIMMs in the Mac Plus, the sizing resistor must be clipped or desoldered and folded back to activate the use of the higher density SIMMs.

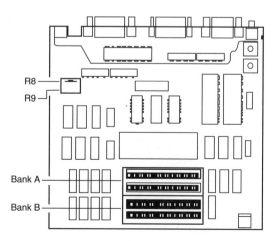

Figure 6.16 Notice the location of the SIMM sockets and sizing resistor on the Macintosh Plus logic board.

SE

The Macintosh SE computer can access a maximum of 4 MB of RAM from its logic board. The stock SE comes with 1 MB (four 256K SIMMs) installed in the four sockets. SIMM upgrades must be loaded into sockets 1 and 2 first; the highest values go first.

Early SEs were made with a logic board that had a sizing resistor similar to the one on the Mac Plus. Later units included a resizing clip or jumper onboard. Both designs are still in circulation.

Jumpered boards allow the unit to be upgraded to 1 MB, 2 MB, 2.5 MB, and 4 MB of RAM. Note that you must place the highest value SIMMs in socket positions 3 and 4 on this particular logic board. A 2.5 MB upgrade to a jumpered logic board will have two 1 MB SIMMs in sockets 3 and 4, and two 256K SIMMs in sockets 1 and 2. This orientation is exactly reverse for the resistor board.

Note

If the Macintosh SE logic board has a RAM size resistor, SIMM placement is exactly the reverse of that for the jumpered board.

To tell the Macintosh how much RAM is installed, you must either remove the RAM size jumper or clip the RAM size resistor on the logic board. It is a common practice to place the unused jumper clip on one of the header posts so that it will not be misplaced and can be used later if needed. Clip or desolder one leg of the sizing resistor and fold it out of the way so that it does not contact the circuit board. Some installers cover the lead with tape or heat-shrink tubing to insulate it (see Figure 6.17).

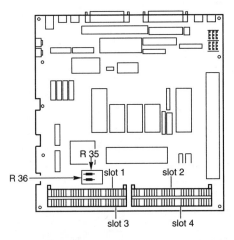

Figure 6.17 Make sure you know which kind of SE logic board you are upgrading. SIMM placement differs for the two boards.

SE/30

Although the SE/30 has eight SIMM sockets onboard, the stock unit comes with 1 MB built from four 256K SIMMs. Fully populated, the SE/30 can access 32 MB of RAM from its logic board.

The SIMM banks must be filled in groups of four with identical SIMMs (see Figure 6.18). Note that the SE/30 is one of the Macs that is not "32-bit clean" and thus requires MODE32 (System <7.1) or the 32-bit enabler (System 7.1) to access more than 8 MB of RAM.

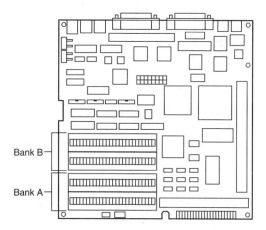

Bank B

Bank A

Figure 6.18 The SE/30 has eight SIMM sockets that must be upgraded in groups of four with matched SIMMs.

Classic

The maximum RAM for a Macintosh Classic is 4 MB. In addition to the 1 MB soldered on the logic board, the Classic provides a RAM card with two sockets that can take 2 MB of memory. The RAM expansion card has one 1 MB soldered onboard as well. A fully populated Classic has two 1 MB SIMMs installed in the expansion card's sockets, which totals 4 MB for the System. The Classic has a memory size jumper that has to be set when upgrades are added (see Figure 6.19).

Note

Macintosh Classics do not work well with the two-chip version of the 1 MB SIMMs. For this reason, the normal eight-chip SIMM is preferred in all Classic upgrades.

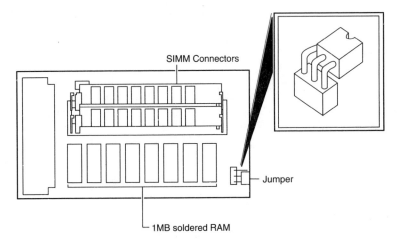

Figure 6.19 The Macintosh Classic uses a RAM expansion card and a sizing jumper to set installed memory.

Classic II

The Classic II can access a total of 10 MB of RAM when its two SIMM sockets are filled with 4 MB SIMMs. 2 MB of RAM is soldered on the logic board at the factory (see Figure 6.20).

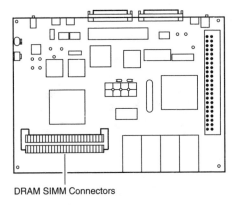

DRAM SIMM Connectors

Figure 6.20 The Macintosh Classic II has 2 MB onboard and two free sockets for expansion.

The Classic II is 32-bit clean so that no 32-bit enabler or MODE32 is required. Be sure to install SIMMs in both slots whenever an upgrade is undertaken.

Color Classic

The Macintosh Color Classic has two SIMM sockets and 4 MB hard-soldered on the logic board. The addition of two 4 MB SIMMs enables the System to use 10 MB of RAM (even though 12 MB is physically present). (See Figure 6.21.) When upgrading the Color Classic, fill the sockets equally and completely.

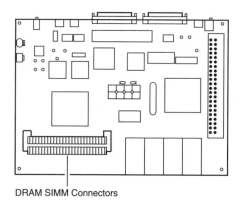

DRAM SIMM Connectors

Figure 6.21   Even though the Color Classic has 12 MB of RAM physically present in the System, it is ROM-locked to address only 10 MB of it.

In addition to the two SIMM sockets, there is an additional VRAM socket on the Color Classic's logic board. A 256K VRAM SIMM can be added to boost the VRAM to 512K. The Color Classic is a 32-bit clean Macintosh.

Mac TV

The Macintosh TV possesses a maximum of 8 MB of RAM and is not upgradeable.

Modular Macs

This section shows you how to add RAM to modular Macs. Use the diagrams to identify important features in each upgrade.

Mac II/IIx

The Macintosh II and IIx models are curious cases that require a special SIMM. Both models use a SIMM with a PAL chip onboard if the SIMMs are greater than 1 MB in size. Various configurations of stock machines were shipped from Apple, resulting in a number of different set-ups found in the field today (see Figure 6.22).

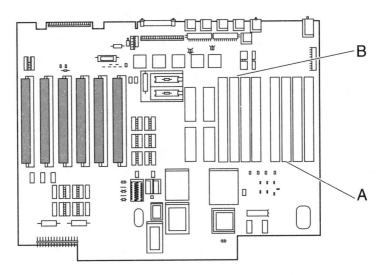

Figure 6.22 Several versions of the Macintosh II logic board exist. Pay close attention to the two banks A and B, which carry the larger SIMMs.

When upgrading the Macintosh II computers with SIMMs greater than 1 MB in size, a special Apple upgrade (M6051/C) is required. A kit is also required to upgrade the ROMs for an FDHD floppy.

A particular problem with the Macintosh II is that it will not accommodate 4 MB SIMMs in bank A of its logic board. The total RAM is thus limited to 20 MB. Furthermore, these Macs are not 32-bit clean, so that MODE32 or the 32-bit Enabler is required. In some cases a PMMU upgrade is required (for the 32-bit Enabler).

According to Apple, there are two different reasons that the Macintosh II and the Macintosh IIx can't support the higher density SIMMs:

- The Macintosh II ROM startup code doesn't understand 4 MB SIMMs and won't start up.

- The Macintosh IIx ROM does understand 4 MB SIMMs, but standard 4 MB SIMMs won't work on the Macintosh IIx. This is because the committee overseeing the standardization of new solid-state devices added an additional built-in test mode to high-density DRAMs after the IIx was developed. This test is invoked by a sequence of electrical signals that were ignored by earlier-generation DRAM. The result is that the current standard 4 MB SIMMs don't work on the Macintosh IIx.

Note

Special 4 MB SIMMs are available that have a PAL chip that you can use in the Macintosh II and IIx. Contact the SIMM vendor or manufacturer to see if they have these special SIMMs.

Mac LC

The Macintosh LC can be upgraded to a maximum 10 MB of RAM using two free SIMM sockets onboard with the 2 MB of RAM soldered to the logic board. Its maximum addressable memory is 10 MB even though the physical RAM is 12 MB (see Figure 6.23).

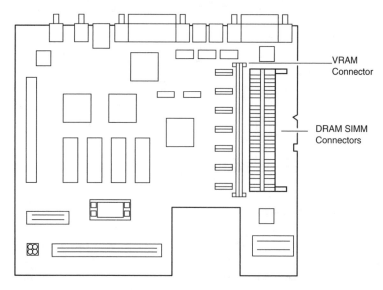

Figure 6.23 The LC can address only 10 MB of its 12 MB installed RAM.

Although no VRAM is provided from the factory, one VRAM socket is onboard that accepts 512K VRAM.

Mac LCII

The Macintosh LCII can be upgraded to a maximum 10 MB of RAM using two free SIMM sockets onboard and the 4 MB of RAM soldered to the logic board (see Figure 6.24). Its maximum addressable memory is 10 MB even though the physical RAM is 12 MB. The two SIMM sockets must be filled with identical SIMMs when upgrading the memory.

The LCII has one VRAM socket with 256K VRAM from the factory; there is no VRAM on the logic board. A VRAM upgrade to 512K is the maximum for this unit.

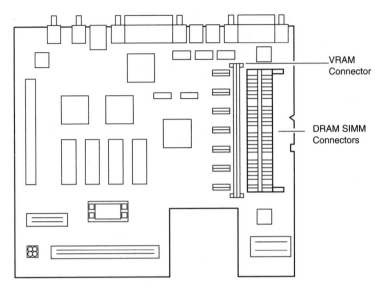

Figure 6.24 The LCII logic board has 4 MB onboard and two free SIMM sockets.

Mac LCIII

LCIII logic boards are available with 2 MB and 4 MB of onboard RAM. Only one SIMM socket exists, but the unit can be expanded to 36 MB (see Figure 6.25).

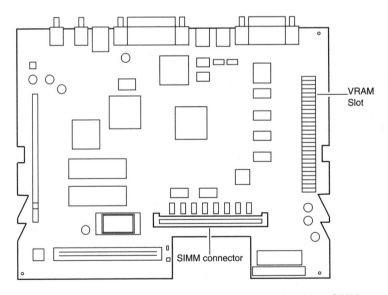

Figure 6.25 The LCIII can access 36 MB of RAM and requires 80 ns SIMMs.

As for VRAM, 512K is onboard and one empty socket is available. Maximum VRAM is 768K with the use of a 256K VRAM SIMM.

LC 475

The LC 475 comes with 4 MB soldered RAM and 1 SIMM socket. It can be expanded to 36 MB of RAM. 80 ns SIMMs are required (see Figure 6.26).

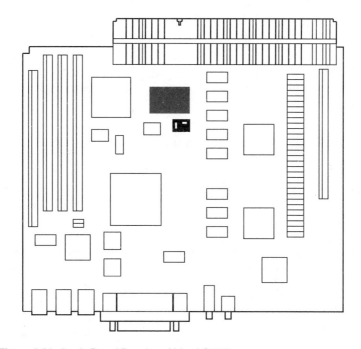

Figure 6.26   Logic Board Drawing of Mac LC 575.

Two VRAM sockets on the LC 475 logic board are capable of handling 1 MB of VRAM (two 512K SIMMs). The LC 475 comes from the factory with two 256K VRAM SIMMs installed. These must be removed to complete the VRAM upgrade.

Mac LC 575, LC 520, LC 550, LC 580, and Performa series models

The LC 575 and related models are based on the LC III. The LC 520 (see Figure 6.27) and 550 are also based on the LCIII.

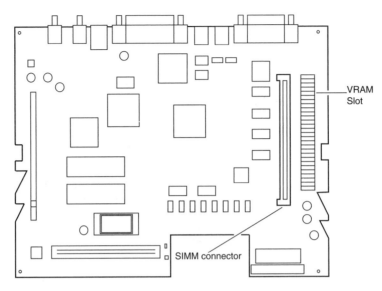

Figure 6.27 Logic Board Drawing of Mac LC520.

Mac IIsi

The Macintosh IIsi can access 17 MB of RAM using the 1 MB of onboard memory and the bank of four 30-pin SIMM sockets. When upgrading, all four sockets must be filled with identical SIMMs (see Figure 6.28). The IIsi uses a RAM-based video System and thus has no VRAM socket.

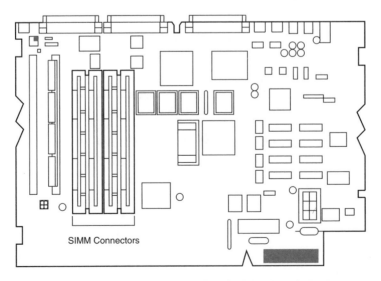

Figure 6.28 The Macintosh IIsi has four 30-pin SIMM sockets that can accommodate 16 MB of RAM. Populate all four sockets identically.

Mac IIcx

The Macintosh IIcx has no RAM installed on the logic board but has 8 SIMM sockets that can handle up to 32 MB (see Figure 6.29). The unit is not 32-bit clean, which means it requires MODE32 or the 32-bit Enabler to access more than 8 MB of RAM. The SIMMs must be loaded in groups of four in this Macintosh.

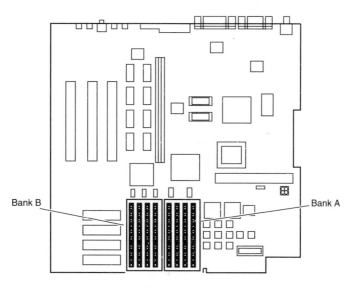

Figure 6.29   The Mac IIcx can be upgraded to 32 MB using the 8 SIMM sockets.

Mac IIci

Two versions of the Macintosh IIci logic board are in circulation. The one normally encountered does no parity checking of RAM. The second, rarer model was designed to do parity checking. The way to tell whether a logic board has parity checking enabled is to check for the parity chip located to the left of the SIMM sockets (see Figure 6.30). For the more common IIci, the pad is blank. If a chip is present, parity checking is enabled and nine chip SIMMs are required. Both IIci models accommodate the same amount of memory whether supporting a parity SIMM or not. SIMMs with the additional parity chip hold the same amount of memory as SIMMs without the parity chip.

In contrast to other Macs, add RAM to the bank A sockets last. All upgrades must be made in groups of four, one bank at a time. Like the Macintosh IIsi, the IIci uses a DRAM-based video buffer. The video is placed in the bank A SIMMs.

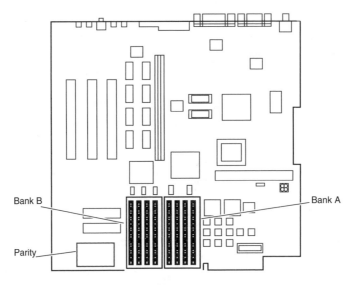

Figure 6.30 The IIci has two versions of the logic board for parity and non-parity RAM. Add SIMMs to bank B sockets first for best results.

Mac IIfx

The Mac IIfx is the oddest of the lot; it uses a special 64-pin SIMM not found in any other Macintosh (see Figure 6.31). The only other device that uses SIMMs resembling the IIfx is the LaserWriter NTX (although they are not the same speed).

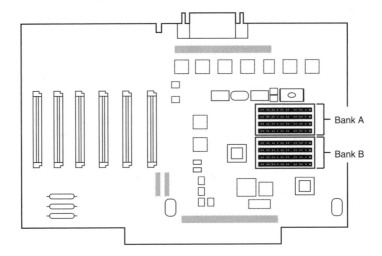

Figure 6.31 The Mac IIfx uses its own special 64-pin SIMM.

The IIfx has eight SIMM sockets and no RAM soldered onboard. Maximum RAM after expansion with 4 MB SIMMs is 32 MB. One of the major drawbacks of this system is that the RAM cannot be used in other Macs. Keep this in mind before investing heavily in an upgrade.

Mac IIvx

The Macintosh IIvx, and its companion IIvi, have 4 MB onboard RAM and four SIMM sockets. They take the older 30-pin SIMMs, accept 16 MB SIMMs, and can accommodate 68 MB of RAM. The maximum VRAM you can add to the IIvx is 1 MB—two 512K SIMMs in its two SIMM sockets (see Figure 6.32).

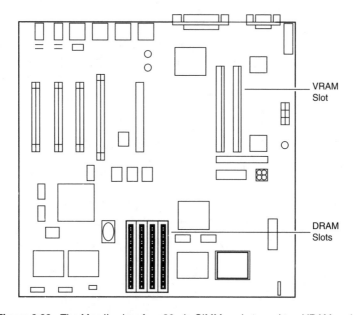

VRAM
Slot

DRAM
Slots

Figure 6.32 The Mac IIvx has four 30-pin SIMM sockets and two VRAM sockets.

Quadra 605

The low-cost Quadra 605 comes with 4 MB installed on the logic board and one 72-pin SIMM socket. It can accommodate a 32 MB SIMM (16 MB SIMMs are hard to find) for a maximum of 36 MB RAM. VRAM on the 605 is held by 2 SIMM sockets that can be upgraded to 1 MB of VRAM. The stock unit comes with two 256K SIMMs, or 512K of VRAM (see Figure 6.33).

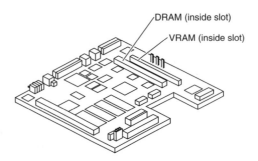

Figure 6.33   The Quadra 605 has 1 SIMM socket and 2 VRAM sockets.

Quadra/Centris 610

The Centris 610 has 4 MB soldered to the logic board and two SIMM sockets. Any supported SIMM size can go into any SIMM socket in any order. The SIMMs can be placed in partially populated banks as well (see Figure 6.34). 1 MB, 2 MB, and 64 MB SIMMs are not supported. Composite SIMMs do not work in the Q610. The two VRAM sockets in the Quadra 610 can hold up to 512K of VRAM.

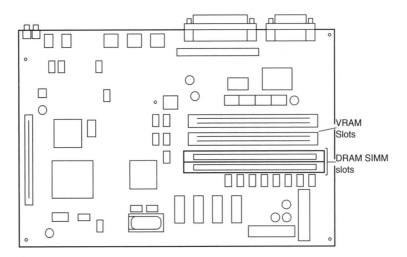

Figure 6.34   The Quadra 610 uses a flexible memory System that allows one SIMM to be installed at a time.

Quadra/Centris 650

The Centris 650 logic board is available in two versions from Apple. One has 4 MB onboard; the other, 8 MB. Because of the differences in factory RAM, the maximum RAM in these systems is 132 MB or 136 MB.

The Quadra 650 is based on the later Centris 650 set-up and has 8 MB onboard. The maximum RAM is 136 MB. Composite SIMMs are not recommended for the Quadra or Centris 650. The Centris and Quadra 650s permit SIMMs to be installed into the SIMM sockets in any order. Partially filled banks are acceptable. 1 MB, 2 MB, and 64 MB SIMMs are not supported in these Macs, however (see Figure 6.35).

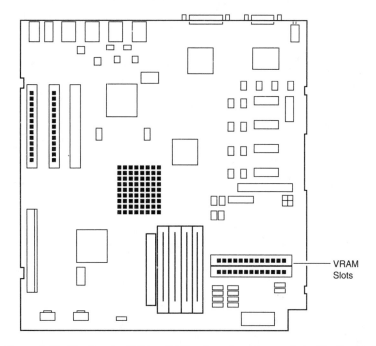

Figure 6.35 The Quadra 650 has 8 MB onboard and four sockets. The Centris 650 has either 4 MB or 8 MB onboard and four sockets.

The Centris and Quadra 650s employ a form of memory interleaving that accesses adjacent pairs of SIMMs concurrently to boost the performance of certain kinds of operations. The net benefit is around a 10 percent performance boost for common tasks.

Two VRAM sockets allow a maximum of 1 MB of VRAM to be added to a fully upgraded Quadra or Centris 650. Normally two 256K VRAM SIMMs are found in the 650s.

Quadra/Centris

The Quadra and Centris 660AVs use a special memory scheme that permits SIMMs to be installed in any socket in any order (see Figure 6.36); even partially filled banks are okay. One deficit is that they do not support 1 MB, 2 MB, or 64 MB SIMMs. Composite SIMMs are not recommended for these Macs.

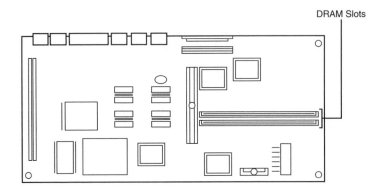

Figure 6.36   The 660AVs do not accept 1 MB, 2 MB, or 64 MB SIMMs, although SIMMs may be installed in any order in the sockets.

Both systems have 4 MB installed on the logic board and two SIMM sockets. The computers are 32-bit mode-only Macs, meaning that there is no option in the Memory control panel to enable 24-bit addressing. The Centris/Quadra has 1 MB of VRAM hard-soldered on the logic board and cannot be expanded.

Quadra 700

The Quadra 700 has four SIMM sockets and 4 MB installed on the logic board. Maximum RAM is 20 MB. 1 MB and 4 MB SIMMs are acceptable. The Quadra 700 uses 30-pin SIMMs and banks must be filled in groups of four, similar to the Quadra 900 and 950.

The Quadra 700 has six VRAM sockets that can hold up to 2 MB of VRAM. When upgrading the VRAM on a Quadra 700, fill the banks on the inside first and move outward (see Figure 6.37).

Quadra 800

The Quadra 800 uses a special memory scheme that permits SIMMs to be installed in any socket in any order (see Figure 6.38); even partially filled banks are okay. One deficit is that it does not support 1 MB, 2 MB, or 64 MB SIMMs. Composite SIMMs are not allowed in these Macs.

The Quadra 800 employs a form of memory interleaving that accesses adjacent pairs of SIMMs concurrently to boost the performance of certain kinds of operations. The net benefit is around a 10 percent performance boost for common tasks. The maximum VRAM is 1 MB—two VRAM sockets with 256K SIMMs.

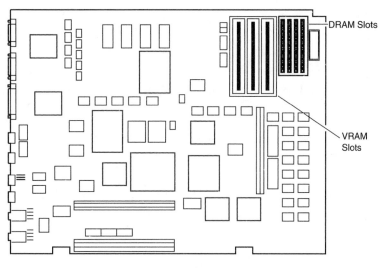

Figure 6.37 The Quadra 700 uses the 30-pin SIMMs. Fill the VRAM sockets from the inside outward when upgrading.

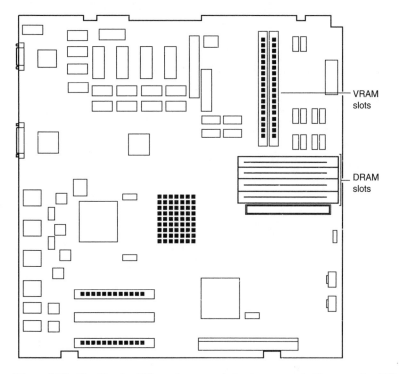

Figure 6.38 The Quadra 800 can be expanded using any socket in any order. Filling one socket or alternating sockets is OK.

Quadra 840AV

The Quadra 840AV uses a special memory scheme that permits SIMMs to be installed in any socket in any order; even partially filled banks are okay. One deficit is that it does not support 1 MB, 2 MB, or 64 MB SIMMs. In addition, no memory is provided on the logic board.

The Quadra 840AV employs a form of memory interleaving that accesses adjacent pairs of SIMMs concurrently to boost the performance of certain kinds of operations. The net benefit is around a 10 percent performance boost for common tasks. Composite SIMMs are not allowed in these Macs. A VRAM expansion of up to 2 MB is possible on the Quadra 840AV using the 1 MB onboard and the four VRAM sockets (see Figure 6.39).

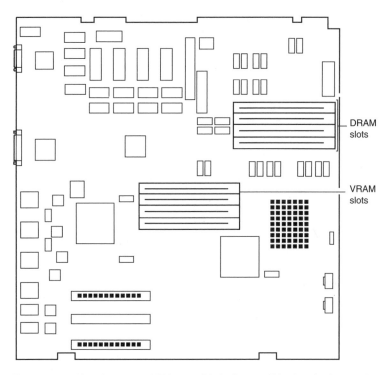

Figure 6.39 A maximum 128 MB is possible in the 840AV using the four sockets provided. 1 MB of VRAM can be added to the four VRAM sockets.

Quadra 900/950

The Quadra 900 and 950 have 16 SIMM sockets on their logic boards. There are four SIMM sockets per bank. Upgrades must fill a bank completely (see Figure 6.40). No memory is soldered on the logic board and the units accept 1 MB, 4 MB SIMMs, and 16 MB SIMMs. These Macs can accommodate up to 64 MB of RAM.

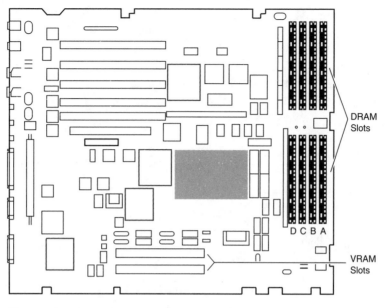

Figure 6.40 Upgrade the 900 and 950 in groups of 4 SIMMs per bank.

The VRAM can be upgraded by adding four 256K SIMMs. This brings the total VRAM to 2 MB.

Power Macintosh 6100/60 and 6100/66

The Power Mac architecture requires that SIMMs be installed in identical pairs in each pair of sockets. If this rule is not followed, the Mac will regard the slower (smaller) SIMM as equal to the faster (bigger), and crashes will result. The use of old SIMMs, like those from the Centris models, is compatible with the Power Macintosh 6100/60, but a matching pair is required for the upgrade.

Note

According to Apple:

Power Macintosh computers use dynamic random-access memory (DRAM) chips. The first 8 MB of RAM is soldered to the main logic board. You can expand the RAM with 72-pin SIMMs that are 80 ns or better (for example, 60 ns) in pairs of 4 MB, 8 MB, 16 MB, and 32 MB.

For example, you can install two 8 MB SIMMs or two 4 MB SIMMs in a 6100. SIMMs of the same size and speed must be installed together in adjacent slots. The 6100 has a total of two SIMM slots on its logic board.

The older Macs have a 32-bit wide memory system; the 72-pin SIMM is 32 bits wide. The Power Macintosh 6100/60 is a 64-bit wide memory system. For this reason, it requires two matching SIMMs (see Figure 6.41).

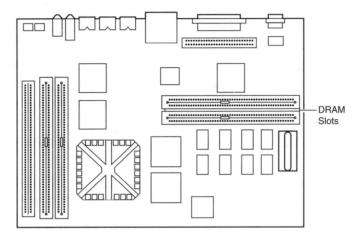

Figure 6.41 Notice that the Power Macs are 64-bit machines and their SIMMs are 32-bit.

If you only install one SIMM, the machine will boot but it will not use the memory because the full 64-bits are not there. The same conditions hold true for the 7100 and 8100 Power Macintosh models.

16-bit video on 14-inch monitors and 8-bit video on 16-inch monitors is achieved in the 6100/60 by the use of a DRAM-based video system that is not expandable.

Power Macintosh 7100/66 and 7100/80

The Power Mac architecture requires that SIMMs be installed in identical pairs in each pair of sockets. If this rule is not followed, the Mac regards the slower (smaller) SIMM as equal to the faster (bigger) SIMM and crashes result. RAM configurations for the 7100 are 8, 16, 24, 32, 40, 48, 72, 80, and 136 MB.

Note

According to Apple:

Power Macintosh computers use dynamic random-access memory (DRAM) chips. The first 8 MB of RAM is soldered to the main logic board. You can expand the RAM with 72-pin SIMMs that are 80 ns or better (for example, 60 ns) in pairs of 4 MB, 8 MB, 16 MB, and 32 MB.

For example, you can install two 8 MB SIMMs in the first two adjoining slots, an additional two 4 MB SIMMs may be added in the next two adjoining slots, and so on. SIMMs of the same size and speed must be installed together in adjacent slots, but you can install different size and speed SIMM pairs in the next adjacent slots.

The use of old SIMMs, like those from the Centris models, is compatible with the Power Macintosh 7100/66, but a matching pair is required for the upgrade. The older Macs have a 32-bit wide memory system; the 72-pin SIMM is 32 bits wide. The Power Macintosh 7100/66, though, is a 64-bit wide memory System. This requires two matching SIMMs for an upgrade (see Figure 6.42). If you only install one SIMM, the machine will boot but it will not use the memory because the full 64-bits are not there.

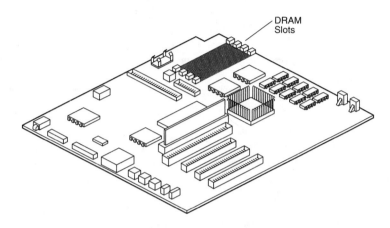

Figure 6.42 The 7100 uses a 64-bit System that requires pairs of 32-bit SIMMs for an upgrade.

The use of the PDS VRAM Expansion Card allows the 7100 to have a second video port with 1 MB of 32-bit VRAM. 2 MB of VRAM are possible in the 7100 if you add four SIMMs to the expansion card. SIMMs used in the 7100 VRAM expansion card have two chips onboard that store 128K × 8 bits of data.

Note

The two matched 32-bit SIMMs used in pairs in the Power Macintosh add their individual densities (MB) to yield the resulting installed memory value for the bank they are in. The sum of the banks constitutes the total installed upgrade. For instance, a Power Macintosh 8100 with four 32 MB SIMMs installed in two banks will have (32 MB + 32 MB) × 2 = 128 MB added to it in addition to its onboard RAM.

Power Macintosh 8100/80, 8100/100, and 8100/110

The Power Mac architecture requires that SIMMs be installed in identical pairs in each pair of sockets. If this rule is not followed, the Mac regards the slower (smaller) SIMM as equal to the faster (bigger) SIMM and crashes result.

Note

According to Apple:

Power Macintosh computers use dynamic random-access memory (DRAM) chips. The first 8 MB of RAM is soldered to the main logic board. You can expand the RAM with 72-pin SIMMs that are 80 ns or better (for example, 60 ns) in pairs of 4 MB, 8 MB, 16 MB, and 32 MB.

For example, you can install two 8 MB SIMMs in the first two adjoining slots, an additional two 4 MB SIMMs may be added in the next two adjoining slots, and so on. SIMMs of the same size and speed must be installed together in adjacent slots, but you can install different size and speed SIMM pairs in the next adjacent slots.

The use of old SIMMs, like those from the Centris models, is compatible with the Power Macintosh 8100/80, but a matching pair is required for the upgrade. The older Macs have a 32-bit wide memory system; the 72-pin SIMM is 32 bits wide. The Power Macintosh 8100/80, however, is a 64-bit wide memory system. This requires two matching SIMMs for an upgrade (see Figure 6.43). If you only install one SIMM, the machine will boot but it will not use the memory because the full 64 bits are not there.

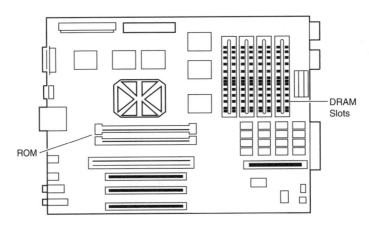

Figure 6.43   The 8100 uses a 64-bit System that requires pairs of 32-bit SIMMs for an upgrade.

Power Macintosh 9500, 8500, 7500, and 7200

The Power Mac architecture requires that DIMMs be installed on the motherboard. If no memory is installed on the motherboard, the Macintosh will not start up. There is no memory soldered to the motherboard. Possible RAM configurations in the 9500, 8500, 7500, and 7200 vary, but can be up to 768 MB. See Table 6.7 for a complete list.

Note

According to Apple:

Power Macintosh computers use dynamic random-access memory (DRAM) chips. No memory is soldered to the main logic board. You can expand the RAM on a 9500, 8500, 7500 or 7200 Mac with 168-pin DIMMs that are 70 ns or better (for example, 60 ns) one at a time or in pairs in increments of 4 MB, 8 MB, 16 MB, and 32 MB.

For example, you can install one 8 MB DIMM in the first slot, an additional 4 MB DIMM may be added in any other available DIMM slot. If you wish to take advantage of memory interleaving, two DIMMs of the same size and speed must be installed together in adjoining slots, but you can install different size and speed DIMMs in any order in any available DIMM slot.

The use of old SIMMs, like those from the Centris models, are NOT compatible with the Power Macintosh 9500, 8500, 7500, or 7200. The older Macs have a 32-bit wide memory System and a 32-bit wide 72-pin SIMM. The PCI Power Macintosh has a 64-bit wide memory system that only works with the 168-pin DIMMs.

Power Macintosh 5200/75 and 6200/75

These Power Mac models require that SIMMs be installed one at a time, not in pairs. Possible RAM configurations in the 5200/75 and 6200/75 are found in Table 6.7. The 5300 and 6300 series Power Macintosh computes follow the same memory rules as the 5200 and 6200 models. The main difference between the two models is that the 5300 and 6300 have a faster processor.

Note

According to Apple:

Power Macintosh computers use dynamic random-access memory (DRAM) chips. You can expand the RAM on a 5200, 5300, 6200, and 6300 with 72-pin SIMMs that are 70 ns or better (for example, 60 ns) one at a time or in pairs in increments of 4 MB, 8 MB, 16 MB, or 32 MB.

For example, you can install one 8 MB SIMM in the first slot. Then an additional 16 MB SIMM may be added in the next slot. If you have two SIMMs of the same size and speed they can be installed together and take advantage of memory interleaving between the two SIMMs.

The use of old SIMMs, like those from the Centris models, is compatible with the Power Macintosh 5200/75, 6200/75, 5300/100, and 6300/100 Macintosh computers.

PowerBook and Portable Mac RAM Configurations

Table 6.8 lists memory specifications for the Macintosh Portables, every PowerBook, and every Duo. Please consult this table for specific configurations and requirements before you upgrade the RAM in a Macintosh portable.

Table 6.8   Macintosh Portable/PowerBook RAM Configurations

Macintosh Model	Possible Expansion Card Sizes (Supported by Apple)	# of SIMM Slots	Min. RAM Speed	RAM Configuration	RAM Expansion Card
Macintosh Portables*	N/A—See below	2	100 ns	1 MB	Soldered to Motherboard
				2 MB to 8 or 9	Add either RAM and/or PDS Card
PowerBook 100	2 MB, 4 MB, 6 MB	1	100 ns	2 MB	Soldered to Motherboard
				4 MB	Add 2 MB Expansion Card
				6 MB	Add 4 MB Expansion Card
				8 MB	Add 6 MB Expansion Card
PowerBook 140, 145	2 MB, 4 MB, 6 MB	1	100 ns	2 MB	Soldered to Motherboard
				4 MB	Add 2 MB Expansion Card
				6 MB	Add 4 MB Expansion Card
				8 MB	Add 6 MB Expansion Card
PowerBook 145B	2 MB, 4 MB	1	100 ns	4 MB	Soldered to Motherboard
				4 MB 6 MB	Add 2 MB Expansion Card
				8 MB	Add 4 MB Expansion Card

Macintosh Model	Possible Expansion Card Sizes (Supported by Apple)	# of SIMM Slots	Min. RAM Speed	RAM Configuration	RAM Expansion Card
PowerBook 160[**]	2 MB, 4 MB, 6 MB, 8 MB, 10 MB	1	100 ns	4 MB	Soldered to Motherboard
				6 MB	Add 2 MB Expansion Card
				8 MB	Add 4 MB Expansion Card
				10 MB	Add 6 MB Expansion Card
				12 MB	Add 8 MB Expansion Card
				14 MB	Add 10 MB Expansion Card
PowerBook 165[***]	2 MB, 4 MB, 6 MB, 8 MB, 10 MB	1	100 ns	4 MB	Soldered to Motherboard
				6 MB	Add 2 MB Expansion Card
				8 MB	Add 4 MB Expansion Card
				10 MB	Add 6 MB Expansion Card
				12 MB	Add 8 MB Expansion Card
				14 MB	Add 10 MB Expansion Card
PowerBook 165c[****]	2 MB, 4 MB, 6 MB	1	85 ns	4 MB	Soldered to Motherboard
				6 MB	Add 2 MB Expansion Card
				8 MB	Add 4 MB Expansion Card

continues

Table 6.8   Macintosh Portable/PowerBook RAM Configurations, CONTINUED

Macintosh Model	Possible Expansion Card Sizes (Supported by Apple)	# of SIMM Slots	Min. RAM Speed	RAM Configuation	RAM Expansion Card
				10 MB	Add 6 MB Expansion Card
				12 MB	Add 8 MB Expansion Card
				14 MB	Add 10 MB Expansion Card
PowerBook 170	2 MB, 4 MB, 6 MB	1	100 ns	2 MB	Soldered to Motherboard
				4 MB	Add 2 MB Expansion Card
				6 MB	Add 4 MB Expansion Card
				8 MB	Add 6 MB Expansion Card
PowerBook 180	2 MB, 4 MB, 6 MB, 8 MB, 10 MB	1	85 ns	4 MB	Soldered to Motherboard
				6 MB	Add 2 MB Expansion Card
				8 MB	Add 4 MB Expansion Card
				10 MB	Add 6 MB Expansion Card
				12 MB	Add 8 MB Expansion Card
				14 MB	Add 10 MB Expansion Card

Macintosh Model	Possible Expansion Card Sizes (Supported by Apple)	# of SIMM Slots	Min. RAM Speed	RAM Configuation	RAM Expansion Card
PowerBook 180c	2 MB, 4 MB, 6 MB, 8 MB, 10 MB	1	85 ns	4 MB	Soldered to Motherboard
				4 MB	
				6 MB	Add 2 MB Expansion Card
				8 MB	Add 4 MB Expansion Card
				10 MB	Add 6 MB Expansion Card
				12 MB	Add 8 MB Expansion Card
				14 MB	Add 10 MB Expansion Card
PowerBk Duo 210	4 MB to 20 MB	1	70 ns	4 MB	Soldered to Motherboard
				8 MB	Add 4 MB Expansion Card
				12 MB	Add 8 MB Expansion Card
PowerBk Duo 230	4 MB	1	70 ns	4 MB	Soldered to Motherboard
				8 MB	Add 4 MB Expansion Card
				12 MB	Add 8 MB Expansion Card
PowerBk Duo 250	4 MB to 20 MB	1	70 ns	4 MB	Soldered to Motherboard
				8 MB	Add 4 MB Expansion Card
				12 MB	Add 8 MB Expansion Card

6

Table 6.8   Macintosh Portable/PowerBook RAM Configurations, CONTINUED

Macintosh Model	Possible Expansion Card Sizes (Supported by Apple)	# of SIMM Slots	Min. RAM Speed	RAM Configuration	RAM Expansion Card
PowerBk Duo 270c 280 280c	4 MB to 28 MB (36M for 280 models)	1	70 ns	4 MB	Soldered to Motherboard
				8 MB	Add 4 MB Expansion Card
				12 MB	Add 8 MB Expansion Card
				20 MB	Add 16 MB Expansion Card
				36 MB	Add 32 MB Expansion Card
PowerBook 540c 540 520c	8 MB, 12 MB, 20 MB, 32 MB	1	70 ns	4 MB	Soldered to Motherboard
				8 MB	Add 4 MB Expansion Card
				12 MB	Add 8 MB Expansion Card
				20 MB	Add 16 MB Expansion Card
				36 MB	Add 32 MB Expansion Card
PowerBook 5300ce/117 5300c/100 5300cs/100	32 MB to 64 MB or 8 MB to 64 MB	1	70 ns	8 or 16 MB	Soldered to Motherboard
				32 MB	Add 16 MB Expansion Card
				64 MB	Add 32 MB Expansion Card

Macintosh Model	Possible Expansion Card Sizes (Supported by Apple)	# of SIMM Slots	Min. RAM Speed	RAM Configuration	RAM Expansion Card
PowerBk Duo 2300c/100	8 MB to 56 MB	1	70 ns	4 MB	Soldered to Motherboard
				16 MB	Add 8 MB Expansion Card
				20 MB	Add 16 MB Expansion Card
				40 MB	Add 32 MB Expansion Card
PowerBk 190cs/66 190/66	4 or 8 MB to 40 MB	1	70 ns	4 MB	Soldered to Motherboard
				32 MB	Add 32 MB Expansion Card (with 8 MB on motherboard)
				40 MB	Add 32 MB Expansion Card (with 8 MB on motherboard)
PowerBook 150	4 MB, 8 MB, 20 MB, 36 MB	1	70 ns	4 MB	Soldered to Motherboard
				8 MB	Add 4 MB Expansion Card
				20 MB	Add 16 MB Expansion Card
				36 MB	Add 32 MB Expansion Card

* *The Macintosh Portables have 1 MB of RAM soldered to the main logic board. The original Portable uses Static RAM and the Backlit uses Pseudo-Static RAM. Additional RAM can be added with an expansion card that is placed in the RAM slot or PDS slot. These expansion cards can have from 1 to 4 MB of RAM.*

** *The PowerBook 160 will access more than 8 MB of memory by using System 7 in 32-bit mode.*

*** *The PowerBook 165 will access more than 8 MB of memory by using System 7 in 32-bit mode.*

continues

Table 6.8   Macintosh Portable/PowerBook RAM Configurations, CONTINUED

**** The PowerBook 165c will access more than 8 MB of memory by using System 7 in 32-bit mode. Memory Expansion Cards larger than 4 MB must have 85 ns fast RAM. 4 MB cards can use 100 ns RAM.

^ The PowerBook 180 will access more than 8 MB of memory by using System 7 in 32-bit mode. Memory Expansion Cards larger than 4 MB must have 85 ns fast RAM. 4 MB cards can use 100 ns RAM.

^^ The PowerBook 180c will access more than 8 MB of memory by using System 7 in 32-bit mode. Memory Expansion Cards larger than 4 MB must have 85 ns fast RAM. 4 MB cards can use 100 ns RAM.

^^^ The PowerBook Duo 210 will access more than 8 MB of memory by using System 7 in 32-bit mode. The PowerBook Duo 210's memory can be expanded to 24 MB by adding a memory expansion card. The 8 and 12 MB configurations are shown as examples.

^^^^ The PowerBook Duo 230 will access more than 8 MB of memory by using System 7 in 32-bit mode. The PowerBook Duo 230's memory can be expanded to 24 MB by adding a memory expansion card. The 8 and 12 MB configurations are shown as examples.

¯ The PowerBook Duo 250 will access more than 8 MB of memory by using System 7 in 32-bit mode. The PowerBook Duo 250's memory can be expanded to 24 MB by adding a memory expansion card. The 8 and 12 MB configurations are shown as examples.

¯¯ The PowerBook Duo 270c will access more than 8 MB of memory by using System 7 in 32-bit mode. The PowerBook Duo 270c's memory can be expanded to 32 MB by adding a memory expansion card. The 8 and 12 MB configurations are shown as examples.

Macintosh Portable

By adding an additional static RAM card to the original Portable, 9 MB is available on this Macintosh. 1 MB is soldered on the logic board, and the pseudo-static RAM card can accept 8 MB. This unit does not have 32-bit clean ROMs (see Figure 6.44).

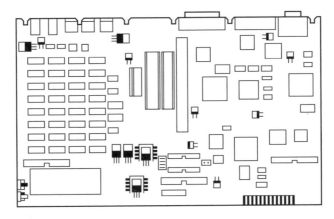

Figure 6.44   Note that the original Portable and Backlit Portable have different memory specifications for upgrades.

PowerBook 100

The PowerBook 100 can be expanded to 8 MB of RAM by adding an additional 6 MB to the logic board (see Figure 6.45).

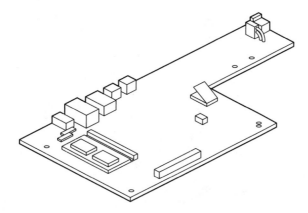

Figure 6.45   The PowerBook 100 takes a RAM module that plugs directly into the circuit board.

PowerBook 140/145/145B

The PowerBooks 140, 145, and 145B can be expanded to 8 MB with the addition of a RAM card. The 140 and 145 both come with 2 MB soldered on the logic board. The 145B has 4 MB onboard (see Figure 6.46).

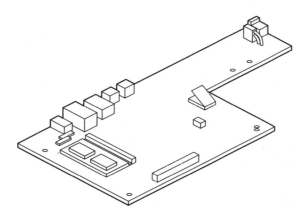

Figure 6.46   Note the position of the RAM expansion header on the circuit board. Check that the connector fit is tight and that the RAM card is parallel to the circuit board.

PowerBook 170

The PowerBook 170 comes with 2 MB on the logic board and can be expanded to 8 MB with the addition of a RAM card (see Figure 6.47).

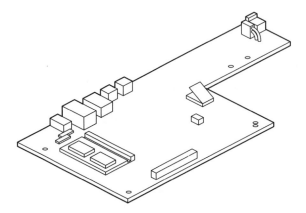

Figure 6.47   Note the position of the RAM expansion header on the circuit board. Check that the connector fit is tight and that the RAM card is parallel to the circuit board.

PowerBook 160/165/180

The PowerBooks 160, 165, and 180 all come with 4 MB soldered to the logic board. A maximum of 14 MB is possible with the addition of a RAM card. The memory card connector is polarized with a key-notch. Do not force the card onto the daughter board; it goes in only one way (see Figure 6.48).

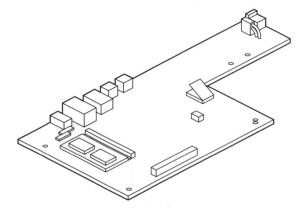

Figure 6.48   Note the position of the RAM expansion header on the circuit board. Do not remove the thermally conductive pads on some of the ICs in the area during the memory upgrade.

Avoid using RAM cards rated at more than 85 ns. The slow memory will add wait states to the System and penalize performance by 10 percent.

PowerBook 165c/180c

The PowerBooks 165c and 180c come with 4 MB soldered to the logic board. A maximum of 14 MB is possible in these models with the addition of an extra RAM card. The memory card connector is polarized with a key-notch. Do not force the card onto the daughter board; it goes in only one way (see Figure 6.49).

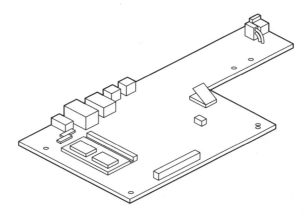

Figure 6.49   Note the position of the RAM expansion header on the circuit board. Do not remove the thermally conductive pads on some of the ICs in the area during the memory upgrade.

Avoid using RAM cards rated at more than 85 ns. The slow memory will add wait states to the System and penalize performance by 10 percent.

Duo 210/230

The Duos 210 and 230 come with 4 MB hard-soldered on their logic boards. Both can be expanded to 24 MB using extra RAM cards (see Figure 6.50).

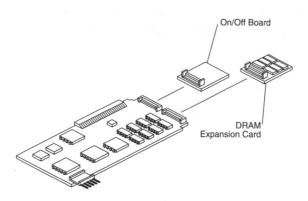

On/Off Board

DRAM
Expansion Card

Figure 6.50   Note the position of the RAM expansion header on the circuit board. The header for the internal modem may be confused with the RAM connector.

Duo 250/270c/280/280c

These Duos have 4 MB soldered to their logic boards. Extra RAM can be added by using an expansion RAM card. The maximum RAM card size for the 250 is 24 MB; for the 270c it is 32 MB; and for the 280 and 280c it is 40 MB (see Figure 6.51).

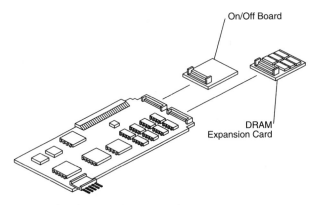

Figure 6.51   Note the position of the RAM expansion header on the circuit board. The header for the internal modem may be confused with the RAM connector.

VRAM

Table 6.9 lists Macintosh VRAM configurations and specifications. Consult this table when you need information on the sizes of VRAM SIMMs, the number of SIMM sockets, VRAM configurations, and compatible upgrades for desktop Macintosh Systems. PCI Power Macs accept VRAM DIMMs that are 32-bit wide, 112 pin fast page mode, and are 70 ns or faster (for example, 60 ns).

Table 6.9   Macintosh VRAM Specifications

Macintosh Model	Onboard (Soldered) VRAM	VRAM SIMM Sizes	# of SIMM Slots	Min. VRAM Speed	VRAM Configuration	Added VRAM # of SIMMs × Size
MODULAR MACS WITH VRAM-BASED VIDEO						
Macintosh Color Classic	256K	256K	1	100 ns	256K / 512K	n/a / 1 × 256K
Macintosh LC	0K	256K, 512K	1	100ns	256K / 1 × 512K	1 × 256K / 512K
Macintosh LCII, Performa 400, 405, 410, 430	0K	256K, 512K	1	100 ns	256K / 512K	1 × 256K / 1 × 512K

Macintosh Model	Onboard (Soldered) VRAM	VRAM SIMM Sizes	# of SIMM Slots	Min. VRAM Speed	VRAM Configuration	Added VRAM # of SIMMs × Size
Macintosh LCIII Performa 450	512K	256K, 512K	1	100 ns	512K 768K	n/a 1 × 256K
Performa 460, 466, 467	512K	256K, 512K	1	100 ns	512K 768K	n/a 1 × 256K
Macintosh LC 475 Performa 475, 476 Quadra 605	0K	256K, 512K	2	80 ns	512K 1 MB	2 × 256K 2 × 512K
Macintosh LC 520 Performa 550	512K	256K	1	80 ns	768K	1 × 256K
Macintosh TV	512K	n/a	0	0	512K	n/a
Macintosh IIvx Performa 600	0K	256K, 512K	2	100 ns	512K 1 MB	2 × 256K 2 × 512K
Centris 610 Quadra 610	512K	256K	2	80 ns	512K 1 MB	n/a 2 × 256K
Centris 650 Quadra 650	512K	256K	2	80 ns	512K 1 MB	n/a 2 × 256K
Centris Quadra	1 MB	n/a	0	n/a	1 MB	n/a
Quadra 700*	512K	256K, 512K*	6	80 ns	512K 1 MB 2 MB	n/a 2 × 256K or 512K 6 × 256K or 512K
Quadra 800	512K	256K	2	80 ns	512K 1 MB	n/a 2 × 256K
Quadra 840AV	1 MB	256K	4	80 ns	1 MB 2 MB	n/a 4 × 256K
Quadra 900, 950*	1 MB	256K, 512K*	4	80 ns	1 MB 2 MB	n/a 4 × 256K or 512K
Power Mac 8500 and 7500	2	1 MB, 2 MB	2	70 ns	2 MB	2 × 2 MB
Power Mac 7200	1	1 MB, 2 MB, 4 MB	2	70 ns	1 MB 2 MB	2 × 1 MB 2 × 2 MB
Macintosh Duo Dock	512K	512K	1	100 ns	512K 1 MB	n/a 1 × 512K

* *You can use 512K VRAM SIMMs, but the CPU will only recognize them as 256K SIMMs.*

continues

Table 6.9 Macintosh VRAM Specifications, CONTINUED

MODULAR MACS THAT USE DRAM-BASED VIDEO

Macintosh IIci
Macintosh IIsi

NUBUS MACS WITH NO VRAM ONBOARD

Macintosh SE/30
Macintosh II
Macintosh IIx
Macintosh IIcx
Macintosh IIfx

COMPACT MACS THAT USE DRAM-BASED VIDEO

Macintosh PlusMacintosh SE
Macintosh Classic
Performa 200
Macintosh Classic II

Hard Drive Replacement

The biggest mistake you can when installing a hard drive is failing to back up your existing drive before the installation. Use whatever media is available; obviously, the bigger the drive, the less likely you'll want to use floppy disks. Before you start playing with any magnetic media, be careful to ground yourself by touching the Mac's metal power supply housing (this only works if the Mac is plugged in) or by using an anti-static wrist strap that clips to a grounded metal source. This section contains general steps you can follow to replace your internal hard drive in your Macintosh computer.

Removing and replacing the drive

The internal hard disk is easily recognizable in a Macintosh; separate power and SCSI cables are plugged into it. Like the floppy mechanisms, the hard disk is a rectangular device with threaded screw holes on its bottom or sides that allow it to be secured to a universal bracket. The bracket fits into the Macintosh computer's chassis. To remove the drive, follow these simple steps:

1. Locate the tabs you must release. Different Macs have different clips; for instance, the 840AV and Power Mac 8100 have a plastic sliding clip allowing front removal of the drive by holding a large tab down and sliding the drive out (see Figure 6.52). The IIci/IIcx, Power Mac 7100, 6100, and Quadra 700 have an aluminum clip that snaps down into the chassis; the Quadra 900/950 has a sled that fits into a tongue and groove and is secured with a screw.

Figure 6.52 In the Quadra 840AV, press the clip and slide the drive forward.

2. After you find the release tabs, unplug the power to the hard drive (the inch-long, 4-pin white plastic connector) and then the SCSI connector (the long, thin gray ribbon cable). Pull both gently from their edges until the cables are free (see Figure 6.53). Do not use a screwdriver or other instrument to dislodge the SCSI cable unless you have to; if so, be extremely careful. The pins on the drive bend easily, and though they are made of soft, pliable metal, getting them straight again can be unbelievably frustrating.

Figure 6.53 Remove the cabling *before* removing the drive from the bay.

3. When the SCSI and power cables are free, unplug the indicator-light cable (the one that runs to the small green/red LED on the front of the Mac) from the front of the drive.

4. After these wires are unplugged, the drive can be removed by unseating it from the Mac's housing using the provided tabs or clip on the bracket. The metal bracket can then be removed by unscrewing it from the bottom of the drive. You can then reuse this bracket with the new internal hard drive.

5. Install the new drive by reversing this process, but not before you check that the SCSI ID number is set to "0" (if this is your primary drive). Attach the bracket from the previous drive and clip it back into the Mac where the old one was (the tabs will "click" when the drive is seated correctly). Make sure that it is seated facing the same direction as the previous drive.

6. Plug the SCSI, power, and indicator cables back into the new drive, being careful not to force anything. Remember that the plugs are "fitted"—if you are forcing them, they are probably upside down.

If the old hard drive still works, it can be used in an external case or housing for more storage. If you're considering selling the old drive, you'll find that even the most antiquated hard drives get snapped up quickly at the right price—most people will sacrifice speed in lieu of a good price per megabyte on a drive.

Adding Internal CD-ROM Drives

Nearly all the new Macs support the use of an internal CD-ROM drive. If you are buying an internal CD-ROM mechanism to put into your Mac, ask the dealer for the correct mounting kit. This kit will include the proper mounting clip, front bezel, and length cables.

Internal CD-ROM Capable Macs:

- Mac IIVX/Performa 600

- Quadra/Centris 610/650

- Quadra 800/840AV

- Quadra 900/950

- All Power Macs

Location and installation

CD-ROM mechanisms install the same as internal hard disks—brackets, SCSI, and power cables. The only difference is popping the Mac's solid bezel and sticking the new plastic CD bezel onto the front of the Mac (with the slot allowing CDs to be inserted). You will want to set the SCSI ID number for the CD-ROM drive to something other than "0"—which is reserved for the internal drive. Apple sets its pre-installed, internal CD-ROM players to SCSI ID 3. Remember not to set the ID number to that of any other existing SCSI device you have on the line; it will confuse the SCSI line and possibly hang the Mac during startup. This won't damage the Mac or the drive, but is a hassle.

Video

Video cards are made with NuBus, PDS, or PCI connectors. These cards can be added to a Macintosh to support a first, second, or third monitor display or can be used to input and output video. Some video cards also have accelerators on them, or work in tandem with a second NuBus or PCI card to provide acceleration.

Macintosh video is a complicated subsystem of the Mac that involves technical complexities with the monitor in addition to video-specific hardware and software. These issues are as intricate as the Macintosh ROMs themselves, which are highly complex chips that you cannot alter. Nevertheless, there are a number of ways to improve video performance and add new capabilities to your Mac.

This section reviews Macintosh monitor upgrades, discusses how a Macintosh draws a picture onscreen, shows you what QuickDraw is, what video standards apply to Macintosh systems, and discusses how you can adapt Macintosh systems to other (foreign) video display systems like VGA monitors and NTSC video monitors and projection systems.

How Macintosh video differs from VGA, CGA, and EGA

The Macintosh handles color differently from CGA (Color Graphics Array), VGA (Video Graphics Array), EGA (Enhanced Graphics Array) color displays. For this reason, you cannot always use PC-type displays on Macs. Nevertheless, later in this section you can read about the wiring and adapter changes you can make to drive a PC-display from a Macintosh.

CGA

CGA (color graphic adapter, color graphics array) is the earliest standard for IBM-type computers. Capable of displaying only four colors at a time from a palette of 16, the maximum resolution of the display is 640 × 200.

PGC

The PGC (professional graphics card) standard was the second to emerge for PCs. It can draw 256 out of 4,096 colors, and provides a screen resolution of 640 × 480. PGC died out when EGA emerged at a better price/performance ratio.

EGA

The EGA (enhanced graphics array) standard can paint 16 colors out of a total of 64, at a resolution of 640 × 480.

VGA

VGA (video graphics array) displays color in three possible modes: two colors at 640 × 480, 16 colors at 640 × 480; and 256 colors at 320 × 200. Total palette size for the 16-color and 256-color modes is 262 and 144 colors.

MS-DOS Color

All the PC video standards often require that different video drivers be used for different applications running on a computer. Five different PCs running five different video cards might require five different drivers to run the same application. There is also no guarantee that monitor resolutions will be the same either. Consistency is not a hallmark of the PC hardware marketplace.

Compatibility issues must also be addressed when a card in one Mac is relocated to another Macintosh computer with a different version of the operating System (for example, 7.1 versus 7.5). Some cards may need to have the ROM on the card upgraded in order to be compatible with a specific version of system software and Mac model. The software installation for the card must be repeated and the driver software may need to be upgraded.

Macintosh color

Macintosh video was designed to provide more consistency, even when changing from monochrome display systems to 24-bit color. Video card developers do not need to adapt to the application because QuickDraw serves as the liaison between the software and hardware. Video drivers as such are unknown in the Macintosh System.

Geometrically all Macintosh displays are approximately 72 pixels per inch. The differences, if any, are small across product lines. This provides one type of constant for Macintosh displays. This has helped in WYSIWYG applications such as typography and graphics, where reproduction and comparison of an image across different workstations is important and must be made identical, if possible. A one-inch by one-inch grid displayed on a Mac Plus should be the same on a Quadra 840AV.

Because QuickDraw is used as the reference for drawing images to the Macintosh screen, the manufacturer of the video card does not affect the geometry of the image. With 32-bit QuickDraw, the Macintosh can display photo-realistic images as a built-in feature.

Macintosh monitors and MS-DOS PCs

Most video cards designed for PC computers will not work with an Apple CPU or RGB monitor. DOS computers use different timing than Apple systems. RGB Apple monitors are locked into specific scan rates that cannot be changed. PCI video cards with Macintosh software drivers will work with Macs, and will most likely have PC equivalents on the market. Apple's multisync monitors, including AV monitors, are designed to work with both Macintosh and Windows PCs.

Macintosh and VGA monitors

It is not uncommon for budget-conscious Macintosh owners to use a VGA monitor on their systems. Most modern Macs can accommodate the VGA monitor. The following Macs can drive the VGA monitor:

LC	Quadra 900
LCII	Quadra 950
LCIII	Quadra 840AV
IIvx	PowerBook 160
Centris 610	PowerBook 165c
Centris 650	PowerBook 180
Centris	PowerBook 180c
Quadra 700	PowerBook Duo 210 & 230 (with MiniDock or Duo Dock)
Quadra 800	

To connect a VGA monitor to the Macintosh, an adapter (cable) is required. Third-party cable vendors and most monitor manufacturers sell these cables. Skilled electronics technicians can even construct their own.

If the monitor is a VGA type, try the following cable pin-outs (see Table 6.10). This common adapter can be used to connect VGA monitors to Macintosh computers. A cable wired as follows might be able to connect many different brands of VGA monitors to a Macintosh Quadra. Test the monitor on the Quadra prior to purchase.

Table 6.10   Typical VGA-to-Mac Adapter

Macintosh Video DB-15	VGA Connector
2 ---------------- Red Video --------- 1	
1 ---------------- Red Ground -------- 6	
9 ---------------- Blue Video -------- 3	
13 ---------------- Blue Ground ------- 8	
5 ---------------- Green Video -------- 2	
6 ---------------- Green Ground ------ 7	
15 ---------------- Hsynch ----------- 13	
12 ---------------- Vsynch ----------- 14	
14 ---------------- Sync Ground ------- 10	
10 ------------- ⌐ Connect 7 and 10 so the sense pin ID	
7 ------------- ⌐ will equal VGA	

VGA monitors from different manufacturers may work differently on the same Macintosh. These monitors have different image quality specifications, which become apparent when placed next to an Apple monitor. Try to compare monitors side by side before deciding which monitor to use. Note that a VGA monitor provides a resolution of 640 × 480. The number of colors supported depends on the amount of VRAM installed in the Macintosh.

Connecting a VGA Monitor to a Macintosh LC-class computer

The Macintosh LC series supports some VGA monitors. There are many different modes/ types of VGA timing, however. The following specifications show the VGA characteristics supported by the Macintosh LC class machines.

Screen/Video Parameter		Timing
Dot clock	=	25.175 MHz
Dot	=	39.722 nsec
Full line	=	31.778 usec
Line rate	=	31.469 KHz
Full frame	=	16.68 msec
Frame rate	=	59.94 Hz

The wiring diagram for the LC-VGA adapter is shown in the following mini-table. To signal that a VGA monitor is connected, connect pins 7 and 10 together. The wiring of the LC always has ID bit 2. Thus, ID# 3 will be grounded, too, and the signal for the VGA monitor will be set.

Macintosh LC Connector
DB-15   *VGA*

```
 2 - - - - - - - - - - - - - - Red Video - - - - - - - - - -  1
 1 - - - - - - - - - - - - - - Red Ground - - - - - - - - -  6
 9 - - - - - - - - - - - - - - Blue Video - - - - - - - - -  3
13 - - - - - - - - - - - - - - Blue Ground  - - - - - - -  8
 5 - - - - - - - - - - - - - - Green Video - - - - - - - -  2
 6 - - - - - - - - - - - - - - Green Ground - - - - - -  7
15 - - - - - - - - - - - - - - Hsynch - - - - - - - - - -13
12 - - - - - - - - - - - - - - Vsynch - - - - - - - - - -14
14 - - - - - - - - - - - - - - Sync Ground - - - - - - -10
10 - - - - - - - - - - - - - -⌐ Connect 7 and 10 so the sense pin ID
 7 - - - - - - - - - - - - - -⌐ will equal VGA
```

The number of colors displayed depends on the amount of VRAM in the LC. Sixteen colors will be displayed with 256K of VRAM. 256 colors can be displayed if 512K of VRAM is installed on the motherboard.

Macintosh Video Overview

A number of video signal standards exist in the video world. Macintosh computers are often interfaced with video devices and peripherals manufactured to these standards. This section discusses these video standards and methods you can use to connect Macs to video devices.

RS-343

The video system designed for Macintosh computers is a variant of the RS-343 standard video signal. The standard RS-343 signal uses a monochrome signal combined with a horizontal and vertical scan control signal. Timing is set for a non-interlaced display that can accommodate a high resolution video display and signal.

According to Apple, the major differences between Macintosh video and the RS-343 standard are:

- Pin three (3) has a separate TTL-level sync signal.

- Separate video lines are used to produce RGB color.

- The vertical scan rate is changed to 66.67 Hz to reduce screen flicker.

- Red and blue signals have a voltage white level of 1 volt; green is 1.3 volts.

Pin 5 on the video connector has the "green signal," which is an analog composite sync. This signal permits the use of a monochrome composite video signal.

RS-170 and NTSC Video

Although largely untrue, RS-170 is still regarded by many as the broadcast standard video signal for North America. RS-170 originated in 1957 as the standard for black-and-white television but has since been left behind as a broadcast standard because of more recent developments. The Macintosh can generate a signal close to true RS-170 but still has minor deviations. The signal generated by the Mac can be displayed on RS-170 monitors but the slightest deviations can cause problems in some video equipment.

It is important to note that NTSC is an outgrowth of RS-170 video. NTSC is the result of combining three RS-170 signals into one encoded color signal. Thus, while largely compatible with NTSC equipment, RS-170 should not be equated with broadcast quality video. Failure to discern this will lead to difficulties in choosing the right equipment.

NTSC and RS-170 Timing Signals

The video standard RS-170 is used in the U.S., Japan, and several other countries for common video distribution. The RS-170 display is based on a 15.75 KHz horizontal and 60 Hz vertical interlaced scan. The RS-170 video frame has 525 lines and is updated 60 times per second. Table 6.11 lists this standard's timing specifications. Because it is interlaced, the even or odd lines are painted to the screen in separate passes. RS-170, like RS-343, is based on the timing of monochrome signals. Color is handled in these systems by combining three signals, each representing red, blue, or green, onto a single signal line. Table 6.12 lists signal values for RS-170.

Table 6.11 Video Timing and Display Specifications for RS-170	
Video Parameter	*RS-170/343 Specified Value*
HORIZONTAL SYNC	
Frequency	35 KHz
Period	1/35 KHz = 28.5714 microseconds
Back Porch	96 dots
Front Porch	64 dots
Sync	64 dots
Active video	640 dots
Blanking	224 dots (back porch + front porch + sync)
Pixel Clock	30.24 MHz (one dot = 1/30.24 MHz = 33.06878 ns)
VERTICAL SYNC	
Frequency	66.67 Hz
Back Porch	39 horizontal scan lines
Front Porch	3 lines
Sync	3 lines
Active	480 lines
Total	525 lines = 15 milliseconds

Lines are derived from 1/ Scan rate = 1/ 35 KHz = 28.5714 microseconds.

Table 6.12 RS-170 Signal Specifications	
Video Parameter	*RS-170/343 Specified Value*
Vertical Even Field Blanked Lines	45 Lines
Video Rise and Fall Times Approx.	5–6 Ns
Video Signal Black Level	0 Volts
Video Signal Green+Csync Black Level	0.3 Volts
Video Signal White Level	1 Volt

If tested at the connector without the 75-ohm terminating resistor in a monitor, the signals should appear to range 0–3 volts.
The signals are for non-interlaced RS-343 video as used in the Apple High Resolution video monitor. Notice that the CSYNC signal does not comply with the RS-343 standard and is a TTL signal.
There are six additional video signals on the connector J3 on the Apple Macintosh video card. J3 is a bank of 14 holes located at the top of the card near the video port.

The RS-170 signal is included in Macintosh video cards so that Macintosh systems can be connected to large-screen video projectors.

NTSC Video (RS-170a)

A variant of the RS-170 standard is RS-170a. This video standard is often referred to as NTSC (National Television Standards Committee) video and was developed at the dawn of broadcast color television to accommodate color TV signals and programming without developing a completely new video system. NTSC-compatible peripherals are an important part of the presenter's and instructor's toolkit. A good example of an NTSC device is a television set. The NTSC signal is not a normal part of the Macintosh computer's video system but it can be generated from available signals.

At the advent of color television, broadcasters had to figure out a way to include color information in a broadcast bandwidth designed for black-and-white television. The solution was to add a sub-carrier modulated onto the luminance signal. The *luminance* signal controls the black and white in the monochrome image; the color signal is called *chrominance*. An NTSC color encoder is performs the sub-carrier modulation and mixing of the colors.

The NTSC encoder requires horizontal sync, vertical sync, blanking period, and red, green, and blue signals in RS-170 format. These signals are available on Apple Macintosh II video cards.

Macintosh II video card pin-outs

This section should help in connecting peripherals and projectors to the Macintosh video card. For most standard projectors and monitors, only an interface cable is required. In some cases the peripheral may need signals not directly supplied by the Macintosh video card. There is another set of signals on the Apple cards that can be accessed for this purpose.

Any third-party video peripheral designed for a Macintosh must meet Macintosh video capability specifications. According to Apple, third party video cards must have:

- Minimum bandwidth of 22 MHz

- Minimum horizontal scan rate of 35 KHz

- Analog RGB video display (for color)

- Ability to receive a negative-going TTL sync signal

The pin-out of the Macintosh DB-15, 15-pin video connector has four video signal pins and four corresponding ground pins. These are shown in the following mini-table.

Pin number	Pin Name	Notes
1	RED VIDEO GROUND	
2	RED	(analog)

continues

Pin number	Pin Name	Notes
3	CSYNC*	(TTL) used by Apple Displays
4	CSYNC GROUND	
5	GREEN + CSYNC	(analog) used for Monochrome; CSYNC not used by Apple displays
6	GREEN CSYNC GROUND	
9	BLUE	(analog)
12	GREEN + CSYNC	(analog) not used
13	BLUE VIDEO GROUND	

* *Composite sync (vertical and horizontal).*
The Apple High Resolution Monochrome Monitor uses the green video and the composite sync signal lines: pins 3, 4, 5, and 6.
The Apple Macintosh video cards produce RS-170 and RS-343 video signals. A description of the video signals and timings are in the following table.

There are six additional video signals on the DB15 connector on Apple Macintosh video cards. These are also similar to J3, also known as 'jumper 3,' which is a bank of 14 holes located at the top of the card near the video port. Pin-out for the DB15 connector are listed in Table 6.13.

Table 6.13   DB15 Pin-outs, Apple Video Cards

Pin number	Function	Description
1	GROUND	
2	GROUND	
3	GROUND	
4	EXT_PBCLCK	(EXTERNAL PIXEL BUS CLOCK)
5	GROUND	
6	CLCK_SEL	(PIXEL BUS CLOCK SELECT)
8	CBLANK⁻	(COMPOSITE BLANKING SIGNAL)
9	GROUND	
10	VSYNC⁻	(VERTICAL SYNC)
11	GROUND	
12	HSYNC⁻	(HORIZONTAL SYNC)
13	VCC	
14	CLCK_SEL⁻	(PIXEL BUS CLOCK SELECT)

* *Pins 1, 2, 3, 5, 7, 9, 11 are tied to ground.*

According to Apple specifications the function of each DB15 signal is as follows:

- **EXT PBCLK.** This signal is found on pin 4 of the connector and is a tri-state clock synchronized from a timing reference on the video card. Its signaling is tri-stated unless an external video device or peripheral is providing the pixel clock timing signal.

- **CLK SEL.** This signal is found on pin 6 of the connector. Its function is to indicate that a display card intends to provide the pixel clock signal. Pin 6 should go to logic level HIGH only when pin 14 goes LOW and an interlace bit has been set on the display card.

- **CBLANK.** The pin 8 connection has the composite blanking information for the video stream.

- **VSYNC.** Pin 10 of the DB15 connector has the vertical sync signal for the video stream. The signal flow is in two directions and can be controlled via software or via a master signal.

- **HSYNC.** Pin 12 of the DB15 connector has the horizontal sync signal for the video stream. The signal flow is in two directions and can be controlled via software or via a master signal.

- **VCC.** Signal processing comes from pin 13. Maximum current drawn from the connection is 100 mA.

- **CLK SEL.** This signal is on pin 14 of the connector. This is the inverted version of the signal found on pin 6.

Some video peripherals require a separate horizontal and vertical sync signal. These can be obtained through DB15 connections.

Making a video cable

Often there is a need to adapt a foreign monitor or video peripheral to a Macintosh, or extend the monitor's distance from the Mac in the workplace. In these cases, the construction of a video cable may be the right idea. Even if the construction of the cable is undertaken by a professional cable manufacturer, it is sometimes necessary to relay the standards to the builders to ensure proper construction and pin-outs.

Cable with an impedance of 75 ohms (RG59) is required, particularly for long distances (over 12 feet). As for the pin assignments in the connectors, pay close attention to grounding each video line, along with the shield, to the appropriate pin on the video device and card. Attach ferrite rings or beads to keep radiation within RFI limits (see comments on RFI and jitter in the section "Notes, common questions, and problems with Macintosh video" later in this chapter).

Overview of sense codes and adapters

Macintosh computers and video cards use "sense" codes in the video cable or connector to determine the resolution of the monitors attached to them. A standard 13- or 14-inch monitor "tells" the Macintosh that it supports 640 × 480, and the Mac responds by providing the appropriate sized screen image (resolution).

A Multiple scan display is smarter. It tells the Mac that it can display a range of screen sizes (resolutions). The Multiscan monitor can step through resolution sizes from 640 × 480 up to 1152 × 870 and selects the desired resolution by generating the sense codes.

Older Macintosh and video cards do not have programmable display drivers that allow resolution switching on-the-fly. A Multiscan monitor connected to an older video card or Macintosh will simply display 640 × 480 resolution. Apple Macintosh CPUs and video cards that cannot switch resolutions on the fly include:

Video Cards: 4•8, 8/24, and 8/24GC
LC, LCII, LCIII
Performa
Quadra 605
PowerBooks
Duo and Mini Dock
Macintosh II series

Sense adapters

Sense code cable adapters enable older Macs and video cards to display higher resolutions on multiple scan displays. The adapters hard-wire a sense code for a particular resolution. This tells the Macintosh that it is hooked to a higher resolution display and is the common technique used to match the resolution of the video card with that of the monitor.

Instead of a sense code adapter, the Macintosh can use a programmable video card to select the desired resolution. The Apple Macintosh Display Card 24AC has this capability. The 24AC can even switch resolutions on-the-fly, without restarting. Older Macintosh systems work were designed for the 24AC card. Many third-party vendors now also support resolution switching on their video cards on mid-range and high-end products.

The proper adapter is essential for the compatibility of a video card and large-screen monitor. Without it the desktop will not display at the proper size or resolution. Tables 6.14 and 6.15 list the pin-outs for two adapters that signal the Macintosh to display images for 832 × 624 and 1152 × 870 screens. You can use this table to build your own adapter.

Table 6.14 832 × 624 Adapter—16-Inch Display

DB-15M	*DB-15F*	*Pin Assignments*
1	1	RED GND
2	2	RED VIDEO
3	3	C SYNC
5	5	GREEN VIDEO
6	6	GREEN GND
9	9	BLUE VIDEO
11	11	C & V SYNC GND
12	12	V SYNC
13	13	BLUE GND
14	14	H SYNC GND
15	15	H SYNC
SHELL	SHELL	

Pins 4 and 10 jumpered together on DB-15 male end.

Table 6.15 1152 × 870 Adapter—21-Inch Display

DB-15M	*DB-15F*	*Pin Assignments*
1	1	RED GND
2	2	RED VIDEO
3	3	C SYNC
5	5	GREEN VIDEO
6	6	GREEN GND
9	9	BLUE VIDEO
12	12	V SYNC
13	13	BLUE GND
14	14	H SYNC GND
15	15	H SYNC
11	11	C & V SYNC GND
SHELL	SHELL	

Pins 4, 7, 10, 11 jumpered together on DB-15 male end.

Display and video pinouts for the Quadra and Centris Macs

The Centris and Quadra Macs determine the resolution of a monitor by inspecting the status of three sense pins. Table 6.19 shows how the three pins should be wired for each of the supported displays. The Quadra and Centris lines should support any display that meets the following specifications. Basic display specifications are listed in Table 6.16.

Table 6.16   Video Sense Pin Specification for Quadra/Centris Macs

Display	Sense Pins 10 7 4	Hor. × Vert (Pixels)	Band Width (MHz)	Vert. Refresh (Hz)	Horiz. Refresh (KHz)
Apple 21 Color	0 0 0	1152 × 870	100	75	68.7
Apple Portrait	0 0 1	640 × 870	57.2832	75	68.9
12-inch AppleColor RGB	0 1 0	512 × 384	15.6672	60.15	24.48
Apple 2-Page Mono	0 1 1	1152 × 870	100	75	68.7
NTSC*	1 0 0	underscan— 512×384	12.2727	59.94	15.7
	1 0 0	overscan— 640×480	12.2727	59.94	15.7
12-inch Apple High-Res Monochrome	1 1 0	640 × 480	30.24	66.7	35.0
13-inch AppleColor High-Res RGB	1 1 0	640 × 480	30.24	66.7	35.0
Apple 16-inch Color Display		832 × 624	57.63	75	49.7
Portrait Color, such as Radius	1 0 1	640 × 870	57.2832	75	68.9

* To produce a color NTSC signal, an RGB-to-NTSC converter is required.

Note

Sense pins 4, 7, and 10 are referred to as MON.ID1, MON.ID2, and MON.ID3 in the Macintosh Quadra pinout table or SENSE0, SENSE1, and SENSE2 in pinout tables for the video connectors. A sense pin value of 0 means that pin should be grounded to the C&VSYNC.GND signal; a value of 1 means do not connect the pin. Extended sense codes will be examined if the sense code 1 1 1 is detected.

The terms underscan and overscan are used to describe the active video resolution for NTSC and PAL modes. *Underscan* means that the active video area appears in a rectangle centered onscreen with a black border. This ensures that the entire active video area always is displayed on all monitors. *Overscan* utilizes the entire possible video area for NTSC or PAL. Most monitors and televisions, however, lose video beyond the edges of the display, so the entire image will not be seen.

The Apple 16-inch Color Display should have pins 4 and 10 tied together and pin 7 should be unconnected. If the Apple 16-inch Color Display is used with a Macintosh Display Card, it also requires the Macintosh Display Card 4•8, 8/24, or 8/24 GC with revised ROMs.

Extended sense codes

Table 6.17 lists Apple specifications for the extended sense codes. Pay close attention to the wiring instructions and do not ground or connect pins in any arrangement not shown in the table.

Note

For systems that use the extended sense codes, refer to this for detailed specifications. Values of 0 mean that the pins should be connected or jumpered together. Values marked as 1 mean do NOT connect. It is recommended to always connect these lines to ground.

	Sense Pins			Hor. × Vert	Band-width	Refresh	Scan
Display	*4-10*	*10-7*	*7-4*	*(Pixels)*	*(MHz)*	*(Hz)*	
16-inch Color, such as E-Machines	0	1	1	832 × 624	57.2832	75	49.7
PAL							
PAL has two wiring options using the extended sense pin configuration. To produce a color PAL signal, an RGB-to-PAL converter is required.							
PAL Option 1	0	0	0	underscan— 640 × 480	14.75	50	15.625
				overscan— 768 × 576	14.75	50	15.625

Table 6.17   Extended Sense Code Specifications

continues

Table 6.17   Extended Sense Code Specifications, CONTINUED

Display	Sense Pins 4-10	10-7	7-4	Hor. × Vert (Pixels)	Band-width (MHz)	Refresh (Hz)	Scan
PAL Option 2	1	1	0	underscan— 640 × 480	14.75	50	15.625
				overscan— 768 × 576	14.75	50	15.625

This sense code also requires a diode between sense pins 10 and 7, with anode toward pin 7, cathode toward pin 10.

NOTE:
The Macintosh Quadra 700 and 900 support PAL Option 1 at up to 8 bpp.
The Macintosh Centris 610, 650, and Quadra 800 support PAL Option 1 at up to 16 bpp.
The Macintosh Quadra 950 supports PAL Option 1 up to millions of colors.

Display	Sense Pins 4-10	10-7	7-4	Hor. × Vert (Pixels)	Band-width (MHz)	Refresh (Hz)	Scan
VGA	1	0	1	640 × 480	25.175	59.95	31.47
Super VGA	1	0	1	800 × 600	36	56	35.16

To enable Super VGA, after configuring and connecting the monitor for VGA, open the monitor's control panel and select Options. Choose Super VGA from the dialog and restart your System.

Display	Sense Pins 4-10	10-7	7-4	Hor. × Vert (Pixels)	Band-width (MHz)	Refresh (Hz)	Scan
19-inch Color	1	1	0	1024 × 768	80	75	60
No external monitor (video halted)	1	1	1				

Video pinouts for Quadra and Centris Macs

The pinouts for Quadra and Centris Macintosh models are listed in Table 6.18. Use this information to help you construct video adapters and for troubleshooting problems with the video System.

Table 6.18   Video Pinouts for the Quadra and Centris Macs

Pin	Signal	Description
1	RED.GND	Red Video Ground
2	RED.VID	Red Video
3	CSYNC⁻	Composite Sync
4	MON.ID1	Monitor ID, Bit 1 (also known as SENSE0)
5	GRN.VID	Green Video
6	GRN.GND	Green Video Ground

Pin	Signal	Description
7	MON.ID2	Monitor ID, Bit 2 (also known as SENSE1)
8	nc	(no connection)
9	BLU.VID	Blue Video
10	MON.ID3	Monitor ID, Bit 3 (also known as SENSE2)
11	C&VSYNC.GND	CSYNC & VSYNC Ground
12	VSYNC⁻	Vertical Sync
13	BLU.GND	Blue Video Ground
14	HSYNC.GND	HSYNC Ground
15	HSYNC⁻	Horizontal Sync
Shell	CHASSIS.GND	Chassis Ground

Note

Apple designs its video circuits to run with its own monitors. It is up to third-party engineers to build monitors according to Apple specifications if they want them to be compatible with Apple computers. Consult the manufacturer of the monitor in question for details concerning compliance with Apple standards.

AV Macs and composite monitors

Many schools and instructional settings use the video-out port on the new AV Macs to drive external TV monitors. A common complaint is that the menu bar and often the right side of the display aren't visible. This is usually caused by the monitor being in overscan mode. For a television, this is normal. As mentioned earlier, a portion of the display is off the screen in overscan mode.

The solution is to generate the signal in underscan mode and send that to the TV monitor. To do this, open the Monitors control panel and select the lower resolution setting of 512 × 384 (via Options). This sets the signal in underscan mode and should display the entire image when it is sent to the TV.

If S-video output is available, a better signal can be sent, although the difference is subtle. Whether the difference is detectable depends greatly on the quality of the monitor.

Macs and NTSC video

The best reason to connect VGA monitors to Macs is the low cost. Another type of monitor you might want to connect is also inexpensive and is available absolutely everywhere: the standard television video monitor. These devices, and the larger projection system, are popular in conference rooms and instructional settings. A popular way to use the Mac with these monitors is to have the Mac drive these peripherals during a display or presentation. Table 6.19

describes the common RCA-type connector that can be fashioned to provide this connection. NTSC monitors should work on Macintosh Quadra and Centris models with this cable. Test the monitor first if possible. The information in this table can also be used to troubleshoot bad connections and faulty wiring.

Table 6.19 Mac-to-NTSC Connection		
Card Connector	*RCA-Type Phono-Connector*	
4	MON.ID1 (sense0) - - - - - ¦	
7	MON.ID2 (sense1) - - - - - ¦	
11	C&VSYNC.GND - - - - - - - ¦	
5	GRN.VID - - - - - - - - - - - - - - ->	Tip (signal)
Shell	CHASSIS.GND - - - - - - - - - -> Sleeve (ground)	

Adjust the RCA-side of the table to whatever type of connector is in use. The sleeve refers to the flange around the outer edge of the connector. This serves as chassis ground in most cases. According to Apple technical documentation, the card-to-connector wiring should follow the layout shown in Table 6.16 when connecting Macs to NTSC video gear.

Grounding pins 4 and 7-11 signal to the Macintosh that an interlaced display is attached. Pin 5 carries the black-and-white signal and connects to the center of the RCA jack. The shell of the connector is usually taken as ground and connects directly to the connector sleeve.

Another approach to this problem is to acquire an NTSC video signal directly from the Macintosh. In this case, an RGB-to-NTSC converter is required. These boxes are available from third-party vendors such as RasterOps, Truevision, NewTek, and Scion.

Macintosh display cards and RGB-to-NTSC converters

The conversion of Macintosh screen data to NTSC video can be accomplished by using one of three basic approaches:

- Several manufacturers make video cards that output an NTSC signal. Examples are RasterOps, Truevision, Focus, and Orange Micro.

- Use an RGB-to-NTSC converter. RasterOps and ComputerVideo make RGB-to-NTSC converter boxes that work directly with existing video cards. Truevision also has an RGB-to-NTSC converter, but it has problems with older Apple video cards.

- Try a scan converter. Companies like RGB Spectrum build scan converters that work with existing video cards and convert the Macintosh output to NTSC.

The NTSC card houses all the circuitry necessary to convert and send the NTSC signal. They are usually simple to install and normally use an RCA plug to connect the Macintosh to a peripheral. Various cards provide a host of options and features, including video overlay and frame grabbing.

Companies such as TechComm and ComputerVideo have NTSC encoder boxes that seem to work well with a variety of video cards. Special cables are sometimes required. RasterOps has a number of video expander products that provide composite and S-video (for S VHS, HiBand 8mm, and ED Beta) outputs. These products may require special cables. In most cases, these devices assume that the signal coming from the Mac is in NTSC interlaced mode.

The best method for converting RGB to NTSC is to use a scan converter. Although more expensive, scan converters create broadcast quality video signals. Scan converters not only convert the signal, they also condition it and remove the screen flicker associated with single pixel scan lines.

Scan converters take the RGB signal directly from the video card, convert it to a buffered digital frame, and reconvert the image to a clean NTSC signal for display. Aspect ratio conversion is also performed on the image. Other features of the scan converter are color bar generation, video mixing, freeze frame, and various video transitions.

NTSC video encoding and the display card 8/24

The Display Cards 8/24 use a special cable to set the video output to NTSC format. Otherwise, a third-party NTSC converter or encoder is required to convert the RGB signal to the NTSC signal.

For 8-bit video, Apple's convolution algorithm provides one of the best ways to eliminate the flicker produced in an NTSC system. For 24-bit images, scan converters are more popular and effective.

NTSC output without a converter box

To configure the Display Card 8/24 in NTSC mode, only a cable is required. Most NTSC devices have an RCA plug on them for signal connections. According to Apple specifications, the following connections provide NTSC output from the 8/24 cards. In Table 6.20, "Tip" refers to the signal wire at the center of the connector; the sleeve is chassis ground.

Table 6.20   NTSC video from the 8/24 card

Card Connector	RCA-Type Phono-Connector
4	MON.ID1 (sense0) - - - - - ¦
7	MON.ID2 (sense1) - - - - - ¦
11	C&VSYNC.GND - - - - - - - ¦
5	GRN.VID - - - - - - - - - - - - - -> Tip (signal)
Shell	CHASSIS.GND - - - - - - - - - - -> Sleeve (ground)

To tell the video card that an interlaced display is attached, ground pins 4 and 7 to 11. Pin 5 carries the black-and-white signal to the tip of the connector. The shell of the video card's connector connects to the RCA jack's sleeve.

If you need a color NTSC signal from any Apple Macintosh display card, use an RGB-to-NTSC converter described earlier.

How to avoid the flicker in NTSC video

Macintosh video displayed on NTSC peripherals often has considerable flicker. Recall that NTSC is an interlaced display: one-pixel scan lines are off the screen half the time for each sweep of the raster. This is what causes the flicker.

The flickering is inherent in NTSC signal processing. A normal image has to have information in both fields at all times. For this reason, a set of horizontal scan lines will always exist in one field or the other. This is not a problem with the Macintosh.

To get around the flicker, a scan converter grabs both lines and holds them for simultaneous display. Extended definition TV works the same way; it displays both scan fields simultaneously so that the one-pixel flicker disappears. Another way around this problem is to use equipment that has a two-pixel line for an image. This is common in television studio equipment.

For routine training and presentations, flicker may be apparent only in a window's title bar. A software correction was developed years ago to mask this problem. A System extension called NeVR was developed that paints the title bar as a solid image instead of in one-pixel lines, and thereby eliminates the flicker from the display.

Simultaneous RGB and NTSC outputs

One useful connection for the Macintosh is to provide simultaneous NTSC and RGB outputs for TV monitors and projector systems (see Figure 6.54). One partially successful technique involves tapping the RGB signal on the Mac and passing it over to the scan converter. This method is only partially successful because it produces a lot of interruptions at the NTSC device.

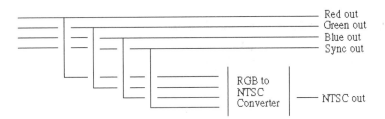

Figure 6.54 Simultaneous RGB and NTSC outputs.

Most video cards do not support simultaneous Macintosh RGB and NTSC. However, some multisync displays and projectors can accommodate NTSC signal timing. If the display device has the capability to sync to the NTSC signal, the Mac's signal can go directly to the display device. Composite NTSC is available for TV monitors. This depends on the timing of the RGB and composite according to the sync of NTSC (see Figure 6.55).

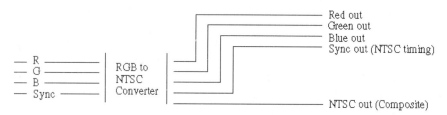

Figure 6.55 NTSC signal timing.

Converters are available that drive the NTSC and RGB devices together with the same image. Some third-party video cards and the Apple 8/24 cards provide this function. The video card is capable of generating NTSC timing to drive the converter. Any RGB devices used this way need to synchronize with the NTSC signal from the video card.

Overview of Macintosh display cards

Apple display cards 4/8 and 8/24 work with all Apple displays and provide a broad range of extra video features. Display card 8/24GC is an enhanced version of the 8/24. The 8/24GC includes a dedicated coprocessor onboard for accelerated graphics.

Display Card 4/8 provides support for up to 256 colors or grays on the Apple 14-inch monitors. It produces up to 16 grays on the Apple Macintosh Portrait Display and the Apple Two-Page Monochrome Monitor.

Display Card 8/24 and 8/24 GC support full 24-bit "true color" reproduction on the Apple color monitors. This allows users to display 16.7 million colors. The combination of true gray-scale and true color reproduction also is perfect for displaying photographic images.

The Macintosh Display Card 8/24 GC runs on an Am29000 RISC microprocessor and a version of QuickDraw that has been optimized for a coprocessor card. The Am29000 and the Macintosh CPU work together to accelerate the QuickDraw processing from 5 to 30 times, depending on the application. As a result, graphics applications run faster and more smoothly, especially when using full 24-bit color.

All three cards—Apple display cards 4/8, 8/24, and 8/24GC—support RS-170 signal processing for compatibility with interlaced video devices. The Macintosh Display Cards 8/24 and 8/24 GC enhance the quality of interlaced video through the use of Apple Convolution.

Color reproduction in video cards

In basic 8-bit video cards, each pixel is represented by an 8-bit color value. The 8-bit value is used as an index for a "color look-up table" (CLUT) of 256 predefined colors. A 24-bit value is derived from the table of 256 preselected colors in the basic scheme. The 24-bit color value is composed of 8-bit values for red, green, and blue. Each color is then processed through one of three 8-bit digital to analog converters (DACs) and made into an analog color signal that is sent to the screen.

8-bit images are painted to the screen by a process of color approximation. The Color Manager compares the 24-bit value to the nearest 8-bit value in the CLUT and chooses the best matching color to display. The 8-bit index of the nearest match is placed in the frame buffer and is used to paint the display area.

The quality of rendered graphic images in 8-bit color depends on the values stored in the CLUT. Complex images lose detail in this system if they are drawn with a large number of approximated colors. This is the primary reason why scanned and reproduced images differ from their originals.

Another problem common in 8-bit systems is referred to as color *blocking*. Blocked colors are shades of a color that are interpreted (and represented) by the CLUT as being the same value or shade. This effect results in loss of shading and detail in the image.

Banding is a different problem, although it has similarities to blocking. In a banded image the reproduction appears as though it is made of only a few basic colors, but with the presence of a great number of variations of those basic colors in the image. A 256 color CLUT does not possess enough colors to handle a very complex image. Whenever one color passes into another in a fine gradation, jumps in color occur that appear as bands. Each band is the CLUT's best attempt at a color match with the true value. The result is a different color than was used to represent the color in the original.

To get around these problems, *dithering* of the color pixels is employed. Dithered colors group several pixels together to produce the illusion of a particular color that does not exist in the CLUT. Given that pixels are small, color mixing is performed by the dithering of pixels onscreen to make colors that cannot be drawn by the CLUT directly. Unfortunately dithering is an approximation and will not reproduce an exact match of the original.

PAL-Compatible versions of Macintosh display cards

Apple Macintosh display cards are available in the PAL video format. To tell whether an 8/24 card is a PAL version, check for a "/A" or "/B" on the label. "/B" is a PAL card; "/A" is NTSC. Display Card 8/24GC is PAL compatible. On other cards, there may be no visible difference.

NTSC or PAL designations are determined by sense pin combinations on the video card. Check with a local Macintosh dealer for information on the latest ROM versions for these cards.

24-Bit Color

Apple documentation occasionally refers to 24-bit color as *direct color*. 24-bit color gets around the problems of 8-bit systems by allowing each component color to possess an 8-bit value. 24-bit color systems can display 16,777,216 RGB combinations normally visible to the human eye.

24-bit color generation does not rely on a CLUT. 24-bit values are generated directly from the video firmware on the video card as three 8-bit components of red, blue, and green. Color values are fed directly to the video DAC on the card for display on-screen.

Grayscale

Grayscale is produced in the 24-bit system by mixing 8-bit values for red, blue, and green in equal amounts. Some cards (like the 8/24) use only the blue signal when driving the larger monochrome displays at 256 gray levels.

Monitor support

Newer video cards use a programmable pixel clock (100 MHz) to accommodate all monitors (up to two pages). Pixel depth is a function of the amount of VRAM present in the System (or on the display card). Most cards have 512K to 1 MB of VRAM onboard.

Apple convolution filter

The flicker caused by interlaced displays is minimized in cards such as the 8/24 by processing every pixel with a convolution calculation of its value. This convolution averages the values of the pixels above and below the scanned pixel to avoid flickering in the display. The calculation is done by the CLUT DAC chip onboard the video card. Convolution results in a blending of the scan lines with the information above and below them, thereby reducing the flicker. A piece of the horizontal line remains onscreen during the display scan to further stabilize the image. The convolution formula used by Apple is 1:2:1. The two represents the active pixel that is weighted twice that of its neighbors.

The Macintosh Display Card 4/8 does not support the convolution filter; the 8/24 card supports the filter at up to 8 bits per pixel. Convolution is disabled in the 8/24 if the card is driving a display in 24-bit mode. For interlaced displays in 8-bit depth or less, convolution is enabled. Convolution is enabled for interlaced displays of 8 bits or less color depth.

Memory organization

Memory organization is the heart of the frame buffer controller. This custom programmable gate array IC performs the address translation that permits cards with only 1 MB onboard to support 24-bit graphics (a 640 × 480 display needs about 1.2 MB VRAM for 24-bit images). To compress the data processed, the 8 bits of data in each pixel that do not possess color information are ignored. This results in a memory requirement of about 900K for a 24-bit image on a 640 × 480 screen. The 8 ignored bits are called the alpha channel, which is used for special effects.

Accelerating graphics

One technique used to speed the drawing of graphic images is to employ a dedicated coprocessor for the screen renderings. This allows the CPU to continue working without having to worry about the drawing and painting of complex screen images. Cards like the 8/24 GC use the Am29000 RISC processor to off-load image processing from the main CPU. The Am29000 was chosen by Apple designers because it can execute complex QuickDraw commands and code directly.

Inter-Process Communication (IPC)

To further optimize the acceleration of video imaging, some video cards such as the Display Card 8/24 GC use a form of inter-process communication that intercepts QuickDraw calls on the Macintosh and passes them to the video card onboard QuickDraw for processing. This removes the overhead associated with QuickDraw processing. The inter-process communication also allows the display card to call specific routines running on the Macintosh to be executed.

NuBus data transfer

The transfer of large images across the NuBus is the biggest bottleneck in the screen rendering system. Typical specifications for data reads are 1000 ns and writes are 500 ns from the Macintosh to the video card. After every 32-bit word is sent, the bus control must be re-arbitrated, or reset to let the Mac know the card is sending data through the slot and motherboard. This slows the System appreciably.

The whole process of drawing a screen can be greatly accelerated if small pieces of data are read across the bus along with the QuickDraw variables. This is how accelerated video cards work. Screen bitmaps can be created on the video card and placed directly into the VRAM buffer. In most cases the contents of the VRAM frame buffer can be read or written to at a rate of about every 66 to 132 ns (for the 8/24GC). Several megabytes of DRAM on the video card can be used to warehouse screen data that is offscreen.

32-bit QuickDraw optimized for the Am29000

Apple engineers have modified several algorithms in QuickDraw to further enhance the processing of graphical images on the 8/24 series video cards. Because of these changes, Display Card 8/24 GC accelerates any Macintosh application that uses QuickDraw. Nothing extra is required of the application to use the features inherent in this card. The Display Card 8/24 AC can enhance the speed of graphics processing by up to 30 times with its improved electronics and software. Keep in mind the 8/24GC card is not compatible with System 7.1 or later and is not supported on Power Macs.

Apple Multiple Scan 17, 1710AV, and 1705 Displays

Multiple scan technology enables you to display multiple resolutions with on-the-fly switching. The three modes supported by the Multiple Scan 17 Display are 640 × 480, 832 × 624, and 1024 × 768 pixels. The 1710AV and 1705 models can display these same resolutions, plus additional modes up to 1152 × 870, and depending on how much VRAM is available to the monitor. Nevertheless, this monitor cannot be used with the Macintosh Display Cards 4/8, 8/24, or 8/24 GC without a third-party adapter. For additional information on Macintosh monitors, see Chapter 4.

You can switch resolutions depending on the application in use. For example, when working on graphics you may need to switch to a lower resolution with larger pixels to edit each pixel. When working on a page layout, you may want the two-page resolution.

Table 6.21 shows the Apple specifications for the video modes supported on each Macintosh computer with the Apple Multiple 17 Display. For the column labeled "Video Available," the following numbers represent one of three resolutions:

1. 640 × 480–14-inch Display

2. 832 × 624–16-inch Display

3. 1024 × 768–19-inch Display

Table 6.21 Resolution Compatibility Table for Macintosh Computers and the Multiple Scan 17 Monitor

Macintosh	Video Available (1)	(2)	(3)	Display Manager Mode Switching?
Power Mac–45 Pin conn	Y	Y	N	Y
Power Mac–AV card	Y	Y	Y	Y
Power Mac–HPV Lite	Y	Y	Y	Y
Power Mac–HPV	Y	Y	Y	Y
Quadra 700	Y	Y	N	Y
Quadra 900	Y	Y	N	Y
Quadra 800	Y	Y	Y	Y
Quadra 950	Y	Y	Y	Y
Quadra 660AV	Y	Y	Y	Y
Quadra 840AV	Y	Y	Y	Y
Quadra 610	Y	Y	Y	Y
Quadra 650	Y	Y	Y	Y
Quadra 605	Y	Y	Y	Y
Centris 610	Y	Y	Y	Y
Centris 650	Y	Y	Y	Y
Mac II ci	Y	N	N	N

continues

Table 6.21   Resolution Compatibility Table for Macintosh Computers and the Multiple Scan 17 Monitor, CONTINUED

Macintosh	Video Available			Display Manager Mode Switching?
	(1)	(2)	(3)	
Mac II si	Y	N	N	N
Mac II vx	Y	N	N	N
Display Card 24AC	Y	Y	Y	Y
8/24	Y	Y	N	N
8/24 GC	Y	Y	N	N
4•8	Y	Y	N	N
Mac II cx	N	N	N	N/A
Mac II	N	N	N	N/A
Mac IIx	N	N	N	N/A
Mac IIfx	N	N	N	N/A
Performa 400	Y	N	N	N
Performa 410	Y	N	N	N
Performa 430	Y	N	N	N
Performa 405	Y	N	N	N
Performa 450	Y	Y	N	N
Performa 460	Y	Y	N	N
Performa 466	Y	Y	N	N
Performa 467	Y	Y	N	N
Performa 475	Y	Y	Y	N
Performa 476	Y	Y	Y	N
Performa 600	Y	N	N	N
Performa 600CD	Y	N	N	N
PowerBook 180	Y	Y	N	N
PowerBook 180c	Y	Y	N	N
PowerBook 165	Y	Y	N	N
PowerBook 165c	Y	Y	N	N
PowerBook 160	Y	Y	N	N
PowerBook 100	N	N	N	N/A
PowerBook 140	N	N	N	N/A
PowerBook 145	N	N	N	N/A
PowerBook 170	N	N	N	N/A
PowerBook Duo 210	N	N	N	N/A
PowerBook Duo 230	N	N	N	N/A
PowerBook Duo 250	N	N	N	N/A

Macintosh	Video Available (1)	(2)	(3)	Display Manager Mode Switching?
PowerBook Duo 270C	N	N	N	N/A
MiniDock	Y	Y	N	N
DUO DOCK	Y	Y	N	N
DUO DOCK II	Y	Y	Y	Y
Mac LC 475	Y	Y	Y	N
Mac LCIII	Y	Y	N	N
Mac LC	Y	N	N	N
Mac LCII	Y	N	N	N

Apple Multiple Scan 20 display

Multiple scan technology enables you to display multiple resolutions with on-the-fly switching. The five modes supported by the Multiple Scan 20 Display are 640 × 480, 832 × 624, 1024 × 768, 640 × 870, and 1152 × 870 pixels. Nevertheless, this monitor cannot be used with the Macintosh Display Cards 4/8, 8/24, or 8/24 GC without a third-party adapter. For additional information on Macintosh monitors, see Chapter 4.

You can switch resolutions depending on the application in use. For example, when working on graphics you may need to switch to a lower resolution with larger pixels to edit each pixel. When working on a page-layout, you may want the two-page resolution.

Table 6.22 shows Apple specifications for video modes supported on each Macintosh computer with the Apple Multiple 20 Display. The numbers in the "Video Available" column correspond to the following displays:

1. 640 × 480–14-inch Display

2. 832 × 624–16-inch Display

3. 1024 × 768–19-inch Display

4. 1152 × 870–21-inch Display

5. 640 × 870–Portrait Display

Table 6.22   Resolution Compatibility Table for Macintosh Computers and the Multiple Scan 20 Monitor

Macintosh	Video Available (1)	(2)	(3)	(4)	(5)	Display Manager Mode Switching?
Power Mac–45 Pin conn	Y	Y	N	N	N	Y
Power Mac–AV card	Y	Y	Y	Y	Y	Y

continues

Table 6.22 Resolution Compatibility Table for Macintosh Computers and the Multiple Scan 20 Monitor, CONTINUED

Macintosh	Video Available (1)	(2)	(3)	(4)	(5)	Display Manager Mode Switching?
Power Mac–HPV Lite	Y	Y	Y	Y	Y	Y
Power Mac–HPV	Y	Y	Y	Y	Y	Y
Quadra 700	Y	Y	N	Y	Y	Y
Quadra 900	Y	Y	N	Y	Y	Y
Quadra 800	Y	Y	Y	Y	Y	Y
Quadra 950	Y	Y	Y	Y	Y	Y
Quadra 660AV	Y	Y	Y	Y	Y	Y
Quadra 840AV	Y	Y	Y	Y	Y	Y
Quadra 610	Y	Y	Y	Y	Y	Y
Quadra 650	Y	Y	Y	Y	Y	Y
Quadra 605	Y	Y	Y	Y	Y	Y
Centris 610	Y	Y	Y	Y	Y	Y
Centris 650	Y	Y	Y	Y	Y	Y
Mac II ci	Y	N	N	N	Y	N
Mac II si	Y	N	N	N	Y	N
Mac II vx	Y	N	N	N	N	N
Display Card 24AC	Y	Y	Y	Y	Y	Y
8/24	Y	Y	N	Y	Y	N
8/24 GC	Y	Y	N	Y	Y	N
4•8	Y	Y	N	Y	Y	N
Mac II cx	N	N	N	N	N	N/A
Mac II	N	N	N	N	N	N/A
Mac IIx	N	N	N	N	N	N/A
Mac IIfx	N	N	N	N	N	N/A
Performa 400	Y	N	N	N	N	N
Performa 410	Y	N	N	N	N	N
Performa 430	Y	N	N	N	N	N
Performa 405	Y	N	N	N	N	N
Performa 450	Y	Y	N	N	Y	N
Performa 460	Y	Y	N	N	Y	N
Performa 466	Y	Y	N	N	Y	N
Performa 467	Y	Y	N	N	Y	N

Macintosh	Video Available (1)	(2)	(3)	(4)	(5)	Display Manager Mode Switching?
Performa 475	Y	Y	Y	Y	Y	N
Performa 476	Y	Y	Y	Y	Y	N
Performa 550	Y	Y	N	N	Y	N
Performa 600	Y	N	N	N	N	N
Performa 600CD	Y	N	N	N	N	N
PowerBook 180	Y	Y	N	N	Y	N
PowerBook 180c	Y	Y	N	N	Y	N
PowerBook 165	Y	Y	N	N	Y	N
PowerBook 165c	Y	Y	N	N	Y	N
PowerBook 160	Y	Y	N	N	Y	N
PowerBook 100	N	N	N	N	N	N/A
PowerBook 140	N	N	N	N	N	N/A
PowerBook 145	N	N	N	N	N	N/A
PowerBook 170	N	N	N	N	N	N/A
PowerBook Duo 210	N	N	N	N	N	N/A
PowerBook Duo 230	N	N	N	N	N	N/A
PowerBook Duo 250	N	N	N	N	N	N/A
PowerBook Duo 270C	N	N	N	N	N	N/A
MiniDock	Y	Y	N	N	Y	N
DUO DOCK	Y	Y	N	N	Y	N
DUO DOCK II	Y	Y	Y	Y	Y	Y
Mac LC 475	Y	Y	Y	Y	Y	N
Mac LCIII	Y	Y	N	N	Y	N
Mac LC	Y	N	N	N	N	N
Mac LCII	Y	N	N	N	N	N

Varying resolution

QuickDraw does not support display systems that have different dots-per-inch specifications when drawing images at the same size. Macintosh and QuickDraw assume that a display resolution of (about) 72 dpi is present (the Apple High Res color display is 69 dpi). This means that calibrated geometric shapes (and all images) should reproduce identically on different displays and different Macs. A 2-inch by 2-inch square displayed on a Macintosh Plus should appear the same on a Quadra 840AV with a 21-inch monitor.

Upgrading VRAM

The most basic video upgrade on the newer Macs is to add VRAM to the System. Specifications for the number of VRAM sockets and the maximum amount of VRAM are discussed earlier in this chapter in the section "Installing RAM." The following sections address the need for VRAM upgrades and discuss the amount of VRAM required to display a particular number of colors on standard Macintosh displays.

A common question at Apple support centers concerning VRAM upgrades goes something like this:

> If I can't run a 21-inch monitor in 24-bit using the full 2 MB of VRAM, and I can run a 16-inch in 24-bit with only 1 MB of VRAM, then what would I use the full 2 MB of VRAM for? A 19-inch monitor, maybe?

The built-in video of some Macs (like the Quadra 700 and Quadra 900, for example) supports 21-inch color and monochrome monitors to 8-bit depth (256 colors/shades) or a 14-inch color monitor to millions of colors (millions colors/shades in the Monitors control panel). Adding VRAM beyond 2 MB has no effect because the System will not recognize the additional VRAM. To get greater depth on a 21-inch monitor, a video card is required. A 19-inch monitor will work only if it has the same operating specifications as another monitor the Mac already supports.

Power Macintosh models 8500, 7500, and 7200 support up to 4 MB of VRAM, with the 8500 and 7500 including 2 MB on the motherboard, and the 7200 1 MB of VRAM. The 6100, 7100, and 8100 models only support VRAM on add-in video cards such as the ones included with the AV or non-AV models. The 9500 does not have any VRAM on its logic board, and requires a video card to support a monitor. Power Mac 5200, 5300, 6200, and 6300 computers have 1 MB of 60 ns VRAM on the logic board; however, it cannot be upgraded or expanded, similar to PowerBooks.

Table 6.23 should help explain the video expansion options available for Macs with built-in video.

Table 6.23 Macintosh Quadra 700 and 900 Built-In Video's Maximum Pixel			
DEPTHS (BITS PER PIXEL) AS A FUNCTION OF VRAM			
Display size	*512K VRAM*	*1 MB VRAM*	*2 MB VRAM*
12-inch landscape 384 × 512, such as 12-inch RGB	8 bpp	24 bpp	24 bpp
12-inch Monochrome 640 × 480	8 bpp	8 bpp	8 bpp
13-inch RGB and VGA 480 × 640	8 bpp	8 bpp	24 bpp

Display size	512K VRAM	1 MB VRAM	2 MB VRAM
Super VGA 800 × 600	8 bpp	8 bpp	24 bpp
15-inch Portrait (b/w) 640 × 870	4 bpp	8 bpp	8 bpp
16-inch Color 832 × 624	8 bpp	8 bpp	24 bpp
2-Page Display (b/w) 870 × 1152	4 bpp	8 bpp	8 bpp
21-inch Color 870 × 1152	4 bpp	8 bpp	8 bpp
PAL with convolution	n.a.	8 bpp	8 bpp
PAL without convolution	8 bpp	8 bpp	24 bpp*
NTSC with convolution	n.a.	8 bpp	8 bpp
NTSC without convolution	8 bpp	8 bpp	24 bpp

  * *Assumes proper sense codes are employed on PAL monitor.*

Notice that 512K of VRAM is the minimum configuration for the Macintosh Quadra 700; for the 900, 1 MB is minimum.

Note

Two methods exist for wiring a PAL monitor to a Macintosh. Only one way, selecting a set of extended sense codes, allows for 24 bits per pixel resolution.

Apple offers VRAM upgrade kits for most Macintosh computers. These kits are not proprietary and can be purchased from a local Apple dealer as upgrade parts for Macintosh computers. Part numbers for Apple VRAM upgrade kits are as follows. Note changes in available kits.

Part Number	Description	Product
M0517LL/A*	Macintosh LC 512K VRAM SIMM	Macintosh LC only
M5951LL/A*	Macintosh VRAM Expansion Kit	Being replaced by M5953LL/A
M5953LL/A*	Macintosh Quadra VRAM Expansion Kit	Macintosh Quadra only
661-0609**	VRAM SIMM, 256K	Use two to upgrade Macintosh Display Card 4•8 only

  * *Order through Finished Goods.*
 ** *Order through Service.*

Exchange information

To exchange defective VRAM modules included as original parts in Apple equipment, use the service part numbers in the following mini-table. Check with a certified Apple repair shop or dealer for information regarding the warranty status of specific systems.

Part Number	Description	Product
661-0609	VRAM SIMM, 256K	Macintosh Display Card 4•8
661-0649	VRAM SIMM, 512K	Macintosh LC only
661-0722	VRAM SIMM, 256K	Macintosh Quadra and LC only

Note

Defective 256K VRAM SIMMs found in Apple equipment can be returned for replacement as either part number 661-0609 or part number 661-0722. The service center must specify the part numbers. Service centers are encouraged to use advanced exchange for these products.

Macintosh Centris and Quadra computers with 1 MB video RAM (VRAM) and a 32,000 color setting may display a horizontal white line just below the middle of the screen. The effect is independent of the monitor used. A faint gray line below the middle of the screen is indicative of a Trinitron monitor.

Errors related to VRAM

The VRAM chips that Apple uses are supplied by multiple vendors. As such, the VRAM chips may have different operating characteristics. If VRAM SIMMs are used in incompatible products or incorrectly, errors will be reported by the System. Obvious display problems will be apparent also.

The Macintosh Centris and Quadra series, for example, require VRAM with a speed of 80 ns or better. 100ns VRAM, such as that found in a Macintosh IIvx, will not work in these machines. Power Macintosh 6100, 7100, 8100, and 9500 do not have VRAM chips or slots on the motherboard, but support NuBus, PDS, or PCI cards which have their own dedicated VRAM on the card. The 5200, 5300, 6200, and 6300, have 1 MB of 60ns VRAM installed on the logic board. The 8500, 7500, and 7200 models support up to 4 MB of 70 ns VRAM on the logic board.

Several common problems related to VRAM are mentioned in the following sections. This is not a comprehensive treatment of all possible errors, but a summary of some common complaints entered in Apple Tech Support files.

Macintosh LC

A few pixels along the left edge of the screen intermittently change colors.

Macintosh Quadra

On large screens, pixels drop.

Macintosh Display Card 4/8

On startup, the 12-inch and 13-inch displays show only 256 colors, instead of the millions the upgrade should provide. The Macintosh also starts up in black-and-white mode. If the Macintosh is restarted, the option for millions of colors becomes available. However, once you shut down the Macintosh, the problem recurs on startup.

Monitor quality

The measure of the distribution of color and brightness over the surface of the video tube is termed the uniformity of the monitor. Because measurements of uniformity are difficult, they must be undertaken in a laboratory. The results are that slight imperfections in the monitor appear as hazy patches onscreen. There is no fixed pattern or predictable location of the spots produced on monitors with poor uniformity. Hazy regions are usually found at the edges of the display.

Factors in the environment also contribute to variations in displayed color. Stray magnetic fields from equipment and lighting fixtures, as well as the earth's magnetic field, affect monitor displays. This is true even if the monitor is degaussed regularly or automatically.

Problems related to the uniformity of brightness are similar to those for color. When viewing a white raster display, the variations in brightness appear as gray patches.

It is normal for monitors to exhibit some color and brightness variances somewhere onscreen. Use a video test program to evaluate the severity of the problem. In cases where there is a slight distortion, CRT replacement should not be considered; large-screen CRTs have design limitations that haven't been corrected completely.

Dot Pitch not applicable for monochrome monitors

The cathode ray tube in every monitor has an electron beam gun that shoots electrons through a perforated metal grid, or grill, to a phosphor coating on the inside of the display area. When the electrons hit the phosphor, the coating emits light over small areas, or spots, called pixels (picture elements).

Aperture in monitor terms refers to perforations in the grid through which the electrons travel before striking the phosphor coating. *Pitch*, or *dot pitch*, is a measure of the distance between pixels onscreen. If pixels are tightly packed, pitch is small. Monitors with smaller dot-pitch appear sharper. Larger dot-pitch monitors appear "grainy" to the viewer.

The terms aperture, pitch, and dot pitch are used interchangeably and refer to the distance between pixels. The number of holes (or apertures) in one row of the metal grid determines the maximum horizontal resolution available to a CRT.

Monochrome monitors do not use dot pitch as a specification. Dot pitch is used only on color monitors because the term refers to the placement of red, green, and blue dots that make up one color pixel. Because a monochrome image is made of only one dot, there is no pitch specification.

Stripe pitch versus dot pitch

A pixel on a CRT can take the shape of a dot (in the case of a conventional monitor) or a stripe (as in the Sony Trinitron tubes). The term *pitch* refers to both types of geometry.

The conventional color display method is to use three dots (red, blue, and green) arranged in a triangular pattern on the tube to create a single color pixel. The *stripe technique* uses a different method; three vertical stripes of phosphor are lined up side-by-side onscreen to produce a color pixel. This method is used in Trinitron displays.

The distance between pixels is defined as *pitch*. In the conventional case, it is the distance between like phosphor dots. For Trinitron tubes, it is a measure of the distance between like phosphor bars.

Multiple monitors via NuBus expander

NuBus slot expanders, such as the expander from Second Wave, Inc., enables 13-inch monitors to be attached to the Macintosh. The expansion chassis uses one slot, leaving five free for video cards. The NuBus expansion chassis can hold eight cards itself. Second Wave warns that all video cards used in their chassis must be 32-bit clean.

The specific configuration of the Mac determines how many monitors you can use at one time. The allocation of System resources in the Macintosh is determined by several managers, including the Memory and Pallet Managers. These memory managers might have problems when more than 32 monitors are used at bit depths greater than 8 bits.

Hardware limitations of the Mac also limit the number of monitors that can display at one time. Parameter RAM on the Mac holds information for six NuBus slots, and the VIA chips have interrupts for only six slots.

No NTSC Video Out on LCs

NTSC video is different from standard composite video in that it is based on half-lines of video information that scan in alternating rows down the screen, not full lines that increment one line at a time down the screen.

To work with NTSC signals, the Mac needs to understand and process half-line screen data. In the case of the LCs, this is impossible because Macintosh LCs are designed to consider one full line across the screen as the basic screen unit.

Cards in the 8/24 series implement NTSC video signals by employing programmable logic in their designs. To do this on the LCs' logic board would require several thousand more transistors in the video ASIC than are currently used. The LC is meant to be a low-cost unit, so this capability was forfeited to production costs.

Upgrading video cards

Users who have older Mac Display Card 8/24 cards can upgrade to the new card, which uses the new Macintosh 21-inch Color Display and the new 16-inch Color Display.

The upgrade is primarily a new PAL for timing corrections on the new monitors. The Macintosh Display Card 8/24 is capable of driving the Macintosh 21-inch Color Display. There is no need to upgrade the ROM to use the Macintosh 21-inch Color Display. A ROM Upgrade is required to support the new 16-inch Color Display, however. The original 8/24 card does not support the 16-inch Color Display.

Users who require the selection of white points in their work are encouraged to get the upgrade by ordering part number 076-0548 through a local Apple certified service center.

When to do In-Situ adjustment

Aging and monitor movement (especially shipping) cause the monitors to drift out of their factory-set alignment. Periodic adjustments are therefore required to restore the unit to its factory configuration.

Monitor adjustments, whether for compact Macs or stand-alone monitors, require the use of a video test program such as Color TPG or Snooper. Both of these programs produce standard test patterns and colors that are used to align the display and calibrate colors.

Warning

Be very careful while working inside a monitor. Various components store charges of deadly intensity.

Remove the monitor cover

Before you adjust anything on a monitor, make sure you have the correct tools. A set of small screwdrivers and plastic television tools are useful. A flexible ruler or tape measure is handy for measuring the screen dimensions. As far as the alignment procedure is concerned, the process is straightforward.

In some cases, the display and alignment controls for a monitor are located under a cover plate at the rear of the monitor. In most cases, however, the rear cover must be removed to access these controls. The cover plate can be removed easily with a small screwdriver to expose the controls. If you have to remove the cabinet back, case screws will need to be removed and the cover will need to be unfastened around its seam with the front bezel. Once open, the chassis will almost always have the adjustment pots facing out along the rear of the unit. The following steps walk you through a safe monitor adjustment:

1. Remove the case or cover from the monitor. Some models have cover plates over the adjustment pots. Check for this first before disassembling the unit.

2. After you have access to the adjustment pots, adjust the width of the display to the monitor's specifications.

3. Next, adjust the height of the display according to specs.

4. Use a test pattern generator to create a focus pattern and adjust the focus of the display.

5. Replace the cover and screws and make sure there are no leftover parts on the work surface. Start the monitor and check that all the adjustments and corrections did not change as you replaced the back cover.

Adjust the width

Adjust the brightness control on the monitor (if it has one) so that it is half its full intensity before correcting the width of the display. Also, set the contrast control to its maximum setting. When these preliminary adjustments are set, launch the video test software that will be used to calibrate the system. Figure 6.56 shows the program Color TPG and its T-square window for setting height and width of the display.

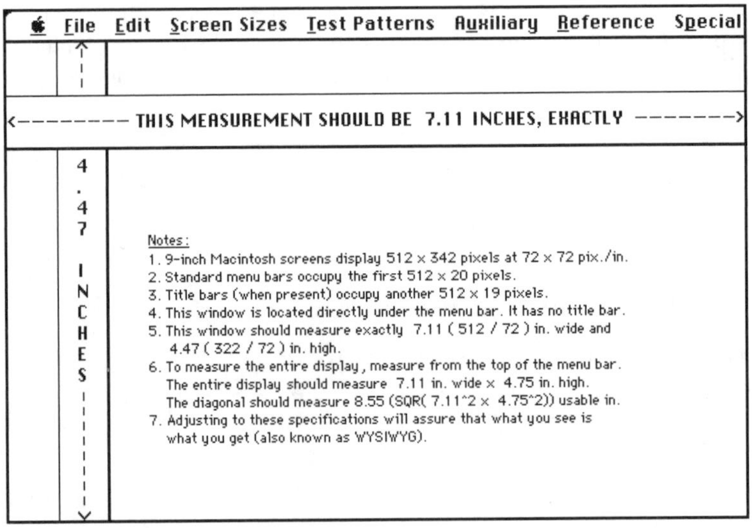

Figure 6.56   The T-square window in ColorTPG is used to align width and height of monitor screens.

The T-square window shows the correct width and height of a display screen for a selected monitor. Custom sizes are supported, too. Use a flexible ruler or tape measure to measure the horizontal and vertical dimensions of the display and adjust the monitor until the settings are correct.

Adjust the width using one of the plastic TV adjustment tools until the dimension matches that indicated on the T-square. Use the tape measure to check the width against the recommended setting.

After the width has been set, flip the tape over and measure the height of the display image. The T-square will have the proper size displayed on it as a guide. Insert the screwdriver or TV adjustment tool in the height adjustment pot and match the dimension with that shown on the T-square. Confirm your settings with the tape measure.

Adjust the focus

The last adjustment to the monitor should be the focus. Clean the screen first. Use a monitor test program to display a focus test pattern onscreen. Color TPG will produce a focus test screen that fills the display with 9- or 12-point characters, as shown in Figure 6.57.

Figure 6.57 Compare the focus in the center with that of the corners and edges.

Look over the display for fuzzy areas that appear out of focus. Pay close attention to the corners relative to the center and the focus of the characters along the diagonals. Switch between the 9-point and 12-point displays for comparison. Adjust the focus pot at the rear of the chassis to balance the focus of the characters across the surface of the display. When the focus is accurate, adjust the contrast of the display so that the text is accentuated.

Compact Mac video alignment aid

The adjustment of a compact Mac's monitor is essentially the same as that of any other monitor, except the case must be removed. A drawing program and a laser printer can be used to construct an alignment tool for the compact Mac monitor. Draw a rectangle that is 7 inches by 4.7 inches using MacPaint or any other drawing program.

Print the drawing on the laser printer using clear transparency sheets. Trim the sheet so that the template fits the screen of the compact Mac. The sheet will stick to the screen thanks to static electricity. Adjust the screen dimensions to match those printed on the template. However, do not use this template for the Color Classic; it is not the correct size for that display.

Notes, common questions, and problems with Macintosh video

Apple Technical Support logs many common problems associated with Apple monitors, new and old. A collection of these popular questions and problems are listed in this section. Look over the list for Systems and configurations that resemble the Macs on which you work. Chances are one of these problems may resemble something that occurred on your Mac.

Macintosh monitor noise at startup

Many Mac monitors make a noise at power-up when the degaussing coil is activated. The sound is simply the coil energizing and is in no way a sign of a problem.

Compatible Systems with the 12-Inch display

Not all Macs support the 12-inch RGB monitor. Macs that support the 12-inch display are:

Macintosh Display Card 4•8 and Macintosh Display Card 8/24
Macintosh IIci built-in video
Macintosh IIsi built-in video
Macintosh LC built-in video
Macintosh LCII built-in video

Video cards prior to the 8/24 do not support the 12-inch RGB. The Macintosh Display Card 8/24 GC does not work with the 12-inch RGB either. The 8/24 GC was designed for high-end systems, not this low-cost display.

Monitors and geometric distortion

Variations and distortions of monitor images may be caused by changes in the Earth's magnetic field from place to place. Such distortions include off-center images, distorted corners, and tilted screens.

Because of the electromagnetic nature of monitors, all are affected to some degree. The extent of the distortion depends on the monitor design and the location. Moving the monitor may change the display dramatically. The suggestions that follow should help you determine whether the monitor is being influenced by environmental factors or is in need of repair.

- Change the monitor location. Move the monitor to another place and note changes to the display. If you notice changes, the environment is the source of the distortion.

- Remove metal objects from the area. Monitors operated in or around large metal objects can suffer from distortions. Try to relocate the monitor, or rearrange the objects around the monitor, until the problem is minimized.

- Look for Other Environmental Influences. Consider the effects of motors, electric appliances, other monitors, and tools in the workplace. If the display jitters, has lines in it, or flickers, this may be signs of environmental interference. Often, two monitors sitting side by side cause a jitter.

- Try turning off appliances to see if the irregularity disappears and the monitor returns to normal. Fluorescent light fixtures are a common source of this kind of problem. Other sources are refrigerators, coffee makers, copy machines, and power tools.

Warning

Do not adjust the monitor to compensate for the effects imposed on it by environmental factors. This will lead to the monitor being adjusted for a specific electromagnetic environment and not according to factory specifications. If adjustments are made to the set under these conditions, relocating the monitor will result in the set being misaligned again. For this reason, alignment under these conditions is not recommended by Apple.

Cause of visible lines in color monitors

An apparent defect in some Apple monitors can be seen when a light-colored background or desktop pattern displays. The "defect" appears as a faint horizontal gray line that extends across the screen just below the middle. Apple 16-inch displays appear to have two of these lines. What are they?

The thin lines running across the bottom of the display are part of the Sony Trinitron design and are not a defect. The 14-inch display has one line running across the display about two-thirds of the way down; the 16-inch monitor has two lines, at one-third of the way down, and at another two-thirds of the way down the display. The following monitors use a Sony Trinitron tube that contains this artifact:

13-inch High Resolution RGB Monitor
14-inch Macintosh Color Display
Macintosh 16-inch Color Display
Macintosh Color Classic

AudioVision 14 Display
Macintosh TV
Macintosh LC 520
Performa 550

The Sony Trinitron has a specially designed grill that produces a sharp image but relies on a support wire to stabilize the aperture grid. The size of the wire is thinner than a human hair.

Note that the faint horizontal line(s) is not a monitor defect. The lines cannot be removed by an adjustment or alignment of the system, nor can they be removed by any repair procedure.

Nearby interference can cause horizontal lines

My Apple monitor has a phantom scan line that scrolls across the screen. What's the cause?

One probable cause of this problem is 60 cycle (Hz) electrical noise somewhere in the vicinity of the monitor. Because the problem is quite noticeable, the scan rate of the monitor is probably around 60 Hz and is susceptible to electrical pickup.

Noise of this kind is usually from electrical lights, appliances, and power tools. Look for sources of magnetic fields in the immediate environment.

Cure for jitters in RGB monitors

Users of the High-Res RGB monitors have encountered a two-prong problem. When a jitter problem is fixed after replacing the logic boards, a serious convergence problem results!

Standard adjustment procedures using V-Twist and H-Stat pots fail to alleviate this problem. Convergence can be off by as much as 1.8-inches vertically. Adjusting V-Twist only partially aligns the image. If the image is correct in the center, it appears off at the edges or at the top and bottom. In addition, distinct red, blue, and green shadowed images are onscreen in different sizes.

To align the unit, adjust pots labeled V-top and V-bottom on the logic board. This should bring the unit back into proper adjustment. The origin of the problem is most likely a jar or bump of that moved the pots.

What you can do to prevent screen interference

If interference is coming from power lines, a power filter is required for the supply lines. If the interference is traceable to electromagnetic interference (EMI) in the environment, the only option is to relocate the monitor. Special shielding placed around the unit can help with EMI problems but is usually not a practical solution.

Shielding suggestions for interference

Several Apple monitors are known to wobble incessantly in the workplace while PC monitors are unaffected and stable. Noise from power lines is the prime suspect, but why are only the Mac monitors affected? Can this interference be shielded?

Electrical lines or arching fluorescent lights are likely the cause of the problem. The reason the VGA monitors appear unaffected is that they operate at a 60 Hz refresh rate, the same as the electrical system. If electrical noise or interruptions occur at the same time the monitor refreshes, the disturbance may be unnoticeable. The Macintosh display refreshes faster than 60 Hz and is subject to the noise.

Find the cause of the noise and try to remove it. There are no practical shielding solutions for a problem like this. The best thing to do is to try to find the source of the noise and remove it or fix it. As far as Apple recommendations are concerned, there is currently no known practical shielding solution for this kind of problem.

Troubleshooting screen flicker in 8/24 cards

The origin of this problem may actually be the 8/24 GC control panel. Restart the computer while holding down the Shift key to disable the extensions. If the flicker goes away, the problem is in the software. Check for cross conflicts with other INITs and CDEVs (extensions and control panels) in the System. Also look for incompatibilities with installed hardware.

Disabling the 8/24 GC CDEV will force the card to function like a standard 8/24 model. If the problem persists, check for EMI problems in the environment.

Degauss adjustment in RGB monitors

When and why should I degauss the monitor?

Degaussing a monitor corrects small patches of color distortion that occur over time as the monitor is used. High EMI enhances the problem. The situation is likely to occur if the monitor is moved while the power is on. To fix a straying or separation of color onscreen, press the degauss switch. Usually only newer Mac monitors have this button.

No sync on green support in LCIII, Q660AV, Q840AV, or Power Macs

Older Macintosh computers sent the video synchronization signal with the green signal. This is referred to as "sync on green" processing. According to Apple technical notes, sync on green was not included in the LCIII, 660AV, 840AV, and Power Macs because of the following:

- The increasingly popular use of PC-multifrequency displays that do not support sync on green has created too many compatibility issues to warrant sync on green in newer Macs.

- Popular standards such as VGA and VESA do not support sync on green.

- Current Apple monitors do not support sync on green.

- Newer power-saving "green" monitors that "sleep" when not in use have separate sync lines to signal the monitor to sleep and save energy. Because separate lines are used anyway, no sync on green is required.

- Signal processing of the sync off the green video adds cost to the system.

If a monitor will not work without sync on green, there is little that can be done to remedy the problem. In fact, this is only a problem with a small number of displays. If the monitor cable does not connect the proper sync signals to the monitor, try replacing the cable (or adapter) with another one properly wired with the correct connections.

Note

In most cases, if sync on green is present in the System, there is no need for cables or adapters to pass the control lines through a physical connection. Because some monitors wind up displaying a greenish tint when separate sync signals are present, not passing them is a sure-fire cure for the problem.

Video monitor screen disappears in Power Macs

AV Power Macs have been known to lose the application Video Monitor's window at full screen suddenly when an external monitor is connected to the HDI-45 port. When the monitor is connected to the DB-15 video port on the AV card, everything is OK. What is the setup for getting the window to appear on the display when the HDI-45 port is used?

The "full screen" setting prompts the Video Manager that there is another display connected to the AV card. This sets the Preferences for the application accordingly. To restore the System to its original state, open the Preferences folder in the System Folder and destroy the Preferences file for the Video Manager.

Video capture

The AV Macs are the first computers capable of capturing video without additional hardware. A new chip onboard the AV Mac handles the video in and out chores. (This chip is also found on the popular VideoSpigot board from SuperMac.) Macintosh AVs have RCA and S-Video inputs, which cover most of the output capabilities of consumer cameras and VCRs. However, any pro-level input would be wasted on the AV's onboard video capabilities.

Although it's amazing for a computer to have any type of built-in video at all, the professional video community will not make much use of the AV's onboard video. Don't be confused by Apple's claim of "full motion video" for the AVs. Although it will transfer incoming video signals directly to the Mac's monitor, capturing video is another story altogether. Full-screen/full-motion/full-color video capture and output takes more than just a chip. Enormously enhanced throughput capabilities are required, along with extremely fast hard disks, accelerated SCSI, disk arrays, and advanced hardware compression. Professional quality video products for Macintosh computers are available from third-party Macintosh vendors such as Avid and Radius.

Apple's own built-in Touchstone technology can input and display "flicker-free" video. Touchstone is built around a convolution algorithm, which creates an interlaced signal like that of standard televisions and video equipment. This interlaced signal is created from a non-interlaced signal, such as the signal generated by the Mac and other computers. This special signal reduces the annoying flicker created by one-pixel lines or contrasting colors. Touchstone is also licensed by Radius Co. for its VideoVision line of display/capture boards.

The software application Apple supplies to use the video capture capability on the AVs is called FusionRecorder; on the Power Macintosh VideoShop—an OEM bundle from Avid—is used. This bundled application can also be used as a front end for audio capture. FusionRecorder has a simple interface consisting of a floating window with a record and a stop button on it. Any QuickTime-capable application can use the clips after they've been captured. Apple's Video Player 1.3 application is also available from Apple's System Update for System 7.5. Apple Video Player is also bundled with Apple's TV Tuner card for the 630, 5200, 6200, and 9500 models.

Another interesting piece of software that uses onboard video capabilities is a bundled application called ESoF2F, from an English company The Electronic Studio. ESoF2F allows AV owners who attach a video camera to videoconference over a network—preferably a high-speed Ethernet network.

ESoF2F also supports AppleTalk and even the rare but extremely fast ISDN line. Of course, the same equipment needs to be used on the other end, but the cash outlay for this kind of system is very low compared to existing solutions that may run more than $3,000–5,000. High-speed networks are preferable because the rate of transfer directly correlates to the quality of the video sent. At best, it will match the playback quality of the AV itself; at worst, video rates can go as low as several minutes per frame with tinny 4-bit noncontiguous sound.

Radius Telecast

Radius' latest multimedia hardware connects variety of video and audio input and output devices to your Macintosh. Telecast supports QuickTime, JPEG compression, CD-quality sound, and Betacam SP input and output. It is also compatible with SMPTE/EBU timecode and can be used with applications to generate frame-accurate video edit lists. This hardware is designed to work with a wide range of software applications bringing broadcast production-level capabilities, such as image effects, mixing, transitions, and similar audio features, to your Macintosh.

Radius, Inc.
215 Moffett Park Drive
Sunnyvale, CA 94089
(408) 541-6100, (800) 227-2795

Graphics

Graphics cards, like video cards, are available in NuBus, PDS, and PCI formats. These cards speed up such graphics technologies as Apple's QuickDraw, QuickDraw 3D, Adobe's PostScript, color synchronization and large image acceleration. Graphics cards enhance the performance of these technologies by dedicating a chip onboard the card.

Monitor technology

One of the major distinctions between Macintosh and other computer systems is that everything in Macintosh is a graphic image. Unlike PCs, which employ one display mode for text and another for graphics, the Mac generates only graphics to accommodate text and images.

In addition, the Macintosh uses a reserved block of memory to map information to the screen for display. This bitmapped display technique works for monochrome and color displays and relies on the contents of the screen buffer for its information. As the video display systems on the Mac increase in complexity, the amount of RAM used as a screen buffer grows. The compact Macs like the Plus and SE used about 22K of RAM to buffer screen contents. Some modern Quadras use 1 MB to 2 MB for their color displays.

Almost everything drawn to the screen of a Macintosh is created by the ROM routines known as *QuickDraw*. QuickDraw was developed by Apple to aid in the drawing of text, graphics, patterns, and colors. QuickDraw is the backbone of the Macintosh computer's drawing and printing capabilities. QuickDraw is one of many components that make up the Macintosh Toolbox, Apple's System software technology which enables the ease-of-use technology on the Macintosh. Much of the Toolbox works with each other. QuickDraw, for example, will commonly interact with the Window Manager (Window Manager is the Toolbox component that controls the Windows on your Mac) and the Menu Manager (Menu Manager is another Toolbox component that controls menu behavior on your Mac).

Creating the Display

The Macintosh display has its picture painted in a manner similar to that used for other computers and television sets. The screen image is composed of thousands of dots arranged over hundreds (or thousands) of parallel lines onscreen. This form of display is referred to as a *raster display* because of the way the image is painted onscreen by the parallel horizontal scan lines. The image itself is created onscreen by an electron beam that energizes a phosphor coating on the video tube that glows for a time after being hit by the beam. The control of the video sweep (electron beam) is managed by the video circuitry in the Macintosh, which scans the screen from the upper left of the display, across the screen to the right, down a pixel repeating the left to right sweep, and ending at the lower right corner of the display. At the end of the scan, the video circuitry returns the beam to the upper left corner and the process begins again to refresh or update the display.

This scan procedure differs from the method used in television sets. In television sets the even-numbered lines are drawn first over the entire screen, and then the screen is updated with the video information for the odd-numbered lines. This method of painting alternate sets of screen information is referred to as *interlacing* the display. Displays that use this technique are referred to as *interlaced displays*.

The speed at which the scanning of a Mac display and TV takes place is referred to as the *frame rate.* The Macintosh SE and Classic have a scan rate of about 1/60 second; that is, they refresh the screen 60 times a second. This figure is often also referred to as the *refresh rate.* The refresh rate is variable and differs for different displays. Table 6.24 lists the different scan rates of early Macintosh models.

Table 6.24 Scan Rates for Some Macintosh Monitors

Model	Vertical (Hz)	Horizontal (KHz)
BUILT-IN MONITORS		
Macintosh 128K	60.15	22.25
Macintosh 512K	60.15	22.25
Macintosh 512Ke	60.15	22.25
Macintosh Plus	60.15	22.25
Macintosh SE	60.15	22.25
Macintosh SE/30	60.15	22.25
Macintosh Classic	60.15	22.25
Macintosh Classic II	60.15	22.25
Macintosh Color Classic	60.15	24.48
Macintosh LC 520	66.70	35.00
MACINTOSH MONITORS		
Apple 21-inch Color Display	75.00	68.70
Apple Two-Page Monitor	75.00	68.70
Apple 16-inch Color Display	75.00	50.00
Apple Portrait Display	75.00	68.90
Apple AudioVision 14 Display	66.70	35.00
Macintosh (14-inch) Color Display	66.70	35.00
Basic (14-inch) Color Monitor	59.94	31.50
Performa Plus Display	66.70	35.00
Performa Display	66.70	35.00
13-inch AppleColor High-Res RGB Monitor	66.70	35.00
12-inch Apple High-Res	66.70	35.00

32-bit QuickDraw

32-Bit QuickDraw is a set of enhancements to the Color QuickDraw routines. Of the three basic operating modes in Color QuickDraw, the standard mode is CLUT (Color Look Up Table) mode. CLUT can generate 1-, 2-, 4-, and 8-bit color values. This mode is commonly referred to as *indirect* mode.

The other two Color QuickDraw modes use RGB values instead of look up tables. Mode two works with 16-bit colors; mode three handles 32-bit values. For mode two, only the first 15 bits are significant. In mode three, only the first 24 bits are significant, hence the confusion over 32-bit QuickDraw being 24-bits in reality. This mode is commonly referred to as *direct* mode.

According to Apple, the key features of 32-Bit QuickDraw are:

- Support for very large frame buffers

- 32-bit addressing of graphics devices

- Support for direct devices

- Pixel values directly specify a color for "Direct" devices, so CLUTs are not used

- Up to 16 million colors per pixel

- Color values contain up to 8 bits for each of the three RGB direct components, with the following:

    - 8 bits of padding, resulting in a maximum of 24 significant bits out of 32
    - Extensions to the PICT file format
    - Support for up to 32 bits per pixel (up to 24 of which are significant)

32-bit QuickDraw's two RGB frames are encoded as 32-bit direct RGB and 16-bit direct RGB. The 32-bit direct RGB value frame is defined as follows:

> 00000000 RRRRRRRR GGGGGGGG BBBBBBBB

The 16-bit direct RGB value frame is defined as follows:

> 0 RRRRR GGGGG BBBBB

Hardware requirements for 32-bit QuickDraw

The benefits of 32-bit QuickDraw depend somewhat on the video card used in the Macintosh System. A direct device video card, when used in a Mac, can access color values directly rather than have to receive a CLUT index value.

The Macintosh Operating System also allows 32-bit images to be created off-screen. Thus, systems that do not employ direct device techniques can still run under 32-bit QuickDraw. In this way, hardware is not a limiting factor in the display of QuickDraw information.

Software issues

32-bit QuickDraw and Color QuickDraw are compatible and do not conflict. Applications do have problems with 32-bit QuickDraw, however; applications usually have trouble when they:

- Draw directly to the screen.

- Fail to put values in all the necessary fields in the pixmap and new gDevice records.

- Manually clone gDevice pixmaps.

- Assume that a pixmap has a CLUT.

Understanding NuBus

NuBus and PDS cards enable you to expand your Macintosh with the addition of features the Mac's built-in hardware cannot support. Common uses for PDS and NuBus cards include high-performance SCSI, additional network connections, complex video display and digitization, and performance acceleration.

Although NuBus and PDS formats both have a slot that accepts special cards, NuBus is more advanced. This format is a well-defined and standardized pathway. PDS cards, on the other hand, integrate directly with the processor's operations. Because PDS cards are forced to operate within the architecture of the processor to which they are attached, a different type of PDS card is required for each Macintosh, and they cannot be used for as wide a range of applications as can NuBus cards.

Each Macintosh model has different configurations of NuBus and PDS slots. The NuBus interface is generally used in larger, more powerful computers; the PDS slot is used most often in compact, low power models. The Macintosh SE, SE/30, and Color Classic have only a PDS slot. The Macintosh II, IIx, IIcx, and IIci only have NuBus slots. The Macintosh IIsi, IIfx, Quadra/Centris 610 and 650, Quadra 700, 800, 900, and 950 feature both PDS and NuBus slots. The Macintosh Classic, Classic II, and PowerBook computers include neither NuBus nor PDS expansion. See Chapters 1 and 2 for details about the exact slot configurations of each Mac.

History of Macintosh expansion

Early Macintosh computers offered little in the way of hardware expansion. The 128K and 512K Macintosh models offered expansion only through two slow serial ports—the modem and printer ports. With the introduction of the Macintosh Plus, the use of the SCSI bus was introduced. Although the SCSI bus provided much faster communication than the serial ports, it wasn't nearly powerful enough to satisfy the demanding needs of high-performance network and video peripherals.

In 1987, Apple released the first Macintosh computers that provided internal expansion. The Macintosh SE featured a PDS, allowing direct connection to the microprocessor. The Macintosh II computer made use of a new industry standard, NuBus, to provide six versatile expansion slots. Since 1987, PDS or NuBus slots have appeared in nearly every Macintosh.

NuBus

The NuBus standard was developed by Texas Instruments and customized by Apple for use in Macintosh computers. NuBus provides general purpose, high-speed communication with the computer, and was designed for the addition of various peripherals.

The major advantage of NuBus is its standard design and interface (see Figure 6.58). This standardization enables NuBus cards to work across multiple Macintosh models and enables your Mac to negotiate the technical needs of the cards, thus removing the need to set large numbers of jumper switches on the card during installation.

Several NuBus configurations have appeared since the Mac II introduced this standard:

- **Standard NuBus.** The standard NuBus card talks to the computer by using a processor-independent N 32-bit-wide pathway. All NuBus cards use Euro-DIN 96-pin connectors, IEEE 1196 standard. The patent for NuBus is owned by its designer, Texas Instruments.

- **NuBus '90.** In 1989, Apple and several other vendors began to expand the NuBus standard. The upgraded standard is known as NuBus '90. Features of the new standard include faster transfers between the computer and cards, power to cards when the machine is off, and compatibility with existing NuBus cards.

  Partial implementations of NuBus '90 first appeared in the Macintosh Quadra 900. Complete implementation began appearing with the Power Macintosh computers.

- **NuBus and Power Macintosh.** According to Apple, the performance of NuBus on the Power Macintosh computers is better than NuBus performance on any other Macintosh except the Quadra 840AV. NuBus performance on the Quadra 840AV is approximately equal to NuBus performance on a Power Macintosh. Most existing NuBus cards work unchanged in a Power Mac, except for those that depend upon certain features of the 68000 processor; these cards require updated drivers.

Note

PDS cards designed for previous Macintosh models do not work in Power Macs because they depend on a specific processor.

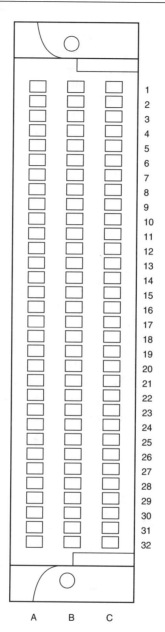

Figure 6.58 NuBus cards use the Euro-DIN 96-pin connector.

6

PDS

PDS is an alternate form of expansion slot available in many Macs. PDS slots are typically used in the more compact Mac models, such as the Classic line. Rather than issue a standard set of commands through a standard interface like NuBus, PDS cards connect directly to the CPU. Because of this direct connection, PDS cards must be designed for the Mac into which they will be added.

Caution

Even though some Macintosh computers have the same physical connectors, they are not the same electronically. Make sure you check with your card's manufacturer before installing a PDS.

68000 and 68020 PDS

A similar PDS interface is used on the Macintosh SE, Macintosh Portable, and Macintosh LC. These three models use a 96-pin connector for PDS cards that is physically identical, but is not electrically identical. Because of the electrical differences, PDS cards for these three Macintosh models are not interchangeable.

68030 PDS

The SE/30, IIfx, and IIsi all use 120-pin connectors for the PDS. The electronic configurations of these cards have some electrical compatibility, but some signals are still specific to each computer. Check with the manufacturer of each card before assuming compatibility.

The 68030 PDS in the LCII and LCIII uses the same 96-pin connector the 68020 LC uses. The PDSs among all three LC models are electrically and physically identical.

68040 PDS

Non-AV Quadra and Centris computers use an 040 PDS with a 140-pin connector. Because the 040 PDS has a different physical and electrical arrangement than previous cards, it isn't compatible with non-Quadra/Centris models.

Note

The AV Macintosh models (Centris/Quadra 660AV/840AV) do not have PDS connectors.

Installing NuBus and PDS cards

Because NuBus cards are installed inside your Macintosh, all standard precautions about opening the case apply. Make sure you carefully read and understand the section earlier in this chapter concerned with opening the case before opening your Macintosh to install a NuBus or PDS card.

After you've opened the case, install the NuBus or PDS card by gently seating the card into its socket. If the card has an external jack (such as a network connection), remove the cover plate on the back of the Mac.

A new Macintosh standard: PCI

NuBus has proven to be a reliable and useful addition to the Macintosh. Nevertheless, the PCI (Peripheral Component Interconnect) standard has been adopted by Apple on its latest Power Macintosh computers. PCI features higher speeds and lower electrical requirements than NuBus and is almost the standard in Intel (x86) and Pentium world. High-end PCI products are already available for Power Macintosh computers. For more information on PCI products for Power Macintosh computers, see Chapter 2.

Apple QuickDraw 3D Accelerator Card

Designed to work in conjunction with Apple's QuickDraw 3D software, the 3D accelerator card accelerates 3D applications such as modeling, interface, and game software.
At press time pricing and availability were not available, nor were slot/card type specifications. Nevertheless, these can be obtained by contacting Apple by phone, or visiting Apple's Web site at www.info.apple.com.

> Apple Computer, Inc.
> One Infinite Loop
> Cupertino, CA 95014
> (408) 996-1010

Radius graphics acceleration

Radius offers five PCI graphics accelerator cards ranging from high-end, high-resolution graphics cards accelerated with DSP chips to entry-level solutions that offer the option of up-grading the amount of VRAM on the card. Radius' graphics acceleration products use the *Thunder* name to identify the graphics acceleration product line.

> Radius, Inc.
> 215 Moffett Park Drive
> Sunnyvale, CA 94089
> (408) 541-6100, (800) 227-2795

ATI Graphics Accelerator

The ATI Graphics Accelerator is the first PCI product in the mach63 family of graphics accelerators available from ATI Technologies. This accelerator combines features such as instant panning, resolution, and color depth changes with an easy-to-use interface that supports Apple Guide.

ATI Technologies, Inc.
33 Commerce Valley Drive East
Thornhill, Ontario, Canada L3T 7N6
(905) 882-2600

YARC Systems Corporation offers PowerPC coprocessor-driven graphics acceleration as well as 3D-specific PCI solutions. Their products are well-known for their incredible performance for PostScript and 3D imaging.

YARC System Corporation
975 Business Center Circle
Newbury Park, CA 91320
800 ASK-YARC, 805 499-9444

Additional PCI graphics products are available from manufacturers such as ATI Technologies, Diamond Multimedia Systems, Weird, Inc., LinoType-Hell Company, and YARC System Corporation. You can now buy PCI-slot products for SCSI, Network, DOS, data acquisition, storage, and PCI-to-NuBus conversion.

Software Upgrades

This chapter covers three types of software upgrades: general System software, new technology System software, and software application upgrades; it also will help you understand the offerings of different System software products, upgrades, and applications, and help you decide whether to invest in some of these technologies. Many of the technologies discussed in this chapter may require that you purchase or install additional memory into your Macintosh, or make more hard drive space available. Upgrading memory is discussed in Chapter 6.

Operating Systems

Macintosh computers require System software in order to access Mac hardware and run software applications. In 1994, with the introduction of System 7.5, Apple gave their Macintosh operating system a name: MacOS. For more information on MacOS, see Chapter 3 and Appendices D and F.

When to upgrade MacOS

Upgrading to a completely new version of System software can involve many changes, including upgrading hardware and software application versions. If you are happy with your current System software features and performance, consider what features are available in a new version of System software or System update release, before purchasing or installing the upgrade. In general, new System software releases offer consistent backward compatibility with most software applications and work on Macintosh computers with at least 4 MB of memory. If you are considering adding more System software to your Mac, make sure you have enough memory and hard drive space available for all System software and any applications you intend to use with the new System software technologies.

System 7.5 supports Macintosh computers from the Mac Plus through the 6100, 7100, and 8100 Power Mac models. If you have System 7.1, a benefit of upgrading to System 7.5 is that all the System Enabler files from System 7.1 are incorporated into the System File. System 7.5 also includes many new features such as Desktop Patterns, General Controls, and WindowShade control panels.

System updates

System updates have been available for Mac computers since System 7.0. System updates are traditionally free and offer performance improvements, bug fixes, and new versions of System software and System software-related products such as printer drivers, QuickDraw GX, and PowerTalk. System updates are available on most online services, and on Apple's ftp site at ftp.info.apple.com. If you aren't sure if you should upgrade to a specific System update version, read the System update ReadMe file for detailed information on what is in a particular System update.

Shared libraries in the System software

Newer Apple technologies, such as OpenTransport and OpenDoc, use software pieces called *shared libraries* to help implement their inherent technologies. Apple develops shared libraries to minimize software needs for memory management. Apple's shared library products include Apple Shared Library Manager 2.0 (also known as ASLM 2.0), and Code Fragment Manager (also known as CFM). Because shared libraries reside in the System Folder, their presence in the System file (as well as existing in System software), may not be used if the technology or software application needing it is not running. However, all shared libraries will take up hard drive space and occupy additional memory when installed in your System Folder. If a shared library is located in your Extension folder or System Folder, it will load with other System software when your Macintosh starts up.

In System 7.5, CFM (Code Fragment Manager) is built into Power Macintosh System software, but not in 680x0-based Macintosh System software. For 68K-based Macintosh Systems, this manager is called CFM 68K. On the Power Macintosh, CFM uses an Interface Library to communicate with System software. The interface library is a separate file located in the System Folder. 68K Macintosh systems using CFM 68K require a 68K version of the Interface Library to work with System software.

System software technologies

The following is a brief discussion of Apple's System software technologies and a summary of memory requirements. These System software technologies extend System software with new functionality. Most of these features are available in software applications created specifically to take advantage of QuickDraw 3D, QuickDraw GX, QuickTime, and other System software technologies.

If you plan to use all of the technologies discussed below, 24 MB of RAM is probably the minimum memory requirement to allow both applications and System software to run optimally. Multimedia System software technologies are Apple's more popular System software. These include Sound Manager 3.1, QuickTime 2.1, and PlainTalk 1.4.1. More information on System software is also available in Chapter 3.

QuickTime 2.1

QuickTime is System software for digital video. It is used by hardware and software applications to integrate digital video with audio, text, and animation. Although QuickTime does not provide complete professional-quality digital video, it is a time and cost-efficient technology used for making movies in Hollywood and in your home. QuickTime is a necessity for most multimedia software, including online applications such as America Online. Version 2.1 offers PCI Power Macintosh compatibility, bug fixes to 2.0, and new features. Version 2.1 also incorporates the Multimedia Tuner extension released for QuickTime 2.0 to fix bugs and improve performance for QuickTime applications. If you have QuickTime 2.1, you no longer need the Multimedia Tuner extension in your system folder.

> 4 MB Memory Requirements w/System software
> 20K Approximate memory when loaded but not in use
> 1 MB Memory when in use (avg)
> 8 MB Recommended amount of memory for use with applications

QuickDraw 3D 1.0.3

QuickDraw 3D is only available for Power Macintosh computers. It adds tremendous 3D interface features and performance using QuickDraw 3D-compatible SimpleText applications or other 3D software. QuickDraw 3D extends System software to support applications that use QuickDraw 3D file formats, image creation, manipulation, and rendering technologies.

> 16 MB Memory Requirements w/System software
> 0K Approximate memory when loaded but not in use
> 2 MB Memory when in use (avg)
> 16 MB Recommended amount of memory for use with applications

OpenTransport 1.1

OpenTransport is Apple's next generation networking software. It is actually a superset of Apple's traditional networking software, including AppleTalk, Ethernet, TCP, and LocalTalk network software drivers and control panels. Initially only available on PCI Power Macintosh Systems, this System software is accelerated for Power Macintosh and enables you to change your TCP and Internet configuration (such as a name server in the OpenTransport software), without restarting your Mac for the changes to take effect. Some initial compatibility problems with OpenTransport 1.0 include SLIP, PPP, and printing problems. Bug fix releases for these problems have been made available on Apple's ftp site at ftp.info.apple.com, and Apple's World Wide Web site at `www.info.apple.com`. OpenTransport 1.1 is expected to reduce the amount of memory OpenTransport uses when it is running with and without AppleTalk, TCP, and other network drivers. (It may also work with many 680×0-based Macintosh computers). At presstime, Apple released OpenTransport version 1.0.8, which is intended to fix the TCP and PPP incompatibilities.

4 MB Memory Requirements w/System software
100K Approximate memory when loaded but not in use
800K Memory when in use (avg. with AppleTalk and TCP on)
8 MB Recommended amount of memory for use with applications

QuickDraw GX 1.1.2

QuickDraw GX is Apple's next generation printing, imaging, and graphics software. Most of this technology is stored in a 1.6 MB extension file. Many of the features of QuickDraw GX are discussed in Chapter 3. QuickDraw GX requires a 68020, 68030, 68040 or Power Mac and System 7.5, with at least 8 MB of memory installed. If you plan to use the latest graphics or desktop publishing software, check out the version of SimpleText that ships with QuickDraw GX, or look into a QuickDraw GX compatible application.

One of the most attractive features of QuickDraw GX is its desktop printing and portable document technologies. Printer icons can be created on your desktop, by opening Chooser in the Apple Menu, selecting the printer driver icon, and selecting the button to create the desktop printer icon. To print a document with QuickDraw GX installed, drag the file to the desired printer icon. Unfortunately, to use the desktop printing feature, you need to have enough memory to run all of QuickDraw GX, which is approximately 2 MB of memory.

8 MB Memory Requirements w/System software
250K Approximate memory when loaded but not in use
2 MB Memory when in use (avg)
12 MB Recommended amount of memory for use with applications

PowerTalk 1.2.3

PowerTalk is Apple's next generation mail and network services technology. It adds a mailbox and catalog to your desktop and includes mail software application and Apple Guide support. If you need mail services for your Macintosh, PowerTalk is included with System 7.5 software. This software comes with its own installation software and provides mail and server access features. Newer versions of PowerTalk are available free from Apple and are a part of Apple's System Update releases for System 7.5 (and newer). For larger networks, a PowerTalk server is recommended.

8 MB Memory Requirements w/System software
250K Approximate memory when loaded but not in use
2 MB Memory when in use (avg)
12 MB Recommended amount of memory for use with applications

PlainTalk 1.4.1

PlainTalk is Apple's speech management technology. First introduced with the AV Macintosh, PlainTalk can read text to you. On AV and Power Macintosh computers, you can speak to your Macintosh and have it speak back, or change your speech into text. Using AppleScript, speech commands also can perform automated tasks on your Mac, such as opening control panels and applications. Several different voices are included with the PlainTalk software that is included on Power Mac and AV hard drives. To use the speech technology, you need Apple's PlainTalk microphone connected to your Mac's microphone port.

8 MB Memory Requirements w/System software
250K Approximate memory when loaded but not in use
2.5 MB Memory when in use (avg)
12 MB Recommended amount of memory for use with applications

Sound Manager 3.1

Sound Manager 3.0 is available in System 7.5. Sound Manager 3.1 is available separately on Apple's ftp and web sites, and also in System update releases for System 7.5. Sound Manager consists of the Sound Manager extension and control panel files. New features in version 3.1 include 4:1 and 2:1 audio compression, improved Power Mac performance (up to 4 to 7 times faster in some cases), and the capability to play sounds asynchronously (that is, to play sounds without tying up the rest of the System). It is backward compatible with previous versions of Sound Manager software.

4 MB Memory Requirements w/System software
10K Approximate memory when loaded but not in use
n/a Memory when in use (avg)
5 MB Recommended amount of memory for use with applications

AppleScript 1.2

AppleScript is also a part of System 7.5. This extension enables you to automate and customize your Macintosh. AppleScript is included with System 7.5 and enables automation of your Macintosh software. Several AppleScript scripts are included with System 7.5 and perform such tasks as selecting the Shutdown menu item and adding items to your Apple menu.

4 MB Memory Requirements w/System software
25K Memory when loaded but not in use

200K Memory when in use (avg)
5 MB Recommended amount of memory for use with applications

Future products

New technologies that Apple has announced, but were not available at press time, are Open Doc 1.0 and System 8. You can expect new technologies to become available as faster CPUs become more readily available, and as more people use computers. In 1995, Apple introduced a variety of new technologies including QuickTime VR, QuickTime Video Conferencing, QuickDraw 3D 1.0, and Open Transport 1.0 and 1.1. These technologies are discussed in this upgrade section.

OpenDoc 1.0

Container and part technology represents a new metaphor for document management on the Macintosh. In essence, you no longer need multiple applications to perform a variety of tasks or need to work with multiple document formats. OpenDoc 1.0 provides a framework for a universal application paradigm. Parts that supply individual or sets of features can be moved into and out of the container framework. Parts can have different file sizes and different memory footprints, and they can be easy to use or sophisticated. Parts also can be simple enough for a relatively new user to create.

Copland

Copland is Apple's fully native System software release for Power Macintosh. Apple has not announced a specific date for its release, however it is the next major release of System software expected from Apple. Software drivers, up to and including every piece of System software will run both 68K and native applications. The Macintosh Toolbox is being rewritten to maintain compatibility with existing software applications, but it will run optimized with PowerPC processors, native System, and application software. The MacOS will also gain a new look and new interface features. Copland can be compared to Apple's System 7.0 transition from System 6.0.x, which upgraded users to a new look and feature set for Macintosh System software.

Software upgrades

Despite what the software companies preach, you don't always need to install every new version of a program. However, waiting too long to buy an upgrade may mean you will miss out on an opportunity for a hot new version at a bargain price.

You can keep up by reading news announcements and product reviews in Macintosh magazines, such as *MacUser, MacWEEK,* and *Macworld.* Advertisements are also a source of information. Some minor upgrades are free and not well-publicized by the software vendors. Also keep in mind that a software purchase is not forever; there may be a time when a competitor's product better meets your needs than an upgrade of your current application.

Types of upgrades

Most applications come out with some sort of upgrade at least once a year, but all upgrades are not created equally. Software manufacturers create upgrades for a variety of reasons, such as fixing defective software and adding new features or compatibility with other software or types of computers. The bigger software companies need a major upgrade every 12 to 18 months to keep up with their competitors, and to take advantage of faster computers. Smaller companies with less mainstream products, such as statistics or accounting packages, come out with major upgrades less frequently.

You can tell if a new version of an application is a major or minor upgrade by looking at its version number. (Some companies use both release and version numbers, such as Release 4 Version 2, but this is more common for UNIX and PC software than for Mac software.) Although not foolproof, the version number will usually tell you if the upgrade is a bug fix, a minor upgrade, or a major upgrade. Version numbers are usually two or three digits, such as 2.0 or 3.2.1. If a company goes from a version 2.5 to a version 4.0, don't assume that you somehow missed version 3.0. Companies will often skip version numbers when issuing a new release of software so they can use the same version number on their Mac and PC versions, or just to make the upgrade sound more important. Macintosh magazines are a good source for determining if a new version is a major or minor upgrade.

Major releases

Major upgrades of software contain whole new groups of functionality and may look and act differently from the previous version, including significant changes in the interface. Major new releases may have been rewritten from the ground up and may use a new file format. This means that older versions of the application may not be able to read files created with the new version. This will require that you upgrade everyone in your group who shares files at the same time. The opposite, *backward compatibility*—the new version can read files created by older versions—is almost always built into the new version. However, this capability may not extend to two or three major versions back.

Major software upgrades are indicated with a version number that ends in zero, such as 2.0 or 4.0. Occasionally, the software company will change the product name slightly and give it a version 1.0 designation, such as going from AcmeWriter 4.5 to AcmeWriter Pro 1.0.

Major upgrades are the most costly types of new software versions. However, the cost of a major upgrade may not end with the upgrade or purchase price. The upgrade may require you to beef up your Mac.

Minor releases

A minor release will add a few new features and capabilities, as well as fix a bug or two. Usually, the interface doesn't change much with this type of upgrade. Minor releases are free to registered users or available for a small fee. Minor releases are usually fairly safe upgrades, in that they usually don't add new problems or require new RAM or hard disk space. If you have to pay for a minor upgrade, make sure the new features are worth the asking price.

You can tell an upgrade is minor when the second or third digit of the version number is increased—version 1.2 would go to a version 1.3 or to 1.2.1. Releases that end in 5, such 2.5 or 3.5, often indicate a more substantial upgrade, with a larger number of new features.

Bug fixes

A bug fix is a minor upgrade to fix a problem in the software—a malfunction that slipped through the company's quality assurance department. A bug in a piece of software doesn't necessarily mean the manufacturer does shoddy work. In just about every software company, some problems slip through every now and then.

Some bugs are small. For example, a certain feature may not work with a certain setting, or may behave incorrectly. Upgrades that fix even minor bugs are worth getting even if you have never encountered any malfunction, because you never know what kind of problem a minor bug will cause later. Other bugs are major, causing your application or Mac to crash. Should you worry about a bug fix causing new problems? This is unlikely if no new features are added.

Because no new features are usually added, a bug fix upgrade is usually considered the most minor upgrade, which is reflected by the version number. A bug fix upgrade is sometimes indicated by a third digit or letter tagged on the end of a two-digit version number, as in 2.0.1 or 5.2a. Sometimes the company will not change the version number at all when issuing a bug fix.

The cost of bug fixes varies. Bug fixes are often free, and the company will send it out to you automatically. Other times, you can obtain a free or inexpensive bug fix or by calling the company. However, this is not always the case. Sometimes, bug fix upgrades are free only to those who encounter the bug and complain about it—otherwise, the company presents the bug fix as just another new version, and requires users to pay for it. Here again, Mac magazines can help let you know when software is broken.

Registration cards: pros and cons

Keeping up with new versions of software starts with filling out the registration card, the little piece of cardboard that comes with electrical appliances such as vacuum cleaners and hair dryers, and computer software. While there are pros and cons to sending in the registration card, there are reasons to send in the card for software. Overall, the pros of sending the registration card back to the manufacturer tend to outweigh the cons.

Some companies will automatically send free copies of upgrades to registered owners, a perk you'd miss out on if your registration card sits unmarked in the box. Another perk offered to registered owners is discounts on major upgrades. If you don't fill out the registration card, you may have to pay full price for a new version. This can be a matter of paying $30 instead of $395.

The biggest drawback to sending in a registration card is that it may increase the amount of junk mail you receive. In addition to information about upgrades to the products you own, the software company will try to sell you its other products with additional brochures you may not be interested in.

How to decide if an upgrade is worth the cost

One of the myths about the latest and greatest version of software is that you need to buy it or else you'll lag hopelessly behind. In fact, the latest version isn't always the greatest for your needs, and the version you already own could serve you for years to come.

To decide whether to upgrade to a new version, you need to judge the cost versus the benefits. First, look at the cost. The price of a major upgrade can be several hundred dollars and that may not be the only cost. If the interface has changed and a large number of new functions are added, there may be training costs involved as well.

Software upgrades also can incur the hidden cost of additional computer resources. A new version may require that you add memory or additional hard disk space to your Mac. In the worst case, a software upgrade may require that you replace your Mac with a newer, faster model. This is because major upgrades to software are often so packed with new features that they run slower than previous versions.

The benefits of a software upgrade should be tangible, enabling you to do something you need to do. This could include more connectivity with other Mac computers, or with PCs, or other computers used in your group. Other benefits would be the automation of multiple tasks that you do frequently, the reduction in the number of steps it takes to accomplish a task, or the ability to improve the quality of the work you do. You should also determine if the upgrade will adversely affect compatibility with other software you use.

Sales brochures alert you that a new version exists, but are poor guides when determining whether to upgrade. The following sections show you what you can do to determine for yourself if the added benefits make up for the cost.

Get your hands on a copy

Magazine reviews are a good source of information, but the best way to see if a new version will add to your productivity is to take a test drive. You can get a demonstration at a software store, a trade show, from a college, or user group. During a software demo, ask if you can run the program yourself. If you succeed in getting your hands on the demo, try the following:

- Do some of the tasks you do with your current version. See if the new version accomplishes the tasks any faster or better than your current version.

- Don't ask for directions at first—try to figure out a new interface yourself. If you can't figure out how to operate the software, there may be some retraining required.

- For new features that require explanation, make sure you follow each step the demonstrator makes and try to repeat them yourself. Software reps know their software forward and backward and can perform a convoluted set of procedures in a flurry of keyboard commands in a second or two.

- Check the amount of memory used by the program by looking at the About this Macintosh box in the Finder (first item in the Apple menu). Often demonstrators will assign large amounts of memory (memory you may not have on your Mac) to make the application run quickly. Also note the Mac model the demonstration is run on—is it a faster model than your Mac?

- If the software crashes, ask if the version that is running on the demo is a beta version (a pre-shipping version that isn't quite finished). If it is, give the software company the benefit of the doubt; most beta software has some bugs that will be fixed when the product finally ships.

If the software company representatives won't let you run the software yourself, ask them for a demonstration copy of the software. Many companies will provide you with a demo version that has some of the functionality of the actual product, but won't let you save a file or is handicapped in some other way.

Getting your hands on a copy of the application is particularly important if you are ordering multiple copies of upgrades for a department or an entire company. You really don't want to be responsible for spending several thousands of dollars of your budget, only to find that the application doesn't meet the needs of your users.

Ask for a list of the new features

Because it is quite likely there are features in the software you have that you never use, it is helpful to see exactly what features are unique to the newer version. Often software companies will print sales brochures listing new features among the features already in the version you have. This is done to overwhelm you with the shear number of features in the product. Ask specifically what you will gain by upgrading to the new version.

Avoid features-for-features sake. Ask yourself how you would use the new features? Are they really helpful or just flashy? Just because something is technologically advanced doesn't mean it's useful.

Study the interface

User interfaces are largely subjective, but a well-designed interface includes some common elements. A well-designed software interface should build on the interface metaphors of previous versions of the software as well as the basic items of Macintosh software. Find out if you can turn off interface features that take up screen real estate, such as toolbars, tool palettes, and status bars. The option to display what you need is a good sign of a flexible application.

A user interface that is substantially different from a previous version may also be more complicated and less easy to use, in spite of fancy-looking buttons. Look for the trade-offs in a new interface to determine whether the tasks you need are easier to accomplish. Also, check to see how the application performs tasks common in other programs you own. If the software company insists on inventing its own way to do things—such as text changes, zoom, page previews, and so forth—this is a good indication that you'll be spending a lot of time learning how to use the new version.

Passing up an upgrade

If the interface of the software upgrade is so different that you do have to retrain, and the new features don't seem particularly useful, you may want to consider other options, such as keeping your current software for a while longer or using a competitor's product. You also can upgrade your software to only some of your computers. For instance, you may want to use an older version (that uses less RAM and hard disk space) on your PowerBook, and use the new version on your desktop Mac.

Keeping your current software may seem low-tech, but can be very practical. The Macintosh is a very backward-compatible machine, so that even the newest Power Mac can run software from the last decade. One thing to keep in mind if you decide not to upgrade is that you may forfeit a good price for a future version of software. For instance, if you hold on to version 3.5 when version 4.0 comes out, the software company probably won't offer you a discount on version 5.0.

This is not a problem if you decide to switch to a competitor's product. Many vendors will periodically offer a trade-in to owners of their competitors' products, so that "upgrading" to the latest version of a competitor's product may not cost more than upgrading to the latest version of the software you own. The same strategies for evaluating a new version of your application apply to switching to a competitor's product: check the product reviews in magazines and get hands-on experience.

You may find yourself in a situation where only some people in the company have switched to a competitor's product, while others have kept the same software. In this case, you can use a file translation utility such as DataViz's MacLinkPlus to convert between the two formats. A file translation tool is also helpful when different people in the company are using different versions of the same software. The users of a newer version will probably be able to read files created with an older version, but the reverse may not be true.

What happens while installing an upgrade

Replacing an application with a new version is an easy process that is usually automated with an installer program. The installer places the various new files where they belong on your hard disk and removes outdated ones. Most application installers begin with a single double-click, asking you to insert the appropriate floppy disks when needed.

The most common installer program is Apple's Installer, used to install all Apple System, application, and server software. Apple's Installer is also included on the installation disks of many third-party software vendors.

When you launch Installer, you have the option of clicking the Easy Install button or performing a Custom Install. The Easy Install option should be the one you choose for most software upgrades. Custom Install is useful if you need to reinstall a specific portion of the software package at some later date.

Most installer programs search your Mac to see what you already have installed, remove some obsolete files, and then copy files and folders from the installation disks to various places inside and outside the System Folder. These System folders typically include the Extensions folder, Control Panels folder, Apple Menu Items folder, Preferences folder, and Fonts folder (if any fonts are installed). Sometimes an application will install its own folder inside the System Folder.

If you are switching to a competitor's product, you may need to remove some files manually. The most important files to delete may be located in the Extensions and Control Panels folders. If Extensions or Control Panels files from two different applications exist and do the same thing, conflicts could interfere with your Mac. Preferences files are less important because they store the settings used in the application. Deleting a preference file will reset the application to its default settings the next time you open it.

Occasionally, certain network management applications will copy invisible files to your hard disk. Invisible files do not have an icon in the Finder, but exist on the hard disk nonetheless. To remove these files, you will need an application that can see invisible files, such as ResEdit from Apple. Some utilities, such as Dayna's ProFiles, enable you to search for and delete invisible files.

For a large-scale upgrade of multiple Macintosh computers in a department or company, you can use a network installer program such as Symantec's NetDistributer Pro or FileWave from Wave Research. These programs enable you to create upgrade packets containing new versions of applications, System software, or third-party extensions and control panels. These packets can install a variety of software with a double-click, or install themselves on users' machines at convenient preset times, such as on weekends or at night.

Like adding RAM, a bigger hard disk, or adding an expansion card, upgrading your software can add new capabilities to your Mac that can help solve problems. Software upgrades can provide you with fixes to bugs, handy new features, and increased productivity, but are by no means required. Free or inexpensive upgrades should be looked at carefully to make sure they aren't going to do any harm to your software setup. Expensive upgrades with major changes in user interface should be evaluated as carefully as the purchase of new software. You should take the plunge and go for a new upgrade only if it can improve the way you use your Mac in a way that is worth the cost.

Selected shareware applications

A few good shareware applications provide a wide range of useful features. This section lists commonly used shareware software, and provides a brief description of what each application does. Popular server sites for these and other Macintosh shareware software include America Online's software library, `ftp.info.apple.com`, and `sumex-aim.stanford.edu` as well as software publisher web sites, eWorld, and CompuServe.

- **Fetch 2.1.2.** If you have an Internet connection, Fetch is an invaluable software application, whose preferences include the most commonly used ftp sites for Macintosh software. Once you download software, Fetch can uncompress and convert the files on your Macintosh hard drive. Fetch is also available as a fat or native application in addition to its 68K version.

- **Netscape 1.1N.** Netscape 1.1 is an extremely easy to use, popular web browser. If you have an Internet connection, launch Netscape to explore a variety of Internet web sites, ftp sites, and download files of information, or new software, or send mail and post questions on Internet newsgroups as you surf the information superhighway. At press time, a 2.0 beta version of Netscape was available for the Internet community that supported some of the Internet's latest "cool stuff," like Java and frames.

- **StuffIt 1.5.1.** StuffIt 1.5.1 was the first Macintosh compression software available, and has since become a software application every user should have. America Online 2.6 and eWorld 1.1 have this software built to uncompress files downloaded from libraries or other online users. StuffIt is also available as a commercial software package, and can also uncompress DOS zip file formats.

- **BinHex 4.0.** If you use SHELL, or don't have Fetch for downloading software from the Internet to your Mac, BinHex 4.0 is a software application that will convert the downloaded BinHex file to a usable file. There is also a BinHex 5.0, which some files may need to be converted for use on a Macintosh. However, most files can be re-converted using version 4.0.

- **ZTerm.** For modem users looking for a telecommunications application for logging into bulletin boards, or for talking to another Macintosh user directly via phone connection, ZTerm is the best choice. This is a must-have if you use your modem often for BBS or Mac-to-Mac phone connections.

- **Telnet 2.6.** If you have a SHELL account on the Internet and need a Macintosh application to log in and get your mail, Telnet is a popular and reliable choice. Telnet also supports dial-in modem connections to Unix, DOS-based servers, and bulletin boards.

- **Alpha 5.81.** If you need a text editor for taking notes, writing source code, or writing outlines, Alpha is a great application. It is most often used by software developers to manage source code, but also makes a great text editor or word processor for those who may not want to invest the memory or hard drive space for commercial software equivalents.

- **Soft FPU 3.x.** For Macintosh systems without a floating point unit, Soft FPU provides software emulation that enables you to launch applications requiring an FPU. Soft FPU consists of a control panel and is easy to use with your System software. Please read the documentation packaged with this software for known incompatibilities with this software, and features of the commercial version.

- **Speedometer 4.01.** This benchmarking software can help identify performance decreases with installed hardware or software. It contains profiles of most existing Macintosh models and is very easy to use.

- **Disinfectant 3.6.** This virus checking tool is a must-have software application that you should run on your Macintosh regularly to check for and kill software viruses. Also, regularly check for new versions of Disinfectant, which is released as new viruses and virus-killing solutions are found.

- **Greg's Buttons.** This utility has a set of features that can alter the fonts and button styles in your Macintosh message dialogs and menus. It has been upgraded frequently over the past year and is relatively stable. If a new System software release is made available, or if you find problems with the current version of the software, check the Macintosh software sites for a newer version.

- **SCSIProbe 3.5.** If you have one or seven SCSI peripherals connected to your Macintosh, SCSIProbe enables you to remount or first time mount a SCSI device without having to restart your Macintosh. This software can be an invaluable timesaver, as well as troubleshooter for checking to see if a SCSI device is visible to your Macintosh.

Commercial add-ins

Commercial software can enhance your System software feature set, or improve overall software performance. These Macintosh solutions are described below, as well as known incompatibilities and things to watch out for when using the products. More information on these products can be found on AOL, eWorld, and publisher web sites as well. Some of these products require a specific Macintosh. SpeedDoubler, for example, only provides performance increases on the first Power Mac up through, but not including, the PCI-based Power Mac or Power Mac PowerBooks. Some of the products below are accelerated for Power Mac, or offer custom software installation options for 68K and Power PC Macintosh computers.

If you have a Power Macintosh, be sure to purchase software applications that are accelerated for Power Macintosh. Although emulated applications will also run on Power Macintosh, almost all native applications have better performance. Most Macintosh applications ship "fat" applications that support both 68K and Power Macintosh CPUs. Keep in mind that a native application cannot run on a 68K Macintosh.

- **Now Utilities 5.0.** This is a group of control panels and extensions that provide a wide range of System software features.

  Compatibility is generally good to great with System 7.5. You may want to look into some of their other personal information management software products.

- **Casady & Greene Conflict Catcher 3.1.** Conflict Catcher is an extensions manager and extension conflict isolation software product. It does its job well, and is extremely popular because most Macintosh users love to use extensions in their System Folder. Like Now Startup Manager, Conflict Catcher enables you to create unique sets of extensions that can be loaded by pressing an alpha character during startup. New features in version 3.0.1 include the capability to display the file name of each extension loading (this can help you identify extensions with generic icons easily), and the option to turn on or off Apple Menu items, fonts, and control strip modules.

- **Connectix RAM Doubler 1.5.2a.** Since its introduction in 1994, RAM Doubler is one of the most popular extensions for the Macintosh. Similar to Apple's Virtual Memory, it is a little faster because it borrows physical memory allocated for other launched applications to the one currently in use. RAM Doubler also has some incompatibilities with applications that have their own virtual memory scheme, such as Photoshop. Sound and video playback may also be slow or jumpy in multimedia games that use QuickTime. Keep in mind that there can be no real software substitute for physical memory, especially in the areas of performance and compatibility.

- **SpeedDoubler 1.0.2.** Connectix introduced SpeedDoubler at Macworld Boston in 1995, and it sold out at the show. SpeedDoubler consists of three software pieces: Speed Access, Speed Copy, and Speed Emulator extensions. Note that these extensions do not have an interface to turn their features on or off. Speed Emulator only works on Power Macintosh systems that cannot use System 7.5.2 (which contains the new DR emulator). Speed Access and Speed Copy work on 68K and Power Macintosh and provide caching and background file copying features (modifying the Finder's copy dialog).

- **Apple Diagnostics 1.1.3.** Apple Diagnostics consists of a set of applications that can identify hardware and software problems on the Macintosh. You can use Apple Diagnostics to run memory tests if you suspect a bad memory SIMM. You can also run diagnostic tests on your hard drive to verify defective sectors or to determine whether the disk in the drive is worth putting data on.

- **Symantec Norton Utilities 3.1.3.** Norton Utilities contains a set of applications that were initially made available for Macintosh years ago. You can use Norton to verify and in most cases fix the file System, optimize the hard drive, restore previously deleted files, and install preventative maintenance software. Norton Utilities has features that Apple's Disk First Aid and Drive Setup do not provide.

- **Symantec S.A.M.** Symantec Anti-Virus for Macintosh (S.A.M.) was introduced shortly after Disinfectant 1.0 when the first Macintosh viruses invaded Macintosh hard drives. Installing S.A.M.'s software into the System Folder enables you to configure the software to check any floppy inserted into the Macintosh, as well as monitor any modification to applications or System files. Some installer applications have installer conflicts with S.A.M. If you are installing software, it is recommended that you start up the Macintosh with the Shift key held down to deactivate extensions before running the installer application.

- **Aladdin StuffIt Deluxe.** StuffIt Deluxe is the big brother version of StuffIt 1.5.1 and includes support for a variety of software compression formats and decompression options. StuffIt enables you to create archives containing files and folders. You can double-click on a folder in a StuffIt archive, and StuffIt will show you all files in the folder. StuffIt and Disk Doubler will show you how much a file was compressed. You can also create compressed files that someone else can decompress without having the StuffIt (or Disk Doubler) application. These are called *self-extracting archives.*

- **Symantec Disk Doubler.** Disk Doubler is file compression software similar to StuffIt Deluxe. If your Mac is running low on hard drive space, or if you have several backups you do not need instant access to, you can use Disk Doubler to compress one or several files, or an entire folder. Disk Doubler has a menu in Finder's menubar giving you easy access to compression features.

- **Apple Remote Access 2.0.** Apple's Remote Access is software that enables a Macintosh to dial into a Macintosh network and access other servers on the network, including the Internet. To use Apple Remote Access, you must have a modem on the Macintosh and the networked Mac, plus the Apple Remote Access server or client software installed on the correct Macintosh (the dial-in Mac is the client; the Mac on the net is the server). This software is especially helpful if you telecommute to work or are traveling and need access to folders at the office.

- **Insignia Soft Windows 2.0.** Cross-platform solutions on the Macintosh are even more popular with the high performance of the Power Macintosh. Soft Windows 2.0 improves upon its 1.0 version that only supported 286 emulation. Version 2.0 emulates 486 processor calls, and for word processing and spreadsheets has great performance. CD and multimedia application performance has been mixed on the 2.0 version, and hardware solutions can outperform this software application. However, Soft Windows requires less time invested in DOS/Windows configuration than its hardware cousins. If you plan to use your Macintosh primarily as a Macintosh and not as a Windows computer, Soft Windows is a low-cost, compatible solution for those with a preference for extending their PC software library with database, games, and other platform-specific software.

Selected software applications

Software applications are the heart of any computer. This section contains many of the applications that have made the Macintosh as popular and useful as it is today. These applications include word processing, page layout, database, graphic and imaging software, as well as software for online services and electronic mail. These products are available through most Macintosh mail order companies, computer software retailers, and directly from the publisher.

- **Kai's Power Tools 3.0.** Kai's Power Tools is a software package that works in conjunction with Adobe Photoshop 2.0 or higher or Fractal Painter 3.0 or higher. Kai's Power Tools are image filters that enable you to create and manipulate all or part of an image file. Other Photoshop and Painter filters are also available from publishers such as Xaos (who creates image filters for Silicon Graphics workstations—a high-end Unix computer platform).

  Kai's Power Tools is published by HSC Software, which also publishes KPT Bryce, a program that enables you to create and render a 3D landscape.

- **Gryphon Morph 2.0.** Morph is Macintosh software that can morph one image to another. This feature is similar to morphing features used on high end Unix workstations for special effects in motion pictures and cartoons (animation).

- **Avid VideoShop and Video Effects.** VideoShop software is bundled with all AV Macintosh Systems. VideoShop has features to view, grab, and compress video images. If you are interested in tinkering with multimedia video, this application is a great low-cost solution.

- **TransJammer Volume 2.** A library of broadcast-quality transitional effects for video editing that can be imported into other video editing software applications such as Avid's VideoShop or Adobe Premiere.

- **ClarisWorks 4.0.** ClarisWorks is a popular all-in-one software application that contains word processing, spreadsheet, database, telecommunications, and drawing applications. It is bundled with all current Performa models.

- **Claris EMailer 1.0.** If you use email on one or several sources such as online services and Internet services and mail accounts, Claris EMailer enables you to log onto any of these servers without having the online service software installed on your Macintosh. It's great if you have limited hard drive space and don't want to spend the extra time logging onto every online and email account one at a time.

- **America Online 2.6.** America Online has over three million users registered, and is recognized as the most popular online service for Macintosh and Windows users. In addition to access to software and hardware vendors, as well as special interest groups, AOL has travel, shopping, and retail services as well as a large number of national magazines and newspapers published and available online. To start an AOL account, you need a starter kit. Billing is $8.95 per month and includes four hours of login time.

- **Hypercard 2.3.** Hypercard Player is bundled on every Macintosh and can play Hypercard stacks. Hypercard began as an easy-to-use software development package. The current version of Hypercard enables you to create standalone applications as well as stacks.

- **Claris Amazing Animation 1.0.** Amazing Animation enables you to manipulate image and sound across time to create animation and stories. Its primary audience is the educational market, but can be a great multimedia tool.

- **Claris FileMaker Pro 2.1v3.** This is a popular flat file database application for both Macintosh and Windows. Its features are similar to those in ClarisWorks 4.0 and are fairly easy to learn and use compared to most other database software. Claris also has a server version of FileMaker Pro that improves network performance and database access.

- **Claris MacWrite Pro 1.5.** Based on the classic, originally bundled software on the first Macintosh, MacWrite Pro 1.5 has a powerful set of features.

- **Adobe Photoshop 3.0.4.** Photoshop is the hallmark application for image editing, especially photographs. Photoshop's open-ended filter design enables you to customize and add new filter features. Keep in mind that the larger the image you use, the more physical memory and free hard drive space you will need.

- **Adobe PageMaker 6.0.** PageMaker was the first desktop publishing application for the Macintosh. It has evolved into a feature-packed publishing package preferred by many publishers. Another desktop publishing application that can be considered as popular as PageMaker is QuarkXPress 3.

- **Adobe Acrobat 2.1.** Acrobat is a universal document reader and document creator. This software package uses Adobe's Adobe Type Manager technology (ATM) to display files without having all the fonts resident on your Macintosh. QuickDraw GX has a similar feature to Acrobat's universal document feature.

- **Macromedia Director 4.0.4.** Director is a popular multimedia software creation tool. It was first created for System 6, but has been updated to take advantage of QuickTime and other System software features. You can create standalone QuickTime or multimedia animation applications using Director.

- **Macromedia MacroModel 1.5.2.** 3D modeling is accelerated for Power Macintosh in MacroModel. Other applications that provide similar features include Infini-D 2.6, Alias Sketch 2.0, and Stratavision's Strata 3D software.

- **Microsoft Office.** Includes the most popular word processor and spreadsheet for Macintosh—Word and Excel—as well as PowerPoint and Microsoft Project. Purchasing Microsoft Office can save you money. Word 6.0.1 and Excel 5.0 use more hard drive space than previous versions (Word 5.1a and Excel 4.0).

Modem, Printing, and Sound Upgrades

This chapter discusses modem, printing, and sound upgrades for Macintosh computers. Modem upgrades include external and internal models. Printer upgrades discussed in this chapter include adding more memory and upgrade notes on selected models. Upgrading sound on your Macintosh includes an overview of digital audio and discusses hardware and software products available for your Macintosh computer.

Modems

Computers talk using binary language—ones and zeros. Unfortunately, telephone lines transmit data using analog signals. Thus, to allow computers to talk over phone lines, a modem needs to convert the digital signals to something that can be transferred over an analog phone line.

Choosing your modem

Modem prices increase proportionally to the speed at which they transmit. Within each class of modem, other features besides price, such as bundled software and cables, distinguish the individual modems.

Generally, modems with faster protocols include support for all the slower protocols. By picking a fast modem, you will be able to connect to older modems with slower speeds. It is best to buy the fastest possible modem you can afford because modem technology moves so quickly that if you buy a low-end modem, you'll quickly be behind the rest of the industry.

After choosing the fastest speed you can afford, you need to decide about error correction and/or compression. Error correction can be quite helpful, particularly if you have noisy phone lines. Data compression isn't as important, particularly if you will use the modem mostly with commercial services such as CompuServe or America Online, because most files available on these services are already compressed. If you're using the modem to dial into your office network, compression isn't an issue at all because the remote access software turns off error compression and error correction.

Modem manufacturers often advertise their modems as having speeds of 38,400 or 57,600 bps (bits per second). These speeds, however, assume ideal compression conditions and don't accurately represent the actual speed of the modem. The speed is usually reduced by line noise or files that don't compress well.

As technology advances, modems and telecommunications will no doubt benefit. As of this writing, the V.Fast standard (V.34) is about to be finalized, making 28.8 bps communication commonplace. In addition, as ISDN (digital networks) become more common, the need for modems may disappear entirely.

External modems

Modems are the hardware gateway to the information superhighway. Modems are available as internal motherboard or expansion slot add-ons, and as external self contained units. External modems are available to support speeds up to 28.8 bps and include common fax and telecommunications software. These applications mimic phones and fax machines, eliminating the need to purchase this expensive equipment.

External modem types range from standard serial connectors, PC cards for PowerBook Macintosh computers, and ADB ports. Apple's external modem solution is GeoPort. GeoPort works like a typical 14.4 modem, but also supports telephony and networking features. GeoPort does not work on all Macintosh models, however. Only the models beginning with the AV and Power Macintosh computers can use GeoPort. The rest of this section highlights recommended modems from a number of manufacturers.

External modems are separate units that connect to your Mac's modem port via a special cable provided with the modem (see Figure 8.1). If your modem didn't come with a Mac cable, check with any of the big Mac mail-order houses to order one.

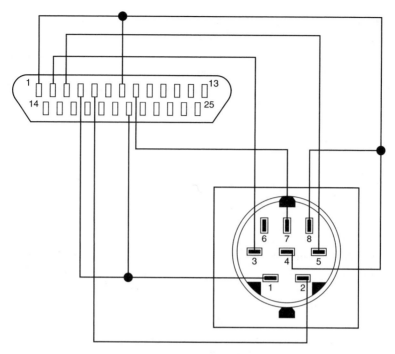

Figure 8.1 An external modem connects to your Macintosh via the serial port using a special cable.

Note

All modem cables are not created equal! Most Macs can send data faster than the modem is able to accept it. To deal with this, the modem has a buffer (similar to your computer's RAM) that stores the data when the modem is busy sending data it already received from the Mac.

When the modem buffer is full (perhaps the error correction circuits had to resend something several times), the modem needs a way to tell the computer to slow down. This is called *flow control.*

Older, slower modems were able to perform flow control using software; today's 9,600 and 14,400 modems do this by connecting to your Macintosh with a special type of modem cable known as a hardware handshaking cable. If the cable that came with your modem isn't a hardware handshaking cable (it should specify), get one. It could save you hours of frustration.

8

Internal modems

Apple has two types of internal modem products: the Express modem for PowerBooks and PowerBook Duos, and internal modems bundled with selected Performa models. Global Village supplies almost all internal modem models that ship with Performa. Apple's GeoPort is an external modem pod that works in conjunction with GeoPort-specific serial ports first introduced on AV and PCI Power Macintosh computers.

PowerBooks

Most PowerBook models have a unique, non-serial expansion slot for an internal modem. Internal modems are especially invaluable on a PowerBook because you don't have to carry around additional hardware for the modem. Standard PowerBook modems are nearly identical to external modems; they're just much smaller and lack the speaker and LEDs normally found on the external models.

Apple's PowerBook modems, known as express modems, are somewhat different from standard modems. The express modems force the computer to do some of the processing work normally done by the modem hardware. The advantage to this setup is that the modem hardware is less complex, resulting in a lower price. The drawback of this setup is that the maximum speed of the modem is somewhat reduced and some software doesn't work properly because the modem isn't behaving quite as expected. As with all tradeoffs, each user must decide if the price savings outweigh the drawbacks in compatibility and speed.

Modem Installation

PowerBook modems connect to the Mac directly inside the PowerBook's case (see Figure 8.2). Installing a modem into a PowerBook is a fairly straightforward process. Once you have the PowerBook case open, the modem simply plugs into the specially designed modem connector located near the back panel.

Warning

Although most PowerBook modems come with instructions on how to install the modem yourself, opening the PowerBook's case voids its warranty. If you're uneasy about opening the PowerBook case, let your local Apple Dealer do it for you. The cost isn't much compared to the anxiety and repair bill caused by a broken PowerBook!

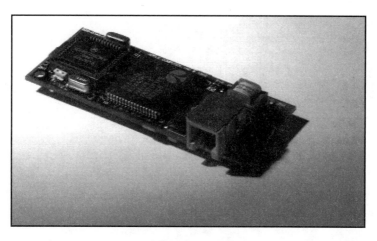

Figure 8.2 A PowerBook modem installs completely inside your PowerBook's case.

After this modem is installed, the only evidence of the modem is a phone jack on the outside of the PowerBook, next to the SCSI port. The modem powers on and off automatically to save battery power. You simply plug a telephone cable in to the phone line and dial. The PowerBook's internal modem connector includes the necessary wiring to provide for hardware handshaking.

GeoPort

Apple's AV and Power Macs (the Quadra and Centris 660AV/840AV and any Power Mac) include a special serial connector called the GeoPort. This new technology takes advantage of the Digital Signal Processing chips in the AV computers, which can act as a modem. To use the GeoPort, you simply use a GeoPort Telecom Adapter to plug your telephone line straight into the GeoPort of the Mac (see Figure 8.3). The GeoPort takes the place of the modem port found in other Macs, yet still performs the same function as a traditional modem port— you can still connect a modem to this port as you can with any other Mac.

The actual GeoPort is an input that closely resembles a basic serial port; however, it has the important addition of another pin that carries power to an external converter box sold by Apple. This box handles the incoming and outgoing phone signals.

To plug into GeoPort, Apple came up with something called the *GeoPort Telecom Adapter* or *Phone Pod,* which looks similar to an ADB mouse with incoming and outgoing phone jacks on the back. The Phone Pod is basically an analog-to-digital converter (and vice versa). It allows the AV Macs to perform fax/modem duties at a respectable 9600 baud rate. This modem can be set even higher, although Apple doesn't recommend it. The modem works just like any regular serial modem, and uses Apple's Express Fax/Modem software as its front end.

8

Figure 8.3   Apple GeoPort Telecom Adapter.

The bundled AplePhone software makes good use of the Phone Pod right out of the box and turns your AV Mac into a capable phone-answering machine and speakerphone. In addition to using the Mac as a modem, this new technology allows your Mac to act as a telephone answering machine. AplePhone is pure Macintosh—easy to use, with a large, colorful screen sporting the same buttons found on any real phone and answering machine, right down to the blinking red lights and the volume controls for recording and playing messages.

Desktop internal modems

Performa models are bundled with Global Village Teleport Bronze modems. These modems use an internal modem port, which in turn occupies the usual external modem port. If you are expecting to use both serial ports for external hardware, you may not want to purchase a desktop or PowerBook Macintosh with an internal modem pre-installed. If you are limited to a small amount of desk or office space, however, the internal modem can help reduce clutter.

Modem software

The most basic modem software is known as a terminal emulation application, or a dumb terminal application. This type of software forces you to deal with technical details of modem communication. More advanced software hides the modem from you, letting you say what you want to do and letting the computer and the modem negotiate the proper commands.

One of the issues that arises when using modem software is modem versus computer speeds. In your communication with a remote computer, you are interested in two speeds: the speed at which your computer talks to the modem, and the speed at which your modem talks to the remote computer.

If you have a data compression modem (MNP 5 or V.42bis), your modem can probably accept data faster than the speed at which it's transmitting (see the earlier note on hardware handshaking cables). To maximize its performance, you should use the communications software to set the speed your computer talks to the modem faster than the speed at which your modem talks to the remote computer. Use Table 8.1 to pick the best computer speed.

Table 8.1 Ideal Modem Speeds	
Modem Speed	*Software Speed*
28,800 bps	76,800 bps
14,400 bps	38,400 bps
9,600 bps	19,200 bps
2,400 bps	4,800 bps

Some older Macs can't keep up when software sets the modem port to speeds faster than the modem is operating. If you have trouble, try changing the settings to select a modem port speed to the actual speed of the modem.

Apple Remote Access

A huge advance in networking is provided by the introduction of Apple Remote Access, usually called ARA. Essentially, ARA allows you to call into a network by using a modem—simulating a network connection through the phone line. During an ARA connection, all network services, including email, printers, and servers, are available to you exactly as they would be if you were in the office.

To use Apple Remote Access, you must have modems on both ends of the connection. Note that an ARA connection is nowhere near the speed of a standard network connection; for this reason, it's best to use the fastest modem you can.

Next, you must choose a computer at the office to be the Remote Access Server. This machine answers the modem and helps your computer simulate its presence. Apple recently released a multiport server, which allows one Mac to handle several phone lines and control several remote communications simultaneously.

Fax/modems

The addition of fax capabilities to modems allows your Mac to act as a fax machine, sending anything you've got onscreen as if you had printed it out, and it allows you to receive faxes and display them onscreen. Nearly every modem currently sold (both external and PowerBook models) now include fax capabilities.

The fax interface

To use your fax/modem, you'll need fax software. This software is nearly always included with the modem. If you don't like the software that came with it, you can purchase additional software from third-party manufacturers.

The interface is different with each software package; nevertheless, fax software has universal similarities. When you have a document onscreen that you would like to fax, you select the Fax option in the File menu, choose the number to send it to, and pick a cover page (see Figure 8.4). Sit back and relax; the remote fax machine won't know the fax came from the computer instead of a regular fax.

To receive faxes, you need to set up your computer and software appropriately. When the phone rings, your modem answers, and the fax software (depending on how you've set it) jumps in and receives the fax and places it in a file on the hard disk. After receiving it, you can display it on-screen or print out the fax. The person who sent you the fax also has no idea that a computer received the fax.

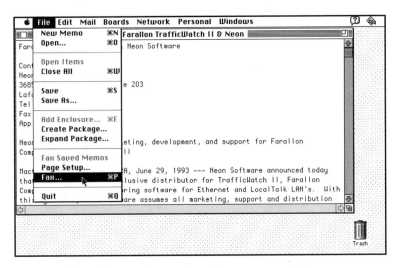

Figure 8.4 Fax software makes sending a fax as easy as printing.

Normally, faxes you receive are converted to graphic files. Because the files you receive are graphical, you can't open them in a word processor. You can only modify the fax as you would any other graphic—using graphic software such as Photoshop. Fax software that includes OCR capabilities converts the graphic file to text that the computer can read (and thus open with a word processor).

Fax/modem uses

Fax/modems can be a useful addition to your office, but they probably won't replace your fax machine because they can't send a pre-printed piece of paper. For example, if you receive a contract in the mail that you'd like to fax to your lawyer, a fax/modem won't help. A standard fax machine, however, is ideal. For documents you've created on the computer and are planning on printing out and then faxing, the fax/modem saves a lot of time and paper.

Note

A fax/modem in a PowerBook is also useful for sending and receiving faxes from hotel rooms while traveling.

Selected modems

Consult Table 8.2 for specifications on a number of recommended modems.

Table 8.2   Specifications of Selected Modems

Manufacturer	Model	Style	Top Data Speed	Top Fax Speed	Special Features
Supra	288	External	v.34	28,800 bps	
	288PB	PowerBook 100 series	V.fast	14,400 bps	
	V.32bis	External	V.32bis	14,400 bps	Upgradable to voicemail capabilities.
	144LC	External	V.32bis	14,400 bps	
	14.4 PB	PowerBook 100 series	V.32bis	14,400 bps	
Zoom	VFX 28.8	External	V.fast	14,400 bps	
	VFX V.32bis	External	V.32 bis	14,400 bps	
	PKT 14.4	External	V.32bis	14,400 bps	Compact modem designed for portable use.
	Pocket14.4	External	V.32 bis	14,400 bps	
	14.4 Internal PowerBook	PowerBook 100 series	V.32 bis	14,400 bps	
	VFX 14.4V voice	External	V.32 bis	14,400 bps	Has voicemail capabilities.
Hayes	Accura 144 +Fax 144	External	V.32 bis	14,400 bps	
	Optima 144 +Fax 144 Pocket Edition	External	V.32 bis	14,400 bps	Compact modem designed for portable use.

continues

Table 8.2   Specifications of Selected Modems, CONTINUED

Manufacturer	Model	Style	Top Data Speed	Top Fax Speed	Special Features
	Accura 96 +Fax 96	External	V.32	9,600 bps	
	Accura 2400	External	V.22 bis	(none)	
Global Village	Teleport Mercury PowerPort Platinum	External Internal External	V.32 terbo v.34	14,400 bps 28,800	Support voice, FAX, and ARA
	PowerPort Mercury	PowerBook 100 series	V.32 terbo	14,400 bps	Bundled with certain models of PowerBook 500 series.
	PowerPort Mercury for PowerBook 500	PowerBook 500 series	V.32 terbo	14,400 bps	Apple includes this modem with selected PBK 500 models in the United States.
	PowerPort Mercury for PowerBook Duo	PowerBook Duo	V.32 terbo	14,400 bps	Only 3rd party DUO modem available.
	Teleport Gold	External	V.32bis	14,400bps	
	PowerPort Gold	PowerBook 100 series	V.32bis	14,400 bps	
	TelePort Silver	External	V.32	9,600 bps	
	PowerPort Silver	PowerBook 100 series	V.32	9,600 bps	
	TelePort Bronze	External	V.22 bis	9,600 bps	
	PowerPort Bronze	PowerBook 100 series	V.22 bis	9,600 bps	
Apple	PowerBook Express Modem	PowerBook	V.32 bis	9,600 bps	
	PowerBook Express Modem for Duo	PowerBook Duo	V.32 bis	14,400 bps	

Upgrading Printers

Upgrade options discussed in this section primarily cover memory upgrades. Many high-end printers also support external hard drives for storing PostScript fonts. Apple also offers a fax upgrade for the LaserWriter 360, and several tray sizes to support extending the standard 8 1/2 × 11 paper size as well as international and legal paper sizes. For more information on hard drives and other Apple printer products, contact Apple or your local Apple authorized dealer.

Printer RAM

Macintosh computers are not the only hardware components that require RAM upgrades. Many printers also need more RAM to help reduce large file processing time and provide extra room for downloaded fonts. This section discusses common Apple printer upgrades.

Whenever you add RAM to a laser printer, remember that the printer driver has to be brought up-to-date. Under LaserWriter Driver 8 or higher, open the Chooser and select the Setup button for the printer. Select Autosetup or Configure to refresh the printer's settings. Check the new RAM amount by viewing the Printer Info.

Personal LaserWriter LS

Right from the factory the Personal LaserWriter LS is configured with 512K of RAM, but it can be upgraded to 1 MB using an optional Apple upgrade kit (see Figure 8.5). The RAM upgrade uses four 256 × 4 DIP modules that plug into sockets on the LS logic board. To signal to the printer that the extra RAM is available, set jumper JP 801 on the controller board. The upgrade kit, Apple part number 334-0114, is available from Apple service centers.

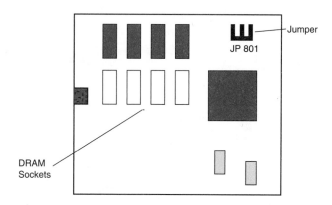

Figure 8.5   The LS can be upgraded to 1 MB with DIP RAM.

Personal LaserWriter NT

Two 4 MB SIMMs, rated at 120 ns or faster, enable the LaserWriter NT to hold up to 8 MB maximum (see Figure 8.6).

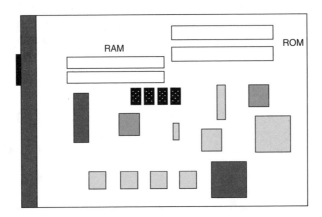

Figure 8.6 The NT has two SIMM sockets for its maximum 8 MB of RAM.

Personal LaserWriter NTR

The LaserWriter NTR can be expanded to a maximum of 4 MB using the lone SIMM socket on the logic board with a 2 MB SIMM. From the factory the unit has a 1 MB SIMM installed in the socket providing 3 MB of RAM. One advantage of this design is that it will accommodate 72-pin SIMMs rated at 80 ns or better (see Figure 8.7).

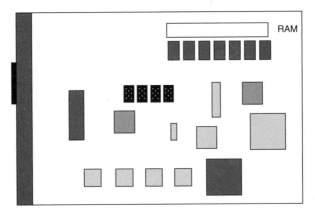

Figure 8.7 The NTR will accept 72-pin SIMMs.

Personal LaserWriter 320

The Personal LaserWriter 320 has two options for memory upgrades: the addition of a 2 MB or 6 MB card. The maximum amount of RAM for the printer is 8 MB. If you purchase this upgrade with an Apple upgrade kit, a Photograde 600 dpi upgrade is included.

LaserWriter IINTX

The LaserWriter IINTX can access 12 MB of RAM maximum. From the factory the printer has 2 MB installed (four 256K SIMMs) using the sockets at banks 0 and 1. Unfortunately, a 6 MB upgrade configuration is not supported by the printer (see Figure 8.8).

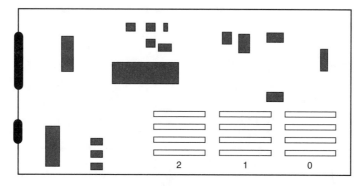

Figure 8.8   The NTX can address 2 MB and 12 MB of RAM but does not accept a 6 MB configuration.

LaserWriter IIf/g

LaserWriters IIf and IIg are among the most expandable printers in the line. They accommodate SIMMs in sizes from 256K to 1 MB and 2 MB. From the factory the IIf comes with 4 MB installed (usually); the IIg usually has 8 MB. Older versions of these printers in circulation can have 2 MB and 5 MB factory RAM configurations. Consult Table 8.3 at the end of this section for available memory upgrades.

A note to the installer: When adding RAM to the IIf and IIg, always start filling bank 0 first (with highest value SIMMs), as shown in Figure 8.9.

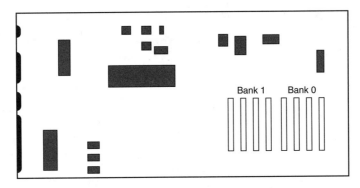

Figure 8.9 Start the RAM upgrade for the IIf and IIg in bank 0 first.

LaserWriter Select 300

The LaserWriter Select 300 can be upgraded to 4.5 MB of RAM with the addition of a 4 MB SIMM (see Figure 8.10). An intermediate upgrade to 1.5 MB is possible with a 1 MB SIMM; the logic board has 512K of RAM hard-soldered onboard.

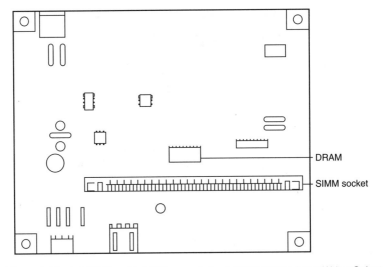

Figure 8.10 A 4.5 MB and 1.5 MB upgrade is available for the LaserWriter Select 320.

LaserWriter Select 310

The LaserWriter Select 310 can be expanded to a maximum of 5.5 MB with the addition of a 4 MB SIMM (see Figure 8.11). Onboard RAM is 1.5 MB and is hard-soldered.

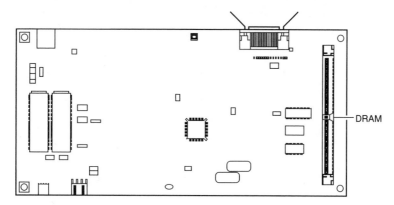

Figure 8.11   The LaserWriter Select 310 can use a 4 MB SIMM to increase RAM to 5.5 MB.

LaserWriter Select 360

The LaserWriter Select 360 can access a maximum of 16 MB of RAM. The 3 MB of onboard RAM can be used in conjunction with a 4 MB 72-pin (80 ns) SIMM. The addition of a 16 MB SIMM in the 360's socket boosts the addressable RAM to 16 MB. Unfortunately, when the 16 MB SIMM is in place, the 3 MB onboard RAM is not accessed by the System (see Figure 8.12).

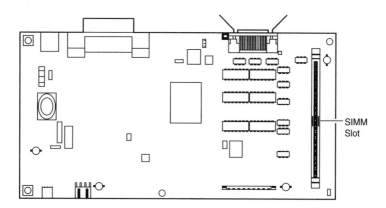

Figure 8.12   The 360's RAM socket can be used to upgrade the unit to 16 MB. If a 16 MB SIMM is used, the system disregards the 3 MB of on-board RAM.

LaserWriter Pro 600/630

The LaserWriter Pro 600 and 630 use the "industry standard" SIMMs (72-pin, 80 ns) in their memory systems. Sizes of 4 MB, 8 MB, and 16 MB are acceptable. From the factory the 600 and 630 have 8 MB installed, although early units were shipped with 4 MB. The 600 and 630 support 8 MB, 16 MB, 20 MB, and 32 MB setups. There are two 72-pin SIMM banks with one socket per bank (see Figure 8.13).

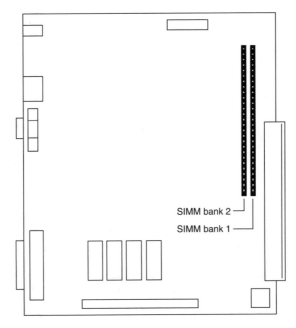

SIMM bank 2
SIMM bank 1

Figure 8.13   LaserWriter Pro 600 and 630 printers use standard 72-pin SIMMs.

LaserWriter Pro 810

The LaserWriter Pro 810 can accept up to 32 MB of RAM, but only Apple RAM cards can be used. 8 MB of RAM are on the logic board. Upgrades are added to the three memory banks in values of 4 MB and 8 MB. Memory configurations shown in the following mini-table are possible.

Total Memory	Logic Board	Bank 1 Memory	Bank 2 Memory	Bank 3 Memory
8 MB	8 MB	0 MB	0 MB	0 MB
12 MB	8 MB	4 MB	0 MB	0 MB
16 MB	8 MB	4 MB	4 MB	0 MB
20 MB	8 MB	4 MB	4 MB	4 MB
24 MB	8 MB	8 MB	4 MB	4 MB
28 MB	8 MB	8 MB	8 MB	4 MB
32 MB	8 MB	8 MB	8 MB	8 MB

Note

When upgrading the RAM in a LaserWriter Pro 810, fill the low numbered banks first. The order of the 4 MB or 8 MB memory card is unimportant provided the lower banks are filled first.

LaserWriter Pro Memory Upgrade Notes

A few notes on the upgrade of the LaserWriter Pro:

- Always fill the low-numbered bank(s) before the higher numbered bank(s). If two sizes of SIMMs are involved in the upgrade, put the bigger SIMM in the low-numbered bank (bank 1).

- Although the LaserWriter Pro printers can use 4 MB, 8 MB, and 16 MB SIMMs, problems could occur if one of the SIMMs is double-sided. If a double-sided SIMM is used, it is treated as two SIMMs by the controller.

- The LaserWriter Pro can address only two banks of memory. Thus, the second socket is unusable in this case, and is usually left empty. Because Apple makes LaserWriter Pro printers with both single- and double-sided 8 MB SIMMs, the 8 MB SIMM must be removed when the System is upgraded.

Table 8.3 lists available memory upgrades for Apple printers.

8

Table 8.3   Quick Reference Chart Apple LaserWriter Configurations

LaserWriter Model	ROM	RAM	Processor/Speed	Page Description
LaserWriter	0.5 MB	1.5 MB	68000/ 12 MBHz	PostScript / Diablo 630
LaserWriter Plus	1 MB	1.5 MB	68000/ 12 MBHz	PostScript / Diablo 630
LaserWriter IISC	16K	1 MB	68000/ 7.45 MBHz	QuickDraw
LaserWriter IINT	1 MB	2 MB	68000/ 11.16 MBHz	PostScript Diablo 630
LaserWriter IINTX	1 MB	2-12 MB	68020/ 16.67 MBHz	PostScript/ Diablo 630 HP-LaserJet
Personal Laser-Writer SC	16K	1 MB	68000/ 7.275 MBHz	QuickDraw
Personal Laser-Writer NT	1.25 MB	2-8 MB[1]	68000/12 MBHz	PostScript / Diablo 630 HP LaserJet
Personal Laser-Writer NTR	2 MB	3-4 MB[2]	AMD29005 RISC/16 MBHz	PostScript HP LaserJet
Personal Laser-Writer LS	none	512K - 1 MB [3]	Uses Mac's Processor	QuickDraw
Personal Laser-Writer 300	none	512K	Uses Mac's Processor	QuickDraw
LaserWriter IIf	2 MB	2- 32 MB[5,6]	68030/20 MBHz	PostScript Level 2/[9] HP LaserJet IIP (PCL4+)
LaserWriter IIg	2 MB	5- 32 MB[5,6]	68030/25 MBHz	PostScript Level 2/[9] HP LaserJet IIP (PCL4+)

Pages Per Min	Communication Interfaces	Cassette Capacity	Minimum Engine Life
8	LocalTalk/ RS-232C	100 pgs	300,000 pgs
8	LocalTalk/ RS-232C	100 pgs	300,000 pgs
8	SCSI, ADB	200 pgs	300,000 pgs
8	LocalTalk RS-232/422 serial ADB (Accessory Port)	200 pgs	300,000 pgs
8	LocalTalk RS-232/422 serial ADB (Accessory Port) SCSI-Ext (Hard Disks)	200 pgs	300,000 pgs
4	SCSI	250 pgs	150,000 pgs
4	LocalTalk RS-232/ RS-422 serial	250 pgs	150,000 pgs
4	LocalTalk RS-232/ RS-422 serial	4	150,000 pgs
4	RS-422 serial	4	150,000 pgs
4	RS-422 serial	100 pgs	100,000 pgs
8	LocalTalk[7] RS-232/422 serial ADB (Accessory Port) SCSI - Ext Hard Disks	200 pgs	300,000 pgs
8	LocalTalk / Ethernet [8] RS-232/422 serial ADB (Accessory Port) SCSI - Ext Hard Disks	200 pgs	300,000 pgs

continues

Table 8.3 Quick Reference Chart Apple LaserWriter Configurations, CONTINUED

LaserWriter Model	ROM	RAM	Processor/Speed	Page Description
LaserWriter Pro 600	2 MB	8 to 32 MB[10]	68030/25 MBHz	PostScript Level 2/[11] HP LaserJet IIP (PCL4+)
LaserWriter Pro 630	2 MB	8 to 32 MB[10]	68030/25 MBHz	PostScript Level 2/[11] HP LaserJet IIP (PCL4+)
LaserWriter Select 300[15]	none	.5 to 4.5 MB[14]	none	QuickDraw
LaserWriter Select 310	2 MB	1.5 to 5.5 MB[14]	AMD Am29205 RISC	PostScript Level 1
LaserWriter Select 360	4 MB	7 to 16 MB[16]	AMD 29200/ 15 MBHz	PostScript Level 2/[18] HP LaserJet III (PCL 5)
LaserWriter Pro 810	3 MB	8 to 32 MB[21]	Weitek 8200	PostScript Level 2/[22] HP LaserJet IIP (PCL4+) (PCL4+)

Pages Per Min	Communication Interfaces	Cassette Capacity	Minimum Engine Life
8	LocalTalk[12] RS-232 / RS-422 serial Centronics Parallel	250 pgs	450,000 pgs
8	LocalTalk / Ethernet[13] RS-232/RS-422 serial Centronics Parallel SCSI - Int or Ext Hard Disks	250 pgs	450,000 pgs
5	RS-422 serial	250 pgs	150,000 pgs
5	RS-422 serial Centronics Parallel	250 pgs	150,000 pgs
10	LocalTalk[19] RS-232/RS-422 serial Centronics Parallel Group 3 Fax (optional)[20]	250 pgs	300,000 pgs
20	LocalTalk[23] RS-232/RS-422 serial Twisted Pair Ethernet[24] Thin Wire Ethernet[24] External SCSI Group 3 Fax (optional)[20]RS-232/RS-422 serial Twisted Pair Ethernet[24] Thin Wire Ethernet[24] External SCSI Group 3 Fax (optional)[20]	250 pgs[25]	600,000 pgs

continues

Table 8.3   **Quick Reference Chart Apple LaserWriter Configurations,** CONTINUED

LaserWriter Model	ROM	RAM	Processor/Speed	Page Description
Color LaserWriter 12/600	n/a PostScript 40 MB	12 to 12/3 color	AMD 29030 RISC LocalTalk, Ethernet Level 2	250 pgs RS-232/RS- (PCL4+)

[1]The Personal LaserWriter NT RAM can be upgraded from 2 to 8 MB. The PLW NT has 2 SIMM sockets that accept 1 or 4 MB 80 ns, 30-pin memory SIMMs.

[2]The Personal LaserWriter NTR RAM can be upgraded from 3 to 4 MB by removing the existing 1 MB SIMM and replacing it with a 2 MB 80 ns, 72-pin SIMM.

[3]The LaserWriter LS comes with 512K of RAM and is upgradeable to 1 MB using a total of four 256K, 120 ns DRAM chips. (Not available from Apple.)

[4]The LaserWriter LS has an optional paper feeder that uses the standard Personal LaserWriter paper/envelope cassette (250 sheets maximum).

[5]The LaserWriter IIf and IIg use 30-pin, 80 ns memory SIMMs of 256K, 1, and 4 MB.

[6]The LaserWriter IIf and IIg must be upgraded to at least 8 MB of RAM to print PhotoGrade images on full legal size paper.

[7]The LaserWriter IIf can have simultaneous connections to LocalTalk, RS-232, and RS-422.

[8]The LaserWriter IIg can have simultaneous connections to Ethernet, LocalTalk, RS-232, and RS-422.

[9]The LaserWriter IIf and IIg use FinePrint. PhotoGrade, which requires 5 MB of memory, gives up to 65 gray levels.

[10]The LaserWriter Pro 600 and 630 use industry standard 72-pin 80 ns memory SIMMs of 4, 8, and 16 MB.

[11]The LaserWriter Pro 600 and 630 are 600 DPI printers that include FinePrint and PhotoGrade (with 91 gray levels). You cannot use PhotoGrade at 600 DPI.

[12]The LaserWriter Pro 600 can have simultaneous connections to LocalTalk and RS-232/RS-422 serial and Centronics parallel ports.

[13]The LaserWriter Pro 630 can have simultaneous connections to EtherTalk, LocalTalk, RS-232/RS-422 serial, and Centronics parallel ports.

Pages Per Min	Communication Interfaces	Cassette Capacity	Minimum Engine Life
n/a			
	422 serial Twisted Pair Ethernet[24] Thin Wire Ethernet[24] External SCSI Group 3 Fax (optional)[20]		

[14]The LaserWriter Select 300 uses 30-pin 80 ns memory SIMMs of 1 or 4 MB; the LaserWriter Select 310 uses 72-pin 100 ns memory SIMMs of 1 or 4 MB.

[15]The LaserWriter Select 300 uses FinePrint. PhotoGrade, with 91 levels of gray, is available with a 4 MB memory upgrade.

[16]The LaserWriter Select 360 is upgraded with a 72-pin, 80 ns 16 MB (4-Mbit × 32-bit) SIMM with 2K Row refresh (11-bit × 11-bit).

[17]The LaserWriter Select 360 can only have a total of 16 MB of memory. If upgraded to 16 MB, it does not use the built-in memory.

[18]The LaserWriter Select 360 prints at 300 or 600 DPI. It uses FinePrint only at 300 DPI.

[19]The LaserWriter Select 360 can have simultaneous connections to LocalTalk and RS-232/RS-422 serial and Centronics parallel ports.

[20]The LaserWriter Pro 810 and the LaserWriter Select 360 can accommodate an optional Group 3 fax send/receive card.

[21]The LaserWriter Pro 810 uses custom memory modules of 4 and 8 MB.

[22]The LaserWriter Pro 810 prints at 300 and 400 DPI native engine resolution. It has controller technology that enables you to use software to select 600 and 800 DPI.

[23]The LaserWriter Pro 810 can have simultaneous connections to LocalTalk, Ethernet, and RS-232/RS-422 serial ports.

[24]The LaserWriter Pro 810 only has one slot for Ethernet interface cards and can only accommodate one type of Ethernet at a time.

[25]The LaserWriter Pro 810 can accommodate three 250-page paper cassettes.

8

Table 8.4 lists supported memory configurations for Apple printers. Printers not included on this list do not support memory upgrades or configurations. Apple Color LaserWriter 12/600 memory configuration information was not available at press time.

Table 8.4   Apple LaserWriter Memory Configurations

LaserWriter Model	RAM Config	RAM Amount		
LaserWriter IINTX	2 MB	Bank 0: 4 × 256K	Bank 1: 4 × 256K	Bank 2: Empty
	3 MB	Bank 0: 4 × 256K	Bank 1: 4 × 256K	Bank 2: 4 × 256K
	4 MB	Bank 0: 4 × 1 MB	Bank 1: Empty	Bank 2: Empty
	5 MB	Bank 0: 4 × 1 MB	Bank 1: 4 × 256K	Bank 2: Empty
	8 MB	Bank 0: 4 × 1 MB	Bank 1: 4 × 1 MB	Bank 2: Empty
	9 MB	Bank 0: 4 × 1 MB	Bank 1: 4 × 1 MB	Bank 2: 4 × 256K
	12 MB	Bank 0: 4 × 1 MB	Bank 1: 4 × 1 MB	Bank 2: 4 × 1 MB
LaserWriter IIf	2 MB	Bank 0: 4 × 256K	Bank 1: 4 × 256K	
	4 MB	Bank 0: 4 × 1 MB	Bank 1: Empty	
	5 MB	Bank 0: 4 × 1 MB	Bank 1: 4 × 256K	
	8 MB	Bank 0: 4 × 1 MB	Bank 1: 4 × 1 MB	
	16 MB	Bank 0: 4 × 4 MB	Bank 1: Empty	
	17 MB	Bank 0: 4 × 4 MB	Bank 1: 4 × 256K	
	20 MB	Bank 0: 4 × 4 MB	Bank 1: 4 × 1 MB	
	32 MB	Bank 0: 4 × 4 MB	Bank 1: 4 × 4 MB	

LaserWriter Model	RAM Config	RAM Amount	
LaserWriter IIg	5 MB	Bank 0: 4 × 1 MB	Bank 1: 4 × 256K
	8 MB	Bank 0: 4 × 1 MB	Bank 1: 4 × 1 MB
	16 MB	Bank 0: 4 × 4 MB	Bank 1: Empty
	17 MB	Bank 0: 4 × 4 MB	Bank 1: 4 × 256K
	20 MB	Bank 0: 4 × 4 MB	Bank 1: 4 × 1 MB
	32 MB	Bank 0: 4 × 4 MB	Bank 1: 4 × 4 MB
LaserWriter Pro 600	8 MB	Bank 0: 1 × 4 MB	Bank 1: 1 × 4 MB
	or	Bank 0: 1 × 8 MB	Bank 1: Empty
	16 MB	Bank 0: 1 × 16 MB	Bank 1: Empty
	20 MB	Bank 0: 1 × 16 MB	Bank 1: 1 × 4 MB
	32 MB	Bank 0: 1 × 16 MB	Bank 1: 1 × 16 MB
LaserWriter Pro 630	8 MB	Bank 0: 1 × 4 MB	Bank 1: 1 × 4 MB
	or	Bank 0: 1 × 8 MB	Bank 1: Empty
	16 MB	Bank 0: 1 × 16 MB	Bank 1: Empty
	20 MB	Bank 0: 1 × 16 MB	Bank 1: 1 × 4 MB
	32 MB	Bank 0: 1 × 16 MB	Bank 1: 1 × 16 MB
LaserWriter Select 300	.5 MB	Built-in	
	1.5 MB	1 × 1 MB	
	4.5 MB	1 × 4 MB	
LaserWriter Select 310	1.5 MB	Built-in	
	2.5 MB	1 × 1 MB	
	5.5 MB	1 × 4 MB	
LaserWriter	7 MB	Built-in: 3 MB[1]	Bank 0: 1 × 4 MB

continues

Table 8.4   Apple LaserWriter Memory Configurations, CONTINUED

LaserWriter Model	RAM Config	RAM Amount			
Select 360	16 MB	Built-in: 3 MB	Bank 0: 16 MB		
LaserWriter Pro 810	8 MB	Bank 1: Empty	Bank 2: Empty	Bank 3: Empty	
	12 MB	Bank 1: 4 MB	Bank 2: Empty	Bank 3: Empty	
	16 MB	Bank 1: 8 MB	Bank 2: Empty	Bank 3: Empty	
	or	Bank 1: 4 MB	Bank 2: 4 MB	Bank 3: Empty	
	20 MB	Bank 1: 8 MB	Bank 2: 4 MB	Bank 3: Empty	
	or	Bank 1: 4 MB	Bank 2: 4 MB	Bank 3: 4 MB	
	24 MB	Bank 1: 8 MB	Bank 2: 8 MB	Bank 3: Empty	
	or	Bank 1: 8 MB	Bank 2: 4 MB	Bank 3: 4 MB	
	28 MB	Bank 1: 8 MB	Bank 2: 8 MB	Bank 3: 4 MB	
	32 MB	Bank 1: 8 MB	Bank 2: 8 MB	Bank 3: 8 MB	

[1]The LaserWriter Select 360 can only have a total of 16 MB of memory. If upgraded to 16 MB, it does not use the built-in memory.

Sound and MIDI

This section briefly reviews the basic concepts of sound and acoustics to help you understand the use of sound and music on the Macintosh. Two principal approaches exist for Macintosh sound—digital audio and MIDI (Musical Instrument Digital Interface). This section includes a discussion of the best methods for incorporating digital audio and MIDI into your work, then explores various ways to use sound on the Mac. You will read about the use of the basic sound chip and onboard speaker all the way up to recent AV and Power Macintosh sound features.

MIDI hardware and software have brought desktop musical composition and performance to the Mac. In this section, you also learn what MIDI does, how it works, and how to configure a MIDI chain. In addition, information is presented on the standard hardware and software used for MIDI. The section on digital audio recording covers both 8-bit and 16-bit sampling and the hardware/software combinations used for digital audio editing. Whether you need to set up a corporate video and multimedia production center or a home-based recording studio, this section points you in the right direction.

Note

The Macintosh audio-visual user interface has always been a friendly environment for the physically challenged; a section on applying the Mac's sound capabilities in assisting people with various kinds of disabilities is included.

To understand music and sound on the Macintosh, you need to know the basic principles of acoustics and human hearing. In physics, sound is mechanical vibration, carried through some medium (usually air). It has three basic properties: frequency, intensity, and spectrum. These properties correspond with the psychological sensations of pitch, loudness, and timbre (or tone color). Human hearing is subjective; what we perceive is not always what we measure with test instruments. By using these two parallel sets of terms, we can distinguish between human perception and mechanical measurement, which provides a basis for a discussion of Mac sound.

Sound is also a series of tiny changes in air pressure. If the changes occur slowly, the frequency of the sound is low; rapid changes are high frequencies. If the amount of change in air pressure is small, the intensity is weak (soft). Larger changes in air pressure equate with greater intensity, or louder sounds. Ears and microphones are sensitive devices for measuring these microscopic variations in air pressure.

The two basic methods of working with sound and music on the Mac (or any computer) are digital audio and MIDI. The difference between these two basic methods is substantial. Digital audio is a recording technique that you use to capture sounds and music as if the computer were a tape recorder. MIDI is more like a player piano. MIDI does not record sound; it only records the data necessary to reproduce it on a MIDI synthesizer.

Digital audio

Digital audio recorders work on the same principle as movies. The digital audio recorder takes a series of snapshots (called samples) of the sound, just as a motion picture camera takes a series of snapshots (the individual frames on the film) of images. If the Mac samples the sound fast enough, the ear won't be able to perceive sounds individually. The human perceptual mechanism merges these "snapshots" into a sensation of sound or motion.

The sampling rate determines the highest frequency the machine can record. According to the *Nyquist Theorem*, the sampling rate must be at least twice as high as the highest frequency you want to record. To record and reproduce the full range of human hearing (20 Hz to 20,000 Hz) on compact discs, the sampling rate must be 44.1 KHz. Often, lower sampling rates will suffice, particularly when storage space is at a premium. For intelligible speech, sampling rates from 16 KHz to 22 KHz are fine.

Quantizing is the process of measuring the intensity of the signal in each sample and assigning a digital number to that measured value. Each time the sampling circuit takes a snapshot, it must measure the intensity of the continuously varying analog signal (as a voltage) at that particular moment. The circuit then must round off the value to the nearest digital number available, because inevitably the measured value will not correspond exactly to one of the digital values. These rounding errors cause noise and distortion. To reduce this effect, you want to have as many digital numbers as possible to represent instantaneous voltage measurements. 16-bit systems, the current standard in the computer audio world, provide a much higher amount of numbers than earlier 8-bit systems. Remember, however, that lower quality saves storage space, and is acceptable for many uses.

Uses and limitations of digital audio

After sound and music is digitized, you can manipulate the recorded data on your Macintosh. Instead of the old cut and splice method of audio tape editing (the trusted razor blade), you can edit down to the individual sample. Random access editing software enables you to assemble a soundtrack for a multimedia production from a library of short excerpts simply by creating a list. You can apply digital filters and other signal processing techniques to the sound, creating a complete digital recording studio on your Mac. You can create CD-quality finished recordings on your hard drive and master them to a CD-ROM.

The amount of storage space required for all this audio data is the main limitation of digital audio. One minute of stereo at a 44.1 KHz sampling rate with 16-bit quantization occupies about 1 MB; for this reason, you should have at least a 500 MB to 1GB hard drive. To permit random access editing, the drives must have an access time of less than 11 ms and support high speed (SCSI-2) transfer rates. In addition, make sure you have backup capabilities so that you can archive old projects and their source materials. Finally, you need a medium to store and transport the finished project; a DAT tape is usually the best choice.

MIDI

The Musical Instrument Digital Interface (MIDI) format began as a method of playing two synthesizers from one keyboard. MIDI captures all the data from every key that is pressed, including how long the key stayed down, how hard it was pressed, and so on, for every controllable parameter of the instrument. It also must capture the exact point in time that each event occurs. The onboard microprocessor converts all this information into a digital data stream and sends it to the other synthesizer. In turn, that instrument's microprocessor sorts out the data and sends each signal to the proper device. Because it all takes place at a rapid rate, everything fits together and the synthesizer plays music, automatically "pressing" the keys and holding them down exactly as they were pressed on the first synthesizer. A method of storing this data stream so that the information could later be played back is now easier than ever with the Mac.

MIDI is an 8-bit system, which means that it can express 256 values for each parameter of the sound that it is describing. The MIDI system transmits those numbers serially (one at a time, in rapid succession) at the rate of 31,250 bits per second. Each 8-bit byte describes the setting of a particular key, knob, button, or switch. Just to keep things straight, serial systems use start and stop bits to tell the microprocessor when each byte begins and ends. MIDI thus adds one extra bit at each end of the byte, turning it into a 10-bit package. The actual data transmission rate in the MIDI cable is 3,125 bytes per second.

MIDI uses two types of bytes: status bytes and data bytes. Every MIDI message begins with the status byte, and is followed by one or two data bytes (depending on what is needed). The status byte tells the receiving unit what control the following data will affect. It could be a Note On message, the setting of a foot pedal, or a change in a patch. To distinguish between the two types, MIDI assigns all data bytes numbers from 0 to 127, and all status bytes numbers from 128 to 255.

A typical stream of MIDI data contains status bytes, followed by one or two (sometimes none) data bytes. The status byte tells the synthesizer, "This data is for the Note On function." The first data byte tells it what pitch to turn on (which key to strike). The second data byte tells it how hard to strike the key. Then the message ends. The next message may contain instructions about which instrumental sound (patch) to use, and so on.

Uses and limitations of MIDI

Because MIDI involves only the data needed to control and play a synthesizer, it generates a fresh performance each time you play back the data. One advantage is that you can alter each performance in real time. You can change the tempo, transpose the music to another key, add a crescendo, or play it with a different set of instrumental sounds. You can edit the MIDI data in much the same way you edit a word processor file. The obvious disadvantage of MIDI is that it cannot record live sounds because it creates sounds by operating synthesizers. MIDI only consists of musical note and instrument data. MIDI does not contain any instrument or sound information as this is stored on the keyboards it communicates with. Digital audio, in contrast, consists of both instrument and musical note content and occupies considerably more hard drive space than MIDI data.

Sound on the Macintosh

The hardware and software architecture of the Macintosh has always included sound as a basic part of the computer. However, its intended uses were mostly for System beeps, game sounds, and an elementary but effective form of speech synthesis called MacInTalk. In fact, when Steve Jobs demonstrated the early 128K Macintosh in public for the first time, he carried it on stage, plugged it in, and it not only displayed the word "hello" onscreen, but the Macintosh also spoke it. In 1984, this simple demonstration captured everyone's attention powerfully and dramatically. Except for some entertainment software, speech synthesis has been ignored until recently, with the advent of the AV versions of Quadras and Power Macs. The reason for this is that acceptable speech requires massive amounts of computational power.

The synthesizer chip in the early Macs was monophonic, but Apple began using a stereo chip in the Mac II series. Although you can make music with the built-in synthesizer chip, you can't do much with it, except accentuate System beeps and game sounds. Conceptually, it contains an oscillator with selectable wave forms, plus a spectrum-shaping filter and an envelope generator (for attack and decay characteristics). With it, software developers can create distinctive sounds to alert users to various problems, or simply to reinforce the fact that you have invoked a particular command. This audio feedback remains one of the Mac's most powerful features.

Game developers, on the other hand, find the synthesizer chip limiting. Unique and attention-getting sounds can mean the difference between a successful game or a failure in the market. For this reason, computer games need striking sound effects. One solution is to use a library of sampled sounds. The concept is similar to the way wave table synthesizers use sampled sounds. Hit a key, and the sampled sound plays back for you (but without pitch changes or other alterations). You can create your sampled sounds in any way. Record natural sounds, develop new sounds on a large synthesizer, alter and manipulate them electronically in various ways, and even play them backwards. When you're finished, simply digitize them and store them as Mac sound files.

Basic digitizer: The MacRecorder

The most widely accepted tool for sound manipulation has been the Farallon MacRecorder (now sold by Macromedia). This is a low-end, inexpensive digital recorder. Its sound quality seems more like a table radio than a high fidelity system, but the storage space requirements are reasonable compared to full CD-quality sound (CDs contain over 600 MB of data). The hardware is contained in a small box that connects to one of the serial ports on your Mac. It accepts line level inputs from mixers, preamps, and synthesizers, and also has a microphone input. The digitizer circuit converts the analog signals into digital data and sends them into your Mac. It can record about 10 seconds for each data file. The software allows you to start and stop the recording, edit the sampled sound, adjust levels, and set the sampling rate.

Because the digitizer works at 8 bits, it has a signal-to-noise ratio of about 54 dB. Also, its maximum sampling rate of 24 KHz means that it can record frequencies only up to about 12 KHz. The trick in using devices such as the MacRecorder is to select a sound that has a narrow dynamic range, and to record it at the highest level possible without distortion. On playback, the sound will rise above the background noise, either on the internal speaker or on small external speakers. If you record at too low a level, the sound will playback noisily; try again at a higher level. Also, select sounds that don't depend on high frequencies for their essential character because MacRecorder will not record anything above 12 KHz.

Newer Macs with microphones

In the Mac IIsi and later models, including the PowerBooks, Apple includes a microphone and System software for digitizing sounds. The more powerful 68040 processor chips in these models eliminate the need for an external digitizer. Some business-oriented applications, such as word processors, spreadsheets, and email, enable you to attach audio notes to your documents. For example, your boss can click on a spreadsheet cell in an expense report and hear a verbal explanation about a certain amount. Another example: you can attach a note to a word processing document to remind yourself to rewrite a section. On a PowerBook, the built-in microphone lets you record random thoughts while you're working on another project. This is a handy way to add items to a To-Do List when you're in a hurry. In applications such as MacWrite Pro, you can adjust the file size and sampling rate (both affect the time length of each audio note).

QuickTime movies also have audio tracks, so don't overlook the possibilities of using sound in them. You can attach QuickTime files to documents in much the same way as audio notes, if the application accepts them. When a QuickTime movie is a Mac-generated animated clip, sound effects and voice-over narration will help you get your point across. Many collections of clip sounds, the audio equivalent of clip art, are available both commercially and as shareware.

When using music and sound effects, be aware of the limitations imposed by copyright laws. Though you can sample a sound bite from a favorite TV show or from a CD, you can't use it in a commercial situation. Personal use, the same as copying a magazine article for your files, is legal. If you're earning money from the use of the sound bite, you must obtain permission from the copyright holder(s). For published and recorded music, the two licensing agencies are the American Society of Composers, Authors, and Publishers (ASCAP), and Broadcast Music, Inc. (BMI). If you're creating a multimedia presentation, an information kiosk, or an in-store demo, don't use copyrighted sounds without obtaining permission.

Although a recorded performance may seem to be intangible, it is also protected. Since 1973, by international agreement, the industry has used the P in a circle symbol to notify users that a sound recording is copyrighted. For example, Scott Joplin's Maple Leaf Rag may be out of copyright, but a recorded performance by Branford Marsalis probably would carry copyright protection. You can perform the Maple Leaf Rag yourself, or record someone else's performance, but you can't use an existing copyrighted recording without permission. Even sound effects can get you into trouble. Don't sample R2D2's cute little bloops and bleeps because those sound effects are part of a copyrighted work. For anything beyond personal use, try to use clip sounds or create your own. The "fair use" doctrine of the copyright laws allows you to sample sounds for "personal use," which would include using the R2D2 sounds as a System beep on your Mac. If you sell it or give it away, you are breaking the law.

Customizing your Mac with sounds

Modifying System sounds with your own sound library can be fun. The standard System sounds from Apple include the familiar Boing, Clink-clank, and Quack; all are available on the Sound control panel. However, these sounds can become boring after a while. You can attach new sounds to the System simply by dragging them into the System Folder, as you do with fonts. Use either MacRecorder or the built-in sound recording capabilities of recent Macs to capture the sounds. Save them as System 7 sound files.

An intriguing audio application is Kaboom! by Nova Development. This commercial version of the old shareware utility, Soundmaster, enables you to add sound effects to every Finder command and change System beeps. It comes with a large library of digitized sound effects, and allows you to record your own. For example, Kaboom! can play the sound of trash cans rattling, flies buzzing, or a toilet flushing every time you empty the Trash. Its sound recording and editing capabilities are similar to the MacRecorder. Kaboom! also saves sound files in nearly every format currently used. This capability allows you to add recorded sounds to multimedia presentations, QuickTime movies, and custom applications. Table 8.5 lists some common Mac sound file formats.

Table 8.5   Typical Mac Sound File Formats

Sound File Format	Description
FSSD	A standard sound file format recognized by most Mac sound editing applications.
System 7	The sound equivalent of fonts, these 8-bit samples are used for System beeps and similar functions.
AIFF	Audio Interchange File Format, another format recognized by most sound editors.
Movie	The sound track portion of a QuickTime movie can also store digitized sounds.

Voice control

Voice control enables you to operate your Mac by speaking to it. Simply speak the commands, and the computer carries them out, just as if you had used a menu or command key. Articulate Systems was the first company to offer voice control for the Mac. You have to train the software to recognize your voice and the way you pronounce each particular command. Their voice control application can store recognition files for several different users, although it only works with one person at a time. This program is especially useful with graphics software; your hands might be occupied with a graphics tablet when you want to save a file, clone an object, move an object, or fill it with a pattern. Coupled with macros, voice control can become a great time saver in some situations.

Voice control is also a great help when you work with sequencer software and your hands are constantly moving from computer keyboard to mouse to one or more synthesizer keyboards. Entering musical notation is a very tedious process; voice control can save tremendous amounts of time when you perform this process. It won't translate singing into written notation—but it will execute a series of commands such as "Quarter note. Middle C. Eighth note E. Quarter note. F. Eighth note. G. Quarter note. D." The notes appear on the onscreen staff as you speak. To convert singing into musical notation, you need a pitch follower.

The AV Macs

The Quadra AV Macs opened a whole new realm to the use of audio and video on the Mac. With an AT&T 3210 Digital Signal Processing (DSP) chip, some modifications in the hardware, and appropriate System software, these Macs became, in effect, hard disk-based digital recorders with performance equal to CDs (16-bit quantization, 44.1 KHz sampling rate). Recently, OSC has introduced Deck II, which allows you to record and mix up to eight tracks of CD-quality digital audio on a Quadra AV.

Can you make your own CDs on the Mac? Well, yes and no. First of all, optical disk drives do not use the CD format. Most of them use Write Once Read Many (WORM) technology, and a data format optimized for storing and retrieving database, word processor, and spreadsheet files quickly. An audio CD drive must read the data at the exact rate the D/A converter requires for re-creating the sound. That rate turns out to be unsuitable for still images and text files, where the goal is to read and display the file as quickly as possible. That's why CD-ROM drives have notoriously slow data access rates. Most of the current models read data files at two or three times the rate of audio files, and shift back to normal speed for audio.

Recently, optical disc drives that record in the CD format have become more affordable and popular for creating audio and data CD-ROMs. Two-speed recorders range in price from $1500–$2000 SRP, and quad-speed recorders in the range of $2500–$4000. Recordable CD media (74-minute discs) range in price from $7–$10 per disc. CD mastering software is fairly easy to use and is more readily available from several vendors including FWB, Sony, and Kodak. Some CD drives support putting data and audio information on the same CD. When the CD is inserted into a Mac, you can access backup data, when inserted into an audio CD player, you can play music tracks from the same CD. All current CD recorders only allow you to write to the CD disc one time only. Another approach is to dump your digital audio files to digital audio tape, then take the tape to a recording studio that offers CD pre-mastering services. They can transfer your DAT to a single copy CD (playable on any CD player) for about $100.

Storing CD-quality digital audio on a hard disk requires a high-capacity drive. If you want to edit it, or back it up, you need more drives. Also, you need a Fast and Wide SCSI-2 interface to handle the vast amounts of data. How big? To record 60 minutes of stereo, you need a one-gigabyte drive. Suddenly that monster 500 MB internal drive on your new Mac becomes rather puny.

To edit you need a place to store the results, namely another high-capacity hard disk. If you have a lot of material to edit, you will need even more high-capacity hard disks so that you have instant random-access editing capabilities. The high-end disk-based editing systems in recording studios generally have a bank of high-capacity, high-speed disk drives connected to them. If you work with relatively short projects (such as radio spots and jingles, individual songs, and audio for short slide shows, training tapes, or store demos) you can work on a 250 or 500 MB drive comfortably.

Other capabilities of the AV Macs include integration of phone, answering machine, voice mail, and fax. Speech recognition (PlainTalk) joins speech synthesis on the AV machines. With PlainTalk, you can implement voice control by means of third-party software. Also, Articulate Systems has developed PowerSecretary, a PlainTalk-based application that will transcribe your verbal thoughts into text on a word processor. Don't get too excited. Right now, speech recognition works about as well as the early Optical Character Recognition (OCR) applications (which translate scanned text into word processor data). Your spell checker will get a healthy workout. However, for circumstances in which you need only short segments of a limited vocabulary, current PlainTalk applications offer a solution.

All Power Macs, except the 5200, 5300, 6200, and 6300 LC models, support 16-bit sound input and output. Power Macs do not have a DSP chip, which is unique to the 660AV and 840AV models. Power Macs rely on the exceptional performance of the PowerPC processors to manage sound data. The 8500 and 7500 PCI models and 5200, 5300, 6200, and 6300 LC models include Megaphone software bundled with the computer and with GeoPort hardware provide telephone answering and telecommunications features.

MIDI Hardware

MIDI synthesizers offer many possibilities for creating music and sound effects with the Mac. Unlike hard-disk based digital audio recording, MIDI synthesizers use control signals from your Mac to play music automatically. Each performance is new, rather than a reproduction of an earlier one. Before you can do this, however, you need a sequencer application running on your Mac to record, store, and send out the MIDI control signals. In addition, you need a MIDI interface to connect your Mac's serial port to a chain of MIDI instruments.

MIDI works in much the same way as LocalTalk and SCSI, in that it can send data to several devices connected together, and route specific data to specific devices. MIDI also lets you capture data from synthesizers and store it as a Mac data file. In other words, when you play music on a synthesizer, your sequencer records the data needed to reproduce that performance exactly as you played it. Using your sequencer application, you can edit the data and alter the performance, add more tracks (corresponding to vocal and instrumental parts), and create a finished composition and performance. At any point, you can play it back to hear how it sounds.

To send signals, MIDI uses serial communications protocols. The wiring used in MIDI systems consists of common off-the-shelf, inexpensive parts. The connector itself is a five-pin DIN connector—widely used in Europe for hi-fi system connections. In the U.S., DIN connectors are used for various special purpose equipment, such as S-Video cabling. At present, MIDI uses only pins 4 and 5 for signal, and pin 2 for ground. The other two pins are available for expanding the MIDI format in the future.

Why does MIDI use DIN connectors? The basic problem in a MIDI system is that you are interconnecting several distinct systems (Mac, audio, video, MIDI), each with its own unique cable connectors and signal levels. The Mac alone uses one set of cables, connectors, and voltages for LocalTalk, another for SCSI devices, another for serial devices, another for ADB devices, and others for connecting video monitors. The reason for all these different ways of connecting equipment is so that you can't make serious mistakes. For example, if you accidentally hook up a hard disk input to a monitor output, a high voltage on a particular pin might cause equipment damage. At the very least, incorrect connections can prevent the system from working.

Similarly, audio systems make distinctions between line-level connections (for tuners, CD players, and tape decks) and power-level connections (for speakers) with different types of connectors. The same is true of video equipment and MIDI equipment. The DIN connectors and cables prevent you from plugging a data line into an audio input and vice versa, because the two types of signals are carried on two completely different sets of cables. In a typical MIDI system, audio, computer, power, and MIDI cables are running all over the place in a confusing web. Different types of connectors not only prevent mistakes, but also simplify the process of setting up a complete system. That becomes important when you take your show on the road.

The MIDI cable is ordinary twisted-pair shielded cable, which is commonly available and relatively inexpensive. In fact, LocalTalk cable for your Mac also is twisted-pair shielded cable. A MIDI cable always has a male DIN connector on each end. The female connectors reside on the equipment. The shielding (wire mesh wrapped around the twisted pair) reduces the possibility of picking up extraneous signals, or Radio Frequency Interference (RFI).

Every wire acts as a radio antenna to some degree, and can pick up interference from nearby radio transmitters (usually CBs, taxis, and police cars). Also, your cables can pick up hum from light dimmers, power transformers, and similar sources. Look for MIDI cables with industrial-strength construction, and strain relief on the connectors. Don't hesitate to replace faulty cables. Always handle cables with care, especially during set up and dismantling. Yanking out the plugs pulls the shielding loose from the ground pin on the connector, leaving the cable wide open to RFI. Also, winding cables tightly into a neat package and tucking in the ends can stress the shielding not only in the middle of the cable, but also at the connectors. You can make your own cables, provided you have the skills and time to do so. The cables you can buy, however, are better than most people can make for themselves. How much do you trust your own solder connections? Unless you play gigs several nights a week, you probably don't need the quality and reliability of professional custom-made cables.

MIDI-to-Mac interface

Every Macintosh needs a MIDI adapter to connect it to a synthesizer. This device connects to one of the serial ports (printer or modem) and provides the electrical interface between the computer and the MIDI System. It has three connectors, labeled In, Out, and Thru. A MIDI interface box serves the same function as a LocalTalk adapter, but operates at a different voltage. A simple, basic MIDI adapter usually costs under $100; you can get one from Apple and many other vendors. A slightly more elaborate version, a MIDI Thru Box, has several Thru ports, each of which sends out an identical copy of the signal. Thru Boxes typically sell for about $500 to $600.

If you have a large and complex MIDI system, consider an "intelligent" or "smart" MIDI interface. Unlike the basic interface, it contains its own microprocessor. A smart MIDI interface can generate its own clock signals and keep the entire system synchronized more effectively than a basic MIDI adapter. In addition, microprocessor-equipped MIDI interfaces usually offer Society of Motion Picture and Television Engineers (SMPTE) Time Code, the industry-standard format for synchronizing multiple audio, video, and film devices. Apple does not make an intelligent MIDI interface, but they are available from Opcode, Mark of the Unicorn, and other companies. Prices vary, but most are $1000 or more, depending on features.

MIDI connections

Connecting your Mac to a single MIDI instrument is simple. Plug the MIDI interface into the modem or printer port. Take a MIDI cable, plug one end into the Out connector on the interface, and the other end into the In connector on your instrument. This connection permits MIDI data to travel from the Mac to the instrument. So far, so good. If you need to send data back to the Mac, you need to connect the Out port on the synthesizer to the In port on the interface. Some MIDI instruments don't have an Out port, however. Sending MIDI data back to the Mac is important because that's how the sequencer records whatever you play on a MIDI instrument. Playing the notes on a MIDI instrument usually is a much easier way to enter musical data than selecting notes from a palette and dragging them onto the staff.

If you have more than two MIDI devices (the Mac with its adapter counts as one), you have more choices to make. In most cases, you will want a daisy chain connection, using the Thru ports instead of the Out ports. Because the MIDI Out port only sends output data from that unit's microprocessor, you won't be able to control the other synthesizers in the chain from the first one (the Mac). The Thru port copies the control signals the unit receives from the Mac, adds the output data from that instrument, and passes them on so the next unit can use them. You can daisy chain as many instruments as you want, subject to some practical limitations. Some instruments route the signal through the microprocessor before copying it and passing it on to the Thru port. This routing process delays the signal slightly. The more times this happens, the longer the delay, commonly known as "MIDI lag." After passing through about four or five such Thru ports, the signal is so late arriving at the next synthesizer that you can hear the delay. It sounds like everyone's playing off beat, and it's quite irritating. Some instruments have a nondelaying Thru port, enabling you to build long daisy chains. Check the owner's manual to see which kind of Thru port your MIDI interface has.

Still another configuration is the star network, which requires either a smart interface, or Thru Box. The Thru Box sends the same signal to all of its Thru ports. The smart interface uses its own onboard microprocessor to receive the control signals from the Mac and send identical copies, all synchronized in time, to each of its Thru ports. This process ensures that all instruments play at exactly the same time, thus preventing "MIDI lag." A Thru Box and a smart interface solve the basic MIDI timing problem. A smart interface extends the synchronization capabilities by generating its own timing signals so that you can control external equipment such as video and audio recorders via SMPTE Time Code. A smart interface can translate MIDI Time Code (MTC) and SMPTE Time Code to synchronize the synthesizers with audio and video recorders (useful for synching music and sound effects with actions on screen in a video production).

Sound and music software

Two major classes of software are available. The first enables you to record and edit digital audio. This software works with and manages actual sound samples. High-end software of this type turns your Mac into a multitrack recording studio. Low-end digital audio software behaves more like an ordinary stereo tape recorder, but with some digital editing capabilities thrown in. Another class of software allows you to work with MIDI data, but not actual sound. These MIDI sequencer applications operate MIDI synthesizers to produce sound. Most sequencer software uses the onscreen metaphor of a multitrack tape deck but only records and plays back MIDI data, rather than sound itself.

The distinction is becoming blurred because many sequencers now allow you to add digital audio tracks to MIDI tracks. For example, you can record a vocal on top of a complex MIDI arrangement so that the synthesizers accompany the voice in perfect synchronization. Obviously, you can record acoustical instruments as well as voices, and add narration to the musical background of a radio or TV ad. In fact, the distinction becomes even more hazy when you look into multimedia software, which blends video, MIDI, and digital audio.

Some other types of musical software don't quite fit into these categories. One valuable addition to any Mac-based musical system is a patch editor/librarian. With one of these, you can create and edit the patches (instrument definitions) on your synthesizer. Advantages to this kind of software include the capability to work on a larger, more legible screen, and to have a dedicated database manager to store and retrieve the patches from a library. Automatic composition and accompaniment programs appeal to many users. Some, such as Band-in-a-Box and Jam, play chords and bass lines with the stereotypical accompaniment figures of a waltz, march, blues, and so on. Others, such as M and Max, create complex musical structures similar to the visual process of a kaleidoscope. Finally, some applications can teach you to play an instrument and tutor you on music theory.

Evaluating notation software

Printing music requires complex software. Entry-level software simply makes a screen dump of the graphics. More advanced applications use PostScript symbols and offer page layout capabilities comparable to PageMaker and QuarkXPress. In fact, because of the intricacies of musical notation, music-printing applications are even more complex than ordinary layout applications. The first solution was to use screen dumps, but bitmapped printouts for music look dreadful. Developers saw the need for a PostScript music typeface, and the Sonata font was introduced. Since then, many developers have created their own music fonts, both in PostScript and TrueType formats. The ability to change the size of the characters without losing resolution makes these formats ideal for musical notation. Obviously, you want a PostScript- or TrueType-compatible laser printer to print music with the necessary clarity.

Some music printing software can extract parts from a full score—a wonderful time-saver. Look for the capability to transpose from scores in C (all instruments written in concert pitch) to the correct key for each instrument (Trumpet in B flat, Clarinet in A, Horn in F, and so on).

If you write for instruments with unusual notation requirements (lute and guitar, harp, and most percussion instruments), be sure that the software will accommodate them. Also, if you write vocal music, you must be able to type the words in precisely the right locations under the notes. Complete flexibility with fonts, point sizes, and type styles, along with hyphenation and positioning, are crucial. Some applications generate lead sheets used in popular music. These sheets have the melody and words only, and all the chords are in shorthand chord notation (C dim 7, A min) and in guitar tablature. Trying to print lead sheets with software lacking this specific capability can be frustrating.

For those who work with nontraditional notation (mostly avant-garde classical and jazz composers), the only answer is to create scores using graphics applications (CAD software, with your own custom library of symbols can be a good approach).

Sound assistance for the physically challenged

In addition to the game sounds and musical capabilities, the Mac's sound can greatly help people with various types of physical disabilities. Most applications fall into the category of either voice input or speech synthesis. Any business attempting to help its employees comply with the Americans with Disabilities Act should investigate all the possibilities available on the Mac; sound is only one of many.

Conversely, developing applications for people with disabilities offers many new opportunities for independent consultants and vertical marketers. With these capabilities, the Mac opens many doors for the physically challenged. In addition, the results of developing applications for the physically challenged can help everyone with their work. For example, speech synthesis helps anyone entering massive amounts of numerical data into a spreadsheet by providing spoken feedback to prevent entry errors.

MacInTalk and the new PlainTalk software allow the Mac to read text. Speech synthesis can help those with impaired vision by reading aloud text that appears onscreen. For people who have difficulties with speaking, speech synthesis can make communication with other office workers more natural. Consider the problems of a hearing impaired person who usually communicates through sign language but who has difficulty speaking. If the individual simply types the words so that the Mac can speak them, he or she can communicate with others in the office much more easily. The same is true for many other people with some form of speech difficulty. Bridging the gap between the market for handicapped people and the general Mac market, Voyager has published many books in Mac form for people to read onscreen (such as during a plane flight). With speech synthesis, the Mac can read these books aloud to the visually impaired.

Clearly, voice control has applications for those who are not able to operate a keyboard. Several years ago, Articulate Systems pioneered speech recognition and voice control on the Mac with a speech recognition program. After you train the software to recognize your speech patterns, you can execute every command in the Finder and any application simply by talking. Apple, through PlainTalk software, now offers similar voice control capabilities on any AV Mac. Recently, Articulate Systems introduced PowerSecretary, which translates spoken language into word processor text. Again, voice control and speech-to-text applications bridge the two markets because they are useful to everyone. People using MIDI sequencers, page layout, and CAD applications frequently like to use voice control so they can keep their hands on the MIDI keyboard or graphics tablet.

Shopping for musical software

For serious MIDI work, consider software such as Master Tracks, Performer, Vision, or Cubase. Many computer stores don't sell this software (the market is too small); you will have to visit a musical instrument store that carries MIDI hardware and software, or buy it through a catalog. Also, professional audio dealers who sell studio-grade digital audio equipment often sell MIDI software. If you have difficulty locating musical applications, call the publishers of the software, and they should be able to recommend dealers in your area, or possibly sell to you directly.

Music software

This brief survey of the most widely known musical applications is not a complete list, but covers most of the popular products. Though computer music is a niche market, it is also technologically advanced. Computer music products change quickly—they must to make the latest, hottest sounds—but other Mac music paraphernalia doesn't change much at all. Read magazines aimed at the computer music market; major Mac magazines focus on business products, and most music and sound manufacturers don't even advertise in them.

Cubase

Cubase Audio integrates a MIDI sequencer, score printing, and digital audio recording into a powerful high-end package. It features a flexible quantization algorithm with six different methods. You can edit on a bar chart or in musical notation and assemble pieces of music in the right order using a list edit window. Cubase also provides a drum editor, MIDI mixer, score printing, wave form editor, and the capability to add digital audio tracks to the MIDI tracks. For digital audio, it supports the Digidesign Audiomedia sound cards.

Cubase Audio 2.0
$995.00 SRP
Steinberg
17700 Raymer St., Suite 101
Northridge, CA 91325
(818) 993-4091 Voice
(818) 701-7452 Fax

Digital Performer

Performer was one of the first serious sequencers, and has gone through many changes to keep it up to date. It is part of a family of related products (notation and printing, etc.) that talk to each other, though it is not formally an integrated application. Digital Performer adds digital audio capability (with the Audiomedia cards or Mark of the Unicorn Digital Waveboard) to the MIDI sequencer.

> Digital Performer 1.4
> $895 SRP
> Mark of the Unicorn
> 1280 Massachusetts Ave.
> Cambridge, MA 02138
> (617) 576-2760 Voice
> (617) 576-3609 Fax

Master Tracks

Encore complements Passport's Master Tracks, providing notation entry and music printing and layout. For musicians who are accustomed to writing music the old-fashioned way (with real notes on a staff), Encore provides all the right tools and layout capabilities to make composing on the computer right at home. When you're finished, you can play the score back through a MIDI instrument or sound card to hear how the music sounds. Encore accepts entry from a MIDI keyboard either by recording a performance in real time, or by the step-entry method (one note at a time from the keyboard). Or, you can select notes from a palette. It includes guitar notation, text insertion, and part extraction and transposition. Encore supports PostScript and TrueType music fonts, includes Anastasia and Frets fonts in both formats, and can export EPS files for use in other applications.

> Encore
> $595 SRP
> Passport Designs, Inc.
> 100 Stone Pine Rd.
> Half Moon Bay, CA 94019
> (415) 726-0280 Voice
> (415) 726-2254 Fax

Finale

Finale takes the notation approach to entering musical data, making it comfortable for composers and arrangers with traditional training. You can use a MIDI keyboard or an onscreen note palette for both entry and editing. Finale offers many notation flexibilities and user-definable symbols to satisfy the needs of experimental and avant-garde composers. It generates lead sheets and will extract and print parts from full scores, breaking multi-bar rests at rehearsal marks automatically. Its page layout, text insertion, and music printing functions are second to none. Finale includes special music fonts in both PostScript and TrueType formats. Finale plays back notated music through MIDI instruments.

Finale 3
$749 SRP
Coda Music Technology
6210 Bury Drive
Eden Prairie, MN 55346
(612) 937-9511 Voice
(612) 937-9760 Fax

Master Tracks Pro 5

Master Tracks Pro 5 provides the sequencer side of the Passport application suite (Encore is the notation side). Master Tracks Pro 5 has been around for a long time and has been refined and improved considerably over the years. The MIDI sequencer handles up to 64 tracks with automated punch-in and punch-out (for editing tracks on the fly), plus an onscreen mixer. An important function for multimedia is a link from MIDI Time Code to SMPTE Time Code, which allows you to synchronize a MIDI sequence with audio and video tape or film. You can edit sequences with event lists or edit graphically. Graphics displays for individual controllers and notes simplifies editing.

Master Tracks Pro 5
$295 SRP
Passport Designs, Inc.
100 Stone Pine Rd.
Half Moon Bay, CA 94019
(415) 726-0280 Voice
(415) 726-2254 Fax

Nightingale

The Nightingale notation program offers many refinements in adjusting symbols. The notes palette contains 86 symbols for note entry and also accepts entry via MIDI in real-time or step-time mode. For vocal music, Nightingale has a Flow In tool that simplifies the process by extracting parts and saving them as separate files. The company is also developing an intriguing OCR application that converts printed music into notation onscreen.

Nightingale 1.3
$495 SRP
Temporal Acuity Product
300 120th Ave. NE
Bldg. 1, Suite 200
Bellevue, WA 98005
(206) 462-1007 Voice
(206) 462-1057 Fax

Studio Vision

Studio Vision gives you all the tools of a high-end MIDI sequencer, including the capability to record up to four digital audio tracks. It supports the Digidesign Audiomedia sound card, and includes SMPTE Time Code for synchronization with audio, video tape, and film. Studio Vision allows you to edit digital audio with Digidesign's editing software. If you're creating radio and TV ads or multimedia productions, or simply need to add live sounds to MIDI sequences, Studio Vision is widely regarded as one of the best applications available.

Studio Vision
$995 SRP
Opcode Systems, Inc.
3950 Fabian Way, Suite 100
Palo Alto, CA 94303
(415) 856-3333 Voice
(415) 856-3332 Fax

TimeBandit

TimeBandit performs a variety of useful functions for high-end users, including time correction for fitting an audio track into the time length of a slightly longer or shorter video track without changing the pitch. Or, it can raise or lower the pitch of an instrument that was out of tune with the other tracks, but without changing the timing. Another capability is harmonization, or the process of thickening the sound by adding one or more parallel tracks just slightly out of tune (to simulate the effect of a chorus or string section). TimeBandit supports AIFF and Sound Designer file formats. It works offline because these bits of magic take time to calculate. If you need these utilities, this is one of the few packages available for the Mac.

TimeBandit 1.5
$495 SRP
Steinberg
17700 Raymer St., Suite 101
Northridge, CA 91325
(818) 993-4091 Voice
(818) 701-7452 Fax

Audioshop

With Audioshop, you can record and edit Macintosh audio by using a familiar CD player-interface. This program allows you to edit a wave form with an onscreen window in which you can cut and paste different parts of the sound, just as if you were editing text. It also plays tracks from CDs on a CD-ROM drive by using a playlist. Audioshop comes with two disks of sound samples.

Audioshop
$89.95 SRP
Opcode Systems, Inc.
3950 Fabian Way, Suite 100
Palo Alto, CA 94303
(415) 856-3333 Voice
(415) 856-3332 Fax

Deck II

With Deck II, you can turn your Quadra 840 AV into an eight-track digital audio recorder. On the 660 AV, this program provides up to six tracks. OSC developed the original software for Digidesign, and now markets its products independently. The original Deck recording software required Audiomedia, a NuBus card with a DSP chip to digitize the sound. This new version takes advantage of the DSP chip on the Quadra AV machines. It also works on other Macs with the Audiomedia card, the RasterOps MediaTime card, and the Spectral Innovations NuMedia card.

Deck allows you to record each digital audio track independently, or in combination, so that you can build a complete musical structure by adding more sounds. Punch-in and punch-out let you start recording in the middle of a previously recorded track to fix fumbles and wrong notes. With track bouncing, you can mix several tracks down to one or two (such as all your vocals, or all your drum tracks) and then use the newly freed tracks for more sounds. Instant access, non-destructive editing lets you assemble all the sections of a piece, as well as edit out glitches and bad notes. The mixing panel controls volume and panning for all channels. Deck II supports QuickTime movies and displays live video in a window, and imports MIDI Files.

Deck II 2.1
$399 SRP
OSC
480 Potrero Ave.
San Francisco, CA 94110
(415) 252-0460 Voice
(415) 252-0560 Fax

Kaboom!

This program enables you to add new and interesting sounds to Finder commands. Kaboom! comes with an extensive library of 8-bit samples. For example, you can have your Mac say "Lucy, I'm home!" instead of chiming at Startup. Or use the Twilight Zone theme for closing a file. It also has a nice 8-bit sound editor that you can use to record your own samples for placement in QuickTime movies and multimedia presentations. You'll need a Mac with a built-in microphone to use the recording feature.

Kaboom!
$50 SRP
Nova Development
23801 Calabasas Rd., Suite 2005
Calabasas, CA 91302
(818) 591-9600 Voice

MacRecorder

MacRecorder combines an external 8-bit digitizer with sound editing software. Originally sold by Farallon, it is now marketed by Macromedia. It's especially useful with older Macs that lack a built-in microphone, but works with any Mac through a serial port. You'll need a microphone to plug into the digitizer box.

MacRecorder
$275 SRP
Macromind
600 Townsend St.
San Francisco, CA 94103
(415) 252-2000, (800) 288-4797

Choosing digital audio and MIDI hardware

To work with CD-quality digital audio on the Mac, you need a sound card. Most of them cost about $1000, though the studio quality and multi-channel models can cost two to three times that amount. Although every Mac ever made has built-in sound capabilities, only the AV models offer the capability to work with CD-quality sound straight out of the box (with the appropriate software). The Quadra AV models have an onboard DSP chip (AT&T 3210), and the Power Macs have enough computing power in the PowerPC chips to carry out DSP functions. Nonetheless, any Mac with a NuBus slot will accept digital audio cards (with their own DSP chips). In addition, Digidesign sells a PDS version of its Audiomedia card that runs on the LCs. For any of these cards you will also need to purchase an amplifier and the best quality speakers you can afford. Desktop "computer speakers" are not suitable for this level of audio production.

To connect MIDI synthesizers to your Mac, the only hardware you need is a MIDI adapter. Basic adapters sell for under $100, but more elaborate types with SMPTE Time Code can cost up to $3000 or more.

If you intend to do intricate multimedia work beyond the level of QuickTime, with several audio and tape decks online, or if you plan to transfer audio tracks to film, you need to consider the benefits of SMPTE Time Code. This format, developed by the Society of Motion Picture and Television Engineers, puts timing signals on tapes and film soundtracks, or embeds them in MIDI sequencer data files. Its purpose is to synchronize every piece of production equipment. A good example of SMPTE Time Code is the synchronization of dialogue with images. Many smart MIDI interfaces include SMPTE synchronization.

Which Mac do you need?

All Macs have built-in sound capabilities, even an old 512K Mac—it can run entry-level software, especially musical applications intended for preschoolers. Many low-end MIDI sequencers and 8-bit sound editors run on a Mac Plus, although you should have more than 1 MB of RAM. If you haven't upgraded to System 7, you should do so, because more and more software requires it. The high-end sequencers, and 16-bit recording and editing applications, generally require System 7 and at least the speed of a IIci and 8 MB of RAM. Applications at this level generally are over 3 MB, and you will probably have more than one audio app open. Also, if you are using a notation application, you need a large screen monitor and at least a IIci and a laser printer.

SCSI accelerators and sound cards

For digital audio recordings, plan to get as much RAM as you can—massive amounts of data will be moving through your Mac. Also, you will need more hard disk capacity than you ever imagined possible. One hour of stereo at a 44.1 KHz sampling rate with 16-bit quantization occupies 600 MB. And you will want to back it up! Beyond that, you must have drives with an access time of 18 ms or less, plus an accelerated SCSI bus. Recent Macs come equipped with SCSI-2; older Macs can be upgraded with a SCSI accelerator card—required for CD quality digital audio work. Without Fast SCSI, your Mac can't transfer data from the hard disk fast enough to play it back.

In addition to the SCSI accelerator, you must have a digital audio card. Its function is to convert analog signals into digital audio data, and it's normally a NuBus card. It will have at least one DSP chip for this purpose. The Digidesign Audiomedia, Sonic Solutions SSP-3, RasterOps MediaTime, and Spectral Innovations NuMedia are common cards. Most available software supports one or more.

A crucial difference between these cards and the DSP chips built into many Intel-based machines is the signal-to-noise ratio. Although a DSP chip may have 16-bit quantization and a 44.1 KHz sampling rate and may be advertised as having CD quality, its actual performance may not be good enough for digital audio recording, editing, and mixing. Less expensive models of these chips suffer from interior digital noise that may reduce their signal-to-noise ratio by as much as 10 dB. So, instead of the 90 dB you might expect from a 16-bit chip, you start at 80 dB.

Why is this important? As you bounce tracks in the overdubbing process, noise starts to build up, just as it does on an analog multitrack recorder. Also, when you mix down 8 or 16 channels, the noise on each track gets added to the stereo mix, reducing the signal-to-noise ratio of your output well below even 80 dB. That's why software developers require a sound card with a good quality DSP chip, such as the Motorola 56001. The Quadra AV machines use an onboard AT&T 3210 chip that delivers similar performance.

Selecting synthesizers

The current trend is away from old-style synthesizers and toward wave table (sampling) synthesizers. Soon, FM synthesizers, such as the Yamaha DX-7 and its successors, will be antiques—as strange and out-of-date as a Moog synthesizer seems today. The popular music market pushes for instruments that are quick to adjust during live performances. Changing patches and fiddling with adjustments takes time. What a rock performer wants is a bank of buttons to push. Also, sampling techniques have improved, and the price of memory has dropped, making sampling synthesizers economically practical and desirable.

Today, a typical wave table system includes one or more black boxes loaded with samples (many units provide space for user-downloaded samples), plus a keyboard to control the sample boxes. Throw in some special effects processors, and you have a modern synthesizer System. Some sample boxes, such as Digidesign's Sample Cell, are actually NuBus cards.

Libraries of samples, many on CD-ROM, are on the shelves at the musical instrument dealers. In a sense, samples on a synthesizer now behave like fonts on a laser printer. Creating a sample has become a specialized skill, similar to creating a typeface. To do it well requires knowledge and skill plus specialized hardware and software.

Keyboard, wind, and string controllers

The keyboard is obviously an important part of a Mac MIDI instrument, particularly for those who learned to play on an acoustic piano. The size, weight, and mechanical resistance of the keys is important to most serious pianists, yet might mean nothing at all to other musicians. A keyboard with advanced features like Velocity-sensitive keys may be one such consideration. Aftertouch, one such program that takes keyboards seriously, even creates data about the way you released the key. Some even have pressure sensitivity for creating effects such as vibrato. Thus, a single master controller keyboard makes sense. Often, they have no sound-generating capabilities, but simply control other instruments. Put all your money into one high-end keyboard, and play your other synthesizers with it through MIDI rather than buy several expensive keyboards.

Alternative controllers designed for string and wind players also are available. They are less common than they were a few years ago, but check the used equipment market. The Intelligent Wind Instrument (IWI), marketed by Akai, was one of the first on the market. Yamaha followed with their WX-11 MII Wind Controller. In addition, guitar synthesizers are available; you can even find MIDI violins and cellos.

No matter what you choose as the ultimate instrument of your dreams, pay attention to the operating controls as well as to the feel of the keyboard. Tiny LCD screens that deliver cryptic information don't make much sense in a dark auditorium during a concert. Banks of buttons smaller than your fingertip and too close together with labels too small to read can drive you batty. Be sure that the human interface makes your job as a player as easy as possible.

Hard-disk based recording

Storing digital audio data on a hard disk rather than on tape has revolutionized the audio industry in many ways. Storing audio on a hard disk has low noise and distortion, allows you to make an exact copy, and provides greater accuracy in editing. In addition, hard disk storage provides one advantage common to all disk based media: nearly instant access to any point in the recording, which makes editing faster. Because all the operations take place on a desktop computer, software can perform all the equalization, compression, mixing, and special effects generation that formerly required an elaborate collection of equipment in a recording studio. Editing digital audio becomes as easy as editing a word processing document. You can make changes without destroying the original, listen to an edit before you commit to it, and even audition several edits before selecting the one that sounds best.

If you've ever edited analog tapes with a razor blade and splicing tape, you know all about the dangers of cutting into a master tape (in analog, you can't work with a copy because of the added noise). Finding the exact location isn't easy. Cut the wrong place and you can destroy the tape. If the performer doesn't like the way you edited the tape, changing it can be difficult, if not impossible.

In digital editing, you can specify where the edit takes place, down to the sample (44,100 of them per second). You can tell the computer to connect Point A to Point D or Point Z without altering your original recording. Also, you can tell the computer to fade in the beginning of Segment 224 while it's fading out the end of Segment 86 (cross-fading), and specify how long the cross-fade should last. This sort of editing is not possible with razor blade editing. In fact, you can assemble a finished production by making a list of all segments you want to use, in the order you need them, and ask the computer to play it back for you as a continuous piece. Because all data is on the hard disk, the software simply reads the appropriate sectors. This process alone has revolutionized film and video production.

MIDI and Sound hardware

The range of digital audio and MIDI hardware for the Mac is as wide as the software. Many 16-bit digital audio cards are available for the Mac, and most manufacturers offer editing software that works with their specific card. Also, special effects cards (such as the Lexicon NuVerb) are beginning to appear on the market. The integrated hardware and software systems usually include SCSI-2 accelerators. The following products are integrated hardware and software systems.

Session 8

Session 8 comes with a 16-bit digital audio card and a SCSI accelerator card, plus the software for direct to hard disk recording. This card requires a IIci or faster. Features include digital mixing, track bouncing, random-access editing, special effects, SMPTE trigger, and MIDI Time Code. Its internal mix mode allows you to mix, edit, and signal process digitally, providing clarity and eliminating noise build-up. An optional hardware mixer/controller provides the feel of a real recording console, and the capability to operate more than one fader at a time.

> Session 8
> $4000 SRP
> Digidesign
> 1360 Willow Rd.
> Menlo Park, CA 94025
> (415) 688-0600 Voice
> (415) 688-0777 Fax

SonicStation II

This card provides 12 tracks of disk playback, with two-channel digital input and output. It includes two NuBus cards and software. The Sonic Solutions equipment is widely used in recording studios, and this is their entry-level package (others approach $100,000). Generally, it is available only from special pro audio dealers, who can help you set up a Mac-based professional studio. SonicStation II offers a high-performance recording solution for those who plan to start a professional studio.

SonicStation II
$4995 SRP
Sonic Solutions
1891 East Francisco Blvd.
San Rafael, CA 94901
(415) 485-4800 Voice
(415) 485-4877 Fax

Sound Cards

Audiomedia II contains a Motorola 56001 DSP chip that digitizes analog audio. Digidesign's Sound Designer II software lets you record, mix, edit, and play back digital audio. The Audiomedia II card offers high quality 16-bit sound at a 44.1 KHz sampling rate. It's available either as a NuBus card or as a PDS card for the LC. The Audiomedia card runs on the LC MAX, which provides slots for up to three other cards.

Audiomedia II
$1295 SRP
Digidesign
1219 West 6th St., Suite 250
Austin, TX 78703
(512) 476-9855 Voice
(512) 476-6399 Fax

Note

Because the LC has only one slot, you can expand it with the LC MAX expansion chassis, available by mail order from DGR Technologies.

NuMedia

Oriented toward QuickTime users, NuMedia delivers 16-bit stereo performance for QuickTime soundtracks. This NuBus card uses the AT&T 3210 DSP chip (see Figure 8.14), and also carries out compression and decompression for audio and video.

NuMedia
$1195 SRP
Spectral Innovations
1885 Lundy Ave.
San Jose, CA 95131
(408) 955-0366 Voice
(408) 955-0370 Fax

Figure 8.14 The NuMedia sound card.

Pro Tools

The Pro Tools digital audio card provides two 56001 DSP chips, and can handle four channels (up to 16 with expansion capabilities). Intended for exacting studio work, it delivers lower noise than the Audiomedia cards, and has balanced line outputs with XLR connectors.

Pro Tools
$6000 SRP
Digidesign
1360 Willow Rd.
Menlo Park, CA 94025
(415) 688-0600 Voice
(415) 688-0777 Fax

Sample Cell II

Sample Cell II stores downloaded sampled sounds on a NuBus card. It handles 32 voices with eight polyphonic outputs, and you can install additional cards for more voices. A CD-ROM with an extensive library of sampled sounds, plus sample editing software comes with it.

Sample Cell II
$1995 SRP
Digidesign
1360 Willow Rd.
Menlo Park, CA 94025
(415) 688-0600 Voice
(415) 688-0777 Fax

NuVerb

NuVerb brings the outstanding quality of Lexicon's famous reverb systems to a NuBus card. It has many other effects, and interfaces with Digidesign.

> NuVerb
> $1795 SRP
> Lexicon
> 100 Beaver St.
> Waltham, MA 02154
> (617) 736-0300 Voice

Vortex

Vortex does for sound what morphing software does for images. This outboard effects processor transforms one sound into another over a specified period of time from 0.01 to 10 seconds. It's great for audio effects that accompany visuals. For example, as an ear of corn becomes a box of cereal, a synchronized sound effect changes along with the image. Vortex has many more capabilities for creating subtle musical effects with various kinds of delay and modulation transformations.

> Vortex
> $479 SRP
> Lexicon
> 100 Beaver St.
> Waltham, MA 02154
> (617) 736-0300 Voice

MIDI Accessories

Apple MIDI Interface

The Apple MIDI Interface connects to one of the Mac's serial ports and provides one MIDI In and one MIDI Out.

> Apple MIDI Interface
> $99.95 SRP
> Apple Computer

MIDI Time Piece II

MIDI Time Piece II includes a 128 channel MIDI interface, with eight independent inputs and outputs, plus SMPTE interface and a MIDI patch bay.

> MIDI Time Piece II
> $595 SRP
> Mark of the Unicorn
> 1280 Massachusetts Ave.
> Cambridge, MA 02138
> (617) 576-2760 Voice
> (617) 576-3609 Fax

MIDI Translator II

This product is an inexpensive, basic 16-channel MIDI interface. MIDI Translator II provides one MIDI In and three MIDI Out, plus LED activity indicators (see Figure 8.15).

> MIDI Translator II
> $59.95 SRP
> Opcode Systems
> 1024 Hamilton Court
> Menlo Park, CA 94025
> (415) 321-8977 Voice

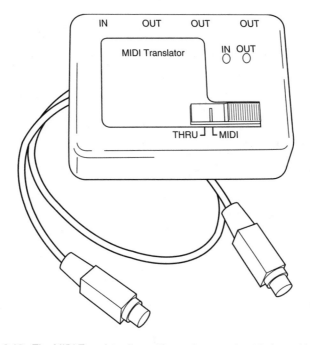

Figure 8.15 The MIDI Translator II provides an inexpensive 16-channel interface.

Studio 3

Studio 3 offers 32 channels, with two MIDI In and six MIDI Out, and an SMPTE Interface Synchronizer.

> Studio 3
> $319.95 SRP
> Opcode Systems
> 1024 Hamilton Court
> Menlo Park, CA 94025
> (415) 321-8977 Voice

Studio 4

Studio 4 offers 128 channels, with 8 MIDI In and 10 MIDI Out, and an SMPTE Interface Synchronizer.

Studio 4
$495.00 SRP
Opcode Systems
1024 Hamilton Court
Menlo Park, CA 94025
(415) 321-8977 Voice

Studio 5

Studio 5 is almost infinitely expandable. It has 240 channels, 15 MIDI In and 15 MIDI Out, activity LEDs, and SMPTE to MIDI Time Code conversion. You can also chain up to 6 Studio 5 LX units together.

Studio 5 LX
$1195 SRP
Opcode Systems
1024 Hamilton Court
Menlo Park, CA 94025
(415) 321-8977 Voice

Troubleshooting Hardware

When your Macintosh appears to be slow or makes an annoying sound, or your hard drive doesn't access files or show window contents as fast as it used to, how do you know whether the problem is normal hardware behavior, a software problem, or something that requires immediate care?

This chapter begins with an overview of the troubleshooting process, followed by scenarios with common problems, possible causes, and expected results for hardware, software, and networks. This chapter can help identify and explain typical and atypical Macintosh behavior. Troubleshooting diagnostic tools are also discussed, and an overview of the technical support process is covered. Learning some of the ins and outs of Macintosh diagnostics can help you keep your Mac running faster for long periods of time. By reading this chapter (and Chapters 10 and 11), you will become familiar with do-it-yourself repairs and learn preventative Macintosh maintenance.

Troubleshooting Methods

Troubleshooting is the process of discovering what's wrong, why it's wrong, and how to fix it. It is important to think logically and clearly about the problem, eliminate what variables you can, and systematically solve the problem. It is also important to be prepared for trouble before it happens. To do this, you need an understanding of what resources you have available and what you must do to make your work easier.

Because no two Macs have exactly the same software installed, and because everyone uses software in a slightly different way, troubleshooting problems that seem to be caused by software can be tricky. That's the bad news. The good news is you have plenty of resources available. The first is common sense. Finding the true source of the problem by eliminating variables is an important early step. It's also important to remain calm and methodical, especially when solutions elude you.

When you experience a problem—an error message appears; software freezes, crashes, or bombs; or your Mac refuses to start up—the first thing to do is find out whether the problem is a one-time occurrence or a true source of trouble. Shut down your Mac (select the Shutdown item from the Special menu) and re-create the problem situation. Turning off the computer resets the software, flushes the memory, and gives you a clean slate. If the problem recurs, it's time to take a closer look.

By using a problem isolation strategy to trim possible problems with software, you will eventually uncover the culprit. Begin your diagnosis by stating the problem you have in specific, concrete terms or steps. It's not enough to say "My Mac won't start"; a better analysis might be "When my Mac starts, it freezes or restarts when control panels and extension icons appear at the bottom of my screen."

Your next task is to find out whether the problem occurs all the time or intermittently. Re-create the conditions or steps that caused the problem. Try to re-create the problem several times, being careful not to change any settings or tasks so that the circumstances are identical each time. If you're stumped by a particularly thorny problem, you may choose to alter conditions slightly (changing one variable at a time) to see what effect these changes have.

When you have a lead on a problem, it's possible to determine what isn't at fault. If, for example, you get a system error only when you open Microsoft Excel, chances are that the trouble is with that program, and not with the printer, the Chooser control panel, or Microsoft Word.

The following sections are divided into hardware, software, and network troubleshooting sections. Hardware troubleshooting covers common monitor, printer, and hard drive troubleshooting. Software troubleshooting covers system software, startup, and extension conflict scenarios. Network and modem troubleshooting discusses common connectivity problems, causes, and expected results.

Hardware problems can be simple oversights, such as incomplete or defective cables or cable connections, or a power switch not turned on. Serious hardware problems are generally more costly repairs that can involve replacing a bad chip on the motherboard, faulty memory SIMM, a hard drive or floppy drive malfunction, or the need to replace the entire motherboard. Many hardware failures are accompanied by smoke or the smell of burnt plastic or metal.

Software problems can be diagnosed much more easily because of a wealth of software tools. These types of problems also are less expensive to repair, although they can take more time to troubleshoot. Software problems can be broken into three main categories: incompatibility, configuration problems, and data corruption. These can affect both system software and application performance, and often cause software freezes, crashes, or unexpected error messages. Software problems can be kept to a minimum by practicing regular preventative maintenance, and being prepared for just such an occasion.

If you are still unable to find a solution to a hardware or software problem, you will have enough information to help online support groups or technical support find an answer. The Macintosh community is rich with information provided by hardware vendors, software publishers, online special interest groups, Macintosh user groups, and Apple authorized dealers.

Before something breaks...

Proper troubleshooting methods are essential when a problem occurs. To know when it's time to break out the books, take a good look at your Mac before anything breaks. Familiarize yourself with what the Mac is supposed to look like so that you can spot when something out of the ordinary occurs. By examining where everything is now, you also will know the location of the major subsystems. You may not have time (or even the temperament) to figure out where to look if your Mac breaks in the middle of an important project.

When your Mac does break, be a detective. As you inspect cables and electronics inside the case, keep an eye out for the unusual—bent parts on the logic board, cables not fully seated in their connectors, RAM SIMMs sitting at a nonuniform angle in their sockets. Is the cover closing smoothly over the expansion cards? Are there any cuts in the internal SCSI cables? Is that a wisp of smoke? Look for what is not there as well, such as empty spaces where screws or parts of something could have fallen out. If a screw is not in its slot, where is it? If it is resting on two leads of a chip, it is probably shorting out the circuitry.

Just as you should familiarize yourself with what a normal Mac looks like, you should familiarize yourself with the normal sounds of your Mac. These include the spinning of the hard drive, the startup sounds, the monitor's subtle high-pitched whine. Turn your Sound control panel up to seven, just to discover what the speaker sounds like when asked to perform at maximum volume.

The Mac should make the same types of sounds day after day; if something changes, something's up. A changing pitch in the spinning of a hard disk can signal the beginning of a drive problem. Listen for grinding noises—nothing should be making that kind of racket. Carefully pick up a malfunctioning Mac, hard drive, or smaller peripheral, and gently rock it from side to side. Hear anything loose? You shouldn't. Also listen for what's not there. The disappearance of a familiar noise can be just as telling as the appearance of an unfamiliar one.

Keep a nose out for the smell of anything burning. Although parts can get warm during normal operation, hard drives, power supplies, cables, expansion cards, monitors, and other parts do not normally combust. A slight burning smell can indicate that something has malfunctioned and is running too hot.

Although these recommendations may seem obvious, it is important to "know" your Mac. By recognizing how it looks and sounds when everything is AOK, you will be able to attack a problem the moment it occurs. Anything out of the ordinary will be immediately recognizable.

9

Using your hardware maintenance logs

Good habits pay off during a crisis. Probably one of the smartest and least troublesome habits you can get into is to regularly enter data into your hardware and software maintenance logs. The more data you provide in your maintenance logs, the better. Always log what you check on each Mac, what and when you run a backup, and list the contents of your hard drive(s). Also keep a running log of content on removable media. You should be able to identify or diagnose hardware problems in the earlier stages by reviewing this information, or isolate hardware or software problems in a shorter amount of time.

Problems you may be able to identify by reviewing maintenance logs include hardware versus software failure, hard drive access defects, CD-ROM software or hardware incompatibilities, unclean internal mechanisms, slow or inconsistent peripheral performance, and any change in the frequency of software errors with specific hardware components.

Hardware logs range in format, style, and content. A minimal log should contain day, date, and year when the Mac was checked, and at least a one-sentence summary of what was checked. If you also note any particularly important files that were backed up, this will help you recover from unexpected emergencies faster. If you have password protection software on your computer, try not to keep this information in your log file. Using a password to access your logs maintains the integrity of your logged information as well as access to some or all of your data on your Macintosh.

Below is an example of a hardware maintenance log:

```
5/2/93    Purchased Quadra 800 16/500 with internal CD player
5/3/93    Connected external hard drive for backups
5/15/93   Installed new application on hard drive
5/21/93   Ran backup on all software on internal drive
5/24/93
          Removed extensions to speed startup
5/25/93   Noticed problem reading audio CD
6/1/93    Added new extensions to
          system software
6/4/93    Looked at Apple CD software and realized I don't have all the
          CD software in my system folder. Reinstalled and audio CDs work
          again.
6/7/93    Backed up system software on hard drive
```

Note

Try to list specific error messages and odd behavior and note any new software installed on your hard drive, especially those installed in the System Folder.

Tools

Though installing Macintosh external peripherals doesn't usually require any tools, it's good to have some ready for an unexpected fix. It's probably not necessary to go out and buy a professional computer repair tool kit for installing peripherals, but you might want to find any specialty tools for your particular Mac.

Integrated, Zero-Footprint (ZFP) Macs (128/512/Plus/SE/Classics) and PowerBooks require a special star head Torx-15 driver tool. PowerBooks require #8 and #10 Torx Drivers (except PB100). For memory changes, the Mac Plus, SE, and Classic require a mini "jaws-of-life" tool called *Mac Cracker* (most mail-order RAM houses sell them and may even include them). Markertek also sells a tool kit for opening integrated Macs. A large, tweezer-like RAM-puller tool will come in handy for memory switch outs, but make sure you first determine if the RAM you have is a 36-pin SIMM or a 72-pin SIMM. An antistatic strap will prevent you from conducting any electricity to your devices and is either free with memory upgrades, or can be found cheaply in any electronics store or catalog—though you absolutely must leave the Mac plugged into the wall for the grounding strap to work.

One repair and upgrade secret is a special conductive contact-enhancing liquid called *Tweek* that comes in a small squeeze bottle. When applied to cable ends and plugs, it actually increases connective surface area. Look for it in electronics magazines, stores, and catalogs. Cans of compressed air to clean the inside of the Mac are also recommended; be sure to have lots of ventilation before doing this; and wear old clothes. A small handyvac vacuum is good to have around for these chores, as well as for cleaning your keyboard.

A decent set of small jewelry-repair screwdrivers and hex wrenches comes in handy for those tiny, nonuniform screw sizes used on many peripheral enclosures. An assorted set of regular size straight-edge and Phillips end drivers will be used more than your other tools.

If you're setting up a comprehensive repair workbench, you're going to need much more, primarily a soldering iron, voltmeter, Torx drivers, a large grounded work surface, point and ambient lights, good ventilation, and a wide assortment of tools, electronic test equipment, and diagnostic machines.

The human factor

While you eliminate possible culprits, make sure the problem you are having is not the result of human error. If, for example, you can't find a document you are certain you created and saved, be sure you saved the file in the proper place. Often, when the Save dialog box appears, the default folder is not the one you want your documents saved to. Use the Find command in System 7 to search for misplaced files (select Find from the File menu, or press ⌘-F).

9

Note

System 7.5 has two Find File window options. Activate the System 7.0 Find File window by holding down the Shift key while pressing ⌘-F, or by selecting Find from the File menu; in System 7.5 hold down the Option key while pressing ⌘-F. If you are using System 6 use the Find File DA.

Human errors often occur when one of the following is ignored or neglected:

- When others use the system and move files and folders to different locations on your hard drive, or mistakenly delete files or folders without notifying you.

- More problems occur if you load a piece of software that isn't compatible with your Macintosh or its system software. A list of hardware and software minimum requirements—on the product packaging, in the documentation, or in Read Me files—may have been ignored. Check these requirements before you panic.

- When you try to take shortcuts, or don't read documentation. Many Mac users avoid manuals because the Mac is so easy to use. When something goes wrong, remember, a wealth of information is available in the software documentation.

Hardware Problems and Answers

Common hardware problems can be anything from having two monitors too close together, a bad power or serial cable, a defective chip on the motherboard, bad power supply, or a hard drive that won't spin up. These problems and their solutions can range from being simple and inexpensive (or even free) to (more commonly) fairly expensive. Many problems, once identified, have easy-to-implement solutions, such as turning on the power switch or using another cable. Other hardware problems, such as a bad motherboard, may be more complex or impossible to fix on your own. However, you can still gather valuable information by performing some initial hardware analysis before contacting a support group for additional help, or before purchasing additional hardware.

The rest of this section contains common hardware problems, possible causes, and some checkpoints to think about before changing your hardware or software configuration. Afterward, a list of expected results is included to compare with your particular results; this helps determine if the problem is fixed correctly.

Note

An explanation of system software and sad Macintosh error codes can be found in Appendix A.

Connecting peripherals

Adding a peripheral device to a Mac demonstrates the best part of these machines: users need to know little or nothing about RAM allocation, drivers, or adapters. In developing the Macintosh, Apple almost perfected the "plug-and-play" machine. Compared to many other computers and platforms, Macintosh computers have relatively few confusing details—you don't need to remember commands, Mac software drivers install themselves, hardware cases and cable ends have matching logos for foolproof connecting, and allocation is set automatically in RAM. Apple has gone to great lengths to make their products easy to use for their customers.

Overview

The same ease-of-use philosophy that is used with Apple's friendly object-oriented Graphical User Interface (GUI) is also incorporated into the process of connecting a peripheral to your Mac system. As one example, the Mac's input ports and cable plug ends have small generic icons to help you figure out what goes where.

Generic cables, however, may not have a symbol at the end of the plug. For faster system setups, savvy users add a sticky dot label, marking it with the same icon as the input port used on the Mac. Refer to Table 9.1 to find out what input port is used as well as to find other input information.

For the most part, you can master the process of adding a Mac peripheral armed only with common sense, a few simple tools, good lighting, patience, and a basic knowledge of electricity.

- The desktop bus connector connects your keyboard and mouse/trackball to your Mac. It is a four-pin connector that plugs into the back of your Macintosh, or into the base of your Apple monitor.

- The Ethernet cable uses an RJ-45 connector for 10BASE-T connections, or a thin coaxial connector. Apple's built-in Ethernet has a custom Ethernet port that connects to either of two transceivers, one for 10BASE-T; the other for Coaxial Ethernet cable.

- Plug a normal RJ-11 phone cable into the modem or GeoPort. LocalTalk drop boxes appear to use the same RJ-11 cable, but the cable must have 4 wires passing through the connectors to communicate with other LocalTalk devices.

- The first Mac microphone used a standard miniplug jack, usually on the back of the Mac. The latest Macintosh models require the more-sensitive PlainTalk microphone, which has a slightly longer mini plug.

9

Table 9.1   Input Capabilities of Desktop Macintosh Models

Model	Modem	Printer	Monitor	ADB	SCSI
Plus/SE/SE30	•	•	n/a	n/a	•
Mac II/IIx	•	•	2	•	•
Mac IIfx	•	•	2	•	•
Classic/II	•	•	n/a	•	•
Color Classic	•	•	n/a	2	•
LC/II/III/475	•	•	•	•	•
IIsi	•	•	•	•	•
IIcx/IIci	•	•	•	2	•
IIvi/IIvx	•	•	•	2	•
Centris 610	•	•	•	2	•
Centris 650	•	•	•	2	•
Quadra 660AV	•	•	•	2	•
Quadra 605	•	•	•	1	•
Quadra 610	•	•	•	2	•
Quadra 650	•	•	•	2	•
Quadra 700	•	•	•	2	•
Quadra 800	•	•	•	2	•
Quadra 840AV	•	•	•	1	•
Quadra 900/950	•	•	•	1	•
Quadra 630	•	•	•	•	•
Power Mac 6100	•	•	•	•	•
Power Mac 7100	•	•	2	•	•
Power Mac 8100	•	•	2	•	•
Power Mac 9500	•	•	w/graphics card	•	•
PowerMac 8500	•	•	•	•	•
PowerMac 7500	•	•	•	•	•
PowerMac 7200	•	•	•	•	•
PowerMac 5200	•	•	•	•	•
PowerMac 5300	•	•	•	•	•
PowerMac 6200	•	•	•	•	•
PowerMac 6300	•	•	•	•	•

Ethernet	Audio I	Video	GeoPort	NuBus/PDS Slot
n/a	n/a	n/a	n/a	1 PDS (SE30 only)
opt	n/a	n/a	n/a	6 NuBus
opt	n/a	n/a	n/a	6 NuBus
n/a	•	n/a	n/a	n/a
opt	•	n/a	n/a	LC PDS
opt	•	n/a	n/a	LC PDS
opt	n/a	n/a	n/a	PDS or NuBus
opt	n/a	n/a	n/a	3 NuBus
opt	•	n/a	n/a	3 NuBus & 1PDS
opt	•	n/a	n/a	1 NuBus or 1PDS
opt	•	n/a	n/a	3 NuBus, 1 PDS
•	•	•	•	1 NuBus
opt	•	n/a	n/a	1 PDS
opt	•	n/a	n/a	1 NuBus or 1 PDS
•	•	n/a	n/a	3 NuBus & 1 PDS
•	•	n/a	n/a	2 NuBus & 1 PDS
•	•	n/a	n/a	3 NuBus & 1 PDS
•	•	•	•	3 NuBus
•	•	•	•	1 NuBus
•	•	•	•	3 NuBus

9

Connection problems

Before working with hardware, be sure to inspect the cable end and input for any wear and bent pins. Make sure the plugs and inputs are free of debris, have no chipped or bent inputs, worn or cracked sleeves, or discoloration. Most Mac specific cables have an extruded D-shaped molded end that corresponds to the same shape input, which makes it quite a bit easier to find the angle of insertion and cable seating to prevent bent pins and possible bad connections.

Note

The metal pins on the inside of Mac cables are hair-thin and will bend easily. Luckily, they are made from soft alloys and can be straightened with thin needle-nose pliers.

Assuming your software drivers (if any) have been loaded into the System Folder, proceed to connect your device. The following list of steps explains how to connect a hardware device to your Macintosh computer.

1. Install software drivers from the floppies included with the peripheral. Look for a TeachText file that may contain the latest bugs and conflicts for the device, or any problem—usually marked READ ME FIRST.

2. Power down the Mac, but leave it plugged in for grounding purposes.

3. Determine the correct angle of insertion of the cable to the input on the peripheral.

4. Gently push the cable into the connectors on the peripheral, feeling for a positive seat, or signs of resistance. Don't force; feel.

5. If you feel resistance, check your angle again, and inspect the plug and input for damage.

6. Repeat steps 3 and 4 until the cable is plugged in.

7. Plug in the power cable of the new device and turn it on.

8. Turn on the Mac, and check your peripheral. You've already installed your device driver, so it should be available where you need it—whether it's from within a backup program trying to locate the tape drive, your paint application looking for a scanner, or from the desktop for CD-ROM or drive icons.

Distributing the wall outlet power among your larger peripherals is a good strategy to avoid overloading any electrical circuits in your workspace. Ideally, your setup will contain a quality power conditioner/uninterruptible power supply (UPS) that "cleans up" the power coming through the walls into your devices; and will filter out or "condition" the power, eliminating harmful voltage spikes, surges, and uneven power. UPS are available for under $500; they can solve many of the riddles that result from hardware gremlins. If a UPS is out of your budget, try to keep your power hungry peripherals broken up over several different circuits—run extensions from other outlets. Loaded circuits add to the problems already found in the raw power stream in office or home outlets. At the very least use surge protected power strips that trip (on/off) fuses instead of blowing out your Mac. For a more in-depth discussion of power, see Chapter 5.

Cable strategies

Cables are a necessary evil in computing. The addition of peripherals means more cables, resulting in more mess, more voltage, and more chances for problems. Though a few companies have made attempts at wireless peripherals, such as mice and tablet stylus pens, there are no all-in-one wireless solutions for a range of Macintosh peripheral devices.

Cables represent the weak link in many systems, and are an expensive afterthought when putting a system together for many new users. Nevertheless, cables should not be thought of lightly. Here are a few guidelines to follow:

- Get the best quality cables you can afford.

- Keep the cables as short as possible.

- Stick with straight, smooth cables.

- Stay away from coiled phone-cord style cables (commonly used for keyboards) that can tangle with all the other cables.

A number of small businesses exist that can custom make cables for your computer. These shops will make all cabling the correct length and will use copper instead of a cheaper alloy found in foreign consumer cables. Custom-made cables are often thicker gauge with better shielding, and many have gold-plated hardware (gold is highly conductive). These custom-made cables take a few days to make, but you will receive quality connectors for not much more than you would pay in a computer store for shoddily constructed generic cables.

Cable routing

You can keep your cables well-organized and away from each other with a cable run. Taped down, routed through tubing, or shield-wrapped and snaked, a cable run is a practical and cheap way of keeping your cables untangled and making the system look more professional. Another benefit of installing a cable run is that it keeps your wires from moving against each other, or getting jammed and torn, resulting in signals straying from their designated paths. A well thought-out cable run will also protect your cabling from any tangling and other potential hazards such as gnawing pets, foot traffic, and environmental moisture.

If you need a cable run, you can put one together using inexpensive items from any hardware and automotive store. Cable runs created from spark plug wire directors, zip ties, or lengths of closed cell pipe insulation all keep your cables running uniformly.

Several large mail order catalogs supply almost every cable, cable accessory, and routing product imaginable. Markertek Video and Audio Supply's catalog (1-800-522-2025) is perhaps the most exhaustive and cost effective.

9

Cable-related problems

Cables are the basic connection between your Mac and most external hardware devices. Some common problems are related to the quality of the cable itself. More common problems are related to incomplete connection of the cable from device to device, particularly with short length cables. Torn, damaged, and missing pins can also cause hardware devices not to be recognized. The following pages cover selected common problems with cables in more detail.

Problem: External SCSI device appears connected to the Macintosh, but is not seen by the computer.

Common SCSI devices include external hard drives, DAT drives, CD-ROM drives, scanners, and removable media drives, such as SyQuest and Zip drives. External SCSI devices can be connected to any Mac, including those with internal IDE hard drives, such as the Quadra/Performa 630 series, PowerBook 150, and Power Macs with PCI expansion slots. The SCSI connector is the most widely used connection for adding peripherals to Macs. Below is a common scenario for SCSI cable connections with SCSI devices connected to a Macintosh computer.

Possible causes

A SCSI cable is not connected completely to either the Macintosh or to the next SCSI device.
SCSI cable is missing connection pins.
SCSI cable is defective.
SCSI cable is not an Apple-quality SCSI cable.
SCSI device is not powered on.
Power cable to the SCSI device is not connected completely.
Power cable to the SCSI device is defective.
Wall outlet SCSI device is connected to may not have power on.

Checkpoints

Swap SCSI or power cables with a SCSI device that works successfully.
Check SCSI cables and make sure all are completely connected to each SCSI device from the Mac to the last SCSI device.
Power down your Macintosh and each SCSI device.
Check each cable and make sure there are no missing metal connectors at each end of the SCSI cable.
Disconnect then reconnect each cable that appears loose.
Turn the power back on to your Macintosh and each SCSI device and use SCSIProbe to see if it can 'see' the hard drive connected to your Macintosh model.
For more information on SCSI, refer to Figure 7.1 or the section on cables in this chapter.

Expected results

After you restart your Macintosh the hard drive should appear on the desktop. Open SCSIProbe and you should see the SCSI device on the SCSI daisy chain.

Identify any improperly functioning cables or hardware components.

Problem: External serial device appears connected to the Macintosh, but is not seen by the computer.

Common serial devices include modems, network connections, serial port switchers, scanners, and graphics tablets.

Possible causes

A serial cable is not connected completely to either the Macintosh or to the next serial device.
Serial cable is missing connection pins.
Serial cable is defective.
Serial device is not powered on.
Power cable to the serial device is not connected completely.
Power cable to the serial device is defective.
Wall outlet serial device is connected to may not have power on.

Checkpoints

If the hardware is a serial device, make sure the serial and power cables are completely connected at the back of you Mac as well as to the serial device.
If the cable is not completely connected, you may want to turn the power off on the serial device before disconnecting and re-connecting it to your Macintosh. You do not need to shut down your Macintosh.

Expected results

Serial device should be able to communicate with the CPU, and be seen by its software counterparts, such as fax, network, and game software.

Problem: No power signal shown on the CPU or peripheral.

Most Macintosh computers and peripheral devices have a red or green indicator light located at the front of the hardware case. When the Macintosh or hardware device is powered on, the indicator light also brightens and stays on until the computer is powered off. Most Macintosh models can be powered on by pressing the power key located at the top right of the keyboard. Some Macintosh computers require you to turn the power switch on by hand. This switch is usually located at the front right or back of the computer case.

9

Possible causes

Power cables inside or outside the hardware unit may not be completely connected to the wall power outlet or to the hardware unit.

The room the computer is in may not have power.

You may have defective or incompatible power cable(s).

Power supply on a particular device may not be connected.

Power supply on a particular device may be damaged.

Checkpoints

Check the room to see if other electrical devices are on.

If the power cable is partially loose or disconnected from a hardware device, check the hardware and make sure it is off. Disconnect and reconnect the power cable into the back of the hardware unit and the wall power outlet.

You may also want to try another power outlet if your power cable does not appear to connect into the power outlet completely or successfully.

Check the hardware device itself to see if the power indicator light is lit, flashing, or if the power supply or fan is moving.

If an external light is visible and lit on the hardware peripheral, the device is receiving power from the wall outlet. It is possible that one of the connecting cables may be insufficient for SCSI or serial communication, or the cable may be damaged or defective. Try swapping connection cables to see if your Macintosh detects the device.

If no red or green lights on the hardware device light up when you power-on the hardware device, listen for a power supply humming sound, or an internal fan. If you can hear an internal device moving, the device may have a nonworking component, or a partially working power supply. Check the device's product warranty for hardware information, contact the product manufacturer. If the product is out of warranty, you may want to seek a consultant, or check with a local Macintosh User Group to see if any information is available on repairing or replacing the hardware device.

Older, larger hard drives often have power supply failures after a year or two of constant use.

Expected results

Power light (usually a green light) will turn on. You should be able to hear a hum or whir indicating the power supply is getting power.

All hardware devices should power up successfully.

Problem: Unable to start CPU with an additional SCSI hardware peripheral connected and powered up.

Possible causes

Incorrect SCSI termination.

If all other devices are visible and usable by the Macintosh, it is possible one of the connecting cables may be insufficient for SCSI communications.

If the hardware device is in the middle of a SCSI chain, or if it is on a network, it is possible the connecting cable may be too long (too much distance across all connecting cables, or between two or more Macs).

If the device is a SCSI device, it is possible you may have a SCSI ID conflict with another SCSI device on the chain.

Checkpoints

Try connecting the hardware device directly to the Macintosh, minus the other hardware devices to see if the Macintosh can see it.

Check additional SCSI, serial, or ADB devices connected to other SCSI or serial ports to see if these devices are functioning correctly.

Most SCSI devices have the ID and a button allowing you to increment or decrement the ID number at the front or back of the SCSI device. Changing the SCSI ID number to a unique number on the SCSI daisy chain will correct the SCSI ID conflict problem.

Try swapping SCSI cables or changing the SCSI ID order.

Decrease the number of SCSI, serial, or ADB devices to see if you can successfully find a defective cable or problematic device.

Problem: Unable to access full features of an internal graphics card, hard drive, scanner, or printer.

Adding new hardware to your Macintosh, such as a graphics card of any card format includes hardware as well as software. Occasionally, a feature may not work due to the incorrect type of cable used to connect the card to another Macintosh peripheral, a broken pin or mis-connection of the cable to the hardware.

Possible causes

If a new hardware device was added to your Macintosh configuration, or if shareware or commercial software was added to the System Folder, or installed on the hard drive, there may be a software conflict with the new software and existing software on your hard drive.

The cable connecting the card to a peripheral device may be damaged, or may be the incorrect cable for one or both products.

A pin may be missing from one or both of the cable connector.

The card may not be seated completely in the NuBus, PDS, or PCI slot in the Macintosh computer.

9

Not all features of the hardware may work with your Macintosh model.

Hardware may need a ROM or software driver upgrade to access new features or attain full system software compatibility.

There might not be enough memory for the software application to access hardware features.

Checkpoints

If you have another similar cable, try swapping the current cable with one which works with a similar device.

Look at the connectors on the cables and make sure all pins and metal connection points are visible and not bent.

Make sure the cable does not have any physical damage, such as cut internal wiring, frayed wiring, or melted cable areas.

You may need to allocate more memory to software applications that access hardware features.

Try to recall the last time you used the hardware and if any new software or hardware has been added to your hardware or software configuration since then.

Check with the hardware vendor's online forum for any product information on the feature you are trying to use with your specific Macintosh model.

Check for known incompatibilities with the hardware product and the version of system software you are using.

Try starting your Macintosh with the Shift key held down to see if the device can be seen using SCSIProbe or—if it is a hard drive—if the icon for the hard drive mounts successfully on the desktop. If the hardware device successfully loads with extensions off, you have an extension conflict in the System Folder.

If you have System 7.5, you can hold down the Spacebar at startup and disable the new software extensions in the Extensions Manager window. Casady & Greene's Conflict Catcher, as well as Now Software's Now Utilities 5.0, Now Startup Manager are commercial software products that provide the same functionality as Extensions Manager, in addition to more user-friendly, customizable features you can use to troubleshoot and configure your Macintosh.

Macs have one-year warranties that include replacement of hardware which is diagnosed as defective or nonfunctional. Apple sends a repair person to your Macintosh location to diagnose and repair the hardware, or if you have a PowerBook, you can send in your PowerBook and Apple will return it next-day air with any necessary hardware changes in place.

If you have a Macintosh under warranty and suspect hardware failure, you can call 1-800-SOS-APPL and contact Apple's support group to walk through some initial troubleshooting and, if necessary, Apple will send a repair person to visit your Macintosh.

Diagnosing problems and Repairing SCSI Devices

Apple was the first large company to pick the Small Computer System Interface (SCSI) protocol as its bus standard for peripherals. Prior to 1986, devices had to be connected to a much slower serial input that could only talk to one device. Today SCSI is at the forefront of all major cutting-edge storage and peripheral device technologies, such as scanners, optical, magneto, DAT, and CD-ROM storage. With SCSI, every Mac can use the same SCSI device—even low-end Macs with a SCSI port.

The SCSI connector has 25 pins in two rows, with a wire clip on each side to fasten the connector to the port on the SCSI device. The other end of the cable connecting to a storage device or scanner can either be a 25-pin connector, or the more common 50-pin ribbon-type connector used in the vast majority of SCSI peripherals. PowerBooks use a unique 5-by-6, 30-pin port, called HDI-30.

Some newer devices use one of two SCSI-2 connectors, a smaller 50-pin connector or the SCSI-2 Wide connector, which has 68 pins.

Chaining SCSI peripherals

SCSI devices can be daisy-chained, allowing one Mac SCSI port to connect five external SCSI peripheral devices. Though a total of seven SCSI address numbers exist, two are taken by the Mac, which sees itself as a SCSI device (and defaults to SCSI 7); the Mac's internal hard drive allocates the other (usually assigned to SCSI 0). You must assign a unique SCSI ID number to each device: between one and six. Most SCSI peripherals have a SCSI number selection switch with a numerical reader on the back on which you can set the number.

If your device does not have a switcher, you can set the SCSI ID number by installing small black *jumpers* (a 1 millimeter sized metal bridge with a plastic jacket), which fit over one of three sets of adjacent but unconnected pins on the controller board of the drive or device. Devices without a hardware switcher usually supply a diagram showing where the ID switching pins are located on its motherboard. As a last resort, technical support at the manufacturer can help you locate the pins by giving you the alpha-numeric code found next to the matched sets of pins on the motherboard, such as "R1, R2, and R3."

Most SCSI devices are configured so that with no jumpers installed, the SCSI will set the device to SCSI ID #0. To configure your device for numbers 1–5, assign a number 1 to the first pin set, 2 to the second, and 4 to the last. If you add the numbers for only the jumpers used, you will arrive at the ID#. These settings may be different for your device, but the spec sheets included with each device detail the location of the SCSI pins and the jumper/SCSI ID correlation. If you have the same SCSI ID number set on two devices, one or both of them will be invisible, or make your hard drive invisible, in which case you will get a blinking question mark when you restart.

Completing a SCSI chain

With its peer-to-peer nature, SCSI devices aren't supposed to care where they belong in the ID number scheme, but eventually you might acquire certain devices that prefer to be at the beginning or the end of the physical SCSI chain. Apple sends out their CPUs with the internal drive set to SCSI ID #0; for this reason, it is recommended that the internal hard disk in your Mac be set the same. Some external devices only have one SCSI input, not two (which is necessary for daisy-chaining). Devices with only one input are often internally terminated, and are meant to be last in the SCSI chain. If they are not internally terminated, you may have to stick a line terminator on the last device—an in-line, double-ended SCSI plug that fits into the lone input of the device.

If you've just installed a SCSI device, and are welcomed with a blinking question mark when you restart the Mac, the SCSI chain is incomplete, and your Mac can't find the SCSI hard drive the System software needs to boot the Mac. If a diagnostic SCSI cable with built-in LED indicators reveals erratic behavior on your SCSI line, restarting is unnecessary. If the blinking question mark appears even after the drive has been terminated (and unique IDs were set for the device), it could mean your drive is damaged or the System software is corrupted (though the latter is less likely to be the problem when you are setting SCSI IDs and termination).

The SCSI system has been designed to be *device independent;* that is, it masks the internal operation of a peripheral from other peripherals and the Mac itself by treating them as logical rather than as physical. All devices on the SCSI bus are treated as equals in terms of their capability to communicate directly with other devices on the bus—making the interface truly peer-to-peer.

Software drivers

Though SCSI allows open compatibility with other devices, many SCSI peripherals have software drivers that must be loaded into the Mac System before the peripheral can be recognized and used. The drivers communicate with the Mac's on-board SCSI Manager—the software traffic cop that allows the Mac to talk to the SCSI device.

Try to follow these recommendations when installing new SCSI device software:

- Keep your peripheral drivers current. If you have a modem, many companies offer a direct line for users to upgrade to the latest drivers as soon as they're released, and sometimes even before so that users can test them.

- Keep your warranty cards in a file by your Mac.

Be forewarned that loading anything into the system—particularly freeware or third-party software Extensions and control panels (INITs and CDEVs) that less adept programmers have written—can create incompatibility problems with your other folder members. The Mac could crash, or run differently. You can prevent most problems by having the latest system software and the latest peripheral drivers. If your Mac is acting funny, pull out the most recent system addition, restart, try to duplicate the problem, and remove the bad software.

Termination and SCSI cable length

External hardware terminator plugs look like SCSI cable ends without the cable, and are plugged into the open SCSI port on the last device in the SCSI line. As simple as this sounds, SCSI termination is the source of many problems with Mac operation. Poorly terminated Macs display inexplicable errors such as write crashes, signal noise, failure to mount a drive or boot the system, and generally erratic operation. Remember that because you are chaining devices together, the Mac needs to see a logical end to the chain; a *terminator resistor* at the beginning and end of the line tells the Mac where the bus begins and ends. The Mac's motherboard SCSI input is terminated; all you need to do is have a SCSI terminator at the end of the chained SCSI bus.

One of the best SCSI external terminators available is built by Granite Digital (510-471-6442): the SCSIvue Diagnostic Terminator. The SCSIvue is well built, with gold connectors and heavier shielding than generic terminators. This innovative terminator also has LED status indicator lights that show you any connection problems or erratic SCSI behavior at the end of the line. These LEDs take much of the guesswork out of solving SCSI problems.

Total cable length should stay under three meters (roughly ten feet) to avoid another type of SCSI termination problem: insufficient power to the terminator. The longer the cables, the more termination power is required; SCSI cables longer than 3 meters require active termination power. The only system that adds externally powered active termination is APS Technology's (1-800-677-3294) SCSI Sentry terminator. It pulls AC power into the line rather than from the potentially more erratic Mac or peripheral power supply.

Macs with unique SCSI requirements

A number of Macs were designed with special SCSI requirements that you need to follow to ensure everything connected runs properly.

Mac Plus and Mac IIfx

The Mac Plus and Mac IIfx are exceptions to the standard Macintosh SCSI spec. Terminators on all other Macs can be either gray or black. The Mac IIfx uses only a single black terminator in a SCSI chain.

The Mac Plus does not support internal hard drives, and does not have an internal SCSI connector. Since it doesn't supply termination power to its external SCSI connector, terminator connectors must always be used on the first and last external devices on a Mac Plus.

The IIfx is more problematic. If this Mac has an internal hard drive that can supply termination at the beginning of the SCSI chain, a specially configured Terminator IIfx external terminator (sold by Apple) must be added that is wired for the fx's peculiar handling of SCSI. The T2 is used at the end of a IIfx SCSI chain just like any normally configured external terminator; this device looks exactly the same as a regular SCSI terminator, except that it is black rather than platinum colored.

9

Warning

Using more than one black terminator on a IIfx can damage the circuitry in the Mac or in the SCSI device. For other Macs, you can use a black terminator with a gray one, but don't use two black terminators together.

If your IIfx has no internal drive, you need to install an internal SCSI Termination block. This internal block is a "pass-through" internal SCSI plug that fits the internal SCSI input on the fx's motherboard and provides internal capacitors that begin the line termination.

PowerBooks and Duos

Apple's portable computers—PowerBooks and Duos—use SCSI to connect peripherals, just as desktop Macs do. The PowerBooks' ports, however, are somewhat different; they require special cables. Termination issues are also different for portables.

All PowerBooks include an internal SCSI hard drive. They also have an external 30-pin, HDI-30 SCSI port on the back. Duos are a bit different; they include internal drives, but only support external SCSI through the Duo Dock, MiniDock, or a third-party dock.

To connect your PowerBook or Duo to an external device, you need an HD-30 cable with either a DB-25 or DB-50 connector on the other end. This cable is a light gray color; SCSI cables are dark gray. Alternatively, you can choose a cable adapter, such as APS Technologies' SCSI Boy, which has an HDI-30 on one end and a 25-pin connector on the other. This arrangement lets you plug the PowerBook or dock into a standard 25-pin SCSI cable, which then connects to an external hard drive or other SCSI device.

Some PowerBooks—100, 160, 165, 165c, 180, and 180c—can be connected to desktop Macs in such a way that their disk drive appears on the other Mac's Desktop. To do this, use an HDI-30 to DB-25 connector, and plug the 25-pin end into the back of the other Mac. Of course, no connections should be made or broken while either computer is turned on. When you turn on both computers, the PowerBook's internal drive appears on the other computer's desktop.

All PowerBooks and Duos have special termination needs because their internal disks are not terminated and they don't include power for termination. If you connect an external SCSI device to a PowerBook, you need to supply powered termination.

You may be able to get external devices connected to a PowerBook to function, but you will probably experience the kind of termination-related trouble discussed in the section, "Termination and SCSI Cable Length." You can either use external devices that provide their own termination power, or purchase a terminator with its own power source, such as APS Technologies' SCSI Sentry, an external device that terminates the chain and provides power to it.

Quadras

The Macintosh Quadra 900 and 950 have a unique SCSI arrangement; these high-end Macs have two separate SCSI buses. Unlike most Macs, which limit you to a total of five external peripherals on a SCSI chain, the Quadra's internal bus allows four more connections.

The Quadra 900/950 case has room for four internal devices: hard drives, a CD-ROM, and/or a removable media drive. These internal devices all share a single SCSI bus. Aside from these connections, you can attach the normal complement of external devices to either Quadra via the external SCSI port because Termination and SCSI ID rules apply separately to each bus. Internal SCSI ports are included because the internal bus is faster, supporting speeds of up to 5 MB per second.

SCSI port problems

The SCSI port is one of the most frustrating areas of Mac troubleshooting. SCSI is the least plug-and-play element of the Mac, and the source of many of the problems you may run into. In theory, you can just plug a SCSI cable into the Mac and it self-configures. Theory also says you can just plug a new SCSI device (up to seven total) into the last device on the SCSI chain.

The reality is that SCSI is a very finicky system, requiring trial and error to work properly, particularly if you have a lot of hard disks in the chain. If hard drives are not showing up on the desktop, chances are the SCSI chain isn't happy about the way you set it up.

SCSIProbe

Troubleshooting a SCSI port requires a utility that gives you some control over the SCSI chain, such as SCSIProbe, a control panel by Robert Polic. SCSIProbe lists the SCSI devices connected to your Mac and tells you their ID numbers. If a device shows up in SCSIProbe but does not show up on the desktop, hit the Mount button, and the drive will miraculously appear. If a drive or two don't show up in SCSIProbe, you probably have a SCSI ID conflict. SCSIProbe will also tell you if your SCSI chain is improperly terminated.

SCSIProbe is so vital to keeping your Mac running that Apple should have included it as part of the System software years ago. Fortunately, SCSIProbe is available free on computer bulletin boards and in many collections of shareware and freeware. It is also included with some storage devices. Some disk utilities, such as Hard Disk Toolkit from FWB, have SCSIProbe's capabilities built in.

Each SCSI device needs to be given an ID number, usually set by a switch on the device. The ID number can be from 0 through 6. Zero is usually the default SCSI ID of an internal hard drive. The Mac itself uses the ID number 7.

If disks are not mounting on the desktop, check the ID numbers of your devices. Two or more devices with the same SCSI ID number can prevent the Mac from seeing the conflicting devices, or from seeing all SCSI devices on the chain.

SCSI hard drive and CD-ROM devices

If your Mac has an internal drive, it is the first device in the SCSI chain, and therefore should be terminated. (You'll still need a terminator connector on the last external device in the chain.) Internal drives usually contain built-in terminating resistors that can be turned on and off either with a switch or in software. (Check your manual to see which type you have.) If you have more than one internal hard disk or CD-ROM drive along with some external devices, only the first internal disk should be terminated. The others must have their terminating resistors removed or turned off. Similarly, if you have multiple internal drives but no external drives, then the first and last internal drives must be terminated.

A problem can occur when the terminator does not get the power it needs from the device it is plugged into. Different devices don't always provide the required five volts to both ports. This lack of power causes disks to disappear from the desktop; SCSIProbe will tell you the chain is not terminated, even when you have terminators on the first and last devices.

The solution is to move the terminators and SCSI cable around to different ports on the device. Try the cable and terminator on separate ports, and on the same port. This is a trial and error process, but it usually works.

Internal termination

Some external SCSI devices include built-in termination and don't require a terminator connector. A few manufacturers put a SCSI termination switch on the outside of the device that enables you to turn it on or off. Other manufacturers require you to set DIP switches; the device's manual lists the settings. In some devices, connectors are soldered in and you cannot turn them off at all. These devices must be the first or last device in the SCSI chain. If in doubt about which type of connector your device has, check the manual or call the tech support department of the manufacturer.

Troubleshooting the Motherboard

This section focuses on tools and troubleshooting methods for locating problems in your Mac's hardware and cabling. Hardware and software tools can reduce the time your Mac spends in the repair shop; this section will show you how to use these tools to isolate problems in specific hardware subsystems. You will read about the Mac's hardware infrastructure, input/output ports, power supply, and logic board. After reading this section you will be able to find the subsystem causing the problem.

Primary hardware diagnostic tools

If your Mac is running, software tools can help you find puzzling problems. No single software utility is sufficient for troubleshooting every conceivable problem; for this reason, try to have several utilities on hand. Some products are better at finding particular problems than others.

Although some of the following utilities can actually fix problems on your Mac, this chapter mainly focuses on products that help locate a problem. This section begins by discussing products that can analyze and diagnose storage disks—a common source of problems and often the first item to suspect when something goes wrong. Many hard drive problems are actually problems with software on the drive, the only way to reach this software is with special utilities. Later in this section you read about the best general purpose hardware diagnostic software you can add to your troubleshooting toolbelt.

Note

Remember to back up your files before using any troubleshooting utility.

MacEKG

MacEKG from MicroMat Computer Systems is a control panel that troubleshoots a variety of hardware problems. At startup, it performs the tests you select—the more tests you turn on in the MacEKG control panel, the longer your Mac's startup time will be. The available tests include those on video, RAM, and SCSI systems, as well as a verification test for disk media and a performance test on CPU logic functions. MacEKG logs test performance results in a histogram that will help you determine if your Mac is sick or old.

Help!

Help! from Technosis is a good tool for detecting problems that are primarily caused by software; nevertheless, it includes some helpful hardware troubleshooting features. Help! produces a report of your entire setup and tells you if you have two or more pieces of software (including extensions, control panels, and applications) that are known to conflict. It does this by comparing your installed software to its own database of known conflicts. For a fee, you can subscribe to quarterly updates to Help!'s database.

To aid in hardware troubleshooting, Help! also gives you a list of your hardware configuration: RAM configuration, SCSI devices, cards, video, and device drivers in addition to software information on versions of system software, fonts, and so on.

MacsBug

If you are a Macintosh power user or programmer, MacsBug 6.5.2 is a debugger that can help isolate software or hardware problems on 68K or Power Macs. MacsBug is placed in the System Folder and loads during startup. By pressing the command-power keys after your Macintosh loads, MacsBug drops your Macintosh into the debugger. There are several books available that discuss debugging and developing software with MacsBug. MacsBug is available from Apple via its Developer Association, APDA which can be reached by telephone at 1-800-282-2732 in the U.S.

Disk First Aid

Disk First Aid comes with Apple's system software disks. This software can diagnose and solve simple problems on floppies and hard drives, whether they are Apple drives or third-party drives. Disk First Aid is a good utility to try first when experiencing disk problems. It's easy to use, and if Disk First Aid can solve the problem, it will do so quickly. Recent versions of Disk First Aid provide information about what is being checked and repaired on the disk.

However, Disk First Aid should not be your only disk troubleshooting tool. The old adage, "You get what you pay for," applies here; Disk First Aid is free. It can't detect or fix many problems, and it cannot recover data. If Disk First Aid (or any other disk utility) repairs a floppy disk, immediately copy your data to another disk and throw the fixed floppy away. Floppy disks don't last forever and are too inexpensive to risk losing data. If the floppy fails again, you could spend an hour trying (perhaps unsuccessfully) to recover the data with another utility. A floppy disk costs at most one dollar, far less than what an hour of your time is worth.

Norton Utilities

Symantec's Norton Utilities for Macintosh is an excellent hard drive troubleshooting application that can diagnose, repair, optimize, and back up hard drives and floppy disks. This program also provides several methods for recovery of data from a crashed disk and from files that have been erased. For problem diagnosis and repair, you select the Norton Disk Doctor portion of the application. The software is easy to use; just click a button, and Disk Doctor runs the diagnostic tests, which are not user-configurable.

Norton Disk Doctor does a good job of bringing damaged disks back to life. You can even use it on disks that won't mount on the desktop. When it finds a problem, the utility gives you a description of the problem and gives you the option to repair or ignore the problem.

One of Norton Disk Doctor's most welcome features is the capability to repair bad boot blocks. *Boot blocks* are portions of the disk active in the early stages of a Mac's startup procedure. This utility checks every file on the disk for anomalies, and can find and recover files that have disappeared. If Norton Disk Doctor detects a problem and tells you it can't fix it, there may be a problem with the drive mechanism.

MacTools DiskFix

Central Point Software's MacTools is a collection of disk utilities and control panels that include disk optimization, backup, and file recovery. MacTools also includes DiskFix, an application for conducting diagnosis and repair of hard drive and floppy disk problems. You can set DiskFix to run one or more of several disk diagnostic tests, including those for bad boot blocks, file problems, and viruses. You can test for individual problems if you suspect one and don't want to run the entire set of tests, which can take a while if your disk is large. You can also set DiskFix to test your hard drive automatically when you are not using it and set it to fix any problems it encounters. DiskFix keeps a record of each repair it makes, so you can "undo" any repair at a later time.

Given these features, is it better to stock your tool chest with Norton Disk Utilities or MacTools with DiskFix? It's actually worth it to have a copy of each. Each program fixes certain problems that the other misses. Both programs come with a bootable emergency disk that you can use in case your hard drive isn't booting or mounting.

Logic Board problems

After tracking down hardware problems with the tools and techniques mentioned in this chapter, you may find that the trail leads you to the Mac's logic board. You can easily replace parts not soldered to the logic board, such as RAM SIMMs, cables, or the lithium battery that maintains the settings in the parameter RAM when the Mac is shut off. A dead battery can manifest itself as an incorrect date and time (often January 1, 1904), the disappearance of text in the Comments field of your Get Info boxes, or mouse speed settings that return to Very Slow.

Aside from these few items, the logic board is where the troubleshooting trail will have to end because there are few things you can do with malfunctioning silicon chips. You need professional help, or you need to replace the logic board. If you want to get a quote for repair of the logic board, be sure to mention the troubleshooting you have done and the subsystem you think is the problem. It is often less expensive to replace the logic board—especially if you can find one used—than it is to repair it. A logic board failure also might be a blessing in disguise: if the only option is to replace the entire board, see if you can purchase a more powerful logic board with extra performance.

Mac power supplies

The power supply takes the high-voltage AC power from the AC socket, and converts it to low-voltage DC power for use by the Mac's hardware components. Power supplies in most Macs are relatively stable, though there were problems with early Macs. Power supplies can be stressed when the total power (measured in watts) used by the expansion boards used in a Mac exceeds the recommended limit for that particular Mac model. Heat is a problem for power supplies; Macs in a hot environment are prone to power supply failure. Power surges from brownouts, blackouts, and lightning storms can also damage a power supply, which is why a surge protector is a good idea. And like power supplies in televisions and other appliances, computer power supplies can fail with age.

Unlike the circuitry on the logic board, power supplies are analog, use less expensive, simpler parts, and can be more easily repaired by trained technicians. The power supplies in most desktop Mac models are contained in a metal casing, and can be easily removed.

Problems on old machines

The first Macs—the 128K, 512K, 512Ke, and Mac Plus—are notorious for using power supplies that eventually go south. The SE fixed many of the problems of the earlier models by adding an internal fan to keep the parts cooler, and by using heavy-duty power supply components with higher temperature and voltage specifications. On the older models, you can tell when a power supply is on its way out when the screen starts shrinking.

Older Mac power supplies on a card

In most models of Macintosh, the power supply is contained inside a metal box. In the first Macs (the Mac 128K, Mac 512K, Mac 512Ke, and the Mac Plus), the power supply was contained on a circuit board known as the analog board, which also contained some of the video circuitry. These were a bit trickier to remove than more recent power supplies, but if you are able to remove it safely, you usually can replace the analog board with another one from a used Mac or another dead Mac. All power supplies in these early Macs are the same.

The following steps walk you through the removal of one of these older analog board power supplies. You can follow these same steps for putting a new power supply circuit board into any of the previously mentioned Macintosh computers, too.

Warning

This procedure is very dangerous and should only be performed by users experienced with sub-component-level hardware repair. If you doubt your proficiency even a bit, seek professional help.

1. Turn the Mac off and unplug it.

2. Place the Mac with the screen facing down. Use a number 15 Torx-head screwdriver with a long neck to remove the screws. Don't forget the screw under the battery cover in the back of the Mac.

3. Open the case with a case spreader to avoid damaging the case. If you can't find a case spreader, you can also use a wide metal device such as a three-inch letter clip. Move the tool around the case and open it little by little. Do not use a screwdriver! It's very easy to damage the case.

4. Pull the case straight up.

Warning

Don't touch the neck of the VCR tube! It may still contain high-voltage energy.

5. Find (**but don't touch**) the high-voltage cable that starts with a connection on the tube that looks like a suction cup and ends on the analog board—the vertical board. (The logic board is perpendicular to the analog board, lying horizontally at the bottom of the Mac.)

6. Discharge the tube at the suction cup with an Apple-approved CRT discharging tool, which has a 10-megohm resistor at the end. If you use a screwdriver without the resistor, you'll get a big spark that can harm both you and the CRT. Rubber gloves are a good idea, and Apple recommends safety goggles for this procedure.

7. Remove the cable running from the analog board to the logic board. Unplug the high-voltage cable that goes from the CRT to the analog board from the CRT.

8. Remove three Phillips head screws from the back of the analog board, and remove the board.

Power supplies in Mac IIcx, IIci, Quadra 700

The Astec power supply used in the Mac IIcx, IIci, and Quadra 700 often fails. One of the symptoms is the inability to start up, and the only way to "fix" it is to temporarily unplug the Mac for a while, then plug it back in later. This is due to the failure of a .0033uf/100vw capacitor at board reference C34, which in turn is caused by the capacitor's proximity to a 5-watt resistor that gets hot and stays hot, even when the Mac is powered down. To fix these power supplies, you need to replace the capacitor, and reposition it farther away from the resistor.

The .0033uf capacitor may generate a high-pitched (12.5 KHz) squeal that some people find excessively annoying. You can substitute a .0022uf/100vw capacitor, which will still work, and will raise the switching frequency of the standby circuit above the range of human hearing.

Mac LC and IIsi problems

Although the power supplies in the Mac LC, LCII (but not the LCIII), and IIsi are generally sound, they are on a tight power budget and are not rated for high-power expansion devices. This is an even greater problem in the original LC. To prevent a power shortage in your Mac that could potentially damage some of its hardware subsystems, you should avoid installing add-ons such as coprocessor cards, RAM disk cards, and multi-gigabyte internal hard disks.

Port problems

Ports are your Mac's way of communicating with the rest of the world. When you are having a problem associated with one of the ports, you need to first determine where the problem lies—with a peripheral, the cable, or the port itself. Isolate the problem by ensuring that two of the three possibilities are functioning correctly. Cabling is the most likely cause of problems; it's a good idea to check it first. The port itself is the least likely of the three to be defective.

First, check to see if the cables are firmly seated in the port. If the cable can be fastened, do so. This is done with a wire clamp or hand screw, depending on the type of cable. A cable that is not fastened can be easily knocked loose.

Next, try replacing the cable with another that is known to work. It's not a bad idea to keep a full set of extra cables on hand to use as troubleshooting tools. Buy them, verify that they work, then keep them together. Do not assume that because a cable fits into the port, it's the correct cable for the job. Cables that look identical can be wired differently internally.

Cabling problems can be a little more complicated on the two ports that are busses: SCSI and ADB. Bus ports can accept multiple devices daisy-chained together. With these ports, the cables themselves could be fine, but the way they are connected may cause problems.

Checking the peripheral is simple if you have other Macs around: just plug it into another Mac and see if it works. This is easy enough for keyboards and modems, but can be a lot of work for a hard drive or a 21-inch monitor. For this reason, make sure your cabling is OK before moving the device to another Mac.

9

You can check the port by plugging in a device that you know works. It doesn't necessarily have to be the same type of device. For example, if you have a scanner plugged into a SCSI port, you can use a small external hard drive to check the port.

Modem and printer (serial) ports

The modem and printer ports are almost identical; the main difference is that you can attach a LocalTalk network to the printer port. Other serial devices (and their cables), including modems and QuickDraw printers, such as the Apple StyleWriter, can be plugged into either port.

If a serial port is not working, make sure the software that controls the device is set to the same port (Modem or Printer) that the device is plugged into. For printers, the setting is often in the Chooser. For modems, you select the port in the settings box of your telecommunications software.

A common problem you may encounter with modems is the cable. Modems that are 9600 bps or faster often use a different cable from slower modems. The high-speed modem cable has wiring that enables hardware handshaking, a type of dialog between modem and Mac. Computer retailers who aren't particularly Mac-aware have been known to sell customers the wrong cable with modems; be sure to ask.

If you are using the printer port to connect to a LocalTalk network, you could have a problem with your LocalTalk connector. Some connectors need to be terminated with a small plug containing a resistor:

- Old Style (DB-9) Connectors. The original Mac 128K, 512K, and 512Ke had 9-pin DB-9 connectors on the two serial ports. DB-9 connectors have a screw on either side of the port to fasten the cable to the port.

- New Style (DIN-8) Connectors. All Macs since the Mac Plus, including PowerBooks, AV Macs, and Power Macs, use the 8-pin DIN-8 connectors. These are roughly the same size as the ADB port; make sure you know which port you are plugging a cable into. Forcing a serial cable into an ADB port can result in bent pins on the cable.

PowerBooks often have internal modems that add another port on the back of the Mac next to the modem port. This internal modem port is identified with a telephone icon. If the modem is completely internal, the telephone port is an RJ-11 port that fits a standard telephone cable. Some older PowerBook modems use a small connector outside of the Mac to attach to the telephone cable. In this case, the telephone port in the PowerBook is round. In either case, the port setting used in telecommunications software is the modem port, although nothing is physically connected to the modem port.

Video ports

Most newer Macs have built-in video ports for standard RGB display monitors. Macs with expansion slots can also accept video cards for larger monitors or for those that support more colors than built-in ports do. The expansion cards also have a video port. Multiple monitors can be used simultaneously when plugged into built-in ports and one or more video cards. You can use the Monitor control panel to select which monitor upon which you want the menu bar to be displayed.

Video cabling is fairly trouble-free on the Mac; it's difficult to configure a video port incorrectly. The standard video Mac port uses a 15-pin connector with hand screws on the edges. If your monitor isn't working, check to see if you're using the cable that came with the monitor. Cables that look the same can be wired differently. Some monitors come with a cable that uses a PC-style connector called HDI-15. Converter connectors are available that enable you to use an HDI-15 cable in your Mac's video port.

Ethernet port

The Ethernet port is a faster networking port than the LocalTalk (printer) port available in some Mac models. If you are not on the network, check to see if you have the correct transceiver connected to the port, and that the transceiver is working. Transceivers can support three different types of network wiring systems—AUI, 10BASE-T, or 10BASE-2. Some transceivers have all three types built in for flexibility, though you can only connect to one network at a time.

If your transceiver looks good but you still have problems getting on the network, go to the Network control panel and select the EtherTalk driver. If EtherTalk refuses to be selected, you probably have a problem with the EtherTalk driver software. Make sure you have the correct EtherTalk file—it should be an Apple file. Some Ethernet card manufacturers have their own EtherTalk drivers that won't work with the Mac's built-in Ethernet port. You can also try reinstalling the driver from your Apple System disks. Select Custom Install, then select EtherTalk.

Audio ports

The speaker and microphone ports are the audio out and in ports, respectively. Most Mac models have a speaker port; fewer models have a microphone port. Both ports use a standard stereo mini-headphone jack. Be sure you know which port you connect to speakers or microphones; plugging in a device to the wrong port can damage the audio circuitry on the logic board.

- Speaker Port. The audio-out port can be used to plug in headphones, powered speakers, or cables to recording devices. The Mac's speaker is disabled when you plug something into this port—a handy feature if you want to use a pair of headphones with a noisy application in a public place, or if you're working in a quiet area.

- Microphone Port. This audio-in port on older Mac models will accept the microphone that comes with some Mac models, as well as third-party microphones and cables from sound producing devices. You can use the Sound control panel in System 7, as well as third-party applications, to create sound files.

The port on some newer Macs, including the AV Macs and Power Macs, use a line-level signal, not a Mic-level signal as was previously used. The microphones from the older Macs will not work on these newer ports, but you can use the newer PlainTalk microphone, or directly connect a VCR, tape deck, or CD player.

ADB ports

The Apple Desktop Bus is part of every Mac model that followed the Mac Plus. (Early Macs used two separate ports for keyboard and mouse.) Many Macs have two ADB ports. The ADB port is used for input devices, including keyboards, mice, trackballs, and pen tablets. The ADB port uses a simple 4-pin connector. It is similar in shape to the serial ports; be careful that you don't try to force the wrong plug into the wrong port, or you may bend pins.

Like SCSI, the ADB port is a bus, in that multiple devices can be connected to a single port by daisy-chaining off each device. Although ADB is made to accept up to 16 devices, ADB is a low-performance bus; for the sake of speed, use only a maximum of three devices per port.

Monitor troubleshooting

Mac monitors have ranged from the original 9-inch black-and-white display to a monstrous 37-inch presentation display. Unlike most of the rest of the computer, which is solid state, electronic, light, and fast; the monitor is a large, fragile, glass vacuum tube that carries tremendous electrical charges.

Why aren't Mac monitors small, solid-state devices? Cost; the first Liquid Crystal Display (LCD) monitors are just hitting the market, and they're expensive and small. Nevertheless, they are great for portable use, with a few caveats. See the topic, "Problems in PowerBooks," later in this section.

Because the monitor is your interface with the computer (along with the keyboard), maintaining it and knowing how it works can make working at the computer considerably more pleasant. A hard drive can be fragmented, a SCSI improperly terminated, and your floppies may be in hopeless disarray; they are peripheral to direct interaction with the computer. Not having a stable, comfortable monitor to work with will be obvious in seconds. A fragmented hard drive does not cause physical discomfort; a distorted monitor certainly does.

You might feel that you need a new monitor, however, rotating it a few degrees, adjusting a window shade or two, and turning off a light can turn an old, washed-out display into a nearly new device. This section starts with the assumption that you haven't set up your monitor at all.

Avoiding screen burn-in

Burn-in used to be a serious problem, but newer display technology has made it less so. In the past, leaving a monitor on for hours and hours would burn the image into the phosphor on the inside of the glass tube. The image was permanent because the phosphor's phosphorescence was literally worn out. Automatic teller machines are prime examples of phosphor burn, where you could see "Welcome to Blank Bank" printed permanently behind "Welcome to Flake Bank," which had just bought Blank Bank.

Fortunately, technology has reduced the chance of burn-in. It would take years for a modern monitor to show significant signs, but if you're still concerned, the simplest way to prevent screen burn-in is to turn down the brightness. This cuts power use by about 20 percent, and it's fast and easy. An alternative is to use a screen saver, which is a lot more interesting.

Changing easily altered settings

A monitor develops a considerable static charge that attracts dust and particulate matter and, if left dirty, will eventually dim the image. Always wipe it down with a soft, nonabrasive cloth, and use monitor cleaner. Always spray the glass cleaner on the cloth, not on the monitor.

If you must point at the monitor, avoid touching the glass, as this will leave an oily fingerprint. If you must touch the glass, an easy way to avoid fingerprints is to turn your palm upward and point with the tip of your fingernail (see Figure 9.1).

Figure 9.1 Touch the monitor with your fingernail, not your finger, to save the monitor coating.

Deepening the color saturation

Do the colors seem pale and weak? Is cobalt blue coming out more like robin's egg? Fixing these problems is as simple as twisting a pair of knobs: brightness and contrast. A low contrast and high brightness setting can turn everything a pale gray; if they're both turned up too high everything will be a bright, pale gray. Follow these steps to find the most saturated (deep and clear) colors as possible:

1. Display an image onscreen that you recognize. If you have a photograph or colorful drawing, scan it in and compare the two.

2. Turn the brightness and contrast all the way down.

3. Gradually turn the contrast up until you have a visible image with deep, rich color, but still a bit dark.

4. Turn the brightness up until the whites are white, not gray.

5. Adjust both knobs a little in either direction until you are satisfied.

Fixing a wandering color

This problem occurs particularly in larger monitors and is a result of the Earth's magnetic field. Sony monitors, for example, are set at the factory in an east-west orientation, just to keep them consistent. When you rotate a monitor, you may notice that whites are no longer white but fuzzy colors, and the edges of the display are out of line. Technically, it's a convergence problem. If the monitor has exterior convergence settings, try them (most large monitors have these settings). If you have to open the case, try the interior settings. If neither of these work, try rotating your monitor and desk 90 degrees.

Ordinary magnetic fields will also affect your monitor. Keep the display away from large appliances, unshielded stereo speakers, and magnets. The little red or green tinge in the corner caused by a standard speaker that you might be using for multimedia will eventually stay there and may throw the whole monitor out of line. (To fix that, see the following section, "Degaussing the Display.")

Apple also includes an application called Gamma with each system. Gamma controls how the monitor displays color and levels of brightness so that you can match your onscreen display as closely as possible to that of your output device and/or the real world. See your Apple manual for its use.

Fixing a monitor that is green

SVGA monitors use different pins in the monitor cable for different things. In particular, some SVGA monitors expect to find a synchronization signal on the same wire as the green signal. Other SVGA monitors have a green cast when they sit on top of some Macs. The following Macs do not use a sync-on-green and should not encounter the problem:

- LCIII/Performa Series

- Centris/Quadra 660AV and 840AV

- All Power Macs

If your monitor suffers from overtly emerald hues, contact Apple Support for a copy of the Basic Color Monitor System Extension. It should fix the green cast in most monitors.

Degaussing the display

If one area on the display is out of focus, or if odd color splotches are on an otherwise normal display, you might need to degauss the monitor. Most modern monitors degauss automatically when you turn them on, but some older and less expensive monitors do not. Why degauss? The powerful magnetic field created by the electron guns in the monitor gradually magnetize the monitor's casing, causing blurring and color splotches. Magnets left near the monitor for long periods of time also can induce color splotches and areas of fuzziness. The monitor's electron gun is literally being thrown out of line by its own magnetized case.

To fix the problem, first check your manual for instructions on how to degauss (it might be a built-in feature). Look for a degaussing button. If you don't know whether it degausses automatically, turn it off and on again quickly. If the screen comes back on waving rapidly with bands of light and color that stop suddenly with an audible click, the screen degaussed.

Any television service shop can handle the job, as can many computer shops. They use a powerful oscillating magnet that cancels out any and all magnetic fields. Just make sure your monitor is far away from any data you need, because a powerful degausser can wipe data off of just about any media from several feet away. Randomizing a magnetic field is another way of erasing an entire disk. This can be a real problem for compact Mac owners. Everything's in the case, and while hard drives are usually well-shielded, do a backup before taking it in. If you borrow a degausser, make sure that you move the monitor into another room, away from your work area.

Using the entire display

You've probably noticed that not all the display area is filled with a computer image. You're no doubt interested in filling this unused area; fortunately, there are two ways to do so. The most elegant is to use either MaxAppleZoom (MAZ), written by Naoto Horii, or Monitor Expander (ME) by Sigurour Asgeirsson. MAZ only works with older Toby cards (on the Mac II) and only on 13- and 14-inch monitors. Named after Toby Farrand of Apple, the Toby display card has a programming anomaly that allows MAZ to display more than the usual 640 × 480 pixels.

MAZ won't work on newer Macs or with most internal video schemes. Monitor Expander has more options and works with either Toby or Apple High Resolution video cards. This software will also work in a multiple-monitor setup. MAZ will only work with the primary monitor; ME checks the slots to see what video cards are available and will fill that unused black band on your secondary display.

Another method, while somewhat less elegant, is to simply stretch the display to cover the available glass area. This method increases the size of all pixels being displayed and makes the image slightly coarser, but not too noticeably. Most monitors have either screws or knobs to accomplish the task. Less expensive models generally have set screws on the back; higher-end models have knobs or digital controls on the face of the monitor. (The Apple Color Plus has two set screws on the back, as does the Apple Basic.)

Compact Macs, such as the SE, SE/30, and Classic rarely need adjustment. Nevertheless, they have two set screws on the inside of the case at the top of the motherboard. There is a special case in which you should adjust them, and you will already have the case open if it occurs. When you add RAM to a compact Mac, it uses some of the power that would have gone to the video subsystem, which in turn makes the display shrink. Add a lot of RAM to, say, an SE/30, and your display area will shrink from 9 inches to almost 8 inches in one fell swoop. There are just as many pixels as before, but they're more tightly packed. Whenever you add or remove RAM in a compact Mac, check your display before closing the case. Please be aware, however, that turning on a computer without the case is dangerous!

All this stretching and filling isn't without its risks, though. Manufacturers sell their monitors based on how much glass is in the box, not on how big the image is. You may have noticed that your 14-inch display isn't really 14 inches and is more like 12.5 inches. Some go as small as 11.9 inches. This apparent shrinking occurs because of convergence and focus, which are discussed later in this section.

Maintaining WYSIWYG

If you alter your monitor's settings, and your work requires a true WYSIWYG (what-you-see-is-what-you-get) display, open an application that uses rulers—Aldus PageMaker or Free-hand, or QuarkXPress—and measure its rulers with your own desk ruler, inch for inch. Do six inches in the applications match six inches on your ruler?

If the final output doesn't really have to look like what you see onscreen, and you really think Monaco font looks better a little narrower (I do), squeeze the display a bit. You might also take into account how your printer handles output. If it tends to print ten percent narrower than your monitor displays, increase your monitor's width by ten percent. To test it, just print out a square that's slightly smaller than a sheet of paper and measure it, comparing the printout to the rulers in the application.

Fixing problems, some inside the case

Opening up a monitor is not a good idea if you're unfamiliar with high-voltage electronics, but there are a number of things you can adjust. For some problems, there's no other way to get to them. Before you crack the case, find out if digital controls are on your monitor that will allow you to adjust some of the following parameters.

Warning

Opening a monitor is dangerous! If you are not familiar with CRT design and components, do not open the case! The capacitors inside carry current for weeks after a display has been unplugged, with enough voltage to cause serious injury or death. Please leave such repairs to service technicians if you are not familiar with CRT design.

Adjusting convergence

When a monitor displays an image, it has to sweep an electron gun back and forth across considerable real estate. The farther from the middle the gun goes, the more likely it is to miss its target. The edges of a display area are quite often out of focus for this very reason, so manufacturers set their monitors to display a smaller area. If you stretch your display, you may discover you have a fuzzy image out on the edge, with colors spilling out in tiny rainbows. Adjusting convergence with your monitor involves re-adjusting settings for the monitor's pixel sharpness and picture quality by making hardware adjustments with software tools (convergence is defined as coming together at a point).

Adjusting convergence usually means opening the monitor's case. Read your manual first, because some monitors have digital controls that allow for many adjustments that aren't obvious. If your monitor doesn't come with convergence software that displays a grid of lines, you can create your own grid using any software capable of drawing vertical and horizontal lines.

Make the lines as narrow as possible, and check each section of the display to see if it's in sharp focus, making sure that no colors spill out of the white and into the black. This test makes it possible to isolate problems even if you don't want to open the case.

Another convergence test involves the General Controls control panel. On a color Mac, set the desktop pattern to solid black except for three pairs of pixels: two red, two blue, and two green. This test covers the entire display, and you will be able to see the same color spillage and out of focus pixels, though it may be harder to track areas that have problems. Move the pixels into vertical and horizontal arrangements to check all alignment directions. If you want, grab a magnifying glass and get a close-up view. It may seem like overkill, but if you do image-editing work, it's important.

If you have to open the case, be aware that the pots that control convergence are often laid out without markings; it may take some time to figure out the arrangement. If it's a really big display, 19 inches or larger, the display area may be broken down into sections, each pot controlling one color in one area.

Adjusting focus

Focus may seem the most obvious, but it is not always the easiest feature to check. If the entire display is out of focus, you may not be able to tell—there's nothing to compare to. Create a grid or a text file that covers your entire display area and compare one area to another. Are all characters sharp and clear? Do any areas of the display seem less than perfectly focused? If you notice an overall lack of focus, pixels aren't quite as sharp as they should be; you may be able to refocus the monitor from the outside.

Some monitors, though not all, have a small, round hole in the case through which you can put a very small screwdriver. Look closely at the sides of the case. It's on the left on many monitors, halfway back, near the bottom. Lower-priced monitors like the Apple Basic do not have an adjustment on the outside and must be opened and adjusted on the inside. The wide variation in focus points is beyond the scope of this book, but a friendly technician can often tell you how this is done.

Focus only adjusts the overall image. If only part of the image is out of focus, it could be a convergence problem, or the monitor could need degaussing.

Monitor tune-ups

Sometimes it takes more than adding an extension or turning a screw to bring things back into line. You may need to climb inside the case with a soldering iron, or need to move the equipment.

Warning

Opening a monitor is dangerous! If you are not familiar with CRT design and components, do not open the case! Capacitors inside carry current for weeks after a display has been unplugged, usually with enough voltage to cause serious injury or death. Please leave such repairs to service technicians if you are not familiar with CRT design.

Fixing a wavy display

If your display is waving like a flag in the wind, it's probably a symptom of one of the following:

- A bad power supply

- Failing solder joints on the motherboard

- Fluctuating current coming out of the wall

- Interference from a nearby electrical device

By far the most common is electrical interference. If your monitor wiggles back and forth as if it were a flag on a windy day, find and remove everything in the area that creates a current, from the clock radio to the external hard drive. Move them as far from the monitor as possible. Even an overhead fluorescent light can interfere (that buzz is the dreaded 60-cycle hum), or an air-conditioning motor. If you have two badly shielded monitors right next to each other, they'll be having a party all their own, wobbling like they've lost their minds. One unshielded monitor can affect or be affected by a relatively well-shielded monitor.

The Plus is renowned for its faulty power supply. If you have a Plus with a waving monitor, do yourself a favor and take it to the service technician. It could be nothing more than annular (ring-shaped) cracks in the solder, which deliver a weakened video signal, but more than likely it's the power supply, which will need to be replaced because it's dying before your eyes.

One particularly insidious wave-creator is bad electricity. The current coming from the wall socket might not be as smooth and stable as it ought to be, giving rise to more than just a wobbly picture. Bad power can cause problems ranging from system errors to hardware failure. Fortunately, power conditioners are available from most computer dealers; they sit in the power line between your equipment and the wall, turning the rough current coming from the power company into smooth current that won't give your monitor such fits. Conditioners have the added advantage of coming with power strips and surge protectors. See "Basic Troubleshooting" in the beginning of this chapter for more information.

In compact Macs, the internal hard drive can interfere with the monitor. After a drive is added, the technician should also add a magnetic shield to keep the drive's activities away from the monitor. If you've recently had a drive installed or changed and have noticed a wavy pattern on the desktop, the technician probably forgot to install (or to reinstall) the shielding.

Ungarbling a garbled image

Newer multisync displays occasionally display a bunch of garbage; seemingly random visual noise with perhaps vague outlines of a desktop. You might have enough of an image to tell that it is a Mac but little more. If you're using an SVGA monitor that wasn't specifically designed for the Mac, you're necessarily also using an adapter to attach its cable to the Mac. The adapter does more than change the shape of the connector at the end of the cable; it changes connections between the wires (pins) in the cable, pins that the monitor uses to communicate with the computer. Your Mac reads the pins in the cable to identify what monitor you're using, its resolution, its size, and a few other details. If the pins aren't what the Mac expects, the display will be a mess.

You can fix a bad adapter in two ways. The first is to go to the retailer who sold you the monitor and describe the problem. Sometimes cables and adapters fail—it's not uncommon for them to just go bad—and a replacement will fix things. Because of the plethora of monitors and associated adapters, it's possible you simply ended up with the wrong adapter. You can build a cable and/or adapter to do the job, but this isn't as easy as it sounds. A bit of solder in the wrong place puts you right back where you started—a garbled image.

Note

Not all monitors were created equal. The Toby card, Apple's original display card, works with almost every monitor sold by Apple. The exception is the Apple Basic Color Monitor, a device with a refresh rate of 60 Hz and a dot pitch of 0.39 mm. It was designed to work with the Performa series; it is not a high-end display, and it won't work with the Toby card. It will work with the internal video of any of the newer Macs as well as that of many of the older Macs. If you plan to use it as a second monitor, however, be aware that you will need an Apple 8024 card or better to drive it. Having a 60 Hz refresh rate at the edge of your peripheral vision (which is highly sensitive to motion) may prove distracting and is likely to give you a headache.

Catching ghosts

If you've noticed *ghosting* on your display—shadowy words and images floating behind their originals—you may have a bad or lengthy cable. The signals going from the Mac to the monitor are remarkably sensitive and are subject to interference. If you're using a long, possibly custom-made monitor cable to keep that Mac at a distance, you may have created your own ghosts. If short cables are in use, the ghosting is generally caused either by interference or by a short-circuit.

For either short or long cables, check your cable route—does it pass any major electrical appliances, such as stereos, stereo speakers, large drives—anything that generates current can annoy the cable shielding that filters out noise. If you can't reroute it, or if you do and the problem persists, try using a more heavily shielded cable. Today's savings of three or four dollars on an inexpensive monitor cable will probably come back to haunt you tomorrow with a regiment of ghosts. The metal weaves that shield cables are not created equal, nor are the connectors at either end.

If you've built or bought a particularly long cable and are sure it's both well shielded and far from electromagnetic influences, the length alone may be the source of your woes. The longer the cable, the greater the chance that video signals will bounce around and lose signal strength. Try to limit monitor cables to less than five feet. Every few inches over that is asking for trouble.

Setting odd resolutions

Some monitors can handle super-high resolutions. Because the multisync is still new in the Mac market, getting it to work may take a little work. Macs used to work only with Mac monitors, but now they'll work with a number of third-party monitors if you can find the right adapter. If you buy a third-party multisync, be sure you buy an adapter that works with it.

For example, Sony owners can use the Sony MacView Cable Adapter to sense and synchronize to any valid resolution for the particular Mac and monitor combination. This adapter has a wheel with 16 and 9 DIP switches. Three of the DIPs select synchronization rates; the rest of the settings select resolutions. This adapter can convince the Mac that it's using any of the following monitors:

- Apple's 14-inch, 16-inch, 19-inch, or 21-inch monitor
- Apple RGB
- Apple portrait
- Apple two-page monochrome (which might turn blue)
- Two PAL resolutions
- Two NTSC resolutions

The MacView Cable Adapter can be used in conjunction with a utility called Monitor Switch, which also alters resolution. Monitor Switch works properly only if the adapter is set to specific resolutions. For example, on the Sony 17se1, if the adapter is set to 1152×870, Monitor Switch can only handle 1024×768. Set to 832×624, Monitor Switch can handle four resolutions.

If you're using a different monitor, you might want to hunt local electronics shops for a similar combination cable/adapter. It switches between four Apple resolutions—14-inch, 16-inch, 19-inch, and 21-inch—if your monitor supports it. You can try Cables-To-Go at 1-800-826-7904.

Bringing back a blank display

A completely dark display could be any number of things. If you turn it on and nothing happens, you might have a bad power supply. If you turn on the Mac and everything seems to work with the single exception of a dark blank monitor, you might have a bad case of annular cracks. Turn on the Mac and, if you can, open a file or two blindly. You'll have to know what's where on the desktop or use keyboard equivalents, but if you can make the drive spin, the machine shut down, or play a sound, you can probably solve the problem.

When a device heats up and cools down, it expands and contracts, and the solder holding its connections has to expand and contract, too. Older Macs, particularly the Plus and 512, have a tendency to develop ring-shaped (annular) cracks in the solder on their motherboards. The cracks are nearly invisible, so don't spend a lot of time looking for them.

> ### Warning
> Don't touch your monitor unless you're already experienced with a soldering iron. You can take a fixable machine and turn it into a doorstop in a matter of seconds.

If the brightness button on your Duo dies, you're not out of luck. If it will respond to software, a copy of CPU 2.0 or similar PowerBook utility should help you along. As for fixing the button itself, send the Duo back to Apple. The number of tiny parts crammed into PowerBook and Duo cases is beyond belief.

Monitor problems you cannot fix

Nothing can be done about certain problems. They have to do with physical design for the most part, or they're too dangerous for folks who aren't service technicians.

In older Apple 13-inch monitors, for example, the most common monitor failure is a high-voltage resistor (or high-voltage block) that sits in series between the flyback transformer and the CRT. This is not a problem you can fix.

Glaring without end

Did you move your workstation, rearrange all the lights, cover the windows, and still see glare? If you have a spherical monitor with a highly polished surface, you may be stuck with it. There are two types of tubes: spherical and cylindrical. The spherical tubes literally bulge like bubbles, have highly curved surfaces, and are typical of less-expensive designs. Cylindrical displays are much flatter because they curve only along a vertical axis. The bulge of the highly curved display tends to catch lights from all angles like a fish-eye lens. For spherical displays, Polarizers will help more than anything else.

9

Flickering monitors

Your monitor may be flickering, especially if it's under a fluorescent light. Flickering is different from waving. To create the image you see, an electron beam literally flicks back and forth across the back of the display's glass at anywhere from 60 Hz to around 90 Hz. Fluorescent lights also flicker; only they do it on and off at 60 Hz. A monitor at 60 Hz is going to have problems in a fluorescent environment; you cannot do much about it except remove either the monitor or the lights. This particular monitor's design has no knobs.

Note

Want to catch your display in the act of refreshing? Eat a few potato chips or carrots (or anything hard and crunchy) while looking at your monitor. The flickering is caused by interference between your eyes' vibration and the screen's refresh rate.

Trinitron display missing pixels

Sony Trinitron displays use a unique technology that provides a sharp image. To produce this image, an image stabilizing wire is required. The wire is horizontal, about two-thirds of the way down the monitor, and it causes a faint line on the screen. It's only visible with a solid white image onscreen. You'll probably have to look for it to find it if you haven't seen it already. On larger monitors there are two of them: one-third of the way down and another two-thirds of the way down. They're normal and should be there.

Bringing back a display from a single dot or a line

Unlike the fully blank display that can sometimes be fixed with a little solder, a monitor that shows only a single, white dot, or a single line can only be fixed by a technician. Major parts of the monitor have failed and a service technician will have to repair the display.

PowerBook display problems

PowerBooks and their LCD displays suffer a number of illnesses that you can't do anything about. Fortunately, none of them are too serious.

- **Dying Pixels**. You can't fix them, but if your PowerBook is under warranty, Apple will replace the display. The criteria for Apple to fix it is one or more pixels stuck on black, or five or more pixels stuck on white. Apple is aware that some PowerBooks have displays with fewer than five pixels stuck on white, but this is much less noticeable than a stuck black pixel. LCD display makers already throw away a large number of their production because of bad pixels; it's still a cutting-edge technology. Apple has decided that five white pixels is an acceptable number for the user to deal with, given the alternative of astronomical prices.

- **Lines That Are (But Shouldn't Be) There**. If you see dark vertical lines on your PowerBook display, you're looking at a problem inherent in passive-matrix displays, particularly on the PowerBook 210 and 230. The lines extend from any vertical lines that are part of your windows or desktop pattern. These displays are remarkably sensitive to changing ambient light. You can temporarily remove the lines by adjusting the display's contrast; unfortunately, if you move to another location they will return. If these lines are truly tiresome, adjust the contrast whenever you sit down to work.

Power Mac monitor concerns

With the introduction of the Power Mac, new architecture and new problems surfaced. Fortunately, these problems can be solved easily.

- **Not Removing the AV Video Board**. A Power Mac's NuBus video board should not be removed. The pins that hold it in and communicate with the rest of the machine are particularly fragile, and the board itself is a NuBus termination that must remain in place when the machine is powered up. If you need to remove the board, see an Apple service representative first. Powering on the machine while the board is disconnected can permanently damage the Mac.

- **Connecting a Standard Monitor to a Power Mac 6100**. The PowerMac 6100 is a little different from the 7100 and 8100 in that it has only one monitor port on the back, which is designed for the AV monitor. If you don't want an AV monitor, you can buy an adapter from Apple for about $30. This adapter allows a standard monitor to display your work. The 7100 and 8100 each have two ports, and the same adapter will handle the AV port if you want to use both with standard monitors.

- **Watching TV on a Power Mac.** It is possible to watch TV on your Power Mac's monitor, but you may see some distortion along the top and bottom of the display. This is caused by the confusion inherent in merging computer and television technologies. When you watch TV on a standard television, you do not see the entire image; the top and bottom of the picture have been intentionally clipped off because they may be carrying anything from unused video (microphones hanging from the ceiling on a talk show) to synchronization signals used by the TV stations. If you see distortion at the top and bottom or notice the frame isn't quite what you thought it would be, you're probably seeing this *overscan*. The computer is unable to differentiate between what should and should not be displayed.

- **Retrieving (and Keeping) a Cursor.** If you have a PowerMac 7100 or 8100 with a standard monitor hooked up to the built-in video (the lower port), you may have noticed that your cursor seems capable of jumping off the edge of the monitor as if another monitor is next to it. The Mac believes there is. It sees the AV card in its slot and assumes a monitor is connected. To find out if your Mac is configured for two monitors, open the Monitors control panel and see if there's a second monitor there. If so, you have two choices: you can buy an AV adapter and put the standard monitor on the AV port, or you can move the nonexistent monitor out of the way electronically.

To hide the nonexistent monitor, open the Monitors control panel and set the two monitors so that they are only touching each other at one corner of their screens in the Monitors control panel. The nonexistent monitor is still out there, but your cursor won't end up offscreen and lost.

Hard Disk Problems and Solutions

Hard drives are by far the most popular Macintosh hardware upgrade. Hard drives generally are not as problematic as other hardware peripherals because of their single-task design and the fact that SCSI hard drives have been in the computer industry since the very first computers were introduced.

Basic troubleshooting

Below are some troubleshooting tips for working with hard drives. Please do not try these suggestions if the hard drive appears to have either damaged a Macintosh while being powered up or connected, or damaged another SCSI or internal Macintosh hardware device. If you see smoke, a hardware failure occurred. Contact the hard drive manufacturer or vendor you purchased the hard drive from for support or troubleshooting help.

The power to the hard drive is on, but I cannot mount one or several of the hard drive's volumes.

Possible causes

This is a symptom of incompatible drivers and System software. System 7.5 shipped with a newer version of hard drive drivers. You should run Apple's HD SC Setup or if you have a PowerMac 630 or PowerBook 150, Drive Setup to update internal or external hard drives with newer drivers so they can be used with Macs running System 7.5.

Incomplete or defective SCSI cable connection (see previous section on troubleshooting SCSI connections).

Improper SCSI termination (see previous section on troubleshooting SCSI connections).

Improper SCSI ID on hard drive(s) (see previous section on troubleshooting SCSI devices).

Improper or dysfunctional SCSI daisy chain to hard drive(s) (see previous section on troubleshooting SCSI devices).

Checkpoints

Check the power outlet and make sure the Mac is plugged in.

Try swapping power cables with another hard drive if you have problems getting the hard drive to power up.

Try swapping SCSI cables with another SCSI device if you have problems seeing the hard drive in a SCSI chain, or directly from your Macintosh.

Check any cables that don't seem to work for missing pins or disconnected wires at the beginning or end of the cable.

If the hard drive is an internal hard drive, try swapping it into another Mac to see if will spin up and/or appear on the desktop. If necessary, boot the Mac with the Disk Tools floppy if no System software is on the hard drive.

If you have an Apple internal or external hard drive you can update the hard drive driver from System 7.x to 7.5 by running Apple's HD SC Setup 7.3.2 on your Macintosh. Select the hard drive to be updated and then select the Update button. If you have hard drive windows open, updating the driver will close and re-open the windows on the desktop. If you have problems copying files on your Macintosh, you may possibly have file system problems, or problems with the System software configuration. Whenever your Macintosh crashes, there is a slim chance your file system (hard drive system for tracking all the files and folders on the drive) may become damaged or corrupted. Apple's Disk First Aid 7.2 (or higher) can help identify and often repair file system problems, as well as Symantec's Norton Utilities software. More information on file system corruption and troubleshooting can be found in the System software troubleshooting section.

Hard drives, like other SCSI devices, require proper connection of the SCSI cable as well as the power cable. If the hard drive is powered up and connected to your Macintosh, but does not appear on the desktop upon startup, try launching SCSI Probe to see if the software can see the hard drive. If SCSI Probe can see the hard drive, select the Mount button located at the bottom of the SCSI Probe control panel. If you have a large hard drive, such as a 700 MB or 1GB or larger drive, mounting may take a few seconds. If the hard drive's light is flashing, your Macintosh is successfully accessing the hard drive volume, and is in the process of mounting the volume on the desktop.

If SCSI Probe cannot see your hard drive, check other SCSI devices and make sure they are not using SCSI ID 0 or 7. If the hard drive is an external hard drive, make sure it is also not using SCSI ID 0 or 7, and that it is not using the same SCSI ID as another SCSI device connected to your Macintosh. Also try shutting down and powering 'off' your Macintosh and all SCSI devices. Then turn your Macintosh and all peripherals 'on' again, and restart your Macintosh. Launch SCSIProbe and see if the hard drive is visible, and if you can mount the volume successfully.

If the hard drive is an older Apple drive, and was formatted, for example with System 6 software drivers, connect the hard drive to your Macintosh and launch Apple's HD SC setup. FWB, LaCie, and Micronet also sell commercial hard drive formatting software that updates hard drive drivers. First try updating the drivers on the hard drive to see if the hard drive is visible to your Macintosh. If you still are not able to see or mount the hard drive, and you have files on the hard drive, back them up. Then reformat the drive with System 7.5-compatible formatting software and try mounting the hard drive with SCSIProbe.

Expected results

All hard drives mount on the desktop.

Sporadic crashes when copying files or running applications from the hard drive.

Possible causes

Extension conflict in System Folder.
This could be a symptom of incompatible hard drive drivers and System software.
Not enough memory available to copy files.
Virus may have infected some hard drive files, or hard drive directory.
Hard drive may be fragmented, or have bad sectors preventing successful copying of files.
Old software drivers on the hard drive.

Checkpoints

Try copying files with Extensions disabled.

Try quitting other open applications, or turning off Extensions at startup to free up more memory in the System.

Check your hard drive for viruses using Disinfectant 3.6 or higher, or another virus protection application.

Try optimizing or checking for hard drive defragmentation using Norton Utilities, Disk Express, or other hard drive defragmentation software.

System 7.5 shipped with a newer version of hard drive drivers that are required for hard drives that will run in a System 7.5 environment. If you have an Apple internal or external hard drive you can update the hard drive driver from System 7.x to 7.5 by running Apple's HD SC Setup 7.3.2 on your Macintosh. Select the hard drive to be updated and then select the Update button. If you have hard drive windows open, updating the driver will close and re-open the windows on the desktop.

If you have problems copying files on your Macintosh, you may possibly have file system problems, or problems with the System software configuration. Whenever your Macintosh crashes, there is a slim chance your file system (hard drive system for tracking all the files and folders on the drive) may be damaged or corrupted.

Apple's Disk First Aid 7.2 (or higher) can help identify and often repair file system problems, as well as Symantec's Norton Utilities software. More information on file system corruption and troubleshooting can be found in the System software troubleshooting section.

Expected results

Successful copying of small or large files to and from the hard drive.

Ability to identify software conflicts, viruses, or software that needs upgrading.

Ability to identify any viruses, file system errors, or hard drive fragmentation problems.

Unable to change the hard drive's name.

Possible causes

Personal File Sharing is on.

Finder Preferences damaged.

File System damage.

Checkpoints

The easiest way to rename a hard drive is to select the hard drive icon, press the Return key, and type the name you want the hard drive to be.

When you press Enter (Return), a box appears around the name of the hard drive. You are now ready to enter text into the hard drive's name field. If this box does not appear, there's a good chance you have personal filesharing turned on in your Sharing Setup control panel.

If File Sharing is on, the status in the File Sharing section of the Sharing Setup control panel will indicate File Sharing is "on," and the File Sharing button reads Stop. To turn file sharing off, click your mouse once on the 'Stop' button, and the button should turn into a "cancel" then "Start" button. Now you should be able to rename your hard drive successfully.

Try moving the Finder Preferences file out of the System Folder and restart your Macintosh.

Try running Apple's Disk First Aid 7.2 or newer to see if any file system errors can be identified and repaired.

Unable to copy software to the hard drive or move files around on the hard drive.

Possible causes

Hard drive is full (has zero K free).

Hard drive is locked.

The System or applications folder is locked.

You do not have write access if the drive is a server volume.

Checkpoints

If you purchase a new hard drive, you should be able to copy, move, create, or delete files and folders on the hard drive.

If you see the icon of a pencil with a diagonal line drawn through it in any of your hard drive windows, this means you either have a Personal File Sharing hard drive network-mounted on the desktop with read-only privileges, or your hard drive has been locked by the person who formatted it so that is a read-only drive. The hard drive may also have been locked using Apple's HD SC Setup or Drive Setup 1.0.2.

To unlock the drive, you can launch the formatting software used to format the hard drive (HD SC Setup or Drive Setup for Apple's internal and external hard drives), and deselect the feature that locks the volume you are trying to use. If the hard drive is a network volume, you need to request write-access from the network administrator who granted you read-access to the hard drive volume.

If you are trying to update a locked file on a hard drive, select the file by clicking on it once, then select Get Info from the File menu. In the lower left corner of the Get Info window, is a checkbox with the word 'Locked' to the right of it. Deselect this box to unlock the file. You can now open and edit the file, replace it with a file of the same name, or throw it away in the trash.

If you are unable to copy the System Folder or Applications folder, check the General Controls control panel and make sure the system and applications "protection" features are not selected.

9

Unable to share the hard drive on a network.

Possible causes

Personal File Sharing not turned on.
Macintosh and Owner name and password not defined in the Sharing Setup control panel.
Hard drive volume does not have correct sharing privileges turned on.
Improper system software installation of Personal File Sharing software.
Extension or other software conflict.

Checkpoints

If you turned File Sharing "on," you should be able to share your internal hard drive automatically provided the person logging on to your Macintosh uses the correct name and password to access the system. If you have an external hard drive, which you may have mounted after startup, and already have File Sharing on, this additional drive can be accessed via file sharing by following these steps:

1. Select the hard drive's icon with file sharing on.

2. Select Sharing from the File menu.

3. Select Share this volume and its contents checkbox.

4. Select OK when the system asks you if you want to save these changes.

5. Log into your Macintosh from another Macintosh and you will see the new volume available on the network.

Open the Users & Groups control panel and make sure guest access if on, if you want guests to log on to your Macintosh computer.
Try turning off all or some extensions except AppleShare, Network, Users & Groups, File Sharing Monitor, and Sharing Setup control panel and restart you Macintosh. Then try to set hard drive access privileges for Personal File Sharing.

File sizes change when files are moved from a small hard drive to a large hard drive.

Possible causes

File System errors can cause this. In addition, if the original drive is smaller in storage capacity than the drive it is being copied to, the file size will grow after being copied to the larger drive. This is normal System software behavior for file system management.

If you have a number of 2K files on your existing drive, and copy them to a larger drive, such as a 700 MB or 1 or 2GB hard drive, you may notice the file sizes do not remain 2K. The 2K file size changes from a 40 MB hard drive to a 700 MB hard drive because the hard drive is formatted for a certain physical hard drive size, but the sector sizes are limited to a minimum file size which is directly related to the size of the hard drive (or how much hard drive space is formatted onto a particular volume).

What does this mean? In general, if you have a 1 or 2 GB drive, and want to keep the minimal file size small, format multiple partitions on the hard drive, with the average size of the partition being approximately 200 MB. This will keep a 2K file on a 40 MB hard drive from becoming a 30K file on a 1 or 2GB hard drive. Most hard drives ship with partitioning options in the formatting software. Most formatting software supports multiple (limited by the amount of hard drive space available per partition volume and size of the physical disk) hard drive partitions.

Expected results

File sizes should change only relative to the size of the drive they originated on, and become larger if the hard drive you are copying to has a larger volume partition.

Error messages when running Apple's Disk First Aid 7.2 or Norton Utilities 3.1.3 (or higher version numbers).

What do the error messages from Apple's Disk First Aid 7.2 or Norton mean when I run this software on my Macintosh?

First off, you should run either of these applications on a regular basis as preventative maintenance for your Macintosh hardware. If you suspect hard drive problems with the file system, you should start up your Macintosh from the Disk Tools or Norton Emergency floppy disk and run the diagnostic checking software from the floppy, and NOT from the hard drive.

If the software finds a problem with your hard drive (both applications should find identical or similar problems if there are errors in your file system), it will tell you if it can repair the damage or problem found. Apple's Disk First Aid has a Repair button, and Norton will prompt you with a dialog asking you if you want to fix the problem now (you should select 'yes' if you have started up from a floppy disk system). After the problem is fixed by the software, you should run the diagnostic check once more, just to make sure the problem does not continue to raise a flag with the software. If the error persists, continue to repair the drive until the error is not detectable.

How do I find out how large my hard drive is?

If you're not sure how many megabytes or space your hard drive can hold, follow these simple steps to find out:

1. Select your hard drive icon. Select Open from the File menu, or double click it.

2. Select View by Name from the Views menu. You should see a sub-menubar appear in the hard drive window listing the number items in the window—MB in disk and MB available.

3. Add the MB in disk and MB available numbers. For example 295 MB in disk, plus 29 MB available total approximately 324 MB. Therefore the drive is a 320 MB hard drive.

Why does the hard drive volume seem smaller than the allowable/physical size of the disk?

If you've ever added up the total storage of all your files and the amount of free storage space left on your hard drive, you may wonder why the files on the disk and free space available do not add up to the advertised total size of the hard drive. When you format a hard drive, system software allocates some of the hard drive space with software drivers and information indicating bad physical sectors on the disk itself, as well as additional software information that is used by both System software and the formatting application software.

The difference should not be more than a few hundred kilobytes. When purchasing a hard drive, you generally want to purchase a drive that doubles or triples your current needs. When you initially format or re-format the hard drive, remember that about 100-200K of hard drive space is pre-allocated by drivers and other software (invisible to you as a hard drive user).

Up-close and personal hard drive troubleshooting topics

Problems with disk drives can result in damaged files and directories. Problems are a result of hardware or media failure, or of sections of the disk that become unrecognizable to the computer and Operating System. Many disk-related problems can be solved with simple procedures, requiring no diagnostic software. In extreme cases, physical reconstruction of the disk may be necessary. In all cases, the first rule of working with troublesome hard disks is *back up regularly.*

Problems with hard disks usually manifest themselves in the form of trouble opening or using files, difficulty booting the computer with the hard disk, or intermittent problems with copying files. Sometimes, it's obvious that the disk is the problem. If you have problems booting the computer with a given hard disk or getting the disk to appear on the desktop, the first thing to do is check your computer's connection to the disk. Turn off the computer and its peripherals and recheck the connections. If the connections are fine and the problem persists, your next line of defense is the SCSI bus. For a full discussion of SCSI hard disk problems and solutions, see the section on SCSI earlier in this chapter.

If the computer won't boot, or the hard drive won't mount despite perfect connections and adherence to the rules of SCSI, the hard disk is probably at fault. If the problem is related to working with files, chances are even better that the disk is the problem.

Damaged directories

The lists of files and folders on your hard disk are called directories. Directories contain the name and attributes of each file, and where the file is stored on the hard disk. Think of a directory as a road map to your hard disk. If the road map becomes damaged or is missing a vital piece, you will have difficulty locating and using files on the disk.

The Macintosh Desktop file (under System 6) and the Desktop DB and DF files (under System 7) are found on every hard disk, floppy disk, or removable media disk. The Desktop file is invisible and contains the disk's directory. You can't double-click on it, copy it, or delete it. It can become damaged if the hard disk's media becomes corrupted, or if contradictory information from two or more files is present. Fortunately, this file is usually easy to fix.

Sometimes your Mac will tell you that a desktop file is damaged and needs to be rebuilt. Rebuilding the desktop removes old information and icons. If you receive this message, you should usually allow the Mac to take care of the problem by clicking on OK. If you haven't backed up the Mac recently, use a disk recovery program to get important data off the damaged disk.

You may also decide to fix the desktop if you notice that the Mac is running more slowly than usual. As you add and delete files from your disks, desktop files enlarge to keep up with the flow of filenames, application attributes, and icons. Deleting a file doesn't get rid of its entry in the Desktop directory.

To rebuild a damaged desktop, do the following:

1. Shut down your Macintosh and all attached hard disks.

2. Restart the Macintosh while holding down the Option and ⌘ keys until a dialog box appears asking if you want to rebuild the desktop file. Click on OK.

3. The Desktop file is rebuilt. This takes a few minutes. When the process is complete, your files and folders should be available to you.

Warning

Rebuilding the Desktop file removes the comments stored in the Get Info box for each file on your disk. For this reason, it's generally not a good idea to store crucial information in the Comments box.

Damaged partition map

Every disk has at least one partition. The partition map allocates space on the disk to the visible partition and to the hidden areas the disk uses to store parameter information. If the partition map becomes damaged, you may be unable to mount the disk normally. The best way to fix a damaged partition map is to use diagnostic software to check and repair the disk. If problems persist, reformat (completely erase and reconstruct) the disk. This re-creates the partition map for you.

9

It may not be obvious that the problem is a damaged partition map. If you experience problems accessing files, or get unexplained disk errors, you may have one of several disk-related problems. Diagnostic software, such as Norton Utilities or MacTools, will uncover the reason behind any inconsistencies.

Optimization software

The hard drives connected to your Macintosh do quite a bit of work during the course of a normal computing session. Information is almost constantly being written, changed, or deleted from the drive.

One side effect of the constant shuffling of data is called *disk fragmentation.* This occurs because of the way computers keep track of used and free space on a disk. When data is first written to a disk, files are placed next to each other in contiguous blocks of space. After files are deleted or modified, holes of free space open up where there used to be data. New files written to the disk are broken up into two or more fragments and placed into these "holes" between other files. Because files are always being added, deleted, and modified, file fragmentation continually gets worse and worse. Eventually, more and more of the files on your hard drive are broken into fragments, and fewer files exist as contiguous blocks. See Figure 9.2 for a representation of a typical disk with numerous fragmented files.

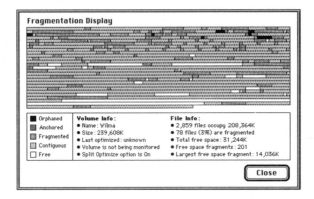

Figure 9.2   Contiguous files are represented by light areas; fragmented files by dark areas. Free space is white.

When the hard drive needs to read a file from disk, the read/write head must be positioned directly above the blocks on the disk that contain data belonging to that file. If the file is broken up into several pieces scattered around the disk, it could take several passes for the drive head to read the entire file. Your Macintosh performance suffers.

Defragmenting the hard drive, or putting all the pieces back together to form contiguous files, is one way to combat the effects of file fragmentation. Software packages that perform this function still leave the free space of a hard disk fragmented, but do rearrange the files that are on the hard disk.

Sometimes, simply defragmenting a drive is not enough. Files that are commonly accessed may exist on opposite sides of the disk, separated by files that never change (such as fonts, applications, and system files). This requires the read/write head to travel an extra distance before the Macintosh can retrieve the data. The reordering of files so that groups of data are stored in the same location is called *optimizing*.

Disk Express II

This powerful control panel does much more than defragment and optimize hard drives. While you work on your Mac, Disk Express II monitors all the files you access, and, depending on their usage, assigns them to one of three categories: active, sporadic, and dormant.

When you perform an optimization using Disk Express II, the software intelligently defragments files and positions them on the hard drive according to their category. By default, active files are placed at the front of the disk, next to the directories. Then the free space is positioned next to these frequently used files to reduce any further fragmentation between optimizations. Next, files that are used only sporadically and those that are considered dormant are placed at the end of the hard drive. See Figure 9.3 for an illustration of Disk Express's default optimization. All other optimization utilities pale in comparison to the feature set and sophistication of Disk Express II.

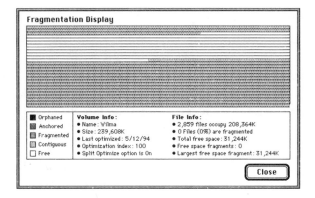

Figure 9.3 Disk Express monitors files and places them on the disk according to their frequency of use.

Disk Express has several features that make it the optimizer of choice for anyone who desires the most efficient hard drives.

- Optimizations can be performed unattended and in the background at scheduled days/times.

- An optimization index can be set from 1 to 100 to specify the "tightness" of the optimization.

- Disk Express can be set to monitor only specific volumes, or any volume that is mounted on the Macintosh (including removable media).

- Optimization can be set to Packed (all files), Split (all files), or Quick (active files only) mode depending on the level of control and file placement desired.

- Disk Express has the option of performing a full disk verification before optimizing files. The program also recognizes when you attempt to regain use of your Macintosh and stops moving files until the System becomes idle again.

- To prevent data loss due to unexpected power failure or other sudden interruption, Disk Express uses a fail-proof method of moving files.

For more information, contact:

AlSoft, Inc.
(713) 343-4090

Note

Some driver-level compression programs recommend not performing disk optimization when they are used.

File recovery

Whether you lost a file because of a hard disk crash or accidentally deleted it from your hard drive, it is sometimes possible to retrieve the lost information. The ability to get a file back depends on how quickly you take action.

When a disk crash causes a file to disappear or to become damaged, the file is actually still on the disk until another file overwrites it or until the disk is formatted. Many crashes simply remove a file from the directory, meaning that if you can let the directory know that the file actually exists, you can once again use it.

Several software packages allow you to look at the contents of your hard disk below the directory level. The software also includes the ability to bring a lost file back to life.

Norton Utilities and MacTools are actually collections of software utilities. Each includes file and disk repair utilities, lost file recovery, and an optimizer/defragmenter to keep your hard disk running its best. The packages differ mostly in style.

Norton Utilities

Norton Utilities, from Symantec, is a disk diagnostic and recovery package. Norton includes several applications that can help you prevent problems with hard disks, and recover from them if disaster strikes. In addition, Norton Utilities includes:

FileSaver
Disk Doctor
UnErase
Volume Recover
Speed Disk

Norton Utilities is a valuable component of your emergency diagnosis and recovery kit. In addition to a full set of tools that can be kept on your hard disk for regular maintenance and troubleshooting, the package includes a bootable floppy for emergencies. If your startup hard disk will not mount, use the Norton emergency disk to get information about your damaged drive, and possibly recover its files.

UnErase, Disk Doctor, Volume Recover, and Speed Disk appear in the program's main window (see Figure 9.4). You'll see this window when you double-click on the Norton Utilities application.

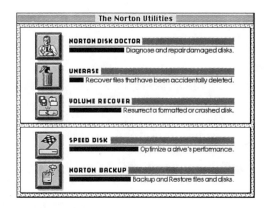

Figure 9.4 Norton Utilities' main window.

Price: $149
Symantec Corp.
10201 Torre Ave.
Cupertino, Ca 95014
(800) 441-7234

Norton FileSaver

When you install Norton Utilities for Macintosh, you have the option of applying a little preventive medicine to your hard drive. FileSaver is a control panel (CDEV under System 6) that keeps a log of files you create, move, and delete from the disk, as well as files found on floppies and removable disks. If a disk crash occurs, FileSaver's record helps Norton's disk recovery utilities find and repair damaged files. FileSaver can also track file activity on more than one currently mounted volume.

The Expert Level configuration (see Figure 9.5) lets you choose to track a specified number of files per volume, and determine whether to maintain finder comments associated with files. The more files you choose to track, the more disk space FileSaver needs for its log.

Figure 9.5   FileSaver's Expert Level dialog box.

Norton Disk Doctor

Disk Doctor is one of Norton's core applications (see Figure 9.6). This diagnostic tool can find and fix many disk and file problems on both hard disks and floppies. You can use Disk Doctor even if there are no known or suspected problems with a disk to find bad resource forks, incorrectly dated files, and other problems that haven't yet caused trouble.

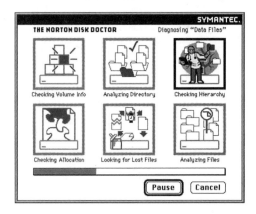

Figure 9.6   Norton Disk Doctor performing a scan of a disk drive. The disk repairman moves from box to box as the scan progresses.

Disk Doctor scans for the following information (you can track his progress graphically):

- *Check Volume Info*: Determines whether the disk can be mounted on your Mac's desktop.

- *Analyze Directory*: Looks for directory inconsistencies, unlocks files that can't be removed, fixes folders that won't open, and generally cleans up the directory structure.

- *Check Hierarchy*: Compares the directory to actual files present on the disk.

- *Check Allocation*: Searches for portions of the disk (blocks) that are improperly allocated to more than one file, then resolves the conflicts.

- *Look for Lost Files*: Finds and fixes sectors of the disk that the directory thinks are being bussed, but which are really available to hold new information.

- *Analyze Files*: Looks for files with missing icons, resource forks, or invalid dates. Identifies and attempts to fix corrupted files.

If Disk Doctor finds problems with the structure of your disk or files, it offers the option of fixing the problem or continuing with the scan. It's usually a good idea to let Disk Doctor fix problems it finds. If you're not sure about a change the software wants to make, click on No when you are asked about a particular file or group of files. Disk Doctor will report on all problems it finds. You may want to run Disk Doctor again after you back up your disk drive.

UnErase

When you use the Empty Trash command to get rid of files you no longer need, information about the files is removed from your hard disk's directory. The file is still stored on your disk, however, until you overwrite it with a new file or use software to erase the file. Because files remain on the disk for a while, you can often retrieve those you accidentally deleted. UnErase provides you with this option and several others (see Figure 9.7):

- *Quick UnErase*: Locates all files and file fragments still on the volume you've selected to search. If you installed Norton FileSaver, the search is quicker and is based on the log FileSaver has created.

- *Search for specific file type*: This option lets you pick from a list of common file types. Each application program you use has its own file type, and using this option lets you search for, say, all Microsoft Word files.

- *Text Search*: As a last resort, you can enter a phrase, word, or other bit of text in the file you're looking for. The Text Search option finds portions of a file, which you must then piece together to recover the entire file. If you can locate all of the pieces, Norton performs the repair for you.

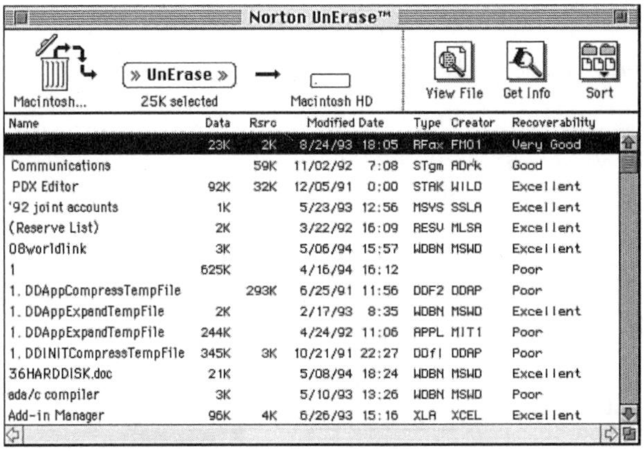

Figure 9.7   Your chances of recovering a file are displayed in the far right column of the UnErase window. Select the file or files you want to recover, and click on UnErase to begin.

Volume recover

If you have a badly damaged or accidentally initialized hard disk, Volume Recover is your best bet. UnErase goes after erased files; Volume Recover reconstructs an entire disk.

Like UnErase, Volume Recover works much better when FileSaver has been installed before a disk crash. When you choose a drive to scan with Volume Recover, the software looks for the FileSaver information associated with the drive.

If you haven't installed FileSaver, you can choose from a Directory Scan or Volume Scan for hard disks, or a Floppy Tags search for floppy disks. If directory information is relatively intact, the Directory Scan option is best. Volume Scan finds and collects file fragments, from which you may be able to piece your files together.

Speed Disk

Speed Disk is primarily a tool for preventive maintenance, although you may want to use it the first time disk trouble occurs or if you feel your hard disk should be performing faster.

Speed Disk optimizes and defragments hard disks and floppies. When you choose Speed Disk from the main Norton menu, you see a "map" of your hard disk (see Figure 9.8). The map shows where data is stored on the disk and how much of it is fragmented or spread across various parts of the disk. When data is fragmented, the hard disk's heads must scan longer to find the data they need. When you copy files onto your hard disk, the information occupies whatever space is available, whether it's contiguous or not. If the file is split over different parts of the disk, the disk is fragmented. Using Speed Disk, you defragment and optimize the disk by moving data into contiguous blocks.

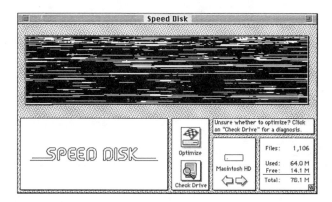

Figure 9.8 Speed Disk's Easy Level window shows a disk in need of optimization.

MacTools

Like Norton Utilities, MacTools, from Central Point Software, is a modular package composed of several disk repair and maintenance utilities. MacTools also includes virus protection and backup software. MacTools' disk fixing and maintenance functions are found in several applications.

MacTools comes on four disks, and includes its own installer program. With this application, you can install the applications and utilities you want, specify where they should be placed, and whether the installer should build bootable emergency and optimization disks (see Figure 9.9).

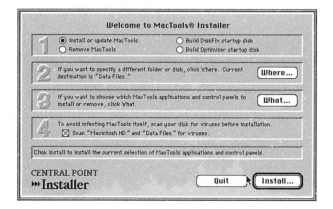

Figure 9.9 The MacTools installer walks you through the installation.

Price: $149.95
For more information, contact:
Central Point Software
15220 N.W. Greenbriar Pkway, Suite 200
Beaverton, OR 97006
(800) 445-4208

DiskFix

The DiskFix application has several functions. You can use it to look for and repair a variety of problems with hard disks, floppies, and removable media. Central Point divides the problems you can fix by their impact on the system:

- *Startup.* Difficulty booting the computer with the affected disk.

- *Disk mounting.* The disk in question doesn't appear on the desktop, or a message tells you that the disk is damaged.

- *File or folders.* Files or folders disappear or won't open.

- *Viruses.*

- *Bad blocks.* Some areas of the disk are damaged, making files stored there unreadable.

- *Cross-linked files.* A single sector on a disk is allocated to more than one file.

- *Damaged desktop.* A disk's master directory (Desktop file) is damaged, so that file hierarchy, icons, dates, and Finder comments are corrupted.

With DiskFix open and all available disks visible in the window, you can run a complete check of a disk's media, file structure, boot blocks, and other parameters, as displayed in Figure 9.10. You can choose which parameters to work with in the Options dialog box.

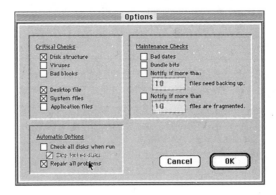

Figure 9.10 The Options dialog box lets you pick and choose among DiskFix's various checks.

If DiskFix finds a problem, it prompts you with a dialog box, asking if you want to have DiskFix repair the problem and continue its check. You may want to choose No if you haven't backed up a disk or are otherwise uncertain of the repair's impact. DiskFix dialogs usually offer an explanation of the pros and cons of making repairs. You can also choose to have DiskFix make a report of the check you've made, and the repairs it completed or deferred. When you've set all these options, you can save the configuration as a Setup file.

Running checks regularly can fix minor problems before they grow. Using DiskFix's AutoCheck and Scheduler features, you can have DiskFix automatically perform checks and repairs unattended. To use this feature, you must be running System 7, or System 6 with MultiFinder. Also, if you didn't build emergency disks when you installed MacTools, DiskFix lets you build them. You might want to create more than one.

Undelete

Undelete can correct your mistakes. If you accidentally throw away a file or folder full of files, Undelete can search your hard disk for them and help you get them back. As discussed earlier, files thrown in the trash are not really deleted until they are overwritten, or until you fill up free space or reformat the disk.

Undelete is MacTools' first line of file recovery. With it, you can scan a disk for files of a certain type or for files that contain a specified text string. You can then restore the files. If you activated the TrashBack extension when you first installed MacTools, you can use this utility to recover files that have accidentally been thrown away.

Undelete may have trouble reconstructing deleted files if they have been partially erased. The Undelete File list tells you whether the chances for recovery are perfect, excellent, good, fair, poor, or destroyed.

FileFix

DiskFix focuses on getting hard disks, floppies, and removable media back in working order; FileFix concentrates on the integrity of individual files. With it, you can scan a whole volume, a folder, or a file to determine whether one of several common file problems have occurred, including:

- Invalid dates
- Bad blocks
- Damaged resource forks
- Incorrectly set bundle bits

The main FileFix window, like the DiskFix window, displays each mounted disk and an icon bar of commands (see Figure 9.11). The Options button lets you pick the problems you want to look for and repair. FileFix lets you scan a whole volume, or just a file or folder. You can then choose to repair problems it finds, and choose how these problems will be reported. If you choose the Repair Automatically option, FileFix's report lets you know what files were fixed.

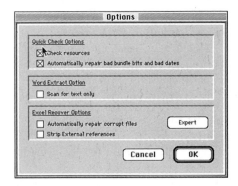

Figure 9.11   FileFix's Options dialog box lets you pick scanning and repair choices.

Note

FileFix includes the unique capability of repairing Microsoft Word and Microsoft Excel files. If you are unable to open a particular Word or Excel file in the normal way, select it in the FileFix window. If the file was created by Microsoft Word, select the Scan For Text Only option in the Options dialog box, and then scan the file. FileFix extracts the text from the file, and prompts you to create a new file that is readable with any word processing program, including Microsoft Word. You lose your Word formatting, but the file will otherwise be intact.

FileFix offers two options for damaged Excel files. First, you can choose to automatically repair corrupt files. Using the Expert button in the Options dialog box gives you more options. If you are having trouble with Excel files that were once linked to other files, use the Strip External References option. The file will then open on its own.

Optimizer

Think of MacTools' Optimizer as a tune-up for your hard disk. Over time, files on the disk become fragmented. As they are saved, moved, and deleted, they become scattered across the disk, requiring the disk head to spend more time looking for the files you need. Optimizer puts file fragments back together, and moves all files on the disk into the same area of the disk.

Of course, any application that moves your files around should be used with caution. Whether you use Optimizer on a regular basis or when the disk's speed is noticeably slow, make sure you back up the disk before optimizing.

Note

Don't optimize a disk if you plan to retrieve deleted files. Moving data around during the optimization process may overwrite all or part of the file you want to undelete.

Optimizer can perform a quick optimization or a full one. Because you can't perform full optimization of a startup disk, or on any other disk with open files, the quick optimize option lets you remove most fragmentation from the media. Use full optimize on non-startup disks with no open files or applications.

Like DiskFix and FileFix, Optimizer presents a window with all available disks and several choices. The Options dialog box (see Figure 9.12) is where you will make most of your choices.

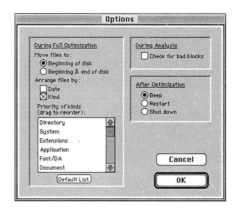

Figure 9.12 Optimizer's options let you decide where files should be located, and which ones should be given priority.

Signs of impending hard disk failure

Some hard disk problems appear all at once: you can't boot the drive, or files can't be opened or copied. Other problems take longer to surface. By taking note of these abnormalities, you may be able to head off disaster before it strikes.

Expected Life Span

A hard disk comprises electronics, mechanical parts, and platters. The mechanical parts and the platters will eventually wear out. Although it is impossible to predict how long a hard disk will last, its longevity really isn't even a concern because you will probably want to replace the drive with a larger or faster one before it ever shows signs of slowing down or crashing.

Warning Signs

Some warning signs of hard disk trouble include:

- Disk crashes intermittently.
- Files will not open normally.

- You are unable to copy files to or from a hard disk.

- You are unable to install software due to disk errors.

- The hard disk makes odd sounds while accessing data.

Solutions

If you experience any of these disk maladies, it's a good idea to take a few general precautions.

- Make sure your disk is completely backed up.

- Check your SCSI connections and termination.

- Use Norton Disk Doctor or MacTools DiskFix to make a quick check of your disk.

- Delete or repair problem files.

- Optimize and defragment your disk.

- Make sure the latest drivers for this hard disk are installed.

Hard disk utilities

Several vendors sell utility packages that can help you manage hard disks. These programs:

- *Format and initialize*: Erasing everything from the disk.

- *Partition*: Dividing a hard disk into sections, which appear on the desktop as totally separate disks.

- *Update disk drivers*: Updating the software on each disk, so that it works at peak efficiency with your Mac and the latest version of the operating system.

Drive7

Casa Blanca Works' Drive7 can format your disk, partition it, and update its driver. Drive7 also includes a control panel (CDEV under System 6) for managing removable disks, such as SyQuests, Bernoulli cartridges, and optical disks.

System 7 caused some problems for Macs with older hard disks. In some cases, the disk's driver needs to be updated so that it can be used with System 7. In others, problems show up when you try to use 24-bit addressing or Virtual Memory. In any case, Drive7's new SCSI driver ensures your disk's compatibility with System 7. Just boot your Mac from the Drive7 floppy, or update your non-startup disks while running the normal startup hard drive. To update the startup drive, you'll need to boot from the floppy.

All versions of the Macintosh Finder include an erase disk command, which works on floppies, hard disks, and removable media. That command, however, isn't as thorough as it should be. If you want to erase all vestiges of the previous contents of your disk, or would like the job done faster, Drive7's formatter is one solution. Formatting also installs the Drive7 driver.

If you hold down the Shift key while clicking on Format in the main Drive7 window, the button changes to Initialize. Initializing a hard disk does not completely erase it, but it does discard directory information. It's also a lot quicker than formatting.

Most Macintosh users have one partition on their hard disk. A *partition* is an area of the disk where your files are stored, which appears as one icon on the Desktop. Some users choose to create multiple partitions as a way of splitting a drive up among people or tasks. You can also partition a drive to run different versions of the Macintosh System, or Apple's A/UX UNIX Operating System (see Figure 9.13).

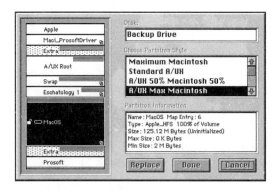

Figure 9.13 Drive7's partition window lets you select from several standard partition styles.

Drive7rem, is a control panel (CDEV under System 6) that is designed to replace control panels for different types of removable drives such as SyQuests, IOmega, and Bernoulli drives. When you open it, Drive7rem presents a picture of your SCSI bus and the devices attached to it. You can also use Drive7rem to alter partition attributes on both removable and hard disks.

> For more information, contact:
> Price: $79.95
> Casa Blanca Works
> 148 Bon Air Center
> Greenbrae, CA 94904
> (415) 461-2227

Hard Disk Toolkit

FWB's Hard Disk Toolkit includes an array of utilities and one of the most comprehensive user manuals around. Its claim to fame is its capability of digging deeply into the inner workings of a hard disk to find problems, or allowing you to customize the disk's operation.

FWB sells two versions of Hard Disk Toolkit: the complete version, and Hard Disk Toolkit Personal Edition. The Personal version does not include benchmarking software, World Control, or HDT Util. The Personal Edition also lacks the extremely detailed user guide, with its multi-chapter explanation of hard disks and SCSI.

HDT's main components are the following:

- HDT Primer
- HDT World Control
- HDT Extension
- HDT Prober

HDT Primer: If you want to get a good look at the top level features of Hard Disk Toolkit, you'll find them in HDT Primer. With Primer, you can format, partition, and update drivers for hard disks and removable media.

HDT Primer's low-level formatting provides more options than most formatters. You have total control of the drive and its attributes. When you format a disk with HDT Primer, the software installs an FWB driver, which gives you access to the rest of Toolkit's special features. You can install the driver without reformatting your hard drive.

Primer includes a disk testing suite (see Figure 9.14). You can configure a quick test, which runs a batch of scans to determine whether the disk contains bad blocks. You can also set up a custom set of tests that verifies the media and tests read, write, and seek integrity.

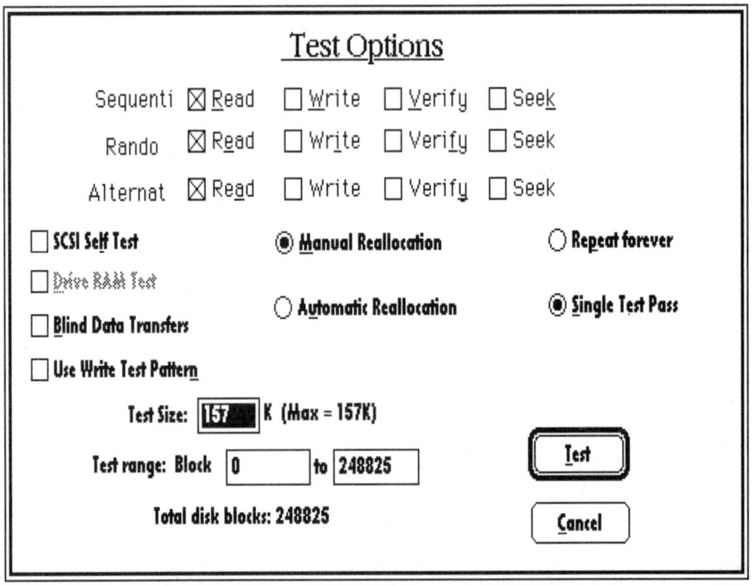

Figure 9.14   HDT Primer includes 13 hard disk tests.

HDT World Control: Opening HDT World Control takes courage. World Control is designed to help disk drive experts set and tune a variety of internal parameters. You shouldn't attempt to use it unless you are sure of what you are doing and have fully backed up your hard disk. World Control lets you view and edit a disk's page parameters, which control the inner workings of disk hardware.

You can use HDT World Control to alter a hard disk's microcode. You do this by modifying the parameters set by the drive's manufacturer. The goal is improved performance. You can manipulate more than 150 SCSI-1 and SCSI-2 parameters. With World Control's caching parameters, you can also alter or optimize the hardware caches within your hard drive. World Control lets you dig deeply into the disk, even locating defects that were present when your drive left the factory. You can scan for new defects, called *grown defects,* as well.

HDT BenchTest: With BenchTest, you can put a disk drive through its paces, comparing its performance to other drives or to previous scans of a given drive. You can also change parameters in World Control based on weaknesses you find when running Bench tests (see Figure 9.15). You can create your own benchmark index by choosing among eight testing parameters.

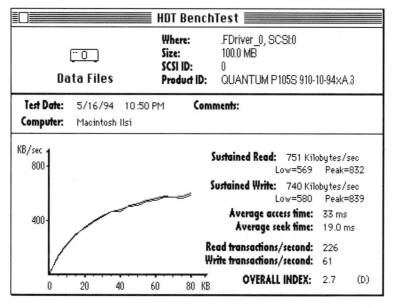

Figure 9.15 BenchTest creates an index of test results based on six tests. You can compare your drive's performance with that of selected FWB products, or other drives you test.

HDT Extension: Removable media, such as SyQuest cartridges and optical disks, do not mount like hard drives when you start up the Mac if there is no media loaded into the drive. HDT Extension is an extension you install into the System Folder. Once installed, HDT Extension mounts drivers when you insert a removable disk into the drive. The extension also compensates for slower (usually older) hard drives, which may not mount properly.

HDT Prober: Prober is a control panel that helps you keep tabs on the SCSI bus (see Figure 9.16). With it, you can view all devices on the SCSI chain, and mount those that didn't mount at startup.

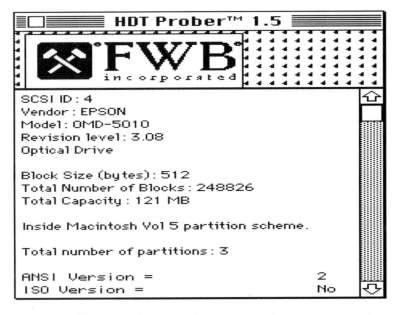

Figure 9.16 HDT Prober gives more information than other SCSI bus control panels, including a drive's block size and partition scheme.

Price: Hard Disk Toolkit Personal Edition: $79
Hard Disk Toolkit: $199
For more information, contact:
FWB. Inc.
2040 Polk Street
San Francisco, CA 94109
(415) 474-8056

Floppy Drive Troubleshooting

Originally, the floppy disk was the sole storage method available to Mac users and the predominant form of storage for users of many other platforms. Disks were as large as 8 inches and were, well... floppy. The 5 1/4-inch floppy disks of old (still popular on DOS machines and used with the Apple II) were encased in a flexible sheath and could be easily damaged or destroyed. Keeping these awfully "floppy" disks flat and safe was a job unto itself, and they were so fragile that writing on one with a ballpoint pen could take it out of action. Fortunately, this wasn't the case with the newer, hard-cased diskettes.

The floppy disk is a popular and convenient way to store and move data; for this reason, you should try to keep your disks and their drive in good shape. This section outlines many of the problems you could have with a floppy disk or its drive. This section lays out what you can do to fix these problems, from simply being aware of the appropriate storage environment through pulling out your toolkit and taking apart the drive.

Floppy disks and preventative maintenance

Standard 3 1/2-inch floppy disks don't look too floppy, and certainly don't seem to be as fragile as the infamous 5 1/4-inch floppy. Unfortunately, 3 1/2 disks can fail too. Floppy diskette drives also can have problems. For this reason, it is a good idea to keep your Macs floppy drive tuned and aligned.

Floppy drive errors signal a problem. They can occur for a number of reasons, ranging from plain dirt to a dead drive. You can correct or prevent most problems yourself.

Cleaning the heads

The simplest way to keep a drive running is to keep it clean. Apple recommends using the 3M floppy cleaning kit whenever the drive begins to misbehave, fails to format, or reads disks improperly. Cleaning will keep oxides from building up on the drive's head. Do not use it too often—the cleaning kit's solution is mildly abrasive and can prematurely wear out read/write heads.

Cleaning consists of putting a little cleaning fluid on a special floppy disk and running it through the drive for a few seconds, allowing the abrasive surface of what would be the disk part of the floppy (but is instead a soft, papery cloth) to wipe the dirt and debris off the heads.

> **Warning**
>
> Writing on a disk with a pencil is potentially damaging. The graphite in the pencil lead can get into the drive and do serious damage to the heads. When you write on a floppy, write with a pen (ballpoint pens are OK to use).

9

Keeping away from magnets

Some Macs generate their own disk-killing electrical fields. A compact Mac's power supply is on the left side of the case. If you have an external floppy drive, keep it on the right side. Leaving the drive or a stack of floppies on the left side of a compact Mac can destroy your data.

The ImageWriter has a magnet in its cover (it tells the printer if the cover's open or not); don't leave floppies on top of it. Old telephones also generate current via their ringers. Stereo system speakers generate powerful magnetic fields: keep floppies away from them. In general, keep your drive and disks away from anything that can generate significant electrical current.

Throwing and bending are bad ideas

Not all offices are networked well; sometimes it is easier to carry a floppy across a room (known as SneakerNet) than it is to pipe something through the network. Not long ago, a few of us used what we called *The Ninja Net*. If someone needed data, he or she would yell across the room, "Hey, give me a floppy with last week's images!" The lucky party would then load the floppy, stand up, and fling the disk like an oriental throwing star. Not surprisingly, we destroyed more than one floppy, although it was a relatively simple, effective, and fun way to transport data. This case may be extreme, but the point is, don't batter your disks.

The danger isn't to the disk itself so much as to the read/write heads inside the drive. A floppy with a bent shutter can jam inside and even shear off the top of the read/write head, which is not easy or cheap to fix. If you have a floppy that contains vital data and has a bent shutter, very carefully remove the shutter, move the data to a safer place, and then "throw" the damaged floppy away.

Drinking around your disks can be dangerous

If you spill water or soft drinks on a disk, your data may survive the event, but don't try to recover the data immediately. Wait a few days. Even if it's critical data, don't put it in your drive unless you're ready to pay for repairs on the drive. Let the floppy dry and then open the shutter and check the media. Only after you've verified that there's no moisture anywhere inside can you put the disk in. Rotate the disk inside its case to look at the entire floppy before putting it in the drive.

In a worst-case scenario, if you really have to have the data, you can pop the floppy's case open and very carefully—without touching the surface of the disk—remove the media and let it dry in the open. Take a second floppy, pop it open, and put the dry disk in the new case, and then tape the whole thing shut and try it in the drive. There are no guarantees—a blob of sugar from a soft drink can still gum up the works—but this is better that having a company collapse for lack of proper accounting data.

Don't force it

Removing a floppy from its drive is usually easy. Hit ⌘-Y or drag the disk image to the Trash. If the drive won't let go or doesn't recognize the disk, here are a few things to try, in this order:

1. Push a paper clip through the manual eject hole.

2. Restart your Mac while holding the mouse button down.

3. Push a paper clip through the manual eject hole while very carefully lifting up the disk with a thin object, such as a letter-opener. This one's dangerous: don't force anything. If it's stuck, it's stuck, and you'll have to take the drive apart.

Never force a disk into a drive. The rack that holds the floppy drive case in place may have slipped or bent. Look through the slot to see if anything is in the way. If it looks like the case of the drive itself is in the way—sort of like an elevator between floors—open the Mac and try to line it up again. (Read about opening the case in the section "Cleaning a Drive" a little later in this chapter.)

Read/write errors and unreadable disks

By far the simplest fix for a disk is to have it in the right format. Did some guy down the hall give you the disk and said that it was formatted? You probably can't even read it, right? First, what kind of computer was he using? If it was a DOS machine, he may have given you a DOS disk, which is an entirely different format. Fortunately, Apple supplies a utility called PC Exchange, which enables your Mac to read and write to DOS disks, as do many third-party utilities such as Access PC and DOS Mounter. They're all extensions, so be sure you have at least one (and not more than one) loaded. Even if the person who gave you the disk was using a Mac, he or she still might have been reading and writing to a DOS disk.

Another, slightly more insidious issue is the gradual change in hardware over time. The 128K, 512K, Plus, and some SEs and Mac IIs can only read 400K and 800K disks. There's no way to make a 128K, 512K, or Plus read the now-popular 1.4 MB disks. An older SE and a Mac II can be taught to read them, but only by buying a new drive for each—the Mac II also requires a new chip on its motherboard. The way to tell if a disk is 1.4 MB is to count the holes in the upper edge of the disk. A double-density (DD) disk holds no more than 800K, although it can be formatted as a 400K disk. It only has one hole. High-density disks hold as much as 1.4 MB and have a second hole on the opposite side.

Remember that if you have an older drive that doesn't recognize 1.4 MB floppies and you put a 1.4 MB floppy in, the Mac will think it's unformatted and ask you if you'd like to format it. Formatting a 1.4 MB disk as an 800K disk can lead to data loss. A quick fix is to cover the second hole with a piece of tape and format away, but it's a hazardous operation that should be used only in emergencies. It won't hurt your drive, but your data might not be saved to the floppy.

Note

If you're thinking about adding a hole to an 800K floppy to make it into a 1.4 MB floppy, it's risky. In a pinch it might hold your data for awhile, but the two use different media designed for different specifications. It will more than likely fail. Format 800K floppies as 800K and 1.4 MB floppies as 1.4 MB unless you're desperate.

It is possible to use a 400K disk as an 800K; if the 400K formats properly the first time it's probably okay. The only difference between an 800K and 400K drive is the number of heads; an 800K has one on top and one on the bottom; the 400K only has one head on the top.

A caveat: If the 400K disk has long been used as a 400K, don't try to make it into an 800K disk. The 400K drives have a pad where the second head would be in an 800K drive, much like a cassette recorder's. It presses the media up into the upper head and wears out the media on the bottom. That lower media hasn't been closely checked by the manufacturer, either. The unused side only has media to keep the floppy from curling up.

Here is something to remember for 128K and 512K Macs HFS disks. Apple changed the way the Mac file system works with the introduction of the Plus, so if you're wondering whether your machine will read HFS disks, Apple very conveniently put a pixel in every window to tell you. It's in the upper left corner at the edge of the double line that separates the window's header info from the icons themselves.

Non-HFS systems are by-and-large pre-SE machines, but check the pixel to be sure. The pixel was no longer used after System 7, which requires the HFS filing system, so rest assured that your Quadra is an HFS machine.

Wandering Alignment

Not all drives behave exactly the same way. A read/write head jumping back and forth madly for hours and hours can gradually move out of alignment. It may not be exactly centered over the tracks that were written when the disk was formatted. One drive may run a little to the inside of the ideal, another to the outside. A disk taken from one machine may not work properly on another. If the machine in question seems to format, read, and write disks that it alone created and modified, and won't read any other disks, its head may be out of alignment.

It is also possible the disk itself has changed. If it was formatted in a cold environment and you're trying to read it in a hot environment, the variance between machines may have been exaggerated just enough by the disk's expansion or contraction to cause an error. Find out where it came from, and then either cool it or warm it and try again.

Failing media

The media on floppy disks isn't permanent and does wear out. Sometimes it comes from the factory with physically bad blocks, but the standard System 7 Finder formatting process marks them so they can't be used. If you're using System 6 or earlier, the Finder will simply tell you the disk is bad, but you may be able to mark the bad blocks with a third-party utility such as MacTools or Symantec Utilities and continue using the disk. Do this only if you really need it because errors tend to propagate. If an error develops after the disk has been formatted, you may have to use an application to retrieve data from the disk. For example, if you insert an often-used disk and the Finder asks if you'd like to format it, don't do so—formatting will destroy all the data on the floppy.

Reformatting will fail in at least one special case. Apple's DiskCopy utility reformats disks to make an exact copy of another disk, and every physical block must be functional for DiskCopy to work. If you're trying to make a copy of a disk and DiskCopy returns with an error -84, it's found a bad block. That doesn't mean the disk is all bad—formatting it with the Finder will mark that bad block (or blocks)—but if you do a lot of DiskCopy work, you might as well label that disk as a -84 and keep it in a separate stack.

Avoiding known PowerBook problems

The PowerBook 140 disk drive does not seem to be properly shielded from its display's backlight. Apple will install a new shield at no charge if you ask, but it's probably easier to simply switch off the back light when you encounter a disk that can't be read. If you suffer a failure with a 1.4 MB disk, you are probably having other problems because 800K disks seem to be the only disks affected by the back light.

Watching time

Disks fail over time. The magnetic media on their surfaces isn't permanently stable, and the data stored on them will eventually randomize. If you have data that you need to keep for several years, don't store it on a disk. In several years you may find you have errors on every one of them—possibly terminal errors. They may last without a problem, but don't count on it. For long-term storage, look into magneto-optical (MO) drives or even CD-ROM, depending on your budget. They remain stable for decades.

Cleaning a drive

This is not meant to be a full repair manual, but if you're handy with a screwdriver, you can clean a floppy drive yourself. It's not for the mechanically challenged, but it can be done. Before you dig in, remember to have a static strap on hand.

1. Start by opening the case. Remove the logic board so you won't accidentally damage it.

2. Remove the four screws on the outside of the drive's metal case. Carefully slide the drive out of the front of the metal case, and give the case a good cleaning. You can blow out a lot of dust with a can of compressed air, but be very careful blowing canned air on the heads; you can knock them out of alignment. Do not use a standard vacuum cleaner: they generate a lot of static electricity that can fry your hardware.

Again, as you pull out the drive, be sure not to touch the drive heads; it's too easy to throw them out of alignment. Head cleaning is best done by your regular cleaning disk, and any dust around the assembly can be blown out, or removed with a very light paint brush.

3. Now that you have the drive, find the drive head, the slider rod, and the worm drive. Viewing the drive from the front, the slider is a smooth, usually polished rod that's below and to the left of the head. The worm drive is to the right. There's also a small pin connected to the worm gear that drives the head laterally over the disk. To the rear and left of the head is an optical switch. A bar on the left of the lower head passes through it and determines where track zero is on the disk.

4. Make sure both the optical switch and the bar that marks track zero are clean. Likewise for the slider and worm gear. If they're dusty, the head will occasionally fail to reach track zero, causing read/write errors. Carefully clean the slider rod and worm with a soft cloth and gentle solvent. The grease used in drives often becomes sticky with age; you may have to pick out clumps of grease from around the moving parts with a cotton swab.

5. After everything's clean, coat the moving parts with a very light layer of Teflon-based lubricant. Duralube will do the job. Do not use graphite; it will destroy your read/write head. To keep the drive clean in the future, you can put on a dust protection sleeve, which is available from Apple (part #076-0439).

6. Reassemble the pieces and put the drive back into the machine. If you put a floppy in the drive and it either fails to slide in easily or won't eject properly, the drive may not be lined up with the slot on the Mac case. You may have to adjust the screws and brackets that hold the drive.

While you're inside the Mac's case and floppy drive, you will probably find piles of dust. The cooling fans on the Mac IIcx, IIci, and Quadra 700 actually draw air through the floppy drive. If you have a vacuum cleaner with a reversible flow, don't use it in your Mac. They create great quantities of static electricity that can fry your hardware. Buy a can or two of compressed air from a computer or photo supply store and clean the computer in a well-ventilated area. (It won't do you much good to blow all the dust out if it settles right back in.)

Before putting in a valuable disk, be sure to clean the drive with a floppy cleaning disk, just in case some lubricant or dust dropped onto the read/write heads. It's also a good idea to put the drive through its paces, reading and writing a noncritical floppy before going back to the daily grind.

How to Hire Consultants and Repair People

Another option for troubleshooting and repairing Macs is to hire a consultant. Consultants can range to specialists or generalists in a particular software genre, or technology for a specific group of people such as a home user or individual, to a person who can provide system administration and help desk services to an entire company, or many groups within a company.

Consultants can be both troubleshooting experts and tutors. However, since each of us has a variety of preferences for how we learn, communicate and solve problems, you should interview, if not have a trial period if you want to consider hiring a consultant. In the interview, you may want to ask if the consultant has worked with problems similar to the ones your are having with your Macintosh, as well as how much time the person has spent with your model of Macintosh, System software and software applications. You should try to find a consultant who has supported as close to a configuration as you own as this will hopefully expedite solving problems as they arise.

Some consultants work at hourly or task-based rates. Others require contracts which can involve any combination of overhead costs, including a block of minimal time the consultant must work in order start troubleshooting a task, set of tasks, or other work. During the interview, if you are seriously considering hiring the person to consult, you should request billing rates, and policies before the consultant begins billing you.

The value of Apple authorized dealers?

Apple authorized dealers are generally computer dealers who have been certified and trained to sell and repair Macintosh computers. These companies will have the latest Macintosh models, as well as information on System software and updates available from Apple. If you purchase your Macintosh from an authorized Apple dealer, they can be an invaluable resource to you as a customer especially if you have questions about your Macintosh hardware or System software.

Buying spare parts for future self fixes

Your Macintosh CPU does not have any parts which require regular replacement. Hard drive, CD-ROM drives, and expansion cards for NuBus, PDS, or PCI also generally do not require any additional parts for replacement. If you do not have another hard drive, or DAT peripheral for backups, you may want to consider having an ample supply of floppies available to backup critical files on your hard drive. However, using floppy disks for backups can be very tedious, and over time, is may be more cost-efficient to do at least a partial backup to another hard drive, or subscribe to a backup service (if one is available in your area). Note that if you use an external source for backups, you may be sacrificing the security or integrity of your information.

Hardware which does have parts which you may want to stock up on include printers, scanners, and removable media. Printers commonly require replacement of ink jet or toner cartridges, in addition to a constant paper supply. Most scanners have a bulb located below the glass table, which may need to be replaced if and when the bulb goes out. Removable media does not generally require parts to be replaced, however, since removable media by nature requires a library of media for backups or storage, you should have at least a small supply of the removable media handy, just in case you want to avoid a possible shortage of removable media during a hasty deadline.

Safety and Work Environment Considerations

The most basic tenet of any electrical area environmental configuring is to keep electricity in the wire, going around and around exactly as it should. If electricity goes where it shouldn't, it could result in disaster. The most important and basic electrical requirement is to ensure that electricity stays in the wire and circulates properly.

To start, keep all liquids away from electronics, especially when you are upgrading or repairing. When the case is off, you can come into direct contact with enough voltage to damage yourself and new equipment. Liquid and electronics just don't mix. Liquids are highly conductive and can fry whatever they touch—a new scanner or a hard drive; or yourself. A fifty-cent cola can ruin a thousand-dollar motherboard, an expensive hard drive, or a print engine.

Avoid excessive environmental moisture and dust, and keep the room at a comfortably cool temperature with a source of fresh air available. (Fluorescents also help to reduce the temperature because they employ charged particle gas that generates little heat, and not hot filaments like a standard bulb.) Fresh air in the room keeps static electricity to a minimum. Though static doesn't usually cause catastrophic damage to the computer, it can create gremlins—inexplicable events that ruin floppies, or cause your machine to lock up. Open windows can add moisture. Keep your eye on the barometer and your Mac away from windows to prevent weather damage.

Tobacco smoke is also something to keep away from electronics. If you must smoke, get a smoke-eating ashtray or at least a fan. Smoke may not kill your computer, but you may have a hard time reselling yellow, tobacco-smell equipment. The platinum and beige plastic casings on Macs and peripherals are notorious for attracting dirt and are nearly impossible to clean once stained.

The tars and resins from smoke collect on your electronics and facilitate air particles to collect on the insides of your computer, which will degrade performance. Dust and particles contain trace amounts of conductive material, liquids, and even live microorganisms—all of which conduct electricity.

Consumer level air filtration devices and negative ion generators are of marginal use; they basically move the air around, remove small amounts of debris, or cause dust to fall to the floor—and on your equipment.

Tables and supports

Many users don't think of their desks as important Mac peripherals. Many computer owners get by with a work table at keyboard/mouse height, makeshift shelving for peripherals, and the floor.

The proper furniture, however, will fix many basic problems that can have a monumental effect on the working relationship with your computer—a science known as ergonomics. An ergonomic desk can fix improper position and angle of the monitor, flexibly gauge the correct proximity of the keyboard and mouse to you, as well as elegantly incorporate a cable run or even power. Environmental factors within the workspace can be the easiest and cheapest ways to minimize or eliminate a potentially hazardous workspace situation.

Though there are many different computer desks, an excellent choice are ScanCo's (800-722-6263) MacTables. They are ergonomic solutions for specific Apple models made by hand using real wood (not veneered plywood and particle board found in many cheaper computer desks). Another excellent Mac furniture product is the Anthro Corp. (503-241-7113) Anthro Cart line of computer furniture. This company's furniture has more than forty accessories to customize it for your setup. A multitude of computer furniture is available now; you only have to imagine your configuration and it is probably sold somewhere near you—check the Yellow Pages under furniture. Don't be surprised to find that most furniture companies and furniture makers feature computer furniture. You can find anything from a highly integrated, rolling single-person desk with built-in cable routing, and sliding keyboard rack with a swinging printer tray and monitor shelf to an electrically grounded, modular, triangular, polymer-extruded, multiuser group workstation hub. Definitely a step up from a door on two filing cabinets!

When shopping for Mac furniture, remember that your computer determines which furniture you can buy. Make sure the Mac desk/table accommodates the specific model you own. With a floor standing Mac like the Quadra 950, you might want to buy a smaller desk with a floor level shelf to hold the tower CPU.

If security is an issue, some desks have integrated steel loops for metal wire security cables and padlocks that lock onto the Mac. Some desks even have integrated power strips and small strip lights under the desk to illuminate your wiring. Regardless of these features, try to find a desk with as low a center of gravity as possible, and stay away from precarious shelves. In addition, make sure you haven't placed heavier peripherals on lighter ones or placed monitors too close together.

For Mac users in California, keeping your Mac safe during an earthquake is a serious concern. A few recommendations:

- Keep your CPU as close to the floor as possible.

- Don't put your Mac underneath anything heavy.

- Leave your SCSI devices plugged in but not screwed in (many SCSI cables have thumb-tighten end screws which secure the cable to the computer). If an earthquake were to strike (or other horizontally disabling event), the device would disconnect and not be dragged to the floor.

- Use lots of Velcro on the feet and undersides of your peripherals, keyboards, and drives; Velcro offers flexible protection for jarring and rolling.

Device proximity problems

Some peripherals can be fussy and problematic when placed too close to each other. Monitors are particularly fussy when placed too close to poorly shielded devices that contain fans or generate magnetism. Monitors in this type of environment display wavy pictures. Sometimes radio frequencies generated by nearby outdoor radio towers can be strong enough to affect your monitor's picture stability. Even a monitor plugged into a power strip that also supplies power to decent-size room fan can be affected. This might be the fault of thinly insulated monitor cables. Shields made by the No-Rad company, designed to cut ELF, are rumored to help prevent monitor picture inconsistencies resulting from emitted radio and low frequency emissions. An inexpensive collar of Ferrite metal beads can be purchased in most computer or electronics stores to clip onto the neck of the cable near the monitor, which will help to eliminate any line RF in either direction.

Scanners and external hard disks generate a decent amount of heat and need fresh air for cooling. Give them 3 to 6 inches at least for healthy operation. Keep them out of the sun and away from each other. In addition, before you tip any devices (such as hard drives) on their sides, make sure you don't block any strategic air input hole or face the air intake directly into the back of other devices that may be emitting hot or positively charged stale air.

Troubleshooting Software

Keep in mind that no software is perfect, all software has problems. Hence, learning to troubleshoot has become an integral part of using a computer. The best way to troubleshoot software problems is to become familiar with your software configurations; get to know your machine—the software that you're running (including version numbers) and the extensions that you have in your System Folder. Write this information down somewhere, because you'll need it in the troubleshooting process.

Software Troubleshooting

The Macintosh Operating System can be the simplest software to use, and, at times, the most complex. System errors can occur when it appears your Macintosh is not performing any work, or when you try to launch a control panel, desk accessory, or file. Other times you may not know why your menu bar flashes, the icons become generic, or your audio CD isn't recognized as a readable disk by the System. This section provides a checklist to help you determine the System software configuration, and identify any potential problem areas. First, let's identify your software configuration:

1. Select About this Macintosh from the Apple Menu to identify which version of System software you are running.

2. Select the System Folder, then select Get Info from the File menu and note how much hard drive space the System software occupies. An Easy Install of System software will take up 5–7 MB of hard drive space. Additional technologies, such as QuickDraw GX, Speech Manager, PowerTalk, QuickDraw 3D, OpenTransport, and OpenDoc take from 2 MB to more than 10 MB of additional hard drive space.

3. Open the Memory Control Panel and see if Virtual Memory is "on" or "off".

4. Open the Sharing Setup Control panel and see if File Sharing is "on" or "off".

5. Check the Extensions folder in the System Folder to see how many extensions exist. Any extension files in this folder will load when you start your Mac.

6. Identify how much free space is available on the hard drive where the System Folder is located.

7. Be sure you have a copy of the System Software Disk Tools disk for either System 7.5, or other System software versions that support the Macintosh model.

8. Back up the System Folder to facilitate troubleshooting and as preventative maintenance.

The System Folder should contain at least a System and Finder File along with the following folders: Apple Menu Items, Control Panels, Extensions, Fonts, Preferences, Startup Items, and Shutdown Items. If you do not see these files in the System Folder, you either have System 6, or the System Folder contents may be damaged.

Common System software problems

Here is a brief list of common System software problems and steps for troubleshooting and repairing System 7 software.

Some or all of my icons have become generic in appearance.

Possible Causes

If you copy and delete many files onto and off your hard drive, the desktop database can run out of room for new icons. As a result, it will show a generic icon, or older icon that shares the same icon number.

Macintosh Easy Open preferences may be damaged.
A previous incomplete build of the desktop may have occurred.
The file System may have errors or be damaged.
Some files may be corrupted.
Possible virus infection.

Checkpoints

If you have System 7.5, or have Macintosh Easy Open installed on the System, open the Macintosh Easy Open control panel and select the Delete Preferences button. Restart your Mac, and the desktop will be rebuilt, returning custom icons to the file System.

You can also rebuild the desktop manually by holding down the command-option keys during startup. A dialog box will appear asking if you really want to rebuild the desktop. Click OK; a progress bar will appear. When this operation is complete, your custom icons should appear. If the progress bar is canceled, some or all of the icons will appear with generic icons because the desktop database will not be properly or completely updated.

10

I get a System error when I try to open a control panel.

Possible causes

Extensions conflict.
File System errors.
Control Panel file damaged.
System software corruption.
Not enough memory to open the control panel.

Checkpoints

Try to remember which control panel created the System error. If all control panels generate a System error, try restarting your Macintosh with the Shift key held down. This deactivates extensions. Then, see if you can open the culprit control panel. If the System error still occurs, try starting up from the Disk Tools floppy to see if the problem goes away. If it does, consider performing a clean installation of the System software.

System 7.5 has a special feature for creating a new system folder. After launching the installer script for system 7.5, press the ⌘-Shift-K keys and a window will appear with two system software installation options. Choose the option to create a new system folder. See the "Easy Fixes" section in this chapter for a more detailed description of system software installation.

I get an out of memory error message when I try to open a folder.

Possible causes

One large software application, or several smaller applications prevent the System from having enough memory to support opening a new folder or window.
Not enough physical memory to open Finder windows or folders.

Checkpoints

This is a known limitation in System software. This can be caused by memory management problems in the System; either an incorrect or insufficient de-allocation of memory when quitting an application, desk accessory, or changing a control panel setting. The easiest (although not always the quickest) way to get rid of this error message is to restart your Macintosh. Be sure to save any documents-in-progress, or other files before restarting or shutting down your Macintosh.

Command-Control-Powerkey is built into system 7.5, and will restart your Macintosh if you are unable to access the Shutdown menu. ⌘-Control-Escape will bring up a debugger if one is installed, and, if not, a blank window will appear. Press the letter g to make the blank window go away.

If you do not have system 7.5, you can install Programmer Key 1.4.1 software to add these features to the system software, or use the hardware switches located on the hardware case to restart or activate the debugger on your Macintosh. Upon restart the "Incorrect Shutdown" error message will appear unless you turn off this message in the General Controls control panel (Select or de-select "Warn me if computer was shutdown improperly.") Install more memory onto your motherboard.

If you don't mind slower performance, turn virtual memory on.

Restart your Macintosh and the problem should go away.

My System runs really slow when I try to play QuickTime movies.

Possible causes

Personal File Sharing is on.
Virtual Memory is on.
Hard drive is fragmented.
Printing a file or files in the background.
Calculate folder sizes is on.
On PowerBooks, hard drive spin down and power conservation settings are too conservative.

Checkpoints

Turn off Virtual Memory and File Sharing and see if QuickTime movies play more smoothly or faster. You may also want to turn off all extensions except for the QuickTime extension(s) to see if performance improves for movie playback. Also, compare playback performance with the movie file on another hard drive or another Mac to see if the problem may just be a poorly recorded QuickTime movie.

My Macintosh only recognizes certain types of CDs.

Possible causes

Incomplete installation of CD-ROM software.
Dirty or scratched CD media.
CD drive improperly connected to Macintosh.

Checkpoints

Apple's CD-ROM software consists of many files that allow System software to correctly identify and read a variety of CD-ROM discs. To play audio CDs with an Apple CD-ROM player, you need the Apple CD-ROM extension, Foreign File, ISO9000, and audio CD access files in the extensions folder. Non-Apple CD players should have similar files for recognizing different types of compact discs. The following Apple CD-ROM software is for version 5.1.2. Run the Apple CD software installer to re-install this software in the System Folder.

Apple CD-ROM extension
Apple Photo Access
Foreign File Access
ISO 9660 File Access
High Sierra File Access
Audio CD Access
Apple CD Player application

When I click on a file, the System says I don't have the application to open the file.

Possible causes

Macintosh Easy Open not installed.
No software applications on hard drive.

Checkpoints

If you have System 7.5 or System 7.1, you don't need the original application to launch the document or file you want to open. System 7.5 ships with Macintosh Easy Open and DataViz translators, which enable you to open files orphaned from their original applications. Macintosh Easy Open 1.1.1 includes three main components: Macintosh Easy Open Control Panel 1.1.1, Document Converter 1.1, and the DataViz folder. This folder contains MacLink Plus files and a Language folder containing language conversion files.

My System appears to crash sporadically and inconsistently.

Possible causes

Extension conflicts.
Too many extensions.
Extensions not 32-bit clean.
Software applications not 32-bit clean.
File System errors or data corruption.
Possible virus attack.

Checkpoints

When you first start your Macintosh, you should create a backup of the System Folder in its 'clean' configuration. This clean folder most likely will not have any built-in extension or other software conflicts. You might want to avoid using compression software or backup software for the System software backup. Unlike previous versions of System software, System 7.5 files are all compressed on floppy and CD-ROM. You need a backup that allows you to access individual files and folders in case you want to restore a partial or complete backup of the System Folder.

To resolve an extension conflict, move half of the System extensions out of the System Folder; then restart your Mac to see if the problem caused by the extension conflict goes away. If the problem goes away, put the extensions you moved out of the System Folder back in one by one until you identify the extension responsible for the software problem. After you know which extension(s) is incompatible, you might want to see if a newer version of the extension is available that fixes the problem. Another option is to find software with similar features that does not cause problems.

I installed more memory on my Macintosh, but the System only sees 8 MB and the System file has grown much larger.

Possible causes

Macintosh is in 24-bit mode.
Memory not completely installed in SIMM slot.
Memory installed partially, or in wrong SIMM slots.

Checkpoints

For your Macintosh to see more than 8 MB of physical memory, it must be in 32-bit mode. This can be set in the Memory control panel. If the System is in 24-bit mode, only 8 MB of physical memory will be recognized, and any additional memory is added to the System file memory. To see how much memory is available on your Macintosh, select About this Macintosh from the Apple menu in the Finder. The amount of built-in memory indicates the total amount of physical DRAM installed on the motherboard.

Troubleshooting the startup process

With a healthy Mac, accessing the desktop is something taken for granted. The startup tone, Happy Mac icon, the familiar "Welcome to Macintosh" greeting, and the parade of icons across the bottom of the screen are certainly reassuring to the user (and the technician!). The more you know about the startup process, the more effectively and efficiently you can address common startup problems.

In this next section, the entire startup sequence from beginning to end is covered in a comprehensive list of all the normal Macintosh startup processes. The two main stages of the startup sequence are discussed, and then each step is explained in detail.

In the second part of this section, common problems you're likely to encounter during startup are revealed—roadblocks on the road to the desktop. The different types of error messages and other signals that the Mac communicates with, can tell you what's wrong.

Finally, this section discusses the infamous "icon parade" software that loads at startup: extensions (or INITs, as they're called under System 6). You will learn what they are, what problems they can cause, and how to manage them.

The Startup sequence

From the time you hit the power switch to the time the Mac reaches the desktop, dozens of processes take place in a specific sequence, known as the startup sequence. With every group of processes, the Mac will provide visual and/or audible cues indicating that a process has succeeded or failed. If you know this sequence, as well as its cues, you know that the Mac is often verbose about its condition. If it's healthy, it will say so. If it's not, it will tell you where it hurts.

The startup sequence has two main stages: Initialization and System Startup. The following sections define these stages and break them down into their component steps.

Stage I: Initialization

In this stage, the Mac checks its hardware and firmware and loads portions of the System from ROM necessary to proceed to the second stage. Initialization means setting variables to their starting values and clearing RAM data in preparation for use. The sequence is as follows:

1. Startup: You hit the power switch or issue a restart command.

2. Logic board test and initialization: The Apple Sound Chip (ASC), Serial Communications Controller (SCC), Small Computer Systems Interface (SCSI) controller, Super Wozniak Integrated Machine (SWIM) or Integrated Woz Machine (IWM), and Versatile Interface Adapter (VIA) chips are all subjected to a series of diagnostic routines. If they pass, they are initialized.

3. Startup tone: On Macs prior to the Mac II, this is a single tone. From the Mac II up to the PowerBooks and Quadras, the Mac plays a three note chime. The PowerBooks and Quadras introduce a new sound, a synthesizer "pad" plays a major chord. The AV Macs play a lower, longer chord with a slightly different synthesizer sound. (No, it's not the regular Quadra sound slowed down.) The Power Macs play a chord of guitar harmonics; for trivia buffs, a chord from jazz guitarist Stanley Jordan.

4. RAM test: A complete RAM test is run at power up. After a Restart, the Mac performs a much shorter test.

5. Start Manager: The Start Manager is initialized. The type and clock speed of the CPU is checked and stored in RAM for use by the OS and applications. (Note that this sequence accommodates accelerators, rather than assumes the Mac will have the CPU that shipped with the unit.) If the Mac has a 68020 or later, the instruction caches are enabled.

6. RAM initialization: Essential RAM values used by the OS are initialized.

7. Memory mode setting: 32-bit Macs prior to the Quadra AVs are set to 24-bit mode by default (or if 24-bit addressing was last selected in the Memory control panel). The AV Macs and Power Macs run only in 32-bit mode.

Note

If you run your Mac in System 7 with 32-bit addressing enabled and have just switched to System 6 without resetting the memory addressing, the Mac will display an error message telling you that it has switched to 24-bit addressing, and it will ask you to restart. This, however, doesn't happen until much later in the boot process. Why? For one thing, the Mac doesn't know what version of the System it's going to be running yet. Also, essential resources necessary to display and process the error haven't been loaded yet, including QuickDraw, the Error Manager, and ADB (Apple Desktop Bus) routines. You won't see this error until after step 12 in the System Startup stage.

8. System heap: The area of RAM used by the System is reserved.

9. Slot Manager: The Slot Manager is initialized; ROMs on NuBus/PDS cards are read and, if applicable, initialized.

10. ADB Manager: The ADB (Apple Desktop Bus) Manager is initialized, except on the Mac Plus and earlier. Mouse tracking is not yet enabled, but keyboard tracking is.

11. Video initialization: In modular Macs, the Start Manager chooses between internal and card-based video for the primary display.

12. QuickDraw is initialized.

13. Gray desktop appears.

14. SCSI, Disk, and Sound Managers are all initialized.

15. Pointer appears on desktop.

Note that we have not yet seen the Happy Mac icon. All this happens very quickly. The RAM test is the longest part of the initialization stage.

Stage II: System startup

In the second stage, the Macintosh Operating System and its extensions are loaded into RAM as follows:

1. Default startup disk: The Mac reads the PRAM to determine the SCSI ID of the device selected in the Startup Disk control panel. If ID is selected, and the Mac finds a drive at that ID, the Mac will wait 15-30 seconds for the drive to spin up. (Fifteen seconds is the default; the wait time is adjustable with numerous SCSI utilities.) Otherwise, it will go directly to step 2.

2. Startup device scan: The Start Manager scans for a startup device in the following order: internal floppy drive(s); external floppy drive; serial (non-SCSI) hard drive; default startup device; and any other valid startup device on the SCSI bus. The Mac scans the SCSI bus in this sequence: First, it checks device ID# 0, and then the Start Manager cycles continuously from ID# 6 down to 0. The floppy drives are also polled during each cycle.

Note

In the first generation of the Mac Plus, the Start Manager cycled through the SCSI addresses only once. Apple fixed this and related bugs in the later ROM revisions.

3. Boot blocks: The Start Manager reads the boot blocks from the startup disk. These contain crucial information required to start up from a volume.

4. SCSI drivers: The SCSI device drivers are loaded by the SCSI manager, starting with the boot drive and continuing in the same order as the Start Manager's scan.

5. The Happy Mac displays as the startup device's SCSI driver loads.

6. System file: The Mac now opens the System file on the startup volume.

7. The Resource Manager, System Error handler, and Font Manager are initialized.

8. Welcome to Macintosh: This message is read from the System's 'DSAT' resource displays.

9. Debugger: If MacsBug or another debugger is present, it loads now and displays a message beneath the System's "Welcome to Macintosh" message to let you know that it's installed.

10. ROM patches: Patches to the ROM are now read from the open System file and loaded into RAM.

11. ADB: On all Macs after the Mac Plus, the ADB routines are loaded into RAM.

12. Mouse tracking is now enabled.

13. NuBus drivers: Driver software for some NuBus cards will load at this time. Other NuBus drivers may be loaded with the extensions.

14. Disk Cache: The Disk Cache in System 7, or "RAM cache" in System 6, is created.

15. Application heap: The area of RAM used for applications is reserved and initialized.

16. Extensions: Extensions containing INIT code are loaded into the System heap in sequence. Most extensions display icons onscreen as they load.

17. Heap adjustment: The System heap is adjusted to account for the extensions loaded.

18. Finder: The Finder loads into memory.

Note

If your Mac is running under System 6 in Finder mode, and you have selected a startup application with the Set Startup dialog, that application will load instead of the Finder. Installer and commercial utility emergency disks use a similar mechanism to launch directly into their applications under System 7.

19. Desktop: Assuming you are running the Finder, the desktop now appears. As volumes mount on the desktop, items appear in their desktop folders.

20. Startup Folder: Any items in the Startup Folder will now open. In MultiFinder under System 6, applications selected in Set Startup will launch after the Finder.

Error handling and the "Stopup sequence"

Now that you know what happens when everything works, how can you apply all this information to troubleshooting? First, you need to understand the basic vocabulary the Mac uses for communicating problems. As you've seen, the Macintosh has some sophisticated methods of testing for problems and for reporting them. To start, familiarize yourself with the error reporting mechanisms of the Macintosh: the error codes, or Sad Mac; and the error sounds, or Death Tones.

The Sad Mac

You'll recall that, during the System Startup stage, the Mac—once it has found a valid startup volume—flashes an icon on screen known as the Happy Mac. In the "Stopup" Sequence (when something isn't working right), you're confronted with the alter ego of the Happy Mac, the Sad Mac. Like the Happy Mac, the Sad Mac is an icon resembling a compact Macintosh that is displayed by the Mac ROM and appears in the center of the screen. The resemblance, however, ends there. First, the icon is obviously different; it has a distinctly somber appearance. Second, the Sad Mac always appears on a black screen, rather than a gray one. Third, the Sad Mac stays on screen until you either restart or turn off the Mac. Finally, the Sad Mac displays beneath it a one or two line hexadecimal error code. That error code tells you a great deal about what's wrong with the Mac; often, it tells you all you need to know.

Sad Mac error codes appear in one of two formats. The first format is a single line, six character error code format. Figure 10.1 illustrates the way Macintosh computers, up to and including the Mac Plus, display errors.

YYZZZZ

Figure 10.1   Sad Mac YY ZZZZ.

The format is YY ZZZZ, where YY is the class code, and ZZZZ is the sub code. The class code indicates the part of the diagnostic program that has identified the error, and the sub class code tells what the error is. In the case of a bad RAM chip, the sub class identifies the bad chip.

Newer Macs use a 32-bit error code format consisting of two lines of eight characters each (see Figure 10.2).

XXXXYYYY
ZZZZZZZZ

Figure 10.2   Sad Mac XXXXYYYY/ZZZZZZZZ.

In the new format, XXXX is information on the internal test manager state; you can ignore this. The YYYY and ZZZZZZZZ codes correspond to their counterparts in the old format, but they cover a considerably wider range of problems, and present more detailed information.

Appendix A contains a complete table of these error codes. Here are the basics:

- In both error formats, if the Y field ends in $01, you have a ROM failure. The Z field is insignificant. ROM failures are relatively rare.

- If the Y field ends in $02–$05, you have a RAM test failure; the Z field identifies the bad chip(s) or, in the case of a value of $0005, a bad address line.

- If the Y field ends in $0F, you have a 680×0 exception, generally—though not always—due to corrupted System or SCSI driver software, or a damaged partition map. The last two characters in the Z field indicate the nature of the exception.

In addition to these general rules, the 32-bit error code format adds the following:

- $0006–$000D represent component failures on the logic board; the Z field is not applicable. Like ROM failures, these errors are rare.

- $000E is a data bus test failure. The Z field indicates the bad bit; this may be due to a bad data bus, but could also be a bad SIMM. This error is also unusual; standard RAM errors are much more common.

A real-world example of a bad SIMM can illustrate how easy it is to use these error codes. On a Mac Plus, you might see the following error code:

030100

The first two digits tell you that the RAM write test has failed; the remaining four tell you which chip has failed—in this case, chip 8. If more than one chip fails, the Sad Mac displays a summed value. For instance, had chips 8 (0100) and 9 (0200) failed, an error code of 030300 would be displayed.

How would the same bad SIMM look on an SE or Mac II? Like this:

00000003
00000100

In this case, the 0003 at the end of the first line indicates that a SIMM in bank B has failed. (Had the SIMM been in bank A, line one would have ended with 0002.) The 0100 at the end of the second line identifies the bad chip.

Another error code format is used for the Macintosh Portable (see Figure 10.3).

XXXXyyYY
ZZZZZZZZ

Figure 10.3   Sad Mac XXXXyyYY/ZZZZZZZZ.

The XXXX field contains various flags that are used by the start up test routines; these can be ignored. The yy field identifies an exception if there has been one, or reads $00 if there hasn't. The YY field identifies the test during which the failure occurred. The Z field contains additional information about the failure. Here's an example of how a memory failure might appear on a Mac Portable:

    00000102
    00003C5B

The first four digits in line one might be anything; it doesn't matter. The 01 tells you that a bus error occurred, and the following 02 tells you that the error occurred during the RAM test. The second line identifies the bits that failed. The Mac Portable uses a single RAM expansion card, so you would just swap the card.

Death tones

From the Mac II on up, when the Mac crashes during startup, it plays an error sound, or combination of sounds. What you hear will vary from model to model. The Mac II series (including the SE/30) plays a minor chord, and then an ascending series of notes that step through a major chord. These notes may be preceded by one or two other notes; their significance is explained in the next section. Quadras and PowerBooks will play the opening four notes of the Twilight Zone theme (yes, it's deliberate). The Power Macs add a charming new voice to the choir: the sound of a car crash, complete with screeching tires and shattering glass.

Depending on the timing of the error tones, the associated symptoms, and even the notes played, you can determine a lot about the nature of the problem—even with nothing on the screen.

Other signs of trouble

When problems fall outside those parameters, however, things get slightly more complicated. Even the Mac can't perform brain surgery on itself while it's in a coma!

Fortunately, you can use other signs to determine the source of these problems. Most of these signs are described on a case-by-case basis in the next section; a couple of universal symptoms, however, indicate obvious signs of trouble.

If you smell anything burning, or a strong scent of ozone, shut down the Mac as soon as possible. This is nearly always indicative of a power supply failure, even if there are no other outward signs. If you hear unusual noises, even if everything is otherwise working properly, be suspicious. Electronic whistling or squealing are common signs of flyback transformer failure in compact Macs. Mechanical squealing or grinding is the hallmark of a hard drive getting ready to fail. If the sounds started recently, make sure your hard drive is backed up!

Sounds, however, can be deceptive. Some older hard drives sound like a death rattle whenever they're accessed, yet they're perfectly fine. Some newer Quantum hard drives emit a high-pitched whine right out of the box; the vendor may replace the unit for a quieter one, but often the whine will fade as the drive is broken in. There are antistatic tabs over the spindle hubs on old Seagate and MiniScribe drives that become worn down and noisy; simply lifting the tab out of the way will solve this. Finally, some frightening sounds can come from fans. The old "rat cage" fans in SEs are notorious for strange sounds. Stray wires can make it sound as if your external drive is ready to explode; all you need to do is pull the wires to the side, and perhaps hold them back with a tie-wrap. Nevertheless, it is safest to assume the worst when dealing with these signs until you can isolate the cause.

Defining the Stopup sequence

Sad Macs, freezes, flashing disk icons, blank screens, discouraging sounds, and smells are all symptoms that eventually surface during startup. Each symptom occurs at a specific point in the startup sequence. If you recognize the symptom, and know what happens immediately before the symptom occurs, troubleshooting becomes much less a shot in the dark.

The following paragraphs set up a second "startup" sequence; only this time, everything is going to fail. Think of this as the startup sequence's evil twin, or a Mac manifestation of the Dark Side of The Force. It's your worst tech support nightmare. Call it the "Stopup" sequence. The steps briefly address the most common symptoms.

Initialization

All that happens prior to the startup tone is a logic board test and initialization. If you don't hear the tone, the problem is hardware: the logic board, the power supply, or something between the power source and the logic board is faulty. Let's look at the most common variations.

Symptom

You hit the power switch, and nothing happens; no lights, no sounds, no smells.

Possible Causes

Check your power cables at both ends, and try a different cable. If you're using a power strip, make sure it's plugged in, turned on, and that its circuit breaker or fuse hasn't blown.

A capacitor in the Astec power supply in a IIcx, IIci, or Quadra 700 has gone bad. Unplugging and then plugging in the power cable causes the power supply to work for a single startup. You can repair this fairly easily if you're handy with a soldering iron.

The lithium batteries on the Mac II or IIx logic board have gone dead. If they test below 3.3v, replace them.

The power supply is dead. It might be just the switch, or it might need major repairs.

Symptom

The LED lights up and/or the fan comes on, but nothing else happens. You do not hear the startup disk.

Possible causes

The logic board in a compact Mac isn't getting power from the power supply. The cable may be broken, the contacts might be bad, solder joints may be cracked, or a technician (surely not you!) might have forgotten to reattach the cable after servicing the board.

The HMMU on a Mac II logic board is damaged or, if it has a PMMU, the chip is either bad or poorly seated. Replace or reseat the chip.

The logic board is dead.

Symptom

On a compact Mac, all you hear is whining, squealing, chirping, buzzing, or flupping (a low, dull, repetitive sound). There is either no video, or there is distorted video. You might smell burning or ozone.

Possible cause

The power supply/analog board is damaged. Any of a large number of components has failed.

Symptom

On a compact Mac, all you see is a pattern of regular horizontal or vertical lines or a checkerboard on screen.

Possible causes

A stuck programmer's switch. Try removing it.

The ROMs are damaged, poorly seated, flipped, or reversed. Try replacing or reseating them.

A clip-on enhancement to the logic board has failed, come loose, or the contacts have gone bad. Try removing or reseating it.

The IC at analog board reference U2 on the Plus, or U1 on the SE and SE/30, has gone bad, resulting in a pattern of thin, clean horizontal lines. Replace it.

Symptom

Immediately after startup, you see a Sad Mac. There is no startup tone.

Possible causes

A logic board component has failed. Check the Sad Mac error code with the table in Appendix A to determine which component has failed.

A bad or badly seated ROM chip or ROM SIMM is in your Mac. If you have a Sad Mac, check to see if the Y field (the first two characters in a one line error code, or last four characters in the top line of a two line error code) ends in $01.

Symptom

There is no startup tone, but everything else appears to be working perfectly.

Possible causes

The wire from the logic board to the speaker is broken or disconnected, or the speaker itself is dead. Check the connections and, if necessary, try another speaker.

After you've repaired all these problems, the Mac plays its startup tone. From here, it proceeds—or tries to proceed—to the RAM test. In this "stopup sequence," of course, it might not even get as far as the test; when it does, it will fail.

Symptom

Immediately after the startup tone plays, the Mac plays an error tone. The display remains dark.

Possible causes

The logic board is shorting out. Check for dust, loose screws, washers, stray solder, or other conductive foreign material on or beneath the logic board. Remove it; be careful to remain grounded so that you do not damage the logic board with a static discharge.

A poorly installed SCSI cable is on the bus. Make sure all cables are securely fastened.

Symptom

Shortly after the startup tone plays, the Macintosh plays an error tone, and/or a Sad Mac appears. If there is no Sad Mac, the screen will be black.

Possible causes

A bad or badly seated SIMM exists. If a Sad Mac appears, you can use the error code and the table in Appendix A to identify the bad SIMM. On any Mac II series computer, a single note preceding the ascending major chord arpeggio indicates a RAM failure in bank A. If two notes sound (playing an ascending fifth) prior to the arpeggio, the RAM failure is in bank B. For details of RAM configuration and installation in all Mac models, see the Chapter 6 section on RAM.

A damaged SIMM socket is in your Mac. This is common on Macs with all-plastic SIMM sockets, especially those with white plastic, as opposed to black. Apple used all-plastic

SIMM sockets in Macs from the Plus up to the early IIci; thereafter, they switched to SIMM sockets with metal clips to hold the SIMMs in place. Even then, it's possible that one of the pins in the socket is bent or broken—look carefully. If a Sad Mac appears, you can use the error code and the table in Appendix A to identify the bad socket, in case you can't already see the damage.

Tip

SIMM sockets cannot be repaired; they must be replaced with new sockets. This is much less expensive than a new logic board, but is still costly and dangerous. You have to solder a new socket to the logic board. Authorized Apple service centers generally won't even perform this service; they only offer board swaps. Often, however, you can solve the problem of a broken clip with a cheap and easy workaround.

Apply a dab of hot glue where the clip meets the SIMM, while holding the SIMM in place until the glue sets (usually about a minute). This is virtually as secure a bond as the original clip, and you can easily remove the glue whenever you want to upgrade RAM. You can find hot glue and glue guns at any good hardware store. Never use epoxy or any other permanent glue!

Symptom

The startup tone plays, but the screen remains dark. There is no error tone.

Possible causes

The monitor is turned off, disconnected, or the brightness is turned all the way down. Check all these things.

The video card, monitor, or monitor cable is defective. Replace each one until you find the culprit.

Passing the RAM test is a major hurdle. The next step is usually a cinch. However, in the stopup sequence, nothing is easy. If it's not RAM, what could it be? Examining the startup sequence makes it clear.

Symptom

After the tone plays, the Mac freezes; there's no display, no disk activity, and no error tones.

Possible causes

There is a problem with an accelerator, and it is frozen at the point where the Start Manager is checking the CPU. Try reseating or removing it.

There is a problem with a NuBus card. The Mac has frozen either at the point where the Slot Manager is reading/initializing the ROM, or where the Start Manager is initializing video. Remove cards to determine which is causing the problem. Check to see if it needs repairs or requires a ROM upgrade.

Symptom

The Mac gets to the gray desktop, but the pointer never appears; the screen remains gray.

Possible causes

A NuBus video card is causing problems as the Start Manager initializes video. In this case, all disk activity will cease when the gray desktop appears. Remove cards to determine which is causing the problem. Check to see whether the culprit needs repairs or requires a ROM upgrade.

The Mac is configured to use more than one display, and you are not viewing the startup monitor. Disk activity continues after the gray desktop appears. You may need to move, reinstall, or attach a monitor to your other video source, or zap the PRAM and restart.

If the Mac gets as far as the gray desktop and pointer, you know that the initialization stage of the startup sequence is complete. Now you and the Mac may proceed to the System startup stage.

System Startup

In this stage, the first thing the Mac does is search for the startup device. This is often a problem area.

Symptom

After the pointer appears, the Mac freezes on the gray desktop or crashes with a Sad Mac.

Possible causes

The boot blocks on the startup drive are corrupted. The drive is spinning normally.

The partition map on the startup drive is corrupted. The drive is spinning normally.

The PRAM is corrupted. Zap the PRAM and restart. For details on how to zap the PRAM under Systems 6 and 7, see Chapters 3 and 8.

You have a drive with a failed SCSI controller, probably a Conner mechanism. You will not hear the usual sound of the drive spinning, nor feel it vibrate.

There is a problem on the SCSI bus. With the Mac and all SCSI devices turned off, make sure all power and SCSI cables (internal and external) are securely fastened, and that termination is properly configured. Make sure all devices have unique SCSI IDs.

Symptom

On the gray desktop, an icon of a floppy disk appears in the center of the screen with a flashing question mark in it.

Possible causes

No hard drive is connected to the Mac, or none of the attached drives has a valid System Folder. Boot from another disk. If a drive is connected, install a System on it.

The boot blocks on the startup drive are corrupted. The drive is spinning normally.

The partition map on the startup drive is corrupted. The drive is spinning normally.
The startup drive is not spinning due to stiction, or other failure of the drive mechanism
or SCSI controller. You will not hear the usual sound of the drive spinning, nor feel it
vibrate. You may hear a clicking or clunking sound.

There is a problem on the SCSI bus. With the Mac and all SCSI devices turned off, make
sure all power and SCSI cables (internal and external) are securely fastened and that
termination is properly configured. Make sure all devices have unique SCSI IDs.

On a Mac Plus, the external hard drive did not come up to speed in time for the Start
Manager's SCSI bus scan. Restart the Mac.

The PRAM is corrupted. Zap the PRAM and restart. See Chapters 3 and 8 for details on
how to zap the PRAM under Systems 6 and 7.

Symptom

When attempting to start from a floppy disk, the Mac spits the disk out. It might or might
not display an icon of a floppy disk with an X on it.

Possible causes

The floppy disk does not contain a valid System Folder. Use a different floppy disk.

The boot blocks on the startup disk are corrupted.

The floppy drive is dirty, damaged, or misaligned. If this is the case, good startup disks will
not work.

The floppy disk is an original, commercial master disk that was produced in a disk
duplicator. These create problems in some Macs. Try making a copy using Apple's
DiskCopy or a similar utility, and boot from the copy.

Symptom

When attempting to start from a floppy disk, the Mac does not recognize the disk, nor
does it eject it. The floppy disk does not spin, and the drive makes no sound. The Mac
displays a flashing question mark, or boots from another attached startup device.

Possible causes

The floppy drive is damaged or disconnected.

After the Mac successfully reads the boot blocks of a startup disk, the System moves on to
the Happy Mac, the loading of the SCSI drivers, and the very beginning of loading the
System file. This is a vulnerable point in the startup sequence, so expect trouble!

Symptom

The Happy Mac appears, then disappears. It may continue to reappear and disappear, or
disappear once and present you with the flashing question mark.

Possible causes

The startup disk has a corrupted System file. Boot from another disk and perform a clean reinstall of the System on the startup disk. See the section on clean reinstalls of System software earlier in this chapter.

The startup disk has a damaged directory or partition map.

Symptom

The Happy Mac icon appears, followed immediately by a crash. The screen will usually display a Sad Mac or go black. Sometimes, garbage appears on screen, and you can hear odd electronic noises.

Possible causes

The startup disk has a corrupted or incompatible SCSI driver. See the section on hard drives for details on SCSI drivers and hard drive utilities.

The startup disk has a damaged directory or partition map.

The startup disk has a corrupted System file. Boot from another disk and perform a clean reinstall of the System on the startup disk. See "Performing a Clean Install," a little later in this chapter.

Tip

Corrupted SCSI drivers can cause problems on any drive, not just the startup drive. To update the driver on the disk, you need to prevent the bad SCSI driver from loading into RAM. There are two ways to do this. The first is to make sure the drive is off when you start up, and only turned on after you begin booting from another disk. This is harder with internal drives, but it can be done. Make sure the four lead power cable—not the SCSI ribbon cable—is unplugged from the drive mechanism when you start up. Plug it back into the mechanism after the Mac begins booting from another drive.

Another method is to hold down ⌘-Option-Shift-Delete when starting up. This key combination will inhibit the SCSI driver for the device at ID# 0, which the Mac presumes to be the internal hard drive. Once you see the Happy Mac, it's safe to release the keys. If this doesn't work, it might be a problem created by a third-party SCSI driver, or a third-party keyboard that can't handle triple modifier keystrokes.

After you get by the Happy Mac icon, the next stop is the "Welcome to Macintosh" message. This message indicates the actual loading of the System file. If there's anything seriously wrong with the System or the directory structures pointing to it, you're unlikely to get past this point.

Symptom

Instead of the Welcome to Macintosh screen, you get an empty, shimmering, rectangular message box.

Possible causes

The startup disk has a corrupted System file. Boot from another disk and perform a clean reinstall of the System on the startup disk.

The startup disk does not have a Finder on it. This is common when people make drag-copies of commercial installers and emergency floppy disks. Use Apple's DiskCopy or a similar utility to make a sector copy of the original disk, and boot from that.

The startup disk has a damaged directory.

Symptom

Welcome to Macintosh appears, followed immediately by a System error or freeze. There are no icons on the bottom of the screen.

Possible causes

The startup disk has a corrupted System file. Boot from another disk and perform a clean reinstall of the System on the startup disk. See "Performing a Clean Install," a little later in this chapter.

The startup disk has a corrupted or incompatible SCSI driver. See earlier sections in this chapter for details on SCSI drivers and hard drive utilities, and the preceding tip on corrupted SCSI drivers.

The startup disk has a damaged directory or partition map.

The startup disk has a corrupted or incompatible debugger installed, or possibly a copy of the old AutoBlack screensaver that installs in the debugger slot, masquerading as MacsBug. Boot from another startup disk and remove the debugger/screensaver.

The first extension to load is corrupted or incompatible. Under System 7, try booting with the Shift key held down. Under System 6, the most dependable method is to boot from another disk and remove the extension.

Symptom

Instead of Welcome to Macintosh, an error message appears telling you that System 6 does not run in 32-bit mode, and the Mac will reboot in 24-bit mode.

Possible cause

The Mac was last booted under System 7 in 32-bit mode, and was not reset to 24-bit mode in the Memory control panel before booting under System 6. Just click Restart, and let the Mac boot again.

Symptom

Instead of Welcome to Macintosh, an error message appears telling you that the Mac you have requires a newer version of the System.

Possible causes

The startup disk has a version of the System installed that predates the Macintosh model you're using. Use another startup disk, or update the System on the one you have.
You are attempting to boot up a System 7.1-dependent Mac with System 7.1, but you do not have the necessary enabler file installed. Boot from a startup disk that has the enabler, and copy that enabler to the System Folder of the problem startup disk.
After you see the first extension icon, problems that crop up from this point forward are nearly always due to extensions.

Symptom

After extensions start to load, the Mac crashes or freezes.

Possible causes

There is a corrupted or conflicting extension. Hold down the Shift key at startup to disable extensions under System 7. Boot from another disk under System 6 and remove the suspect extension(s).
The startup disk has a corrupted System file. Boot from another disk and perform a clean reinstall of the System.
The startup disk has a damaged directory.
The last extension icon appears, the screen clears, the desktop shows up; but don't get your hopes up yet. You're still not out of the woods!

Symptom

Right after the desktop appears, you get a System error.

Possible causes

The Finder is corrupted. Perform a clean reinstallation of the System.
There is a corrupted or conflicting extension. Hold down the Shift key at startup to disable extensions under System 7. Boot from another disk under System 6 and remove the suspect extension(s).
The startup disk has a damaged directory.
The startup disk has a corrupted Desktop file: rebuild the Desktop.
Insufficient memory to accommodate the entire contents of the System heap. Start up with extensions off, remove some extensions, or install more RAM.
A corrupted or incompatible program is in the Startup Items folder under System 7, or configured as a startup application under System 6. Remove or re-install the program.

That ends the "stopup sequence"; you made it to the desktop! Unfortunately, this scenario does not anticipate every possible problem. By following this guide, however, you can quickly identify and resolve the vast majority of startup sequence problems.
You probably noticed that many of these symptoms stem from the failure of a few specific hardware and software components: power supplies, logic boards, disk drives, SIMMs; SCSI drivers, System files, and extensions. You can also add in the popular corrupted PRAM. Even when the symptoms don't match anything discussed earlier, you can't go too wrong by assuming it was one of these components.

Easy fixes

If you work with Macs, you will eventually have to rebuild the Desktop and reinstall the System. You will probably do both many times. Rebuilding the Desktop is the number one antidote for generic icons and the Application not found alert; System reinstallation is the cure for a whole catalog of ills. Both operations are easy and effective. Although this section is lengthy, when you know the procedures, it takes less time and effort to do them than it does to read about them (or write them!). Familiarize yourself with the routines that follow. The time spent will more than pay for itself in time saved troubleshooting the problems they address.

Rebuilding the Desktop

The Finder has a great deal to remember. It has to keep track of icons, aliases, file types and their parent applications, window positions and views, and more. Because this vital information is different from Mac to Mac, disk to disk, and day to day, the Finder needs a good place to store all this data. This place is the Desktop database.

Under System 6, there is a single, invisible Desktop file per volume, and it stores much of its information as resources. This worked fine for smaller volumes with limited numbers of files, but larger volumes posed a problem due to limitations of the Resource Manager. Apple addressed this first in AppleShare 2.0, their file server software, by including an extension called the Desktop Manager. The Desktop Manager stores all this Finder information in two invisible data files per volume: Desktop DB and Desktop DF. By switching from resource to data format, Apple eliminated the old limitations. (As an added bonus, the new Desktop files are also impervious to viral infection.) They then rolled the Desktop Manager into System 7 as an integrated component rather than an extension.

Tip

Every time you switch between System 6 and System 7, if you have done anything in the Finder at all, the Desktop files will be rebuilt. If you need to switch Systems often and want to avoid excessive Desktop rebuilding, you can install the Desktop Manager extension from AppleShare 2.0.x into the System 6 System Folder. The two Systems will then use the same Desktop file format. Apple does not sanction this, and there is no official source of the Desktop Manager extension other than an old copy of AppleShare, but many people have used this method successfully.

Because these files are constantly open and modified by the Finder, they are highly susceptible to corruption, which can manifest itself in any number of ways: file icons disappearing, files not opening their parent applications when double-clicked, sluggish behavior, and crashes in the Finder. When these files are corrupted, you need to be able to regenerate the data and correct the errors that cause these problems. This process is called rebuilding the Desktop.

Even if your Mac is not having any problems, it's a good idea to rebuild the Desktop files every month or so. When you're having problems you can't figure out, zapping the Desktop files—along with zapping the PRAM—should be one of the first things to try. It may not solve the problem, but it usually doesn't hurt.

Warning

When you have a disk from which you need to recover data, or that is having problems and is not completely backed up, do not rebuild the desktop until the data is secure. If a disk has directory damage or is having trouble with SCSI transfers, any write operation, including Desktop rebuilding, runs the risk of overwriting valid data and further complicating existing directory corruption. If you have any doubts, verify the disk with Apple's Disk First Aid or a commercial disk utility program before proceeding.

Apple's sanctioned method of rebuilding the Desktop is fairly simple. During startup, hold down the Command and Option keys simultaneously until disks start to mount in the Finder. The Finder will then present you with a dialog asking if you're sure you want to rebuild the desktop. If you click OK, the Finder will scan the disk(s) and fix the problems.

Sometimes, Apple's method isn't good enough. Some types of Desktop file corruption are resistant to this method used in the Finder's standard rebuild routine. To get around this, the best thing to do is delete (or "zap") the old Desktop files altogether and have the Finder build new ones from scratch. There are several ways to do this. You can use a utility such as ResEdit to make the Desktop files visible, then drag them to the trash and restart. Under System 7, you can create a folder named Desktop at the root level of the drive, and the Finder—thinking you've recently been running System 6—will build new System 7 Desktop files on restart. Several utilities also are designed to handle this problem. The best of these is MicroMat's freeware TechTool, which enables you to choose the disks that will have their Desktop files rebuilt.

A clean install

When a System file is corrupted, or you want to install a later version of the System, the correct procedure is to run the Installer. If you do a normal install, this will replace or update files in your existing System Folder. A clean install is different. Rather than update the current System Folder, it creates a new one, leaving your old files in place in the old System Folder.

A clean install helps you avoid future corruption problems. Installing over the old System runs the risk of retaining, and even compounding, any corruption. Brand new files are safer. You can be more certain that if a problem is not resolved it is not due to any residual corruption. A normal install doesn't necessarily update all files associated with the System; it might fail to replace a problematic component. Clean installs replace everything. Some forms of directory damage also can cause problems with specific folders. By performing a clean install, you create a new folder, sidestepping any such damage. In addition to these direct benefits, a clean install tends to encourage general housekeeping, which is beneficial in keeping the System stable.

Apple recommends the normal install under normal circumstances, and the clean install specifically for troubleshooting. The author recommends the clean install for all System installations. Why? System corruption is not always obvious; the clean install is a good preemptive strike against future problems. Also, in some circumstances, a normal install can actually create corruption where none was before, especially if the Installer is run while third-party extensions are active.

Performing a clean install

Several methods are available for performing a clean install; the following procedure is thorough and reliable. Before you begin, make sure you have the correct disks for your Macintosh. If you have a Mac with an 800K drive, make sure you have 800K disks. In addition, use a version of the System known to be compatible with your Macintosh model. This includes being sure you have an Install disk with the proper enabler if your Mac requires one. When upgrading to System 7, make sure you have sufficient RAM installed; 4 MB is a realistic minimum. Always use original master disks, or sector copies made with Apple's DiskCopy or a similar utility; don't use Finder copies. Always keep the Installer disks locked.

If you're ready (disks are correct, updated System version, sufficient RAM) follow these steps for a clean install:

1. Start up from the Disk Tools disk, or another startup disk with a clean, Apple-only System, Disk First Aid, and (for an Apple brand hard drive) HD SC Setup. Because of the way extensions patch the System in RAM, they can interfere with any software installation.

2. Run Disk First Aid to make sure there are no problems with the target disk's directory. You also can run one or more current third-party disk utilities such as Norton Utilities, Public Utilities, or MacTools, these programs can find some things that Disk First Aid will miss. You do not want to suffer from or compound an existing directory problem. In addition, check the drive with a current antivirus utility.

Warning

Always back up data on the drive before attempting any directory repairs! If Disk First Aid finds and fixes—or fails to fix—a problem, always verify with another utility. If you cannot get them to agree that the drive is completely fixed, reformat the drive.

3. Make sure the hard drive's SCSI driver is current. If it is an Apple hard drive, use a compatible version of HD SC Setup—preferably the latest available. A suitable version is on the Apple Disk Tools disk, but there may be a more recent version posted online, or on a support disk such as Apple's System Update distribution disks. If you use a third-party formatter, find out what version it is. This step is especially crucial when

upgrading to System 7; older SCSI drivers can cause severe problems that can lead to data loss. Older drives may require that you reformat to install a current driver. Make sure you are backed up before reformatting or "taking over" a drive previously formatted with another product.

4. Make sure at least 5 MB free space is available on the target disk.

5. Move the Finder to another folder, or onto the Desktop. Rename it "Old Finder."

6. Rename the System Folder to "Old System Folder." You should see that the System Folder's icon has changed from its usual, unique icon to that of a regular folder.

7. Restart the Mac. You should see a flashing question mark icon. If the Mac boots from the target disk instead, another System folder is on the disk. Use the Finder's Find feature to find it, move that folder's Finder to the desktop, then place everything in the trash. If there are any others, throw them away too.

8. Restart from an Install disk (System 7) or System Tools disk (System 6). If you're installing System 7.1 on a Mac with an 800K drive, you will need to boot from a hard disk other than the target disk with a clean System (no extensions).

9. Install the System by following the instructions given by the Installer. If the target disk is to be used with one Macintosh, it's preferable to do a Custom Install for that model Mac, adding printer drivers and network software by hand.

10. If you are installing System 7.0 or 7.0.1, the next thing you should do is install System 7 Tune-Up 1.1.1. If you are installing System 7.1.x, you should install the latest System Update. As of this writing, version 3.0 is current.

11. After performing a clean install, verify that you have resolved the problem before adding anything back to the System Folder. Adding items to the new System folder before resolving the problem will defeat the purpose of performing the clean install.

12. After you confirm that the install is successful, you can reinstall or recover all your non-Apple software. Reinstalling is "cleaner," and always recommended. Still, you can drag extensions, preferences, fonts, and so on, from your Old System Folder to the new one, if you prefer. Do not replace anything that is in your new System folder, only add items that are not already there.

13. You can open the old System suitcase by double-clicking on it to see if you can recover resources in System 7, or use Font/DA Mover to do this under System 6; nevertheless, this is not advisable, especially when you are addressing System corruption. You may want to check the System file, however, so that you know what you need to reinstall.

14. After you are sure you have recovered everything of value from the Old System Folder, throw it and the Old Finder away.

Tip

If you need to install Systems frequently, having a hard drive, partition, or removable cartridge set aside and configured for this purpose can be a real time saver. Make sure you have a volume with a valid, "virgin" System Folder. Next, create a folder called "Net Install Folder" (or whatever else you prefer). Insert each of the disks in the set and drag its icon onto the icon of the Net Install Folder. A new folder with the exact same name as the disk will be created within the Net Install folder. Do not rename these new folders! You can now use these folders in lieu of a set of System disks, without needing to swap any floppies or put up with slow floppy i/o.

Some people use a similar method to perform a clean install called the *image* install. To perform a clean install this way, use a utility to mount disk images created by Apple's DiskCopy. These images then behave as virtual floppies, with all the advantages of the Net Install. Unfortunately, this isn't recommended because image mounting has proven to be rather unreliable in the field. If you can't be talked out of it, you are much better off using a registered copy of the shareware utility DiskDup+ than the freeware extension MountImage. DiskDup+ is more reliable, allows you to mount an unlimited number of images, and works without any extensions. MountImage, by working as an extension, is counter to the whole idea of the clean install.

Extensions

Extensions are the boon and bane of Macintosh existence. Virtually anything you might want to do to customize and enhance the Mac OS, you can do with extensions. Because of the way they patch the operating System, they are extremely powerful. They are also extremely subject to conflicts. To learn how to control these animals, you need to know more about how they operate and how they break.

A brief history of extensions

Extensions started life as INITs, or initialization resources, so named because they initialize at startup along with the System. They are also known as startup documents, which is how the Finder identifies them in list views up through System 6. INITs were Apple's answer to terminate-and-stay-resident programs, or TSRs, in the DOS world.

When developers first started writing them, the only way to use INITs was to have an application install them directly into the System file. This is not a great idea; the risk of System corruption is high, and identifying and disabling installed INITs is difficult. In System 3.2, Apple introduced a mechanism called INIT 31. This is an INIT in the System file that, when run, searches for extensions in the System folder to load. INIT 31 identifies each INIT by file type.

In System 4.0, Apple introduced control panel devices, or CDEVs. These provide a control interface accessed in a newer, modular version of Apple's Control Panel DA. Some CDEVs contain INIT code; the controls are used to change the behavior of the INIT. Others, such as the System's General CDEV, contain no INIT code, and may be used to control System parameters, hardware peripherals, and so on. Today, the term INITs refers to INITs and CDEVs (whether they contain INIT code).

With the release of System 7, many things changed. First, the nomenclature is different. Apple introduced the term extensions to be used in place of INITs. Similarly, CDEVs are now control panels. The old Control Panel DA is gone; individual control panels can be launched. Extensions are also organized differently. In System 6, they are all stored in the System Folder, and loaded in alphabetical order. In System 7, they are divided into two subfolders: the Extensions folder and the Control Panels folder. Load order is as follows: Extensions folder in alphabetical order; Control Panels folder in alphabetical order; System folder in alphabetical order.

Note

Regarding the order extensions load, there is one exception: extensions of type 'scri' will load alphabetically ahead of all other extensions. Apple has reserved this file type for critical extensions. The first was the System 7 Tuner extension in System 7 Tune-Up; another 'scri' extension is the System Update extension.

Several other kinds of extensions are not INITs. INITs show up in the Finder as System extensions, as do files of type 'adev', 'ddev', and 'thng', for example. All these are stored in the Extensions folder, and so are printer drivers and network drivers, which show up as Chooser extensions because they are accessed through the Chooser DA. Tools used by the Communications Toolbox are stored in the Extensions folder. Under System 7.0.x, PostScript font files are treated as extensions. In System 7.1, they are stored in the Fonts folder, and treated as a separate class.

Apple acknowledges the problem of extension conflicts by including a bypass mechanism in System 7. Now, holding down the Shift key at startup will disable all extensions, including Apple's extensions. Beneath the message "Welcome To Macintosh," you'll see another message: "Extensions off."

How extensions work and fail

As the name implies, extensions are small programs that extend the capabilities of the Mac. Extensions modify System routines used by all applications; as a result, they provide global services to all applications. They do this using a number of methods. The most significant is the application of patches to code in ROM called *traps*. Programs use these traps to access standard System toolbox routines. When an extension patches a trap, the extension's code is substituted for the original ROM code whenever a program makes use of that trap. Most conflicts arise from two or more extensions patching the same trap, specifically if one or more of them applies its patch improperly. This is why reordering extensions is so crucial in resolving conflicts; the order in which patches are applied to the same trap can be the difference between repeated crashing and stable performance.

The other likely cause of conflicts involves low memory globals. These values are stored in RAM by the System; some extensions work their magic by changing one or more of them. If two extensions change the same low memory global, you can run into trouble.

During the startup sequence, the Mac sets aside an area of RAM for the System known as the System heap; the System later loads extensions into this area. Each extension can occupy anywhere from 1K to over 400K of RAM. Depending on how many extensions you load, their memory requirements can really add up. If the Mac runs low on memory, crashes are likely to occur. If your Macintosh has a limited amount of RAM to spare, run a limited number of extensions.

Another factor in the successful execution of extensions is the method they use to request memory. Most extensions have a System zone expansion ('sysz') resource, which they use to tell the System how much RAM they need. The System reads the 'sysz', expands the heap accordingly, and loads the extension into the newly reserved RAM. If an extension lacks a 'sysz' resource, or requests an insufficient amount of memory with it, problems can arise.

Furthermore, some extensions request more memory after the startup sequence. If such an extension does not properly reserve this memory in advance, that memory may not be available when the extension needs it. System 7 is very good about expanding the heap to accommodate requests for additional RAM and releasing that RAM when it is no longer needed. System 6 is not as reliable: MultiFinder will expand, but not contract, and even that expansion is less reliable than System 7's. System 6 in Finder mode and previous System versions offer no post-startup heap expansion at all. In System 6, therefore, it is often wise to take precautions and reserve some extra heap space for the System.

Extension management

Despite all these problems, extensions are more popular than ever. Part of this is due to the increasing quality of both extension programmers and the System; extensions today under System 7.1 are more stable than even a couple of years ago under System 7.0. Even so, there are still plenty of conflicts, and this proliferation of extensions demands an effective management System for juggling and troubleshooting.

When INIT files were introduced in System 3.2, there was only one way to manage them: pull them out of the System Folder and reboot. This time honored method still works today, of course, but even then, it was apparent that a more convenient method of enabling and disabling extensions was needed. Enter the extension manager.

Extension managers

The following extension managers are not the only ones in use today; others may be comparable in quality, but these are the most popular and important ones.

Extensions Manager

Extensions Manager is a freeware program from Ricardo Batista, and is currently installed with System 7.5. It lacks many of the features common in its commercial brethren, but it's still very popular.

Extensions Manager introduces the concept of the disabled folder. Rather than changing file types or file flags of extensions, or using any other heavy-handed and invisible method of controlling them, Extensions Manager expands on the concept of Apple's Extensions folder and Control Panels folder. It creates parallel folders named Extensions (Disabled) and Control Panels (Disabled); it's simple, it's clear, it's unobtrusive, and it works. This is now the method of controlling extensions, and all contemporary extension managers use it.

Extensions Manager extends this control to other types of files. It manages startup items, it manages Apple Menu items, it manages fonts, and it even manages items loose in the System folder.

Extensions Manager also gives you sets; allows you to easily customize the file types it will recognize and control; lets you bring up the control panel at startup to change your extensions on-the-fly; and it recovers extensions modified by previous extension managers using the old, file-modifying methods. One especially impressive feature is that you can create a set called Network, and Extensions Manager will automatically load that set when it detects the presence of a network at startup (see Figure 10.4). This is terrific for PowerBook owners!

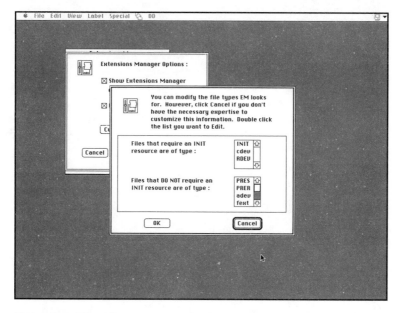

Figure 10.4 The ability to customize the file types that can be controlled is just one of Extensions Manager's unique features.

So, what don't you get? You get no reordering, no links, no extension analysis or information, no crash protection, and no support for aliasing extensions. These omissions keep Extensions Manager from being a power user's tool. However, it is the top choice to replace primitive extension managers in the System folders of novices and intermediate end users.

Extensions Manager works with System 6 and System 7.

Symbionts 2.4.

B. Kevin Hardman's shareware Symbionts picks up where Extensions Manager leaves off, omitting only the Network set and Extension recovery features, and adding some significant new ones. You still don't get reordering or links. However, Symbionts gives you plenty of information on your extensions, and in a completely unique way: it displays the names and memory usage of extensions beneath their icons as they load at startup. You can even pause the startup sequence with the Caps Lock key so that you have time to read everything. Symbionts also displays icons for all extensions, regardless of whether they have code to display them, and it wraps icons onscreen—in its own inimitable fashion—so you're sure to see them all.

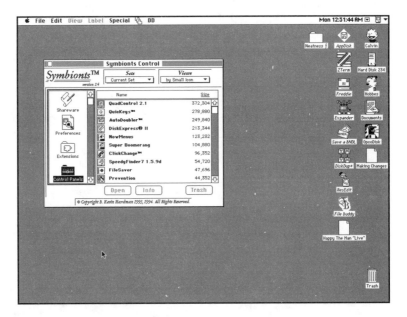

Figure 10.5 Symbionts' unique "By Size" view lets you identify the RAM guzzlers at a glance.

Symbionts has separate extension and control panel files. The extension is named !Symbionts so it will load early; "!" is the first visible character in the Mac's alphabet, and Hardman wants the user to see the leading character, rather than using a space. Also, under System 7.1 or later, Symbionts will change its file type from 'INIT' to 'scri' in order to load earlier.

Symbionts works with System 6 and System 7.

Startup Manager 5.0.

Now Software's Now Utilities has a reputation not only for cramming the maximum number of features into a reasonably priced package, but also for implementing those features well and thoroughly. Startup Manager, the extension manager in the Now Utilities package, lives up to the reputation, which accounts for its great popularity (see Figure 10.6).

Startup Manager

Figure 10.6   Startup Manager icon.

Startup Manager displays the amount of memory used by each extension. If you need more information, Now Profile, another Now Utilities component, can prepare as detailed a report as you want. You can even switch startup volumes on-the-fly. As of version 5.0, it uses the disabled folder method; earlier versions change file types.

Startup Manager 4.0.x works only with System 7; System 6 users need to use version 3.0.2. In an unusual move, Now software is pursuing parallel development of versions 3.0.x and version 5; they have announced that v3.0.3 is in beta as of this writing.

Conflict Catcher 3, version 3.1

Casady & Greene's Conflict Catcher 3 (and its previous incarnation Conflict Catcher II) has emerged as the preeminent extension manager of the day. Start with everything that Startup Manager does, add the ability to lock extensions, control fonts, recover modified extensions, and load aliased extensions—even from a networked volume—and you've got yourself one powerful extension manager. It's even the first extension manager available in native PowerPC code, and it can report the impact on performance of non-native extensions. It doesn't control Apple Menu items, but why quibble? It does do one thing that no other extension manager does: it actually does the grunt work in testing for and resolving extension conflicts. This is how it earns its name and a great deal of admiration (see Figure 10.7).

Conflict Extension™   **Conflict Catcher™**

Figure 10.7   Conflict Extension and Conflict Catcher icons.

When running a Conflict Test, Conflict Catcher will configure your extensions, ask you to check for the existence of the problem, and then restart, reconfiguring your extensions as it goes until it finds your conflict by process of elimination. It can even track down those nasty three-way or more-way conflicts that defy human tolerance. If you're concerned that Conflict Catcher itself might be part of the problem, you can disable the portions of it that patch traps, and test without them. Until somebody comes out with a product that can isolate bugs by reading them right out of RAM, Conflict Catcher belongs in every troubleshooter's gig bag.

Basic Software Troubleshooting

Almost all applications include the ability to create and read document files. Some applications work with extension software to communicate and get information from hardware components or other software pieces. Other applications use shared libraries to reduce the amount of memory required to run the application.

Common problems with application software include file corruption, which can be caused by defects in the software (such as a crash), viruses, or poor media formats (such as bad floppy disks). Because many applications require a minimum amount of memory in order to launch, error messages relating to not enough memory and not enough hard drive space commonly occur, especially if you use your Macintosh often, and need access to a large number of files. The following are some troubleshooting tips for software applications, and some common scenarios related to incorrect software application configurations or incompatibilities. Here are some questions you should ask yourself when a problem occurs:

1. Does the problem occur with extensions 'off', or with only the extensions needed to use the product?

2. Does the problem occur with other software applications running on the same Macintosh?

3. Have you tried re-installing the software from original disks to correct the problem?

4. Does the problem occur if the same tasks are performed on another Macintosh with the same versions of System software and application software?

5. What is the order of tasks you did that created the software problem?

In order to fix the problem, there are some things you'll need to know in order to troubleshoot correctly. Here are the basics; specific problems will be discussed later in this section.

1. If you receive an error message while using the software applications, write down the error message and any steps you took to arrive at the error message.

2. If the application used to run without generating any error messages or compatibility problems, try to recall if you added any additional software to the System that might have coincided with any new error messages or odd software behavior.

10

Also, try re-installing a backup of the original software to see if the error messages go away.

3. If your application crashes, start from your Disk Tools disk and run Apple's Disk First Aid 7.2 to make sure your file System is not damaged.

4. If others have access to the Macintosh you're using, or if you downloaded or used software that might not have been checked with virus software, run Disinfectant 3.6 on your application and System software to make sure your drive is virus free.

Software application solutions

Following is a list of solutions to some of the more common software problems out there today.

I can't launch the application on my Macintosh; the error message says I need an FPU.

Possible causes

Damaged software application.
On Power Macs, emulator may have a software conflict.
Hardware lacks FPU chip.
Extension conflict.
Possible virus infection.
File System errors.

Checkpoints

Many Macintoshes have a 68030 with a socket to add an FPU chip, or a 68L040 processor, which must be replaced with a 68040 processor to add FPU capabilities. Soft FPU is shareware available on most Macintosh ftp sites that emulates FPU calls in 68K or Power Macintosh System software. A commercial version of the software is also available that increases emulation performance, and fixes bugs in the shareware version of the software.

Although the error message indicates you need an FPU, it may also indicate the software may have an extension conflict or may be corrupted. Try re-installing the software, or if it was downloaded, try downloading it again with most extensions turned off. Most software does not require an FPU chip in order to launch. Software that commonly uses an FPU include CAD, 3D graphics, and math-intensive applications. You may want to contact the software publisher to see if a specific software application requires an FPU in your Mac.

When I try to launch the application, I get an error message saying it is only for PowerPC.

Possible causes

You have a 68000, 68020, 68030, 68LC040 or 68040 Macintosh.
Incorrect installation of software application to hard drive or 68K Macintosh.

Checkpoints

PowerPC applications only launch on Power Macs. If the application contains both 68K and PowerPC code (also known as a fat application), it will launch on any Macintosh.

When I'm using an application, my Mac freezes.

Possible causes

Software application damaged.
System Software conflict.
Extension conflict.
Not enough memory to run application.
Out of hard drive space.
Application memory allocation partition set too low.
Application version incompatible with hardware or System software.

Checkpoints

Open your Memory Control Panel. If you have a Power Macintosh, try turning the Modern Memory Manager "off" to see if the problem stops. If it stops, the application may have an incompatibility problem with the modern memory manager, which only runs on Power Macintoshes. If you have a Macintosh that supports 24- and 32-bit modes (most LC and Quadra, plus earlier Macintoshes), try setting the System to 24-bit mode. Keep in mind that physical memory over 8M will not be recognized in this mode. If the freeze or crash problem does not occur with the application with the System set to 24-bit mode, it is possible the application is not 32-bit clean. Check with the software publisher for an update, or if the application is shareware, check an online service or Macintosh ftp site for a newer version of the software.

Try to recall the exact tasks, or steps you performed before the Macintosh froze. If you can't (or do not want to), try to reproduce the problem. Write down as much information as possible to see if the problem might be solved by re-installing the application, related product files, or by turning off extensions.

Also, if you notice other applications exhibiting the same behavior, try to note what you are doing when the Macintosh freezes, and see if there is a common task such as saving a file or printing that may be setting off the freeze.

After I run the application, my sound won't work.

Possible causes

Sound Control Panel settings need to be adjusted.
Headphone connected to sound output port.
External speakers not on.
Application sound settings need to be adjusted.
Check sound settings on front of case.

Checkpoints

If the application required all the available memory on the System to run, it is possible your sound playback may have been affected after quitting the application. Try restarting your Macintosh to see if your sound playback works correctly. If the System is low on memory, try disabling all extensions at startup to see if sound playback still works after quitting the application.

Do I need any of the Rescued Items in the Trash?

Possible causes

System software crashed, and Macintosh had to force restart, or power down and power up Macintosh.
Macintosh was turned off with the power switch, not with the Shutdown menu item in the Special menu.

Checkpoints

Check the hard drive with Apple's Disk First Aid to make sure the file System was not damaged by the crash.

Check the hard drive for viruses using Disinfectant or other virus protection software.

I get an error type 11 when launching or running an application on Power Macintosh.

Possible causes

Extension conflict.
Application damaged.
System software damaged.

Checkpoints

Try restarting your Macintosh to see if you can reproduce the problem.

Check for upgrades or update for application or System software.

Log as much information about the problem and if you cannot find a workaround, contact Apple's or software applications' technical support group.

I get an error type 1 and cannot launch an application.

Possible causes

Application is not 32-bit clean.
Application is not compatible with System software.
Application not compatible with hardware or Macintosh model.
Extension conflict.
Application damaged.

Checkpoints

Check documentation for compatibility or System requirements.
Check for newer versions of the software.
Check for upgrades to software.
Re-install application from a duplicate of original floppies or from CD-ROM.

I can't launch an application because I don't have enough disk space.

Possible causes

RAM disk may be too small, Virtual Memory can free up space. Need to backup and clear hard drive of unneeded files.
Personal File Sharing on.
Virtual Memory on.

Checkpoints

Turn off RAM Disk, Virtual Memory, FileSharing and make sure no background printing is occuring on your Macintosh.
Back up files you are no longer using and remove them from the hard drive.

When the Basics Don't Work

Knowing and practicing the basics can save you a considerable amount of time and money if you have backups of your software, and keep track of what you're adding to the System software, as well as to application software. With many problems, however, the basics just won't work, and these problems can range to problems many other customers are having, or problems that are isolated to your specific configuration. Almost all software and hardware companies have technical support groups, whose main job is to help their customers use their products. Many companies also have online forums that are monitored by support or engineering staff, and are available to anyone with access to the online service.

The nature of software

Software problems usually fall into one of several categories:

- Incompatibility
- Data corruption
- Configuration problems

Software incompatibilities are particularly noticeable at startup. The System software, control panels (CDEVs), and extensions that load when you start the computer can often clash with others loading in the same sequence. Software vendors don't always write the programs in accordance with Apple's guidelines, and even when they do, the sheer number of startup files available means that not every product has been tested with every other product.

Incompatibilities also occur between applications, but they are less of a problem because, unlike startup files, applications aren't constantly running in the background, interacting with the operating System. The solution to software incompatibility is usually to eliminate a problem program from your startup routine.

Corrupted or damaged software can lead to crashed and frozen computers. Software can become corrupted by defective media (hard disks or floppies) or at the time of a crash. You may have corrupted files or applications. The solution is usually to replace the problem file. If you're having trouble with application software, getting a fresh copy from your original program disks is your best bet. If it's a data file, or a file that supports a software application (like a preferences file), you should use a backup copy to replace it.

Older Macintosh software can often be loaded onto your hard disk simply by dragging an icon from a floppy to the disk. In the past few years, however, setting up a large application has meant running an installer program, which puts the program and supporting files in special locations, with the proper folder names. Misplacing a component file can cause a software problem.

Another configuration woe is memory. Using the Get Info box for each application on your Mac, you can see how much memory the program uses and needs. Often, the default memory setting isn't enough to reliably run the software. If you're having problems opening files or you're experiencing application errors, use Get Info, as shown in Figure 10.8, to boost the memory allocation.

Figure 10.8 In the Finder, click once on an application program's icon and choose Get Info from the File menu. Increasing the amount of memory available for the application may stave off some errors.

Using documentation

Getting your list of possible causes down to a manageable number makes the next important task easier. You need to look for help, from your software documentation, vendor technical support, or another source.

Many software manuals do a fine job of explaining the program's features, but troubleshooting is usually a big weakness. Many do not print the error codes you see when a problem crops up, making those codes pretty useless. Others don't organize their troubleshooting sections very well. Still others, perhaps on the theory that Mac users don't read documentation, omit problem solving altogether. Apple's user manuals, of course, are only useful if you have trouble with System software. Even if the troubleshooting section of a software manual is poor, a good glossary of terms or index can often help you find reasons for odd behavior.

Emergency preparations

If you experience serious problems—so serious that you're unable to boot the Macintosh normally—it's essential that you find a way to get the computer working again so that you can solve the problem. The best way to do this is to create one or more emergency startup disks. Booting the Mac from an emergency floppy also allows you to perform diagnostics and repairs on a startup hard drive.

Minimal System

If you have looked at the System Folder lately, you know that it contains lots of files. The System Folder is probably more than 2 MB, and could be as much as 5 MB, in size. You can't get that much information onto a floppy disk. High density floppies have a maximum capacity of 1.4 MB, while the older double-density variety can hold 800K. Getting a working System Folder onto a floppy is called creating a minimal System. To create it, you must eliminate any unnecessary files from the System folder.

There are several ways to create a minimal System disk:

- Use Disk Tools disks. Macintosh Systems include a floppy disk called Disk Tools. This disk contains a stripped-down version of the System and two Apple utilities for repairing damaged Macs. You can do little more than run this software, but it may be enough to get your normal startup disk back in working condition.

- Use the Installer. The Apple Installer disks, which came with your Mac, can put a fresh copy of the Operating System on your hard disk. If you choose to install a minimal System, you can place it on a high density floppy for use as a startup disk. When you use the Installer, be sure to select the minimal System configuration that is specific to your Macintosh. Different Macs require different software to start up properly.

- Use a Diagnostic Tool. Diagnostic tools such as Apple Personal Diagnostics, Norton Utilities, MacTools, and others include emergency disks with minimal versions of the Operating System, as well as their diagnostic applications.

- Create your own startup disk. If you use System 6, it may be possible for you to drag the files you need for a minimal System disk onto a blank floppy, along with the diagnostic software of your choice. System 6 and its accompanying files are much smaller than those associated with System 7. If you take this approach, be sure that the copy of the System and Finder you drag to the blank disk are not corrupted. To make the file fit, you may have to remove fonts and desk accessories with the Font/DA Mover, available on your Apple-supplied System disks.

Disk First Aid

Apple includes Disk First Aid with every Macintosh. You find it on the Disk Tools disk. Disk First Aid takes a cursory look at the System and directory structure and makes minor repairs. Using the copy of Disk First Aid on your Disk Tools disk, you can repair a damaged startup drive when booting from the Disk Tools floppy.

Disk First Aid lets you verify your hard disk—check to see that the media is without defects that could corrupt files—and check the structure of the disk's directory. If Disk First Aid finds problems, you can repair them.

You can run Disk First Aid on any disk (hard disk, floppy, or removable media). The program does not possess the advanced features of commercial disk diagnostic software, but it's a good first step as you work to eliminate possible causes of difficulty.

HD SC Setup

HD SC Setup is another Apple utility found on your Disk Tools disk. With it, you can test or partition your hard disk. Partitioning the disk divides it into as many volumes as you like, making it appear that you have several disks. This is useful for organizing your files or using multiple copies of the Macintosh System at the same time. HD SC Setup does not have the sophisticated partitioning features of tools like FWB's Hard Disk Toolkit, but it can create basic partitions and perform a quick test of your hard disk's integrity. Use HD SC Setup if you're having trouble mounting or using hard disks with your Mac. For the Power Macintosh, HS SC Setup is replaced by Drive Setup 1.0.2.

Virus protection programs

Computer viruses can, unfortunately, find their way into your computer when you copy files from a friend, or even when you install new software. A virus may corrupt data, cause your computer to crash, or erase your hard disk. It may also lie dormant until something triggers it. Because a virus's actions can't be predicted or easily cured, it's important to defend the System against them.

Virus detection and protection software loads when your Mac starts up. Some programs scan disks as you insert or mount them, and some allow you to perform a virus scan at any time. The software looks for corrupted files or files with viruses attached to them.

If you experience unusual problems with your Mac that can't be traced or that seem intermittent, you may have a virus. If you do have virus checking software installed, use it to scan your disks (particularly your startup hard disk) while the System is in use. If you find viruses, let the software remove them, or follow the software's instructions for deleting problem files.

Serious virus attacks affect multiple files and folders. If the System becomes infected, it's a good idea to reinstall the System and software, even if the infection has been eliminated by a virus checker. The System software is a particular target of virus writers. Fortunately, it's easy to reinstall. If you have a good backup of your disk, try reinitializing (erasing) the disk and reinstalling everything. If you do this, be sure that your backup is not infected by viruses.

Because new viruses are created and found on a regular basis, virus detection software must frequently be updated. If you buy a commercial package, like SAM, the vendor will make updates available regularly. Two freeware virus checkers, Disinfectant by John Norstad and GateKeeper by Chris Johnson, are also very popular, and are updated as new viruses are discovered. If you have an account on an online service like CompuServe or America Online, you may be able to download updates of commercial and freeware programs soon after they become available. For more information on virus detection, see Appendix G.

Seeking outside help

If the user manual doesn't contain the answer you need, it may have one last bit of information to offer: the phone number or electronic mail address of the company's technical support staff. It may be tempting to call tech support the minute you suspect trouble with software, but your call will be much more productive if you try to solve the problem yourself before calling. First of all, the process of finding out where the problem actually lies is similar to the questions you are asked by a technical support representative. You need to know details about the configuration of your Mac, the versions of System and application software you are using, when the problem appeared, and so on. You spend less time on the phone (and probably save long distance charges) if you do your homework and use the resources you already have to solve problems, before taking them to technical support. This is even more relevant as software companies' tech support lines become busier, and as a few companies begin charging users for support.

Most major Macintosh software vendors maintain a presence on one or more online services, such as America Online, eWorld, CompuServe, GEnie, or AppleLink. If you have an account on one of these services, you may find that reading through messages posted in the software vendor's forum or bulletin board area can answer many of your questions. If not, post the problem and await the solutions. This process may take awhile, depending upon how well-staffed the online area is and how much other traffic is there.

You do have other technical support options. Many consultants specialize in recommending and installing Macintosh products and solving Mac problems. A consultant can take the time to work through a problem with you, and evaluate it in the context of your whole System. The consultant may advise you on the phone or in person, and may even solve the problem for you, with know-how and/or diagnostic tools. This personal service usually comes at a high price: between $50 and $100 an hour.

A less costly way to get hands-on support is through a local user group: people who gather to share the joys and problems of Mac ownership. User group members may have experienced problems similar to yours. Like online technical support, though, a user group does not provide instantaneous help.

But hopefully, things will never get that bad, and you'll be able to solve all the problems yourself. The next chapter discusses troubleshooting your networks, communications hardware, and printing problems. While these problems are both hardware and software related, this kind of topic deserves its own chapter due to its complexity.

Troubleshooting Printing, Networking, and Communications

Printers and networks have general straightforward configurations. Printers usually require their own printer driver to work with Macintosh system software. The benefit of buying an Apple printer is that most drivers are updated with each new system software release. Most non-Apple printer companies, like Hewlett-Packard, Brother, and Panasonic, also upgrade their printer software drivers. However, to locate their latest software you may need to call them or check with the computer dealer who sold you the printer. Configuring and troubleshooting networks is also fairly straightforward when following some basic steps. This chapter discusses common printer and network problems and basic configuration steps.

Printer Problems and Solutions

Most printers today share similar hardware mechanisms for printing. The primary differences between today's printers are the software drivers created for them and the features of the printer driver and software applications bundled with the printer. Common printing problems include:

- Not seeing the printer from your Macintosh
- Sending but not having the printer print your document
- Having parts of the page cut off at the edges
- Printing the wrong font
- Ink (single color or multi-color) printing problems

First steps

When you set up your printer with your Macintosh, you will use one of several connections, which might include power, serial (either direct or via network), EtherTalk (a faster networking protocol), SCSI (very few of today's printers use SCSI), or Expansion card. Be sure the printer cable is completely connected to your Macintosh's expansion port as well as to the back of the printer. Then install the printer's software onto your Macintosh. If you did not receive printer software with your printer, you may want to see if the printer manufacturer has an ftp site or online forum with its software. Apple's printer software usually includes software for both System 6.0.7 and System 7.5. Make sure all tape and packaging is removed from the printer before turning on the power to the printer.

Success with power?

If you do not see a light, or if the light is flashing when you power on the printer, the power cable may not be completely connected, or a piece of the printer's packaging may be inside the printer case, preventing the printer from performing its hardware diagnostics. Some ink jet printers require synchronization of the printer heads before you can print. LaserWriters need to have a toner cartridge inserted into the printing mechanism to print. Your LaserWriter printer should include a toner cartridge with the packaging. Directions (generally with pictures) for installing the toner cartridge are usually located on the inside panel of the printer. Aside from this, dot matrix and LaserWriter printers do not have moving parts, and do not need any synchronization to power-up correctly or print.

If you have a PostScript printer and have System 7.5, LaserWriter 8.0 will already be installed on your Macintosh; in lieu of installing the newer version of the LaserWriter 8 driver, open your Chooser desk accessory (located in your Apple menu) and select the LaserWriter 8 icon in the upper left window of the Chooser window. Your PostScript printer's name should appear in the right window.

Proper fonts installed?

PostScript, TrueType, screen fonts, and a variety of shareware font formats interact with the monitor and printer. Current LaserWriter printers can print PostScript Level 1 and 2 fonts with the LaserWriter 8.0 printer driver. PostScript is font imaging and printing technology created by Adobe for high-end publishers who need quality graphics and printer output. PostScript font files must be placed either in the Font folder or in the System Folder to be recognized by the printer.

Printers that do not use PostScript can use TrueType fonts—font technology created by Apple Computer, Inc. TrueType fonts can be scaled to a wide range of sizes; however, the image quality of smaller size fonts is not as crisp as PostScript fonts. TrueType fonts are sold by Apple in a font kit, and if you purchase an Apple printer you automatically receive all of Apple's TrueType fonts. Hundreds if not thousands of font types are available for Macintosh. PostScript fonts are commercial fonts. TrueType fonts can be created using software such as Fontographer, or several shareware applications.

System 7.5 includes several fonts that are automatically installed with an Easy Install of System Software—Chicago, Courier, Geneva, Helvetica, Monaco, New York, Palatino, Times, and Symbol. Each font family is stored in a font suitcase titled with the font family's name. A font suitcase can contain TrueType or PostScript screen fonts from one or many font families.

Finder suggestions for Happy Printing

If you have a problem printing a page to your printer, go to the Finder and try to print the contents of a window as a test to see if the printer can print this correctly. To Print the contents of a window, select a window, or open your hard drive icon. Select Print Window from the File menu. Check the application menu at the far right of the menubar and select Print Monitor when it appears in the application menu. If you can see the window content in the Print Monitor window and the file prints successfully, you probably do not have a hardware problem with your printer. The problem may be a setting or memory-related problem with the file or software application on your Macintosh.

Some printers can also receive and send facsimiles via a modem port. Make sure any additional cable connections are made for the fax hardware features and install any additional software that supports the fax features.

Because the best solution for problems is to avoid them, the following sections outline settings to keep you on the right path, as well as some solutions when things go wrong. Printing problems fall into eight categories: drivers, the Chooser, Page Setup, the Print dialog box, printer languages, spoolers, hardware, and color.

Printing basics

To print, your Macintosh must have a driver for your printer. A *driver* is a computer file installed in the System Folder that sends instructions to a specific type of printer. Without it, your Macintosh can't identify a printer or transmit instructions. Even the most basic task, printing an active window (⌘+Shift+4), will not work without a driver.

The disks used to install the System software include some drivers for specific printers. You must specify printing choices in the Chooser, the Page Setup dialog box, the Print dialog box, and sometimes a Document Setup dialog box. Your printer must be accessible via a proper connector (usually a cable) to download your printing choices. Some printers are connected only to a specific Macintosh, while others are shared by multiple Macintoshes over a network.

Understanding drivers

Not all System installation disks contain the same drivers. For example, the single System Disk that came with the original Macintosh 128K in 1984 contained only an ImageWriter driver for the single printer then available. Now System 7's Printing disk contains nine printer drivers, as shown in Figure 11.1.

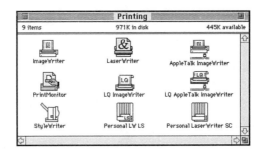

Figure 11.1   The print drivers supplied with System 7.

Additional drivers are available from third-party suppliers, including files for printers designed to work with IBM-compatible computers and high-end typesetters used in the publishing industry. If you need a special driver, try contacting the manufacturer of the printer. If that doesn't produce results, local retailers and mail-order houses sell driver/cable packages.

Make sure you use the right driver. The ImageWriter driver, for example, is meant to be used when that printer is directly connected to a single Macintosh, and the AppleTalk ImageWriter driver is used for an ImageWriter modified to be shared on a network. Similarly, the LQ ImageWriter driver is used with that printer connected directly to a single Macintosh and the LQ AppleTalk ImageWriter driver is for use on a network.

The driver in the System file may be the right one for your printer, but the wrong version. Drivers with the same names are sometimes updated with new System versions. For example, the ImageWriter file that came with the Macintosh 128K is the original version; the file provided with System 7.1 is up to version 7.0.1 and the LaserWriter driver is 7.1.2.

Failing to update printer drivers along with the System file can be a source of printing problems. Drivers are often optimized to work with specific System versions. To check a driver's version number, select it and choose Get Info (⌘+I) from the File menu. A window opens containing the version number, as in Figure 11.2.

Figure 11.2   Checking the version number of a printer driver.

Be aware, however, this doesn't mean the System and printer driver will have the same version number. System 6.0.7, for example, comes with two LaserWriter drivers, versions 5.2 and 6.0.2, an ImageWriter 2.7 driver, and the LQ ImageWriter 2.0 driver. When in doubt about printer driver versions, check the version numbers on the Printing disk that came with the package used to install the System file.

When a printer such as a LaserWriter is shared on a network, all the Macs on the network should use the same version of the LaserWriter file. If not, the first Macintosh to use the printer will set it to be used only with the version of the LaserWriter and Laser Prep files on that Macintosh.

When another Macintosh with a different driver version attempts to print, it will be greeted with an error message. The printer must then be reset (usually by turning it off and on again) before that Macintosh can print. The newest printer driver for System 7, LaserWriter 8.0, however, does not appear to have this problem.

Using the Chooser

After a driver (or drivers) has been installed on your Macintosh, you must specify which driver the Mac will use. This is done in the Chooser, a program installed in the System Folder and available under the Apple menu.

Non-networked printing

When a non-networked printer is selected, two icons appear in the right-side Chooser window. One is a printer icon and the other is a telephone icon. They correspond to the two serial ports on the back of your Macintosh.

When setting up a printer, the usual choice is to select the printer icon in the Chooser. This requires that the cable from your printer be plugged into the corresponding printer-icon port on the Macintosh. If the cable is plugged into the telephone-icon port, and the printer-icon port is selected in the Chooser (or vice versa), any print commands will simply be lost.

Using two types of printers

Using the telephone-icon port is impossible if a modem is to be used with the Macintosh. If no modem is connected, however, the port can be used to access a non-networked printer while a printer or printers remain available on a network through the printer port.

Simply connect a non-networked printer to the modem port and the network cable to the printer port. Then select the appropriate non-network printer driver and the modem port. The non-networked printer will be accessible only from the Macintosh to which it is connected. This way, you can print on either the non-networked printer or on a networked printer by selecting the appropriate driver in the Chooser.

Alternatively, if a modem is to be used, a simple A-B box can be connected to the telephone-icon port and be used to switch between the non-networked printer or the modem. The Chooser procedures are the same.

My port changed

One of the most frustrating experiences for novice users is the discovery that even when a printer driver and the printer port are selected, printing suddenly isn't possible. The printing process appears normal on the Macintosh screen, but the printer doesn't respond.

If this happens to you, open the Chooser and select your print driver. You may discover that the port selection has mysteriously switched from the printer port to the modem port. However, this change really isn't a mystery for two reasons:

- Multiple networked and non-networked printer drivers have been installed in the System Folder, regardless of whether you have those printers. You or another user may have selected a networked printer driver and then switched back to the non-networked driver.

- On some early System file versions, disconnecting the printer cable from a Macintosh, perhaps while moving the machine, will also switch the port selection to the modem port.

Because networked printer drivers always claim the printer port, selecting one automatically moves non-networked printers to the modem port. This makes possible the two-printer configuration described previously. A frustrating experience like this is a good argument for installing only the printer drivers that are needed. Then no one will be tempted to experiment with driver changes that can cause problems.

Networked printing

Most LaserWriters are networked printers, whether this is a single Macintosh connected to a LaserWriter or an entire production facility. In a network, there's no need for separate LaserWriter and AppleTalk LaserWriter drivers such as the ImageWriter and AppleTalk ImageWriter.

An exception to this rule are some low-end LaserWriters like the Personal LaserWriter SC, which cannot be networked. If you're not sure whether your printer is networkable, consult the owner's manual; if it supports AppleTalk, it's a networked printer. Some non-networked printers can later be upgraded to support AppleTalk. In this case, they require networked printer drivers.

When a networked printer driver is selected in the Chooser, several options become available; an error in any one of them can cause problems:

- The box on the right side of the Chooser contains the names of the printer or printers that are available, as shown in Figure 11.3. If only one printer is available, it will appear in the upper left window and must be selected prior to printing from an application. If more printers are available, all of them will appear in the upper left window, and only one can be selected at any given time.

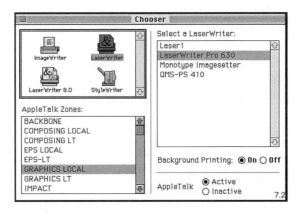

Figure 11.3 Choose the correct printer in the Chooser window.

If you select the wrong printer, of course, your output will be somewhere other than what you expected. If you deselect the printers so none is specified, a dialog box appears instead of printed results, as shown in Figure 11.4.

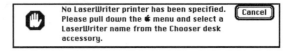

Figure 11.4 A dialog box that appears when no printer name is selected.

- Background printing becomes available. This involves the PrintMonitor file, which is discussed later in this chapter. If you turn off background printing, your Macintosh will be tied up until each print job ends.

- In Choosers before System 7, a user name can be specified in the box provided. It's a good idea to use your name or the name assigned to your Macintosh. The name you choose identifies your Macintosh on a network, and makes it easier for other network users to see who is using a printer.

- AppleTalk can manually be made inactive. This simply disconnects your Macintosh from the network and makes the printers on the network unavailable. You should always leave the Active button selected.

When a non-networked printer driver has been assigned to the printer port, switching to a networked driver produces an alert box reminding you to be sure a network is connected.

Similarly, switching from a networked to a non-networked driver warns you that AppleTalk will be made inactive and suggests that you remove any network connections. As we have seen, removing the network connections is not necessary if a non-networked printer is connected to the modem port.

When a print job is being processed by a non-network driver assigned to the printer port, it ties up that port. Consequently, switching to a network driver may not be possible until the job finishes. Figure 11.5 shows one of the less alarming messages that appears in this situation. Unfortunately, some alert boxes with less clear messages may be displayed in certain situations. The bottom line, however, is that the printer port is tied up.

Figure 11.5   An alert box notifying you that the printer port is busy.

In the simplest situations, the solution is to wait until the print job finishes and the printer port is again free. In more serious situations, perhaps due to an INIT conflict or insufficient RAM, the Macintosh may crash and have to be restarted. To be safe, save your work frequently!

Understanding Page Setup

The Page Setup command is available in the File menu of most applications. This command calls up a dialog box in which you can make important specifications about your printed output. The choices that appear in the dialog box depend on the System version in use and the printer driver selected in the Chooser. Notice in Figure 11.6 that the printer driver involved is specified at the top of the dialog box along with its version number. Other standard Page Setup dialog boxes are available with other printer drivers.

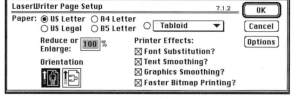

Figure 11.6 Page Setup dialog boxes for the standard System 7.0 LaserWriter driver and for the newest LaserWriter version 8.0.

In addition to the standard Page Setup dialog boxes available with each type of printer driver, some applications make their own modifications. For example, the LaserWriter Page Setup dialog box for Aldus Freehand and QuarkXPress are shown in Figure 11.7. This box contains advanced features specific to those programs.

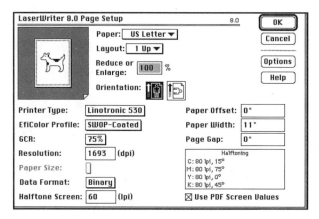

Figure 11.7 The Modified LaserWriter 8.0 Page Setup dialog box for QuarkXPress. Note the advanced features not available on standard dialog boxes.

The purpose of the Page Setup dialog box is to control the paper you are using to print. You can specify the size of the paper to be used, whether the type will print horizontally or vertically, enable some special effects, and even enlarge the printable area of the paper.

Some applications only need the standard Page Setup dialog box, but others, like Aldus Freehand and QuarkXPress, provide separate Document Setup dialog boxes that control the placement of the image on a page. Put another way, Page Setup defines the printer's paper stock in relation to the image; Document Setup defines the image in relation to the paper stock. This is a critical distinction and the source of much confusion and many printing problems.

Although some programs don't have a Document Setup dialog box, they do allow adjusting margins, either onscreen or in a modified Page Setup dialog box. For proper printing, the document and Page Setup specifications must be compatible. As an example, a document could be created to fit on U.S. Legal (14 inch) paper but U.S. Letter (11 inches) might be specified in the Page Setup dialog box. The result would be a document that stops at 11 inches on the first legal-length sheet and continues on a second sheet.

Some common Page Setup problems

Image is too small or too big

Check the percentage enlargement or reduction in the LaserWriter Page Setup dialog box. This setting affects the entire printed image, unlike the Scale command in some applications which is often used to enlarge or reduce portions of an image. Non-network printers like the ImageWriter and Personal LaserWriter SC allow only preset reductions.

Image doesn't print vertically

Specify the orientation of the page that you want in the Page Setup dialog box. The default setting prints across the narrow portion of a page, but clicking the other icon flips the paper on its side before printing.

Images appear distorted

Because printers output at different resolutions, a graphic that appears fine on one printer may need adjustment on another. Special adjustments are provided in Page Setup dialog boxes to address this problem, including Tall Adjusted, Text Smoothing, Graphics Smoothing, and Precision Bitmap Alignment (also called Exact Bit Images).

Tip

If you are using MacInTax with an ImageWriter, always specify Tall Adjusted for best results when printing official IRS tax forms.

Special tricks may resolve some problems

No Gaps Between Pages

Non-networked printers often use continuous-feed paper instead of individual sheets. This option eliminates the top and bottom margins that would otherwise appear on a printed page, which is useful for printing items like banners.

Font Substitution

This is useful when a document is prepared using a bitmap font like Geneva. Such a font does not print well on LaserWriter, so this option enables the substitution of a true LaserWriter font like Helvetica. Be careful, however, if you use special characters in your text such as characters from the bitmap Chicago font.

Flip Horizontal, Flip Vertical

The LaserWriter dialog box contains an Options button, which opens the dialog box shown in Figure 11.8. These commands flip a document's image.

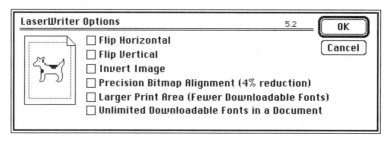

Figure 11.8 The LaserWriter Options dialog box.

Invert Image

Turns white areas black and vice versa for a negative effect.

The LaserWriter clipped my document

Sometimes an image is only partially printed on a LaserWriter, as in Figure 11.9. Common results are missing top, bottom, and side edges.

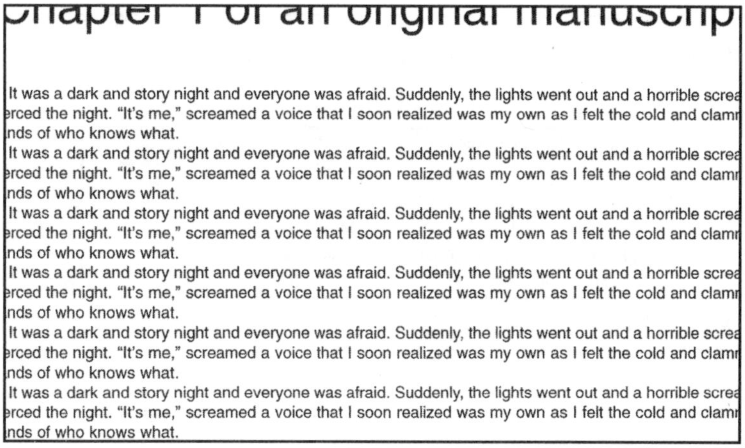

Chapter 1 of an original manuscrip

It was a dark and story night and everyone was afraid. Suddenly, the lights went out and a horrible scre erced the night. "It's me," screamed a voice that I soon realized was my own as I felt the cold and clamr nds of who knows what.
It was a dark and story night and everyone was afraid. Suddenly, the lights went out and a horrible scre erced the night. "It's me," screamed a voice that I soon realized was my own as I felt the cold and clamr nds of who knows what.
It was a dark and story night and everyone was afraid. Suddenly, the lights went out and a horrible scre erced the night. "It's me," screamed a voice that I soon realized was my own as I felt the cold and clamr nds of who knows what.
It was a dark and story night and everyone was afraid. Suddenly, the lights went out and a horrible scre erced the night. "It's me," screamed a voice that I soon realized was my own as I felt the cold and clamr nds of who knows what.
It was a dark and story night and everyone was afraid. Suddenly, the lights went out and a horrible scre erced the night. "It's me," screamed a voice that I soon realized was my own as I felt the cold and clamr nds of who knows what.
It was a dark and story night and everyone was afraid. Suddenly, the lights went out and a horrible scre erced the night. "It's me," screamed a voice that I soon realized was my own as I felt the cold and clamr nds of who knows what.

Figure 11.9 A clipped page.

Some common causes of this ugly problem are the following:

- Specifying margins that are too narrow. By default, a LaserWriter requires a document to have margins no smaller than 1/2 inch. However, this can be reduced to 1/4 inch by selecting Larger Print Area in the LaserWriter Options dialog box. As the command line indicates, selecting this option means using a smaller mix of fonts in a document.

- Specifying a different printer from the one specified in the Chooser. Depending on the selection, this error may send the wrong instructions to the printer and may generate a PostScript error.

- Specifying the wrong PPD file in a modified Print dialog box. The Print dialog box is covered in the next section.

The Print dialog box: quicksand for the unwary

The Print command from the File menu in most applications displays a dialog box that, like Page Setup, varies depending on the printer driver selected in the Chooser. It also may be modified by some applications (see Figures 11.10, 11.11, and 11.12).

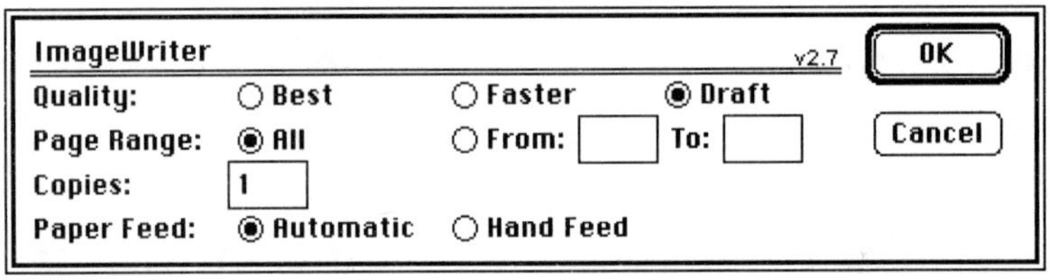

Figure 11.10   The standard ImageWriter Print dialog box.

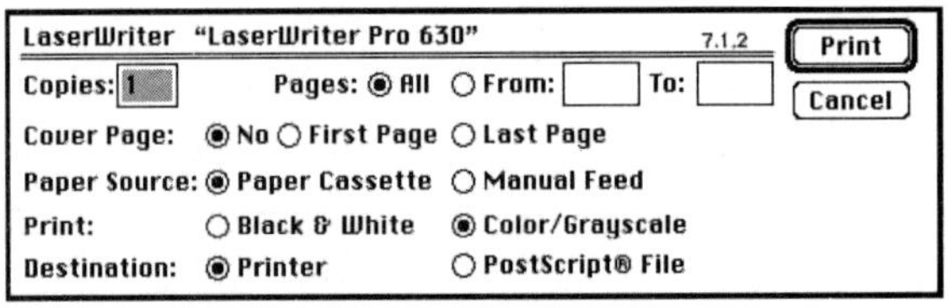

Figure 11.11   Standard Print dialog box for a LaserWriter Pro 630.

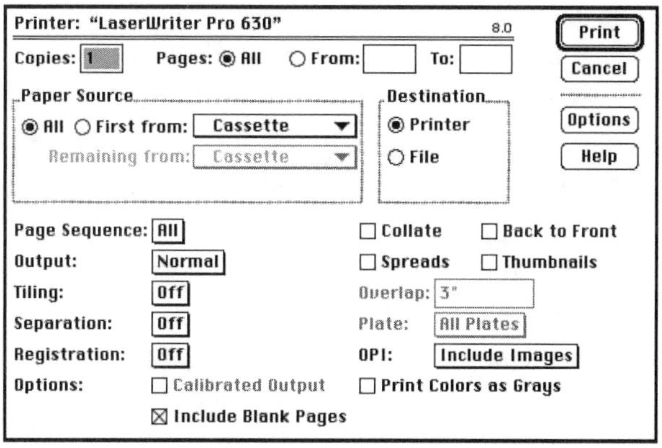

```
Printer: "LaserWriter Pro 630"                    8.0    ┌─────────┐
                                                         │  Print  │
Copies: 1      Pages: ◉ All   ○ From:      To:           └─────────┘
                                                         ┌─────────┐
┌─Paper Source──────────────────┐  ┌─Destination─────┐   │ Cancel  │
│ ◉ All  ○ First from:  Cassette ▼│  │ ◉ Printer      │  └─────────┘
│        Remaining from: Cassette ▼│  │ ○ File         │  ┌─────────┐
│                               │  │                 │   │ Options │
└───────────────────────────────┘  └─────────────────┘   └─────────┘
                                                         ┌─────────┐
                                                         │  Help   │
                                                         └─────────┘
Page Sequence: All        □ Collate    □ Back to Front
Output:        Normal      □ Spreads    □ Thumbnails
Tiling:        Off        Overlap: 3"
Separation:    Off        Plate:   All Plates
Registration:  Off        OPI:     Include Images
Options:       □ Calibrated Output  □ Print Colors as Grays
               ⊠ Include Blank Pages
```

Figure 11.12 Modified LaserWriter 8.0 Print dialog box for QuarkXPress and Aldus Freehand.

As with Page Setup, the Print dialog box displays the name of the printer driver selected at the top left and the version number of the driver. In addition, the LaserWriter dialog box shows the name of the printer selected. With instructions for the placement of the image on the page already specified, the Print dialog box is for final instructions on print quality. Here is where you specify which pages are to be printed, the number of copies, and how the paper will be fed into your printer. Many other instructions can be specified here, depending on the application.

This section looks at some of the options that may give you difficulties, including:

- If you are using an application that allows you to change page numbers, notice that the page specifications apply to the physical order of the pages, not the page numbers you have set.

  A document that begins with page 5 and ends with page 10, for example, has six physical pages. Page 5 would be the first page and page 10 would be the sixth page. To print only pages 7 and 8, you would need to specify "From 3 To 4" in the dialog box.

- Although the standard ImageWriter dialog box allows three levels of quality, some applications may not allow the Faster mode, so be prepared to wait for a document to print in Best mode or to accept Draft quality. Generally, applications with no "faster" mode are meant to be used mostly with high-end typesetters.

- The Cover Page option in the LaserWriter dialog box enables you to print a cover page before or after a document. With LaserWriter driver 8.0, this option lists the name of the Macintosh in use, the application in use, the name of the document, the date and time, the name of the printer, and the number of pages printed.

- Some LaserWriters come with only a paper cassette for U.S. Letter paper. If you need to use legal-size paper, you can hand-feed sheets or purchase a legal-size cassette.

- The Tabloid size that can be set in the Page Setup dialog box is available only on printers that can handle paper in that size. Most such printers also offer higher resolutions than standard LaserWriters.

- The Black & White option in the LaserWriter dialog box is the default and provides just what it says—only black and white. (If color toner is used in your LaserWriter, of course, the choice would be white and whatever color is used.)

  The Color/GrayScale settings are meant for printers that produce colors or halftones and for documents that contain colors or shades of gray.

  The Color/GrayScale setting can be used with standard LaserWriters, but the results may be less than satisfactory. LaserWriter printer driver 8.0 offers an additional option, Calibrated Color/GrayScale, for printers that support PostScript Level 2.

- The option to create a PostScript file rather than print a document produces a text document containing codes that can be opened by any word processing program.

  LaserWriter drivers before System 7.0 don't contain this option, but a PostScript file can be created by executing ⌘+F immediately after clicking the OK button in the Print dialog box. Hold the ⌘ and F keys down until a dialog box reports that a PostScript file is being created. The first PostScript file will be named PostScript0, followed by PostScript1 and so on up to PostScript9. If you have difficulty finding them, use the Find command in the Finder.

Understanding print resolution

Print resolution is expressed in dots per inch, or dpi. In general, the higher the dpi, the better the print quality, although the paper stock being used also affects quality. Low-end printers like the ImageWriter provide 144 dpi, which results in type and graphics with ragged edges. Most LaserWriters are 300 dpi printers, although 600 dpi is becoming increasingly common. High-end typesetters used in the publishing industry can provide more than 2,000 dpi.

Most people consider text and line drawings produced at 300 dpi as good as professionally printed materials, and few can tell any difference at 600 dpi. However, resolutions above 1,000 dpi produce much better halftones, which are common in photos and paintings.

Although most printers produce "square" resolutions, or 300 dpi horizontally and vertically, some "turbo" models are not "square" and can be troublesome. For example, a printer that prints at 300 dpi horizontally and 600 dpi vertically can produce noticeable lines (or dot gaps) in patterns. The simplest solution for this problem is to turn off the "turbo" feature, if possible.

Jagged edges

The low resolution of printers like the ImageWriter produces images with jagged edges. However, you can produce rough text and images on a high-resolution printer if the wrong images and fonts are used. Here are two examples:

- Images produced by "paint" applications such as MacPaint and by low-resolution scanners are bitmap images. They are made up of relatively large square dots that can be difficult to smooth.

  Such images can be improved somewhat with the Graphics Smoothing and Precision Bitmap Alignment specifications in the LaserWriter Page Setup dialog box. But for best results, PICT and EPS images are better choices.

- The use of bitmapped fonts such as Chicago and Geneva may produce rough type if the Font Substitution option in the LaserWriter Page Setup dialog box is not checked. Be aware, however, that selecting this option may have unexpected results because the substituted font may not match the onscreen spacing of the bitmapped font.

Lines per inch

The Lines Per Inch, or lpi, setting is normally preset at 60 lpi for 300 dpi printers and at 85 lpi for 600 dpi printers. Some applications, such as Aldus Freehand, allow adjustment of the lpi setting. Here are some guidelines for use with the LaserWriter driver:

- Most LaserWriters with 300 dpi cannot handle more than 60 lpi. Specifying fewer lines per inch increases the spacing between the lines of dots and generally degrades image quality. However, this can be useful for special effects where a lesser quality is desired.

- For higher-resolution printers, the optimum lpi setting depends on the paper that will be used. If your printed image will be reproduced in a magazine or newsletter, make your settings based on the paper stock to be used for the magazine or newsletter.

  The glossier the final paper stock, the higher the lpi setting that can be used. A high setting for an image to be used on coarse stock like newsprint, however, may produce too fine an image for good reproduction.

QuickDraw: slower printing

Most printers used with the Macintosh fall into three categories based on language: native language, QuickDraw, and PostScript. Native-language printers tend to be those developed for computers other than the Macintosh. This section focuses on QuickDraw and PostScript printers, which are more commonly used with Macintosh computers.

QuickDraw is the language the Macintosh uses to draw screen images. Printers that use this language simply accept fully processed images from the Macintosh. Examples of such printers are the ImageWriter, ImageWriter LQ, and the Personal LaserWriter SC. Until recently, such printers cost far less than PostScript printers.

There are two major disadvantages to using QuickDraw printers:

- The Macintosh must do all the processing of an image to be printed. This can tie up a Macintosh during the processing. Large files and files with graphics tend to take longer than a one-page document containing only text.

Special problems may appear with applications such as Adobe Illustrator, which bypass QuickDraw and use the PostScript language to draw onscreen. In this case, the translation back to QuickDraw for printing may be less than perfect and what you see onscreen may differ from the printed output.

- Print quality may be noticeably less than on a PostScript printer, depending on the document. However, text can be improved by using a utility such as Adobe System's ATM program and the TrueType fonts provided with recent Macintosh System disks. A simple rule of thumb is that if an image can be improved onscreen, it will be improved on the printed copy.

PostScript: faster printing and smoother images

PostScript is a computer language developed for printers by Adobe Systems and used on most LaserWriters and high-end typesetters. Essentially, it translates the onscreen QuickDraw image into the PostScript language using the Laser Prep file installed in the System Folder. That language is then sent to a PostScript printer, where the image is processed and then printed.

Several advantages to this System include:

- The Macintosh is not tied up during processing of the file because that work is handled by the printer. Assembling an image in PostScript also tends to be faster than QuickDraw.

- PostScript draws "cleaner" images because it adapts to different printer resolutions. It will print just as well on a 300 dpi LaserWriter as on a 2,000 dpi typesetter. QuickDraw is limited in part by the screen resolution of the Macintosh.

Thus, a PICT circle drawn on a Macintosh Plus with 72 dpi screen resolution will print cleanly on any PostScript machine, but will be slightly jagged on any printer with more than 72 dpi resolution.

Clone PostScript: some problems

Although PostScript was developed and is maintained by Adobe Systems, the language itself has been placed in the public domain. That means that not all PostScript printers use Adobe PostScript. There are a number of printers available with cloned PostScript, and though they work well most of the time, they sometimes create printing problems:

- At one time, only Adobe PostScript could print fonts from Adobe Systems correctly, particularly in small sizes. While this problem has largely been eliminated in recent years, some sites might still be using older technology where this may be a problem. The solution is to upgrade the equipment.

- Because clones are a derivative of Adobe's PostScript, problems in cloning sometimes appear when applications like Aldus FreeHand are updated to take advantage of previously unused capabilities in PostScript, or when Adobe PostScript itself is updated. The solution is either to limit purchases to Adobe PostScript printers, or ask the clone supplier to provide updates.

Spoolers: how to reduce printing time

To print a file on the Macintosh, an application must create a temporary file on disk and feed that file to the printer. While this takes place, the Macintosh can be tied up. To reduce the waiting time when using the LaserWriter printer driver, Systems since version 5.0 have come with PrintMonitor, a print spooler that is installed in the System Folder. It works with MultiFinder.

When a print job is ordered, a temporary disk file is created in a folder inside the System Folder. Then the file is fed to the printer in the background, freeing the Macintosh to perform other tasks.

PrintMonitor doesn't work with non-networked printer drivers such as the ImageWriter; nevertheless, a number of commercial spoolers are available that work with those drivers.

Common spooler problems

I printed a number of documents, but not all of them came out.

PrintMonitor works just like other applications, requiring and allocating a section of RAM on startup. Your files may be too large to fit into the amount of RAM PrintMonitor claims. Increase the amount of RAM PrintMonitor allocates at startup.

Close PrintMonitor and select it in the System Folder. Open its Get Info (⌘+I) window and increase the number in the Application Memory Size box shown in Figure 11.13. The Suggested Memory Size is 72K, but the number can be enlarged. Doing so allows bigger documents to be queued for printing.

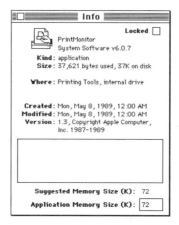

Figure 11.13 The PrintMonitor Info window.

I started a print job 10 minutes ago and nothing has come out.

A slight delay is normal when using a print spooler, but if the time seems excessive, check your application menu to see if the spooler has loaded. If it has not, you may have too many applications open hogging all the RAM.

If there isn't enough RAM available, spoolers will not load. Close one of your applications (preferably the last one opened); this may clear enough RAM for the spooler to load and begin printing. If PrintMonitor has loaded, check its menu to be sure printing hasn't been turned off by a previous user.

Another network user may be tying up the printer with a long print job or that user's Macintosh has crashed during printing. The PrintMonitor monitoring box should display a message telling you who is using the printer.

PostScript Errors

Sometimes a document can't be printed because of a PostScript error. When this happens, a message to that effect may appear in PrintMonitor. The PostScript Language Reference Manual is helpful in interpreting the codes shown in the message. However, most are triggered by errors in the Page Setup and Print dialog boxes already discussed.

Make sure the specifications in these boxes are correct. For example, specifying different printers in the Chooser and the Page Setup dialog box in QuarkXPress can trigger a PostScript error and halt printing.

Keeping your printer running correctly

Most printers with print resolutions at or below 600 dpi require little maintenance beyond loading paper, clearing paper jams, and changing the print cartridge or ribbon once in a while. Non-laser printers may also require occasional lubrication and cleaning of the print head as outlined in the owner's manual. An exception, however, is the Varityper VT600W, one of the first laser printers to support 600 dpi and Tabloid paper stock. For optimum performance, a service contract with an outside vendor is a good idea.

Typesetters above 600 dpi are often limited to professional print shops not only because of their cost, but because they require constant maintenance. Aside from routine maintenance, a few problems occasionally appear:

My printer's name no longer appears in the Chooser.

There are three likely causes. The first is a break in the network, perhaps a loose cable, that is interrupting printer as well as file-sharing traffic. Contact the network administrator for help.

Another reason is a change in the printer's settings so that it no longer recognizes the network protocol you are using. For example, if the printer was used temporarily on an IBM network, it may not have been reset to AppleTalk.

The third reason the name is missing in the Chooser could be because the printer may have crashed and is not accepting network signals. Initializing the printer, usually by turning it off and then on again, should clear this problem.

Printed output is not acceptable.

Check to see if the cartridge or the ribbon needs to be replaced. If the cartridge is OK on a laser printer that has received high use over a long period, open it up and check the rollers; they could be disintegrating.

Problems with color

Color printing on the Macintosh has recently taken off with the introduction of Apple's first color LaserWriter. Nevertheless, it's still not economical to print multiple copies of a single document on new color printers. Most output on the color LaserWriter and other high-end color printers is original documents and color proofs for commercial printing.

Most color problems occur when outputting color proofs; resolving them requires an understanding of the color systems used on computers and for printing.

An overview of color

A computer uses colors created by light, called *additive* colors, that are red, green, and blue (hence the term RGB monitors). Combining all three colors produces white, and other colors are a combination of the three base colors. For example, combining red and green produces yellow; combining green and blue produces cyan; and combining red and blue produces magenta.

The human eye, however, perceives print colors only when light shines on them. Such colors are *subtractive*, and the major components are yellow, magenta, and cyan. Combining all three colors produces black. Combining yellow and magenta produces red; combining magenta and cyan produces blue; and combining cyan and yellow produces green.

Varying the combination of the base colors in both additive and subtractive models produces a nearly complete spectrum of colors.

Matching screen and print colors

A number of solutions have been advanced to bridge the gap between screen and print colors, however, none is totally satisfactory. A decision to use one of these systems should be based on how exacting your color requirements are. Although some solutions are better than others, some users may find indexing the best route to successful color printing.

Basic Networking Troubleshooting

Networks are essentially phone cables, or variations of phone cables that allow Macintosh computers to talk to each other, as well as with other computers, telephones, and printers. AppleTalk software enables System software to use network capabilities.

If your Mac requires network System software such as the Communications Toolbox, you should always run the installer script to install the software components. The installer installs resources, in addition to the Communications Toolbox file, which can be installed in the System file as well as the System Folder. Apple has a Network Software Installer floppy disk that you can also run to upgrade network software on your Macintosh computer. Correctly installing network system software on your Mac is the best starting point for troubleshooting network problems that may be software-related.

Understanding networks

Networking is perhaps one of the most complicated and least understood areas within the field of personal computers. Fortunately, the way computers speak on a network can be fairly easily understood by thinking of intercomputer communication in terms of a human conversation.

For two computers to communicate, they must have many things in common. First, a common language (protocol) is chosen. Then each computer is given a name (node #). The multiple members in one location are joined into a community, which is assigned a name (network #). Communication takes place via several independent messages (packets). To send a message, the sender must simply label the message with his address (node & network #) and the address of the recipient.

Network communication is accomplished through a set of rules known as *protocols*. Each task that each type of computer performs has its own set of protocols. To aid in understanding the vast proliferation of network protocols, the International Standards Organization (ISO) created a general model of protocols called the OSI (Open Systems Interconnection). Yes, the ISO created the OSI to simplify terminology.

The OSI separates network protocols into seven conceptual layers. Apple simplifies the OSI model by describing protocols as belonging to one of three layers. A detailed discussion of the various protocols and their placement within the various layers is beyond the scope of this book.

Networking problems and solutions

LocalTalk networks support up to 32 Macintosh or LocalTalk devices on a LocalTalk 'chain.' This includes printers as well as Macs and other computer platforms totaling at most 32 devices sending information across the LocalTalk cabling. Exceeding this threshold of LocalTalk devices can degrade network performance, and possibly force devices to "drop" off the network. If you need more than 32 devices per LocalTalk network, you need to add additional network devices to improve communication efficiency across a wider networked area.

Common pitfalls to LocalTalk networks include improperly terminated LocalTalk transceivers, defective cables and transceiver boxes, and loose Macintosh printer port connections. If a number of people are using the network, you should regularly check all LocalTalk connections and physical integrity of the Macintosh computers to which they are connected. Checking hardware connectivity and integrity is the best preventative maintenance for networks.

LocalTalk devices must be terminated at the beginning and end of the 'chain.' Most LocalTalk connectors ship with an RJ-11 cable-less connector. This is a terminator, and if this is not connected to the empty LocalTalk port at the beginning or end of the chain, noticeable network performance problems and inconsistent appearance of hardware on the network will occur.

EtherTalk is the standard protocol for Internet as well as inter-office connectivity because of its high transfer rate and throughput. Two types of Ethernet formats are commonly used in offices today: ThinNet and 10BASE-T. Each requires a specific transceiver to support successful communications with other devices on the EtherTalk network. Both formats must be terminated at the beginning and end of the Ethernet chain. Apple's Ethernet transceivers have termination built into them, and termination plugs are not needed for ThinNet or 10BASE-T transceivers or their expansion ports.

Current Macintosh computers either have Ethernet ports as a default configuration, or as an option for an upgrade. Transceivers are less likely to disconnect from Ethernet ports because of their more integrated connectors, which are found in the Macintosh case, or on the network card. It is still good practice to check ThinNet cable connections if a performance problem occurs because cable connections can be loosened or not completely connected to the network card.

I can't see another printer on my network.

Possible Causes

Incomplete network connection to printer or other network nodes.
Defective network cables, or transceivers.
Improper configuration of software application.
Improper configuration of Chooser.
Lack of network software on Macintosh.
Incorrect printer driver on Macintosh.

Checkpoints

Check the network connection on the back of the printer and make sure the network cabling is completely connected to the network port of the printer. If the printer supports LocalTalk and Ethernet ports, both can be connected (even to separate LocalTalk and Ethernet zones) and the printer should be accessible on the network. If connections are solid, turn off the printer for a few minutes, then turn it back on. If the printer is a LaserWriter, try accessing the LaserWriter application software to see if you can see the printer and possibly rename it or reset it.

If you still can't "see" the printer, you may want to try to connect the printer directly to your Macintosh to see if shows up in Chooser. If it shows up in Chooser, you may have an incomplete network connection between your Macintosh and the printer, or a defective network port on the printer. Contact the printer manufacturer or the network administrator to further diagnose any suspected hardware problems with networked hardware.

I can't see another Macintosh on my network.

Possible Causes

Incomplete network connection to printer or other network nodes.
Defective network cables or transceivers.
Improper configuration of software application.
Improper configuration of Chooser.
Lack of network software on Macintosh.

Checkpoints

Many of the steps outlined for network printer problems can be applied to a Macintosh that is not visible on the network. It is also possible the network may have been improperly configured, and the Macintosh may have been left out of the network chain (or loop). If the Macintosh you want to connect to has File Sharing on, try turning it off, then restarting the System. Turn File Sharing on on your Macintosh, and see if you can log on to your Macintosh from the other System you initially had problems seeing.

If you are successful at logging on to your original Mac, you most likely do not have a network configuration problem. It is more likely the System software on the problem Macintosh may be misconfigured, or may have an extension or other software conflict. Notify the network administrator, or see the System software troubleshooting section in Chapter 10 for more information.

I can't see another server on my network.

Possible Causes

Incorrect network configuration.
Server is not powered up.
Improper Macintosh network software configuration.
Defective network cable on the network.

Checkpoints

Servers on a network can either be a Macintosh running AppleShare software, a Novell NetWare server, or a Unix or Windows NT computer. If you are not able to see a server from your Macintosh, try accessing the server from another Macintosh, or if possible another computer platform. If another system can access the server, the network may not be connected to your Macintosh, or software may be missing on your Macintosh that allows access to AppleTalk networks.

I can't connect to a DOS/Windows PC on the network.

Possible Causes

Unix, DOS, or Windows server not configured to support AppleTalk network.
Incorrect network configuration.
Server is not powered up.
Improper Macintosh network software configuration.
Defective network cable on the network.

Checkpoints

Connecting to another computer platform on a network is similar to connecting to another Macintosh on a network. The main difference is you won't have the Macintosh Operating System as common software to configure on both computers. If the other computer platform supports AppleTalk network protocols, make sure all the appropriate software is installed and try to access the Macintosh from the other computer platforms' software. Now try to access the other computer platform on the network from the Macintosh. It should be visible in the right-most Chooser window.

My network is slow.

Whenever I try to copy files or log in to another Macintosh, the network appears to freeze, and it takes twice as long as usual to complete the task.

Possible Causes

This can be caused by many of the hardware misconnection scenarios mentioned earlier. Network performance can also be affected if each Macintosh is incorrectly connected to other Macintosh computers.
Improper Macintosh network software configuration.
Defective network cable on the network.
Network cable length is too long.

Checkpoints

Avoid branching cabling from one Ethernet or LocalTalk transceiver. This creates a sub-loop within the main network chain or loop, which can cause network packets to take longer to travel from one point on the network to another. Redundant looping can also force your Macintosh to send more packets than are necessary across the network cabling. If the network's Macs are spread far apart across a large surface area, you may want to consider breaking up the areas into separate network zones. A Macintosh running router software can be positioned between two different network areas to create zones. The router will track, allow additional network zone access, and strengthen the network signal being sent across zones and separate signals sent within a zone. For more information on network routers and network configuration, refer to a network consultant or network administration references.

Network security

Network security schemes largely are designed to hide data and resources from users who are not authorized access to them. It may seem that you can never have too much security. The more you protect your data, however, the greater the chance of it becoming unrecoverable. Each form of computer security has a different compromise between security and accessibility; you must weigh your need for security against the potential for data loss.

Tip

The best way to keep data accessible and continue to provide a high level of security is to perform thorough and frequent backups of all system information.

User station security

At the individual user's computer, security concerns center around the information and resources this user can access. One form of this is *inactive user security*. This type of security protects the system from unauthorized entry when a user temporarily leaves the computer. Inactive user security is most commonly a part of a screen saver package that clears the display on the monitor after a set period of inactivity.

The downside of this type of security is that by restarting the computer, the security is reset, leaving the computer vulnerable to entry. Fortunately, this hole is easily plugged by adding the next class of software: Startup user security.

Note

Screen savers that are application based (such as Dark Side of the Mac), use less memory, and suffer few compatibility troubles; nevertheless, they are less secure than applications with extensions or control panels (such as After Dark).

Startup user security

Startup user security is designed to prevent unauthorized users from accessing a computer's files after a warm or cold boot (restart or complete shutdown). As with idle user security, startup security depends on passwords to identify the proper owner of the equipment. Startup security is generally implemented through special features of a hard disk formatter or utility software (such as DiskLock by Fifth Generation Systems).

Warning

Startup security protects the Mac at a low system level: the hard disk driver. This driver is so crucial to Mac operation that if the user forgets his or her password or if the protection software becomes damaged, it can become impossible to recover the hard disk's files!

Server security

A computer that stores files, mail, databases, or other types of information holds the data that users share on a network. Each individual user can only access the data that the server allows from his or her computer, but the same user surprisingly can access all the information from the server itself. For this reason, it is important to ensure the actual physical server is secure; use inactive system security and startup user security continuously. In addition, make sure the server is behind locked doors or is tied in with an alarm system.

Network maintenance

Network maintenance is the ongoing support of users and computers on the network. This task will be made much easier if you establish and discuss a thorough network policy with your users.

The physical wiring and configuration of the network will require occasional maintenance, but most of your work will involve maintaining the network software you install.

File server maintenance—lists and backups

The main task of file server maintenance is to maintain the server's internal list of users so that it matches the physical and employee configurations of the company. In addition, the person maintaining the file server needs to make sure the server operates efficiently and that it has sufficient storage resources.

Email maintenance is similar to file server maintenance. The main task is to keep the email server's list of users current. In addition, you'll probably need to perform periodic diagnostics and cleanups of the mail files, as required by the software you're using.

If you're using a network-wide backup scheme, you need to periodically check on this machine to ensure that it's actually backing up the items it thinks it is, and that it always has sufficient backup media to perform scheduled backups. If you choose not to perform backups centrally, you should periodically check to ensure that users are performing their own backups.

Wiring maintenance

Network wiring does not require frequent maintenance. Wiring is often the first source of blame for network problems, but if it is properly installed, it is rarely the actual cause of the problem. Check the wiring periodically when it is working to spot intermittent connections. This will help you recognize any differences after things stop working properly.

To test network wiring, special software sends short messages ("pings") to different spots on the network, and times the amount of time it takes to reply. Periodic quick checks around the network will find areas with long response times, which will give you an idea of the overall status of your wiring condition. This preventative maintenance usually will rule out wiring conditions as the source of network troubles.

Note

Network wiring can be one of the most difficult and most frustrating things to trouble-shoot after it's installed. For this reason, plan the network carefully and use high-quality network wiring.

Tools for network maintenance

Performing the setup and maintenance described in this section would seem to be an insurmountable task. Fortunately, many software tools are available to help ease the task of network maintenance. These tools provide the capability to perform maintenance tasks from a variety of locations on (and off) the network.

The most accessible file server maintenance software available is the software included with your file server package. AppleShare, for example, makes use of the "AppleShare Admin" software to perform updates to user lists and access privileges. Third-party software tools such as GraceLan Server Manager or Sonic System's Server Sentry enable you to perform similar tasks, but also allow you to maintain the network from any computer on the network. With this capability, you can configure multiple file servers from one location.

Network inspection tools

A few of the most popular software packages that test network integrity are GraceLan Network manager, Sonic System's Radar, and Apple's Inter•Poll. These tools use test signals to show you how quickly and accurately each computer on the network can send and receive messages. In addition, these packages can give you information about the hardware in use at each network station.

Inter•Poll
Apple Computer, Inc.
20525 Mariani Ave.
Cupertino, CA 95014
(800) 776-2333

GraceLan Network Manager
Technology Works
4030 Braker Ln. W Ste 350
Austin, TX 78759
(800) 688-7466

Radar 4.0
Sonic Systems, Inc.
1150 Kifer Rd, #201
Sunnyvale, CA 94086
(800) 437-1518

Software update tools

When you need to upgrade common software packages on a number of networked computers, programs such as GraceLan Update Manager or Sonic System's Radar can be immensely helpful. These packages allow the network administrator to prepare and perform updates to all stations from one central location.

Remote Access

Apple's Remote Access (ARA) isn't a network management tool; it is software that uses modems to trick your computer and a remote network into thinking you're physically connected. Combining ARA with any of the above tools enables you to perform network administration tasks from virtually anywhere.

> *Warning*
> ___
>
> Don't use Apple Remote Access connections to perform network configuration changes that could affect the network status of the machine controlling the ARA connection. You could be disconnected in the middle of your changes and be unable to reconnect!

Modem Problems and Solutions

Common problems with modems often result from general misconceptions about the exact purpose of modems and how they work when compared with telephone and fax machines. Modem software ranges in number of features and quality of feature implementation from vendor to vendor. Knowledge of the different types of modem-related error messages and Internet, network, or Web site error messages can make a world of difference in getting the best performance from your modem. Before you dig into nitty gritty modem troubleshooting, try to answer these questions, which will help lead you to simple modem fixes:

1. When the modem is plugged into a power outlet, do any of the lights light up? (Try another power outlet if no lights appear.)

2. Are the modem cables missing any pins either connecting to the modem or Macintosh side of the cable?

3. Are all cables connected in the correct port?

4. Are all cables firmly connected into each port?

5. Are you able to dial out and log in to any service successfully?

My printer won't print with my modem software.

Possible Causes

Software conflict with fax/modem software.
Extension conflict in System Folder.
Serial port switcher software or hardware conflict.
Improper cable connections to printer or modem.

Checkpoints

If you have installed fax software for your modem on your Macintosh in addition to your printer software, you may need to turn off your fax software before printing. You may also want to look into using a different fax software product that supports your modem model and speed and works in tandem with your printer. Some fax software has an 'off' switch in its software interface. Turning 'off' your software (versus moving the extension out of the System Folder and restarting) may be all you need to do to let the Mac talk to the printer. Try turning off all other extensions except the printer driver and networking software to see if you can print successfully.

Try removing the serial port switcher if you have one attached to the serial port.

Check for complete power and serial cables connecting the Mac and the printer and modem.

I can't connect to another modem.

Possible Causes

Incorrect phone number for high speed access to online service.
Phone cable is not connected to phone outlet completely.
Modem is not turned on.
Modem is not configured correctly to connect to the other modem.
Fast bps not supported by service you want to log in to.
Hardware incompatibility with two modems made by the same manufacturer.
Hardware incompatibility with two modems made by two different manufacturers.

Checkpoints

Not all modems are made equal. One of the more difficult tasks is for two identical model modems to connect to each other. Two different modem models from different manufacturers may have no problem communicating or connecting at even the highest bps rates. If you are setting up an in-house high-speed modem-to-modem configuration (that is, for use with Apple's Remote Access software), you should contact the modem manufacturer or your modem vendor to see if other customers have been able to connect and communicate between the modem model you are looking at purchasing.

The modem maker might have a forum on an online service, such as eWorld, America Online, CompuServe, or Prodigy. Check here for the latest conflict information and solutions. Popular modem makers include Global Village, SupraModem, US Robotics, Hayden, and Telebit.

I can't see or use Web pages with my modem software.

Possible Causes

Improper TCP, SLIP, or PPP connection to your Macintosh and to the Internet.
Incorrect configuration of Internet or internal nameserver.
Damage to the Web client software.
Modem hardware throughput is too slow.

Checkpoints

If you are able to log in to an Internet service and get your mail from the Internet server, you will also want to eventually access World Wide Web pages. Using your modem to connect to Web sites requires software written specifically to access Web pages. Netscape 1.1 and Mosaic are both free to users to access World Wide Web pages on the Internet. Using a Web page requires a name server, similar to using news services on the Internet. Your Internet service provider should be able to provide you with your name server location when you receive access to your Internet service account.

Access to World Wide Web sites can also be accomplished by using eWorld 1.1 or America Online 2.6. Neither currently use the Netscape browser, and some users have requested faster Web page access. However, access to Web pages and Internet news is much simpler to configure and connect to using online services.

I can't access other services at the fastest speed my modem supports.

Possible Causes

Incorrect phone number for high speed access to online service.
Fast bps not supported by service you want to log in to.
Slower access rate selected in your online service software.

Checkpoints

Even though your modem can support 14.4 or 28.8, you will only be able to take advantage of these transfer rates if you log in to a service supporting these faster speeds. Most bulletin board services support 28.8, but online services currently support only 14.4 access rates. Over time, online services will upgrade to the fastest modem speeds available; however, larger services tend to upgrade transfer rates slower due to hardware costs, and the amount of time necessary to test performance and efficiency of the hardware changes. Most external modems have a display that will show what the bps is at any given time. This can vary depending on signal, network, and cabling integrity as well as how big of a workload the server and modem System is handling, and pending any unforeseen performance problems, System crashes, or power outages.

How do I turn the modem sounds off?

Possible Causes

Incorrect AT command in use.
Software settings in modem software not set correctly.
Hardware may not have any sound support.
Hardware may have defective sound components.

Checkpoints

Modems can be controlled using a number of non-user friendly command strings. This includes a string that can turn off the modem sounds. Apple's Express modem software has a control panel that enables you to toggle this feature without typing the command string. You may want the modem sounds to be audible if you have trouble communicating or connecting to an online service or modem. The presence or absence of modem sounds can tell you quite a bit about where in the login process your modem might be floundering.

I can't connect to an online service with my modem model

Possible Causes

The modem is not supported by the online service you are using.
Online service software is not properly configured for your modem.
Missing files from online software package that allow your modem to log in to the service.

Checkpoints

All online services have modem model-specific files that tell the online software how to talk between your modem and the online service's host computer at the other end of the phone line. Most online software has configuration settings that you must set before attempting to log in to an online service. If your specific modem model is not available in the list of supported models, try selecting a model close to the one you have by the same modem manufacturer. Most online services have a toll-free 800 number, which you can also call to either have the service send you the correct connection file(s), or tell you where you can download the connection file for your modem.

Modem configurations are set in the online services setup window. This usually contains the phone number for connecting to the service, and phone-specific settings for dialing out with your modem. Make sure your modem model is selected in the setup window before attempting to dial into the service.

The online software might be improperly installed. Try reinstalling or redownloading the software from a backup to see if your modem software is supported in the setup window. And if all else fails, it might be time to upgrade your operating system or even your hardware. The next chapter will discuss when it's time to upgrade.

When to Replace the OS, Software, or Hardware

The nature of the computer industry is such that hardware and software technology eventually become obsolete. Macintosh is not excluded from this rule; if you own a Mac, you will eventually encounter faster, more interesting, and innovative software requiring more memory and hard drive space. If you take the time to fine-tune and create a custom, stable software environment that is integrated into every-day software use, you will be better prepared for upgrading, repairing, and eventually replacing your Macintosh. A full section on budget is the core of this chapter, discussing accounting issues in light of changing technology.

Stability and the Art of Denial

It does not matter if you have the top-of-the line Macintosh, the smallest PowerBook, or the slowest LC model. These Macs may not need to be replaced if they run efficiently and allow you to be productive. On the other hand, if you have one or more Macs with some form of a custom environment that you can never get to work efficiently, it may be difficult to acknowledge that your equipment may need to be replaced. If you find yourself increasingly restoring files from backups, cleaning hardware so that it will be recognized by the rest of the System, or returning to older versions of System software to maintain stability, it may be time to consider replacing hardware, System software, or software applications.

Common hardware replacements include floppy disks, removable media, CD-ROM disks, keyboards, mice, cables, and buttons. These items are generally low cost and do not require extensive technical knowledge to replace. More expensive items to replace are memory, hard drives, removable media drives, CD-ROM players, monitors, and the CPU itself. The biggest compatibility hit you may face is replacing your Macintosh. If you have many peripherals and software applications, the need to use new hardware and System software may create new headaches.

Learning to replace the software

By knowing how to replace hardware and software when a problem occurs you can save yourself a lot of time, and even money. You don't need to keep an inventory of spare parts to prepare for hardware replacement. These can be ordered as needed, unless you have an older model Mac for which nearby stores or mail order companies do not keep inventory. If you are forced to keep spares around, they should be stored in a static-free bag in a dust-free and water-free environment. Software should be duplicated and backed up in its original state, and regularly as an entire folder or with other updated files. Updating and replacing internal hardware pieces is best learned by hands-on experience or training from a certified technician.

Software replacement is simpler and requires a floppy disk or CD-ROM player and hard drive or other peripheral backup mechanism. The most important thing to remember is that when you replace application software, be sure the older preferences are not in the System Folder before launching the application. This can help avoid software problems, and make the software replacement process go forward with fewer flaws.

System software and most applications come with software installers that allow you to install a configuration suitable for your work. System software is generally stable when run without addition of extensions and application software extensions. A 'clean' install is preferred when replacing System software. These steps are outlined in the OS troubleshooting section in Chapter 10. Performa System software can be replaced by restoring a backup of the System on floppy disks. A clean install for Performa System software involves renaming the System Folder to any name except "System Folder," and moving the System file out of the System Folder before restoring the backup. This creates a newly created System Folder on the hard drive.

Software applications offer a wide range of installers. Some software application installers are decompression archives created by applications such as StuffIt Deluxe, or Aladdin's ShrinkWrap software. Other installers are more complex and show you how much hard drive space the application folder will occupy, the option of installing a Power Mac-only, 68K, or fat application, as well as de-installing the application from the hard drive. Running the application's de-installer deletes all known installed files from the hard drive. Some de-installers also remove the preferences file from the System Folder.

If you have an internal CD-ROM, you may want to consider purchasing the CD version of software products and their updates. CD media lasts longer and is less susceptible to corruption and damage compared to floppy disks. Try to keep master and duplicate media stored in a dry, cool place away from magnetic sources. Also, try to keep track of the number of software updates, upgrades, and new versions you manage over time. If you feel you are not being productive, it may be that you are spending too much time troubleshooting or replacing software. You may want to consider a larger backup system, accelerator or CPU upgrade, or faster Macintosh in lieu of spending large amounts of time with smaller size media and inferior applications.

Note

If you want System software that does not bottleneck (slow down) your hardware or application performance, keep a minimal set of extensions for regular System software use. This will shorten your System's startup time, free up hard drive space, and shorten application launch times. Extension Managers, such as Apple's Extensions Manager, Now's Startup Manager, and the ever-helpful Conflict Catcher 3, can help you create minimal and every-day extension configurations to facilitate troubleshooting. Conflict Catcher can also help you identify extension and control panel software conflicts without the need to manually move files out of the System Folder.

Replacement and Upgrade Budgeting 101

At some point in the ownership of a Macintosh System, the owner or manager will have to address the issue of whether to upgrade an old Mac or replace it with a new model. In most cases the decision to upgrade a System is based largely on money. In many cases an upgrade might be inexpensive, such as when adding VRAM or a small amount of RAM. Clearly the decision to upgrade the ROM and FDHD (floppy drive, high density) on a Mac II is more difficult and more expensive. Keep in mind that System-wide logic board upgrades offered by Apple to convert machines to higher levels within the product line often include compatibility advantages and added functional specifications because of newer ROMs. Some types of accelerators and partial upgrades do not include upgraded ROMs.

Another issue to address is whether to buy one of Apple's System upgrades—convert the old Mac to a newer, speedier model—or use one of many excellent third-party accelerator boards to enhance the performance of the System. This chapter addresses the issue of upgrading a Macintosh using Apple-designed System conversions or Logic Board Upgrades (LBU). These upgrades are furnished by Apple Dealers as upgrade paths for owners who desire more performance from their existing Macintosh models while extending their investments in their current hardware. The net effect of these upgrades is to convert a (lower-level) Macintosh to a higher one within the Macintosh product line. Examples of this kind of upgrade are discussed in detail in the following sections. The upgrade kits and the Macs for which these kits are designed are listed. Other options, such as the addition of RAM, video cards, and CPU accelerators are addressed in other chapters.

Legal and accounting issues

Before undertaking any upgrade of a Macintosh or its components, you may want to inquire about the warranty risk associated with the upgrade and any financial advantage (or disadvantage) of pursuing that option. The next section discusses these factors and addresses some typical examples.

Opening the case voids warranty

All the hardware upgrades described in this chapter involve converting one kind of Macintosh to another, which requires partial or complete disassembly of the computer. To protect any warranty on the computer, an Apple Certified Technician is required to perform these upgrades. Please consult a local Apple Dealer for information on the installation of these logic board upgrades. Some third-party vendors offer these upgrades from reclaimed parts, but they will certainly not be honored by Apple as warranty items.

Depreciation of Computer Hardware

The business user who faces the decision to upgrade has a more complicated situation than the personal user. When should the Mac be retired, and should it be sold outright or traded-in for a new one? How can the unit be depreciated? Does it pay to upgrade first and extend the life of the System before trading it in for a new one? Please keep in mind that this chapter's discussion of these options is not necessarily a detailed treatment of tax law or your tax situation. Please consult a qualified accountant or CPA for advice specific to your situation and the current tax laws.

The Internal Revenue Service (IRS) has taken a big bite out of possible deductions for personal computers used in the home; nevertheless, this deduction should be not be considered frivolous. Under the current stringent guidelines few people qualify for tax deductions who are not running a business or are required by their employer to have and operate a computer as part of their jobs.

To depreciate the cost of personal computer equipment, it must be acquired and used for the purposes of the business or for the convenience of the employer. If owned personally by an employee, the Mac must be required for the job and must be shown to benefit the employer and not just make the employee's life easier or more enjoyable.

These basic tests apply only to an employee's use of a personal computer. If the computer is used 100 percent of the time in a business, and if the expenses are reasonable and ordinary, the expenses are deductible. Please consult a qualified accountant or CPA for an analysis of your situation to assess if you qualify for a deduction and to predict the amount of the deduction.

Section 179 Deduction

As with all equipment purchased to aid a business, an expense may be deducted under Section 179 of the tax code for amounts up to $17,500 (currently). That is, you may write-off up to $17,500 in expenses for business equipment immediately without the need to depreciate the cost over the required five-year period. Once again, this deduction requires that the equipment be used exclusively for business at a regular business establishment or a qualified home office. If the computer is not used exclusively for business, then the percentage of business use may be deducted as an expense. Consult an accountant for details.

Given that the cost of personal computer equipment (and especially Macintosh computers) has decreased dramatically in the recent past, the Section 179 deduction is the simplest and possibly the most popular deduction method for standard office equipment like a new Macintosh. It is a one-time write-off for the entire amount and requires no complicated depreciation schedule or bookkeeping; nevertheless, adequate records of purchase and ownership are required.

Depreciating Computer Equipment on a Schedule

If the financial structure and organization of your company are considered complex, traditional depreciation methods may be required. This section can help you set up a detailed, realistic depreciation schedule for Macintosh upgrades. The following three scenarios illustrate the financial elements of a Macintosh upgrade; they do not help in deciding whether upgrades or replacement is the best choice.

Scenario I: Buy a Mac and trade-in after 5 years for new model

One common situation in business ownership of a Macintosh involves trading in an old Mac for a new one. Under the current tax guidelines, the exchange of business or investment property for similar business or investment property is allowed as a nontaxable exchange. That is, if you trade the old Mac in (presumably for a discount on the new system), the amount gained in the trade-in is not taxable. This is referred to as *like kind exchange* and is not the same as selling the system outright and applying the money toward the purchase of a new Macintosh.

Refer to Table 12.1 for information on how the basis remaining in the system changes with time. In this scenario, a group of five Macs is to be purchased for use in a small company. Notice the trade-in value ($900 per system) is applied to the cost of the new systems, resulting in a net cost of $20,500.

Table 12.1   Depreciation Schedule for Five Systems for Five Years

Invoice Cost: $25,000
Trade-in value: $4,500
Asset value: $20,500

Year	Depreciation %	Depreciation $	Total Dep $	Basis $	Basis %	Total Deprec'd %
year 1 (half yr)	20.00	4,100.00	4,100.00	16,400.00	65.60	34.40
year 2	32.00	6,560.00	10,660.00	9,840.00	39.36	60.64
year 3	19.20	3,936.00	14,596.00	5,904.00	23.62	76.38
year 4	11.52	2,361.60	16,957.60	3,542.40	14.17	85.83
year 5	11.52	2,361.60	19,319.20	1,180.80	4.72	95.28
year 6 (half yr)	5.76	1,180.80	20,500.00	0.00	0.00	100.00
Total	100.00	20,500.00				

Because of the half-year convention used in calculating the first and last years in the five-year depreciation, the actual period of depreciation is over six years. Basis refers to the value remaining in the asset after the depreciation expense is deducted from the cost. Thus, after four years, the Macintosh System has a basis of $3542.40 remaining in it for the owner. At the end of the depreciation schedule the basis is zero.

Keep an eye on the basis left in the computer as an index of when to upgrade. If the owner of this system decides to trade the system in after three years (as many are tempted to do because of rapid expansion in the Macintosh line), he or she will have to apply the remaining basis to the cost of the new system for the depreciation of the new system. In most cases it is advisable to wait until the fifth year before retiring a system.

Tip

Often the most economical and easiest method to remember is to keep systems for five years, then buy a new system.

Scenario II: Buy a Mac and trade-in after 2 years for new model

Most power users choose to move up to new Macs every two years. With the rapid advance of Macintosh systems, the ideal system of two years ago is impossible to tolerate for those concerned with processing performance. If you're this way too, an upgrade to a new, faster system is required.

The first part of this scenario assumes that new Macs are purchased as a group with no other equipment offered in trade. There is no residual basis to transfer to the purchase because no other equipment is involved.

Luckily, at the time of the system upgrade the dealer offers a hefty trade-in for the old system to offset the cost. The total outlay for the final systems is $63,867 compared to an initial investment of $25,000.

Table 12.2   Depreciation Schedule for Five Systems with Major Upgrades

PURCHASE OF ORIGINAL EQUIPMENT

Invoice Cost: $25,000
Asset value: $25,000

Year	Depreciation %	Depreciation $	Total Dep $	Basis $	Basis %	Total Deprec'd %
year 1 (half yr)	20.00	5,000.00	5,000.00	20,000.00	80.00	20.00
year 2	32.00	8,000.00	13,000.00	12,000.00	48.00	52.00

year 3	19.20	4,800.00	17,800.00	7,200.00	28.80	71.20
year 4	11.52	2,880.00	20,680.00	4,320.00	17.28	82.72
year 5	11.52	2,880.00	23,560.00	1,440.00	5.76	94.24
year 6 (half yr)	5.76	1,440.00	25,000.00	0.00	0.00	100.00
Total	100.00	$25,000.00				

UPGRADE OF PREVIOUS SYSTEM AFTER TWO YEARS OF USE

Invoice Cost: $40,000
Trade-in value: $8,333
Basis from old: $12,000
Final cost: $43,667
Total outlay: $68,667

Year	Depreciation %	Depreciation $	Total Dep $	Basis $	Basis %	Total Deprec'd %
year 1 (half yr)	20.00	8,733.33	8,733.33	34,933.33	80.00	20.00
year 2	32.00	13,973.33	22,706.67	20,960.00	48.00	52.00
year 3	19.20	8,384.00	31,090.67	12,576.00	28.80	71.20
year 4	11.52	5,030.40	36,121.07	7,545.60	17.28	82.72
year 5	11.52	5,030.40	41,151.47	2,515.20	5.76	94.24
year 6 (half yr)	5.76	2,515.20	43,666.67	0.00	0.00	100.00
Total	100.00	$43,667.00				

Scenario III: Buy a Mac, upgrade, and trade-in after 5 years

In this situation, the owner of a small company decides to upgrade a group of five Macs with either a logic board upgrade or some other kind of interim upgrade, before finally retiring the group in a purchase of new Macs.

At the start, each system is valued at $5,000. At the second year, an upgrade of $1,200 per Mac is applied to the five systems. The existing basis at that time is $12,000 for the collection. This is added to the upgrade value of $6,000, resulting in a new basis of $18,000. The total cash outlay for the system with the upgrade is now $31,000, an increase of cost of 24 percent over the initial price of the system.

This upgrade carries the new Macs another two years until it is once again decided that new machines are called for. The five Macs are retired at a trade-in value of $1,400 each, carrying over an old basis of $8,640 from the previous schedule. The resulting value is $41,640. The total cash outlay so far on these Macs is $64,000, more than two times the value of the original system.

Table 12.3   Depreciation Schedule for Five Systems with Upgrades and Trade-ins

BUY 5 NEW MACS

Invoice Cost:	$25,000
Asset value:	$25,000

Year	Depreciation %	Depreciation $	Total Dep $	Basis $	Basis %	Total Deprec'd %
year 1 (half yr)	20.00	5,000.00	5,000.00	20,000.00	80.00	20.00
year 2	32.00	8,000.00	13,000.00	12,000.00	48.00	52.00
year 3	19.20	4,800.00	17,800.00	7,200.00	28.80	71.20
year 4	11.52	2,880.00	20,680.00	4,320.00	17.28	82.72
year 5	11.52	2,880.00	23,560.00	1,440.00	5.76	94.24
year 6 (half yr)	5.76	1,440.00	25,000.00	0.00	0.00	100.00
Total	100.00	$25,000.00				

ADD 5 UPGRADES TO PREVIOUS SYSTEMS

Invoice Cost of Upgrade:	$6,000
Basis from old:	$12,000
New Basis:	$18,000
Total Outlay:	$31,000

Year	Depreciation %	Depreciation $	Total Dep $	Basis $	Basis %	Total Deprec'd %
year 1 (half yr)	20.00	3,600.00	3,600.00	1,4400.00	80.00	20.00
year 2	32.00	5,760.00	9,360.00	8,640.00	48.00	52.00
year 3	19.20	3,456.00	12,816.00	5,184.00	28.80	71.20
year 4	11.52	2,073.60	14,889.60	3,110.40	17.28	82.72
year 5	11.52	2,073.60	16,963.20	1,036.80	5.76	94.24
year 6 (half yr)	5.76	1,036.80	18,000.00	0.00	0.00	100.00
Total	100.00	$18,000.00				

RETIRE PREVIOUS SYSTEMS AND UPGRADE TO 5 NEW MACS

Invoice Cost:	$40,000	
Basis from old:	$8,640	
Trade-in value:	$7,000	
Final cost:	$41,640	
Total Outlay:	$64,000	

Year	Depreciation %	Depreciation $	Total Dep $	Basis $	Basis %	Total Deprec'd %
year 1 (half yr)	20.00	8,328.00	8,328.00	33,312.00	80.00	20.00
year 2	32.00	13,324.80	21,652.80	19,987.20	48.00	52.00
year 3	19.20	7,994.88	29,647.68	11,992.32	28.80	71.20
year 4	11.52	4,796.93	34,444.61	7,195.39	17.28	82.72
year 5	11.52	4,796.93	39,241.54	2,398.46	5.76	94.24
year 6 (half yr)	5.76	2,398.46	41,640.00	0.00	0.00	100.00

As illustrated in these examples, the true cost of ownership can be greatly inflated if upgrades are undertaken at the wrong time or to the wrong degree. This leads many to conclude that it is wisest to purchase the most Mac possible at the start to extend the life of the system. In other words, if the buyer of these systems had chosen to "buy-up" at the start and purchased better systems than might have been originally needed, the overall useful life of the purchase might have been extended, thereby eliminating the need for the interim upgrade altogether.

On the other hand, the interim upgrade can provide considerable performance boosts to older systems that allow currently owned Macs to be used until the price of advanced systems comes down to more approachable levels.

Cost accounting of time saved due to upgrade versus upgrade cost

Another area of business upgrade decisions is whether the cost of the proposed upgrade can be recovered through the increased performance gained by the new system. Table 12.4 illustrates a type of analysis the buyer may want to consider to determine the practicality of a major upgrade.

Table 12.4   Upgrade Cost Benefits and Time Savings

Basic System	Mac hrs per day	%WP small	%WP long	%SS simple	%SS complex	%Graphics simple
Clerical use	6	50				
Basic business	4	50		50	50	
Adv business	6	20		20	20	
Basic GA	4	5				40
Adv GA	6	5				20
Basic DTP	4	40	30			25
Adv DTP	6	10	70			10
Basic tech	4	20	5	5	5	5
Adv tech	6	10	5	5	5	5
Major upgrade	50					
Net Gain		5	25	5	10	20
Time saved (hrs)						
Basic clerical use		0.150	0.000	0.150	0.000	0.000
Basic business		0.100	0.000	0.000	0.200	0.000
Adv business		0.060	0.000	0.060	0.120	0.000
Basic GA		0.010	0.000	0.000	0.000	0.320
Adv GA		0.015	0.000	0.000	0.000	0.240
Basic DTP		0.080	0.300	0.000	0.000	0.200
Adv DTP		0.030	1.050	0.000	0.000	0.120
Basic tech		0.040	0.050	0.020	0.020	0.040
Adv tech		0.030	0.075	0.015	0.030	0.060

TOTALS	TIME SAVED	$ HR	$ DAY	$ YR
Basic clerical use	0.300	30	9.00	3,069.00
Basic business	0.300	40	12.00	4,092.00
Adv business	1.040	50	52.00	17,732.00
Basic GA	1.063	30	31.90	10,877.90
Adv GA	1.755	60	105.30	35,907.30
Basic DTP	0.647	30	19.40	6,615.40
Adv DTP	1.400	60	84.00	28,644.00
Basic tech	0.877	40	35.07	11,957.73
Adv tech	1.570	80	125.60	42,829.60

Basic System	%Graphics complex	%DB simple	%DB complex	Other special	Total	
Clerical use					100	
Basic business					100	
Adv business			40		100	
Basic GA	55				100	
Adv GA	75				100	
Basic DTP	5				100	
Adv DTP	10				100	
Basic tech		5		50	100	
Adv tech		5		65	100	
Major upgrade						
Net Gain	33	20	33	33		
Time saved (hrs)					*hours*	*mins*
Basic clerical use	0.000	0.000	0.000	0.000	0.300	18.0
Basic business	0.000	0.000	0.000	0.000	0.300	18.0
Adv business	0.000	0.000	0.800	0.000	1.040	62.4
Basic GA	0.733	0.000	0.000	0.000	1.063	63.8
Adv GA	1.500	0.000	0.000	0.000	1.755	105.3
Basic DTP	0.067	0.000	0.000	0.000	0.647	38.8
Adv DTP	0.200	0.000	0.000	0.000	1.400	84.0
Basic tech	0.000	0.040	0.000	0.667	0.877	52.6
Adv tech	0.000	0.000	0.000	1.300	1.570	94.2

TOTALS	**TIME SAVED**	**$ HR**	**$ DAY**	**$ YR**
Basic clerical use	0.300	30	9.00	3,069.00
Basic business	0.300	40	12.00	4,092.00
Adv business	1.040	50	52.00	17,732.00
Basic GA	1.063	30	31.90	10,877.90
Adv GA	1.755	60	105.30	35,907.30
Basic DTP	0.647	30	19.40	6,615.40
Adv DTP	1.400	60	84.00	28,644.00
Basic tech	0.877	40	35.07	11,957.73
Adv tech	1.570	80	125.60	42,829.60

In this example, nine different fictitious Macintosh users are listed with an estimate of the number of hours they spend on their Macs and the tasks they employ in an average day. You should design your own chart to weigh the amount and type of usage in your organization.

In this example, a basic clerical employee uses his Macintosh exclusively for light word processing and simple spreadsheets. This might cover such situations as short letters, memos, email, and some expense reports. Other users in the company use their Macs for long document preparations, annual reports, retouching photos, and CAD, and as such are entered differently in the table for other applications.

Next, a value for (or degree of) the proposed upgrade is assigned to the system. In this case a 50 percent upgrade is selected; that is, the performance of the system is increased 1.5 times over the baseline to see what savings will result. A net gain or net benefit factor is then assigned to each different computer task or application. This example assumes a 50 percent increase in overall system performance will be translated to some other (lesser) factor in actual net efficiency or productivity in the workplace. "Light" use of the Macintosh—and the applications used for this purpose—will not benefit as greatly from a major upgrade as "heavier," more serious, applications. You should substitute your own employees and Macs in the chart to judge the benefits of a "buy-up" approach.

Table 12.5   Comparison of Performance and Costs for Apple LBUs

Baseline Model	Disk	CPU	Fl. Pt.	Video	Upgrade Model
128k					Mac Plus
512k					Mac Plus
512Ke					Mac Plus
SE	2.5	0.8	0.6	1	SE/30
Classic	2.5	0.8	0.6	6	Classic II
LC					LCIII
LCII (P400...)		7.6	3.8	4.7	5
Mac II	6.5	5.4	68	5	Mac IIfx
Mac IIx					Mac IIfx
Mac IIcx					Mac IIci
Mac IIci	10.7	8.3	129	9	Quadra 650
Mac IIci	10.7	8.3	129	9	Quadra 700
LC 520					Mac IIvx
Mac IIvx(P600)	10.2	7.3	151	9	Quadra 650

Based on these numbers, estimates of time saved per Macintosh workday are generated. The basic clerical employee saves 18 minutes per day; high-end graphics and engineering users save more than an hour a day because of the faster Macintosh System. Depending on the value of the billable hours for these employees, the savings or gains for the employer can be considerable. If these savings can be directly transferred to more jobs processed by the employer, the cost of the upgrade can be recaptured directly in a short time.

Upgrading an Older Mac

Table 12.5 lists upgrade paths and options for desktop Macintosh Systems. Along with upgrades offered by Apple, many third-party manufacturers offer their own accelerator or upgrade kits to enhance the performance of older systems. The logic board upgrades (LBU) provided by Apple are the only boards discussed in this chapter. These upgrades allow the user to convert an older Mac to a speedier and more capable model. Other upgrade options are discussed in subsequent chapters.

Disk	CPU	Fl. Pt.	Video	Cost of Upgrade	Vendor
				$100	Shreve Systems
				$100	Shreve Systems
				$100	Shreve Systems
				$400	Shreve Systems
7.6	3.8	4.6	5.8	$700	Apple
10	10	10	10	$1,700	Apple
10	10	10	10	$1,700	Apple
9.2	18	240	8	$1,299	
9.2	18	240	8	$1,299	
10.7	8.3	129	9	$400	
18.2	42	406	23	$1,400	Shreve Systems
					Apple
10.2	7.3	151	9		Apple
18.2	42	406	23		Apple

continues

Table 12.5 Comparison of Performance and Costs for Apple LBUs, CONTINUED					
Baseline Model	Disk	CPU	Fl. Pt.	Video	Upgrade Model
Centris 610					6100/60
Centris 650					7100/66
Centris 660AV	16	32	307	22	6100/60AV
Quadra 610	18.4	31	307	18	6100/60
Quadra 650	18.2	42	406	23	7100/66
Quadra 660AV	16	32	307	22	6100/60AV
Quadra 800	19	42	410	25	8100/80
Quadra 840AV	19	49	476	30	8100/80AV
Quadra 900					Quadra 950
Quadra 950	16	41	400	27	

The overall performance figures given for each Macintosh use the Macintosh Classic as a reference point or a value of 1 for comparison. For example, a Mac Plus is considered 80 percent the performer of a Classic; the Centris 650 is roughly 10.6 times faster. A table of conversion kits and logic board upgrades follows. Not all possible upgrades are still offered by Apple. Those offered by third-party vendors are marked. The buyer interested in these upgrades should compare the price of the LBU to the cost of a new Macintosh. Given that the street price of a Quadra 605 is currently below $990, the attractiveness of LBU upgrades has diminished markedly in recent months.

Upgrade paths

A description of the upgrade paths for various Macintosh models is given in this section. Keep in mind that not all LBUs are currently available; the buyer may have to invest in third-party hardware. Where possible, model numbers for Apple upgrades are given. Consult a local Apple Dealer for more information on these upgrades and current pricing. Refer to Table 12.5 for a list of which particular Macs have upgrade options to other models and what the resulting performance and features benefits should be. In many cases upgrades benefit more than just the speed of the machine. Expanded features like built-in video, color, maximum RAM, and built-in Ethernet are such examples.

Upgrades for the 128K, 512K, and the 512Ke Macs

Early pre-Mac Plus models are not common candidates for upgrades. Largely replaced by faster Macs, they are often still maintained by their (original) owners for sentimental reasons and not because of their general utility. In most cases the original Apple upgrades can still be purchased through local Apple dealers. There are still third-party sources of these upgrades, too, although they are less common each year.

Disk	CPU	Fl. Pt.	Video	Cost of Upgrade	Vendor
20	112	3220	25	$1,600	Apple
21	166	4185	34	$2,000	Apple
20	151	3292	18	$2,000	Apple
20	112	3220	25	$1,600	Apple
21	166	4185	34	$2,000	Apple
20	151	3292	18	$1,900	Apple
22	202	4339	35	$3,000	Apple
				$3,000	Apple
16	41	400	27		Apple

As far as Apple upgrades are concerned, one option for a 128K or 512Ke Mac is to buy the newer 128K ROM and replace the original 64K ROM chips. Apple offered a two-part upgrade to a Mac Plus for these earlier models that included a ROM upgrade and an 800K internal floppy disk drive. The 512Ke model already has the 128K ROMs and floppy drive.

The second part of the upgrade from Apple involves installing the Macintosh Plus logic board, which replaces the original logic board. The Mac Plus upgrade provides a SCSI port and 1 MB of onboard RAM as part of the basic kit. The 128K ROM upgrade must accompany this upgrade because the SCSI port and floppy disk require the code in the new ROMs to operate. Currently a 512Ke to Mac Plus upgrade is around $100.

Upgrades for the Plus, SE, and SE/30

Apple-approved logic board upgrades for the Mac Plus are not available. As such, the usual upgrade path is to add RAM, buy a third-party accelerator, or sell the unit outright and apply the money to a new Mac. All these options are addressed in later sections.

The Macintosh SE, on the other hand, can be upgraded to the SE/30. This upgrade is mostly a logic board swap of the original 68000 SE logic board with the SE/30's 16 MHz 68030 board. Otherwise the units are the same; the official Apple upgrade kit includes only a new bezel for the converted SE/30 and a metal chassis for old SEs that might need a replacement. Although the SE/30 supports the Superdrive directly, no drive unit is included in the upgrade kit. The Superdrive must be purchased separately to complete the upgrade. The Superdrive can be added to the SE without an SE/30 logic board if a drive upgrade is the only thing needed. Keep in mind that because the SE/30 has a different expansion slot from the SE, all cards used in the SE will have to be replaced with SE/30-compatible versions after completing the upgrade. RAM is directly transferable to the new SE/30.

Besides CPU speed, two big advantages the SE/30 has over the SE are the wider and faster data bus and the support of color video in its ROM (a PDS video card must be used). The SE/30 also supports up to 128 MB of RAM, compared to 4 MB in the SE. The original price of the Apple SE/30 upgrade kit was $1,699. Recently the street price of this upgrade kit was around $700 and a single SE/30 logic board may be purchased for around $400.

The SE/30, however, has no logic board upgrade to any other Macintosh model. See the chapters on accelerators and RAM for upgrade options for this Macintosh.

Macintosh Classic to Classic II Upgrade

The Macintosh Classic can be upgraded to the Classic II by purchasing the Classic II LBU. The part number is M1545LL/A.

Like the SE-to-SE/30 upgrade, the Classic II has a faster data bus and supports 10 MB of RAM instead of 4 MB in the Classic. The Classic II has 2 MB of hard-soldered RAM onboard; the Classic has 1 MB. Because the Classic II uses a 68030, a PMMU is present for Virtual Memory.

Upgrades for the Mac II, IIx, and IIcx Models

The original Mac II and IIx are still loved by their owners because of the hefty power supply and six NuBus slots. In addition to these options, the II and IIx have eight 30-pin SIMM slots for memory upgrades. The big differences between the Mac II and IIx are that the II has a 16 MHz 020 processor in contrast to the IIx's 16 MHz 030; the Mac IIx also has a PMMU and Superdrive support built in.

Apple offered a Mac II to IIx conversion kit (originally priced at $2,199) that involved a logic board swap and installation of the Superdrive mechanism. Third-party upgrade kits are available for the logic board at around $400. The Superdrive upgrade for the Mac II is also available at around $250 (ROMs only) not including the cost of the new floppy drive mechanism (around $200).

Another (less popular) upgrade for the Mac II or IIx converts either machine to a Macintosh IIfx. The logic board upgrade and SIMM swap is available as an Apple upgrade kit or through third-party vendors as a logic board upgrade.

An original Mac II or IIx is upgraded to a Macintosh IIfx by changing the logic board, adding new (fx-specific) 64-pin SIMMs, and a Superdrive floppy mechanism. There is no need to upgrade a Mac II to a IIx first since the logic board upgrade is all-inclusive and the other components in the System, like the power supply for instance, remain the same.

The Mac IIfx logic board provides a 40 MHz 68030 with FPU and built-in PMMU. A 32K static RAM cache is included along with the SWIM controller for the 1.44 MB Superdrive. The 512K ROM is in a SIMM socket (in contrast to older Macs that use DIP socketed ROMs). Currently the cost of a IIfx conversion is around $2,200 from Apple.

The most popular approach to upgrading an original Mac II is to upgrade the floppy drive(s) to Superdrive capability and employ a third-party accelerator for the performance boost. The upgrade procedure for the Superdrive involves ROM and SWIM chip replacements on the Mac II logic board.

Upgrade for IIcx Models

An official Apple upgrade for the Macintosh IIcx converts it to a Macintosh IIci. The form factor of the two computers is the same, so the upgrade is a logic board swap. The IIcx has the Superdrive by default so that upgrade is unnecessary. Things to look out for in this upgrade include checking to see if the 30-pin SIMMs being placed in the (new) IIci are 80 ns or faster. If the IIci's built-in video is to be used, make sure that the fast (80 ns) SIMMs are in SIMM bank A for best results. The upgrade to a Mac IIci provides the user with a 25 MHz 68030 processor with built-in PMMU and FPU onboard. An onboard 120-pin connector accommodates cache cards and accelerators. Similar to the IIfx, the IIci includes a 512K ROM in a SIMM; the IIcx uses a 256K ROM hard-soldered on the logic board. Currently the cost (from a third-party vendor) of a Macintosh IIci logic board is around $400.

Macintosh IIci Upgrade Path

There is a discontinued Apple-approved upgrade of the Macintosh IIci to the Quadra 700. The Quadra 700 is an 040-based Macintosh that offers better than twice the performance of the IIci. In addition, the Quadra 700 sports a much better video system. See Table 12.5 for comparisons. Although this Apple upgrade is discontinued, third-party upgrades of the IIci to the Quadra 700 are available.

Macintosh IIvx Upgrade Path

Apple has announced an upgrade path for owners of the Macintosh IIvx to an 040-based system. For owners of this Mac, Apple provides an LBU for the Mac IIvx to a Quadra 650. The part number for the upgrade kit is M1330LL/A. This upgrade kit can also be used with the Performa 600 and 600CD models.

In addition to the 040 upgrade, Apple has prepared another upgrade option for the IIvx owner to the Power Macintosh 7100/66. Power Macintosh upgrades and part numbers are detailed later in this chapter.

Macintosh LCII LBU for the Macintosh LC

The Macintosh LC is upgradeable to the LCII via LBU kit M1710LL/A. This kit includes the LCII logic board (with 4 MB RAM installed), System 7.1, documentation, and a new cover for the computer. No HyperCard is included in the kit.

Macintosh LCIII LBU for the Macintosh LC

All LCs and LCIIs are upgradeable to the LCIII via Apple upgrade M1386LL/A. This kit can also be used with Performa models 400, 405, 410, and 430. The LCIII has a 25 MHz 030 along with a wider and faster data bus. A PMMU is present. The coprocessor (FPU) is optional. Maximum RAM in an LCIII is 36 MB in contrast to the 10 MB limit in the LC and LCII. The LCIII also has improved video specifications over the LC and LCII.

Upgrade for the LCII and LCIII Macintoshes

A Macintosh model LCII or LCIII can be upgraded to a Macintosh LC 475 with Apple-provided LBU kit M2139. This kit can also be used for the Performa models 400, 405, 410, 430, 450, 460, 466, and 467. Note that there is currently no direct upgrade for a Macintosh LC to a Mac LC 475.

This kit includes: Macintosh LC 475 logic board which has a 68LC040 processor, name badge, Getting Started Manual, Install Me First disk, Disk Tools disk, Agency approval label, Resource Guide, and product return form. Note that this kit does not include System software. Owners who do not have System 7.1 will need to buy it.

Performa 400, 405, 410, and 430 to Performa 450 Upgrade

Performa models 400, 405, 410, and 430 can be upgraded directly to the Performa 450 by purchasing the LCIII LBU kit number M1386LL/A from an Apple dealer. The Performa 450 is identical to the LCIII, both of which use a 68030 processor.

Upgrade for the LC 520 (and Performa 550)

A LBU kit from Apple converts the Mac LC 520 or Performa 550 to an LC 575, which has a 68LC040 processor. The Apple part number for this kit is M2479LL/A.

Macintosh Quadra 900 or Quadra 950 Upgrade to the AWS 95

Quadra models 900 and 950 have an upgrade kit to the Apple Workgroup Server 95, which has a 33MHz 68040 processor, using Apple part number M6940ZA. This is referred to as the AWS 95 PDS Card Upgrade Kit in the Apple parts catalog.

Upgrades to the PowerPC

A number of PowerPC (PPC) upgrades for current Macintosh models are emerging. These upgrades mostly apply to 040-based Macs, although there are exceptions. A list of the currently available PPC Upgrade Cards and Logic Board Upgrades follows. Consult Table 12.5 in this chapter to see if your Mac qualifies for a PPC upgrade. These upgrades include System software version 7, complete setup, learning and reference documentation, and a limited Apple warranty.

PowerBook upgrades to PowerPC models are also available for PowerBook and Duo models. These upgrade the 680LC040 processor to a 603e PowerPC processor. PowerBook Duo 200 series models keep the screen they originally shipped with, but are replaced with the Power Mac motherboard. Upgrades from the PowerBook series to the 5300 Power Mac have the option of replacing the screen in addition to the motherboard. PowerBook users can also upgrade to the 190/66, which has a 33MHz 68LC040 processor.

Power Macintosh Upgrade Card

Part number M2843LL/A Power Macintosh Upgrade Card includes all necessary hardware for installation and complete instructions. A photograph of the Apple PPC Upgrade Card is shown in Figure 12.1. For more information on Power Macintosh upgrade card product requirements and compatibility, see Chapter 6.

Figure 12.1   Power Macintosh Upgrade Card.

- Power Macintosh 6100/66 LBU. Order number M2343LL/A. This kit comes with 8 MB of RAM and a Power Macintosh Display Adapter.

- Power Macintosh 6100/60AV LBU. Order number M2901LL/A. This kit comes with 8 MB of RAM and a cable for S-video to composite video.

- Power Macintosh 7100/66 LBU. Order number M2474LL/A. This kit comes with 8 MB of RAM and 1 MB VRAM.

- Power Macintosh 7100/66AV LBU. Order number M2840LL/A. This kit comes with 8 MB of RAM, a cable for S-video to composite video, and 2 MB of VRAM.

- Power Macintosh 8100/80 LBU. Order number M2344LL/A. This kit comes with 8 MB of RAM and 2 MB of VRAM.

- Power Macintosh 8100/80AV LBU. Order number M2902LL/A. This kit comes with 8 MB of RAM, a cable for S-video to composite video conversion, and 2 MB of VRAM.

Internal CD-ROM Upgrades for Power Macintosh

In addition to the System upgrades, a number of CD-ROM upgrades apply to Macintosh models with a 5.25-inch drive bay. For example, the Mac IIvx, Centris/Quadra 610, Centris/Quadra 650, Quadra 800, Quadra 900, and Quadra 950 all qualify. Consult an Apple dealer for more information on specific internal CD-ROM upgrade features.

- The AppleCD 300i Plus internal CD-ROM drive kit: order Apple part number M3152LL/A.

- Apple 600e external CD ROMs are part number M3958LL/A.

- The adapter kit for Power Macintosh 6100/60 or 6100/60AV: order Apple part number M2846LL/A.

- The adapter kit for Power Macintosh 7100/66 or 6100/66AV: order Apple part number M3126LL/A.

- The adapter kit for Power Macintosh 8100/80 or 8100/80AV: order Apple part number M2847LL/A.

When to Buy, When to Trade—The Basic Questions

The decision to upgrade a Macintosh system is the product of a long series of questions and lengthy analysis. Sometimes the solution to upgrade is easy, such as when the current system clearly lacks a specific feature or capability that is needed to complete day-to-day tasks. Other times the elusive "speed" questions pop up and the user must assess what value an extra measure of time is worth in his or her day. To help evaluate the type and timing of the upgrade, the following section addresses some of the basic questions surrounding upgrades and the best time to purchase a new Mac.

In the course of deciding when to upgrade and what to upgrade to, the Macintosh user or manager should address the following:

- What am I unable to do now that an upgrade will permit?

- What are the new features and performance worth?

- Do I need a complete system upgrade, or will an enhancement to a specific subsystem (Ethernet card, SCSI accelerator, faster hard drive) suffice?

- What are the advantages and disadvantages of using an accelerator?

- What are the advantages and disadvantages of a logic board upgrade?

- Should I just buy a new Mac (and perhaps sell the old)?

Most of these issues have been addressed in this chapter, such as possible logic board upgrades and the performance boosts that accompany them. The tables presented in this chapter list Macintosh products which offer upgrade potential for older systems. The preceding sections have also addressed some of the financial elements of upgrading, including cost benefits derived from using faster systems in the workplace. Finally, when to buy and how to time a purchase of a new system is highlighted to help you get the most bang for your buck.

When to buy—product life-cycle

Recently the rate of new Macintosh arrivals has made users cautious of buying a Macintosh too soon or without due need. Mac IIvx owners, for example, were treated to a cathartic drop in price that still has some owners shaking; in addition, the Centris models are almost a footnote in the Macintosh genealogy.

Consider the history of the Mac IIci. Revered as the Old Faithful of midrange Macs, this model was on the price list from September 1989 to February 1993. After the Mac IIci was on the market for a year, the price dropped 15 percent. The Mac IIfx was released on or about March 1990. Shortly thereafter, the Mac IIci price dropped another 20 percent from its previous value. After October 1990 the price remained reasonably stable, although decaying slightly. At the time of its discontinuation, its street value was around $2000 (roughly 30 percent of its original value) and now it can be had for under $1000.

The behavior of the resale price of an older Macintosh model provides some clue of what to expect after you buy a new Mac. Don't buy too soon: give the model enough time to mature, and keep an ear to the ground for upcoming models and chips that might nudge its place in the line-up, as the IIfx did to the IIci. Second, assuming the model is stable, wait for the first price drop after the excitement of its release. If the model is a winner, it will hold its value reasonably well for a time, and then probably get nudged out of line by a newer model or be discontinued outright by Apple while demand (and its value) is still high. Keep an eye open for upcoming models or abrupt changes in price that might herald a change in the product line, and try to sell before the value of the system takes too large a hit.

Recently the product life-cycles have been so short that strategically timing the purchase of a new Mac is similar to predicting stock or commodities prices. Many Macintosh power users and fanatics are trading in gear every nine months or so to remain current. As a general rule, avoid buying a new model within the first 90 days of its introduction unless you are looking for the bleeding-edge technology and don't mind paying the extra for the early lead.

Another important recommendation is to look for Macs that have upgrade paths. It appears that Apple has an interest in providing users with long-term value in their investment by providing more logic board upgrades to new and existing models. Because PowerPC is central to the business plan for Apple, most modern Macs will be given some kind of upgrade to the PowerPC chip. Otherwise, use the following tips to plan your purchase for long-term value from your Macintosh system.

Buy-up for greatest long-term value

Popular opinion among many long time Mac users is to buy the most computer you can afford for long-term value. Try to provide yourself and your users with enough elbow room in features and performance to accommodate the expansion in software requirements along with future hardware and storage needs.

Plan for the long-term

Software developers are developing their wares to run on next year's Macs, not on the LCIII. System software is growing at a pace equal to the arrival of new Macs and is targeted at the new machines and new processors, not those from years past. There is no way to avoid having to buy or upgrade a new Mac, but hopefully by choosing your Mac wisely you can avoid having to upgrade too soon or as frequently as less astute buyers.

Mac models and upgrades

Table 12.6 lists Macintosh specifications and upgrades. In it you will find a compilation of Apple approved upgrades along with possible buy-up options. In some cases, more than one Apple upgrade may be possible for a specific model; in most cases, more than one buy-up model is available if price is no option. In most cases, the next Mac up the ladder of performance is included, in case you decide to "buy-up" to the higher model Mac.

Use Table 12.6 to cross-check the upgrade against added features and performance. Use this table also to assess the cost/performance benefit of a complete conversion. Keep in mind that, in contrast to other upgrades, these will result in ownership of a completely new Macintosh. In many cases, more than the speed of the CPU changes. Performance of major subsystems such as the SCSI port and video system may change as well and are reflected in the data in the table.

Table 12.6   Macintosh Specifications and Upgrades

	128K	512K	Plus	512Ke
GENERAL SPECS				
Date introduced	Jan-84	Sep-84	Jan-86	Apr-86
Date discontinued	Apr-86	Apr-86	Oct-90	Aug-86
Product Lifetime	2.25	1.58	4.75	0.33
Overall perf. (rel. Classic)	0.8	0.8	0.8	0.8
Effective MIPS rating	0.7	0.7	0.7	0.7
Used Price	100	150	350	200
PROCESSOR SPECS				
Model	68000	68000	68000	68000
Clock speed	8	8	8	8
Data path (speed/ size)	8/16	8/16	8/16	8/16
Coprocessor	none	none	none	none
PMMU	none	none	none	none
MEMORY SPECS				
Hard-soldered RAM	128K	512K	0	512K
Memory cache	none	none	none	none
Maximum RAM	128K	512K	4 MB	512K
No. SIMM sockets	n/a	n/a	4	n/a
SIMM type	DIP	DIP	30-pin	DIP
Minimum RAM speed (ns)	150	150	150	150
VIDEO SPECS				
Built-in video	mono	mono	mono	mono
Standard VRAM	0	0	0	0
Maximum VRAM	0	0	0	0
VRAM sockets	0	0	0	0
Standard color	B&W	B&W	B&W	B&W
Maximum colors	0	0	0	0
Maximum monitor size 8-bit	n/a	n/a	n/a	n/a
Maximum monitor size 16-bit	n/a	n/a	n/a	n/a

	SE	SE/30	Classic	Classic II (P200)
GENERAL SPECS				
Date introduced	Mar-87	Jan-89	Oct-90	Oct-91
Date discontinued	Oct-90	Oct-91	Sep-92	Sep-93
Product Lifetime	3.59	2.75	1.92	1.92
Overall perf. (rel. Classic)	1	3.2	1	1.8
Effective MIPS rating	3.9	0.7	3.9	0.7
Used Price	450	650	450	600
PROCESSOR SPECS				
Model	68000	68030	68000	68030
Clock speed	8	16	8	16
Data path (speed/ size)	8/16	16/32	8/16	16/16
Coprocessor	none	68882	none	opt.
PMMU	none	yes	none	yes
MEMORY SPECS				
Hard-soldered RAM	0	0	1 MB	2 MB
Memory cache	0	0	0	0
Maximum RAM	4 MB	128 MB	4 MB	10 MB
No. SIMM sockets	4	8	2 on bd.	2
SIMM type	30-pin	30-pin	30-pin	30-pin
Minimum RAM speed (ns)	150	120	120	100
VIDEO SPECS				
Built-in video	mono	mono	mono	mono
Standard VRAM	0	0	0	0
Maximum VRAM	0	0	0	0
VRAM sockets	0	0	0	0
Standard color	B&W	B&W	B&W	B&W
Maximum colors	0	0	0	0
Maximum monitor	n/a	n/a	n/a	n/a
Maximum monitor size 16-bit	n/a	n/a	n/a	n/a

continues

Table 12.6   Macintosh Specifications and Upgrades, CONTINUED

	128K	512K	Plus	512Ke
SLOT & PORT SPECS				
NuBus slots	0	0	0	0
PDS slot	0	0	0	0
Cache slot	0	0	0	0
Sound port	0	0	out	0
Video port				
Serial (RS-232/-422)	2	2	2	2
ADB				
Max SCSI transfer (MB/s)	0	0	1.25	0
Networking				
Superdrive	No	No	No	No
Power supply (W)	60	60	60	60
Official Apple LBU	Mac Plus kit	Mac Plus kit	none	Mac Plus kit
Currently offered by Apple?	No	No	No	No
"Buy-up" or other upgrade options	512 512Ke			

	Color Classic	LC	LCII (P400,&c.)	LCIII (P450)
GENERAL SPECS				
Date introduced	Feb-93	Nov-90	Mar-92	Feb-93
Date discontinued	Feb-94	Mar-92	Mar-93	
Product Lifetime	1.00	1.33	1.00	current
Overall perf. (rel. Classic)	1.7	1.8	1.7	3.6
Effective MIPS rating	6.3	3.9	2.6	6.3
Used Price	700	350	500	600
PROCESSOR SPECS				
Model	68030	68020	68030	68030
Clock speed	16	16	16	25
Data path (speed/ size)	16/16	16/16	16/16	25/32
Coprocessor	optional	optional	optional	optional
PMMU	yes	none	yes	yes
MEMORY SPECS				
Hard-soldered RAM	4 MB	2 MB	4 MB	4 MB
Memory cache	0	0	0	0

	SE	SE/30	Classic	Classic II (P200)
SLOT & PORT SPECS				
NuBus slots	0	0	0	0
PDS slot	1	1	0	0
Cache slot	0	0	0	0
Sound port	0	0	0	2
Video port				
Serial (RS-232/-422)	2	2	2	2
ADB	2	2	1	1
Max SCSI transfer (MB/s)	1.25	1.25	1.25	1.25
Networking				
Superdrive	Later models	Yes	Yes	Yes
Power supply (W)	100	75	76	100
Official Apple LBU	SE/30	none	Classic II LBU	none
Currently offered by Apple?	No	No	Yes	
"Buy-up" or other upgrade options	LCIII	LCIII	LCIII	LCIII

	II	IIx	IIcx	IIci
GENERAL SPECS				
Date introduced	Mar-87	Oct-88	Mar-89	Sep-89
Date discontinued	Jan-90	Oct-90	Mar-91	Feb-93
Product Lifetime	2.84	2.00	2.00	3.42
Overall perf. (rel. Classic)	2.4	2.9	2.9	4.3
Effective MIPS rating	2.6	3.9	3.9	6.3
Used Price	500	650	550	800
PROCESSOR SPECS				
Model	68020	68030	68030	68030
Clock speed	16	16	16	25
Data path (speed/ size)	16/32	16/32	16/32	25/32
Coprocessor	68881	68882	68882	68882
PMMU	option	yes	yes	yes
MEMORY SPECS				
Hard-soldered RAM	0	0	0	0
Memory cache	0	0	0	0

continues

Table 12.6   Macintosh Specifications and Upgrades, CONTINUED

	Color Classic	LC	LCII (P400,&c.)	LCIII (P450)
Maximum RAM	10 MB	10 MB	10 MB	36 MB
No. SIMM sockets	2	2	2	1
SIMM type	30-pin	30-pin	30-pin	72-pin
Minimum RAM speed (ns)	100	100	100	80
VIDEO SPECS				
Built-in video	color	color	color	color
Standard VRAM	256K	256K	256K/512K	512K
Maximum VRAM	512K	512K	512K	768K
VRAM sockets	1	1	1	1
Standard color	256	16	16	256
Maximum colors	32,768	256	256	32,768
Maximum monitor size 8-bit	n/a	14 inch	14 inch	16 inch
Maximum monitor size 16-bit	n/a	n/a	n/a	14 inch
SLOT & PORT SPECS				
NuBus slots	0	0	0	0
PDS slot	1	1	1	1
Cache slot	0	0	0	0
Sound port	1	2	2	2
Video port				
Serial (RS-232/-422)	2	2	2	2
ADB	2	1	1	1
Max SCSI transfer (MB/s)	1.25	1.5	1.5	1.5
Networking				
Superdrive	Yes	Yes	Yes	Yes
Power supply (W)	100	50	50	50
Official Apple LBU	none	LCIII LBU	LCIII LBU	LC475 LBU
Currently offered by Apple?		No	No	No
"Buy-up" or other upgrade options	LCIII		LC475 LBU	Mac IIvx LC520

	II	*IIx*	*IIcx*	*IIci*
Maximum RAM	68 MB	128 MB	128 MB	128 MB
No. SIMM sockets	8	8	8	8
SIMM type	30-pin	30-pin	30-pin	30-pin
Minimum RAM speed (ns)	120	120	120	80
VIDEO SPECS				
Built-in video	No	No	No	color
Standard VRAM	n/a	n/a	n/a	0
Maximum VRAM	n/a	n/a	n/a	0
VRAM sockets	0	0	0	0
Standard color	n/a	n/a	n/a	256
Maximum colors	n/a	n/a	n/a	256
Maximum monitor size 8-bit	n/a	n/a	n/a	14 inch
Maximum monitor size 16-bit	n/a	n/a	n/a	14 inch
SLOT & PORT SPECS				
NuBus slots	6	6	3	3
PDS slot	0	0	0	1
Cache slot	0	0	0	1
Sound port	1	1	1	1
Video port				
Serial (RS-232/-422)	2	2	2	2
ADB	2	2	2	2
Max SCSI transfer (MB/s)	1.25	1.25	1.25	1.25
Networking				
Superdrive	option	Yes	Yes	Yes
Power supply (W)	230	230	230	90
Official Apple LBU	Mac IIfx	Mac IIfx	IIci, Q700	Q700
Currently offered by Apple?	No	No	No	No
"Buy-up" or other upgrade options	Q605/ Q610	Q610/ Q650/Q800	Q605/ Q610	Q610/Q650/ Q800

continues

Table 12.6 Macintosh Specifications and Upgrades, CONTINUED

	IIsi	LC520	IIvx (P600)	Color Classic II
GENERAL SPECS				
Date introduced	Oct-90	Jun-93	Oct-92	Oct-93
Date discontinued	Mar-93	Feb-94	Oct-93	
Product Lifetime	2.42	0.7	1.00	current
Overall perf. (rel. Classic)	2.9	3.7	4	4.6
Effective MIPS rating	5	6.3	7	8.3
Used Price	600	1650	875	700
PROCESSOR SPECS				
Model	68030	68030	68030	68030
Clock speed	20	25	32	33
Data path (speed/size)	20/32	25/32	16/32	33/32
Coprocessor	option	option	68882(opt)	option
PMMU	yes	yes	yes	yes
MEMORY SPECS				
Hard-soldered RAM	1	4	4	4
Memory cache	0	0	32K	0
Maximum RAM	65 MB	36 MB	68 MB	36 MB
No. SIMM sockets	4	1	4	*unknown*
SIMM type	30-pin	30-pin	30-pin	*unknown*
Minimum RAM speed (ns)	80	80	80	*unknown*
VIDEO SPECS				
Built-in video	color	color	color	*unknown*
Standard VRAM	0	0	512K(0K)	512K
Maximum VRAM	0	256K	1 MB	1 MB
VRAM sockets	0	1	2	1
Standard color	256	256	256	256
Maximum colors	256	32,768	32,768	32,768
Maximum monitor size 8-bit	14 inch	14 inch	14 inch	n/a
Maximum monitor size 16-bit	n/a	n/a	14 inch	n/a

	LC550	P460	P466	P467
GENERAL SPECS				
Date introduced	Feb-94	Oct-93	Oct-93	Oct-93
Date discontinued	Mar-95			
Product Lifetime	0.9			
Overall perf. (rel. Classic)	4.6	4.6	4.6	4.6
Effective MIPS rating	8.3	8.3	8.3	8.3
Used Price		1075	1200	1200
PROCESSOR SPECS				
Model	68030	68030	68030	68030
Clock speed	33	33	33	33
Data path (speed/ size)	33/32	33/32	33/32	33/32
Coprocessor	option	option	option	option
PMMU	yes	yes	yes	yes
MEMORY SPECS				
Hard-soldered RAM	4	4	4	4
Memory cache	0	0	0	0
Maximum RAM	36 MB	36 MB	36 MB	36 MB
No. SIMM sockets	1	1	1	1
SIMM type	72-pin	72-pin	72-pin	72-pin
Minimum RAM speed (ns)	80	80	80	80
VIDEO SPECS				
Built-in video	color	color	color	color
Standard VRAM	512K	512K	512K	512K
Maximum VRAM	768K	1 MB	1 MB	1 MB
VRAM sockets	1	1	1	1
Standard color	256	256	256	256
Maximum colors	32,768	32,768	32,768	32,768
Maximum monitor size 8-bit	14 inch	14 inch	14 inch	14 inch
Maximum monitor size 16-bit	14	14	14 inch	14

continues

Table 12.6 Macintosh Specifications and Upgrades, CONTINUED

	IIsi	LC520	IIvx (P600)	Color Classic II
SLOT & PORT SPECS				
NuBus slots	0	0	3	0
PDS slot	1	1	0	1
Cache slot	0	0	1	0
Sound port	1	2	2	1
Video port		built-in 14 inch		
Serial (RS-232/-422)	2	2	2	2
ADB	2	2	2	2
Max SCSI transfer (MB/s)	1.25	1.5	1.5	1.25
Networking		LT		
Superdrive	Yes	Yes	Yes	Yes
Power supply (W)	90	60	112	100
Official Apple LBU	none		7100/66	none
Currently offered by Apple?			Yes	
"Buy up" or other upgrade options	Q605/ Q610		Mac IIvx	Q650
	P550	P560	C610	C650
GENERAL SPECS				
Date introduced	Oct-93		Feb-93	Feb-93
Date discontinued			Oct-93	Oct-93
Product Lifetime			0.66	0.66
Overall perf. (rel. Classic)	4.6		7.7	10.6
Effective MIPS rating	8.3		17.6	22
Used Price	1725		875	1200
PROCESSOR SPECS				
Model	68030		68040	68040
Clock speed	33		20	25
Data path (speed/ size)	33/32		20/32	25/32
Coprocessor	option		none	yes

	LC550	P460	P466	P467
SLOT & PORT SPECS				
NuBus slots	0	0	0	0
PDS slot	1	1	1	1
Cache slot	0	0	0	0
Sound port	2	2	2	2
Video port				
Serial (RS-232/-422)	2	2	2	2
ADB	1	1	1	1
Max SCSI transfer (MB/s)				
Networking	LT			
Superdrive	Yes	Yes	Yes	Yes
Power supply (W)	60	50	50	50
Official Apple LBU	PPC			
Currently offered by Apple?	Yes—via 575 LBU			

	C660AV	LC475	IIfx	P475
GENERAL SPECS				
Date introduced	Jul-93	Oct-93	Mar-90	Oct-93
Date discontinued	Oct-93		Apr-92	
Product Lifetime	0.25		2.09	
Overall perf. (rel. Classic)	10.6	10.6	6.8	10.6
Effective MIPS rating	22	22	10	22
Used Price	1475	1350	1100	1450
PROCESSOR SPECS				
Model	68040	68040	68030	68040
Clock speed	25	25	40	25
Data path (speed/ size)	25/32	25/32	40/32	25/32
Coprocessor	yes	none	68882	none

continues

Table 12.6   Macintosh Specifications and Upgrades, CONTINUED

	P550	P560	C610	C650
PMMU	yes		yes	yes
MEMORY SPECS				
Hard-soldered RAM	4		4	8
Memory cache	0		8K	8K
Maximum RAM	36 MB		68 MB	136 MB
No. SIMM sockets	1		2	4
SIMM type	72-pin		72-pin	72-pin
Minimum RAM speed (ns)	80		80	80
VIDEO SPECS				
Built-in video	color		color	color
Standard VRAM	512K		512K	512K
Maximum VRAM	768K		1 MB	1 MB
VRAM sockets	1		2	2
Standard color	256		256	256
Maximum colors	32,768		32,768	32,768
Maximum monitor size 8-bit	14 inch		21 inch	21 inch
Maximum monitor size 16-bit	14 inch		16 inch	16 inch
SLOT & PORT SPECS				
NuBus slots	0	opt.	0	3
PDS slot	1		1	1
Cache slot	0		0	0
Sound port	1		1	1
Video port				1
Serial (RS-232/-422)	2	2	2	2
ADB	2	2	2	2
Max SCSI transfer (MB/s)			5	5
Networking				
Superdrive	Yes		Yes	Yes
Power supply (W)	60		86	112
Official Apple LBU			6100/60	7100/66
Currently offered by Apple?			Yes	Yes
"Buy-up" or other upgrade options			PPC Upgr Card C660AV LBU	PPC Upgr Card Q660AV

	C660AV	LC475	IIfx	P475
PMMU	yes	yes	yes	yes
Hard-soldered RAM	4	4	0	4
Memory cache	8K	8K	32K	8K
Maximum RAM	68	36	128	36
No. SIMM sockets	2	1	8	1
SIMM type	72-pin	72-pin	64-pin	72-pin
Minimum RAM speed (ns)	80	80	80	80
VIDEO SPECS				
Built-in video	color	color	No	color
Standard VRAM	1 MB	512K	n/a	512K
Maximum VRAM	1 MB	1 MB	n/a	1 MB
VRAM sockets	0	2	0	2
Standard color	256	256	n/a	256
Maximum colors	32,768	32,768	n/a	32,768
Maximum monitor	21 inch size 8-bit	21 inch	n/a	14 inch
Maximum monitor size 16-bit	16 inch	16 inch	n/a	14 inch
SLOT & PORT SPECS				
NuBus slots	1 opt.	0	6	0
PDS slot	1	1	1	1
Cache slot	0	0	0	0
Sound port	2	2	0	2
Video port	2	1	0	0
Serial (RS-232/-422)	2	2	2	2
ADB	2	1		1
Max SCSI transfer (MB/s)	5	5	3	
Networking	LT & EN	LT		LT
Superdrive	Yes	Yes	Yes	Yes
Power supply (W)	86	30	230	30
Official Apple LBU	6100/60AV		none	
Currently offered by Apple?	Yes			
"Buy-up" or other upgrade options	6100/60 Q800 Q840AV	Q610		

continues

Table 12.6 Macintosh Specifications and Upgrades, CONTINUED

	P476	LC575	Q700	Q605
GENERAL SPECS				
Date introduced	Oct-93	Feb-94	Oct-91	Oct-93
Date discontinued		Apr-95	Mar-93	Oct-94
Product Lifetime		0.50	1.42	1.00
Overall perf. (rel. Classic)	10.6	20	10	10
Effective MIPS rating	22	29	22	22
Used Price	1525		1350	725
PROCESSOR SPECS				
Model	68040	68040	68040	68040
Clock speed	25	33	25	25
Data path (speed/ size)	25/32	33/32	25/32	25/32
Coprocessor	none	none	yes	none
PMMU	yes	yes	yes	yes
MEMORY SPECS				
Hard-soldered RAM	4	4	4	4
Memory cache	8K	8K	8K	8K
Maximum RAM	36	36	64	36
No. SIMM sockets	1	1	4	1
SIMM type	72-pin	72-pin	30-pin	72-pin
Minimum RAM speed (ns)	80	80	80	80
VIDEO SPECS				
Built-in video	color	color	color	color
Standard VRAM	512K	512K	512K	512K
Maximum VRAM	1 MB	1 MB	2 MB	1 MB
VRAM sockets	2	2	6	2
Standard color	256	256	256	256
Maximum colors	32,768	32,768	16.7 million	32,768
Maximum monitor size 8-bit	14 inch	14 inch	21 inch	21 inch
Maximum monitor size 16-bit	14 inch	14 inch	n/a	16 inch

	Q610	Q610 DOS	Q900	Q650
GENERAL SPECS				
Date introduced	Oct-93	Oct-93	Oct-91	Oct-93
Date discontinued	Jul-94	Jun-94	May-92	Sep-94
Product Lifetime	0.8	0.75	0.58	0.9
Overall perf. (rel. Classic)	10	10	10	10
Effective MIPS rating	22	22	22	22
Used Price	1100	1400	2300	1750
PROCESSOR SPECS				
Model	68040	68040	68040	68040
Clock speed	25	25	25	33
Data path (speed/ size)	25/32	25/32	25/32	33/32
Coprocessor	option	none	yes	yes
PMMU	yes	yes	yes	yes
MEMORY SPECS				
Hard-soldered RAM	4	4	0	4
Memory cache	8K	8K	8K	8K
Maximum RAM	68	68	256	136
No. SIMM sockets	2	2	16	4
SIMM type	72-pin	72-pin	30-pin	72-pin
Minimum RAM speed (ns)	80	80	80	80
VIDEO SPECS				
Built-in video	color	color	color	color
Standard VRAM	512K	512K	1 MB	512K
Maximum VRAM	1 MB	1 MB	2 MB	1 MB
VRAM sockets	2	2	4	2
Standard color	256	256	256	256
Maximum colors	32,768	32,768	16.7 million	32,768
Maximum monitor size 8-bit	21 inch	21 inch	21 inch	21 inch
Maximum monitor size 16-bit	16inch	16inch	n/a	16 inch

continues

Table 12.6   Macintosh Specifications and Upgrades, CONTINUED

	P476	LC575	Q700	Q605
SLOT & PORT SPECS				
NuBus slots	0	0	2	0
PDS slot	1	1	1	1
Cache slot	0	0	0	0
Sound port	2	2	1	2
Video port	0	0		
Serial (RS-232/-422)	2	2	2	2
ADB	1	2	2	2
Max SCSI transfer (MB/s)			5	5
Networking	LT	LT	LT & EN	LT
Superdrive	Yes	Yes	Yes	Yes
Power supply (W)	30	60	130	30
Official Apple LBU		PPC Upgr Card	none	
Currently offered by Apple?			Yes	
"Buy-up" or other upgrade options				Q610

Q660AV	Q950	Q800	Q840AV
GENERAL SPECS			
Date introduced	Oct-93	Oct-91	Feb-93	Jul-93
Date discontinued		May-92		
Product Lifetime	current	0.58	current	current
Overall perf. (rel. Classic)	10	10	13.5	16.5
Effective MIPS rating	22	22	29	35
Used Price	1600	3000	1850	2400

	Q610	Q610 DOS	Q900	Q650
SLOT & PORT SPECS				
NuBus slots	0	0	5	3
PDS slot	1	1	1	1
Cache slot	0	0	0	0
Sound port	2	1	1	1
Video port				
Serial (RS-232/-422)	2	2	2	2
ADB	2	2	1	2
Max SCSI transfer (MB/s)	5	5	5	5
Networking	LT & EN	LT & EN	LT & EN	LT & EN
Superdrive	Yes	Yes	Yes	Yes
Power supply (W)	86	210	303	112
Official Apple LBU	PPC	PPC Upgr Card	7100/66	
Currently offered by Apple?	Yes		Yes	Yes
"Buy-up" or other upgrade options	Q660AV LBU Q660AV LBU 486 DOS card		Q950LBU Card Q840AV	PPC Upgr Q66AV, Q800

	6100/60	60AV	7100/66	7100/66AV
GENERAL SPECS				
Date introduced	Mar-94	Mar-94	Mar-94	Mar-94
Date discontinued	Jan-95	Sep-94	Jan-95	Jan-95
Product Lifetime	0.75	0.50	0.75	0.75
Overall perf. (rel. Classic)	22.5	22.5		
Effective MIPS rating	48	48		
Used Price				

continues

Table 12.6   Macintosh Specifications and Upgrades, CONTINUED

	Q660AV	Q950	Q800	Q840AV
PROCESSOR SPECS				
Model	68040	68040	68040	68040
Clock speed	25	33	33	40
Data path (speed/ size)	25/32	33/32	33/32	40/32
Coprocessor	yes	yes	yes	yes
PMMU	yes	yes	yes	yes
MEMORY SPECS				
Hard-soldered RAM	4	0	8	8
Memory cache	8K	8K	8K	8K
Maximum RAM	68	256	136	128
No. SIMM sockets	2	16	4	4
SIMM type	72-pin	30-pin	72-pin	72-pin
Minimum RAM speed (ns)	70	80	70	70
VIDEO SPECS				
Built-in video	color	color	color	color
Standard VRAM	1 MB	1 MB	512K	1 MB
Maximum VRAM	1 MB	2 MB	1 MB	2 MB
VRAM sockets	0	4	2	4
Standard color	256	256	256	256
Maximum colors	32,768	16.7 million	32,768	16.7 million
Maximum monitor size 8-bit	16 inch	21 inch	21 inch	21 inch
Maximum monitor size 16-bit	n/a	19 inch	16 inch	19 inch
SLOT & PORT SPECS				
NuBus slots	1 w/adapt.	5	3	3
PDS slot	1	1	1	0
Cache slot	0	0	0	0
Sound port	2	1	1	1
Video port	2			
Serial (RS-232/-422)	2	2	2	2
ADB	2	1	2	2

	6100/60	60AV	7100/66	7100/66AV
PROCESSOR SPECS				
Model	PPC 601	PPC 601	PPC 601	PPC 601
Clock speed	60	60	66	66
Data path (speed/ size)	30/64	30/64	33/64	33/64
Coprocessor	none	none	none	none
PMMU	none	none	none	none
MEMORY SPECS				
Hard-soldered RAM	8	8	8	8
Memory cache	L2, 256K opt.	opt. 32K	opt. 32K	opt. 32K
Maximum RAM	72	72	136	136
No. SIMM sockets	2	2	4	4
SIMM type	72-pin	72-pin	72-pin	72-pin
Minimum RAM speed (ns)	80	80	80	80
VIDEO SPECS				
Built-in video	color	color	color	
Standard VRAM	640K DRAM	640K DRAM	640K DRAM	
Maximum VRAM	n/a	n/a	2 MB	
VRAM sockets	n/a	n/a		
Standard color	32,768		256	
Maximum colors	32,768		16.7 million	
Maximum monitor size 8-bit	16 inch		16 inch	
Maximum monitor size 16-bit	14 inch		14 inch	
SLOT & PORT SPECS				
NuBus slots	1 w/o PDS	0	3	3
PDS slot	1 w/o NuBus		0	
Cache slot	1		1	
Sound port	2		2	
Video port				
Serial (RS-232/-422)	2 & Geo	2 & Geo	2 & Geo	2 & Geo
ADB	1	1	1	1

continues

Table 12.6   Macintosh Specifications and Upgrades, CONTINUED

	Q660AV	Q950	Q800	Q840AV
Max SCSI transfer (MB/s)	5	5	5	5
Networking	LT & EN			LT & EN
Superdrive	Yes	Yes	Yes	Yes
Power supply (W)	86	303	200	200
Official Apple LBU	6100/60AV	PPC Upgr Card	8100/80	8100/80AV
System Offered by Apple?	Yes	Yes	Yes	Yes
"Buy-up" or other upgrade options	6100/60 Q800, Q840AV		PPC Upgr Card Q840AV LBU Q950	

	8100/80	8100/80AV
GENERAL SPECS		
Date introduced	Mar-94	Mar-94
Date discontinued	Jan-95	Jan-95
Product Lifetime	0.75	0.75
Overall perf. (rel. Classic)		28.4
Effective MIPS rating		60
Used Price		
PROCESSOR SPECS		
Model	PPC 601	PPC 601
Clock speed	80	80
Data path (speed/ size)	40/64	40/64
Coprocessor	none	none
PMMU	none	none
MEMORY SPECS		
Hard-soldered RAM	8	8
Memory cache	32K	32K
Maximum RAM	264	264
No. SIMM sockets	8	8
SIMM type	72-pin	72-pin
Minimum RAM speed (ns)	80	80

	6100/60	60AV	7100/66	7100/66AV
Max SCSI transfer (MB/s)				
Networking	LT & EN	LT & EN	LT & EN	LT & EN
Superdrive	Yes	Yes	Yes	Yes
Power supply (W)	210	210	325	325

	6100/66 & 66AV	7100/80 &80AV	8100/100	8100/110/AV
GENERAL SPECS				
Date introduced	Jan-95	Jan-95	Jan-95	Feb-95
Date discontinued				
Product Lifetime	current	current	current	current
Overall perf. (rel. Classic)	n/a	n/a	n/a	n/a
Effective MIPS rating	n/a	n/a	n/a	n/a
Used Price				
PROCESSOR SPECS				
Model	PPC 601	PPC 601	PPC 601	PPC 601
Clock speed	66	80	100	110
Data path (speed/ size)	33/64	40/64	33/64	36/64
Coprocessor	none	none	none	none
PMMU	none	none	none	none
MEMORY SPECS				
Hard-soldered RAM	8	8	8	8
Memory cache	L2, 256K	32K	32K	32K
Maximum RAM	72	136	264	264
No. SIMM sockets	2	4	8	8
SIMM type	72-pin	72-pin	72-pin	72-pin
Minimum RAM speed (ns)	80	80	80	80

continues

Table 12.6   Macintosh Specifications and Upgrades, CONTINUED

	8100/80	8100/80AV
VIDEO SPECS		
Built-in video	color*	color*
Standard VRAM	640K DRAM	640K DRAM
Maximum VRAM	4 MB	4 MB
VRAM sockets		
Standard color	32,768	16.7 million
Maximum colors	32,768	16.7 million
Maximum monitor size 8-bit	16 inch	16 inch
Maximum monitor size 16-bit	14 inch	14 inch
SLOT & PORT SPECS		
NuBus slots	3	3
PDS slot	1	1
Cache slot	1	1
Sound port	2	2
VIDEO PORT		
Serial (RS-232/-422)	2 & Geo	2 & Geo
ADB	1	1
Max SCSI transfer (MB/s)		
Networking	LT & EN	LT & EN
Superdrive	Yes	Yes
Power supply (W)	454	454
Official Apple LBU		
Currently offered by Apple?		
"Buy-up" or other upgrade options		

	7200/75	7200/90	7500/100	8500/120
GENERAL SPECS				
Date introduced	Aug-95	Aug-95	Aug-95	Aug-95
Date discontinued				
Product Lifetime	current	current	current	current

	6100/66 & 66AV	7100/80 &80AV	8100/100	8100/110AV
VIDEO SPECS				
Built-in video	color	color	color	
Standard VRAM	640K DRAM	640K DRAM	640K DRAM	
Maximum VRAM	n/a	2MB	4 MB	4 MB
VRAM sockets	n/a	n/a		
Standard color	32,768	256	32,768	32,768
Maximum colors	16.7 million	16.7 million	16.7 million	
Maximum monitor size 8-bit	16 inch	20 inch	20 inch	20 inch
Maximum monitor size 16-bit	14 inch	14 inch	14 inch	14 inch
SLOT & PORT SPECS				
NuBus slots	1 w/o PDS	3	3	3
PDS slot	1 w/o NuBus	0	0	0
Cache slot	1	1	1	1
Sound port	2	2	2	2
VIDEO PORT				
Serial (RS-232/-422)	2 & Geo	2 & Geo	2 & Geo	2 & Geo
ADB	1	1	1	1
Max SCSI transfer (MB/s)				
Networking	LT & EN	LT & EN	LT & EN	LT & EN
Superdrive	Yes	Yes	Yes	Yes
Power supply (W)	210	325	454	454

	9500/132&120	5200/75& 5300/100	6200/75& 6300/100	
GENERAL SPECS				
Date introduced	Jun-95	Apr/Sept-95	Apr/Sept-95	
Date discontinued				
Product Lifetime	current	current	current	current

continues

Table 12.6 Macintosh Specifications and Upgrades, CONTINUED

	7200/75	7200/90	7500/100	8500/120
Overall perf. (rel. Classic)	n/a	n/a	n/a	n/a
Effective MIPS rating	n/a	n/a	n/a	n/a
Used Price				
PROCESSOR SPECS				
Model	PPC 601	PPC 601	PPC 601	PPC 604
Clock speed	75	90	100	120
Data path (speed/ size)	n/a	n/a	n/a	n/a
Coprocessor	none	none	none	none
PMMU	none	none	none	none
MEMORY SPECS				
Hard-soldered RAM	8	8	8	8
Memory cache	n/a	n/a	n/a	n/a
Maximum RAM	256	256	512	512
No. SIMM sockets	4	4	8	8
SIMM type	168-pin	168-pin	168-pin	168-pin
Minimum RAM speed (ns)	70	70	70	70
VIDEO SPECS				
Built-in video	color	color	color	color
Standard VRAM	1MB VRAM	1MB VRAM	2MB VRAM	2MB VRAM
Maximum VRAM	4MB	4MB	4 MB	4MB
VRAM sockets	2	2	2	2
Standard color	256	256	32,768	32,768
Maximum colors	32,768	32,768	16.7 million	16.7 million
Maximum monitor size 8-bit	20 inch		20 inch	
Maximum monitor size 16-bit	n/a	n/a	n/a	n/a
SLOT & PORT SPECS				
PCI slots	3	3	3	3
PDS slot	0	0	0	0
Cache slot	n/a	n/a	n/a	n/a
Sound port	2	2	2	2

	9500/132&120	*5200/75&* *5300/100*	*6200/75&* *6300/100*	
Overall perf. (rel. Classic)	n/a	n/a	n/a	n/a
Effective MIPS rating	n/a	n/a	n/a	n/a
Used Price				
PROCESSOR SPECS				
Model	PPC 604	PPC 603	PPC 603	PPC 603
Clock speed	132 &120	75/100	75	100
Data path (speed/ size)	n/a	n/a	n/a	n/a
Coprocessor	none	none	none	none
PMMU	none	none	none	none
MEMORY SPECS				
Hard-soldered RAM	8	8	8	8
Memory cache	n/a	n/a	n/a	n/a
Maximum RAM	256	256	512	512
No. SIMM sockets	12	2	2	2
SIMM type	168-pin	72-pin	72-pin	72-pin
Minimum RAM speed (ns)	70	70	70	70
VIDEO SPECS				
Built-in video	color	color	color	color
Standard VRAM	0K	1MB VRAM	1MB VRAM	1MB VRAM
Maximum VRAM	n/a	1MB	1MB	1MB
VRAM sockets	n/a	none	none	none
Standard color	n/a	256	256	256
Maximum colors	n/a	Thousands	Thousands	Thousands
Maximum monitor size 8-bit	n/a	n/a	n/a	n/a
Maximum monitor size 16-bit	n/a	n/a	n/a	n/a
SLOT & PORT SPECS				
NuBus/PCI slots	6	0	0	0
PDS slot	1	1	1	1
Cache slot	1	0	0	0
Sound port	2	2	2	2

continues

Table 12.6   Macintosh Specifications and Upgrades, CONTINUED

	7200/75	*7200/90*	*7500/100*	*8500/120*
VIDEO PORT				
Serial (RS-232/-422)	2 & Geo	2 & Geo	2 & Geo	2 & Geo
ADB	1	1	1	1
Max SCSI transfer (MB/s)				
Networking	LT & EN	LT & EN	LT & EN	LT & EN
Superdrive	Yes	Yes	Yes	Yes
Power supply (W)	325	325	325	454

	5300/117&100		*190/66*	*2300/100*
GENERAL SPECS				
Date introduced	Aug-95	Aug-95	Aug-95	Aug-95
Date discontinued				
Product Lifetime	current	current	current	current
Overall perf. (rel. Classic)	22.5	22.5		
Effective MIPS rating	48	48		
Used Price				
PROCESSOR SPECS				
Model	PPC 603e	PPC 603e	68LC040	PPC 603e
Clock speed	117	100	33	100
Data path (speed/ size)	n/a	n/a	n/a	n/a
Coprocessor	none	none	none	none
PMMU	none	none	none	none
MEMORY SPECS				
Hard-soldered RAM	16	8 or 16	4 or 8	8
Memory cache	n/a	n/a	n/a	n/a
Maximum RAM	64	64	40	56
No. SIMM sockets	1	1	1	1
SIMM type	PowerBook	PowerBook	PowerBook	PB Duo
Minimum RAM speed (ns)	n/a	n/a	n/a	n/a

	9500/132&120	*5200/75& 5300/100*	*6200/75& 6300/100*	
VIDEOPORT				
Serial (RS-232/-422)	2 & Geo	1	1	1
ADB	1	1	1	1
Max SCSI transfer (MB/s)				
Networking	LT & EN	LT & EN	LT & EN	LT & EN
Superdrive	Yes	Yes	Yes	Yes
Power supply (W)	520	200	200	200

continues

Table 12.6   Macintosh Specifications and Upgrades, CONTINUED

	5300/117&100	190/66	2300/100	
VIDEO SPECS				
Built-in video	color	color	color	
Standard VRAM	n/a	n/a	n/a	n/a
Maximum VRAM	n/a	n/a	n/a	n/a
VRAM sockets	n/a	n/a	n/a	n/a
Standard color	32,768	32,768	16-256	256
Maximum colors	Thousands	256-Thousands	256	256
Maximum monitor size 8-bit	16 inch		16 inch	
Maximum monitor size 16-bit	14 inch		14 inch	
SLOT & PORT SPECS				
NuBus slots	n/a	n/a	n/a	n/a
PDS slot	n/a	n/a	n/a	n/a
Cache slot	n/a	n/a	n/a	n/a
Sound port	1	1	1	1
VIDEO PORT				
Serial (RS-232/-422)	1	1	1	1
ADB	1	1	1	0
Max SCSI transfer (MB/s)				
Networking (Duo Dock only)	LT, IR, EN (PC Card)	LT, IR, EN (PC Card)	LT, IR, EN (PC Card)	LT & EN
Superdrive	Yes	Yes	Yes	No
Power supply (W)	40	40	40	36

Error Codes and What They Really Mean

Positive ID Codes

DS Error Table

1	dsBusError	Bus error
2	dsAddressErr	Address error
3	0dsILLInstErr	Illegal instruction error
4	dsZeroDivErr	Zero divide error
5	dsChkErr	Check trap error
6	dsOvflowErr	Overflow trap error
7	dsPrivErr	Privilege violation error
8	dsTraceErr	Trace mode error
9	dsLineAerr	Line 1010 trap error
10	dsLineFErr	Line 1111 trap error
11	dsMiscErr	Miscellaneous hardware exception error
12	dsCoreErr	Unimplemented core routine error
13	dsIrqErr	Uninstalled interrupt error
14	dsIOCoreErr	IO core error
15	dsLoadErr	Segment loader error
16	dsFPErr	Floating point error
17	dsNoPackErr	Package 0 not present [List Manager]
18	dsNoPk1	Package 1 not present [Reserved by Apple]
19	dsNoPk2	Package 2 not present [Disk Initialization]
20	dsNoPk3	Package 3 not present [Standard File]
21	dsNoPk4	Package 4 not present [Floating-Point Arithmetic]
22	dsNoPk5	Package 5 not present [Transcendental Functions]

23	dsNoPk6	Package 6 not present [International Utilities]
24	dsNoPk7	Package 7 not present [Binary/Decimal Conversion]
25	dsMemFullErr	Out of memory!
26	dsBadLaunch	Can't launch file
27	dsFSErr	File system map has been trashed
28	dsStknHeap	Stack has moved into application heap
30	dsReinsert	Request user to reinsert offline volume
31	dsNotThe1	Not the disk I wanted (obsolete)
33	negZcbFreeErr	ZcbFree has gone negative
40	dsGreeting	Welcome to Macintosh greeting
41	dsFinderErr	Can't load the Finder error
42	shutDownAlert	Handled like a shutdown error (obsolete)
43	dsSystemFileErr	Can't find system file to open (sad Mac only)
51	dsBadSlotInt	Unserviceable slot interrupt
81	dsBadSANEopcode	Bad opcode given to SANE Pack4
83	dsBadPatchHeader	SetTrapAddress saw the "come-from" header
84	menuPrgErr	Happens when a menu is purged
85	dsMBarNfnd	SysErr—cannot find MBDF
86	dsHmenuFindErr	SysErr—recursively defined Hmenus
87	dsWDEFNotFnd	Could not load WDEF
88	dsCDEFNotFnd	Could not load CDEF
89	dsMDEFNotFnd	Could not load MDEF
90	dsNoFPU	An FPU instruction was executed and the machine doesn't have one
98	dsNoPatch	Can't patch for particular Model Mac
99	dsBadPatch	Can't load patch resource
101	dsParityErr	Memory parity error
102	dsOldSystem	System is too old for this ROM
103	ds32BitMode	Booting in 32-bit on a 24-bit system
104	dsNeedToWriteBootBlocks	Need to write new boot blocks
105	dsNotEnoughRAMToBoot	Must have at least 1.5 MB of RAM to boot 7.0
106	dsBufPtrTooLow	bufPtr moved too far during boot
1011	dMixedModeFailure	Bad shared library
20000	dsShutDownOrRestart	User choice between ShutDown and Restart
20001	dsSwitchOffOrRestart	User choice between switching off and Restart
20002	dsForcedQuit	Allow the user to ExitToShell, return if Cancel

20003	dsRemoveDisk	Request user to remove disk from manual eject drive
20004	dsDirtyDisk	Request user to return a manually ejected dirty disk
20109	dsShutDownOrResume	Allow user to return to Finder or ShutDown
20010	dsSCSIWarn	Portable SCSI adapter warning
32767	dsSysErr	General system error (catch-all used in SAT)

Negative System Error Codes

System Errors (VBL Mgr, Queue, and so on)

0	noErr	0 for success
OR		
0	smNotTruncated	No truncation necessary
−1	qErr	Queue element not found during deletion
OR		
−1	smTruncErr	Truncation indicator alone is wider than the specified width
−2	vTypErr	Invalid queue element
−3	corErr	Core routine number out of range
−4	unimpErr	Unimplemented core routine
−5	SlpTypeErr	Invalid queue element
−8	seNoDB	No debugger installed to handle debugger command

Color Manager Errors

−9	iTabPurgErr	From Color2Index/ITabMatch
−10	noColMatch	From Color2Index/ITabMatch
−11	qAllocErr	From MakelTable
−12	tblAllocErr	From MakelTable
−13	overRun	From MakelTable
−14	noRoomErr	From MakelTable
−15	seOutOfRange	From SetEntry
−16	seProtErr	From SetEntry

−17	i2CRangeErr	From SetEntry
−18	gdBadDev	From SetEntry
−19	reRangeErr	From SetEntry
−20	seInvRequest	From SetEntry
−21	seNoMemErr	From SetEntry

I/O System Errors

−17	controlErr	Driver can't respond to Control call
−18	statusErr	Driver can't respond to Status call
−19	readErr	Driver can't respond to Read call
−20	writErr	Driver can't respond to Write call
−21	badUnitErr	Driver ref num doesn't match unit table
−22	unitEmptyErr	Driver ref num specifies NIL handle in unit table
−23	openErr	Requested read/write permission doesn't match driver's open permission, or Attempt to open RAM serial Driver failed
−24	closErr	Close failed; Permission to close .MPP driver was denied
−25	dRemovErr	Tried to remove an open driver
-26	dInstErr	DrvrInstall couldn't find driver in resources
−27	abortErr	IO call aborted by Kill0; publisher has written a new edition
OR		
−27	iIOAbortErr	IO abort error (Printing Manager)
−28	notOpenErr	Couldn't rd/wr/ctl/sts because driver not opened
−29	unitTblFullErr	Unit table has no more entries
−30	dceExtErr	dce extension error

File System Errors

−33	dirFulErr	Directory full
−34	dskFulErr	Disk Full
−35	nsvErr	No such volume; volume not found
−36	ioErr	I/O error (bummers)
−37	bdNamErr	Bad file name
−38	fnOpnErr	File not open
−39	eofErr	End of file; no additional data in the format
−40	posErr	Tried to position to before start of file (r/w)

-41	mFulErr	Memory full (open) or file won't fit (load)
-42	tmfoErr	Too many files open
-43	fnfErr	File not found; folder not found; edition container not found; target not found
-44	wPrErr	Disk is write protected; volume is locked through hardware
-45	fLckdErr	File is locked
-45	fLckdErr	Publisher writing to an edition
-46	vLckdErr	Volume is locked through software
-47	fBsyErr	File is busy (delete); section doing I/O
-48	dupFNErr	Duplicate file name (rename); file found instead of folder
-49	opWrErr	File already open with write permission
-50	paramErr	Error in user parameter list
-51	rfNumErr	Reference number invalid
-52	gfpErr	Get file position error
-53	volOffLinErr	Volume is offline; was ejected
-54	permErr	Software lock on file; not a subscriber [permissions error on file open]
-55	volOnLinErr	Drive volume already online at MountVol
-56	nsDrvErr	No such drive (tried to mount a bad drive num)
-57	noMacDskErr	Not a Mac disk (sig bytes are wrong)
-58	extFSErr	External file system—file system identifier is nonzero; volume in question belongs to an external fs
-59	fsRnErr	File system internal error; during rename the old entry was deleted but could not be restored
-60	badMDBErr	Bad master directory block
-61	wrPermErr	Write permissions error; not a publisher

Font Manager Errors

-64	fontDecError	Error during font declaration
-65	fontNotDeclared	Font not declared
-66	fontSubErr	Font substitution occurred

Disk, Serial Port, Clock Specific Errors

-64	lastDskErr	I/O System error
-64	noDriveErr	Drive not installed
-65	offLinErr	R/W request for an offline drive
-66	noNybErr	Couldn't find 5 nibbles in 200 tries

−67	noAdrMkErr	Couldn't find valid addr mark
−68	dataVerErr	Read and verify compare failed
−69	badCksmErr	Addr mark checksum didn't check
−70	badBtSlpErr	Bad addr mark bit slip nibbles
−71	noDtaMkErr	Couldn't find a data mark header
−72	badDCksum	Bad data mark checksum
−73	badDBtSlp	Bad data mark bit slip nibbles
−74	wrUnderrun	Write underrun occurred
−75	cantStepErr	Step handshake failed
−76	tkOBadErr	Track 0 detect doesn't change
−77	initIWMErr	Unable to initialize IWM
−78	twoSideErr	Tried to read second side on a one-sided drive
−79	spdAdjErr	Unable to correctly adjust disk speed
−80	seekErr	Track number wrong on address mark
−81	sectNFErr	Sector number never found on a track
−82	fmt1Err	Can't find sector 0 after track format
−83	fmt2Err	Can't get enough sync
−84	verErr	Track failed to verify
−84	firstDskErr	I/O System Error
−85	clkRdErr	Unable to read same clock value twice
−86	clkWrErr	Time written did not verify
−87	prWrErr	Parameter RAM written didn't read-verify
−88	prInitErr	InitUtil found the parameter RAM uninitialized
−89	rcvrErr	SCC receiver error (framing, parity, OR)
−90	breakRecd	Break received (SCC)

AppleTalk Errors

−91	ddpSktErr	Error opening socket, error in socket number
OR		
−91	eMultiErr	Invalid address or table is full
−92	ddpLenErr	Data length too big
OR		
−92	eLenErr	Packet too large or first entry of the write data structure did not contain the full 14-byte header
−93	noBridgeErr	No network bridge available [for non-local send]
−94	lapProtErr	Error in attaching/detaching protocol
OR		

−94	LAPProtErr	Protocol handler is already attached, node's protocol table is full, protocol not attached, or protocol handler pointer was not 0
−95	excessCollsns	Hardware error [excessive collusions on write]
−97	portInUse	Driver Open error code (port is in use)
−98	portNotCf	Driver Open error code (parameter RAM not configured for this connection)
−99	memROZEErr	Hard error in ROZ
−99	memROZEError	Hard error in ROZ
−99	memROZWarn	Soft error in ROZ

Scrap Manager Errors

−100	noScrapErr	No scrap exists error
−102	noTypeErr	Format not available [no object of that type in scrap] Storage Allocator Errors
−108	memFullErr	Ran out of memory [not enough room in heap zone]
−109	nolHandleErr	GetHandleSize fails on baseText or substitutionText; NIL Master Pointer [Master Pointer was NIL in HandleZone or other]
−110	memAdrErr	Address was odd or out of range
−111	memWZErr	Attempted to operate on a free block; GetHandleSize fails on baseText or substitutionText [WhichZone failed (applied to free block)]
−112	memPurErr	Trying to purge a locked or non-purgeable block
−113	memAZErr	Address in Zone Check failed
−114	memPCErr	Pointer Check failed
−115	memBCErr	Block Check failed
−116	memSCErr	Size Check failed
−117	memLockedErr	Trying to move a locked block (MoveHHI)

HFS Errors

−120	dirNFErr	Directory not found
−121	tmwdoErr	No free WDCB available
−122	badMovErr	Move into offspring error
−123	wrgVolTypErr	Not an HFS volume [wrong volume type error or (obsolete) operation not supported for MFS]

−124	volGoneErr	Server volume has been disconnected
−125	updPixMemErr	Insufficient memory to update a pixmap
−127	fsDSIntErr	Internal file system error

Menu Manager Errors

−126	dsMBarNFnd	System error code for MBDF not found
−127	dsHMenuFindErr	Could not find Hmenu's parent in MenuKey
−128	userCanceledErr	User canceled an operation

HFS File ID Errors

−130	fidNotFound	No file thread exists
−131	fidNotAFile	Directory specified
−132	fidExists	File id already exists

Color QuickDraw & Color Manager Errors

-145	noMemForPictPlaybackErr	unknown
-147	rgnOverflowErr	unknown
−147	regionTooBigError	Region too big or complex
−148	pixMapTooDeepErr	Pixel map record is deeper than 1 bit per pixel [passed pixel map is too large]
−149	notEnoughStack	Not enough stack space for the necessary buffers
OR		
−149	nsStackErr	Insufficient stackOffScreen QuickDraw Errors
−150	cMatchErr	Color2Index failed to find an index
−151	cTempMemErr	Failed to allocate memory for temporary structures
−152	cNoMemErr	Failed to allocate memory for structure
−153	cRangeErr	Range error on colorTable request
−154	cProtectErr	ColorTable entry protection violation
−155	cDevErr	Invalid type of graphics device
−156	cResErr	Invalid resolution for MakeITable
−157	cDepthErr	Invalid pixel depth
−158	cParmErr	Invalid parameter

Resource Manager Errors (other than I/O Errors)

−185	badExtResource	Extended resource has a bad format
−186	CantDecompress	Resource bent ("the bends"): can't decompress a compressed resource
−188	resourceInMemory	Resource already in memory

−189	writingPastEnd	Writing past end of file
−190	inputOutOfBounds	Offset of count out of bounds
−192	resNotFound	Resource not found
−193	resFnotFound	Resource file not found
−194	addResFailed	AddResource failed
−195	addRefFailed	AddReference failed
−196	rmvResFailed	RmveResource failed
−197	rmvRefFailed	Remove reference failed
−198	resAttrErr	Attribute inconsistent with operation
−199	mapReadErr	Map inconsistent with operation

Sound Manager Errors

−200	noHardware	Required sound hardware not available [no hardware support for the specified synthesizer]
−201	notEnoughHardware	Insufficient hardware available [no more channels for the specified synthesizer]
−203	queueFull	No room in the queue
−204	resProblem	Problem loading the resource
−205	badChannel	Channel is corrupt or unusable [invalid channel queue length]
−206	badFormat	Resource is corrupt or unusable
−207	notEnoughBufferSpace	Insufficient memory available
−208	badFileFormat	File is corrupted or unusable or not AIFF or AIFF-C
−209	channelBusy	Channel is busy (the Channel is being used for a PFD already)
−210	buffersTooSmall	Buffer is too small
−211	channelNotBusy	Channel not currently used
−212	noMoreRealTime	Not enough CPU time available (not enough CPU cycles left to add another task)
−213	badParam	A parameter is incorrect
−220	siNoSoundInHardware	No sound input hardware available
−221	siBadSoundInDevice	Invalid sound input device (invalid index passed to SoundInGetIndexedDevice)
−222	siNoBufferSpecified	No buffer specified (returned by synchronous SPBRecord if nil buffer passed)
−223	siInvalidCompression	Invalid compression type
−224	siHardDiskTooSlow	Hard drive too slow to record to disk
−225	siInvalidSampleRate	Invalid sample rate
−226	siInvalidSampleSize	Invalid sample size

−227	siDeviceBusyErr	Sound input device is busy
−228	siBadDevice Name	Invalid device name (input device could not be opened)
−229	siBadRefNum	Invalid input device reference number
−230	siInputDeviceErr	Input device hardware failure
−231	siUnknownInfoType	Invalid info type selector (returned by driver)
−232	siUnknownQuality	Invalid quality selector (returned by driver)

Speech Manager Errors

−240	noSynthFound	Synthesizer not found
−241	synthOpenFailed	Unable to open synthesizer
−242	synthNotReady	Synthesizer unavailable, or not ready
-243	bufTooSmall	Buffer size too small
-244	voiceNotFound	Unable to find voice
-245	incompatibleVoice	Voice selected incompatible
-246	badDictFormat	Unable to read diction format
-247	badInputText	Input text unreadable

MIDI Manager Errors

−250	midiNoClientErr	No client with that ID found
−251	midiNoPortErr	No port with that ID found
−252	midiTooManyPortsErr	Too many ports already installed in the system
−253	midiTooManyConsErr	Too many connections made
−254	midiVConnectErr	Pending virtual connection created
−255	midiVConnectMade	Pending virtual connection resolved
−256	midiVConnectRmvd	Pending virtual connection removed
−257	midiNoConErr	No connection exits between specified ports
−258	midiWriteErr	MIDIWritePacket couldn't write to all connected ports
−259	midiNameLenErr	Name supplied is longer than 31 characters
−260	midiDuplDErr	Duplicate client ID
−261	midiInvalidCmdErr	Command not supported for port type Notification Manager Errors
−299	nmTypeErr	Wrong qType—must be ORD (nmType)
1	siInitSDTblErr	Slot int dispatch table could not be initialized
2	siInitVBLQsErr	VBLqueues for all slots could not be initialized
3	siInitSPTblErr	Slot Priority Table could not be initialized
10	sdmJTInitErr	SDM Jump Table could not be initialized

11	sdmInitErr	SDM could not be initialized
13	sdmPRAMInitErr	Slot PRAM could not be initialized
14	sdmPriInitErr	Cards could not be initialized

Start Manager Errors

−290	smSDMInitErr	SDM could not be initialized
−291	smSRTInitErr	Slot Resource Table could not be initialized
−292	smPRAMInitErr	Slot Resource Table could not be initialized
−293	smPriInitErr	Cards could not be initialized
−300	smEmptySlot	No card in slot
−301	smCRCFail	CRC check failed for declaration data
−302	smFormatErr	FHeader Format is not Apple's
−303	smRevisionErr	Wrong revision level
−304	smNoDir	Directory offset is Nil
−305	smDisabledSlot	This slot is disabled; Long Word test field <> $5A932BC7; formerly smLWTstBad
−306	smNosInfoArray	No sInfoArray; memory Mgr error
−307	smResrvErr	Fatal reserved error; reserved field <> 0
−308	smUnExBusErr	Unexpected Bus Error
−309	smBLFieldBad	ByteLanes field was bad
−310	smFHBlockRdErr	Error occurred during _sGetFHeader
−311	smFHBlkDispErr	Error occurred during _sDisposePtr (Dispose of FHeader block)
−312	smDisposePErr	_DisposePointer error
−313	smNoBoardsRsrc	No Board sResource
−314	smGetPRErr	Error occurred during _sGetPRAMRec (see SIMStatus)
−315	smNoBoardId	No board ID
−316	smIntStatVErr	The initStatusV field was negative after primary or secondary init
−317	smIntTblVErr	An error occurred while trying to initialize the Slot Resource Table
−318	smNoJmpTbl	SDM jump table could not be created
OR		
−318	smReservedSlot	Slot is reserved, VM should not use this address space
−319	smBadBoardId	BoardId was wrong, re-init the PRAM record
−320	smBusErrTO	BusError time out
−330	smBadRefld	Reference Id not found in list
−331	smBadsList	Bad sResource [sList] structure: Id1<Id2<Id3 ... format is not followed

A

−332	smReservedErr	Reserved field not zero
−333	smCodeRevErr	Code revision is wrong
−334	smCPUErr	Code revision is wrong
−335	smsPointerNil	LPointer is nil {From sOffset Data; if this error occurs, check sInfo rec for more information}
−336	smNilsBlockErr	Nil sBlock error {Don't allocate and try to use a nil sBlock}
−337	smSlotOOBErr	Slot out of bounds error
−338	smSelOOBerr	Selector out of bounds error; function not implemented
−339	smNewPErr	_NewPtr error
−340	smBlkMoveErr	_BlockMove error
−341	smCkStatusErr	Status of slot = fail
−342	smGetDrvrNamErr	Error occurred during _sGetDrvrName
−343	smDisDrvrNamErr	Error occurred during _sDisDrvrName
−344	smNoMoresRsrcs	No more sResources
OR		
−344	smNoMoresResources	Specified sResource data structure not found
−345	smsGetDrvrErr	Error occurred during _sGetDriver
−346	smBadsPtrErr	Bad pointer was passed to sCalcsPointer function
−347	smByteLanesErr	ByteLanes field in card's format block was determined to be zero
−348	smOffsetErr	Offset was too big (temporary error)
−349	smNoGoodOpens	No opens were successful in the loop
−350	smSRTOvrFlErr	SRT over flow
−351	smRecNotFnd	Record not found in the SRT

Misc. Device Manager Errors

| −360 | slotNumErr | Invalid slot # error |
| −400 | gcrOnMFMErr | gcr format on high density media error |

Dictionary Manager Errors

−410	notBTree	The file is not a dictionary
−413	btNoSpace	Can't allocate disk space
−414	btDupRecErr	Record already exists
−415	btRecNotFnd	Record cannot be found
−416	btKeyLenErr	Maximum key length is too long or equal to zero
−417	btKeyAttrErr	There is no such key attribute
−20000	unknownInsertModeErr	There is no such insert mode

–20001	recordDataTooBigErr	The record data is bigger than buffer size (1024 bytes)
–20002	invalidIndexErr	The recordIndex parameter is not valid

Edition Manager Errors

–450	editionMgrInitErr	Manager not initialized or could not load package by this application
–451	badSectionErr	Not a valid SectionRecord
–452	notRegisteredSectionErr	Not a registered SectionRecord
-453	badEditionFileErr	Edition file is corrupt
–454	badSubPartErr	Cannot use sub parts in this release
–460	multiplePublisherWrn	Publisher is already registered for that container
–461	containerNotFoundWrn	Alias was not resolved or could not find editionContainer at this time
-462	containerAlreadyOpenWrn	container already opened by this section
–463	notThePublisherWrn	Not the first registered publisher for that container

SCSI Manager Errors

–470	scsiBadPBErr	Invalid field(s) in the parameter block
–471	scsiOverrunErr	Attempted to transfer too many bytes
–472	scsiTransferErr	Write flag conflicts with data transfer phase
–473	scsiBusTOErr	Bus error during transfer
–474	scsiSelectTOErr	scsiSelTO exceeded (selection failed)
–475	scsiTimeOutErr	scsiReqTO exceeded
–476	scsiBusResetErr	Bus was reset, so your request was aborted
–477	scsiBadStatus	Non-zero (not "Good") status returned
–478	scsiNoStatusErr	Device did not go through a status phase
–479	scsiLinkFailErr	Linked command never executed
–489	scsiUnimpVctErr	Unimplemented routine was called

DeBugger Errors

(SysErrs used instead of inline $A9FF & $ABFF)

–490	userBreak	User debugger break
–491	strUserBreak	User debugger break—display string on stack
–492	exUserBreak	User debugger break—execute commands on stack

Misc. QuickDraw, TextEdit, and O/S ErrUCors

−500	rgnTooBigErr	Bit map would convert into a region greater than 64K
−501	teScrapSizeErr	Scrap item too big for text edit record
−502	hwParamrErr	Bad selector for _HWPriv

Process Manager Errors

−600	procNotFound	No eligible process with specified process serial number
−601	memFragErr	Not enough room to launch application with special requirements
−602	appModeErr	Memory mode is 32-bit, but application is not 32-bit clean
−603	protocolErr	App made module calls in improper order
−604	hardwareConfigErr	Hardware configuration not correct for call
−605	appMemFullErr	Partition size specified in 'SIZE' resource is not big enough for launch
−606	appIsDaemon	Application is background-only
−607	bufferIsSmall	Buffer is too small
−608	noOutstandingHLE	No outstanding high-level event
−609	connectionInvalid	Connection is invalid
−610	noUserInteractionAllowed	Attempted PostHighLevelEvent from background and no session yet established

Thread Manager Errors

−617	threadTooManyReqsErr	Unknown
−618	threadNotFoundErr	Unknown
−619	threadProtocolErr	Unknown

Virtual Memory Dispatch Errors

−620	notEnoughMemoryErr	Insufficient physical memory
−621	notHeldErr	Specified range of memory is not held
−622	cannotMakeContiguousErr	Cannot make specified range contiguous
−623	notLockedErr	Specified range of memory is not locked
−624	interruptsMaskedErr	Called with interrupts masked
−625	cannotDeferErr	Unable to defer additional user functions
−626	noMMUErr	No MMU present

Database Access (PACK13) Errors

−800	rcDBNull	The data item was NULL
−801	rcDBValue	Data available or successfully retrieved

−802	rcDBError	Error executing function
−803	rcDBBadType	Next data item not of requested data type
−804	rcDBBreak	Function timed out
−805	rcDBExec	Query currently executing
−806	rcDBBadSessID	Session ID is invalid
−807	rcDBBadSessNum	Invalid session number
−808	rcDBBadDDEV	Couldn't find the specified database extension, or error occurred in opening database extension
−809	rcDBAsyncNotSupp	Database extension does not support asynchronous calls
−810	rcDBBadAsyncPB	Invalid parameter block specified
−811	rcDBNoHandler	No handler for this data type installed for the current application
−812	rcDBWrongVersion	Wrong version number
−813	rcDBPackNotInited	InitDBPack function has not yet been called

Balloon Help Manager Errors

−850	hmHelpDisabled	Help balloons are not enabled
−851	hmResNotFound	Unknown
−852	hmMemFullErr	Unknown
−853	hmBalloonAborted	Because of constant cursor movement, the help balloon wasn't displayed
−854	hmSameAsLastBalloon	Menu and item are same as previous menu and item
−855	hmHelpManager	NotInited Help menu not set up
−856	hmBadSelector	Unknown
−857	hmSkippedBalloon	No balloon content to fill in
−858	hmWrongVersion	Wrong version of Help Manager resource
−859	hmUnknownHelpType	Help message record contained a bad type
−860	hmCouldNotLoadPackage	Unknown
−861	hmOperationUnsupported	Bad method parameter
−862	hmNoBalloonUp	No balloon showing
−863	hmCloseViewActive	User using Close View won't let you remove balloon

AppleTalk PPC Toolbox Errors

−900	notInitErr	PPC Toolbox has not been initialized yet
−902	nameTypeErr	Invalid or inappropriate locationKindSelector in location name
−903	noPortErr	Invalid port name; unable to open port or bad port reference number

−904	noGlobalsErr	System unable to allocate memory, critical error
−905	localOnlyErr	Network activity is currently disabled
−906	destPortErr	Port does not exist at destination
−907	sessTableErr	PPC Toolbox is unable to create a session
−908	noSessionErr	Invalid session reference number
−909	badReqErr	Bad parameter or invalid state for this operation
−910	portNameExistsErr	Another port is already open with this name
−911	noUserNameErr	User name unknown on destination machine
−912	userRejectErr	Destination rejected the session request
−915	noResponseErr	Unable to contact application
−916	portClosedErr	The port was closed
−917	sessClosedErr	The session has closed
−919	badPortNameErr	PPC port record is invalid
−922	noDefaultUserErr	User has not specified owner name in Sharing Setup control panel
−923	notLoggedInErr	Default user reference number does not yet exist
−924	noUserRefErr	Unable to create a new user reference number
−925	networkErr	An error has occurred in the network
−926	noInformErr	PPCStart failed because target application did not have an inform pending
−927	authFailErr	User's password is wrong
−928	noUserRecErr	Invalid user reference number
−930	badServiceMethodErr	Service method is other than ppcServiceRealTime
−931	badLocNameErr	Location name is invalid
−932	guestNotAllowedErr	Destination port requires authentication

AppleTalk NBP Errors

−1024	nbpBuffOvr	Buffer overflow in LookupName
−1025	nbpNoConfirm	Name not confirmed on ConfirmName
−1026	nbpConfDiff	Name confirmed at different socket
−1027	nbpDuplicate	Duplicate name exists already
−1028	nbpNotFound	Name not found on remove
−1029	nbpNISErr	Error trying to open the NIS

AppleTalk ASP (XPP Driver) Errors

−1066	aspBadVersNum	Server cannot support this ASP version
−1067	aspBufTooSmall	Buffer too small
−1068	aspNoMoreSess	No more sessions on server
−1069	aspNoServers	No servers at that address
−1070	aspParamErr	Parameter error
−1071	aspServerBusy	Server cannot open another session
−1072	aspSessClosed	Session closed
−1073	aspSizeErr	Command block too big
−1074	aspTooMany	Too many clients (server error)
−1075	aspNoAck	No ack (acknowledgement) on attention request (server error)

AppleTalk ATP Errors

−1096	reqFailed	Request to contact router failed: retry count exceeded
−1097	tooManyReqs	Too many concurrent requests
−1098	tooManySkts	Too many concurrent-responding sockets
−1099	badATPSkt	Bad ATP-responding socket
−1100	badBuffNum	Bad response buffer number specified
−1101	noRelErr	No release received
−1102	cbNotFound	Control Block not found; no pending asynchronous calls
−1103	noSendResp	Add Response issued without SendResponse
−1104	noDataArea	No data area for request to MPP
−1105	reqAborted	ERdCancel function called for this ERead [SendRequest aborted by RelTCB] AppleTalk DSP Errors
−1273	errOpenDenied	Open request denied by recipient
−1274	errDSPQueueSize	Read or write queue is too small
−1275	errFwdReset	Read terminated by forward reset
−1276	errAttention	Attention message too long
−1277	errOpening	Attempt to open connection failed
−1278	errState	Bad connection state for this operation
−1279	errAborted	Control call aborted
−1280	errRefNum	Bad connection reference number

A

New HFS Errors

−1300	fidNotFound	File ID not found [No file thread exists]
−1301	fidExists	File ID already exists
−1302	notAFileErr	Specified file is a directory [directory specified]
−1303	diffVolErr	Files on different volumes
−1304	catChangedErr	Catalog has changed and CatPosition may be invalid
−1305	desktopDamagedErr	The desktop database has become corrupted; the Finder will fix this, but if your application is not running with the Finder, use DTReset or DTDelete
−1306	sameFileErr	Can't exchange a file with itself
−1307	badFidErr	File id is dangling or doesn't match with the file number
−1308	notARemountErr	When _Mount allows only remounts and doesn't get one
−1309	fileBoundsErr	File's EOF, offset, mark or size is too big
−1310	fsDataTooBigErr	File or volume is too big for system

AppleEvent Errors

−1700	errAECoercionFail	Unable to coerce data supplied
−1701	errAEDescNotFound	Descriptor record was not found
−1702	errAECorruptData	Data in an Apple event could not be read
−1703	errAEWrongDataType	Wrong descriptor type
−1704	errAENotAEDesc	Not a valid descriptor record
−1705	errAEBadListItem	Operation involving a list item failed
−1706	errAENewerVersion	Need a newer version of the Apple Event Manager
−1707	errAENotAppleEvent	Event is not an Apple event
−1708	errAEEventNotHandled	Event wasn't handled by an Apple event handler
−1709	errAEReplyNotValid	AEResetTimer was passed an invalid reply
−1710	errAEUnknownSendMode	Invalid sending mode was passed
−1711	errAEWaitCanceled	User canceled out of wait loop for reply or receipt
−1712	errAETimeout	Apple event timed out
−1713	errAENoUserInteraction	No user interaction allowed
−1714	errAENotASpecialFunction	No special function for keyword
−1715	errAEParamMissed	Handler did not get all required parameters
−1716	errAEUnknownAddressType	Unknown Apple event address type
−1717	errAEHandlerNotFound	No handler found for an Apple event or a coercion

| −1718 | errAEReplyNotArrived | Reply has not yet arrived |
| −1719 | errAEIllegalIndex | Not a valid list index |

Apple Event Manager Errors

−1720	errAEImpossibleRange	A range like 3rd to 2nd, or 1st to all
−1721	errAEWrongNumberArgs	Logical op kAENOT used with other than 1 term
−1723	errAEAccessorNotFound	Accessor proc matching wantClass and containerType or wildcards not found
−1725	errAENoSuchLogical	Something other than AND, OR, or NOT
−1726	errAEBadTestKey	Test is neither typeLogicalDescriptor nor typeCompDescriptor
−1727	errAENotAnObjSpec	Param to AEResolve not of type 'obj'
−1728	errAENoSuchObject	specifier asked for the 3rd, but there are only 2
−1729	errAENegativeCount	CountProc returned negative value
−1730	errAEEmptyListContainer	Attempt to pass empty list as container to accessor
−1731	errAEUnknownObjectType	Available only in version 1.0.1 or greater
−1732	errAERecordingIsAlreadyOn	Available only in version 1.0.1 or greater
−1750	errOSASystemError	API Error
−1751	errOSAInvalidID	API Error
−1752	errOSABadStorageType	API Error
−1753	errOSAScriptError	API Error
−1754	errOSABadSelector	API Error
−1756	errOSASourceNotAvailable	API Error
−1757	errOSANoSuchDialect	API Error
−1758	errOSADataFormatObsolete	API Error
−1759	errOSADataFormatTooNew	API Error
−1761	errOSAComponentMismatch	Parameters are from 2 different components
−1762	errOSACantOpenComponent	Can't connect to scripting system with that ID

QuickTime Errors

−2000	couldNotResolveDataRef	Could not resolve data reference
−2001	badImageDescription	Unable to read image description
−2002	badPublicMovieAtom	Unable to read public movie atom

A

−2003	cantFindHandler	Unable to locate handler
−2004	cantOpenHandler	Unable to open handler
−2005	badComponentType	Unable to recognize component
−2006	noMediaHandler	Media handler not found
−2007	noDataHandler	Data handler not found
−2008	invalidMedia	Invalid media
−2009	invalidTrack	Invalid track
−2010	invalidMovie	Invalid movie
−2011	invalidSampleTable	Invalid sample table
−2012	invalidDataRef	Invalid data reference
−2013	invalidHandler	Invalid handler
−2014	invalidDuration	Invalid duration
−2015	invalidTime	Invalid time
−2016	cantPutPublicMovieAtom	Unable to use public movie atom
−2017	badEditList	Unable to access edit list
−2018	mediaTypeDontMatch	Media types do not match
−2019	progressProcAborted	Progress procedure aborted
−2020	movieToolboxUnitialized	Movie toolbox unitialized
−2021	wFileNotFound	Unable to locate file
−2022	cantCreateSingleForkFile	Failed to create a single fork file
−2023	invalidEditState	Invalid edit state
−2024	nonMatchingEditState	Invalid matching edit state
−2025	staleEditState	Edit State not updates
−2026	userDataItemNotFound	Unable to find data item
−2027	maxSizeToGrowTooSmall	Grow size is too small for maximum size
−2028	badTrackIndex	Invalid track index
−2029	trackIDNotFound	Unable to find track ID
−2030	trackNotInMovie	Invalid track in movie
−2031	timeNotInTrack	Invalid time in track
−2032	timeNotInMedia	Invalid time in media
−2033	badEditIndex	Invalid index edit
−2034	internalQuickTimeError	Internal QuickTime error
−2035	canEnableTrack	unknown
−2036	invalidRect	Invalid rectangle
−2037	invalidSampleNum	Invalid sample number
−2038	invalidChunkNum	Invalid chunk number
−2039	invalidSampleDescIndex	Invalid sample description index
−2040	invalidChunkCache	Invalid chunk cache
−2041	invalidSampleDescription	Invalid sample description
−2042	dataNotOpenForRead	Unable to access data to be read
−2043	dataNotOpenForWrite	Unable to access data to be opened
−2044	dataAlreadyOpenForWrite	Data already open for write

−2045	dataAlreadyClosed	Data already closed
−2046	endOfDataReached	End of data reached
−2047	dataNoDataRef	Unable to reference data
−2048	noMovieFound	Movie not found
−2049	invalidDataRefContainer	Invalid data reference container
−2050	badDataRefIndex	Unable to access data reference index
−2051	noDefaultDataRef	Unable to access default data reference
−2052	couldNotUseAnExistingSample	Unable to use an existing sample
−2053	featureUnsupported	Feature unsupported
−2057	unsupportedAuxiliaryImport Data	Auxiliary data for import unsupported
−2058	auxiliaryExportDataUnavailable	Export data already in use or unavailable
−2059	samplesAlreadyInMediaErr	Sample already in media
−2062	movieTextNotFoundErr	Unable to locate movie text
−2201	digiUnimpErr	Feature unimplemented
−2202	qtParamErr	Bad input parameter (out of range, and so on)
−2203	matrixErr	Bad matrix, digitizer did nothing
−2204	notExactMatrixErr	Warning of bad matrix, digitizer did its best
−2205	noMoreKeyColorsErr	All key indexes in use
−2206	notExactSizeErr	Can't do exact size requested
−2207	badDepthErr	Can't digitize into this depth
−2208	noDMAErr	Can't do DMA digitizing (that is, can't go to requested destination)
−2209	badCallOrderErr	Usually due to a status call being called prior to being set up first

Translation Manager Errors

−3025	invalidTranslationPathErr	Source type to destination type not a valid path
−3026	couldNotParseSourceFileErr	Source document does not contain source type
−3030	noTranslationPathErr	Check sum error
−3031	badTranslationSpecErr	
−3032	noPrefAppErr	AppleTalk ATP Errors
−3101	buf2SmallErr	Packet too large for buffer; partial data returned
−3102	noMPPErr	No MPP error
−3103	ckSumErr	Check sum error

−3104	extractErr	Extraction error
−3105	readQErr	Read queue error
−3106	atpLenErr	ATP length error
−3107	atpBadRsp	ATP bad response error
−3108	recNotFnd	Record not found
−3109	sktClosedErr	Socket closed error

Print Manager with LaserWriter Errors

−4096	Unknown	No free Connect Control Blocks available
−4097	Unknown	Bad connection reference number
−4098	Unknown	Request already active
−4099	Unknown	Write request too big
−4100	Unknown	Connection just closed
−4101	Unknown	Printer not found, or closed

File Manager Extension and AppleTalk AFP Errors

−5000	accessDenied	Incorrect access for this file/folder
−5006	DenyConflict	Permission/Deny mode conflicts with the current mode in which this fork is already open
−5015	NoMoreLocks	Byte range locking failure from Server
−5020	RangeNotLocked	Attempt to unlock an already unlocked range
−5021	RangeOverlap	Attempt to lock some of an already locked range

Appletalk AFP Errors

−5000	afpAccessDenied	AFP Access denied
−5001	afpAuthContinue	AFP Authorization continue
−5002	afpBadUAM	AFP Bad UAM
−5003	afpBadVersNum	AFP Bad version number
−5004	afpBitmapErr	AFP Bit map error
−5005	afpCantMove	AFP Can't move error
−5006	afpDenyConflict	AFP Deny conflict
−5007	afpDirNotEmpty	AFP Dir not empty
−5008	afpDiskFull	AFP Disk full
−5009	afpEofError	AFP End-of-File error
−5010	afpFileBusy	AFP File busy
−5011	afpFlatVo	AFP Flat volume
−5012	afpItemNotFound	AFP Information not found
−5013	afpLockErr	AFP Lock error
−5014	afpMiscErr	AFP Misc error

−5015	afpNoMoreLocks	AFP No more locks
−5016	afpNoServer	AFP No server
−5017	afpObjectExists	AFP Object already exists
−5018	afpObjectNotFound	AFP Object not found
−5019	afpParmErr	AFP Parm error
−5020	afpRangeNotLocked	AFP Range not locked
−5021	afpRangeOverlap	AFP Range overlap
−5022	afpSessClosed	AFP Session closed
−5023	afpUserNotAuth	AFP User not authorized
−5024	afpCallNotSupported	AFP Call not supported
−5025	afpObjectTypeErr	AFP Object-type error
−5026	afpTooManyFilesOpen	AFP Too many files open
−5027	afpServerGoingDown	AFP Server going down
−5028	afpCantRename	AFP Can't rename
−5029	afpDirNotFound	AFP Directory not found
−5030	afpIconTypeError	Size of new icon and one it replaces don't match
−5031	afpVolLocked	Volume is Read-Only
−5032	afpObjectLocked	Object is M/R/D/W inhibited

Negative ID Codes

SysEnvirons Errors

−5500	envNotPresent	SysEnvirons trap not present—returned by glue
−5501	envBadVers	Version non-positive
−5502	envVersTooBig	Version bigger than call can handle

Gestalt Errors

−5550	gestaltUnknownErr	Could not obtain the response
−5551	gestaltUndefSelectorErr	Undefined selector
−5552	gestaltDupSelectorErr	Selector already exists
−5553	gestaltLocationErr	Function not in system heap

LaserWriter Driver Errors

−8132	Unknown	Manual Feed time out
−8133	Unknown	General PostScript Error
−8150	Unknown	No LaserWriter chosen
−8151	Unknown	Version mismatch between LaserPrep dictionaries
−8150	Unknown	No LaserPrep dictionary installed

| –8160 | Unknown | Zoom scale factor out of range |

PictInfo Errors

–11000	pictInfoVersionErr	Version number not zero (Wrong version of the PictInfo structure)
–11001	pictInfoIDErr	Invalid PictInfo ID (the internal consistency check for the PictInfoID is wrong)
–11002	pictInfoVerbErr	Invalid verb combination specified (the passed verb was invalid)
–11003	cantLoadPickMethodErr	Custom pick method not in resource chain (unable to load the custom pick proc)
–11004	colorsRequestedErr	Number out of range or greater than passed to NewPictInfo
–11005	pictureDataErr	Invalid picture data

Power Manager Errors

–13000	pmBusyErr	Power Manager IC stuck busy
–13001	pmReplyTOErr	Timed out waiting to begin reply handshake
–13002	pmSendStartErr	Power Manager IC did not start handshake
–13003	pmSendEndErr	During send, Power Manager did not finish handshake
–13004	pmRecvStartErr	During receive, Power Manager did not start handshake
–13005	pmRecvEndErr	During receive, Power Manager did not finish handshake

MacTCP Errors

–23000	ipBadLapErr	Bad network configuration
–23001	ipBadCnfgErr	Bad IP configuration error
–23002	ipNoCnfgErr	Missing IP or LAP configuration error
–23003	ipLoadErr	Error in MacTCP load
–23004	ipBadAddr	Error in getting address
–23005	connectionClosing	Connection in closing
–23006	invalidLength	Unknown
–23007	connectionExists	Request conflicts with existing connection
–23008	connectionDoesntExist	Connection does not exist
–23009	insufficientResources	Insufficient resources to perform request
–23010	invalidStreamPtr	Unknown
–23011	streamAlreadyOpen	Unknown
–23012	connectionTerminated	Unknown
–23013	invalidBufPtr	Unknown
–23014	invalidRDS	Unknown

−23014	invalidWDS	Unknown
−23015	openFailed	Unknown
−23016	commandTimeout	Unknown
−23017	duplicateSocket	Unknown
−23030	ipOpenProtErr	Can't open new protocol, table full
−23031	ipCloseProtErr	Can't find protocol to close
−23032	ipDontFragErr	Packet too large to send w/o fragmenting
−23033	ipDestDeadErr	Destination not responding
−23034	ipBadWDSErr	Error in WDS format
−23035	icmpEchoTimeoutErr	ICMP echo timed out
−23036	ipNoFragMemErr	No memory to send fragmented pkt
−23037	ipRouteErr	Can't route packet off-net
−23041	nameSyntaxErr	Unknown
−23042	cacheFault	Unknown
−23043	noResultProc	Unknown
−23044	noNameServer	Unknown
−23045	authNameErr	Unknown
−23046	noAnsErr	Unknown
−23047	dnrErr	Unknown
−23048	outOfMemory	Unknown

Slot Manager Primary or Secondary Init Code Errors

32768	svTempDisable	Temporarily disable card but run primary init
−32640	svDisabled	Reserve −32640 to −32768 for Apple temp disables

Hardware Error Codes—Sad Mac on the Original ROMs (128K, 512K, 512Ke, Plus)

Pressing the interrupt button on the side of your Macintosh when booting should produce a sad Mac icon with '0F000D' and some bits cycling under the icon indicating it is performing a memory test.

This numeric code is in two parts: the first two characters are the subcode. The class code tells what part of the diagnostic program found the error and the sub class code tells what the error was. In the case of a bad RAM chip, the sub class identifies the bad chip (this was very helpful to homegrown upgraders).

Class Code	*Sub Code*
1 = ROM test failed	Meaningless
2 = Memory test—bus subtest	Identifies bad chips
3 = Memory test—byte write	Identifies bad chips

4 = Memory test—Mod3 test   Identifies bad chips
5 = Memory test—address uniqueness   Identifies bad chips

Data Bit	Location	Sub Code Bits
0	F5	0001
1	F6	0002
2	F7	0004
3	F8	0008
4	F9	0010
5	F10	0020
6	F11	0040
7	F12	0080
8	G5	0100
9	G6	0200
10	G7	0400
11	G8	0800
12	G9	1000
13	G10	2000
14	G11	4000
15	G12	8000

Class Code	Sub Code
F = Exception	0001 Bus error
	0002 Address error
	0003 Illegal instruction
	0004 Zero divide
	0005 Check instruction
	0006 Traps instruction
	0007 Privilege violation
	0008 Trace
	0009 Line 1010
	000A Line 1111
	000B Other exception
	000C Nothing
	000D NMI (normal indication)
	0064 Couldn't read system file into Memory

Macintosh SE and Macintosh II ROMs

The sad Mac error codes have been changed to incorporate additional power for testing and to support the 32-bit world. Generally, the same codes are used for 68000 exceptions as the Macintosh; however, they are displayed differently. The traditional Macintosh error codes are displayed like this:

Sad Mac error codes appear in one of two formats. The first format is a single line, six character error code format. All Macs up to and including the Mac Plus use this format to display errors:

YY ZZZZ

YY is the class code, and ZZZZ is the sub code. The class code indicates the part of the Mac's diagnostic program that has identified the error, and the subclass code tells what the error is. In the case of a bad RAM chip, the sub class identifies the bad chip.

Newer Macs use a 32-bit error code format consisting of two lines of eight characters each.

XXXXYYYY

ZZZZZZZZ

In the new format, XXXX is information on the internal test manager state; you can ignore this. The YYYY and ZZZZZZZZ codes correspond to their counterparts in the old format, but they cover a considerably wider range of problems, and present more detailed information. Here are the essentials to help you understand this format:

- In both error formats, if the Y field ends in $01, you have a ROM failure. The Z field is insignificant. ROM failures are relatively rare.

- If the Y field ends in $02–$05, you have a RAM test failure; the Z field identifies the bad chip(s) or, in the case of a value of $0005, a bad address line.

- If the Y field ends in $0F, you have a 680x0 exception, generally—though not always—due to corrupted System or SCSI driver software, or a damaged partition map. The last two characters in the Z field indicate the nature of the exception.

In addition to these general rules, the 32-bit error code format adds the following:

- $0006–$000D represent component failures on the logic board; the Z field is not applicable. Like ROM failures, these errors are rare.

- $000E is a data bus test failure; the Z field indicates the bad bit; this may be due to a bad data bus, but could also be a bad SIMM. This error is also unusual; standard RAM errors are much more common.

A real-world example of a bad SIMM can illustrate how easy it is to use these error codes. On a Mac Plus, you might see the following error code:

030100

The first two digits tell you that the RAM write test has failed; the remaining four tell you which chip has failed—in this case, chip 8. If more than one chip fails, the sad Mac displays a summed value. For instance, had chips 8 (0100) and 9 (0200) failed, an error code of 030300 would have displayed.

How would the same bad SIMM look on an SE or Mac II? Like this:

00000003

00000100

In this case, the 0003 at the end of the first line indicates that a SIMM in bank B has failed. (Had the SIMM been in bank A, line one would have ended with 0002.) The 0100 at the end of the second line identifies the bad chip.

YYYY Error Codes

$0001	The ROM checksum test failed. Ignore the Z field.
$0002	The first small chunk of RAM to be tested failed. The Z field indicates which RAM Bit(s) failed. This small chunk of RAM is always in bank B. Example: $AABBCCDD AA=8-bit mask for bits 31–24 BB=8-bit mask for bits 23–16 CC=8-bit mask for bits 15–8 DD=8-bit mask for bits 7–0
$0003	The RAM test failed while testing bank B, after passing the chunk tested for code $0002. The Z field indicates which bits failed as in code $0002.
$0004	The RAM test failed while testing bank A. The Z field indicates which bits failed as in code $0002.
$0005	The RAM External addressing test failed. The Z field indicates a failed address line.
$0006	Unable to properly address the VIA1 chip. The Z field is not applicable.
$0007	Unable to properly address the VIA2 chip (Macintosh II only). The Z field is not applicable.
$0008	Unable to properly access the Front Desk Bus. The Z field is not applicable.
$0009	Unable to properly access the MMU. The Z field is not applicable.
$000A	Unable to properly access NuBus. The Z field is not applicable.
$000B	Unable to properly access the SCSI Chip. The Z field is not applicable.
$000C	Unable to properly access the IWM chip. The Z field is not applicable.
$000D	Unable to properly access the SCC Chip. The Z field is not applicable.

$000E	Failed data bus test. The Z field indicated the bad bit(s) as a 32-bit mask for bits 0–31. This may indicate either a bad SIMM or data bus failure.
$000F	Reserved for Macintosh compatibility.
$FFxx	A 680xx exception occurred during power on testing. The xx indicates the exception:

$01 — Bus Error
$02 — Address Error
$03 — Illegal Instruction Error
$04 — Zero Divide
$05 — Check Instruction
$06 — cpTrapCC, Trap CC, Trap V
$07 — Privilege violation
$08 — Trace
$09 — Line A
$0A — Line F
$0B — Unassigned
$0C — CP protocol violation
$0D — Format exception
$0E — Spurious interrupt
$0F — Trap 0–15 exception
$10 — Interrupt Level 1
$11 — Interrupt Level 2
$12 — Interrupt Level 3
$13 — Interrupt Level 4
$14 — Interrupt Level 5
$15 — Interrupt Level 6
$16 — Interrupt Level 7
$17 — FPCP bra or set on unordered condition
$18 — FPCP inexact result
$19 — FPCP divide by zero
$1A — FPCP underflow
$1B — FPCP operand error
$1C — FPCP overflow
$1D — FPCP signalling NAN
$1E — PMMU configuration
$1F — PMMU illegal operation
$20 — PMMU access level violation

A

Macintosh Portable ROMs

The bootup code in the Macintosh Portable contains a series of startup tests that are run to ensure that the fundamental operations of the machine are working properly. If any of those tests fail, a sad Mac icon appears onscreen with a code below that describes what failure occurred. The Macintosh Portable uses a different error code format:

XXXXyyYY

ZZZZZZZZ

The XXXX field contains various flags that are used by the start-up test routines; these can be ignored. The yy field identifies an exception if there has been one, or reads $00 if there hasn't. The YY field identifies the test during which the failure occurred. The Z field contains additional information about the failure. Here's an example of how a memory failure might appear on a Mac Portable:

00000102

00003C5B

The first four digits in line one might be anything; it doesn't matter. The 01 tells you that a bus error occurred, the following 02 tells you that the error occurred during the RAM test. The second line identifies the bits that failed. The Mac Portable uses a single RAM expansion card, so you would just swap the card.

Major Error Codes

Below is a brief description of the various test codes that might appear in the major error code:

Warning

Some of these codes may mean slightly different things in Macintosh models other than the Macintosh Portable. These descriptions describe specifically how they are used in the Macintosh Portable.

$01	-ROM test failed. Minor error code is $FFFF, means nothing.
$02	-RAM test failed. Minor error code indicates which RAM bits failed.
$05	-RAM external addressing test failed. Minor error code indicates a failed address line.
$06	-Unable to properly access the VIA 1 chip during VIA initialization. Minor error code not applicable.
$08	-Data bus test at location eight bytes off of top of memory failed. Minor error code indicates the bad bits as a 16-bit mask for bits 15–00. This may indicate either a bad RAM chip or data bus failure.
$0B	-Unable to properly access the SCSI chip. Minor error code not applicable.

$0C	-Unable to properly access the IWM (or SWIM) chip. Minor error code not applicable.
$0D	-Not applicable to Macintosh Portable. Unable to properly access the SCC chip. Minor error code not applicable.
$0E	-Data bus test at location $0 failed. Minor error code indicates the bad bits as a 16-bit mask for bits 15–00. This may indicate either a bad RAM chip or data bus failure.
$10	-Video RAM test failed. Minor error code indicates which RAM bits failed.
$11	-Video RAM addressing test failed. Minor error code contains the following:

upper word   =   failed address (16-bit)
msb of lower word =   data written
lsb of lower word =   data read
Data value written also indicates which address line is being actively tested.

$12	-Deleted
$13	-Deleted
$14	-Power Manager processor was unable to turn on all the power to the board. This may have been due to a communication problem with the Power Manager. If so, the minor error code contains a Power Manager error code, explained in the next section.
$15	-Power Manager failed its self-test. Minor error code contains the following: msw = Error status of transmission to power manager. lsw = Power Manager self-test results (0 means it, non-zero means it failed)
$16	-A failure occurred while trying to size and configure the RAM. Minor error code not applicable.

Minor Error Codes—Power Manager Processor Failures

If a communication problem occurs during communication with the Power Manager, the following error codes appear somewhere in the minor error code (usually in the lower half of the code but not always):

$CD38	Power Manager was never ready to start handshake.
$CD37	Timed out waiting for reply to initial handshake.
$CD36	During a send, Power Manager did not start a handshake.
$CD35	During a send, Power Manager did not finish a handshake.
$CD34	During a receive, Power Manager did not start a handshake.
$CD33	During a receive, Power Manager did not finish a handshake.

Diagnostic Code Summary

The following list summarizes the sad Mac error codes:

Test Codes

$01	ROM checksum test
$02	RAM test
$05	RAM addressing test
$06	VIA 1 chip access
$08	Data bus test at top of memory
$0B	SCSI chip access
$0C	IWM (or SWIM) chip access
$0D	Not applicable to Macintosh Portable. SCC chip access
$0E	Data bus test at location $0
$10	Video RAM test
$11	Video RAM addressing test
$14	Power Manager board power on
$15	Power Manager self-test
$16	RAM sizing

Power Manager Communication Error Codes

$CD38	Initial handshake
$CD37	No reply to initial handshake
$CD36	During a send, no start of a handshake
$CD35	During a send, no finish of a handshake
$CD34	During a receive, no start of a handshake
$CD33	During a receive, no finish of a handshake

CPU Exception Codes (As Used by the Startup Tests)

$0100	Bus error exception code
$0200	Address error exception code
$0300	Illegal error exception code
$0400	Zero divide error exception code
$0500	Check inst error exception code
$0600	cpTrapcc,Trapcc,TrapV exception code
$0700	Privilege violation exception code
$0800	Trace exception code
$0900	Line A exception code
$0A00	Line F exception code
$0B00	Unassigned exception code
$0C00	CP protocol violation
$0D00	Format exception

$0E00	Spurious interrupt exception code
$0F00	Trap inst exception code
$1000	Interrupt level 1
$1100	Interrupt level 2
$1200	Interrupt level 3
$1300	Interrupt level 4
$1400	Interrupt level 5
$1500	Interrupt level 6
$1600	Interrupt level 7

A

Guides to Macintosh Maintenance

The Quick Guide to Software Maintenance

To keep your Macintosh in top shape, try to perform each of these steps regularly:

- Keep at least one backup of your software, preferably three copies of important files and applications.

- Run virus protection software (Disinfectant 3.6, SAM).

- Run Apple Disk First Aid 7.2 or Norton 3.1or higher.

- Shut down your Macintosh using the Special Menu's Shutdown menu item.

- Deactivate unused system software extensions. If your system appears to run slowly, or if you have extensions loading at startup that you do not want to use, move them out of your System Folder.

- Organize files in folders, or move files no longer used off the hard drive to free up hard drive space.

- Rebuild the desktop. If generic icons are being used for files or folders on the desktop, hold down the ⌘-Option keys during startup and a dialog will appear asking you if you want to rebuild the desktop. Select OK and allow the progress bar to complete its task, and the icons should return. Rebuilding the desktop can help your Macintosh desktop free up icons no longer used with files on the hard drive, and enable more icons to be supported by the desktop database (this is where icons are stored).

- Check for new updates to software applications from online services, magazines, or Web sites to stay current with software updates and new software.

- Move unused preferences files for applications you no longer use out of the System Folder. Most are named after the application; some are not. The name of the preferences file is sometimes documented in the software application manual. If your Mac is running low on hard drive space, or maintaining files in the System Folder, you can save a few kilobytes of hard drive space by removing unnecessary preference files from the System Folder and hard drive.

- Remove unused aliases to servers, files, and folders on the hard drive. As you create new folders, or delete them from the hard drive, remember to dispose of any aliases you may have created.

- If you install application software regularly, check for an Installer Temp folder in your System Folder, and make sure it is empty. If it has contents you need, back it up first before throwing it away and deleting it from your hard drive.

The Quick Guide to Hardware Maintenance

To keep your Macintosh hardware in tip top shape, perform these maintenance suggestions regularly:

- Clean or dust monitor screen(s).

- Clean/dust external casings of external peripherals and the CPU.

- Check cables for secure connection for both connecting ends.

- Listen for irregular sounds originating from the hard drive, power supply or other peripherals.

- Run performance software, or observe any performance changes.

- Check for software updates to printer drivers and peripherals.

- Run optimization software on internal and external hard drives.

- Check for system software updates that may improve hardware performance or fix hardware-related bugs.

- Check for and move any magnetic devices that may be situated near a computer and remove if affecting monitor integrity.

- Check for any pests that may be situated nearby any hardware and spray the area if necessary. Be sure to turn off all electrical equipment before spraying to avoid electrical conflicts. Also, check periodically to make sure your internal case is bug and dust-free.

The Quick Guide to Networking Maintenance

To keep your Macintosh network humming nicely, perform these maintenance suggestions regularly:

- Check backup servers and network clients on the network to make sure they are running and properly connected before starting a network-based backup session. Archive old or unused files and back up work in progress and valuable files.

Note

Server refers to a Macintosh running personal filesharing as well as a Macintosh running AppleShare or Apple Remote Access software. **Client** refers to a Macintosh connected to another Macintosh running personal filesharing software.

- Run network integrity software. Try to locate network systems that may have loose cable connections, appear to be losing packets, or have high packet traffic.

- Check external network modem for correct configuration and operation. Also verify that external mail can be sent correctly across the modem from the Internet or other network to the local network.

- Check physical LocalTalk and EtherTalk connections for complete connections to printers, servers, and computers.

- Check network connectivity to hardware such as transceivers, as well as to hubs, repeaters, and routers to make sure all are functioning. Focus and most Farallon LocalTalk and Ethernet transceivers have lights that turn green if connected to a net, and red if no connection is registered within the transceiver.

- Remove any network users or groups who do not need access to servers or client Macs on the network.

- Change passwords for server and client systems (as admin and user).

- Check with original vendor support sites for network hardware and software upgrades for the network.

- Check for new system and network software network updates from Apple that may improve performance, support new Macs, or fix any relevant bugs for your site.

- Check with other network users for feedback on network performance, integrity, and problem areas.

Apple Upgrade Index

This Appendix contains selected Apple parts and upgrades by category.

Apple Cables

Product	*Description*
SCSI CABLES	
M0206	Apple SCSI System Cable
	Connects CPU to the first SCSI peripheral.
M2538LL/A	Apple HDI-30 SCSI System Cable
	Connects a PowerBook, Duo Dock, or Duo MiniDock to a SCSI device.
M2539LL/A	Apple HDI-30 SCSI Disk Adapter
M0207	Apple SCSI Peripheral Interface Cable
	Connects any two SCSI peripherals together.
M0208LL/B	Apple SCSI Cable Extender
	Extends SCSI cables by one meter.
M3503LL/A	Apple SCSI Cable Terminator
	Filters noise on SCSI cabling. One terminator is required between each CPU and the first (and last) SCSI peripheral.
M5871G/A	Apple SCSI Cable Terminator II (black)
	For connecting a hard disk to the LaserWriter Pro 630 external SCSI port — also requires HDI-30 SCSI System Cable (M2538LL/A).

LOCALTALK CABLES

Product	Description
M2066LL/B	LocalTalk Locking Cable Kit—10 meter *Includes 10 meters of LocalTalk cable and one cable extender plug.*
M20681LL/B	LocalTalk Locking Connector Kit—din8 *Includes one LocalTalk connector with mini-circular 8-pin plug, one 2-meter LocalTalk cable for Apple IIGS, Macintosh Plus and later, and the LaserWriter IINT, IINTX, IIf, IIg, Personal LaserWriter NT, NTR, or LaserWriter Pro 600 or 630.*
M1657Z/A	LocalTalk RJ11 Connector Kit—DB9 *Includes one LocalTalk UTP Connector with mini-circular 8-pin plug, one 2-meter UTP cable, and one terminating resistor for Apple IIGS, Macintosh Plus and later, LaserWriter IINT, IINTX, IIf, IIg, Personal LaserWriter NT, NTR, or LaserWriter Pro 600 or 630.*
M2065	LocalTalk Locking Connector Kit—DB9 *Includes one LocalTalk connector with DB9 plug, one 2-meter LocalTalk cable, and one cable extender plug for Macintosh 512K, LocalTalk PC Card, LaserWriter, LaserWriter Plus.*
M1661Z/A	LocalTalk RJ11 Connector Kit—DB9 *Includes one LocalTalk Unshielded Twisted Pair (UTP) Connector with DB9 plug, one 2-meter UTP cable, and one terminating resistor for Macintosh 512K, LaserWriter, LaserWriter Plus, or LocalTalk PC Card.*
M2069	LocalTalk Locking Cable Kit—25 meter *Includes one 25-meter LocalTalk cable, 20 preassembled plugs, 20 cable-splicing mechanisms, and 4 cable extender plugs.*

PRINTER/MODEM CABLES

Product	Description
A2C0312	Apple II Modem—8 Cable *Connects the Apple Personal Modem to Apple IIe and Apple IIGS equipped with a Super Serial Card. Connects ImageWriter II to Macintosh XL and Apple III. Connects AppleLine to Macintosh Plus, II, or SE. Connects ImageWriter I to Apple IIc Plus.*
A9C0314/b	Apple II Printer—8 Cable *Connects the ImageWriter II or LQ to Apple II+, Apple IIe, and Apple IIGS equipped with a Super Serial Card.*
M0196	Macintosh Peripheral—8 Cable *Connects the ImageWriter II or Apple modems to Macintosh 512K.*
M0197LL/B	Apple System Peripheral—8 Cable *Connects ImageWriter II or LQ and Apple modems to Apple IIGS,*

Apple IIc Plus, (and AppleFax modem to) Macintosh (except 512K). Connects Personal LaserWriter LS and StyleWriter to Macintosh.

M1099   Macintosh Peripheral Adapter
When connected to Macintosh (except 512K), this adapter (circular 8 to DB9) will enable use of peripherals and cables that require a DB9.

Apple Scanner and Peripherals

Product	Description
B0634LL/D	Apple OneScanner with Accessory Kit *(requires appropriate SCSI cables)*
B0842LL/B	Apple OneScanner with Accessory Kit *(for Windows)* *Includes SCSI Card, Cable, and Terminator.*
A9M0338	Apple Scanner Replacement Lamp
B0993LL/A	Apple Color OneScanner with Accessory Kit

Macintosh Memory (DRAM) Product Description

Product	Description
M2091LL/A	Macintosh IIci 1MB Memory Exp. Kit (four 256K SIMMs)
M0219	Macintosh 2 MB Memory Exp. Kit (two 1 MB SIMMs) *(Plus, SE, LC, 2 MB Classic, Classic II only)*
M5952LL/A	Macintosh 4MB Memory Exp. Kit (four 1 MB SIMMs) *(SE/30, II, IIx, IIcx, IIci, IIvx, IIsi, Quadra 700, 900, 950, LaserWriter IIf & IIg)*
N1507LL/A	Macintosh 4 MB Memory Exp. Kit (one 4 MB SIMMs) *(LC III, Centris/Quadra 610, 650, 660AV, Quadra 605, 800, 840AV, AWS 60 & 80, Power Macintosh) Required: 2 SIMMs for use in Power Macintosh.*
M0294LL/A	Macintosh IIci 4 MB Parity Memory Exp. Kit (four 1 MB Party SIMMs)
M1508LL/A	Macintosh 8 MB Memory Exp. Kit (one 8 MB SIMM) *(LC III, Centris/Quadra 610, 650, 660AV, Quadra 605, 800, 840AV, AWS 60 & 80, Power Macintosh) Requires 2 SIMMs for use in Power Macintosh.*
M3372LL/A	16 MB Memory Expansion Kit (one 16 MB SIMM)

C

Second-Level Memory Cache and DRAM

These products require installation by an authorized Apple Service Provider.

The Workgroup Servers 60 and 80 use the same memory as the Centris 610 and Quadra 800.

Product	Description
M6810Z/A	Workgroup Server 95 128K/Tag Second-level Memory Cache Upgrade Kit *Adds two SRAM SIMMs to the Workgroup Server 95 PDS Card. Brings total second-level memory cache on the Workgroup Server 95 PDS Card.*
M6815Z/A	Workgroup Server 95 16 MB Parity Memory Exp. Kit (4-4 MB Parity SIMMs)

Macintosh Accessories

Product	Description
A9M0103	Apple MIDI Interface *Connects Apple IIGS or Macintosh CPUs to MIDI equipped musical instruments. Cables included.*
M2896LL/B	Apple TV/Video System (Macintosh Quadra/Performa 63X only)
M2895LL/A	Apple Presentation System
M2706LL/A	Apple DeskTop Bus Mouse IIM14811LL/A Apple Omni-Directional MicrophoneM3261LL/A AppleDesign Powered Speakers II (compact)
M4475LL/B	AppleDesign Powered Speakers
M8168LL/A	1 MB Apple Double-Sided Disks (double-density 10/bx)
M8169LL/A	2 MB Apple Double-Sided Disks (high-density 10/bx)
M9060Z/A	Apple PlainTalk Microphone (for Quadra 605 and Power Macintosh) *Already included with all AV configurations.*
M3790LL/A	Apple QuickTake 150 for Macintosh (with software for Power Macintosh)
M1644LL/A	Apple QuickTake 100 for Macintosh *Software for Power Macintosh compatibility.*
M2851LL/A	AC Adapter for QuickTake
M2655G/A	Apple QuickTake Battery Booster Pack
M2848G/A	Apple QuickTake Travel Case
M1867LL/A	Apple Headphone *Also for use with CD-ROM drive or external speakers equipped with an audio-out jack.*

All peripherals should be ordered with the appropriate cable.

Macintosh Upgrades

These products require installation by an authorized Apple Service Provider unless otherwise noted. As outlined in the Apple Authorized Service Provider Agreement, all Apple authorized service providers can perform repair service and upgrades on the Performa product line. System software is provided by reseller unless otherwise noted.

Product	Description

MACINTOSH ENTRY LEVEL UPGRADES

Product	Description
M2139LL/A	Macintosh LC 475 Logic Board Upgrade *To upgrade Macintosh LCII or LCIII to Macintosh LC 475. Also includes 4 MB RAM and name plate.*
M1386LL/A	Macintosh LCIII Logic Board Upgrade *To upgrade Macintosh LC or LCII to Macintosh LCIII. Also includes 4 MB DRAM, 512K VRAM, System software, and case.*
M6775LL/A	Macintosh Math Coprocessor *(for Macintosh LC III and Color Classic)*
M1545LL/A	Macintosh Classic II Logic Board Upgrade *To upgrade Macintosh Classic to Macintosh Classic II. Also includes 2 MB RAM, System software, microphone and new case. System software requires hard disk (not included).*
M6052/B	Macintosh SE SuperDrive Upgrade Kit *To upgrade Macintosh SE to Macintosh SuperDrive SE. Includes Macintosh SE SuperDrive Rom Kit (M0242), and Internal SuperDrive (M0247).*
M0444LL/D	Apple IIe Card for Macintosh LC v2.2 *Compatible only with the Apple 5.25 drive A9M0107 and Apple UniDisk 3.5 drive-A2M2053. Supports internal Macintosh LC drives and up to three external drives (maximum combination of up to two Apple 5 1/4-inch drives and one UniDisk 3 1/2-inch drive). Customer installable.*
M1222LL/C	Apple IIe Card Upgrade Package *(software to upgrade prior versions to v2.2). Customer installable.*

Product	Description

MACINTOSH II UPGRADES

Product	Description
M6051/C	Macintosh II SuperDrive Upgrade Kit *Includes Internal SuperDrive (M0247) and ROM/SWIM Kit (0244).*
M0375LL/B	Macintosh IIfx Logic Board Upgrade *To upgrade Macintosh II (w/M2047) or IIx to Macintosh IIfx. DRAM is required (4 MB) and must be purchased separately.*

C

M0326LL/B	Macintosh IIci Cache Card *(Customer installable)*
M0480LL/B	Macintosh IIsi 030 Direct Slot Adapter Card *(Customer installable)*
	Allows addition of one 030 Direct Slot Expansion Card. Includes 68882 floating point math coprocessor.
M0481LL/A	Macintosh IIsi NuBus Adapter Card *(Customer installable)*
	Allows addition of one NuBus Expansion Card. Includes 68882 floating point math coprocessor.
M1330LL/A	Macintosh Centris 650 Logic Board Upgrade
	To upgrade Macintosh IIvx to a Macintosh Centris 650. Also includes 8 MB DRAM, 512K VRAM, Ethernet, and FPU.

Product	Description

MACINTOSH CENTRIS/QUADRA UPGRADES

M1402LL/A	Macintosh Centris/Quadra 610 NuBus Adapter Card
	For addition of NuBus cards up to 7 inches in length. Customer installable.
M3397LL/A	Macintosh Processor Upgrade Card
M1534LL/A	Macintosh Quadra 660AV Logic Board Upgrade
	To upgrade Centris/Quadra 610 to a Quadra 660AV. Also includes 4 MB DRAM, System 7.1, Apple PlainTalk Microphone, and name plate.
M9049LL/A	Macintosh Centris/Quadra 660AV NuBus Adapter Card
	For addition of NuBus cards up to 7 inches in length. Customer installable.
M1848LL/A	Macintosh Quadra 840 AV Logic Board Upgrade
	To upgrade Quadra 800 to a Quadra 840AV. Uses same DRAM as Quadra 800. Also includes 8 MB DRAM, System 7.1, Apple PlainTalk Microphone, and front panel assembly.
M2843LL/A	Power Macintosh Upgrade Card *(Customer installable)*
	To upgrade Macintosh Quadra/Centris 610, 650 or Quadra 700, 800, 900, 950. Includes Upgrade Card and System software.
M2343LL/A	Power Macintosh 6100/60 Logic Board Upgrade
	To upgrade Macintosh Quadra/Centris 610, 660AV. Also includes System software, 8 MB DRAM, name plate, and Power Macintosh Display Adapter.
M2901LL/A	Power Macintosh 6100/60AV Logic Board Upgrade
	To upgrade Macintosh Quadra/Centris 610, 660AV. Also includes System software, 8 MB DRAM, 1 MB VRAM, PlainTalk Microphone, cables for S-video to composite video, and name plate.

M2474LL/A   Power Macintosh 7100/66 Logic Board Upgrade
To upgrade Macintosh IIvx, Performa 600, Quadra/Centris 650. Also includes System software, 8 MB DRAM, 1 MB VRAM, and new top cover.

M2840LL/A   Power Macintosh 7100/66AV Logic Board Upgrade
To upgrade Macintosh IIvx, Performa 600, Quadra/Centris 650. Also includes System software, 8 MB DRAM, 2 MB VRAM, PlainTalk Microphone, cables for S-video to composite video, and new top cover.

M2344LL/A   Power Macintosh 8100/80 Logic Board Upgrade
To upgrade Macintosh Quadra 800, 840AV. Also includes System software, 8 MB DRAM, 2 MB VRAM, and new top cover.

M2902LL/A   Power Macintosh 8100/80AV Logic Board Upgrade
To upgrade Macintosh Quadra 800, 840AV. Also includes System software, 8 MB DRAM, 2 MB VRAM, PlainTalk Microphone, cables for S-video to composite video, and new top cover.

Product	Description

POWERBOOKS AND POWERBOOK UPGRADES

M3530LL/A   Macintosh PowerBook 190/66 4MB Hard Disk 500MB Grayscale

M3531LL/A   Macintosh PowerBook 190/66 8MB Hard Disk 500MB Grayscale

M4072LL/A   Macintosh PowerBook 190cs/66 4MB 500MB Color

M4073LL/A   Macintosh PowerBook 190cs/66 8MB 750MB Color

M4221LL/A   Macintosh PowerBook Duo 2300c/100 20MB Hard Disk 1.1GB Color

M3824LL/A   Macintosh PowerBook 5300cs/100 16MB Hard Disk 750MB Color

M3828LL/A   Macintosh PowerBook 5300ce/117 (SVGA) 32MB Hard Disk 1.1GB Color

M2995LL/B   PCMCIA Expansion Module

M3881LL/A   Macintosh PowerBook Logic Board Upgrade Kit with PowerPC 603e for Macintosh PowerBook 190 series

M3170LL/A   Macintosh PowerBook Logic Board Upgrade Kit with PowerPC 603e for Macintosh PowerBook 200 series

M4071LL/A   Macintosh PowerBook Infrared Upgrade Kit for Macintosh PowerBook 190 series

M3743LL/A   Macintosh PowerBook 8-bit Color Video-out Upgrade Kit for Macintosh PowerBook 190 series

M3747LL/A   Macintosh PowerBook Power Adapter for Macintosh PowerBook 5300 series and 190 series

C

M3748LL/A	Macintosh PowerBook Rechargeable Lithium-Ion Battery for Macintosh PowerBook 5300 series and 190 series
M3750LL/A	Macintosh PowerBook 8 MB RAM Expansion Card for Macintosh PowerBook 5300 and 190 Series
M3746LL/A	Macintosh PowerBook 10.4" Active-Matrix Color Display upgrade Kit for Macintosh PowerBook 5300 series
M4088LL/B	Macintosh PowerBook 150 4 MB Hard drive 250 MB
M3179LL/A	Macintosh PowerBook 150 Memory Adapter Kit
M4662LL/A	Macintosh PowerBook AC Adapter
M4664LL/A	Macintosh PowerBook 4MB Memory Expansion Kit
M1027LL/A	Macintosh PowerBook Battery Recharger
M3927LL/A	Macintosh PowerBook Video Adapter Cable
M4286LL/A	Macintosh PowerBook Express Modem Kit (for PowerBook Duo 200 series)
M1921LL/A	Macintosh PowerBook Duo Dock Plus (1MB VRAM) with Ethernet
M4181LL/A	Macintosh PowerBook Duo MiniDock
M4180LL/A	Macintosh PowerBook Duo Floppy Adapter
M2780LL/A	Macintosh PowerBook Duo Rechargeble Battery, High-Capacity Type III
M4178LL/B	Macintosh PowerBook Duo Battery Recharger (uses AC Adapter)
M4174LL/B	Macintosh PowerBook Duo AC Adapter (280, 280c, and prior)
M1910LL/A	Macintosh PowerBook 500 Series AC Adapter
M1908LL/A	Macintosh PowerBook 500 Series Intelligent Battery

Product	*Description*

POWER MACINTOSH AND POWER MACINTOSH UPGRADES

M3093LL/A	Power Macintosh 9500/132 16 MB Hard Disk 2GB Internal Quad-speed CD-ROM
M3680LL/A	Power Macintosh 8100/100AV 16 MB Hard Disk 1GB Internal CD-ROM and AV Card
M3105LL/A	Power Macintosh 8500/120 16 MB Hard Disk 2GB Internal Quad-speed CD-ROM
M3102LL/A	Power Macintosh 7500/100 16 MB Hard Disk 1GB Internal Quad-speed CD-ROM
M4082LL/A	Power Macintosh 7200/90 8 MB Hard Disk 500MB Internal Quad-speed CD-ROM
M3947LL/A	Power Macintosh 5200/75 LC 8 MB Hard Disk 500MB Internal Quad-speed CD-ROM
M4107LL/A	Macintosh Performa 5215CD 8 MB Hard Disk 1GB Internal Quad-speed CD-ROM

M4103LL/A	Macintosh Performa 6230CD (MPEG/VI) 16 MB Hard Disk 1GB Internal Quad-speed CD-ROM
M3939LL/A	Macintosh Performa 640CD DOS Compatible 12 MB Hard Disk 500 MB Internal CD-ROM
M2337LL/A	Power Macintosh 6100/60 NuBus Adapter Card *(Customer installable)*
M2385LL/A	Power Macintosh 256K Cache Card *(6100/60 and AV, 7100/66 and AV only)*
M3447LL/A	Power Macintosh AV Card *(customer installable for Power Macintosh 6100 and Performa 61XX only)*
M3581LL/A	DOS Compatibility Card

Workgroup Server Products

Workgroup Server 60 CPUs

Includes System 7.1 and AppleShare 4.0 preinstalled, Ethernet, online and hard-copy documentation. Keyboard, display, and appropriate Ethernet transceiver sold separately.

| M1780LL/B | Workgroup Server 60 8 MB hard disk 230 CPU |
| M1781LL/B | Workgroup Server 60 8 MB hard disk 500 CPU w/CD-ROM |

Workgroup Server 80 CPUs

Includes System 7.1 and AppleShare 4.0 preinstalled, Ethernet, FPU, online and hard-copy documentation. Retrospect Remote backup software included in configurations with DAT Tape Backup with compression. Keyboard, display, and appropriate Ethernet transceiver sold separately.

| M1681LL/A | Workgroup Server 80 16MB Hard Disk 1000 CPU withDAT Drive |
| M1685LL/A | Workgroup Server 80 16MB Hard Disk 1000 CPU with DAT Drive and CD-ROM |

Workgroup Server 95 CPUs

CPUs include preinstalled, tuned server version of A/UX 3.1 operating system. Also included are A/UX backup software, Parity DRAM, Ethernet, FPU, online and hard-copy documentation, and Retrospect Remote. Some configurations also include DAT Tape Backup Drive with compression. Keyboard, display, and appropriate Ethernet transceiver sold separately. Server Applications, such as AppleShare Pro, sold separately unless otherwise noted. CD-ROM drive required to reinstall the A/UX system software.

| M16855LL/A | Workgroup Server 95 16 MB Hard Disk 230 CPU *(128K second-level memory cache)* |

File/Print Environment

M3074LL/A   Workgroup Server 95 32 MB Hard Disk 2000 CPU w/DAT
                   Drive *(512K second-level memory cache)*

Database Environment

M6895LL/A   Workgroup Server 95 48 MB Hard Disk 230 and Hard Disk
                   1000 CPU with DAT Drive *(512K second-level memory cache)*
M3075LL/A   Workgroup Server 95 48 MB Hard Disk 250 and Hard Disk
                   1000 CPU with DAT Drive *(512K second-level memory cache)*

Workgroup Server 95 Upgrade Kits

Kits require installation by an authorized Apple Service Provider.

Overall system performance may vary depending on CPU being upgraded and/or hard disk
drive selection. Each Kit includes Processor Direct Slot (PDS) card with 128K second-level
memory cache, documentation, and CD-ROM containing system software, online documentation, and Retrospect Remote backup software. CD-ROM drive needed to install system
software.

M6940Z/A   Workgroup Server 95 PDS Card Upgrade Kit
                   *To upgrade a Macintosh Quadra 900 or 950 to a Workgroup
                   Server 95.*
M6945Z/A   Workgroup Server 95 PDS Card/DDS-DC Drive Upgrade Kit
                   *To upgrade a Macintosh Quadra 900 or 950 to a Workgroup Server
                   95 with internal DDS-DC backup drive.*

PowerPC Processor Workgroup Server Products

RAID software (included with PowerPC-based Workgroups Servers and logic board upgrades) ships separately. Be sure to return your warranty card for fastest delivery.

Workgroup Server 6150 CPUs

The Workgroup Server 6150 runs the PowerPC 601 processor at 60 and 66MHz. Includes
System 7.5 or 7.5.1 preinstalled, 256K second-level cache, Ethernet, FPU, online and hard-
copy documentation. Also includes RAID software for disk mirroring to protect data (RAID
level 1) or data stripping to improve disk throughput (RAID level 0). Use of either RAID
feature requires the addition of an approved external disk drive or drives (for a fax of approved drives, call 1-800-462-4396). Keyboard, display, and appropriate Ethernet transceiver
sold separately.

M3358LL.A   Workgroup Server 6150 8 MB Hard Disk 500 CPU with CD-ROM with AppleShare 4.0.2 preinstalled.

M4066LL/A   Workgroup Server 6150/66 16 MB, 700 MB Hard Disk, Quad Speed CD-ROM with AppleShare 4.1

Workgroup Server 8150 CPUs

The Workgroup Server 8150 runs the PowerPC 601 processor at 80 and 110 MHz. Includes System 7.5 or 7.5.1 preinstalled. 256K second-level cache, Ethernet, FPU, online and hard-copy documentation. Also includes RAID software for disk mirroring to protect data (RAID level 1) or data stripping to improve disk throughput (RAID level 0). Use of either RAID feature requires the addition of approved external disk drive or drives (for a fax of approved drives, call 1-800-462-4396). Retrospect Remote backup software included and 120-meter DAT drive with DDS-2 data compression. Keyboard, display, and appropriate Ethernet transceiver sold separately.

M3300LL/A   Workgroup Server 8150 16 MB Hard Disk 1000 CPU with DAT Drive and CD-ROM.

M3359LL/A   Workgroup Server 8150 16 MB Hard Disk 1000 CPU with DAT Drive and CD-ROM with AppleShare 4.0.2 preinstalled.

M4042LL/A   Workgroup Server 8150/110 16 MB Hard Disk 1000 CPU with Quad-speed CD-ROM

M4043LL/A   Workgroup Server 8150/110 8 MB Quad CD-ROM Built to Order

Workgroup Server 9150 CPUs

The Workgroup Server 9150 runs the PowerPC 601 processor at 80 MHz. Includes System 7.1.2 preinstalled, 512K second-level cache, Ethernet, FPU, online and hard-copy documentation. Also includes RAID software for disk mirroring to protect data (RAID level 1) or data stripping to improve disk throughput (RAID level 0). Retrospect Remote backup software included and 120-meter DAT drive with DDS-2 data compression. Keyboard, display, and appropriate Ethernet transceiver sold separately.

M3272LL/A   Workgroup Server 9150 16 MB with two Hard Disks 1000 CPU with DAT Drive and CD-ROM.

M3357LL/A   Workgroup Server 9150 16 MB with two Hard Disks 1000 CPU with DAT Drive and CD-ROM with AppleShare 4.0.2 preinstalled.

Workgroup Server PowerPC Logic Board 9150 CPUs

These products require installation by an authorized Apple Service Provider. Overall system performance may vary depending on server application.

The Workgroup Server 95 running A/UX requires a separate PowerPC processor upgrade path to include migration of Unix applications and data—details to be released at a future date.

M2913LL/A   Workgroup Server 6150 Logic Board Upgrade
To upgrade a Workgroup Server 60 to a Workgroup Server 6150. Includes System software, AppleShare 4.0.2 update kit, 8 MB DRAM, 256K second-level cache, RAID 0/1 software, name plate, and Power Macintosh Display Adapter.

M2915LL/A   Workgroup Server 8150 Logic Board Upgrade
To upgrade a Workgroup Server 80 to a Workgroup Server 8150. Includes System software, AppleShare 4.0.2 update kit, 8 MB DRAM, 256K second-level cache, RAID 0/1 software, Retrospect Remote upgrade, new top cover, and Power Macintosh Display Adapter.

M3262LL/A   Workgroup Server 9150 Logic Board Upgrade
To upgrade a Quadra 900 or Quadra 950 to a Workgroup Server 9150. Includes System software, 8 MB DRAM, 512K second-level cache, RAID 0/1 software, and new top cover. Quadra 900/950 DRAM is not compatible with this Workgroup Server 9150 logic board upgrade. The updated Workgroup Server 9150 requires Power Macintosh DRAM (M15071LL/A or M1508LL/A). For customers with AppleShare 4 and Retrospect Remote, upgrade kits are available separately.

Networking and Communications Products

Apple Development Products are available from APDA (AppleLink path: Developer Support>Developer Services->APDA).

Telecommunications hardware

M1694LL/A   Apple GeoPort Adapter (Centris/Quadra 660AV and Quadra 840AV only)
Enables data and fax send/receive at up to 14.4 kbps. For use with analog telephone lines only. Includes disk (with GeoPort and Express Modem software) and phone cable. Communications software not included.

M3127LL/A   Apple GeoPort Adapter (Power Macintosh)
M0417LL/B   Apple Ethernet NB Card (transceiver required)
Requires a NuBus Adapter Card when used with the IIsi and Centris 610.

M3345Z/A	Apple Ethernet NB Thin Coax Connection
	Includes Ethernet NB Card and Thin Coax Transceiver for use with Macintosh computers with a NuBus slot. NuBus adapter required for Macintosh IIsi, Centris/Quadra 610, and Power Macintosh 6100/60.
M1768Z/A	Apple Ethernet NB Twisted-Pair Card (for use with a 10BASE-T compatible hub)
	Network cable not included. Separate transceiver not required. Requires NuBus Adapter Card when used with the IIsi and Centris/ Quadra 610.
M0443LL/C	Apple Ethernet LC Card (transceiver required)
M3346Z/A	Apple Ethernet LC Thin Coax Connection
	Includes Ethernet LC Card and Thin Coax Transceiver for use with Macintosh computers with an LC PDS Slot (such as Color Classic, LC, and Quadra 605).
M2406Z/A	Apple Ethernet LC Twisted-Pair Card (for use with 10BASE-T compatible hub)
	Network cable not included. Separate transceiver not required.
M3348Z/A	Apple Ethernet 3-Meter Twisted-Pair Cable (for use with 10BASE-T compatible hub)
	Industry standard Category 3 cable for use with Twisted Pair Transceiver, Ethernet LC or NB card.
M3349Z/A*	Apple Ethernet 7-Meter Twisted-Pair Cable
M3350Z/A*	Apple Ethernet 13-Meter Twisted-Pair Cable
M0437Z/B	Apple Ethernet Twisted-Pair Transceiver
M0329Z/B	Apple Ethernet Thin Coax Transceiver (cable not included)
M3347Z/A	Apple Ethernet 2-Meter Thin Coax Self-Terminating Cable
M0833LL/B	Apple Ethernet 5-Meter Thin Coax Cable
M0436LL/B	Apple Ethernet 13-Meter Thin Coax Plenum Cable
M0432LL/A	Apple Ethernet AUI Adapter
A2B2088	Apple II Workstation Card

Network Software

See the Workgroup Server Products section for Client/Server software.

A2D2059	Aristotle (requires AppleShare)
M8101Z/B	MacX.400 Single Domain v1.1
M8062Z/D	MacX25 v1.2
M8068Z/A	MacX25 Router Extensions
	Requires Basic Connectivity Package (M0502Z/B) and MacX25 v1.2 (M0711Z/D).
M8096Z/B	OSI Connection for Macintosh v1.1
M0502Z/B	Apple Internet Router Basic Connectivity Package v.3.0.1
M8112Z/A	Apple Internet Router AppleTalk/IP Wide Area Extension
	Requires Basic Connectivity Package (M0502Z/B).

C

M8111Z/A	Apple Internet Router AppleTalk/X.25 Wide Area Extension
	Includes MacX25 software. Requires Basic Connectivity Package (M0502Z/B).
M8066Z/A	AppleTalk Administration for Macintosh
M8069Z/A	AppleTalk Connection for Macintosh
M8065Z/A	AppleTalk Connection for Macintosh, 20-user license
	Requires AppleTalk Connection for Macintosh (M8069Z/A).
M8114Z/A	TCP/IP Administration for Macintosh
M8113Z/A	TCP/IP Connection for Macintosh
M8115Z/A	TCP/IP Connection for Macintosh, 20-user license
	Requires TCP/IP Connection for Macintosh (M8113Z/A).

System Enablers and System 7.5.x

This Appendix lists all of the available System Enablers for the Macintosh. It also includes a listing of Extensions and Control Panels that are installed when you install System 7.5.x. Using all of these correctly will help you get the most out of your current system.

Apple System Enablers

The Plus, SE, SE/30, Classic, Classic II, LC, LCII, Mac II, IIx, IIcx, IIsi, IIci, IIfx, PB 100/ 140/145/170, Quadra 700, 900, and 950 **DO NOT** need a System Enabler. Also, the Performa 200, 400, 405, 430, and 410 **DO NOT** require a System Enabler.

System Enablers—All Models

Macintosh	System Enabler Used	Current Version	Note
Macintosh Centris 610	System Enabler 040	1.1	D
Macintosh Centris 650	System Enabler 040	1.1	D
Macintosh Centris 660AV	System Enabler 088	1.2	D
Macintosh Color Classic	System Enabler 401	1.0.5	D
Macintosh IIvi	System Enabler 001	1.0.1	D
Macintosh IIvx	System Enabler 001	1.0.1	D
Macintosh LCIII	System Enabler 003	1.1	D
Macintosh LC 475	System Enabler 065	1.2	D
Macintosh LC 520	System Enabler 403	1.0.2	D
Macintosh LC 550	System Enabler 403	1.0.2	D
Macintosh LC 575	System Enabler 065	1.2	D

Macintosh LC 630	System Enabler 405	1.0	D
Macintosh PowerBook 150	PowerBook 150 Enabler	1.1	D
Macintosh PowerBook 160	System Enabler 131	1.0.3	A
Macintosh PowerBook 165	System Enabler 131	1.0.3	A
Macintosh PowerBook 165c	System Enabler 131	1.0.3	A
Macintosh PowerBook 180	System Enabler 131	1.0.3	A
Macintosh PowerBook 180c	System Enabler 131	1.0.3	A
Macintosh PowerBook 520	PBook 500 Series Enabler	1.0.2	D
Macintosh PowerBook 520c	PBook 500 Series Enabler	1.0.2	D
Macintosh PowerBook 540	PBook 500 Series Enabler	1.0.2	D
Macintosh PowerBook 540c	PBook 500 Series Enabler	1.0.2	D
Macintosh PowerBook Duo 210	PowerBook Duo Enabler	1.0	B
Macintosh PowerBook Duo 230	PowerBook Duo Enabler	1.0	B
Macintosh PowerBook Duo 250	PowerBook Duo Enabler	1.0	B
Macintosh PowerBook Duo 270c	PowerBook Duo Enabler	1.0	D
Macintosh PowerBook Duo 280	PowerBook Duo Enabler	2.0	C
Macintosh PowerBook Duo 280c	PowerBook Duo Enabler	2.0	C
Macintosh Quadra 605	System Enabler 065	1.2	D
Macintosh Quadra 610	System Enabler 040	1.1	D
Macintosh Quadra 630	System Enabler 405	1.0	D
Macintosh Quadra 650	System Enabler 040	1.1	D
Macintosh Quadra 660AV	System Enabler 088	1.2	D
Macintosh Quadra 800	System Enabler 040	1.1	D
Macintosh Quadra 840AV	System Enabler 088	1.2	D
Macintosh TV	System Enabler 404	1.0	D
Performa 600	System Enabler 304	1.0.1	D
Performa 450, 460, 466/7	System Enabler 308	1.0	D
Performa 475, 476, 575, 577/8	System Enabler 364	1.1	D
Performa 550, 560	System Enabler 332	1.1	D
Performa 630, 635CD	System Enabler 405	1.0	D
Performa 611x	Requires System 7.5		D
Performa 5200CD	System Enabler 406	1.0	
Power Macintosh 5200/75LC	System Enabler 406	1.0	
Power Macintosh 6100/60	PowerPC Enabler	1.0.2	D
Power Macintosh 7100/66	PowerPC Enabler	1.0.2	D
Power Macintosh 8100/80	PowerPC Enabler	1.0.2	D
Power Macintosh 8100/110	PowerPC Enabler	1.1.1	E
Power Macintosh 6100/66	PowerPC Enabler	1.1.1	E

Power Macintosh 7100/80	PowerPC Enabler	1.1.1	E
Power Macintosh 8100/100	PowerPC Enabler	1.1.1	E
Power Macintosh Upgrade	PowerPC Upgrade CD Enabler	1.0.1	D
Power Macintosh 9500/120	System Enabler 701	1.0	
Power Macintosh 9500/132	System Enabler 701	1.0	

Legend for Notes Column

A. System Enabler 131 replaces System Enabler 111 and System Enabler 121.

B. Express Modem users should also install the Duo Battery Patch (Extension).

C. Requires System Software version 7.1.1 or later. System Software 7.1.1 and PowerBook Duo Enabler 2.0 ship with the PowerBook Duo 280 and 280c.

D. No System Enabler is required for this Macintosh under System 7.5.

E. Power Macintosh 6100/66, 7100/80, 8100/100, and 8100/110 require System 7.5 and Finder 7.1.5.

Enabler Change History

PowerBook 150 Enabler

1.1 First release.

PowerBook 500 Series Enabler

1.0.2 First release.

PowerBook Duo Enabler

1.0 First release. Replaced System Enabler 201.

2.0 Includes support for type III batteries, better support for dual monitors, and multiple resolution support for color displays. Added support for PowerBook Duo 280 and 280c.

PowerPC Enabler

1.0 First release.

1.0.1 Fixes some video and serial communications problems.

1.0.2 Improved Energy Star compatibility for certain monitors connected to the built-in video port.

1.1 Manufacturing release only.

1.1.1 Added support for speed bumped Power Macintosh. Requires Finder 7.1.5.

PowerPC Upgrade Card Enabler

1.0 First release.

1.0.1 Includes Communications Toolbox 1.1

System Enabler 001

1.0 First release.

1.0.1 Improved support for high speed serial communications and improved accuracy of the system clock. Also addressed a rare problem in which floppies may not be ejected properly at shutdown.

System Enabler 003

1.0 First release.

1.1 Updated in System Update 3.0. Minor bug fix for compatibility.

System Enabler 040

1.0 First release.

1.1 Added support for Quadra 610 and Quadra 650.

System Enabler 065

1.0 First release for Macintosh LC 475 and Macintosh Quadra 605.

1.1 Added support for Macintosh LC 575.

1.2 Minor bug fix for compatibility.

System Enabler 088

1.0 First release.

1.0.1 Required for System 7 Pro 7.1.1 support.

1.1 Added support for Quadra 660AV.

1.2 Corrects problems with serial port, involving printing to LaserWriter 310. The system would crash in certain instances when receiving a fax and network traffic is high.

System Enabler 131

1.0 First release to support the PowerBook 180c. Replaced System Enabler 121 (supporting 165c) as well as System Enabler 111 (supporting 160 and 180).

1.0.2 Corrected a problem involving the serial driver. If a user has the serial driver open, but is not transmitting, and then puts the PowerBook to sleep, any attempt to transmit on waking would cause the system to hang.

1.0.3 Added support for the PowerBook 165.

System Enabler 401

1.0.4 First release.

1.0.5 Fixed a problem involving erratic mouse movement with Apple II mouse-based applications running on the Apple IIe card installed in the PDS.

System Enabler 403

1.0 First release for Macintosh LC 520.

1.0.1 Manufacturing release only.

1.0.2 Added support for Macintosh LC 550.

System Enabler 404

1.0 First release.

System Enabler 405

1.0 First release.

System Enabler 406

1.0 First Release

System Software 7.5 Control Panel and Extensions

This section briefly describes all the Control Panels and Extensions that are installed with a full installation of System 7.5. Disabling the some of the Extensions and Control Panels that you do not use will clear up RAM for use with other applications.

Control Panels

System 7.5 Control Panels

File Name	Explanation of the File and Other Files Needed
Apple Menu Options	When it is "on" enables hierarchical menus, and can create up to three folders in the Apple menu for Recent Documents, Folders and Servers. System Update 7.5, version 1.0, has version 1.0.2 of this control panel.

Auto Power On/Off	Version 1.0 enables some Macintosh models, such as the AV and Power Macs, to set on and off times for your Macintosh.
AutoRemounter	A PowerBook control panel for handling AppleShare servers when the PowerBook goes to sleep. Version 1.2.
Brightness	Only works with specific Macs. If you cannot open this control panel, you do not need to have this in your System Folder. Version 7.0.1.
Color	Version 7.1. This control panel enables you to set the highlight color of selected text items, and Window border colors.
Control Strip	Version 1.1 is for easy access to System software features on PowerBooks. A newer version is available for PCI Power Macintosh computers.
Date & Time	Version 7.5. Set your date, time, and clock options.
Extensions Manger	Version 3.0. Works with the EM extension file to enable you to select which extensions in your System Folder are loaded on your Macintosh at startup.
File Sharing Monitor	Version 7.1. Works with the Users and Groups Control Panel along with AppleShare, Network, and FileSharing extensions to provide Personal FileSharing features.
General Controls	Version 7.5 has been modified for System 7.5, and includes many features formerly found in the Performa Control Panel.
Keyboard	Version 7.1. Select different keyboard layouts, set your keyboard repeat and delay repeat rates.
Labels	Version 7.1 Rename and reselect colors that appear in the Labels Menu in Finder.
Launcher	Version 2.4 originated from Performas and works with a folder with aliases to simplify launching applications from Finder.
Macintosh Easy Open	Version 1.1. Works with PC Exchange and offers document to application translation options for a number of file formats.
Map	Version 7.5 is similar to previous versions of this control panel. This panel shows a map of the world and the latitude and longitude of major cities in the world. This works in conjunction with the Date & Time control panel settings.
Memory	Version 7.5 holds feature settings for cache sizes, virtual memory, and RAM Disks. Earlier Macintosh models have 24 or 32-bit mode selection options. Power Macs can select between Modern Memory Manager and traditional Memory Manager.

Monitors	Version 7.5 lets you set the bit depth of the monitor; if you have a multisync display, you can change the screen size of the desktop. This and the sound control panel are replaced by the EZAV control panel on PCI Power Macs.
Mouse	Version 7.3 enables you to set mouse movement and click preferences.
Network	Version 3.0.2 lets you select between available network protocols such as LocalTalk, Ethernet and Token Ring. If your Macintosh is not on a network, and you do not have one or more printers, you do not need this control panel.
Numbers	Version 7.1 lets you select number formats.
PC Exchange	Version 2.0.2 enables System software to mount PC/DOS/Windows formatted floppies onto your desktop and move files to your Macintosh. Works in conjunction with Macintosh Easy Open to translate and open documents from other platforms with Macintosh-compatible applications.
Power Macintosh Card	Version 1.0. If you have a Power Macintosh card, you must use this control panel to turn the card "on." The Macintosh must be completely shut down before turning the card on or off.
PowerBook	Version 7.3.1. PowerBook-only software for setting PowerBook feature settings.
PowerBook Setup	Version 7.3.1. Another PowerBook-only control panel.
PowerBook Display	Version 7.5. For setting display options on PowerBooks.
Screen	Version 1.0.4. Enables you to select screen brightness on all-in-one Macintosh models. If this control panel does not open on your Macintosh, you can move it out of your System Folder.
Serial Switch	Version 1.2. Originally created for the IIfx and also functional on some newer models, this control panel enables setting serial port settings. If it does not open on your Macintosh model, move it out of your System Folder.
Sharing Setup	Version 7.1. This is where you give your Macintosh its network name and password. You can turn Personal FileSharing on and off as well as Program Linking. It works in conjunction with the File Sharing Monitor and Users & Groups Control Panels plus AppleShare, Network and File Sharing extensions. System 7.5, Update 1.0 has a newer version of personal File Sharing software.

Sound	Version 8.0.3 is also available in Sound Manager 3.0 software. This control panel is where you select your system beep sound, volume settings, record sounds, and if you have an internal CD-ROM player, playthrough settings. The latest version of Sound Manager is version 3.1 and consists of a Sound extension and control panel.
Startup Disk	Version 7.3.2 lets you select which hard drive you want to start your Macintosh with. Hard drives must be mounted on your desktop to be selectable.
Text	Version 7.1 lets you select text behavior settings and language for your System software. If you have additional languages installed in your System software, you may also want to change settings in your Date & Time, Keyboard, and Numbers Control Panels. WorldScript extensions are also required to run additional languages with System software.
Users & Groups	System 7.1. Works with Personal File Sharing. Lets you create users and groups who can access your Macintosh. To grant access to a file, folder, or hard drive volume on your Macintosh, you must turn FileSharing on in the Sharing Setup control panel; select the file, folder, or hard drive; and select users and access options in the Sharing menu item in the File menu.
Views	Version 7.1 lets you change the font size for all files and folders and the information that appears in the finder windows. You can also set icon sizes in View by Name list modes in Finder windows, and turn icon views on and off.
WindowShade	Version 1.3 is new software to System 7.5, but has been Macintosh shareware previously. It lets you hide a window's contents by double or triple-clicking on the top of a window. If you do not use this feature, you can move this control panel out of your System Folder.

Extensions

The following table is a quick summary of the evolution of Macintosh System software releases and System and finder versions.

System 7.5 Extensions

File Name	Explanation of the File and Other Files Needed
EM Extension	The Extension Manager extension version 3.0 lets you control which Extensions load when your computer starts up. Works with the Extension Manager control panel.

A/ROSE	Enables communication between the Macintosh main logic board and Macintosh Coprocessor Platform (MCP) based NuBus cards that run the Apple Real-Time Operating System, such as Apple Token Ring 4/16 NB or the Apple Serial NB card.
Apple CD-ROM	The driver software for any installed Apple CD-ROM drive.
Apple Photo Access	Part of the CD-ROM software that lets you view Kodak PhotoCDs.
Audio CD Access	Part of the CD-ROM software that lets you play audio CDs through the internal or external CD-ROM drive. It requires the AppleCD Audio Player or equivalent to control the CD.
Foreign File Access	Part of the CD-ROM software that lets you mount non-Macintosh file system CDs such as ISO 9660 or High Sierra formats.
High Sierra File Access	Part of the CD-ROM software that lets you view non-Macintosh file system CDs created in the High Sierra format.
ISO 9660 File Access	Part of the CD-ROM software that lets you view non-Macintosh file system CDs created in the ISO 9660 format.
Apple Guide	Apple Guide is Apple's integrated help system.
About Apple Guide	The guide file that provides information about AppleGuide. When in the Finder, you can read the contents of this file by selecting About Apple Guide under the question mark icon in the upper right corner of the screen.
	Another system update build is expected to be released this year with additional bug fixes and performance enhancements for all Macintosh models.
Macintosh Guide	Apple Guide database describing Macintosh.
PowerBook Guide	Apple Guide database describing PowerBook related topics.
Additions	Apple Guide database describing Finder Shortcuts.
Shortcuts	Speech Guide
Speech Guide Additions	Mix-In for Apple Guide describing speech.
AppleScript	AppleScript enables you to automate repetitive tasks within scriptable applications.
Finder Scripting Extension	Provides support for scripting of the Finder through AppleScript.
AppleScriptLib	AppleScriptLib implements the AppleScript Open Scripting Architecture (OSA) component.

D

Scripting Additions	Extend the AppleScript language with special features, such as finding the date or time of day. With scripting additions installed, AppleScript acts as if these features are part of the language. Scripting additions are required only when a script uses them (many scripts use them). If you have Apple Event Manager 1.0.3, you can move it out of your System Folder because this code is built into the Scripting Additions extension file. Apple Event Manger 1.0.3 was a bug fix release for AppleScript 1.1.
Video Guide Additions	Mix-in for Apple Guide describing video.
AppleShare	Lets you access shared network volumes through the Chooser.
EtherTalk Phase 2	Enables a Macintosh to connect to an Ethernet network.
File Sharing Extension	Lets you share part or all of your Mac's hard drive with others on a network.
Network Extension	Version 7.1.3. Used by AppleShare and Personal File Sharing to select network options.
TokenTalk Phase 2	Driver for Token Ring Card.
TokenTalk Prep	Support for TokenTalk Phase II.
MacTCP Token Ring Extension	For customers who have standardized on TCP/IP over Token Ring.
AppleTalk ImageWriter	The printer driver for a networked ImageWriter printer.
Assistant Toolbox	Base extension for Auto Remounter (for PowerBook computers) enables file synchronization, battery management, and easy mobile computing. Provides support for "Persistent RAM disk" and deferred printing. Has a conflict with the Select 310 printer driver, and can block printing. The workaround is to turn off background printing.
Caps Lock	Provides caps lock function for PowerBooks (the keyboards do not have Caps lock key). When the caps lock function is active, an "up" arrow is displayed in the menu bar next to the Balloon Help icon.
Clipping Extension	Lets Drag & Drop create clipping files on the desktop.
Color Picker	Presents a standard interface for color selection. With this dialog, any application can ask the user to choose a color.

Color Sync	Version 1.0.5 helps synchronize colors across monitors and printers.
Find File Extension	The Find File extension enables the enhanced Find File desk accessory in System 7.5. Extension is version 1.0.
Finder Help	Provides the support for Balloon Help for the Finder. Version 7.1.4.
IIci/IIsi Monitors	Hardware specific information for the Monitor Control Panel that describes the capabilities of the built in video card for the IIci and IIsi. Version 7.5. Removing this file has no effect on the capability of the Macintosh to use the built-in video card or to select the bit depth. Options in the "option" section of the Monitor Control Panel may not be available, however (gamma settings, for example).
ImageWriter	Version 7.0.1 is the ImageWriter print driver.
LaserWriter	LaserWriter print driver version 7.2. A newer version of this driver is LaserWriter 8.
LaserWriter 300	Version 1.2 is included with System 7.5.
LaserWriter 8	LaserWriter print driver version 8.x. If you are using the LaserWriter 8.1.1 driver, you do not need the LaserWriter 7.2 driver in the System Folder. Newer versions of the LaserWriter 8 driver are available in System Updates.
LC Monitors Extension	Version 7.5 for LC Macintosh computers. Removing this file has no effect on the capability of the Macintosh to use the built-in video card or to select the bit depth. Options in the "option" section of the Monitor Control Panel may not be available, however (gamma settings, for example).
MacinTalk Pro	Lets a Macintosh computer read text documents in human-like voices.
My Speech Macros	Support for Speech Macro Editor.
Speech Recognition	Provides support for speech recognition.
SR Monitor	Extension used to monitor and interpret speech.
System Speech Rules	Supports the voices/dialect of speech.
Mailbox Extension	Provides Mailbox support under PowerTalk.
Object Support Library	A library developers use to implement the OSA object model—for example, how to refer to a word in a paragraph.
Personal LaserWriter SC	The Personal LaserWriter SC print driver.

D

PowerBook Monitors Extension	Hardware-specific information for the Monitor Control Panel that describes the capabilities of the Video system for the PowerBooks. Removing this file has no effect on the capability of the Macintosh to use the built-in video card or to select the bit depth. Options in the "option" section of the Monitor Control Panel may not be available, however (gamma settings, for example).
PowerPC Finder Update	Extends the width of the "About This Macintosh" dialog box (under the Apple Menu). This extension prevents the Macintosh Name from being clipped. The names of the Power Macintosh computers are longer than the standard Macintosh names, and part of the name was not displayed in the standard About This Macintosh dialog box.
PowerPC Monitors Extension	Support for AudioVision 14" Monitor.
PowerTalk Extension	Provides support for the PowerTalk services. Also has information that the keychain uses.
PowerTalk Guide	Apple Guide database describing PowerTalk.
PowerTalk Manager	Provides management of the AOCE Mailbox and services.
Printer Descriptions	Contains descriptions for a many printers used by the LaserWriter 8 driver.
Printer Share	Provides the capability to share non-network printers (such as StyleWriter II, Color StyleWriter 2400, and Pro) across a network.
PrintMonitor	Handles the printing process when you have Background Printing enabled.
Quadra AV Monitors Extension	Hardware specific information for the Monitor control panel that describes the capabilities of the built-in video card for the Quadra and Centris AV systems. Removing this file has no effect on the capability of the Macintosh to use the built-in video card or to select the bit depth, but options found in the "option" section of the Monitor control panel may not be available (gamma settings, for example).

Quadra Monitors Extension	Hardware specific information for the Monitors control panel that describes the capabilities of the built in video card for the Quadra & Centris Computers.
	Removing this file has no effect on the capability of the Macintosh to use the built-in video card or to select the bit depth, but options found in the "option" section of the Monitor control panel may not be available (gamma settings, for example).
QuickTime	Lets you play QuickTime movies within any application that supports QuickTime.
QuickTime PowerPlug	Provides native support of QuickTime for Power Macintosh computers when used in combination with QuickTime 2.0. It, by itself, is not a fully functional version of QuickTime, but an extension that must be used in addition to QuickTime 2.0.
QuickTime Musical Instruments	Supports 30 Roland Standard MIDI sound samples that can be accessed by QuickTime applications with no additional MIDI equipment.
SCSI Manager 4.3	An update to the driver software used by the Macintosh to access hard drives. It is coded into the ROM in the Power Macintosh computers.
StyleWriter II	The print driver for the StyleWriter II. Newer versions of StyleWriter drivers also support the StyleWriter I & II printers. Try printing with the newer driver before moving the older driver out of the System Folder.
WorldScript Power Adapter	Support for Language Kits on Power Macintosh computers. Works with the Date & Time, Keyboard, Numbers, and Text control panels.
Video Startup	Extension used by Apple Video Player.

System Update 1.0 for System 7.5

File Name	Explanation of the File and Other Files Needed
Finder Update	Updates resources in the Finder code.
ThreadsLib	ThreadManager resource.
System Update	Adds System software updates to System file.

System Extensions for System 7.5.2

File Name	Explanation of the File and Other Files Needed
9500 Guide Additions	Mix-in for Apple Guide describing the Power Macintosh 9500.
Apple Color SW Pro CMM	ColorSync 2.0 color-matching method file for maintaining consistent color information between documents.
AV Setup	Extension used by Sound & Displays control panel included in the second release of System 7.5.2.
Color SW 2000 Series CMM	ColorSync 2.0 color-matching method file for maintaining consistent color information between documents.
Color SW 2400	The print driver for the Color StyleWriter 2400.
Color SW Pro	The print driver for the Color StyleWriter Pro.
ColorSync	Resources for color matching between different hardware and applications.
Ethernet (Built-In)	Open Transport code resource to allow access to built-in Ethernet port.
Graphics Accelerator	Provides video acceleration for the PCI video card.
MacinTalk 3	Speech generation extension included in the second release of System 7.5.2.
Open Tpt AppleTalk Library	Open Transport code resource for AppleTalk communication protocol.
Open Tpt Internet Library	Open Transport code resource for TCP/IP communication protocol.
Open Transport Library	Open Transport code resource.
OpenTptAppleTalkLib	Open Transport code resource for AppleTalk communication protocol.
OpenTptInternetLib	Open Transport code resource for TCP/IP communication protocol.
OpenTransportLib	Open Transport code resource.
Serial (Built-In)	Open Transport code resource to allow access to built-in serial port.
SystemAV	Audio-video input extension included in the second release of System 7.5.2.
Tutorial Items	Files used when running the Macintosh Tutorial under the Apple Guide menu.

Virus Index

This appendix lists known Macintosh Viruses. Thanks to John Norstad's excellent Disinfectant Program for some of the Virus information used here.

HC

This virus infects only HyperCard stacks and can spread only through HyperCard stacks. When an infected stack is run, the Macintosh may hum strangely and HyperCard painting tool symbols appear on random parts of the screen.

The Scores Virus

The Scores virus was written by a disgruntled programmer. It attacks only two applications that were under development at his former company. Neither of the two applications were ever released to the general public. Scores was first discovered in the spring of 1988. Scores is also sometimes referred to as the "Eric," "Vult," "NASA," and "San Jose Flu" virus.

There is an easy way to see if you have a Scores infection. Open the System Folder and check the icons (View by Icon under the Views menu) for the Note Pad and Scrapbook files. They should have distinctive icons under System 7 or look like little Macintoshes under System 6. If instead the icons look like blank sheets of paper with turned-down corners, there is a good chance your software may have been infected by Scores.

It is possible to be only partially infected by the Scores virus and still have normal Note Pad and Scrapbook icons. Nevertheless, run Disinfectant to make sure your Macintosh is not infected.

Scores infects the System, Note Pad, and Scrapbook system files. It also creates two invisible files in the System Folder named "Scores" and "Desktop." You cannot see invisible files without the aid of ResEdit (available from most online services). Do not confuse Scores' invisible Desktop file with the Finder's invisible Desktop file; they have nothing to do with each other.

The Finder's Desktop file lives at the root level on the disk, outside the System Folder; Scores' Desktop file lives inside the System Folder. Also, Scores' Desktop file has an extra space character at the end of its name.

Scores cannot and does not infect or modify document files—only applications and system files. Scores gets its name from the invisible "Scores" document it creates. Two days after the System becomes infected, Scores begins to spread to each application you run. The infection occurs between two and three minutes after you begin the application. The Finder and DA Handler usually also become infected. For technical reasons, some applications are immune to infection.

Scores does not intentionally try to do any damage other than to spread itself and attack two specific applications (never released to the public). It does occupy memory and disk space, however, and this can cause problems all by itself. People have reported errors in printing and using MacDraw and Excel. There are also several errors in Scores that could cause System crashes or other erroneous behavior.

A serious conflict occurs between Scores and Apple's System Software release 6.0.4 and later System 6 releases. In System 6.0.4, Apple began using some resources with the same type ID as those used by Scores. When Scores infects the system file, it replaces Apple's versions of these resources with the Scores viral versions of the resources. Once the virus has been deleted you should immediately replace the System with an original "clean" copy of the System file.

The nVIR Virus

The nVIR virus first appeared in Europe in 1987 and in the United States in early 1988. At least one variation of the virus was written. Two strains are known: "nVIR A" and "nVIR B." This virus is also known as Hpat, nFLU, AIDS, MEV#, nCAM, and prod. The nVIR virus got its name because one of the viral resources added to infected files is resource type "nVIR."

There are reports of an earlier version of nVIR that was malicious. It destroyed files in the System Folder. This earlier version appears to be extinct; anti-virus programmers have been unable to obtain a copy.

nVIR is simpler than Scores. It infects the System file, but it does not infect the Note Pad or Scrapbook files and does not create any invisible files. nVIR begins spreading to other applications immediately, without the two-day delay of the Scores virus. Whenever a new application is run, it becomes infected immediately. As with Scores, some applications are immune to infection; the Finder and DA Handler usually become infected, and document files are not infected or modified.

At first nVIR A and B only replicate. When the System file is first infected, a counter is initialized to 1000. The counter is decremented by one each time the System is started up and it is decremented by two each time an infected application is run.

When the counter reaches zero, nVIR A will sometimes either say "Don't panic" (if MacinTalk is installed in the System Folder) or beep. This will happen on System startup with a probability of 1:16. It will also happen, with a probability of 15:128, when an infected application is run. In addition, when an infected application is run, nVIR A may say "Don't panic" or beep twice with a probability of 1:256.

When the counter reaches zero, nVIR B will sometimes beep. On System startup, the probability of this beep is 1:8. A single beep occurs (probability of 7:32) or double-beep occurs (probability of 1:64) when an infected application is run.

It is possible for nVIR A and nVIR B to mate and reproduce, resulting in new viruses combining parts of their parents. Unlike Scores, there is no way to tell that you have an nVIR virus unless you run an anti-virus program.

The INIT 29 Virus

The INIT 29 virus appeared in late 1988; not much is known about its origin. INIT 29 is extremely virulent, and it spreads very rapidly. Unlike Scores and nVIR, you do not have to run an application for it to become infected. INIT 29 also will infect almost any file, including applications, System files, and document files. Document files are only infected; they are not contagious. The virus spreads only through System files and application files. One of the viral resources added to infected files by INIT 29 has the resource type "INIT" and the resource ID 29, after which the virus was named.

INIT 29 has one side effect that reveals its presence. If you try to insert a locked floppy disk on a system infected by INIT 29, you get the following alert:

The disk "xxxxxx" needs minor repairs.

Do you want to repair it?

If you see this alert whenever you insert a locked floppy, it is a good indication that the system is infected by INIT 29.

As with Scores and nVIR, INIT 29 does not intentionally try to do any damage other than spread itself. Nevertheless, it can cause problems. In particular, some people have reported problems printing on systems infected with INIT 29. Users have also experienced many system crashes, problems with MultiFinder under System 6, and incompatibilities with several startup documents.

The ANTI Virus

Two known strains of the ANTI virus were first discovered in France. The ANTI A strain was discovered in February 1989, followed by the ANTI B strain discovered in September 1990. The string "ANTI" appears within the virus, giving it its name.

ANTI does not infect the System file. It only infects applications and other files that resemble applications, such as Finder. ANTI does not infect document files. It is less contagious than the INIT 29 virus, but more contagious than the Scores and nVIR viruses. It is possible for an application to become infected even if it is never run.

Due to a technical quirk, ANTI does not spread at all under System 7 or under System 6 when MultiFinder is in use. It only spreads when Finder is used under System 6. Nevertheless, an error in ANTI slightly damages applications. Usually Disinfectant or other anti-virus programs can repair them, but not perfectly. If you experience problems with the application it should be replaced with a clean copy.

The error in ANTI clears all the resource attributes of the CODE 1 resource. Disinfectant has no way of knowing the values of the original attributes, so it leaves them cleared on the repaired application. The only effect of this error is that repaired applications may use memory less efficiently than the original version, especially on old Macintoshes with the 64K ROMs.

As with other viruses, ANTI does not intentionally attempt to do any damage other than spread itself. As with all viruses, however, it can still cause problems.

Even though the B strain of ANTI was not discovered until about 19 months after the A strain, it appears that the B strain was actually written before the A strain. The A strain of the virus contains a special code that neutralizes any copies of the B strain it encounters. It is possible for an application to be infected by both the neutralized version of the B strain and by the A strain. Other than this special code in the A strain, only minor technical differences exist between the two versions of the virus.

The MacMag Virus

The MacMag virus appeared in December 1987. This virus is also known as "Drew," "Brandow," "Aldus," and "Peace." It was named after the Montreal offices of *MacMag* magazine from where it originated.

Unlike the other viruses, MacMag only infects System files. It originated as a HyperCard stack named "New Apple Products." The stack contained several poorly digitized pictures of the then new Apple scanner. When the stack was run, the virus spread to the currently active System file. When other floppy disks containing System files were subsequently inserted in a floppy disk drive, the virus spread to the system files on the floppies.

Because applications are not infected by MacMag, it spreads much more slowly than the other viruses (people share System files much less frequently than they share applications). Even though the virus originated on a HyperCard stack, it does not spread to other stacks—only to System files.

MacMag was programmed to wait until March 2, 1988, the anniversary of the introduction of the Mac II. The first time the system was started on March 2, 1988, the virus displayed a message of peace onscreen and then deleted itself from the System file.

Because MacMag was programmed to self-destruct, it is unlikely that your software is infected with this virus. There are two slightly different versions of MacMag, with minor differences; both versions were programmed to behave identically.

The WDEF Virus

The WDEF virus was first discovered in December 1989 in Belgium and at Northwestern University. Since the initial discovery, it has also been reported at many other locations and seems to be widespread. Two strains of the virus are known: "WDEF A" and "WDEF B."

WDEF infects only the invisible "Desktop" files used by Finder. With a few exceptions, every Macintosh disk contains one of these files. WDEF does not infect applications, document files, or other System files. Unlike the other viruses, it is not spread through the sharing of applications, but rather through the sharing and distribution of disks (usually floppy disks). WDEF spreads from disk to disk very rapidly. It is not necessary to run an application for the virus to spread. Fortunately System 7 is completely immune to the WDEF virus.

The WDEF A and WDEF B strains are very similar. The only significant difference is that WDEF B beeps every time it infects a new Desktop file; WDEF A does not beep.

Although the virus does not intentionally try to do any damage, WDEF contains errors that can cause serious problems. In particular, the virus causes newer Mac models to crash almost immediately after insertion of an infected floppy (IIci and later computers). The virus also causes other Macs to crash more frequently than usual and it can damage disks. The virus also causes problems with the proper display of font styles. In particular, it often causes problems with the "outline" font style. Many other symptoms have also been reported and it appears that the errors in the virus can cause almost any kind of problem with the proper functioning of your Macintosh.

You can remove a WDEF infection from a disk by rebuilding the desktop. This is also the only way to get rid of a WDEF infection under System 7.

Even though AppleShare servers do not use the normal Finder Desktop file, many servers have an unused copy of this file. If the AppleShare administrator has granted the "make changes" privilege to the root directory on the server, any infected user of the server can infect the Desktop file on the server. If a server Desktop file becomes infected, performance on the network will be severely degraded. For this reason, administrators should never grant the "make changes" privilege on server root directories. In addition, the Desktop file should be deleted if it exists. It does not appear that the virus can spread from an AppleShare server to other Macs on the network.

The WDEF virus can spread from a TOPS server, however, to a TOPS client if a published volume's Desktop file is infected and the client mounts the infected volume. It does not appear that the virus can spread from a TOPS client to a TOPS server.

If you use ResEdit to search for WDEF resources, do not be alarmed if you find them in files other than the Finder Desktop files. WDEF resources are a normal part of the Macintosh operating system. Any WDEF resource in a Finder Desktop file, however, is cause for concern.

The ZUC Virus

Three known strains of the ZUC virus have been discovered (all in Italy). The virus is named after the reported discoverer of the first strain, Don Ernesto Zucchini. ZUC A was discovered in March 1990, ZUC B in November 1990, and ZUC C in June 1991. ZUC only infects applications. It does not infect System files or document files. Applications do not have to be run to become infected.

ZUC A and B were timed to activate on March 2, 1990, or two weeks after an application becomes infected, whichever is later. Before that date, they only spread from application to application. After that date, approximately 90 seconds after an infected application is run, the cursor begins to behave unusually whenever the mouse button is held down. The cursor moves diagonally across the screen, changing direction and bouncing like a billiard ball whenever it reaches any of the four sides of the screen. The cursor stops moving when the mouse button is released. Except for this unusual cursor behavior, ZUC does not attempt to do any damage.

ZUC C is similar to ZUC A and B. The only significant differences are that ZUC C was timed to cause the unusual cursor behavior only during the period between 13 and 26 days after an application becomes infected but not earlier than August 13, 1990. ZUC C causes the cursor to behave unusually approximately 67 seconds rather than 90 seconds after an infected application is run.

The behavior of the ZUC virus is similar to that of a desk accessory named "Bouncy." The virus and the desk accessory are different and should not be confused. The desk accessory does not spread and it is not a virus.

ZUC has two noticeable side effects. On some Macs, the A and B strains can cause the desktop pattern to change. All three strains can also sometimes cause long delays and an unusually large amount of disk activity when infected applications are opened. The virus also adds 1256 bytes of code to the end of the first executed CODE resource.

ZUC can spread over a network from individual Macs to servers and from servers to individual Macs. ZUC does not change the last modification date when it infects a file, so it is almost impossible to trace its source.

The MDEF Virus

Four known strains of the MDEF virus have been discovered in Ithaca, New York. The MDEF A strain was discovered in May 1990 and is also sometimes called the "Garfield" virus; MDEF B was discovered in August 1990 and is sometimes called the "Top Cat" virus. The C and D strains were discovered in October 1990 and January 1991, respectively. The MDEF, WDEF, and CDEF viruses have similar names, but they are completely different and should not be confused with each other.

Prompt action by computer security personnel and investigators of the New York State Police resulted in the identification of the author. The author, a juvenile, was released into the custody of his parents after consultation with the district attorney. The same person was responsible for writing the CDEF virus.

The A, B, and C strains of MDEF infect applications and the System file. They can also infect document files, other System files, Finder Desktop files, the finder, and DA Handler. The System file is infected as soon as an infected application is run. Other applications become infected as soon as they are run on an infected system.

The D strain of MDEF infects only applications, not System files or document files. Applications can become infected even if they are never run. An application infected by MDEF D beeps every time it is run. The D strain of MDEF seems to have never been released to the public.

The MDEF viruses do not intentionally attempt to do any damage, yet they can be harmful. They do not display any messages or pictures. The MDEF B and C strains attempt to bypass some of the popular protection INITs. The MDEF C strain contains a serious error that can cause crashes and other problems. The MDEF D virus can damage some applications in such a way that they cannot be repaired. You should delete any infected applications you have and replace them with a clean copy.

The MDEF viruses are named after the type of resource they use to infect files. MDEF resources are a normal part of the Macintosh system; do not be alarmed if you see them with ResEdit.

The Frankie Virus

The Frankie virus is very rare. Frankie affects only some kinds of Macintosh emulators running on Atari computers. Reports have said that it was targeted against pirated versions of the Aladdin emulator. It does not affect the Spectre emulator, nor does it spread or cause any damage to regular Apple Macintosh computers.

After a time delay, Frankie draws a bomb icon and the message "Frankie says: No more piracy!" at the top of the Atari screen, then proceeds to crash the Atari.

Frankie infects only applications, not System files or document files. The Finder also usually becomes infected. Applications do not have to be run to become infected. For technical reasons, the virus only spreads under Finder, not MultiFinder.

The CDEF Virus

The CDEF virus was first discovered in Ithaca, New York, in August 1990. The same person who wrote the MDEF virus also wrote the CDEF virus. (See the description of the MDEF virus for details.) The CDEF virus is quite widespread. A new version of the CDEF virus was discovered in February 1993. There are only minor technical differences between the new version and the original virus.

CDEF is similar to the WDEF virus. It only infects the invisible "Desktop" files used by the Finder. It does not infect applications, document files, or other System files. It spreads from disk to disk very rapidly. Fortunately, System 7 is completely immune to the CDEF virus. Although the behavior of the CDEF virus is similar to that of the WDEF virus, it is not a clone of WDEF. It is a completely different virus.

The virus does not intentionally try to do any damage. As with all viruses, however, the CDEF virus is still dangerous. Problems on CDEF-infected systems have been reported. As with the WDEF, you can remove a CDEF infection from a disk by rebuilding the desktop.

The CDEF virus is named after the type of resource it uses to infect files. CDEF resources are a normal part of the Macintosh operating system; do not be alarmed if you see them with ResEdit or some other tool. Any CDEF resource in a Finder Desktop file is cause for concern.

The MBDF Virus

The MBDF virus was first discovered in Wales in February 1992. Several popular Internet archive sites contained some infected games for a short period of time, so a number of people around the world were affected. The games were named "10 Tile Puzzle" and "Obnoxious Tetris." In addition to these two games, a third game named "Tetricycle" or "Tetris-rotating" was a Trojan Horse that installed the virus. The MBDF virus is named after the type of resource it uses to infect files.

There are two known strains of the MBDF virus: MBDF A and MBDF B. No significant differences exist between the two strains. MBDF resources are a normal part of the Macintosh system, so you should not become alarmed if you see them with ResEdit.

Two undergraduate students at Cornell University were quickly apprehended shortly after the virus was discovered. They pleaded guilty to charges of second-degree computer tampering for writing and spreading the MBDF virus. They were sentenced to community service and restitution of damages. A third student at Cornell also pleaded guilty to a charge for helping to spread the virus and was sentenced to community service.

The MBDF virus infects both applications and the System file. It also usually infects the Finder and several other System files. The System file is infected as soon as an infected application is run. Other applications become infected as soon as they are run on an infected system.

The MBDF virus is non-malicious, but it can cause damage. In particular, the virus takes quite a long time to infect the System file when it first attacks a system. The delay is so long that people often think that their Mac is hung, so they do a restart. Restarting the Mac while the virus is in the process of writing the System file very often results in a damaged System file that cannot be repaired. The only solution is to reinstall a new System file from scratch. There are also reports that the MBDF virus causes problems with the BeHierarchic shareware program and reports of other menu-related problems on infected systems.

Special thanks go out to the people at Claris who included self-check code in their Macintosh software products. Their foresight resulted in an early detection of the virus and has thus helped the entire Mac community. It is strongly encouraged that other vendors consider doing the same with their products.

The INIT 1984 Virus

The INIT 1984 virus was discovered in the Netherlands and in several locations in the U.S. in March 1992. INIT 1984 is a malicious virus that is designed to trigger an infected system if it is restarted on any Friday the 13th in 1991 or later years. The virus damages a large number of folders and files. File and folder names are changed to random 1–8 character strings. File creators and file types are changed to random 4–character strings. This changes the icons associated with the files and destroys the relationships between programs and their documents. Creation and modification dates are changed to Jan. 1, 1904. In addition, the virus can delete a small percentage (less than 2 percent) of files.

The virus caused significant damage to the hard drives of several users on Friday, March 13, 1992. Because only a relatively small number of reports of damage were received, the virus does not seem to be widespread.

The virus only infects INITs (known as startup documents or system extensions). It does not infect the System file, desktop files, control panel files, applications, or document files. Because INIT files are shared less frequently than programs, the INIT 1984 virus does not spread as rapidly as most other viruses. The virus spreads from INIT to INIT at startup time.

The virus affects all types of Macintoshes. It spreads and causes damage under both System 6 and System 7. On very old Macs (the Mac 128K, 512K, and XL), the virus will cause a crash at startup.

The CODE 252 Virus

The CODE 252 virus was discovered in California in April 1992. The virus is designed to trigger if an infected application is run or an infected system is started up between June 6 and December 31 of any year, inclusive. When triggered, the virus displays the following message:

```
You have a virus

Ha Ha Ha Ha Ha Ha Ha

Now erasing all disks…

Ha Ha Ha Ha Ha Ha Ha

P.S. Have a nice day

Ha Ha Ha Ha Ha Ha Ha
```

(Click to continue…)

Despite this message, no files or directories are deleted by the virus. However, a worried user might turn off or restart a Macintosh upon seeing this message, which could corrupt the disk and lead to significant damage.

Between January 1 and June 5 of any year, inclusive, the virus simply spreads from applications to System files and then on to other application files. Due to errors in the virus, it only spreads to new applications under System 6 without MultiFinder; the Finder is also usually infected. Under System 6 with MultiFinder the virus infects the System file and the "MultiFinder" file and spreads to new applications.

Under System 7, the virus infects the System file, but it does not spread to new applications. An error in the virus can cause crashes or damaged files under System 7. Under any System, the virus infects the System file, and it can and will trigger the message shown earlier. The virus contains a number of additional errors that can cause crashes, damage, or other problems on any system.

The T4 Virus

The T4 virus was discovered in several locations around the world in June 1992. The virus was included in versions 2.0 and 2.1 of the game GoMoku. Copies of this game were posted to the Usenet newsgroup comp.binaries.mac and to a number of popular bulletin boards and anonymous FTP archive sites.

The games were distributed under a false name. The name used in the posting and embedded in the game's About box is that of a completely uninvolved person. Please do not use this person's name in reference to the virus. The actual virus author is unknown, and probably used this person's name as a form of harassment.

The virus spreads to other applications and to the Finder. It also attempts to alter the System file. When the virus infects an application, it damages it in such a way that the application cannot be repaired. The change to the System file results in alterations to the startup code under both.

Under System 6 and System 7.0, the change results in INIT files and system extensions not loading. Under System 7.0.1, the change may render the System unbootable or cause crashes in unpredictable circumstances. The System file cannot be repaired and has to be reinstalled with a clean System file.

If the System suddenly stops loading INITs and system extensions for no good reason, it is a good indication that you may have been attacked by the T4 virus.

The virus masquerades as Disinfectant in an attempt to bypass general-purpose suspicious activity monitors like Gatekeeper. If you see an alert from such an anti-viral tool telling you that "Disinfectant" is trying to make some change to a file, and if Disinfectant is not running, it is a good indication that T4 is attacking the system. The virus also sometimes actually re-names files to "Disinfectant."

Once installed and active, the virus does not appear to perform any other overt damage. The virus may display the following message:

```
Application is infected with the T4 virus.
```

Four known strains of the T4 virus exist: T4-A (contained in GoMoku 2.0), T4-B (contained in GoMoku 2.1), T4-C (discovered in February 1993), and a version that appears to have been used for testing, T4-beta. The strains are very similar. The only significant difference is the trigger date. The trigger date for T4-A is August 15, 1992, while the trigger date for T4-B is June 26, 1992. The virus does not do anything before its trigger date. After the trigger date, the virus begins to spread to other files and attempts to alter the system file. The T4-C virus has no trigger date; T4-C begins spreading immediately.

The INIT 17 Virus

The INIT 17 virus was discovered in New Brunswick, Canada, in April 1993. The virus infects both the System file and application files. It does not infect document files. The virus displays the message From the depths of Cyberspace the first time an infected Macintosh is restarted after 6:06:06 A.M. on October 31, 1993. After this message has been displayed once, it is not displayed again.

The virus contains many errors that can cause crashes and other problems. In particular, it causes crashes on Macintoshes with the 68000 processor such as the Mac Plus, SE, and Classic. For technical reasons, the virus does not infect some applications; on some systems, it does not spread at all. It does, however, spread under both System 6 and System 7.

The INIT-M Virus

The INIT-M virus was discovered at Dartmouth College in April 1993. INIT-M is a malicious virus that is designed to trigger on any Friday the 13th. The virus severely damages a

E

large number of folders and files. File names are changed to random 8-character strings. Folder names are changed to random 1–8 character strings. This changes the icons associated with the files and destroys the relationship between programs and their documents. File creation and modification dates are changed to January 1, 1904.

The virus infects all kinds of files, including extensions, applications, preference files, and document files. The virus creates a file named "FSV Prefs" in the Preferences folder. In some cases, one file or folder on a disk may be renamed to "Virus MindCime." In some very rare circumstances, the virus may also delete a file or files. The virus can also sometimes cause problems with the proper display of windows. The virus only spreads and attacks under System 7.0 or later. It does not spread or attack Systems earlier than System 6.

The damage caused by the INIT-M virus is very similar to that caused by the INIT 1984 virus. Despite the similarity, the two viruses are very different in other respects and should not be confused.

The CODE 1 Virus

The CODE 1 virus was discovered at several colleges and universities on the East Coast of the United States in November 1993. The virus infects both applications and the System file. It does not infect document files. It spreads under both System 6 and System 7.

The virus renames the System hard drive to "Trent Saburo" whenever an infected Mac is restarted on any October 31. Although the virus does not contain any other intentionally destructive code, it can cause crashes and other problems.

The INIT 9403 Virus

The INIT 9403 virus was discovered in Italy in March 1994. Unlike most of the other Mac viruses, INIT 9403 is very destructive. After a certain number of other files have been infected, the virus will erase disks connected to the system; it attempts to destroy disk information on all connected hard drives (greater than 16 MB) and attempts to completely erase the boot volume.

The virus spreads only under the Italian version of the Mac system. It appears that the virus was initially spread by an altered version of some pirated software. The software, when run, installs the virus on the affected system. Once present, the virus alters the Finder file, and may insert copies of itself in various compaction, compression, and archive programs. These infected files then spread the virus to other Macs. The virus spreads under both System 6 and System 7.

Trojan Horses

The following is a list of all known Trojan Horses. A *Trojan Horse* is a program that seems useful and may be functional but does damage to the System behind the scenes (much like the mythical Trojan Horse).

- **Font Finder.** Before the trigger date, February 10, 1990, this application would display fonts and point sizes located in the System file under System 6. On or after the date this Trojan Horse destroys directories of all currently mounted volumes, thus destroying all your data.

- **MOSAIC.** This will mount all available SCSI hard drives and destroy the directories, rendering them useless, then renaming the disks "Gotcha."

- **STEROID.** Steroid claims to install an extension (INIT under System 6) that increases QuickTime performance on Macs with 9-inch screens. What it did instead was destroy data on all available hard disks.

- **Unamed PostScript Hack.** For those who don't know, PostScript is the "programming language" of most laser printers. It's the raw data your Macintosh sends to the printer to tell it what should be on the paper. Apparently, this "hack" renders your printer useless and requires the replacement of a chip on the printer logic board.

- **Tetricycle or TetrisRotating.** Claims to be a game, but Tetricycle instead installs the MBDF virus (see the MBDF virus earlier in this appendix).

- **ChinaT.** ChinaT claims to be an extension (INIT under System 6) that can produce an oriental voice through Macintalk. It has nothing to do with Macintalk though; instead, it erases all available hard disks.

- **CPro 1.41.** CPro 1.41 claims to be a new version of Compact Pro (1.41). This is not an upgrade. It'll erase the startup volume and any disk inserted in drive one. It contains a 312K ' snd' resource called "Log Jingle." Please note, though, that Compact Pro is a legitimate file compression program that is popular in the Macintosh world. Only an application masquerading as Compact Pro version 1.41 is the Trojan Horse. All other versions are known to be the legitimate Compact Pro compression software.

History of System Software

The following table is a quick summary of the evolution of Macintosh System software releases and System and finder versions.

Year	History
1983	System 0.97, a pre-release of the original System. Familiar components such as the Shutdown command didn't yet exist, and CDEVs, INITs, and extensions weren't even glimmers in programmers' eyes.
1984	System 1.0 and Finder 1.1, released with the 128K.
	System 2.0 Finder 1.1g, released with the 128K and the 512K.
1985	System 2.0 and Finder 4.1, an updated Finder for the 512K.
1986	System 3.0 (179K) Finder 5.0 (55K), released with the Plus and considered unstable by most. The Shutdown command arrives.
	System 3.1 and Finder 5.2, an update for Plus. Still unstable.
	System 3.2 (186K) and Finder 5.3 (55K), the most stable and widely used System and Finder combination.
1986-1987	System 3.3 and Finder 5.4, a slightly updated version of System 3.2 and Finder 5.3.
	System 4.1 (311K) and Finder 5.5 (78K), released with SE and Mac II. It wasn't particularly stable. INITs and CDEVs in the System Folder.
	System 4.2 (312K) and Finder 6.0 (97K), also referred to as System Release 5.0. It ushered in the use of CDEVs and INITs. The last version where Switcher, a proto-MultiFinder, still functions.

1988	System 6.0 (361K) and Finder 6.1 (103K), the first System 6 release and renowned for its instability. It introduced MultiFinder and stable color for the Mac II. 4.1's "extensions" won't work anymore, but 6.0 introduced startup documents, the beginnings of INITs, CDEVs, and extensions. System 6 also has modular control panels instead of a single window. System 6.0.1 bug-fix update, released with the IIx. System 6.0.2 (245K) and Finder 6.1.2 (107K), mostly a bug-fix. System 6.0.3 (246K) and Finder 6.1.3 (107K), released with the SE and the SE/30 and known as the first stable version of System 6.0.x System 6.0.4 (279K) and Finder 6.1.4 (107K), released with the IIci and the Portable.
1989	System 6.0.5 (328K) and Finder 6.1.5 (107K), released with the IIfx.
1990	System 6.0.6 and Classic, the LC, and the IIsi. It was so unstable that Apple almost simultaneously released 6.0.7. System 6.0.7 (490K) and Finder 6.1.7 (107K), a bug-fix for the ill-fated 6.1.6. System 6.0.8 and Finder 6.1.8 were updates to 6.0.7 making System 6.0.x compatible with System 7.
1991	System 7.0 and Finder 7.0, the first major rewrite of Mac System in years. Its size and those afterward depend on how many features are installed. System 7.0.1 and Finder 7.0.1, an upgrade of 7.0. System 7.0.1P and Finder 7.0.1P, a smaller version of System 7 for Performas.
1992	System 7.1 and Finder 7.1, an almost-major upgrade of System 7.0. System 7.1P and Finder 7.1P, a smaller version of System 7.1 for Performas.
1994	System 7.1.2 and Finder 7.1.2, a rewrite of System 7.1 for the Power Macs. 7.1.1 is System 7 Pro. 7.1.2 does not include System 7 Pro; it's only a modification of 7.1 for use with the Power Macs. 7.5 is released in late summer of 1994. It features all System enabler files released after system 7.1. Finder is version 7.1.4. Performa System 7.5 software available on new Performa models.

F

1995   7.5.1, System Update 4.0 for System 7.5, the first system update for System 7.5. Modifications to the system are in a System Update Enabler file. This version fixed many bugs and included upgraded versions of QuickDraw GX and PowerTalk. This is a free update.

Performa 7.5.1 system software available on new Performa models.

7.5.2, System Software for PCI Power Macintosh computers. Available first on the 9500 model shipped in June of 1995. Apple announced it is working on Copland, the next major system software release.

An additional system update build is expected to be released Late 1995/Early 1996 with additional bug-fixes and performance enhancements for all Macintosh models.

Software Updates, Content Summary, and Version Numbers

The following sections detail the System 7.5 structure of Apple Software Updates and areas available on commercial online services and Apple Internet sites.

Software update availability

- AppleLink (path: Software Sampler -> Apple SW Updates)

- eWorld (shortcut: support; path: Computer Center -> Apple Customer Center -> Apple Technical Support)

- ftp.support.apple.com (path: pub -> Apple Software Updates)

- ftp.info.apple.com (formerly ftp.austin.apple.com) (path: Apple.Support.Area -> Apple.Software.Updates)

- info.hed.apple.com (Apple Higher Education gopher server) (path: Apple.Support.Area -> Apple.Software.Updates)

Note

Apple's Support Forum on CompuServe (GO: APLSUP) has a different structure because CompuServe does not support subdirectories (folders) within each library.

Finding Software on Apple's Sites

There are now five top-level folders inside Apple Software updates:

- About Apple Software Updates (Titled "New Files" on eWorld)

- DOS & Windows

- Apple II

- Macintosh

- Newton

The following sections summarize the current folder and file structure of Apple's software updates. Folders are marked with bullets •; files are marked with asterisks (*).

Apple II

- Apple II Supplemental

    * Apple II SCSI Utilities

    * Apple II System Disk 3.2

    * Apple II Video Overlay Card

    * Apple IIGS CD Setup 5.1

- Apple IIGS System 6.0.1

    * Disk 1 of 7 - Install

    * Disk 2 of 7 - System.Disk

    * Disk 3 of 7 - SystemTools1

    * Disk 4 of 7 - SystemTools2

    * Disk 5 of 7 - Fonts

    * Disk 6 of 7 - synthLAB

    * Disk 7 of 7 - Apple II Setup

- HyperCard IIGS

    * HCIIGS (1.1 - Disk 1 of 6)

    * HCIIGS (1.1 - Disk 2 of 6)

    * HCIIGS (1.1 - Disk 3 of 6)

    * HCIIGS (1.1 - Disk 4 of 6)

    * HCIIGS (1.1 - Disk 5 of 6)

    * HCIIGS (1.1 - Disk 6 of 6)

    * HyperMover.Mac

    * HyperMover.IIGS

F

- DOS & Windows
  - * LaserWriter Pro 810 for Windows
  - * LW Printer SW for Windows (three disks)
  - * LaserWriter SW 3.0 for Windows.zip (one large zip file)
  - * LaserWriter SW 3.0 for Windows.sea (three disk images compressed into three .sea files)
  - * LWSEL310.zip (LaserWriter Select 310 for Windows software in zip file format)
  - * LWPRO810.zip (LaserWriter Pro 810 for Windows software in zip file format)
  - * PLWNTR.zip (Personal LaserWriter NTR for Windows software in zip file format)
  - * QuickTime for Windows 2.0 to 2.01 Patch.sea -> DOS & Windows (Macintosh .sea file)
  - * QuickTime for Windows 2.0 to 2.01 Patch.zip -> DOS & Windows (zip file format)

Macintosh

- Display and Peripheral Software
  - * Ofoto Version 2 Update 2.0.2 Now Available
  - * 8*24 GC Software 7.0.1
  - * Apple IIe Card 2.2.1
  - * AppleScan 1.0.2
  - * AudioVision Installer 1.0.2
  - * Basic Color Monitor 1.0
  - * CD-ROM Setup 5.0.1
  - * CD-ROM Setup 5.1.1
  - * Display Card 24AC 1.2
  - * Display Software 1.2
  - * HyperScan 2.0.1
  - * ISO 9660 File Access 5.0.2
  - * Monitor Energy Saver 1.1
  - * PowerCD Setup 1.0.1

* QuickTake for Power Mac 1.0

* Scanner 2.0 (system extension)

* Scanner 3.0 (system extension)

Network and Communications

- Apple Remote Access

- ARA 1.0 Original Scripts

  * Abaton Interfax 24/96

  * Apple Modem 2400

  * DSI 9624LE

  * DSI 9624LE Plus

  * Farallon Remote V.32

  * Global Village Teleport

  * Hayes Smartmodem 2400

  * Hayes Ultra 96

  * MicroCom MacModem V.32

  * Microcom MicroPorte 1042

  * MultiTech MultiModemV32

  * Practical Peripherals 2400SA

  * Practical Peripherals 9600SA (Updated)

  * Prometheus ProModem 2400

  * Prometheus ProModem Plus

  * Prometheus ProModem Ultima

  * Supra SupraModem 2400

  * Telebit T1600

  * US Robotics Courier 2400e

  * US Robotics Courier V.32bis

- ARA 1.0 User Scripts

  * AppleTalk Remote Access: Sample V.32/Slower Script

  * AppleTalk Remote Access: Sample V.32bis Script

  * Digicom Scout+ 1.0

  * Direct Connect 1.0

  * Hayes Accura 144 1.0

  * Hayes Optima 144 2.0

  * Maya V.32

  * Microcom QX/4232bis

  * PSI ComStation V

  * Telebit T3000/WorldBlazer V.32bis 1.0.4

  * Telebit QBlazer 2.0.1

  * UDS V.3227

- ARA 2.0 Original Scripts (currently empty)

- ARA 2.0 User Scripts

  * Motorola V3400

  * Motorola FasTalk II

  * Motorola Codex 3260Fast

  * Motorola Cellect Wireline

  * Motorola Cellect Cellular

- Other ARA Software

  * Apple Remote Access 1.0 Client Enabler

- Security Stack

  * Security Info

  * Security Stack

- AppleShare

  * Apple II Setup Disk 2.2

  * AppleShare Tune-Up 4.0.1

  * AppleShare 3.0.3 Patch - Read Me First

* AppleShare 3.0.3 Patch - English

* AppleShare 3.0.3 Patch - French

* AppleShare 3.0.3 Patch - Japanese

* AppleShare 3.0.3 Patch - Spanish

* AppleShare 3.0.3 Change History

* AppleShare 4.0 Upgrade Kit

* AppleShare 4.0.2 Information

* AppleShare 4.1 Update Kit Info

* DataClub to AppleShare Upgrades

* PC Net Exchange 1.0

- Apple Telecom

  * Apple Telecom 2.1 (2 1.44 MB disk image files)

- Communications Toolbox

  * Basic Connectivity Set 1.1.1 - Read Me First

  * Basic Connectivity Set 1.1.1 (Contains All Files)

  * Text Tool (1.0.1)

  * TTY Tool (1.0.1)

  * ADSP (1.5.1)

  * Apple Modem Tool (1.5.3)

  * AppleTalk ADSP Tool (1.0)

  * Serial Tool (1.0.2)

  * TTYFont (1.0)

  * VT102 Tool (1.0.2)

  * VT102Font (1.0.1)

  * XMODEM Tool (1.1)

Network Software Installer

- Network Software Installer (1.4.4)

- Network Software Installer (ZM-1.4.5)

- Network Software Installer (ZM-1.5.1)

Other N&C Software

- Using Express Modem SW with PowerBook Fax/Data Modem
- AppleSearch 1.0.1 Patch
- AWS 95 Tune-Up (1.0)
- AWS 95 Tune-Up (2.0)
- Express Modem 1.5.5
- GeoPort for 660AV/840AV (1.2.2)
- GeoPort for Power Mac (1.0.2)
- GlobalFax 2.5.2P Update
- Apple Internet Router 3.0.1 Patch
- Invisible AWS 95 Fix (elap)
- MacTCP 2.0.4 Update
- MacTCP 2.0.6 Update
- MacTCP Token Ring Extension 1.0
- MacX25 1.2 Patch
- Open Transport 1.0.1 Patch
- Network Launch Fix (1.0.2)
- SNA*ps 3270 1.1.2 Patch
- TextEditor (1.3a1)
- X11 Server Update for A/UX 3.0

System Software

- 6.0.8 800K

  * System 6.0.8 Information
  * Disk 1 of 4 - System Tools
  * Disk 2 of 4 - Utilities 1
  * Disk 3 of 4 - Utilities 2
  * Disk 4 of 4 - Printing Tools

- 6.0.8 - 1.4MB

  * System 6.0.8 Information

  * System Startup

  * System Additions

- 7.0

  * Disk 1 of 8 - Install

  * Disk 2 of 8 - Install 2

  * Disk 3 of 8 - Install 3

  * Disk 4 of 8 - Fonts

  * Disk 5 of 8 - Printing

  * Disk 6 of 8 - Tidbits

  * Disk 7 of 8 - More Tidbits

  * Disk 8 of 8 - Disk Tools

- 7.0.1

  * Disk 1 of 6 - Install 1

  * Disk 2 of 6 - Install 2

  * Disk 3 of 6 - Tidbits

  * Disk 4 of 6 - Printing

  * Disk 5 of 6 - Fonts

  * Disk 6 of 6 - Disk Tools

- Other System Software

  * 040 VM Update (1.0)

  * 32-Bit System Enabler (1.0.3)

  * 950 Color Addition 1.0

  * Apple Event Manager (1.0.3)

  * Apple Menu Options 1.0.2

  * Apple Multimedia Tuner 2.0.1

  * AV Serial Extension (1.0)

  * Cache Switch 7.0.1

* Chinese Language Kit Updater 1.0 - updates CLK to version 1.1.1

* Color Classic Update (1.0)

* ColorSync 2.0 Rev.

* Drive Firmware Update 1.2

* Duo Battery Patch (1.0)

* EM Sound Update (1.0)

* Finder Scripting Extensions (1.2)

* Information about QuickTime 2.0

* Intelligent Battery Update

* Japanese Language Kit Updater (for System 7.5.1)

* Macintosh Drag and Drop (1.1)

* Macintosh Easy Open 1.1.1

* Mount IDE Drive (1.0)

* PCMCIA Updater 1.0.1

* PC Setup 1.0.2

* PC Setup 1.0.3

* PC Setup 1.0.5

* Portable Control Panel (1.3)

* PowerBook PCMCIA 1.0

* Power Macintosh AV Update (1.0) - Bootable Disk

* Power Macintosh AV Update (1.0) - Extension Only

* QuickTime Musical Instruments

* Screen 1.0.6

* Serial Switch 1.1

* Sound Manager 3.1

* System 7 Tune-Up 1.1.1

* System Update 3.0 (1.4MB Disks)

* System Update 3.0 (800K Disk)

* Telephone Manager (1.1.1)

* Thread Manager (2.0.1)

* TV Setup (1.0.2)

* Video Software Installer 1.0.4

- QuickDraw GX

    * QuickDraw GX 1.1.2 Read Me

    * QuickDraw GX 1.1.2 (1 of 4)

    * QuickDraw GX 1.1.2 (2 of 4)

    * QuickDraw GX 1.1.2 (3 of 4)

    * QuickDraw GX 1.1.2 (4 of 4)

    * QuickDraw GX 1.1.2 Net Install

- PlainTalk (1.2.1)

    * PlainTalk (1.2.1) Disk 1 of 5

    * PlainTalk 2 (1.2.1) Disk 2 of 5

    * PlainTalk 3 (1.2.1) Disk 3 of 5

    * PlainTalk 4 (1.2.1) Disk 4 of 5

    * PlainTalk 5 (1.2.1) Disk 5 of 5

    * PlainTalk User Guide

    * QuicKeys Test Drive

- PlainTalk (1.3)

    * PlainTalk Software Information - Read Me First

    * PlainTalk (1.3) Disk 1 of 5

    * PlainTalk 2 (1.3) Disk 2 of 5

    * PlainTalk 3 (1.3) Disk 3 of 5

    * PlainTalk 4 (1.3) Disk 4 of 5

    * PlainTalk 5 (1.3) Disk 5 of 5

    * PlainTalk User Guide

    * QuicKeys Test Drive

F

- PowerTalk
  - * PowerTalk Information
  - * PowerTalk Gateways
  - * PowerTalk Guided Tour 1.1
  - * PowerTalk Solutions Guide
  - * PowerTalk for Power Macintosh (1.0.2)
  - * PowerTalk for Power Macintosh (1.0.2 For France)
  - * PowerTalk Direct Dialup (1.0.1)
  - * Direct Dialup (1.1.1)
- System Enablers
  - * System Enablers - Read Me First
  - * PowerBook 150 Enabler (1.1)
  - * PowerBook 500 Series Enabler (1.0.2)
  - * PowerBook Duo Enabler (1.0)
  - * PowerBook Duo Enabler (2.0)
  - * PowerPC Enabler (1.0.2)
  - * PowerPC Enabler (1.1.1)
  - * PowerPC Upgrade Card Enabler (1.0.1)
  - * System Enabler 001 (1.0.1)
  - * System Enabler 003 (1.1)
  - * System Enabler 040 (1.1)
  - * System Enabler 065 (1.2)
  - * System Enabler 088 (1.2)
  - * System Enabler 131 (1.0.3)
  - * System Enabler 401 (1.0.5)
  - * System Enabler 403 (1.0.1)
  - * System Enabler 404 (1.0)
  - * System Enabler 405 (1.0)
  - * System Enabler 406 (1.0)

- System 7.5 Update
    - * 7.5 Update 1.0/APD 1.1/Pwr Mac Note
    - * System 7.5 Update 1.0 Read Me
    - * System 7.5 Update 1.0 (1 of 4)
    - * System 7.5 Update 1.0 (2 of 4)
    - * System 7.5 Update 1.0 (3 of 4)
    - * System 7.5 Update 1.0 (4 of 4)
    - * System 7.5 Update 1.0 Net Install
- TrueType Fonts & Software
    - * Courier
    - * Courier (bold)
    - * Font/DA Mover 4.1
    - * Helvetica
    - * Helvetica (bold)
    - * Symbol
    - * Times
    - * Times (bold)
    - * Times (bold, italic)
    - * Times (italic)
    - * TrueType 1.0 (System Extension)
- Printing
- LaserWriter Software
    - * Apple Printer Utility 2.0
    - * LaserWriter Fax Tune-Up 1.0
    - * LaserWriter Software Information (Read Me)
    - * LaserWriter Fax Utility 8.1.2
    - * LaserWriter Pro Font Tune-Up Disk
    - * LaserWriter Pro Energy Star Software
    - * LW Pro 810 Utility Solaris

F

* Personal LaserWriter SC 7.0.1

* Backgrounder 1.3

* Chooser 7.3

* Laser Prep 7.1.2

* Laser Prep 7.2

* LaserWriter 7.1.2

* LaserWriter 7.2

* LaserWriter 300 1.2

* LaserWriter 8.2.2f

* LaserWriter 8.3 (3 disks, includes PPDs)

* LW Select 310 7.0

* LW Select 360 Fax SW 1.0.1

* PANTONE Files for LW 12/600

* Personal LW LS 7.2

* Personal LW LS Prep 1.0

* PrintMonitor 7.0.1

* PrintMonitor 7.1

• Other Printing Software

* Apple Color Printer 1.0

* Apple Color SW Pro CMM 1.0

* AppleTalk ImageWriter 7.0.1

* ASFU Fixer 1.0.1

* Color StyleWriter Pro 1.5.2

* Color StyleWriter 2400 1.6.1

* DT (Desktop) Printer Spooler 1.0.2

* GrayShare Update 1.0

* ImageWriter 7.0.1

* LQ AppleTalk ImageWriter 7.0.1

* LQ ImageWriter 7.0.1

* Portable StyleWriter 1.0.1

* Printer Share 1.1.2

* PrintMonitor 7.1.2

* SpoolLauncher 2.1.1a

* SpoolMaster 2.1.1a

* StyleWriter 7.2.3

* StyleWriter 1200 2.0

* StyleWriter II (1.2)

* The Namer (7.0)

• Utilities

* Adobe Acrobat Reader 2.0.1

* Apple Guide Authoring Kit Offer

* Apple DocViewer (1.1.1)

* Apple HD SC Setup 7.3.2

* AMK (Apple Media Kit) Spinning Cursor Bug-Fix

* APD (Apple Personal Diagnostics) 1.1.3 Update

* AppleShareSetup 1.0.1

* Backlight Control 1.0

* Color Tools 2.3.1 Update (for HyperCard 2.3)

* Compatibility Checker 2.0

* DART 1.5.3

* Disk Copy 4.2

* Disk First Aid 7.2

* Extensions Manager 2.0.1

* Internal HD Format 1.3

* Macintosh Basics 5.0.3

* Macintosh Tutorial 1.2

* MacsBug 6.5d12

* MoviePlayer 1.0

* Mouse Basics 4.5

* Network Access Disk 7.5

* Remote Control & Server Controller 1.0

* Rename Rescue 1.0

* ResEdit 2.1.3

* SIMM Stack 4.6 (Requires HyperCard 2.2)

* SIMM Stack 4.6-App (HyperCard Player Embedded)

* SimpleText 1.3

* UnmountIt 1.0

Unsupported Software

* Assistant Toolbox 1.0.1d1

* ApplePhone 1.0.1

* Apple LAN Utility 1.0b3

* Ignore Dialtone 1.0fc1

* IIe Startup 2.2.2d1

* MacTCP Ping 2.0.2

* MovieShop 1.2.1

* Video Monitor 1.0.1

* VideoSync 1.0

* VideoSync II

Newton

* Modem Enabler 1.0

* MP100 Update 1.3 414313

  (For installation with Newton Connection Kit for Macintosh)

* MP100 Update 1.3 414313.zip

  (For installation with Newton Connection Kit for Windows)

* MP110 Update 1.3 345025

  (For installation with Newton Connection Kit for Macintosh)

- MP110 Update 1.3 345025.zip

  (For installation with Newton Connection Kit for Windows)

- NewtonMail Modules 1.0

- System Update 1.05

- System Update 1.11

- System Update 1.3 (344052)

Macintosh Model Specifications

This section begins by describing in detail the latest Macintosh models, then goes back to the first Mac introduced for that particular CPU's form factor (the design of the Mac case). In this Appendix, information for each Macintosh includes a brief summary of the model, internal system information specific to the motherboard, and a detailed list of that model's hardware components.

Power Mac 9500/132, 9500/120

As Apple's top-of-the-line Macintosh model, the 9500 has the fastest processor available. This processor can be upgraded to an even faster CPU. The 9500 also has the maximum number of expansion slots available for a Mac, the maximum number of built-in ports for a wide range of peripherals, and includes 16-bit stereo audio input and output ports. In addition, the 120MHz model has a graphics accelerator card (2 MB expandable to 4 MB).

PowerMac 9500/132, 9500/120

GENERAL PRODUCT INFORMATION

Introduction date	5/1/95
Discontinuation date	
Processor	604
Clock speed	132 or 120 MHz
MIPS rating	n/a
Display resolution	640×480 to 1024×768 or card dependent
	The 9500/120 comes with a video card, the 9500/132 does not.
Color depth	up to millions with card
Display size	card dependent
Systems supported	7.5.2, Enabler 701 version 1.0

INTERNAL SYSTEMS

RAM (min and max)	16 to 768 MB-168 pin DIMMs
RAM speed	70 ns
RAM slots	12 slots, install 1 SIMM at a time
VRAM (standard)	requires video card
PCI slots	6
PDS slots	none
SCSI transfer rate	5.0 MB/second
Power supply	Int'l
Maximum wattage	520 Watts
Bus width	n/a
FPU	built-in
MMU	built-in
ROM size	4 MB
Memory cache	n/a

EXTERNAL STORAGE SYSTEMS

Hard drive	2GB internal and external
Floppy drive	1.4 MB, 800K, 400K
CD-ROM	4x internal or external 600i
Serial ports	two
ADB ports	one
Sound input	16-bit stereo
Sound output	stereo
Network availability	LocalTalk or EtherTalk

Power Macintosh 8500/120

The 8500/120 shares the same 120 MHz 604 processor as the 9500/120, and includes the following multimedia hardware and software:

- Near-broadcast quality video input and output capability built-in

- High-resolution graphics (up to 1,280 by 1,024 pixels)

- CD-quality stereo sound input and output

One example of the Power Macintosh 8500/120: it can capture quarter-screen video in real time. Combine this capability with Apple's QuickTime software, and you can capture and edit video media easier and faster than ever.

PowerMac 8500

GENERAL PRODUCT INFORMATION

Introduction date	8/95
Discontinuation date	
Processor	604
Clock speed	120 MHz
MIPS rating	n/a
Display resolution	640×480 to 1024×768 or card dependent
Color depth	up to millions on built-in video
Display size	14" through 21" OR card dependent
Systems supported	7.5.2, Enabler 701 version 1.1

INTERNAL SYSTEMS

RAM (min and max)	16 to 768 MB-168 pin DIMM
RAM speed	70 ns
RAM slots	8 slots, install 1 DIMM at a time
VRAM (standard)	2 MB, expandable to 4 MB
PCI slots	3
PDS slots	one—holds CPU upgradable
SCSI transfer rate	5.0 MB/second
Power supply	Int'l
Maximum wattage	n/a
Bus width	n/a
FPU	built-in
MMU	built-in
ROM size	4 MB
Memory cache	n/a

EXTERNAL STORAGE SYSTEMS

Hard drive	500 MB–2GB internal and external
Floppy drive	1.4 MB, 800K, 400K
CD-ROM	4x internal or external
Serial ports	two
ADB ports	one
Sound input	16-bit stereo
Sound output	stereo
Network availability	LocalTalk or EtherTalk

Power Macintosh 7500/100

The 7500/100 is a professional Power Macintosh with new architecture and more flexibility than previous models. built-in video input, high-resolution graphics (up to 1,280 × 1,024 pixels), and CD-quality stereo sound are just a few of this Mac's features. The Power Macintosh 7500/100 also optimizes the transfer of video data between a network and the computer's display monitor, making this an ideal system for videoconferencing—Apple's QuickTime Conferencing software is even included. Connecting your computer to an Ethernet network is easier than ever with the Power Macintosh 7500 because it includes both AAUI and 10BASE-T connectors.

PowerMac 7500/100

GENERAL PRODUCT INFORMATION

Introduction date	8/95
Discontinuation date	
Processor	601
Clock speed	100 MHz
MIPS rating	n/a
Display resolution	640×480 to 1024×768 or card dependent
Color depth	up to millions on built-in video
Display size	14" through 21" OR card dependent
Systems supported	7.5.2, Enabler 701 version 1.1

INTERNAL SYSTEMS

RAM (min and max)	16 to 768 MB–168 pin DIMM
RAM speed	70 ns
RAM slots	8 slots, install 1 DIMM at a time
VRAM (standard)	2 MB
PCI slots	3
PDS slots	one
SCSI transfer rate	5.0 MB/second
Power supply	Int'l
Maximum wattage	n/a
Bus width	n/a
FPU	built-in
MMU	built-in
ROM size	4 MB
Memory cache	n/a

EXTERNAL STORAGE SYSTEMS

Hard drive	500 MB–1GB internal and external
Floppy drive	1.4 MB, 800K, 400K

CD-ROM	4ξ internal or external
Serial ports	two
ADB ports	one
Sound input	16-bit stereo
Sound output	stereo
Network availability	LocalTalk or EtherTalk

Power Macintosh 7200/75 and 7200/90

These two Power Macs are perfect for small and medium-size businesses and home offices. Both models support screen resolutions of up to 1,280 × 1,024 pixels. Both models also come with Apple's GeoPort Fax and GeoPort Telephony software (requires GeoPort Telecom Adapter). Graphics, telephony, and expansion capabilities can be accessed with Mac's renowned plug-and-play simplicity.

Another nifty feature of these two models: they can both be upgraded to a Power Macintosh 7500 system.

PowerMac 7200/75, 7200/90

GENERAL PRODUCT INFORMATION

Introduction date	8/95
Discontinuation date	
Processor	601
Clock speed	75 and 90 MHz
MIPS rating	n/a
Display resolution	640×480 to 1024×768 or card dependent
Color depth	up to millions on built-in video
Display size	14" through 21" OR card dependent
Systems supported	7.5.2, enabler 701 version 1.1

INTERNAL SYSTEMS

RAM (min and max)	16 to 768 MB–168 pin DIMM
RAM speed	70 ns
RAM slots	4 slots, install 2 SIMMs at a time
VRAM (standard)	1 MB
PCI slots	3
PDS slots	none
SCSI transfer rate	5.0 MB/second
Power supply	Int'l
Maximum wattage	n/a

Bus width	n/a
FPU	built-in
MMU	built-in
ROM size	4 MB
Memory cache	n/a

EXTERNAL STORAGE SYSTEMS

Hard drive	500 MB internal and external
Floppy drive	1.4 MB, 800K, 400K
CD-ROM	4x internal or external
Serial ports	two
ADB ports	one
Sound input	16-bit stereo
Sound output	stereo
Network availability	LocalTalk or EtherTalk

LC 6200

GENERAL PRODUCT INFORMATION

Introduction date	5/1/95
Discontinuation date	
Processor	603
Clock speed	75 MHz
MIPS rating	n/a
Display resolution	640×480 to 832×624
Color depth	up to millions on built-in video
Display size	14, 15, or 17" RGB or multisync
Systems supported	7.5.1, enabler 406

INTERNAL SYSTEMS

RAM (min and max)	8 to 64 MB-72 pin
RAM speed	70 ns
RAM slots	4 slots, install 2 SIMMs at a time
VRAM (standard)	none
NuBus slots	none
PDS slots	one LC, comm, TV
SCSI transfer rate	5.0 MB/second
Power supply	Int'l
Maximum wattage	200 Watts
Bus width	37.5 MHz, 64-bit/64-bit
FPU	built-in
MMU	built-in
ROM size	4 MB
Memory cache	none

EXTERNAL STORAGE SYSTEMS

Hard drive	500 MB IDE internal and external
Floppy drive	1.4 MB, 800K, 400K
CD-ROM	4x internal or external
Serial ports	two
ADB ports	one
Sound input	mono
Sound output	stereo
Network availability	LocalTalk or EtherTalk

LC 5200

GENERAL PRODUCT INFORMATION

Introduction date	4/3/95
Discontinuation date	
Processor	603e
Clock speed	75 MHz
MIPS rating	n/a
Display resolution	640×480 to 832×624
Color depth	up to millions on built-in video
Display size	15" Multisync
Systems supported	7.5.1, enabler 406

INTERNAL SYSTEMS

RAM (min and max)	8 to 64 MB–72 pin
RAM speed	70 ns
RAM slots	4 slots, install 2 SIMMs at a time
VRAM (standard)	none
NuBus slots	none
PDS slots	one LC, comm, TV
SCSI transfer rate	5.0 MB/second
Power supply	Int'l
Maximum wattage	200 Watts
Bus width	37.5 MHz, 64-bit/64-bit
FPU	built-in
MMU	built-in
ROM size	4 MB
Memory cache	none

EXTERNAL STORAGE SYSTEMS

Hard drive	500 MB IDE internal and external
Floppy drive	1.4 MB, 800K, 400K
CD-ROM	4x internal or external
Serial ports	two

ADB ports	one
Sound input	mono
Sound output	stereo
Network availability	LocalTalk or EtherTalk

LC5300

GENERAL PRODUCT INFORMATION

Introduction date	
Discontinuation date	
Processor	603e
Clock speed	100 MHz
MIPS rating	n/a
Display resolution	640×480 to 832×624
Color depth	up to millions on built-in video
Display size	15" Multisync
Systems supported	7.5.1, Enabler 406

INTERNAL SYSTEMS

RAM (min and max)	8 to 64 MB-72 pin
RAM speed	70 ns
RAM slots	4 slots, install 2 SIMMs at a time
VRAM (standard)	none
NuBus slots	none
PDS slots	one LC, comm, TV
SCSI transfer rate	5.0 MB/second
Power supply	Int'l
Maximum wattage	200 Watts
Bus width	37.5 MHz, 64-bit/64-bit
FPU	built-in
MMU	built-in
ROM size	4 MB
Memory cache	none

EXTERNAL STORAGE SYSTEMS

Hard drive	500MB IDE internal and external
Floppy drive	1.4MB, 800K, 400K
CD-ROM	4x internal or external
Serial ports	two
ADB ports	one
Sound input	mono
Sound output	stereo
Network availability	LocalTalk or EtherTalk

LC6300

GENERAL PRODUCT INFORMATION

Introduction date	
Discontinuation date	
Processor	603
Clock speed	100 MHz
MIPS rating	n/a
Display resolution	640×480 to 832×624
Color depth	up to millions on built-in video
Display size	14, 15, or 17" RGB or multisync
Systems supported	7.5.1, Enabler 406

INTERNAL SYSTEMS

RAM (min and max)	8 to 64 MB–72 pin
RAM speed	70 ns
RAM slots	4 slots, install 2 SIMMs at a time
VRAM (standard)	none
NuBus slots	none
PDS slots	one LC, comm, TV
SCSI transfer rate	5.0 MB/second
Power supply	Int'l
Maximum wattage	200 Watts
Bus width	37.5 MHz, 64-bit/64-bit
FPU	built-in
MMU	built-in
ROM size	4 MB
Memory cache	none

EXTERNAL STORAGE SYSTEMS

Hard drive	500 MB IDE internal and external
Floppy drive	1.4 MB, 800K, 400K
CD-ROM	4x internal or external
Serial ports	two
ADB ports	one
Sound input	mono
Sound output	stereo
Network availability	LocalTalk or EtherTalk

PowerBook 5300ce, 5300c, 5300cs, 5300

GENERAL PRODUCT INFORMATION

Introduction date	8/28/95
Discontinuation date	
Processor	603
Clock speed	117 and 100MHz; only ce model has 117 MHz processor
MIPS rating	
Display resolution	640×480
Color depth	16 levels of gray to thousands of colors
Display size	9.5 inch dual scan—10.4 inch backlit dual scan or active matrix coloronly ce model has active matrix color display
Systems supported	7.5.2, enabler PowerBook 5300 version 1.1

INTERNAL SYSTEMS

RAM (min and max)	8 MB –64 MB; models vary as to how much memory is soldered on the motherboard
RAM speed	70 ns
RAM slots	1 slot, install 1 SIMM at a time
VRAM (standard)	none
PC card slots	2
PDS slots	none
SCSI transfer rate	5.0 MB/second
Power supply	Int'l
Maximum wattage	40 Watts
Bus width	n/a
FPU	built-in
MMU	built-in
ROM size	4 MB
Memory cache	none

EXTERNAL STORAGE SYSTEMS

Hard drive	500 MB-1.1GB IDE internal
Floppy drive	1.4MB, 800K, 400K
CD-ROM	3.5" CD internal or external
Serial ports	one
ADB ports	one
Sound input	16-bit stereo
Sound output	stereo
Network availability	LocalTalk or EtherTalk

PowerBook 190, 190cs

GENERAL PRODUCT INFORMATION

Introduction date	8/28/95
Discontinuation date	
Processor	68040
Clock speed	33 MHz
MIPS rating	
Display resolution	640×480 pixels
Color depth	16 levels of gray to 256colors
Display size	9.5 inch dual scan—10.4 inch backlit dual scan color
Systems supported	7.5.2, Enabler PowerBook 190

INTERNAL SYSTEMS

RAM (min and max)	4-14 MB, 4 MB, or 8–36 MB, or 40 MB
RAM speed	70 ns
RAM slots	1 slot, install SIMM at a time
VRAM (standard)	none
PC Card slots	2
PDS slots	none
SCSI transfer rate	5.0 MB/second
Power supply	Int'l
Maximum wattage	40 Watts
Bus width	n/a
FPU	built-in
MMU	built-in
ROM size	4 MB
Memory cache	n/a

EXTERNAL STORAGE SYSTEMS

Hard drive	500 MB IDE internal
Floppy drive	1.4 MB, 800K, 400K
CD-ROM	3.5" CD internal or external
Serial ports	one
ADB ports	one
Sound input	none
Sound output	stereo
Network availability	LocalTalk or EtherTalk

PowerBook 2300c/100

GENERAL PRODUCT INFORMATION

Introduction date	8/28/95
Discontinuation date	
Processor	603e
Clock speed	100 MHz
MIPS rating	n/a
Display resolution	640×480 or 640×400
Color depth	256 colors
Display size	9.5-inch backlit active matrix color
Systems supported	7.5.2, Enabler PowerBook Duo 2300 1.0

INTERNAL SYSTEMS

RAM (min and max)	8 or 20 MB to 56 MB
RAM speed	70 ns
RAM slots	1 slot, install 1 SIMM module
VRAM (standard)	none
NuBus slots	none
PDS slots	one (Duo Dock)
SCSI transfer rate	5.0 MB/second
Power supply	Int'l
Maximum wattage	25 Watts
Bus width	n/a
FPU	built-in
MMU	built-in
ROM size	4 MB
Memory cache	none

EXTERNAL STORAGE SYSTEMS

Hard drive	700 MB or 1.1GB IDE internal
Floppy drive	external only
CD-ROM	external only
Serial ports	one
ADB ports	one
Sound input	16-bit stereo
Sound output	stereo
Network availability	LocalTalk

PowerMac 6100/60, Performa 6110, 6112, 6115, 6116, 6117, 6118

GENERAL PRODUCT INFORMATION

Introduction date	3/14/94
Discontinuation date	1/3/95
Processor	601
Clock speed	60 MHz
MIPS rating	
Display resolution	640×480 to 1024×768 or card dependent
Color depth	up to millions on built-in video
Display size	built-in 13" through 21" OR card dependent
Systems supported	7.1.2, enabler PPC v1.0

INTERNAL SYSTEMS

RAM (min and max)	4 to 72 MB–72 pin
RAM speed	80 ns
RAM slots	2 slots, install 2 SIMMs at a time
VRAM (standard)	none
NuBus slots	one 7" or PDS
PDS slots	one 7" or PDS
SCSI transfer rate	5.0 MB/second
Power supply	Int'l
Maximum wattage	202 Watts
Bus width	30 MHz, 64-bit/64-bit
FPU	built-in
MMU	built-in
ROM size	4 MB
Memory cache	256K optional

EXTERNAL STORAGE SYSTEMS

Hard drive	160 to 250 MB internal and external
Floppy drive	1.4 MB, 800K, 400K
CD-ROM	2X internal or external
Serial ports	two
ADB ports	one
Sound input	stereo
Sound output	stereo
Network availability	LocalTalk or EtherTalk

PowerMac 6100/60AV

GENERAL PRODUCT INFORMATION

Introduction date	3/14/94
Discontinuation date	9/12/94
Processor	601
Clock speed	60 MHz
MIPS rating	
Display resolution	640×480 to 1024×768 or card dependent
Color depth	up to millions on built-in video
Display size	built-in 13" through 21" OR card dependent
Systems supported	7.1.2, enabler PPC v1.0

INTERNAL SYSTEMS

RAM (min and max)	4 to 72 MB-72 pin
RAM speed	80 ns
RAM slots	2 slots, install 2 SIMMs at a time
VRAM (standard)	2 MB on card
NuBus slots	none
PDS slots	one—filled
SCSI transfer rate	5.0 MB/second
Power supply	Int'l
Maximum wattage	202 Watts
Bus width	30 MHz, 64-bit/64-bit
FPU	built-in
MMU	built-in
ROM size	4 MB
Memory cache	256K optional

EXTERNAL STORAGE SYSTEMS

Hard drive	160 to 250 MB internal and external
Floppy drive	1.4 MB, 800K, 400K
CD-ROM	2X internal or external
Serial ports	two
ADB ports	one
Sound input	stereo
Sound output	stereo
Network availability	LocalTalk or EtherTalk

PowerMac 7100/66

GENERAL PRODUCT INFORMATION

Introduction date	3/14/94
Discontinuation date	1/3/95
Processor	601
Clock speed	66 MHz
MIPS rating	n/a
Display resolution	640×480 to 1024×768 or card dependent
Color depth	up to millions on built-in video
Display size	built-in 13" through 21" OR card dependent
Systems supported	7.1.2, enabler PowerMac

INTERNAL SYSTEMS

RAM (min and max)	4 to 72 MB-72 pin
RAM speed	80 ns
RAM slots	4 slots, install 2 SIMMs at a time
VRAM (standard)	none
NuBus slots	3
PDS slots	one
SCSI transfer rate	5.0 MB/second
Power supply	Int'l
Maximum wattage	86 Watts
Bus width	33 MHz, 64-bit/64-bit
FPU	built-in
MMU	built-in
ROM size	4 MB
Memory cache	256K optional

EXTERNAL STORAGE SYSTEMS

Hard drive	250 to 500 MB internal and external
Floppy drive	1.4 MB, 800K, 400K
CD-ROM	2X internal or external
Serial ports	two
ADB ports	one
Sound input	stereo
Sound output	stereo
Network availability	LocalTalk or EtherTalk

PowerMac 7100/66AV

GENERAL PRODUCT INFORMATION

Introduction date	3/14/94
Discontinuation date	1/3/95
Processor	601
Clock speed	66 MHz
MIPS rating	n/a
Display resolution	640×480 to 1024×768 or card dependent
Color depth	up to millions on built-in video
Display size	built-in 13" through 21" OR card dependent
Systems supported	7.1.2, enabler PowerMac

INTERNAL SYSTEMS

RAM (min and max)	4 to 72 MB-72 pin
RAM speed	80 ns
RAM slots	4 slots, install 2 SIMMs at a time
VRAM (standard)	2MB on card
NuBus slots	3
PDS slots	one—filled
SCSI transfer rate	5.0 MB/second
Power supply	Int'l
Maximum wattage	230 Watts
Bus width	33 MHz, 64-bit/64-bit
FPU	built-in
MMU	built-in
ROM size	4 MB
Memory cache	256K optional

EXTERNAL STORAGE SYSTEMS

Hard drive	250 to 500 MB internal and external
Floppy drive	1.4 MB, 800K, 400K
CD-ROM	2X internal or external
Serial ports	two
ADB ports	one
Sound input	stereo
Sound output	stereo
Network availability	LocalTalk or EtherTalk

PowerMac 8100/80

GENERAL PRODUCT INFORMATION

Introduction date	3/14/94
Discontinuation date	1/3/95
Processor	601
Clock speed	80 MHz
MIPS rating	n/a
Display resolution	640×480 to 1024×768 or card dependent
Color depth	up to millions on built-in video
Display size	built-in 13" through 21" OR card dependent
Systems supported	7.1.2, enabler PowerMac

INTERNAL SYSTEMS

RAM (min and max)	4 to 264MB-72 pin
RAM speed	80 ns
RAM slots	8 slots, install 2 SIMMs at a time
VRAM (standard)	none
NuBus slots	3
PDS slots	one
SCSI transfer rate	5.0 MB/second
Power supply	Int'l
Maximum wattage	200 Watts
Bus width	40 MHz, 32-bit/64-bit
FPU	built-in
MMU	built-in
ROM size	4 MB
Memory cache	256K optional

EXTERNAL STORAGE SYSTEMS

Hard drive	250 to 1GB internal and external
Floppy drive	1.4 MB, 800K, 400K
CD-ROM	2X internal or external
Serial ports	two
ADB ports	one
Sound input	stereo
Sound output	stereo
Network availability	LocalTalk or EtherTalk

8100/80 AV

GENERAL PRODUCT INFORMATION

Introduction date	3/14/94
Discontinuation date	1/3/95
Processor	601
Clock speed	80 MHz
MIPS rating	n/a
Display resolution	640×480 to 1024×768 or card dependent
Color depth	up to millions on built-in video
Display size	built-in 13" through 21" OR card dependent
Systems supported	7.1.2, enabler PowerMac

INTERNAL SYSTEMS

RAM (min and max)	4 to 264 MB-72 pin
RAM speed	80 ns
RAM slots	8 slots, install 2 SIMMs at a time
VRAM (standard)	2 MB on card
NuBus slots	3
PDS slots	one—filled
SCSI transfer rate	5.0 MB/second
Power supply	Int'l
Maximum wattage	200 Watts
Bus width	40 MHz, 32-bit/64-bit
FPU	built-in
MMU	built-in
ROM size	4 MB
Memory cache	256K optional

EXTERNAL STORAGE SYSTEMS

Hard drive	250 to 1GB internal and external
Floppy drive	1.4 MB, 800K, 400K
CD-ROM	2X internal or external
Serial ports	two
ADB ports	one
Sound input	stereo
Sound output	stereo
Network availability	LocalTalk or EtherTalk

PowerMac 8100/100 and 8100/110, 8115/110

GENERAL PRODUCT INFORMATION

Introduction date	1/3/1995, 2/23/95 (8115/110)
Discontinuation date	
Processor	601
Clock speed	100 or 110 MHz
MIPS rating	n/a
Display resolution	640×480 to 1024×768 or card dependent
Color depth	up to millions on built-in video
Display size	built-in 13" through 21" OR card dependent
Systems supported	7.5, enabler PPC 1.1.1

INTERNAL SYSTEMS

RAM (min and max)	4 to 264MB-72 pin
RAM speed	80 ns
RAM slots	8 slots, install 2 SIMMs at a time
VRAM (standard)	2MB
NuBus slots	3
PDS slots	one—filled
SCSI transfer rate	5.0 MB/second
Power supply	Int'l
Maximum wattage	200 Watts
Bus width	36.7 MHz, 32-bit/64-bit
FPU	built-in
MMU	built-in
ROM size	4 MB
Memory cache	256K optional

EXTERNAL STORAGE SYSTEMS

Hard drive	250 to 1GB internal and external
Floppy drive	1.4 MB, 800K, 400K
CD-ROM	2X internal or external
Serial ports	two
ADB ports	one
Sound input	stereo
Sound output	stereo
Network availability	LocalTalk or EtherTalk

PowerMac7100/80, 711/80AV (2 MB VRAM)

GENERAL PRODUCT INFORMATION

Introduction date	1/3/95
Discontinuation date	
Processor	601
Clock speed	80 MHz
MIPS rating	n/a
Display resolution	640×480 to 1024×768 or card dependent
Color depth	up to millions on built-in video
Display size	built-in 13" through 21" OR card dependent
Systems supported	7.5, enabler PPC 1.1.1

INTERNAL SYSTEMS

RAM (min and max)	4 to 136 MB-72 pin
RAM speed	80 ns
RAM slots	4 slots, install 2 SIMMs at a time
VRAM (standard)	1MB
NuBus slots	3
PDS slots	one—filled
SCSI transfer rate	5.0 MB/second
Power supply	Int'l
Maximum wattage	230 Watts
Bus width	40 MHz, 32-bit/64-bit
FPU	built-in
MMU	built-in
ROM size	4 MB
Memory cache	256K optional

EXTERNAL STORAGE SYSTEMS

Hard drive	350 to 700 MB internal and external
Floppy drive	1.4 MB, 800K, 400K
CD-ROM	2X internal or external
Serial ports	two
ADB ports	one
Sound input	stereo
Sound output	stereo
Network availability	LocalTalk or EtherTalk

PowerMac6100/66, 6100/66AV (2 MB VRAM)

GENERAL PRODUCT INFORMATION

Introduction date	1/3/95
Discontinuation date	
Processor	601
Clock speed	66 MHz
MIPS rating	n/a
Display resolution	640×480 to 1024×768 or card dependent
Color depth	up to millions on built-in video
Display size	built-in 13" through 21" OR card dependent
Systems supported	7.5, enabler PPC 1.1.1

INTERNAL SYSTEMS

RAM (min and max)	4 to 136 MB-72 pin
RAM speed	80 ns
RAM slots	2 slots, install 2 SIMMs at a time
VRAM (standard)	1 MB
NuBus slots	none
PDS slots	one—filled, optional 486DX-66
SCSI transfer rate	5.0 MB/second
Power supply	Int'l
Maximum wattage	230 Watts
Bus width	33 MHz, 32-bit/64-bit
FPU	built-in
MMU	built-in
ROM size	4 MB
Memory cache	none

EXTERNAL STORAGE SYSTEMS

Hard drive	350 to 500 MB internal and external
Floppy drive	1.4 MB, 800K, 400K
CD-ROM	2X internal or external
Serial ports	two
ADB ports	one
Sound input	stereo
Sound output	stereo
Network availability	LocalTalk or EtherTalk

LC630, Quadra 630, Performa 630 series

LC 630, Quadra630, Performa 630, 631, 635, 636, 637, 638

GENERAL PRODUCT INFORMATION

Introduction date	7/1/94
Discontinuation date	8/11/95
Processor	68LC040
Clock speed	33/66 MHz
MIPS rating	29
Display resolution	640×480
Color depth	up to millions
Display size	14" to 17" RGB
Systems supported	7.1.2P, enabler 405

INTERNAL SYSTEMS

RAM (min and max)	4 to 36 MB-72-pin
RAM speed	80 ns
RAM slots	1 slot, install 1 SIMM at a time
VRAM (standard)	512K
NuBus slots	none
PDS slots	one—LC/comm/TV, optional 486DX2, 66MHz
SCSI transfer rate	1.5 MB/second
Power supply	Int'l
Maximum wattage	45
Bus width	33 MHz, 32-bit/32-bit
FPU	none
MMU	built-in
ROM size	1024K
Memory cache	none

EXTERNAL STORAGE SYSTEMS

Hard drive	40 to 80 MB internal and external
Floppy drive	1.4 MB, 800K, 400K
CD-ROM	2X internal or external
Serial ports	two
ADB ports	one
Sound input	mono
Sound output	stereo
Network availability	LocalTalk or EtherTalk

LC 580

GENERAL PRODUCT INFORMATION

Introduction date	4/3/95
Discontinuation date	
Processor	68LC040
Clock speed	33/66 MHz
MIPS rating	29
Display resolution	640×480
Color depth	up to millions on built-in video
Display size	14"
Systems supported	7.5

INTERNAL SYSTEMS

RAM (min and max)	4 to 52 MB-72 pin
RAM speed	80 ns
RAM slots	4 slots, install 1 SIMM at a time
VRAM (standard)	none
NuBus slots	none
PDS slots	one LC PDS, comm, video
SCSI transfer rate	5.0 MB/second
Power supply	Int'l
Maximum wattage	60
Bus width	33 MHz, 32-bit/32-bit
FPU	none
MMU	built-in
ROM size	1024K
Memory cache	none

EXTERNAL STORAGE SYSTEMS

Hard drive	160 to 320 MB internal and external
Floppy drive	1.4 MB, 800K, 400K
CD-ROM	2X internal or external
Serial ports	two
ADB ports	one
Sound input	mono
Sound output	stereo
Network availability	LocalTalk or EtherTalk

LC 575, Performa 575, 577, 578

GENERAL PRODUCT INFORMATION

Introduction date	10/18/93
Discontinuation date	4/3/95
Processor	68LC040
Clock speed	33/66 MHz
MIPS rating	29
Display resolution	640×480
Color depth	up to millions on built-in video
Display size	14"
Systems supported	7.1, 065 or 7.1P3, enabler 364

INTERNAL SYSTEMS

RAM (min and max)	4 to 36 MB-72 pin
RAM speed	80 ns
RAM slots	4 slots, install 1 SIMM at a time
VRAM (standard)	512K
NuBus slots	none
PDS slots	one LC PDS, comm.
SCSI transfer rate	5.0 MB/second
Power supply	Int'l
Maximum wattage	60
Bus width	33 MHz, 32-bit/32-bit
FPU	none
MMU	built-in
ROM size	1024K
Memory cache	none

EXTERNAL STORAGE SYSTEMS

Hard drive	160 to 320 MB internal and external
Floppy drive	1.4 MB, 800K, 400K
CD-ROM	2X internal or external
Serial ports	two
ADB ports	one
Sound input	mono
Sound output	stereo
Network availability	LocalTalk or EtherTalk

LC550, Performa 550, 550CD, 560

GENERAL PRODUCT INFORMATION

Introduction date	10/18/1993, 1/1/94 (56)
Discontinuation date	3/23/95
Processor	68030
Clock speed	25/50MHz
MIPS rating	8.3
Display resolution	640×480
Color depth	up to thousands on built-in video
Display size	built-in 13" monitor
Systems supported	7.1, enabler 332

INTERNAL SYSTEMS

RAM (min and max)	4 to 36 MB-72 pin
RAM speed	80 ns
RAM slots	1 slot, install 1 SIMM at a time
VRAM (standard)	512K
NuBus slots	none
PDS slots	one (LC PDS)
SCSI transfer rate	5.0 MB/second
Power supply	Int'l
Maximum wattage	86
Bus width	25 MHz, 32-bit/32-bit
FPU	MC68882 optional
MMU	built-in
ROM size	1024K
Memory cache	none

EXTERNAL STORAGE SYSTEMS

Hard drive	80 to 160 MB internal and external
Floppy drive	1.4 MB, 800K, 400K
CD-ROM	2X internal or external
Serial ports	two
ADB ports	two
Sound input	mono
Sound output	mono
Network availability	LocalTalk, EtherTalk w/card

The Macintosh LC520 and Performa 520

The LC520 and Performa 520 are based on the LCIII Macintosh, which is the most sold all-in-one Macintosh ever made. The 520 was the first all-in-one Macintosh to include a built-in 14" color RGB monitor. The 520 series also has a built-in microphone, CD-ROM player, floppy disk and hard disk drives and one PDS expansion slot. This computer is ideal for home use or areas with a limited amount of space.

LC520, Performa 520

GENERAL PRODUCT INFORMATION

Introduction date	6/28/93
Discontinuation date	2/2/94
Processor	68030
Clock speed	25/50MHz
MIPS rating	6.3
Display resolution	640×480
Color depth	up to thousands on built-in video
Display size	built-in 13" support
Systems supported	7.1, enabler 403

INTERNAL SYSTEMS

RAM (min and max)	4 to 36 MB-72 pin
RAM speed	80 ns
RAM slots	1 slot, install 1 SIMM at a time
VRAM (standard)	512K
NuBus slots	none
PDS slots	one LC PDS
SCSI transfer rate	1.5 MB/second
Power supply	Int'l
Maximum wattage	60
Bus width	25 MHz, 32-bit/32-bit
FPU	MC68882 optional
MMU	built-in
ROM size	1024K
Memory cache	none

EXTERNAL STORAGE SYSTEMS

Hard drive	80 to 160 MB internal and external
Floppy drive	1.4 MB, 800K, 400K
CD-ROM	external only
Serial ports	two
ADB ports	two
Sound input	mono
Sound output	mono
Network availability	LocalTalk, EtherTalk w/card

Macintosh TV

Only 10,000 Macintosh TV models were built. Its motherboard was borrowed from the IIvx, but only supported a maximum of 8 MB of memory. With this Mac the user could press the command-space keys to switch from the Macintosh desktop to the television tuner. A unique trivia fact: the Macintosh TV has a flat black case, unlike all other Macintoshes.

PowerBook 540

Courtesy of Apple Computer, Inc.

Figure G.1　If you can afford it, the PowerBook 540c gives you an excellent color display.

PowerBook 540c

GENERAL PRODUCT INFORMATION

Introduction date	5/16/94
Discontinuation date	
Processor	68LC040
Clock speed	33/66MHz
MIPS rating	29
Display resolution	640×480
Color depth	up to 8-bit color
Display size	9.5"
Systems supported	7.1, PB500 v 1.0

INTERNAL SYSTEMS

RAM (min and max)	2 to 36 MB–PB5xx pin
RAM speed	70 ns
RAM slots	one
VRAM (standard)	512K
NuBus slots	none
PDS slots	modem/PCMCIA optional
SCSI transfer rate	1.5 MB/second
Power supply	Int'l
Maximum wattage	40
Bus width	33 MHz, 32-bit/32-bit
FPU	none
MMU	built-in
ROM size	2MB
Memory cache	none

EXTERNAL STORAGE SYSTEMS

Hard drive	240 MB internal and external
Floppy drive	1.4 MB, 800K, 400K
CD-ROM	external only
Serial ports	one
ADB ports	one
Sound input	mono
Sound output	stereo
Network availability	LocalTalk or EtherTalk

Courtesy of Apple Computer, Inc.

Figure G.2   The PowerBook 540's active matrix display is perfect for long flights.

PowerBook 540

GENERAL PRODUCT INFORMATION

Introduction date	5/16/94
Discontinuation date	10/17/94
Processor	68LC040
Clock speed	33MHz
MIPS rating	29
Display resolution	640×480
Color depth	up to 8-bit color
Display size	9.5"
Systems supported	7.1, PB500 v 1.0

INTERNAL SYSTEMS

RAM (min and max)	4 to 36 MB-PB5xx pin
RAM speed	70 ns
RAM slots	one
VRAM (standard)	512K
NuBus slots	none
PDS slots	modem/PCMCIA optional
SCSI transfer rate	1.5 MB/second
Power supply	Int'l
Maximum wattage	40
Bus width	33 MHz, 32-bit/32-bit
FPU	none
MMU	built-in
ROM size	2MB
Memory cache	none

EXTERNAL STORAGE SYSTEMS

Hard drive	240 MB internal and external
Floppy drive	1.4 MB, 800K, 400K
CD-ROM	external only
Serial ports	one
ADB ports	one
Sound input	mono
Sound output	stereo
Network availability	LocalTalk or EtherTalk

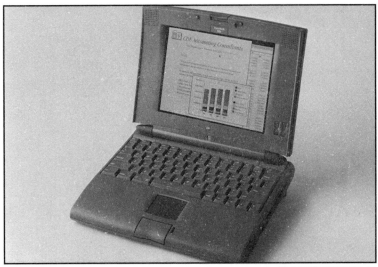

Courtesy of Apple Computer, Inc.

Figure G.3 The PowerBook 520c.

PowerBook 520c

GENERAL PRODUCT INFORMATION

Introduction date	5/16/94
Discontinuation date	6/10/95
Processor	68LC040
Clock speed	25MHz
MIPS rating	22
Display resolution	640×480
Color depth	up to 8-bit color
Display size	9.5"
Systems supported	7.1, PB500 v 1.0

INTERNAL SYSTEMS

RAM (min and max)	4 to 36 MB-PB5xx pin
RAM speed	70 ns
RAM slots	one
VRAM (standard)	512K
NuBus slots	none
PDS slots	modem/PCMCIA optional
SCSI transfer rate	1.5 MB/second
Power supply	Int'l
Maximum wattage	40
Bus width	25 MHz, 32-bit/32-bit

FPU	none
MMU	built-in
ROM size	2 MB
Memory cache	none

EXTERNAL STORAGE SYSTEMS

Hard drive	160 to 320 MB internal and external
Floppy drive	1.4 MB, 800K, 400K
CD-ROM	external only
Serial ports	one
ADB ports	one
Sound input	mono
Sound output	stereo
Network availability	LocalTalk or EtherTalk

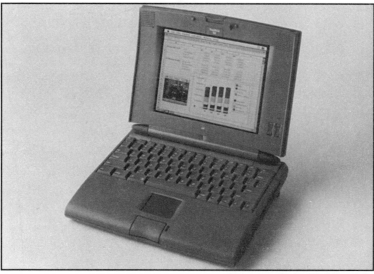

Courtesy of Apple Computer, Inc.

Figure G.4   The PowerBook 520 is very capable, and is reasonably priced.

PowerBook 520

GENERAL PRODUCT INFORMATION

Introduction date	5/16/94
Discontinuation date	6/10/95
Processor	68LC040
Clock speed	25MHz
MIPS rating	22

Display resolution	640×480
Color depth	4-bit grayscale
Display size	9.5"
Systems supported	7.1, PB500 v 1.0

INTERNAL SYSTEMS

RAM (min and max)	4 to 36 MB-PB5xx pin
RAM speed	70 ns
RAM slots	one
VRAM (standard)	512K
NuBus slots	none
PDS slots	modem/PCMCIA optional
SCSI transfer rate	1.5 MB/second
Power supply	Int'l
Maximum wattage	40
Bus width	25 MHz, 32-bit/32-bit
FPU	none
MMU	built-in
ROM size	2MB
Memory cache	none

EXTERNAL STORAGE SYSTEMS

Hard drive	160 to 240 MB internal and external
Floppy drive	1.4 MB, 800K, 400K
CD-ROM	external only
Serial ports	one
ADB ports	one
Sound input	mono
Sound output	stereo
Network availability	LocalTalk or EtherTalk

PowerBook Duo 280c

GENERAL PRODUCT INFORMATION

Introduction date	5/16/94
Discontinuation date	10/1/95
Processor	68030
Clock speed	33MHz
MIPS rating	8.3
Display resolution	640×480
Color depth	8-bit color, 32-bit QD
Display size	10"
Systems supported	7.1, Enabler 201, Duo Enabler

INTERNAL SYSTEMS

RAM (min and max)	4 to 24 MB–PBDUO
RAM speed	70 ns
RAM slots	1 slot, install 1 SIMM at a time
VRAM (standard)	512K
NuBus slots	none
PDS slots	one, plus modem slot
SCSI transfer rate	1.5 MB/second
Power supply	Int'l
Maximum wattage	25
Bus width	33 MHz, 32-bit/32-bit
FPU	none
MMU	built-in
ROM size	1024K
Memory cache	none

EXTERNAL STORAGE SYSTEMS

Hard drive	80 to 160 MB internal and external
Floppy drive	external only
CD-ROM	external only
Serial ports	one
ADB ports	none
Sound input	mono
Sound output	mono
Network availability	LocalTalk

PowerBook Duo 280

GENERAL PRODUCT INFORMATION

Introduction date	5/16/94
Discontinuation date	11/14/94
Processor	68030
Clock speed	33MHz
MIPS rating	8.3
Display resolution	640×480
Color depth	8-bit grayscale, 32-bit QD
Display size	10"
Systems supported	7.1, Enabler 201, Duo Enabler

INTERNAL SYSTEMS

RAM (min and max)	4 to 24 MB-PBDUO
RAM speed	70 ns
RAM slots	1 slot, install 1 SIMM at a time
VRAM (standard)	512K
NuBus slots	none

PDS slots   one, plus modem slot
SCSI transfer rate   1.5 MB/second
Power supply   Int'l
Maximum wattage   25
Bus width   33 MHz, 32-bit/32-bit
FPU   none
MMU   built-in
ROM size   1024K
Memory cache   none

EXTERNAL STORAGE SYSTEMS

Hard drive   80 to 160 MB internal and external
Floppy drive   external only
CD-ROM   external only
Serial ports   one
ADB ports   none
Sound input   mono
Sound output   mono
Network availability   LocalTalk

PowerBook Duo 250	*PowerBook 270, 270c*

GENERAL PRODUCT INFORMATION

Introduction date		
Discontinuation date		
Processor	68030	68030
Clock speed	25MHz	33MHz
MIPS rating	8.3	8.3
Display resolution	640×480	640×480
Color depth	4-bit grayscale	4-bit grayscale or color
Display size	10"	10"
Systems supported	7.1, Enabler 201, Duo Enabler	7.1, Enabler 201, Duo Enabler

INTERNAL SYSTEMS

RAM (min and max)	4 to 24 MB-PBDUO	4 to 24 MB-PBDUO
RAM speed	70 ns	70 ns
RAM slots	1 slot, install 1 SIMM at a time	1 slot, install 1 SIMM at a time
VRAM (standard)	512K	512K
NuBus slots	none	none
PDS slots	one, plus modem slot	one, plus modem slot
SCSI transfer rate	1.5 MB/second	1.5 MB/second
Power supply	Int'l	Int'l

Maximum wattage	25	25
Bus width	33 MHz, 32-bit/32-bit	33 MHz, 32-bit/32-bit
FPU	none	none
MMU	built-in	built-in
ROM size	1024K	1024K
Memory cache	none	none

EXTERNAL STORAGE SYSTEMS

Hard drive	80 to 160 MB internal and external	80 to 160 MB internal and external
Floppy drive	external only	external only
CD-ROM	external only	external only
Serial ports	one	one
ADB ports	none	none
Sound input	mono	mono
Sound output	mono	mono
Network availability	LocalTalk	LocalTalk

Courtesy of Apple Computer, Inc.

Figure G.5 The PowerBook Duo 230.

Duo 230

GENERAL PRODUCT INFORMATION

Introduction date	10/19/92
Discontinuation date	7/18/94
Processor	68030
Clock speed	33MHz
MIPS rating	8.3
Display resolution	640×400
Color depth	4-bit grayscale, 32-bit QD
Display size	10"
Systems supported	7.1, Enabler 201, Duo Enabler

INTERNAL SYSTEMS

RAM (min and max)	4 to 24 MB-PBDUO
RAM speed	70 ns
RAM slots	1 slot, install 1 SIMM at a time
VRAM (standard)	512K
NuBus slots	none
PDS slots	one, plus modem slot
SCSI transfer rate	1.5 MB/second
Power supply	Int'l
Maximum wattage	25
Bus width	33 MHz, 32-bit/32-bit
FPU	none
MMU	built-in
ROM size	1024K
Memory cache	none

EXTERNAL STORAGE SYSTEMS

Hard drive	80 to 160 MB internal and external
Floppy drive	external only
CD-ROM	external only
Serial ports	one
ADB ports	none
Sound input	mono
Sound output	mono
Network availability	LocalTalk

Courtesy of Apple Computer, Inc.

Figure G.6   Macintosh Duo 210 and docking station.

Duo210

GENERAL PRODUCT INFORMATION

Introduction date	10/19/92
Discontinuation date	10/21/93
Processor	68030
Clock speed	25MHz
MIPS rating	6.3
Display resolution	640×400
Color depth	4-bit grayscale, 32-bit QD
Display size	10"
Systems supported	7.1, Enabler 201, Duo Enabler

INTERNAL SYSTEMS

RAM (min and max)	4 to 24 MB-DUO
RAM speed	70 ns
RAM slots	1 slot, install 1 SIMM at a time
VRAM (standard)	512K
NuBus slots	none
PDS slots	one, plus modem slot
SCSI transfer rate	1.5 MB/second
Power supply	Int'l
Maximum wattage	25

Bus width	25 MHz, 32-bit/32-bit
FPU	none
MMU	built-in
ROM size	1024K
Memory cache	none

EXTERNAL STORAGE SYSTEMS

Hard drive	80 to 160 MB internal and external
Floppy drive	external only
CD-ROM	external only
Serial ports	one
ADB ports	none
Sound input	mono
Sound output	mono
Network availability	LocalTalk

PowerBook 150

GENERAL PRODUCT INFORMATION

Introduction date	7/18/94
Discontinuation date	
Processor	68030
Clock speed	33MHz
MIPS rating	8.3
Display resolution	640×400
Color depth	8-bit grayscale
Display size	640×480
Systems supported	7.1, Enabler PB150

INTERNAL SYSTEMS

RAM (min and max)	4 to 40 MB-Duo
RAM speed	70 ns
RAM slots	1 slot, install 1 SIMM at a time
VRAM (standard)	512K
NuBus slots	none
PDS slots	none, modem slot
SCSI transfer rate	1.5 MB/second
Power supply	Int'l
Maximum wattage	17
Bus width	25 MHz, 32-bit/32-bit
FPU	none
MMU	built-in
ROM size	256K
Memory cache	none

EXTERNAL STORAGE SYSTEMS

Hard drive	120 to 250 MB IDE internal and external
Floppy drive	1.4 MB, 800K, 400K
CD-ROM	external only
Serial ports	none
ADB ports	none
Sound input	mono
Sound output	mono
Network availability	LocalTalk

Courtesy of Apple Computer, Inc.

Figure G.7 Macintosh PowerBook 160.

PowerBook 165c   *PowerBook 180c, 180, 165*

GENERAL PRODUCT INFORMATION

Introduction date	2/10/93
Discontinuation date	12/1/193
Processor	68030
Clock speed	33MHz
MIPS rating	8.3
Display resolution	640×400
Color depth	8-bit color
Display size	10"
Systems supported	7.1, 121

INTERNAL SYSTEMS

RAM (min and max)	4 to 14 MB–PB1xx pin
RAM speed	85 ns
RAM slots	1 slot, install 1 SIMM at a time
VRAM (standard)	32K
NuBus slots	none
PDS slots	none, modem slot
SCSI transfer rate	1.5 MB/second
Power supply	Int'l
Maximum wattage	24
Bus width	33 MHz, 32-bit/32-bit
FPU	68882
MMU	built-in
ROM size	1024K
Memory cache	none

EXTERNAL STORAGE SYSTEMS

Hard drive	40 to 80 MB internal and external
Floppy drive	1.4 MB, 800K, 400K
CD-ROM	external only
Serial ports	two
ADB ports	one
Sound input	mono
Sound output	stereo
Network availability	LocalTalk

Courtesy of Apple Computer, Inc.

Figure G.8   Macintosh PowerBook 170.

	PowerBook 170	PowerBook 140

GENERAL PRODUCT INFORMATION

Introduction date	10/21/91	10/21/91
Discontinuation date	10/19/92	10/19/92
Processor	68030	68030
Clock speed	25MHz	20MHz
MIPS rating	6.3	6.3
Display resolution	640×400 active	640×400 passive
Color depth	1-bit	1-bit
Display size	10"	10"
Systems supported	7.0.1 and higher with enough memory	7.0.1 and higher with enough memory

INTERNAL SYSTEMS

RAM (min and max)	2 to 8MB–PB1xx pin	2 to 8 MB–PB1xx pin
RAM speed	100 ns	100 ns
RAM slots	1 slot, install 1 SIMM at a time	1 slot, install 1 SIMM at a time
VRAM (standard)	32K	32K
NuBus slots	none	none
PDS slots	none, modem slot	none, modem slot
SCSI transfer rate	1.5 MB/second	1.5 MB/second
Power supply	Int'l	Int'l
Maximum wattage	17	17
Bus width	25 MHz, 32-bit/32-bit	25 MHz, 32-bit/32-bit
FPU	none	none
MMU	built-in	built-in
ROM size	256K	256K
Memory cache	none	none

EXTERNAL STORAGE SYSTEMS

Hard drive	40 to 80 MB internal and external	40 to 80 MB internal and external
Floppy drive	1.4 MB, 800K, 400K	1.4 MB, 800K, 400K
CD-ROM	external only	external only
Serial ports	two	two
ADB ports	one	one
Sound input	mono	mono
Sound output	mono	mono
Network availability	LocalTalk	LocalTalk

Courtesy of Apple Computer, Inc.

Figure G.9   The PowerBook 145B.

PowerBook 145B

GENERAL PRODUCT INFORMATION

Introduction date	6/7/93
Discontinuation date	7/18/94
Processor	68030
Clock speed	25MHz
MIPS rating	6.3
Display resolution	640×400
Color depth	1-bit
Display size	10"
Systems supported	7.1

INTERNAL SYSTEMS

RAM (min and max)	2 to 8 MB-PB1xx pin
RAM speed	100 ns
RAM slots	1 slot, install 1 SIMM at a time
VRAM (standard)	32K
NuBus slots	none
PDS slots	none, modem slot
SCSI transfer rate	1.5 MB/second
Power supply	Int'l
Maximum wattage	17
Bus width	25 MHz, 32-bit/32-bit
FPU	none

MMU	built-in
ROM size	256K
Memory cache	none

EXTERNAL STORAGE SYSTEMS

Hard drive	40 to 80 MB internal and external
Floppy drive	1.4 MB, 800K, 400K
CD-ROM	external only
Serial ports	two
ADB ports	one
Sound input	mono
Sound output	mono
Network availability	LocalTalk

Courtesy of Apple Computer, Inc.

Figure G.10   The Quadra 840AV: the fastest 68040-based Macintosh

Quadra 840AV

GENERAL PRODUCT INFORMATION

Introduction date	7/29/93
Discontinuation date	7/18/94
Processor	68040
Clock speed	40/80MHz
MIPS rating	35
Display resolution	640×480 to 1024×768 or card dependent
Color depth	up to millions on built-in video
Display size	built-in 13" through 21" OR card dependent
Systems supported	7.1, Enabler 040 v1.0

INTERNAL SYSTEMS

RAM (min and max)	4 to 128MB–72 pin
RAM speed	80 ns
RAM slots	4 slots, install 1 SIMM at a time
VRAM (standard)	512K
NuBus slots	3
PDS slots	one
SCSI transfer rate	5.0 MB/second
Power supply	Int'l
Maximum wattage	200
Bus width	40 MHz, 32-bit/32-bit
FPU	MC68882
MMU	built-in
ROM size	1024K
Memory cache	none

EXTERNAL STORAGE SYSTEMS

Hard drive	230 to 1GB internal and external
Floppy drive	1.4 MB, 800K, 400K
CD-ROM	external only
Serial ports	two
ADB ports	one
Sound input	stereo
Sound output	stereo
Network availability	LocalTalk or EtherTalk

Courtesy of Apple Computer, Inc.

Figure G.11   The Quadra 660AV is a low-cost introduction to Apple's AV Technologies.

Quadra 660AV, Centris 660AV

GENERAL PRODUCT INFORMATION

Introduction date	
Discontinuation date	
Processor	68040
Clock speed	33/66MHz
MIPS rating	29
Display resolution	640×480 to 1024×768 or card dependent
Color depth	up to millions on built-in video
Display size	built-in 13" through 21" OR card dependent
Systems supported	7.1, Enabler 040 v1.0

INTERNAL SYSTEMS

RAM (min and max)	4 to 136 MB–72 pin
RAM speed	80 ns
RAM slots	4 slots, install 1 SIMM at a time
VRAM (standard)	512K
NuBus slots	3
PDS slots	one
SCSI transfer rate	5.0 MB/second
Power supply	Int'l
Maximum wattage	202
Bus width	33 MHz, 32-bit/32-bit
FPU	built-in
MMU	built-in
ROM size	1024K
Memory cache	none

EXTERNAL STORAGE SYSTEMS

Hard drive	230 to 1GB internal and external
Floppy drive	1.4 MB, 800K, 400K
CD-ROM	2X internal or external
Serial ports	two
ADB ports	one
Sound input	stereo
Sound output	stereo
Network availability	LocalTalk or EtherTalk

Quadra 800

GENERAL PRODUCT INFORMATION

Introduction date	2/10/93
Discontinuation date	3/14/94
Processor	68040
Clock speed	33/66MHz
MIPS rating	29
Display resolution	640×480 to 1024×768 or card dependent
Color depth	up to millions on built-in video
Display size	built-in 13" through 21" OR card dependent
Systems supported	7.1, enabler 040 v1.0

INTERNAL SYSTEMS

RAM (min and max)	4 to 136 MB–72-pin
RAM speed	80 ns
RAM slots	4 slots, install 1 SIMM at a time
VRAM (standard)	512 or 1024K
NuBus slots	3
PDS slots	one
SCSI transfer rate	5.0 MB/second
Power supply	Int'l
Maximum wattage	200
Bus width	33 MHz, 32-bit/32-bit
FPU	built-in
MMU	built-in
ROM size	1024K
Memory cache	none

EXTERNAL STORAGE SYSTEMS

Hard drive	230 to 1GB internal and external
Floppy drive	1.4 MB, 800K, 400K
CD-ROM	2X internal or external
Serial ports	two
ADB ports	one
Sound input	mono
Sound output	stereo
Network availability	LocalTalk or EtherTalk

Courtesy of Apple Computer, Inc.

Figure G.12 The Quadra 950's tower design and excellent expandability make it a favorite platform for high-end graphics professionals.

Quadra 950

GENERAL PRODUCT INFORMATION

Introduction date	
Discontinuation date	
Processor	68040
Clock speed	25/50MHz
MIPS rating	22
Display resolution	640×480 to 1024×768 or card dependent
Color depth	up to millions on built-in video
Display size	built-in 13" through 21" OR card dependent
Systems supported	7.0.1 and higher with enough memory

INTERNAL SYSTEMS

RAM (min and max)	4 to 256 MB-30 pin
RAM speed	80 ns
RAM slots	16 slots, install 4 SIMMs at a time
VRAM (standard)	1024K
NuBus slots	5
PDS slots	one
SCSI transfer rate	5.0 MB/second
Power supply	Int'l

Maximum wattage	303
Bus width	25 MHz, 32-bit/32-bit
FPU	built-in
MMU	built-in
ROM size	1024K
Memory cache	none

EXTERNAL STORAGE SYSTEMS

Hard drive	40 to 400 MB internal and external
Floppy drive	1.4 MB, 800K, 400K
CD-ROM	2X internal or external
Serial ports	two
ADB ports	two
Sound input	mono
Sound output	stereo
Network availability	LocalTalk or EtherTalk

Quadra 900

GENERAL PRODUCT INFORMATION

Introduction date	10/21/91
Discontinuation date	5/18/92
Processor	68040
Clock speed	25/50MHz
MIPS rating	22
Display resolution	640×480 to 1024×768 or card dependent
Color depth	up to millions on built-in video
Display size	built-in 13" through 21" OR card dependent
Systems supported	7.0.1 and higher with enough memory

INTERNAL SYSTEMS

RAM (min and max)	4 to 256 MB-30 pin
RAM speed	80 ns
RAM slots	16 slots, install 4 SIMMs at a time
VRAM (standard)	1024K
NuBus slots	5
PDS slots	one
SCSI transfer rate	5.0 MB/second
Power supply	Int'l
Maximum wattage	303
Bus width	25 MHz, 32-bit/32-bit
FPU	built-in
MMU	built-in
ROM size	1024K
Memory cache	none

EXTERNAL STORAGE SYSTEMS

Hard drive	80 to 160MB internal and external
Floppy drive	1.4MB, 800K, 400K
CD-ROM	external only
Serial ports	two
ADB ports	one
Sound input	mono
Sound output	stereo
Network availability	LocalTalk or EtherTalk

Courtesy of Apple Computer, Inc.

Figure G.13 Macintosh Quadra 700.

Quadra 700

GENERAL PRODUCT INFORMATION

Introduction date	10/21/91
Discontinuation date	3/15/93
Processor	68040
Clock speed	25/50MHz
MIPS rating	22
Display resolution	640×480 to 1024×768 or card dependent
Color depth	up to millions on built-in video
Display size	built-in 13" through 21" OR card dependent
Systems supported	7.0.1 and higher with enough memory

INTERNAL SYSTEMS

RAM (min and max)	4 to 68 MB-30 pin
RAM speed	80 ns
RAM slots	4 slots, install 4 SIMMs at a time
VRAM (standard)	512K
NuBus slots	2
PDS slots	one
SCSI transfer rate	5.0 MB/second
Power supply	Int'l
Maximum wattage	130
Bus width	25 MHz, 32-bit/32-bit
FPU	built-in
MMU	built-in
ROM size	1024K
Memory cache	none

EXTERNAL STORAGE SYSTEMS

Hard drive	40 to 400 MB internal and external
Floppy drive	1.4 MB, 800K, 400K
CD-ROM	external only
Serial ports	two
ADB ports	two
Sound input	mono
Sound output	stereo
Network availability	LocalTalk or EtherTalk

Courtesy of Apple Computer, Inc.

Figure G.14 The three-slot Quadra 650 can accept full-size NuBus cards.

Quadra 650

GENERAL PRODUCT INFORMATION

Introduction date	10/21/93
Discontinuation date	9/12/94
Processor	68040
Clock speed	33/66MHz
MIPS rating	29
Display resolution	640×480 to 1024×768 or card dependent
Color depth	up to millions on built-in video
Display size	built-in 13" through 21" OR card dependent
Systems supported	7.1, enabler 040 v1.1

INTERNAL SYSTEMS

RAM (min and max)	4 to 136 MB–72 pin
RAM speed	80 ns
RAM slots	4 slots, install 1 SIMM at a time
VRAM (standard)	512K
NuBus slots	3
PDS slots	one
SCSI transfer rate	5.0 MB/second
Power supply	Int'l
Maximum wattage	230
Bus width	33 MHz, 32-bit/32-bit
FPU	MC68882
MMU	built-in
ROM size	1024K
Memory cache	none

EXTERNAL STORAGE SYSTEMS

Hard drive	230 to 500 MB internal and external
Floppy drive	1.4MB, 800K, 400K
CD-ROM	2X internal or external
Serial ports	two
ADB ports	two
Sound input	mono
Sound output	stereo
Network availability	LocalTalk or EtherTalk

Courtesy of Apple Computer, Inc.

Figure G.15 The Quadra 610 is a low-cost Macintosh that includes built-in Ethernet.

Quadra 610

GENERAL PRODUCT INFORMATION

Introduction date	10/21/93
Discontinued	7/18/94
Processor	68040
Clock speed	25/50MHz
MIPS rating	22
Display resolution	640×480 to 1024×768 or card dependent
Color depth	up to millions on built-in video
Display size	built-in 13" through 21" OR card dependent
Systems supported	7.1, enabler 040 v1.1

INTERNAL SYSTEMS

RAM (min and max)	4 to 68 MB–72 pin
RAM speed	80 ns
RAM slots	4 slots, install 1 SIMM at a time
VRAM (standard)	512K
NuBus slots	1 7" NuBus or PDS
PDS slots	1 7" NuBus or PDS
SCSI transfer rate	5.0 MB/second
Power supply	Int'l
Maximum wattage	202

Bus width	25 MHz, 32-bit/32-bit
FPU	MC68882
MMU	built-in
ROM size	1024K
Memory cache	none

EXTERNAL STORAGE SYSTEMS

Hard drive	80 to 500 MB internal and external
Floppy drive	1.4 MB, 800K, 400K
CD-ROM	2x internal or external
Serial ports	two
ADB ports	two
Sound input	mono
Sound output	stereo
Network availability	LocalTalk or EtherTalk

Courtesy of Apple Computer, Inc.

Figure G.16 The Centris 610 and Centris 650.

	Centris 650	Centris 610
GENERAL PRODUCT INFORMATION		
Introduction date	2/10/93	2/10/93
Discontinued	10/21/93	10/21/93
Processor	68040	68LC040
Clock speed	25/50 MHz	20/40 MHz
MIPS rating	22	17.6
Display resolution	640×480 to 1024×768 or card dependent	640×480 to 1024×768 or card dependent
Color depth	up to millions on built-in video	up to millions on built-in video
Display size	built-in 13" through 21" OR card dependent	built-in 13" through 21" OR card dependent
Systems supported	7.1, Enabler 040 v1.0	7.1, Enabler 040 v1.0
INTERNAL SYSTEMS		
RAM (min and max)	4 to 136 MB-72 pin	4 to 68 MB-72 pin
RAM speed	80 ns	80 ns
RAM slots	4 slots, install 1 SIMM at a time	2 slots, install 1 SIMM at a time
VRAM (standard)	512K	512K
NuBus slots	3	17" NuBus or PDS
PDS slots	one	17" NuBus or PDS
SCSI transfer rate	5.0 MB/second	5.0 MB/second
Power supply	Int'l	Int'l
Maximum wattage	112	86
Bus width	25 MHz, 32-bit/32-bit	20 MHz, 32-bit/32-bit
FPU	MC68882	MC68882
MMU	built-in	built-in
ROM size	1024K	1024K
Memory cache	none	none
EXTERNAL STORAGE SYSTEMS		
Hard drive	80 to 500 MB internal and external	40 to 400 MB internal and external
Floppy drive	1.4 MB, 800K, 400K	1.4 MB, 800K, 400K
CD-ROM	2x internal or external	2x internal or external
Serial ports	two	two
ADB ports	two	two
Sound input	mono	mono
Sound output	stereo	stereo
Network availability	LocalTalk or EtherTalk	LocalTalk or EtherTalk

Courtesy of Apple Computer, Inc.

Figure G.17   Macintosh IIvx.

IIvx

GENERAL PRODUCT INFORMATION

Introduction date	10/19/92
Discontinued	10/21/93
Processor	68030
Clock speed	32 MHz
MIPS rating	7
Display resolution	640×480
Color depth	up to thousands
Display size	13" to portrait, no 17" or higher without card
Systems supported	7.1, enabler 001

INTERNAL SYSTEMS

RAM (min and max)	4 to 68 MB–30 pin
RAM speed	80 ns
RAM slots	4 slots, install 4 SIMMs at a time
VRAM (standard)	256K
NuBus slots	3
PDS slots	one
SCSI transfer rate	1.5 MB/second
Power supply	Int'l
Maximum wattage	230
Bus width	16 MHz, 32-bit/32-bit
FPU	MC68882 optional

MMU	built-in
ROM size	1024K
Memory cache	none (32K card optional)

EXTERNAL STORAGE SYSTEMS

Hard drive	40 to 400 MB internal and external
Floppy drive	1.4 MB, 800K, 400K
CD-ROM	2x internal or external
Serial ports	two
ADB ports	two
Sound input	mono
Sound output	mono
Network availability	LocalTalk, EtherTalk w/card

IIvi

GENERAL PRODUCT INFORMATION

Introduction date	10/19/92
Discontinued	2/1/93
Processor	68030
Clock speed	16 MHz
MIPS rating	4.3
Display resolution	640×480
Color depth	up to thousands
Display size	13" to portrait, no 17" or higher w/o card
Systems supported	7.1P, enabler 001

INTERNAL SYSTEMS

RAM (min and max)	4 to 68 MB–30 pin
RAM speed	80 ns
RAM slots	4 slots, install 4 SIMMs at a time
VRAM (standard)	256K
NuBus slots	3
PDS slots	one
SCSI transfer rate	1.5 MB/second
Power supply	Int'l
Maximum wattage	112
Bus width	16 MHz, 32-bit/32-bit
FPU	MC68882 optional
MMU	built-in
ROM size	1024K
Memory cache	none (32K card optional)

EXTERNAL STORAGE SYSTEMS

Hard drive	40 to 400 MB internal and external
Floppy drive	1.4 MB, 800K, 400K
CD-ROM	2x internal or external
Serial ports	two
ADB ports	two
Sound input	mono
Sound output	mono
Network availability	LocalTalk, EtherTalk w/card

Courtesy of Apple Computer, Inc.

Figure G.18 Macintosh IIsi.

IIsi

GENERAL PRODUCT INFORMATION

Introduction date	10/15/90
Discontinued	3/15/93
Processor	68030
Clock speed	20 MHz
MIPS rating	5
Display resolution	card dependent
Color depth	up to millions
Display size	card dependent
Systems supported	6.0.7 and higher with enough memory

INTERNAL SYSTEMS

RAM (min and max)	1 to 17 MB–30 pin
RAM speed	100 ns
RAM slots	4 slots, install 4 SIMMs at a time
VRAM (standard)	none
NuBus slots	1
PDS slots	one
SCSI transfer rate	1.25 MB/second
Power supply	Int'l
Maximum wattage	90
Bus width	20 MHz, 32-bit/32-bit
FPU	MC68882 optional
MMU	built-in
ROM size	512K
Memory cache	none

EXTERNAL STORAGE SYSTEMS

Hard drive	40 to 80 MB internal and external
Floppy drive	1.4 MB, 800K, 400K
CD-ROM	external only
Serial ports	two
ADB ports	one
Sound input	mono
Sound output	stereo
Network availability	LocalTalk, EtherTalk w/card

Quadra 605, LC 475, Performa 475, 476

GENERAL PRODUCT INFORMATION

Introduction date	10/18/93
Discontinued	10/17/94
Processor	68LC040
Clock speed	25/50 MHz
MIPS rating	22
Display resolution	640×480 to 1024×768 or card dependent
Color depth	up to millions on built-in video
Display size	built-in 13" through 21" OR card dependent
Systems supported	7.1, 065 or 7.1P3, Enabler 364

INTERNAL SYSTEMS

RAM (min and max)	4 to 36 MB-72 pin
RAM speed	80 ns
RAM slots	4 slots, install 1 SIMM at a time
VRAM (standard)	512K

NuBus slots	none
PDS slots	one LC PDS
SCSI transfer rate	5.0 MB/second
Power supply	Int'l
Maximum wattage	30 (53 for 605)
Bus width	25 MHz, 32-bit/32-bit
FPU	none
MMU	built-in
ROM size	1024K
Memory cache	none

EXTERNAL STORAGE SYSTEMS

Hard drive	80 to 230 MB internal and external
Floppy drive	1.4 MB, 800K, 400K
CD-ROM	external only
Serial ports	two
ADB ports	one
Sound input	mono
Sound output	stereo
Network availability	LocalTalk or EtherTalk

LCIII

GENERAL PRODUCT INFORMATION

Introduction date	2/10/93
Discontinued	2/14/94
Processor	68030
Clock speed	25/50 MHz
MIPS rating	8.3
Display resolution	640×480
Color depth	up to thousands on built-in video
Display size	built-in 13" support
Systems supported	7.1, Enabler 003

INTERNAL SYSTEMS

RAM (min and max)	4 to 36 MB-72 pin
RAM speed	80 ns
RAM slots	1 slot, install 1 SIMM at a time
VRAM (standard)	512K
NuBus slots	none
PDS slots	one LCIII PDS
SCSI transfer rate	1.5 MB/second
Power supply	Int'l
Maximum wattage	86

Bus width	25 MHz, 32-bit/32-bit
FPU	MC68882 optional
MMU	built-in
ROM size	1024K
Memory cache	none

EXTERNAL STORAGE SYSTEMS

Hard drive	230 to 1GB internal and external
Floppy drive	1.4 MB, 800K, 400K
CD-ROM	external only
Serial ports	two
ADB ports	one
Sound input	mono
Sound output	mono
Network availability	LocalTalk, EtherTalk w/card

Performa 460, 466, 467

GENERAL PRODUCT INFORMATION

Introduction date	
Discontinued	
Processor	68030
Clock speed	25/50 MHz
MIPS rating	8.3
Display resolution	640×480
Color depth	up to thousands on built-in video
Display size	built-in 13" support
Systems supported	7.1P3, Enabler 308

INTERNAL SYSTEMS

RAM (min and max)	4 to 36 MB-72 pin
RAM speed	80 ns
RAM slots	1 slot, install 1 SIMM at a time
VRAM (standard)	512K
NuBus slots	none
PDS slots	one LCIII PDS
SCSI transfer rate	1.5 MB/second
Power supply	Int'l
Maximum wattage	86
Bus width	25 MHz, 32-bit/32-bit
FPU	MC68882 optional
MMU	built-in
ROM size	1024K
Memory cache	none

EXTERNAL STORAGE SYSTEMS

Hard drive	230 MB to 1GB internal and external
Floppy drive	1.4 MB, 800K, 400K
CD-ROM	external only
Serial ports	two
ADB ports	one
Sound input	mono
Sound output	mono
Network availability	LocalTalk, EtherTalk w/card

Performa 410

GENERAL PRODUCT INFORMATION

Introduction date	10/18/93
Discontinued	
Processor	68030
Clock speed	16 MHz
MIPS rating	3.9
Display resolution	640×480
Color depth	up to thousands
Display size	13"
Systems supported	7.0.1P

INTERNAL SYSTEMS

RAM (min and max)	4 to 10 MB–30 pin
RAM speed	100 ns
RAM slots	2 slots, install 2 SIMMs at a time
VRAM (standard)	256K
NuBus slots	none
PDS slots	one
SCSI transfer rate	1.5 MB/second
Power supply	Int'l
Maximum wattage	50
Bus width	16 MHz, 16-bit/32-bit
FPU	MC68882 optional
MMU	built-in
ROM size	512K
Memory cache	none

EXTERNAL STORAGE SYSTEMS

Hard drive	80 MB internal and external
Floppy drive	1.4 MB, 800K, 400K
CD-ROM	external only
Serial ports	two

ADB ports	one
Sound input	mono
Sound output	mono
Network availability	LocalTalk, EtherTalk w/card

Courtesy of Apple Computer, Inc.

Figure G.19   Macintosh Performa 600.

Performa 600

GENERAL PRODUCT INFORMATION

Introduction date	9/14/92
Discontinued	10/18/93
Processor	68030
Clock speed	32 MHz
MIPS rating	6.5
Display resolution	640×480
Color depth	up to thousands
Display size	13" to portrait, no 17" or higher without card
Systems supported	7.1P, enabler 304

INTERNAL SYSTEMS

RAM (min and max)	4 to 68 MB–30 pin
RAM speed	80 ns
RAM slots	4 slots, install 4 SIMMs at a time

VRAM (standard)	256K
NuBus slots	3
PDS slots	one
SCSI transfer rate	1.5 MB/second
Power supply	Int'l
Maximum wattage	112
Bus width	16 MHz, 32-bit/32-bit
FPU	MC68882 optional
MMU	built-in
ROM size	1024K
Memory cache	none (32K card optional)

EXTERNAL STORAGE SYSTEMS

Hard drive	160 MB internal and external
Floppy drive	1.4 MB, 800K, 400K
CD-ROM	2x internal or external
Serial ports	two
ADB ports	two
Sound input	mono
Sound output	mono
Network availability	LocalTalk, EtherTalk w/card

Courtesy of Apple Computer, Inc.

Figure G.20   Macintosh Performa 400.

GENERAL PRODUCT INFORMATION

Introduction date	9/14/92
Discontinued	10/18/93
Processor	68030
Clock speed	16 MHz
MIPS rating	3.9
Display resolution	640×480
Color depth	up to thousands
Display size	12"
Systems supported	7.0.1P and higher with enough memory

INTERNAL SYSTEMS

RAM (min and max)	4 to 10 MB-30 pin
RAM speed	100 ns
RAM slots	2 slots, install 2 SIMMs at a time
VRAM (standard)	256K
NuBus slots	none
PDS slots	one
SCSI transfer rate	1.5 MB/second
Power supply	Int'l
Maximum wattage	50
Bus width	16 MHz, 16-bit/32-bit
FPU	MC68882 optional
MMU	built-in
ROM size	512K
Memory cache	none

EXTERNAL STORAGE SYSTEMS

Hard drive	80 to 120 MB internal and external
Floppy drive	1.4 MB, 800K, 400K
CD-ROM	external only
Serial ports	two
ADB ports	one
Sound input	mono
Sound output	mono
Network availability	LocalTalk, EtherTalk w/card

Courtesy of Apple Computer, Inc.

Figure G.21   Macintosh Performa 200.

Performa 200

GENERAL PRODUCT INFORMATION

Introduction date	9/14/92
Discontinued	10/18/93
Processor	68030
Clock speed	16 MHz
MIPS rating	3.9
Display resolution	512×342
Color depth	1-bit
Display size	9"
Systems supported	7.0.1P and higher with enough memory

INTERNAL SYSTEMS

RAM (min and max)	2 to 10 MB-30 pin
RAM speed	100 ns
RAM slots	2 slots, install 2 SIMMs at a time
VRAM (standard)	none
NuBus slots	none
PDS slots	none
SCSI transfer rate	1.25 MB/second
Power supply	U.S. only
Maximum wattage	76
Bus width	16 MHz, 16-bit/32-bit

FPU	MC68882 optional
MMU	built-in
ROM size	512K
Memory cache	none

EXTERNAL STORAGE SYSTEMS

Hard drive	40 to 80 MB internal and external
Floppy drive	1.4 MB, 800K, 400K
CD-ROM	external only
Serial ports	two
ADB ports	one
Sound input	mono
Sound output	mono
Network availability	LocalTalk

Courtesy of Apple Computer, Inc.

Figure G.22   Macintosh LCII.

LCII

GENERAL PRODUCT INFORMATION

Introduction date	3/23/92
Discontinued	3/15/93
Processor	68030
Clock speed	16 MHz
MIPS rating	3.9
Display resolution	640×480
Color depth	up to thousands
Display size	13"
Systems supported	7.0.1 and higher with enough memory

INTERNAL SYSTEMS

RAM (min and max)	4 to 10 MB-30 pin
RAM speed	100 ns
RAM slots	2 slots, install 2 SIMMs at a time
VRAM (standard)	256K
NuBus slots	none
PDS slots	one
SCSI transfer rate	1.5 MB/second
Power supply	Int'l
Maximum wattage	50
Bus width	16 MHz, 16-bit/32-bit
FPU	MC68882 optional
MMU	built-in
ROM size	512K
Memory cache	none

EXTERNAL STORAGE SYSTEMS

Hard drive	80 MB internal and external
Floppy drive	1.4 MB, 800K, 400K
CD-ROM	external only
Serial ports	two
ADB ports	one
Sound input	mono
Sound output	mono
Network availability	LocalTalk, EtherTalk with card

Courtesy of Apple Computer, Inc.

Figure G.23 Macintosh LC.

LC

GENERAL PRODUCT INFORMATION

Introduction date	10/15/90
Discontinued	3/23/92
Processor	68020
Clock speed	16 MHz
MIPS rating	2.6
Display resolution	card dependent
Color depth	up to thousands
Display size	card dependent
Systems supported	6.0.7 and higher with enough memory

INTERNAL SYSTEMS

RAM (min and max)	2 to 10 MB-30 pin
RAM speed	100 ns
RAM slots	2 slots, install 2 SIMMs at a time
VRAM (standard)	256K
NuBus slots	none
PDS slots	one
SCSI transfer rate	1.25 MB/second
Power supply	Int'l
Maximum wattage	50
Bus width	16 MHz, 16-bit/32-bit
FPU	MC68881 optional
MMU	built-in
ROM size	512K
Memory cache	none

EXTERNAL STORAGE SYSTEMS

Hard drive	80 MB internal and external
Floppy drive	1.4 MB, 800K, 400K
CD-ROM	external only
Serial ports	two
ADB ports	one
Sound input	mono
Sound output	mono
Network availability	LocalTalk, EtherTalk with card

Color Classic, Performa 250

GENERAL PRODUCT INFORMATION

Introduction date	2/10/93
Discontinued	5/16/94
Processor	68030
Clock speed	16 MHz
MIPS rating	3.9
Display resolution	512×384
Color depth	8-bit
Display size	10"
Systems supported	7.1, Enabler 401

INTERNAL SYSTEMS

RAM (min and max)	4 to 10 MB-30 pin
RAM speed	100 ns
RAM slots	2 slots, install 2 SIMMs at a time
VRAM (standard)	none
NuBus slots	none
PDS slots	one LC PDS
SCSI transfer rate	1.25 MB/second
Power supply	Int'l
Maximum wattage	100
Bus width	16 MHz, 16-bit/32-bit
FPU	MC68882 optional
MMU	built-in
ROM size	1024K
Memory cache	none

EXTERNAL STORAGE SYSTEMS

Hard drive	40 to 160 MB internal and external
Floppy drive	1.4 MB, 800K, 400K
CD-ROM	external only
Serial ports	two
ADB ports	two
Sound input	mono
Sound output	mono
Network availability	LocalTalk
	Only sold in Japan.

Color Classic II (Japan only)

GENERAL PRODUCT INFORMATION

Introduction date	10/21/93
Discontinued	
Processor	68030
Clock speed	33 MHz
MIPS rating	3.9
Display resolution	640×480
Color depth	1-bit
Display size	10"
Systems supported	7.1J, Enabler 403

INTERNAL SYSTEMS

RAM (min and max)	4 to 36 MB-72 pin
RAM speed	80 ns
RAM slots	1 slot, install 1 SIMM at a time
VRAM (standard)	256K
NuBus slots	none
PDS slots	1 LC PDS
SCSI transfer rate	1.5 MB/second
Power supply	Int'l only
Maximum wattage	100
Bus width	33 MHz, 32-bit/32-bit
FPU	MC68882 optional
MMU	built-in
ROM size	512K
Memory cache	none

EXTERNAL STORAGE SYSTEMS

Hard drive	40 to 80 MB internal and external
Floppy drive	1.4 MB, 800K, 400K
CD-ROM	external only
Serial ports	two
ADB ports	one
Sound input	mono
Sound output	mono
Network availability	LocalTalk

Figure G.24 The Mac Classic II shares the same case as the Performa 200. The only difference is the name tag.

Classic II

GENERAL PRODUCT INFORMATION

Introduction date	10/21/91
Discontinued	9/13/93
Processor	68030
Clock speed	16 MHz
MIPS rating	3.9
Display resolution	512×342
Color depth	1-bit
Display size	9"
Systems supported	7.0.1 and higher with enough memory

INTERNAL SYSTEMS

RAM (min and max)	2 to 10 MB-30 pin
RAM speed	100 ns
RAM slots	2 slots, install 2 SIMMs at a time
VRAM (standard)	none
NuBus slots	none
PDS slots	none
SCSI transfer rate	1.25 MB/second
Power supply	U.S. only
Maximum wattage	76

Bus width	16 MHz, 16-bit/32-bit
FPU	MC68882 optional
MMU	built-in
ROM size	512K
Memory cache	none

EXTERNAL STORAGE SYSTEMS

Hard drive	40 to 80 MB internal and external
Floppy drive	1.4 MB, 800K, 400K
CD-ROM	external only
Serial ports	two
ADB ports	one
Sound input	mono
Sound output	mono
Network availability	LocalTalk

Classic

GENERAL PRODUCT INFORMATION

Introduction date	10/15/90
Discontinued	9/14/92
Processor	68000
Clock speed	8 MHz
MIPS rating	0.7
Display resolution	512×342
Color depth	1-bit
Display size	9"
Systems supported	6.0.7 and up with enough memory

INTERNAL SYSTEMS

RAM (min and max)	1 to 5 MB–30 pin
RAM speed	120ns
RAM slots	2 slots, install 2 SIMMs at a time
VRAM (standard)	none
NuBus slots	none
PDS slots	none
SCSI transfer rate	1.25 MB/second
Power supply	Int'l
Maximum wattage	76
Bus width	8 MHz, 16-bit/24-bit only
FPU	none
MMU	none
ROM size	512K
Memory cache	none

EXTERNAL STORAGE SYSTEMS

Hard drive	40 or 80 MB internal and external
Floppy drive	400K, 800K, or 1.4MB
CD-ROM	external
Serial ports	two
ADB ports	one
Sound input	none
Sound output	mono
Network availability	LocalTalk

Courtesy of Apple Computer, Inc.

Figure G.26 Macintosh SE/30.

SE/30

GENERAL PRODUCT INFORMATION

Introduction date	1/19/89
Discontinued	10/21/90
Processor	68030
Clock speed	16 MHz
MIPS rating	3.9
Display resolution	512×342
Color depth	1-bit (8-bit QuickDraw built-in)
Display size	9"
Systems supported	6.0.3 and higher with enough memory

INTERNAL SYSTEMS

RAM (min and max)	1 to 32 MB-30 pin
RAM speed	120 ns
RAM slots	8 slots, install 4 SIMMs at a time
VRAM (standard)	64K
NuBus slots	none
PDS slots	1
SCSI transfer rate	1.25 MB/second
Power supply	Int'l
Maximum wattage	75
Bus width	16 MHz, 32-bit/24-bit
FPU	MC68882
MMU	built-in
ROM size	256K
Memory cache	none

EXTERNAL STORAGE SYSTEMS

Hard drive	40 or 80 MB internal and external
Floppy drive	1.4 MB, 800K, 400K
CD-ROM	external only
Serial ports	two
ADB ports	two
Sound input	none
Sound output	stereo
Network availability	LocalTalk, EtherTalk w/card

Courtesy of Apple Computer, Inc.

Figure G.27 Macintosh IIfx.

IIfx

GENERAL PRODUCT INFORMATION

Introduction date	3/19/90
Discontinued	4/15/92
Processor	68030
Clock speed	40 MHz
MIPS rating	9.1
Display resolution	card dependent
Color depth	up to millions
Display size	card dependent
Systems supported	6.0.4 and higher with enough memory

INTERNAL SYSTEMS

RAM (min and max)	4 to 128 MB-64 pin
RAM speed	80 ns
RAM slots	8 slots, install 4 SIMMs at a time
VRAM (standard)	none
NuBus slots	6
PDS slots	one
SCSI transfer rate	3.0 MB/second
Power supply	Int'l
Maximum wattage	230
Bus width	40 MHz, 32-bit/32-bit
FPU	MC68882
MMU	built-in
ROM size	512K
Memory cache	32K

EXTERNAL STORAGE SYSTEMS

Hard drive	40 to 160MB internal and external
Floppy drive	1.4 MB, 800K, 400K
CD-ROM	external only
Serial ports	two
ADB ports	two
Sound input	none
Sound output	stereo
Network availability	LocalTalk, EtherTalk w/card

IIci, IIcx

GENERAL PRODUCT INFORMATION

Introduction date	9/20/89	3/7/89
Discontinued	2/10/93	3/11/91
Processor	68030	68030
Clock speed	25 MHz	16 MHz
MIPS rating	6.3	3.9
Display resolution	card dependent	card dependent
Color depth	up to millions	up to millions
Display size	card dependent	card dependent
Systems supported	6.0.4 and higher with enough memory	6.0.3 and higher with enough memory

INTERNAL SYSTEMS

RAM (min and max)	1 to 32 MB-30 pin	1 to 32 MB-30 pin
RAM speed	80 ns	120 ns
RAM slots	8 slots, install 4 SIMMs at a time	8 slots, install 4 SIMMs at a time
VRAM (standard)	none	none
NuBus slots	3	3
PDS slots	none	none
SCSI transfer rate	1.25 MB/second	1.25 MB/second
Power supply	Int'l	Int'l
Maximum wattage	90	90
Bus width	25 MHz, 32-bit/24-bit	16 MHz, 32-bit/24-bit
FPU	MC68882	MC68882
MMU	built-in	built-in
ROM size	512K	256K
Memory cache	32K (optional on early models, standard later)	none

EXTERNAL STORAGE SYSTEMS

Hard drive	40 or 80 MB internal and external	40 or 80 MB internal and external
Floppy drive	1.4 MB, 800K, 400K	1.4 MB, 800K, 400K
CD-ROM	external only	external only
Serial ports	two	two
ADB ports	two	two
Sound input	none	none
Sound output	stereo	stereo
Network availability	LocalTalk, EtherTalk with card	LocalTalk, EtherTalk with card

IIx

GENERAL PRODUCT INFORMATION

Introduction date	9/19/88
Discontinued	10/15/90
Processor	68030
Clock speed	16 MHz
MIPS rating	3.9
Display resolution	card dependent
Color depth	up to millions
Display size	card dependent
Systems supported	6.0.2 and higher with enough memory

INTERNAL SYSTEMS

RAM (min and max)	1 to 32 MB-30 pin
RAM speed	120 ns
RAM slots	8 slots, install 4 SIMMs at a time
VRAM (standard)	256K
NuBus slots	6
PDS slots	none
SCSI transfer rate	1.25 MB/second
Power supply	Int'l
Maximum wattage	230
Bus width	16 MHz, 32-bit/24-bit
FPU	MC68882
MMU	built-in
ROM size	256K
Memory cache	none

EXTERNAL STORAGE SYSTEMS

Hard drive	40 or 80 MB internal and external
Floppy drive	800K, 400K, and 1.4 MB
CD-ROM	external only
Serial ports	two
ADB ports	two
Sound input	none
Sound output	stereo
Network availability	LocalTalk, EtherTalk w/card

II

GENERAL PRODUCT INFORMATION

Introduction date	3/1/87
Discontinued	1/1/90
Processor	68020
Clock speed	16 MHz
MIPS rating	3.4
Display resolution	card-dependent
Color depth	up to millions
Display size	card dependent
Systems supported	4.0.1 and up with enough memory

INTERNAL SYSTEMS

RAM (min and max)	1 to 20 MB-30 pin
RAM speed	120ns
RAM slots	8 slots, install 4 SIMMs at a time
VRAM (standard)	256K
NuBus slots	6
PDS slots	none
SCSI transfer rate	1.25 MB/second
Power supply	Int'l
Maximum wattage	230
Bus width	16 MHz,32-bit/24-bit
FPU	68881
MMU	68851 optional
ROM size	256K
Memory cache	none

EXTERNAL STORAGE SYSTEMS

Hard drive	40 or 80 MB internal and external
Floppy drive	800K, 400K, 1.4 MB
CD-ROM	external only
Serial ports	two
ADB ports	two
Sound input	none
Sound output	mono
Network availability	LocalTalk, EtherTalk with card

Cross-Platform Macintosh Computers

Power Macintosh 6100/66 DOS

Power Macintosh 6100/66 DOS

GENERAL PRODUCT INFORMATION

Introduction date	2/28/94
Discontinued	6/13/94
Processor	68040/486SX–25
Clock speed	25 MHz
MIPS rating	22
Display resolution	640×480 to 1024×768 or card dependent
Color depth	up to millions on built-in video
Display size	built-in 13" through 21" OR card dependent
Systems supported	7.1, Enabler 040 v1.1

INTERNAL SYSTEMS

RAM (min and max)	4 to 68 MB–72 pin
RAM speed	80 ns
RAM slots	2 slots, install 1 SIMM at a time
VRAM (standard)	512K
NuBus slots	none
PDS slots	Filled—486SX-25
SCSI transfer rate	5.0 MB/second
Power supply	Int'l
Maximum wattage	202
Bus width	25 MHz, 32-bit/32-bit
FPU	MC68882
MMU	built-in
ROM size	1024K
Memory cache	none

EXTERNAL STORAGE SYSTEMS

Hard drive	230 to 1GB internal and external
Floppy drive	1.4 MB, 800K, 400K
CD-ROM	2x internal or external
Serial ports	two
ADB ports	two
Sound input	mono
Sound output	stereo
Network availability	LocalTalk or EtherTalk

Quadra 640

Quadra640 DOS

GENERAL PRODUCT INFORMATION

Introduction date	2/28/94
Discontinued	6/13/94
Processor	68040/486SX–25
Clock speed	25 MHz
MIPS rating	22
Display resolution	640×480 to 1024×768 or card dependent
Color depth	up to millions on built-in video
Display size	built-in 13" through 21" OR card dependent
Systems supported	7.1, Enabler 040 v1.1

INTERNAL SYSTEMS

RAM (min and max)	4 to 68MB-72 pin
RAM speed	80 ns
RAM slots	2 slots, install 1 SIMM at a time
VRAM (standard)	512K
NuBus slots	none
PDS slots	Filled—486SX-25
SCSI transfer rate	5.0 MB/second
Power supply	Int'l
Maximum wattage	202
Bus width	25 MHz, 32-bit/32-bit
FPU	MC68882
MMU	built-in
ROM size	1024K
Memory cache	none

EXTERNAL STORAGE SYSTEMS

Hard drive	230 to 1GB internal and external
Floppy drive	1.4 MB, 800K, 400K
CD-ROM	2x internal or external
Serial ports	two
ADB ports	two
Sound input	mono
Sound output	stereo
Network availability	LocalTalk or EtherTalk

Quadra610 DOS

GENERAL PRODUCT INFORMATION

Introduction date	2/28/94
Discontinued	6/13/94
Processor	68040/486SX–25
Clock speed	25 MHz
MIPS rating	22
Display resolution	640×480 to 1024×768 or card dependent
Color depth	up to millions on built-in video
Display size	built-in 13" through 21" OR card dependent
Systems supported	7.1, Enabler 040 v1.1

INTERNAL SYSTEMS

RAM (min and max)	4 to 68 MB-72 pin
RAM speed	80 ns
RAM slots	2 slots, install 1 SIMM at a time
VRAM (standard)	512K
NuBus slots	none
PDS slots	Filled—486SX-25
SCSI transfer rate	5.0 MB/second
Power supply	Int'l
Maximum wattage	202
Bus width	25 MHz, 32-bit/32-bit
FPU	MC68882
MMU	built-in
ROM size	1024K
Memory cache	none

EXTERNAL STORAGE SYSTEMS

Hard drive	230 to 1GB internal and external
Floppy drive	1.4 MB, 800K, 400K
CD-ROM	2x internal or external
Serial ports	two
ADB ports	two
Sound input	mono
Sound output	stereo
Network availability	LocalTalk or EtherTalk

GLOSSARY

Actuator. The motor that moves the read/write head over the platters. Voice coil actuators are used in better drives; cheaper drives often use a clumsy Stepper-motor based actuator. Stepper motors cannot provide the fine control of a voice coil actuator.

ADB (Apple Desktop Bus). The Apple Desktop Bus is a serial interface designed for connecting input devices to the Mac. Pass-through connectors on each device (if present) enable you to chain several devices together. The ADB handles data signals and the electrical power supply. Nearly all types of input devices conform to the ADB standard, except graphics tablets, which require a faster data rate than the ADB port.

Aspect Ratio. The aspect ratio of a monitor is measured in number of pixels wide by number of pixels high. For instance, the Applecolor 13-inch monitor's aspect ratio is 640×480 pixels, or 72 dpi. A higher aspect ratio does not mean better visual quality. A monitor displaying a higher aspect ratio on the same 13-inch display does not make a sharper image—just more working area. It is the same as opening a camera lens wider; you can see more, but at smaller sizes. A high aspect ratio can come in handy in some applications, such as desktop publishing, when you need to look at different views of a page.

AT commands. Modems speak to your computer using their own language. The words in this language are based on the "Hayes standard," which consists of lines of commands that begin with the letters AT (for attention). Basic commands are standard across modems (see Table 1); more advanced commands, such as error control, data compression, and selection of high speeds, are specific to each manufacturer. Many manufacturers provide a list of the proper commands. Check the modem's manuals for details about your modem's special commands.

Fortunately, most modem software can either automatically sense the type of modem you have or will ask you to specify the modem and can then provide the necessary AT commands automatically.

Table 1   Basic AT Commands

Command	Function	Comments
A	Answer phone	
DT n	Tone Dial	n = number to dial, use commas for pauses
DP n	Pulse Dial	n = number to dial, use commas for pauses
Hn	Hook	H0 hangs up, H1 answers phone
Mn	Speaker	M0 turns off, M1 turns on
Z	Reset	Sets modem to power-on settings
+++	Command	Returns modem to command state
O	Online	Returns to on-line (opposite of +++)
S0= n	Answer Rings	Sets ring # to answer phone
S7= n	Wait time	Time to wait for remote modem

Preface each command with AT.

You may combine multiple commands into one command (e.g., AT M0 DT 1234). For example, to disable call waiting, preface the number you're dialing with *70, (e.g., ATDT *70,555-1212).

AV. Audio/Video, or Audio/Visual.

BPS (bits per second). The speed at which your modem communicates determines how much you can get done and how quickly. The rate at which the modem's speed is measured is bits per second (bps): the number of 0s and 1s that go across the phone line per second.

In real world terms, a 100K spreadsheet file would take about seven minutes to send at 2,400 bps; at 14,400 bps the same file could be sent in one minute. Because most on-line services charge by the minute (your local phone company certainly does), a faster modem can help cut down on bills.

Bus. The connections (wires, etc.) over which electrical signals are transmitted. Mac drives use the Mac's SCSI bus, and some SCSI accelerator cards use the Mac's NuBus.

Carpal Tunnel Syndrome. Carpal tunnel syndrome results from bending the wrist while typing; this is the most common repetitive stress injury affecting the hand. Pain can extend from the fingers to the shoulders, but usually is most noticeable in the wrist. Failure to seek medical attention can increase the severity and result in long-term effects.

Note

The term "baud" is used to describe modem speed, but for technical reasons is no longer accurate. Use "bps" to describe modem speed.

CCD. Charge Coupled Devices perform various electronic tasks. They are the sensing devices most commonly used in flatbed scanners, and convert light energy into electrical energy. They were used in the early digital delay lines for audio because they could retain a charge (a digital "on") for a brief period of time.

Chording Keyboard. Chording keyboards use only a few keys or buttons to enter alphanumeric characters, instead of a separate key for each character. You press combinations of keys (like playing chords on the piano) to enter letters and numbers.

CMYK. In four-color printing, the three primary colors are not the familiar red, green, and blue, but (C)yan, (M)agenta, and (Y)ellow, with Blac(K) added for convenience in printing text. The distinction between RGB and CMYK is important because light reflected from a printed page is not the same as light emerging from a video monitor. For example, when you see a red area on a printed page, the ink absorbs all colors except red, and reflects only red light. In contrast, when the light comes directly from a monitor, you see only the actual color of the light it produces. As a consequence, the color separator must produce transparencies containing shades of cyan, magenta, and yellow. When printed with ink on paper, these colors mix together to produce the original colors as reflected light.

Command Overhead. This is a measurement of the time it takes for the computer's command to be interpreted and acted upon by the controller.

Composite Video. In broadcast television signals, the transmitter bundles many different components into a composite signal. The composite video signal may include monophonic audio, stereo audio, black and white, and color information. High end home video recorders provide separate signals for the intensity of each color (S-Video); computers frequently output red, green, and blue separately.

Controller. The electronics on the hard drive that allow the drive to process data independently of the Mac's CPU. This circuitry controls the spindle motor's spin up and speed, actuator movement, and some housekeeping utilities.

CPU. Central Processing Unit, or main chip found on the computer's logic board processor. The CPU in Centris, Quadra, and AV Macs is the 68040; Power Macs use the PowerPC 601, 603, 603e, and 604 CPUs.

Data Compression. Data compression allows a modem to compress transmitted data in a manner similar to compression utilities used with a hard disk. This effectively speeds up transmission of data, by reducing the amount of 1s and 0s the computer actually has to send for a file. Note that data compression protocols are used in conjunction with error correction protocols. The types of compression a modem supports are described by its compression protocols. See Table 2 for an overview of compression protocols.

Table 2 Data Compression Protocols	
Protocol	*Comments*
MNP 5	max. compression 2:1. (requires MNP 4)
CCITT V.42bis	max. compression 4:1. (requires V.42)

Data Link. The data link is a subdivision of the network protocol that provides details about how and at what speed computers will communicate. LocalTalk and Ethernet are common data links used on the Macintosh.

Dot Matrix. Dot matrix printers take page description instructions from the Mac and use an impact head and ink ribbon to shuffle back and forth across the page—line by line and dot by dot—impacting the ink ribbon and the paper.

Dot Pitch. Dot pitch is the space between the pixels, which are the tiny points of light in rows across and down the screen. Smaller dots enable a monitor to display more detailed and sharper images—if the monitor is calibrated correctly. High-quality monitors have a dot pitch of 0.28 mm or less. A low dot pitch is necessary for fine detail work with images and CAD/CAM work, where accuracy is very important. Because smaller pixels can be moved more densely together, a higher degree of detail can be achieved on-screen. Poor dot pitch ratings—in the high .30 and even .40+ mm range—are not recommended for exacting Mac work.

Drivers. The software that translates Macintosh system requests into SCSI commands to the hard drive.

Drum Scanner. Drum scanners use a rapidly spinning drum to scan artwork wrapped around the drum; a scanning head moves down the length of the drum during the scan. Generally, drum scanners use photomultiplier tubes (PMTs), which have a greater range of intensity values than other sensing devices. Because of the use of PMTs, and the fact that the sensing head can be within millimeters of the artwork, drum scanners generally provide the highest quality image.

DSP. Digital Signal Processor chipset that can process incoming signals in real time independently of another onboard CPU.

Duty Cycles. Maintenance of a printer is defined by its duty cycles. The duty cycle of the printer's most used (and abused) parts is the amount of time—usually measured in pages—that a part will last. Parts include ink, toner, or wax refills and replacement, periodic part and print head replacement, necessary cleaning of internal parts, or paper tray refills. Obviously, printers that can be cleaned and serviced by the user are preferable to printers that require service from an authorized service center.

Duty cycles are similar to gas mileage. Some of the sleekest, fastest cars are the worst gas hogs and are difficult to maintain without special knowledge or a lot of money. The same is true with a printer—the fastest, most vivid, most realistic, or biggest format printers are fussy, media intensive, and require special technicians to keep them running. Dye Sublimation printers, for example, can only print a hundred pages before they need new media.

Monochrome inkjet printers are among the easiest to maintain. When the ink runs out, open the cover, pop the old cartridge out, pop the new one in, close the cover, and it's ready to go.

Dvorak Keyboard. An alternative arrangement of the standard QWERTY keyboard layout on a typewriter or computer keyboard. The Dvorak keyboard layout facilitates rapid data entry.

Dye Sublimation. Dye sublimation printing is the most accurate continuous tone color reproduction printing available for the Mac. Mixed color dye is printed on special (read: expensive) paper; the average per-page cost can exceed $3 to $5. Dye sublimation printers can print near-photographic quality prints.

Edit Decision List. Video editing systems that permit random access editing enable the user to create an Edit Decision List (EDL). This set of instructions tells the computer where to enter and exit each video clip as it assembles a complete program or program segment.

EnergyStar Rating. Low power consumption is a key consideration when evaluating monitors. Less power means less energy consumed—saving money on electricity. The EPA's new EnergyStar rating of equipment that requires less than 15 watts of power is the latest stamp of politically correct hardware usage. Few monitors actually meet the standard unless they go into a sleep mode during inactive periods. Software such as Display Power Management Signaling from NEC induces this mode.

Ergonomics. Ergonomics, or "human engineering," seeks to find designs and interfaces that both enhance productivity and decrease discomfort and injury resulting from the use of different products.

Error Correction. Error correction insures that random static on the telephone line doesn't interfere with data transfer. Correction circuits constantly monitor communications looking for errors. When these circuits detect an error in transmission, they ask the remote modem to resend information.

The type of correction a modem supports is described by its correction protocols. See Table 3 for a description of error correction protocols.

Table 3	Error Correction Protocols
Protocol	*Comments*
MNP 4	Basic error control
V.42	More advanced error control (includes MNP 4)
MNP 10	Designed for cellular modems

Flatbed Scanner. Flatbed scanners look like the typical office copy machine. After you place the artwork on a flat glass plate and close the cover, a scanning head moves down the page. Some color scanners make three passes—each pass with a different color filter—and others make only a single pass, capturing all three colors at once. Neither design is inherently superior or faster than the other.

FPUs and Floating Point Math. The floating point unit (FPU) or math coprocessor is mostly used in CAD and 3-D rendering programs. Sometimes the FPU is used in complex spreadsheets—statistical and scientific calculations that use trigonometric functions and square roots. Macs use SANE routines to process numeric calculations. An FPU can speed calculations because SANE traps built into programs route mathematical processes and instructions away from the ROM code to the FPU. SANE routines are more accurate (they exceed the accuracy recommended by the IEEE standards), but FPU routines are fine for most applications.

The advantage of the FPU is speed when floating point calculations are required. If an FPU is to be added to a system, clock speeds of the FPU and CPU should match. Typical increases in floating point performance are in the range of 400 to 800 percent depending on cards and clock speeds.

Graphics Tablet. Graphics tablets contain a wire grid that senses where the stylus moves and translates the data into screen positions. You simply draw on the surface of the tablet with a stylus. Graphics tablets are designed for computer illustrators.

Handheld Scanner. Handheld scanners are small, portable devices usually about half the width of a letter size page. They use motorized rubber wheels to move down the page, but require assistance from the operator to keep them at right angles with the margin.

Home Keys. On a Mac QWERTY keyboard, the D and K keys are the home keys for touch typing. Frequently, they have little bumps on them so that the typist can find them by touch.

Hot Switching. A printer that features hot switching capabilities can print from multiple platforms simultaneously, intelligently spooling the incoming jobs and automatically switching the input languages to match the page description language.

Imagesetter. Imagesetters are high-density Postscript printers that can print at resolutions in excess of 5000+ dots per inch. Photosensitive paper film is etched with laser light and develops like a picture. Imagesetters are the prepress link to the Macintosh. Most professional color publishing done on the Mac is sent to imagesetters for the highest black-and-white resolution, or to produce color-separated halftones for traditional 4-color print reproduction.

Inkjet. Inkjet printers "jet," or spray, ink in small dots as a fast-traveling print head moves in both directions.

Interactive Media. Interactive media enable the user to choose the order and content of a presentation. Interactive instructional materials permit a user to branch off to ask for more detailed explanations, or to select more remedial topics. Interactive entertainment media enable users to make choices about plot lines, character development, and so on.

Interlaced and Noninterlaced. These terms are used in reference to the display method used by the monitor. *Interlaced* monitors are NTSC monitors—like televisions and standard television technology—that produce an image on-screen by passing from the top to the bottom of the screen twice in 1/60 of a second. The first pass creates 50% of the image; the second pass fills in every other line in the image—the second pass is *interlaced* with the first. They write 60 separate "fields" per second to the screen in an odd/even sequence; each field contains the odd (followed by the even) lines, which, when combined, make a full frame. *Noninterlaced* displays (used on computers) display 30 full-sized frames per second.

Internetwork. When a large number of LANs are connected, but they don't cover large geographical distances, the LANs are referred to as an *internetwork*. Note that this is completely different from the much-publicized Internet network, which is actually a Wide Area Network (WAN).

Joystick. Joysticks resemble the steering control found in airplanes and are most frequently used for playing computer games and flight simulators. Joysticks move the cursor around on-screen by means of a vertical handle, instead of a rolling ball. Usually, joysticks have one or more buttons for activating various game functions.

Kiosk. A kiosk is a free-standing display or booth that provides information to the general public through interactive media. Touch screens are frequently used to allow browsers to touch an area of the screen to activate a command or ask for information on a particular subject. Kiosks are often used for directories of hotel services, tourist information, demonstrating products, and giving directions to local points of interest.

Laser Printer. Laser printers use a laser that reads the data stream from the print description source—the PostScript or QuickDraw bytes streaming from the print controller— and "etches" an electrostatic image on a spinning metal drum. This image attracts and applies positively charged dry black toner to the paper as the paper is rolled under the rotating drum. From there, the paper makes its way under a hot fuser that dries and permanently solidifies the toner on the page.

Latency Time. The time it takes for the spinning platters to move the specific platter to the read/write head. Some drive manufacturers now have two actuators—each mounted on opposite sides of the platter—to reduce by half the time it takes the platter to get to the read/write head.

Local Area Network (LAN). Computers, printers, and other computer devices in one location that are connected by networking hardware and software.

Macro. A short execution script triggered by an input function; i.e. speech recognition.

Megabyte/Gigabyte. A megabyte is 1,000,000 bytes of information; this is the most common measuring stick of hard drive capacity. Larger drives are measured in gigabytes—1,000 megabytes equals one gigabyte.

Modulation Protocols. The speed at which your modem can communicate is determined by modulation protocols. Some protocols are designed by specific modem manufacturers; others are an industry standard that are compatible with most modems. See Table 4 for an overview of the most common modulation protocols.

Mouse. A mouse uses a rolling ball on the bottom, and an optical sensor to determine relative position of a cursor on-screen. The mouse enables you to move the cursor around the screen and to select various items. The mouse button enables you to select items the cursor is physically over or has highlighted.

Multi-Processing. Technology utilized by AV Macs to process events apart from the main CPU chip. Apple uses a chipset from AT&T and another from Philips electronics to process speech, video, and telephone on the AV Macs.

Negotiation. Two modems can only talk to each other using speed, correction, and compression protocols that they share. Immediately upon connection, modems "negotiate" with each other to determine the highest speed and best error correction and compression protocols they can share.

Table 4   Modulation Protocols

Protocol	Speed	Comments
Bell 103	300 bps	U.S. standard
Bell 212A	1,200 bps	U.S. standard
V.22	1,200 bps	Standard outside U.S.
V.22 bis	2,400 bps	International standard
V.32	9,600 & 4,800 bps	International standard
V.32 bis	14,400 bps	International standard
U.S. Robotics HST	9,600/14,400/16,800	U.S. Robotics modems only
Telebit PEP	14,400	Telebit modems only
Hayes Express 96	9,600	Hayes modems only
V.fast/V.terbo/V.34	19,200-28,800 bps	Proprietary/not yet finalized

If you have trouble getting your modem to connect with a particular remote modem, check the manual for ways to disable auto-negotiation and to force a particular speed and/or correction protocol that you know both sides share.

Network Protocol. Network protocols are a set of rules computers agree to use when speaking to each other.

Node. An individual device (computer, printer, network modem, and so on) on a network is referred to as a network node.

NTSC. NTSC stands for National Television Standards Committee, an industry group that evaluated the various systems proposed for color television in the 1950s. The system they recommended to the FCC, and which that group ultimately approved, is called the NTSC format. The NTSC format (525 lines, interlaced at 1/60 second) is used in the U.S. and Japan.

NuBus. NuBus is the most common type of expansion slot used on the Mac. Because NuBus cards use a standard set of commands to communicate with the computer, NuBus cards generally work in any Macintosh model that has a NuBus slot.

NuBus '90. NuBus '90 is an upwardly compatible redesign of the NuBus interface. Increased speed and more versatile power handling are some of NuBus '90s new features.

OCR. Optical Character Recognition (OCR) software translates a scanned image of a printed page into word processor text.

OnLine/OffLine. Online refers to the state of the modem or Mac when it is connected to another modem. Offline is the state of the modem or Mac when it's not connected to another computer.

Optical Resolution. The optical resolution of a scanner is a measure of how many dots per inch (dpi) it actually can capture. Through software interpolation scanners offer still greater resolution. Regardless, optical resolution is more important when high-quality is necessary; the better the optical resolution, the better the interpolated resolution.

OSI. The OSI (Open Systems Interconnection) is a seven layer conceptual model of network protocols developed by the International Standards Organization.

Packet. The individual pieces of data sent between computers on a network are referred to as packets.

PAL. PAL is the color broadcast format widely used in Europe. The primary difference from the American format is that it operates at 50 Hz, rather than 60 Hz. As a result, this standard has a more noticeable flicker.

Parallel Port. A parallel port sends and receives data by using one wire for every bit in the data byte. The data is sent in parallel, rather than in series, enabling more data to be transmitted in less time.

PCI. PCI is an open standard for expansion cards jointly developed by over 150 companies. The PCI standard is popular on Intel (x86) platforms because it offers high speeds (greater than NuBus or NuBus '90) and low power requirements.

PDS. PDS is an alternative form of expansion slot available in many Macs. PDS cards connect directly to the CPU in the Mac, instead of through a standard interface like the NuBus. Because of this direct connection, PDS cards must be designed for each type of Mac model.

PhoneNET. PhoneNET is the networking scheme that uses unshielded twisted-pair wiring to connect Macs; LocalTalk is the data link.

Photo CD. Kodak's Photo CD format stores traditional photographs on special-format CD-ROMs. These discs are readable in nearly all CD-ROM drives, and in many audio CD players that are Photo CD-compatible. When you visit your photofinisher and request the "prints" in Photo CD format, the prints are returned on a Photo CD. You can load these images into your Mac or view them on a TV set with the proper Photo CD player. The images are stored in five different resolutions to accommodate a variety of needs.

Photodiode. Photodiodes convert light energy into electrical energy, and are used in high-end flatbed scanners. Their performance lies somewhere between Charged Coupled Devices (CCDs) and Photo Multiplier Tubes (PMTs).

Pixel. A pixel, or "picture element," is the smallest dot of information that a monitor can display and a scanner can scan. The more pixels a monitor can display, the higher the resolution.

PlainTalk. Apple technology that was written to understand speech as an input device. PlainTalk will perform functions based on speech, such as when you say "Open" a macro executes that goes to the file menu and pulls down "Open." This type of input replaces traditional mouse input.

Platters. The spinning disk(s) within the hard drive mechanism that are used to hold information.

PMT. Photomultiplier tubes (PMTs) are the sensing devices typically used on high-end drum scanners. They offer greater dynamic range (more shades of color) than other sensing devices.

PostScript and QuickDraw. PostScript and QuickDraw are page description languages used by the software on your Mac. When you want to print your work, the software you are using outputs the PostScript or QuickDraw file to the printer. The file is then interpreted by the printer if the printer is capable of reading that particular language. PostScript is licensed by Adobe Corporation to software and hardware companies; QuickDraw is the Mac's built-in, or native, page description language.

PostScript-capable Macintosh printers can read QuickDraw, but not the other way around. Some software, such as Adobe Illustrator and FreeHand, are PostScript software packages that work with PostScript printers or machines running a clone of the PostScript interpreter language.

Adobe licensing costs and the larger memory needed by on-board PostScript printers raises the price of PostScript-compatible printers; QuickDraw-only printers always cost less. Nevertheless, PostScript is used throughout high-end publishing and printing industries. A PostScript printer is one of the requirements of an effective proofing system, and helps in prepress work. By looking at laser proofs, you can discover print anomalies before you take your files to a service bureau for expensive high-resolution imagesetter output.

Pressure-Sensitive Pen. Some graphics tablets offer a pressure sensitive stylus, which mimics the behavior of a pen, brush, or pencil on a surface. By pressing harder, you can make the stroke width wider or increase the color density.

Protocol. The languages that computers use to speak to each other.

QuickTime. Apple Computer's format for video compression and playback. QuickTime also accommodates multiple digital audio tracks.

QWERTY Keyboard. The standard arrangement of keys on a typewriter or computer keyboard. Originally developed for use on early typewriters, this layout intentionally slows typists to prevent the typewriter keys from jamming. It is named QWERTY because of the first few keys in the top row.

RAID. Redundant Array of Inexpensive Disks.

H

RAM Cache Boards. A RAM cache stores frequently used instructions and data in a special area of RAM so that the CPU can access the data quickly when it is needed. Under System 7, the Memory control panel is used to set the amount of cache; System 6 provides cache settings in its General control panel.

The application of cache is more important today because the microprocessors in modern Macs greatly exceeds the speed of memory and hard drive components. Apple recommends that 32K of cache be reserved for system use for every 1 MB of RAM installed. This is a controversial number, however, and some users report that the Mac, due to a poor search algorithm, will actually slow down when large caches are set. Other users report that a particular cache setting results in specific programs "feeling" faster. Experimentation is the key to resolving the exact setting suitable for your work.

Refresh Rate. The refresh rate is the speed at which the electron gun inside the monitor draws the screen—quickly scanning a beam sequentially from top to bottom. The faster the electron gun can write, the more stable and flicker-free the screen appears, and the higher the screen refresh rate. Poorer quality monitors have lower refresh rate and produce a flicker similar to a fluorescent light. This flicker is very hard on your eyes.

Repetitive Stress Injuries. Repetitive stress injuries result from performing the same action(s) over and over, with little or no variation. This type of injury is common among computer users, musicians, athletes, and assembly line workers.

Resolution. Printer resolution directly affects the visible quality of documents and artwork. Resolution is measured in dots per inch (dpi)—horizontally and vertically. Higher resolution printers usually cost more because of the increased memory storage necessary to hold the higher resolution images, as well as increased consumables. For instance, a 600 × 600 dpi laser uses twice the toner of a 300 × 300 dpi laser.

RGB. When working with light, the three primary colors are (R)ed, (G)reen, and (B)lue. Color monitors are called RGB monitors. (See also CMYK.)

RISC. Reduced Instruction Set Computer chips are used in Power Macs. RISC chips can execute far faster than standard CISC (Complex Instruction Set Computer) chips used in PCs and pre-Power Macs.

SCSI. Small Computer System Interface (SCSI) is a standard for how computers and peripherals communicate. SCSI is Apple's primary hard drive bus interface.

SECAM. SECAM is the color video format used in France and Russia. It provides the best picture quality of the three standards (NTSC, PAL, and SECAM), but requires relatively expensive video switchers because it uses time delay.

Sector. A physical subdivision of each track on the hard disk platter. Sector size is determined by the amount of data a particular type of Mac can read at a time. In many cases 512 bytes is the sector size for Macs.

Seek Time. The time it takes for the read/write head to locate the appropriate sector on the spinning platter that contains the information required by the CPU.

Serial Port. A serial port provides a means of transmitting and receiving data over a single pair of wires. The communication protocol sends the data one byte at a time, in a prescribed order.

SMPTE Time Code. Developed by the Society of Motion Picture and Television Engineers, SMPTE Time Code enables you to synchronize multiple audio, video, and film devices with a high degree of precision. It records a continuous series of timing pulses on the tape or film, with absolute addressing, so that you can access a specific frame on the tape or film quickly and accurately.

Spindle Speed. This measurement helps determine a hard drive's overall speed. The spindle that spins the platters is turned by a brushless dc (direct current) motor—like the motor on an audio turntable. These motors spin the disks in revolutions per minute (RPM). The higher the RPM of the motor, the more quickly data can be retrieved by the CPU. The faster the spindle speed, the more noisy and hot the mechanism will be—and the greater the chance for drive error.

Spindle speeds of average-performance hard drives are 3600 and 4800 RPMs; high-end drives spin at 5400 RPMs to 7200 RPMs.

SR. Speech Recognition (SR) technology found on the AV Macs.

Sync. A shortened term for Synchronize. Describes a device's capability to conform to an incoming signal and process it correctly.

Telephony. The telephone features that a computer can mimic, enhance, or manipulate.

Termination. Related to the SCSI bus. Termination is the physical closing off of a circuit to dampen signal resonance and to keep lines free of performance robbing echos that travel down the SCSI line. Termination also matches the impedance of the lines—crucial for daisy chaining multiple devices with the increased cable length that needs to be filled.

Thermal Wax Printer. A thermal wax printer is similar to an inkjet printer but uses melted black or colored dyed wax as the media. Unlike inkjets, thermal wax printed pages don't smear or feel soaked.

Topology. The physical layout of network cables is known as the topology. Common topologies are bus, passive star, and active star. Not all topologies can be used with all transmission media or data links.

Touch Screen. Touch screens are another type of input device for controlling a computer. A transparent screen, with embedded sensors, fits over the computer monitor so that the user can simply touch buttons on-screen to activate a command, or drag an object from one place to another.

Trackball. Another type of input device that resembles a mouse on its back. With a trackball you move the ball in its stationary holder to move the cursor around the screen. Roll the trackball in the desired direction, and the cursor moves accordingly.

Tracks. The magnetic grooves on hard disk platters where information is stored.

Transfer Protocols. File transfer protocols ensure reliability and maximize transmission speed. Older protocols sent text files at full speed ignoring errors. Newer protocols handle error correction, and enable you to specify multiple files to be sent or received in a session. The addition of MacBinary to any protocol allows Mac-specific file information (such as icons) to be transmitted. See Table 5.

If you are using an error correcting modem and the computer you're calling supports it, ZMODEM is the protocol of choice. ZMODEM's capability to resume interrupted transfers is priceless. If ZMODEM isn't available, try YMODEM-G. If you don't have an error correcting modem, use YMODEM or XMODEM-1K.

Transmission Medium. The physical means by which network signals are sent between computers on a network.

TTS. "Text-to-Speech" translation. TTS functions on the AVs can vocalize written text through the Mac speaker.

Wide Area Network (WAN). For computers to communicate over great distances, a WAN must be formed. A WAN is generally composed of several LANs connected by some form of long distance communication.

Table 5   File Transfer Protocols

Protocol	Speed	Error Correction	Comments
ASCII	Fast	None	Text only
XMODEM	Slow	Simple Checksum	Most widely used
XMODEM-1K	Medium	CRC	Sometimes called YMODEM, YMODEM1X with batch transfer
YMODEM	Fast	none	Use only with error correcting modem
ZMODEM	Fast	none	Use only with error correcting modem. Allows canceled download to be restarted.

INDEX